Sacred Theology

Abraham Kuyper

Sovereign Grace Publishers, Inc.
P.O. Box 4998
Lafayette, IN 47903

ISBN 1-58960-057-6

Printed In the United States of America
By Lightning Source, Inc.

sacred theology

abraham kuyper

ASSOCIATED PUBLISHERS AND AUTHORS

CONTENTS

FIRST DIVISION

THEOLOGICAL ENCYCLOPEDIA
CHAPTER I.

CHAPTER II.

CHAPTER III.

CHAPTER IV.

SECOND DIVISION

THE ORGANISM OF SCIENCE
CHAPTER I.

CHAPTER II.

CHAPTER III.

CHAPTER IV.

THIRD DIVISION

THEOLOGY
CHAPTER I.

CHAPTER II.

CHAPTER III.

CHAPTER IV.

CHAPTER V.

CONCERNING ABRAHAM KUYPER

Those who are unfortunate enough to be unfamiliar with the Dutch language are dependent on the remarkably small proportion of Abraham Kuyper's voluminous writings which have been translated into English. By far the most important of these is the translation by the Rev. J. Hendrik de Vries of Kuyper's monumental *Encyclopedia of Sacred Theology*, first published in English in 1898. The original edition contained a *Preface* by Kuyper himself and an *Introduction* by B. B. Warfield, the substance of which are included with additional material in the present brief biographical and introductory outline.

Born in the riverside town of Classluis in 1837, Abraham Kuyper was the son of a minister of the state church in Heiddelburg, the capital and chief sea-port of the Zeeland district. Educated at first by his parents at home, he later attended high school in Leiden and then spent eight years at the University there, until 1861, when the degree of Doctor of Theology was conferred upon him, in part for his contribution to the study of John a Lasco.

It was during a brief country pastorate in the village of Beesd that Kuyper was converted to Biblical Christianity. Rationalistic and liberal in his theology through the influence of his teacher Dr. J. H. Scholten, he was nevertheless powerfully affected by a group of strongly orthodox saints in the vicinity of Beesd. One of them, a middle-aged woman by the name of Pietronella Baltus, impressed Kuyper strongly with her uncompromising faith in the eternal truths of sovereign grace and her consistent world-view. Kuyper's own honesty about his personal convictions led him through the long discussions and arguments with these solid Calvinists of an earlier generation, to a full and firm orthodoxy, as he progressively gave up the mediating and vacillating theology into which he had drifted during his student days.

While he was a Pastor in Utrecht, Kuyper developed more completely his convictions concerning a fuller independence of the Church from the State. In 1869 he became an associate-editor of *The Herald,* a religious and political weekly oriented towards the Antirevolutionary Voter's Club which had been inspired and led by Groen van Prinsterer. In the following year he became Pastor of the Amsterdam state church and therefore head of a city-wide complex of ten local churches and some twenty-eight ministers, with other elders and deacons. It became clear to him that a full reformation of the state church would have to proceed from Amsterdam, and he embarked on an extensive educational program in support of such a reformation. His program for solving this vexed question of the relation between the State and the Church was set forth in a small book, partly as a personal testimony and partly apologetic, entitled *Confidentially* and published in 1873. During the following year he took a seat in the Second Chamber of Parliament. In the meantime, *The Herald* expanded into a daily paper called *The Standard* in which the original religious weekly appeared as a Saturday supplement. Kuyper was editor of both and set out on the journalistic program which enabled him to capture so many of his countrymen for the Anti-revolutionary Party. Up to his death in 1920 he produced thousands of editorial columns, leading articles, and meditations for these newspapers, many of which ran in series, and when printed separately formed sizable volumes. Many individual articles were quickly reprinted as political pamphlets and were widely distributed at critical moments such as so often precede important elections. It was in these editorials that Kuyper developed his full-scale Calvinistic world-view, including a Christian re-interpretation of politics, art, industry, literary criticism, and the sciences. It was his endeavour to capture all these areas of culture for Christ as Lord. For Kuyper, this was nothing but the inevitable result of accepting the full sovereignty of God, and of men's actual (if not acknowledged) dependence upon God for meaning during the flow and development of history.

As a member of Parliament, Kuyper soon became leader of the *Anti- revolutionary Party*. Through skilful support of other parties at selected moments, he was able to see much legislation through to law. It especially advanced the opportunities of non-state schools to provide realistically at last for the education of those who wished their children to be free from the secularizing philosophies of the state school system. Kuyper's dream of a Christian University began to be realized through legislation that first made the founding of independent universities possible, and then accepted those so founded on an equal footing with the state-controlled ones. In 1880 the Free University of Amsterdam was opened, with Kuyper as the principal lecturer in Theology. On October 20, 1881, he handed his position over to Dr. F. L. Rutgers and delivered an address concerning "Present-day Biblical Criticism in its Destructive Impact on the Church of the Living God," an address which indicates his fearless and open opposition to the then popular critical views of Abraham Kuenen.

Kuyper's printed lectures of 1888 on *Calvinism and Art* give one an idea of what his lectures on Aesthetics must have been like, and a series of editorial leaders in *The Herald* were eventually printed in 1889 as the book on *The Work of The Holy Spirit*.

In 1886, Dr. Kuyper was a leader in an attempt to reform the state church in the matter of accepting liberal ministers on an equal footing with those who continued to believe in the doctrinal standards of the church. Kuyper wanted a full disestablishment; but the result was only the formation of a free and independent Reformed Church.

The years 1893 and 1894 saw the production of the monumental *Encyclopedia of Sacred Theology,* the fruit of university lectures on the structure of theological science. The 1890's also saw the growth and influence of the Free University of Amsterdam and of Kuyper's determination to prove that Christian Apologetics should be an aggressive force in every area of intellectual and cultural endeavour. To raise the banner of a sovereign Lord was to challenge the basis of all which the natural man could achieve in his presumed independence of God.

Kuyper's genius as a teacher of the ordinary Christian in the midst of the everyday world is proven by his four-volume commentary on the *Heidelberg Catechism* published during 1892 to 1895, and by the volumes of collected devotional meditations appearing in the newspapers of which he was editor.

After serving his country as Prime Minister from 1901 to 1905, Kuyper became an "elder statesman" and continued to lead the Anti-revolutionary Party until shortly before his death in 1920.

COMMON GRACE

In 1895 Kuyper began a series of articles in *The Herald* which ran until 1901. These were soon afterward published in three volumes entitled *Common Grace*. Distinct from the "special" grace which results in the salvation of its recipient, "common" or general grace is God's attitude, acts of mercy and providence toward all sinners, in restraining and controlling the results of the Fall and its curse within the structure of an orderly universe. Many gifts and abilities are given to men through this common grace regardless of their status before God. This general grace is thus the source of all that is good, true, and beautiful in the lives of the unredeemed. It is expressed in the order of family and state, through the science, art, philosophy and general culture of the non-redeemed world. It makes civilization and education possible despite the corruption of the natural man and the world's subjection to the curse of sin. As history unfolds God's plan for his creation, the area of common grace becomes progressively smaller in the life of the individual until in Hell nothing remains of it for the unsaved while in Heaven all its benefits have been absorbed into the saving or special grace, to be inherited for eternity by the redeemed of the Lord.

It was John Calvin who gave this doctrine to the world as a legitimate part of systematic theology, but it was Kuyper who developed it into a full-orbed pattern of truth, linking science, art, philosophy, and theology into one system of general culture for the Christian. *Common Grace* forms much of the basis for what follows in Kuyper's exposition of *Theological Encyclopedia*.

Theological Encyclopedia

The modern term encyclopedia refers primarily to a *book* listing alphabetically the basic general knowledge of an introductory nature covering what is known about everything. Kuyper uses the term in an organic sense, holding that we must have a concept of science as a subject in itself, rather than as merely the aggregate of the various sciences and arts. For Kuyper *"Encyclopedia"* is the scientific study of science itself, of its proper basis and structure, and provides a foundation for interdisciplinary studies. Far from seeking to swallow up all the sciences as mere departments of theology, *Encyclopedia* includes the study of the interrelationships between all the sciences, including theology. *Encyclopedia* deals not with the content, but with the organic structure of the various sciences and therefore with science as a living and growing whole. It is thus philosophic in nature, and is not intended to replace introduction to the content of individual disciplines.

Volume One of the *Encyclopedia of Sacred Theology* was introductory, containing some five hundred pages of history of theological science. Volume Two treated the subject generally, showing how theological Encyclopedia develops from its fundamental *principium* or organic principle. Motivated by the regeneration of the heart of man, theological science has Scripture as its organic *principium* and so determines the view of reality which is opened up to the regenerate consciousness in submission to God in Christ by the illumination of the Holy Spirit.

The third volume, yet untranslated into English, treats the structure of the science of Theology itself, showing how its divisions develop naturally from the starting-point in what Calvin called the *semen religionis*, the *sensus divinitas*, which all men have by virtue of their being created in the divine image. This "seed of religion," the "sense of divinity," expresses itself through man's reaction from God and his misinterpretation of himself and the world of experience with himself as the reference-point. There can be no neutral ground upon which a world-view can be based, for the sinner and the saint have necessarily divergent starting-points and presuppositions in interpreting what they separately conceive reality to be. All human interpretation either proceeds in submission to God and his Revelation or it does not. But because of common grace, no unbeliever manages to act consistently with his own principles, for he has contradictory principles of chance and logic involved in all that he says. He can never be fully rational (as logic requires him to be) nor fully irrational (as chance would have him be) because his own human-ness revolts at the results of both. A balance is therefore struck at some point between an absolute unity and an absolute diversity, with his own presumed antonomy of personality as the final arbiter. The variety of unregenerate systems and schemes for seeking this balance is endless and each one can be shown to be unstable, depending as it must on arbitrary absolutes and limited data. Standards of judgement are inevitably tenuous and elusive for the unbeliever, and the problem of subjectivity is unavoidable.

SPHERE-SOVEREIGNTY

Kuyper's concept of distinct spheres of law within the created order became the instrument that he hoped would transform the Reformed Christian from acquiescent passivity or apathetic indifference to aggressive witness to God's interpretation of reality and to his sovereign Lord's claims upon all in each and every area of experience. It was his hope that despite all worldly opposition, God's holy ordinances would again be established in the home, the school, and the state, for the good of the people.

Religion is common to all men by virtue of their being created in God's image and so a common root of religious consciousness is found in the human "heart" or concentration-point of man's being. This is not an organ or faculty or feeling, but is the point where God himself begins to act in man's soul; it is the point of man's awareness of the break between the finiteness of his own being and the infinity of God's being. It is also the point of origin of our sense of antithesis, making the distinction between unity and diversity possible. Because God is Creator in the Scriptural sense, God's sovereignty is the unifying principle of Christian thought. Every aspect of the creation is therefore furnished with a pattern of created laws which give it its character and structure and enables it to be part of a *uni*-verse, the *cosmos*. All of the life-experience of the Christian must be dedicated to God's glory. Even the spheres of politics and society have their law-structures imposed upon them by God. These law-spheres are therefore sovereign within themselves, but God is sovereign over all of them as they are co-ordinated together. The law-spheres cooperate but cannot be reduced to one another; each has an element of uniqueness, given it by God.

The individual is to find his relationship to these spheres through his "calling" under God, but in each area he must obey the law-structure with which he is interacting at any moment. As an office-bearer under God, man is limited by the Christian concept of obedience as well as by his own finiteness. The individual finds meaning (in the sense of knowledge) by accepting the interpretation of reality which God makes possible through faith in his Revelation, developing this interpretation in the course of acting out his calling. Likewise, he finds meaning (in the sense of purpose) in the fact that God's plan for creation includes him in particular. His significance as an individual personality derives from his place in this comprehensive plan of God, rather than from a presumed antonomy from God's control. For the Christian individual, freedom is ethical submission to God and is expressed in practice through obedience in one's calling.

Kuyper's theory of sovereign law-spheres, each with its own God-given rights, duties, and responsibilities, included the idea that man must express God's will in each sphere, without transgressing the boundary lines or subordinating one sphere to another. The state, for example, has as much power as God bestows on it, no more and no less. It must, as a divinely-ordained office, take its place not above but beside the other law-spheres. Finite authority as expressed within each sphere is delegated by God and is therefore responsible to him.

Kuyper saw that for the Calvinist, the variety of callings among men are given unity by man's covenantal relation to God; the basis of civilization is the cultural mandate received by Adam at the hand of his Creator. However, because of sin, an abnormal universe is in need of illumination from God in order to dispel the darkness, and Biblical Revelation is the light. Because of sin, man and then society as a whole, stands in need of regeneration through this Word of Life, to be effected by the Holy Spirit. This is true in the scientific, cultural, and political areas as much as in the individual's Christian life. Through the obedience of the individual Christian in his own calling, regeneration and its fruit is to extend to all areas of culture, thus redeeming civilization from the effects of the Fall.

There is therefore an antithesis between apostate and Christian culture, science, and philosophy, arising from the light of Revelation being shed in the darkness of an abnormal world. Because there is a two-fold point of departure for science, arising as it must from *either* the regenerate *or* the unregenerate heart, there are two kinds of science just as much as there are two kinds of people in the world. The entire range of Christian sciences must therefore be contrasted with the entire range of non-christian sciences. The antithesis is thus complete between the Christian and the apostate view-points, and the whole directions and content of life and culture is under dispute between them. *Both* claim the entire scope of the domain of human knowledge.

DIVISION I

THEOLOGICAL ENCYCLOPEDIA

CHAPTER I

THE NAME ENCYCLOPEDIA

Clarity demands that we begin an investigation of the significance of the term "encyclopedia" by the definition of the general conception. An etymological explanation is of some help because as a rule there is history in a name, which it will not do to pass by. In the Greek classics, the first trace of the word is discovered in Galen, the physician and philosopher who died about 200 years after the birth of Christ. He uses the term for the totality of the instruction by which a boy is educated to become a man. Aristotle uses the term to refer to the measure of instruction or knowledge which was deemed indispensible for normally-developed Athenian citizens. To the Greeks therefore, the term did not refer to a group of sciences which formed an abstract whole, nor even "everyday matters of knowledge," but to the union which such sciences had in relation to the forming of the young Greek. The principle which unified the separated parts of human knowledge so making a united circle of the content of education, was one's life-circle or "world-view."

Among the fathers of the Christian church a transition began to take place. When the higher knowledge of the Christian religion came out of Israel into the Greco-Roman world, it was but natural that Christian scholars should class the entire heathen classical development with what was lower and common in antithesis to the higher knowledge of the Scriptures. The term "encyclopedia" came to mean the entire circle of the heathen classical life, over against which stood theological theory as "higher knowledge." Encyclopedia no longer signified the common instruction given to the ordinary citizen, but the whole realm of worldly science in distinction from Sancta Theologia, Holy Theology.

Only after the rise of humanism in the sixteenth century does the term begin to appear again. During the period of the Reformation, by the beginning of the seventeenth century the term began to refer not only to the *world* of science but to the *book* in which this world of science was contained. The effort to give manuals of this sort of methodical arrangement met with increasing success. A good example is the work of John Henry Alstedt published in 1608 and thereafter in 1620 with the title Cursus Philosophical Encyclopediae. For many years it was the standard work for the study of general science, and in 1649 was reprinted at Leyden in four octavo volumes. Perusal of this work soon makes it evident that under the name "encyclopedia," Alstedt embraced all the sciences, and was bent on establishing them mutually in technical relations. It was evidently his purpose to exhibit before our eyes the body of the sciences as a whole. He does not only describe the members of the body, but also on the other hand the network of nerves and veins that unite these parts.

After the seventeenth century a large variety of works were compiled including one in Germany between 1732 and 1750 in sixty-eight volumes. The idea soon appeared of keeping people informed of the continual progress of scientific investigation. A supplement was provided each year to an alphabetic encyclopedia bringing each department of science up to date. By this time the antithesis between theological and secular encyclopedia was utterly lost from view.

In the nineteenth century, the idea of a logically-structured body of knowledge was increasingly abandoned. From its very nature an encyclopedia needed only to be an accumulation of knowledge. The term now meant nothing but the *book*. Later still, under the influence of rationalism (especially as evidenced in the philosophies of Fichte and Hegel), *science as such* now became an object of scientific investigation. The *word* encyclopedia became the name of an independent *science* which had for its object the investigation of all other sciences.

CHAPTER TWO

THE IDEA OF ENCYCLOPEDIA

The development of the idea of the encyclopedia did not necessarily coincide with the development of the name. There lies a majesty in the mind and by virtue of which it can not rest until it has acquired a full dominion in the world of thought. It cannot bear the suggestion that there should still be something in that world of thought that has withdrawn itself from the power of its sceptre. An atomistic science offends the mind's sense of unity, and by pulverizing the cosmos, robs the mind of confidence of step. The history of thought shows that increasing harmony and unity have been sought by those seeking to present knowledge in its totality. For example, Bacon (in 1620) divided the sciences organically, that is, after a principle derived from these sciences themselves. Yet even in those days the material to be collected began to be too extensive for the handling of it all, and for the deeper study of its relations to lie within the individual reach of single scholars.

The victory of the organic idea was first manifest in the writings of Fichte, who wrote numerous monographs for his classes in Berlin, in which he marked *knowing itself* as the object of an independent science. The truth had come to light that the "knowledge" of man forms a world by itself, and that without unity of principle this world of our knowledge remains unintelligible. From now on, there was a necessary relation between (1) the man who knows, (2) knowledge as such, and (3) that which is known and explained organically from this one principle.

A break, however, came in the process of the development of encyclopedic knowledge, because of the practical problem of introducing students of a given university faculty to their own science. The sad tendency was for university faculties to develop within themselves, without relationship to parallel or related developments in another faculty. This development in encyclopedical study has an undeniable disadvantage. In the first place, the jurist, the theologian, the physician, or student of languages may readily fall short of philosophical unity and power of thought. Secondly, instead of the principle of science itself, the historical division of the faculties has become the motive of division. Thirdly, the practical purpose has tempted the production of convenient manuals rather than the writing of fully scientific encyclopedia. Finally, the old custom of introducing the students to the universe of science as a whole and then into their own department, has been more and more neglected. In the universities and theological seminaries, the fragmentation of knowledge has led irresistibly to a loss of the unity of truth.

CHAPTER THREE

THE CONCEPTION OF ENCYCLOPEDIA

The conception of encyclopedia is not cast up by us arbitrarily, but germinates of necessity and defines itself. The germ was already prepared, when the first impulse began to work in the human mind, from which sprang all encyclopedic study. Suddenly, with a clear insight, we grasp the thought that impels us. Originally in the human mind there lurks the need of bringing a certain order into the chaos of its knowledge, not arbitrarily but in agreement with a certain distinguishing principle that forces itself upon it.

In forming this definition of the concept we must work critically. Because of a great variety of matter exhibited under this label, no unity is obvious. We have noticed that after the effort to establish order was made by placing the several departments of knowledge in a certain logical relation, finally the attempt was made to penetrate the organism itself, which science, taken as a whole, represents. Encyclopedic necessity therefore arises from the antithesis of chaos and order. The question must be put as to what it is that compels us logically to take this order in this way and not in another, and by what right a succeeding generation seeks to improve upon the efforts of a bygone generation. The question also arises as to whether this logical necessity of our thinking has its ground in our thinking itself alone, or whether it proceeds from data outside of our thinking. Or if you like, does the unity arise naturally from the data, or do we impose it on the data? The tendency in the natural sciences is for the human spirit to both claim to be inventing a certain order for knowledge, while at the same time seeking out and indicating the order which is already there.

Encyclopedic study becomes truly scientific only when it is seen that we need not bring order into our knowledge, but must merely trace out the order which is already in it. From the investigation into a mechanical arrangement, it now becomes the study of an organic life-relation.

Encyclopedic science has undoubtedly been productive of fruits for writing compendia and manuals, and is entitled to the distinction that the writers of such books deal with its results, but as a science it must be studied for its own sake. Its aim must always be to grasp the inner organism of science as such. All encyclopedic study is therefore philosophical, and forms a subdivision of philosophy. It will be related to methodology and introduction, which although often taken for each other are sharply distinguishable. Introduction assumes that the way is there, that it has been used, and points it out. Methodology on the other hand, is the science which decides *how* the way is to be laid, and approves or disapproves of the way that has been laid, even seeking to improve upon it or to justify each step.

The study of knowledge is to be clearly distinguished from knowledge itself. "Knowledge" and "Science" are different things. Knowledge itself is a phenomenon in the human mind, and assumes a living, thinking person who knows. A city emptied of its people would contain no knowledge, but there would still be science to be found in the city, if the books in its library could be found. It would then be the task of encyclopedia to furnish us a knowledge of that science as an organic whole. Botany treats of the vegetable kingdom which itself exists organically. Likewise it is the task of encyclopedia to treat of science as a whole organically. If it is true therefore that encyclopedia intends self-consciously to give a clear account of what it understands by the organism of science itself, it becomes self-evident that it cannot allow itself to be governed by the practical university division into faculties, but that it must rather examine them critically and correct them.

From the fact that the object is still incomplete, flows of necessity the incompleteness of encyclopedia itself. In the field of knowledge, some ground is not broken and other parts are but imperfectly known. And yet encyclopedia must not wait until its object is completely ready, since science is in need of her assistance to get itself ready. Since, however, the field of knowledge is only known in part and the psychological sciences are still at variance with each other, and since in every department tendencies and schools are still in the heat of combat, no writer of encyclopedia can carry an argument, save from the view-point which he himself occupies, and except he start out from the hypothesis upon which his general presentation is founded. There is of course nothing wrong with this, since every science proceeds in the same way. But it remains necessary, for each separate science to beware lest it find itself being interpreted in terms of another, so losing its own integrity and distinctive contribution. This is what happens when in a University, a theological faculty originally oriented to the historic conception of theology, is converted arbitrarily into a department for the study of religion in general or of comparative religion, an entirely different science.

A three-fold task therefore presents itself to us. It is the task of encyclopedia to investigate the organism of science physiologically and anatomically and pathologically. Physiologically, in order to enter into the nature of the life of every science and to trace out and to define the function of each member in the body of sciences. Anatomically, in order to exhibit the exact boundaries, divisions and relations of the several departments. And pathologically, in order to bring to light the imperfection in the functioning of every science to show its lack of accuracy in the fixing of its different relations, and to watch lest some of its parts develop out of proper proportion. Its methods will begin with the study of historical development of the special sciences as they now are, and from this endeavor to form for itself an image of the development of science in general. Encyclopedia does not build the body of science, neither does it produce it, but it begins by viewing this body of science as given already. Its task is therefore purely formal in the sense that it does not deal with the material of each science, but uses the content in any particular case simply to illustrate a general structure.

CHAPTER FOUR

THE CONCEPTION OF THEOLOGICAL ENCYCLOPEDIA

Two difficulties present themselves when we begin to apply the idea of general encyclopedia to theology. First, the scientific character of theology is disputed by many, and secondly, those who do not dispute this are still disagreed as to what is to be understood by theology itself. As a result the general theology is exhibited which is simply that particular theology to which the theologian has committed himself, and back of this beautiful exterior, the subjective view-point lurks which was said to be avoided, and yet governs the entire exposition.

Doubt concerning the scientific character of theology does not spring from the still imperfect development of this science, but finds its origin in the peculiar character it bears in distinction from all other sciences. To answer the objection, the theologian must not only show that theology subordinates its activity to the conception of "science," but also that the parts of theology are mutually related organically, allowing it to stand in organic relation to the rest of the organism of science.

The second difficulty should be considered somewhat more at length. There are Greek, Roman, Lutheran, Reformed and Modern theologies. Frequently one theology investigates a different object from another. One theology may deny the very existence of the object which another theology investigates. This springs from the fact that the object of theology lies closely interwoven with our subjectivity, and is therefore incapable of being absolutely objectified. A blind man is no more able to furnish a scientific study of the phenomenon of color, or a deaf person to develop the theory of music, than a scholar whose organ for the world of the divine has become inactive or devected is capable of furnishing a theological study, simply because he has none other than a hearsay knowledge of the object which theology investigates. Hence no escape is here possible from the refraction of subjectivity. If a scientific investigator and then the writer of an encyclopedia, could investigate his object without himself believing in the existence of his object, it might be possible for the encyclopedist at least to keep himself outside of this difference. But this is out of the question. Faith in the existence of the object to be investigated is the condition sine qua non of all scientific investigation. It is evident, therefore, that the theological encyclopedist cannot possibly furnish anything but an encyclopedia of *his own* theology. For though this may be denied, the outcome always shows that in reality the writer claims universal validity for his theology.

This is a self-deception which nevertheless contains a germ of truth. What we claim to be valid must also be valid for everyone else. This is no presumption, but only the immediate result of the firmness of conviction which is the motive for scientific investigation. All sceptism causes science to wither. But from this there flows an obligation: to point out in the other theologies what is untenable and inconsequent, to appreciate what is relatively true, and to a certain extent show the necessity of their existence. No one theology can claim to be all-sided and completely developed. This is not possible, because every theology has to deal with an object that is not susceptible to an abstract intellectual treatment, and which can therefore only be known in connection with its historic development in life. A theology can therefore be onesided without being heretical or an aberation. A theologian can acknowledge truth in another position, without recognizing the truth of the position as a whole. The start is taken from one's conviction, with an open eye to one's own imperfections so as sincerely to appreciate the labors and efforts of others, and to be bent upon the assimilation of their results.

The view-point taken in this work purposely avoids therefore every appearance of neutrality, which is after all bound to be dishonest at heart; and makes no secret of what will appear from every page that the Reformed theology is here accepted as *the* theology, in its very purest form. This declaration intends simply to make it clearly known, that the theologian himself cannot stand indifferently to his own personal faith, and to his consequent confession concerning the object of theology, and therefore does not hesitate to state it as his conviction that the Reformed theology with respect to this object has grasped the truth most firmly.

The task of theological encyclopedia is therefore fourfold. First, it must vindicate scientific character of theology. Secondly, it must explain the relation between theological science and the other sciences. Thirdly, in its own choice of the object of theology it must exhibit the error in the choice of others, and appreciate what is right in the efforts of others and so appropriate it for itself. Finally, it must do for theology what it is the task of general encyclopedia to do for science in general.

The aim of theological encyclopedia is in itself purely scientific. Philosophically, its aim is to exhibit its organic coherence in relationships. But its aim is equally strong to bring theology itself to self-consciousness. No more than in any other science does theology begin with knowing what it wants. Practical interests, necessity, and unconscious impulse bring it to its development. But with this it cannot remain satisfied. For its own honor's sake theology must given an account of its nature and its calling. This is the more necessary since in our times theology as a whole is no longer studied by hardly anyone, and the various theologians choose for themselves but a part of the great task. The fragmentation of non-Christian thought virtually dominates Christian theology today. Therefore in the third place, the aim of encyclopedia of theology is defensive or apologetic. And fourthly, its aim must be for the sake of non-theologians, to declare in scientifically connected terms, *what theology is.*

In conclusion therefore, we have before us the scientific investigation of the organic nature and relations of theology in itself and as an integral part of the organism of science. Belonging to the science of philosophy, theological encyclopedia as such is formal and must not be allowed to become material, as if it were its duty to collect its theological content into a manual.

DIVISION II

THE ORGANISM OF SCIENCE

CHAPTER I

THE CONCEPTION OF SCIENCE

In studying theology we face a phenomenon that extends across the ages, and has engaged many persons, and therefore cannot be the out-come of a whim or notion, nor yet of an agreement or common contract, but is governed by a motive of its own, which has worked upon these persons in all ages. Further, this motive by which the human mind is impelled to theological investigation, not only formally demands such an investigation, but is bound to govern the content and tendency of these studies. This impulse is certainly exhibited in special theological studies, but never exhausts itself in them. It lies behind and about its temporal and individual revelations. It is not the work of an individual man, but men have found it in the human mind. Neither is it found as an indifferent something, but as something definite in essence and in tendency. There can be no clearness, therefore, in an encyclopedical exposition until it is definitely stated what the writer understands by his science and by its prosecution in general. For this reason this investigation into the nature of theology begins with a summary treatment of science and its prosecution.

Etymologically, it is fairly certain that *to know* as an intellectual conception is derived from the sensual conception *to see;* and more particularly from seeing something one was looking for in a sense of *finding*. As a result, there is both a naive and a deeper sense of knowing just as there is a naive and a deeper sense of seeing. We may "see" without particularly "looking," or "look" without "seeing," and as a result we may "know" without "understanding," or understand without a complete knowledge. Again, the accepted use of the verb *to know* has both a general and a limited sense. To know that the mailboat has suffered shipwreck, is simply to have heard that it has. If on the other hand, I say "Do you know that this is so?", then to know is taken in a stricter sense and means: Can you vouch for it? In general, to have knowledge of a thing is also synonomous with having certainty of it, which of itself implies that such a presentation of the matter or fact has been obtained that it can be taken up into our consciousness. And further, it is knowledge only when besides this presentation in my consciousness, I also have the sense that this presentation corresponds to an existing reality.

For many centuries the conception of science and its corresponding forms in other languages was entirely free from sceptical confusion, and carried no other impression than of studies which were able to impart real knowledge of all sorts of things, so that by it one knew what before one did not know.

On the other hand, the word "science" is not synonomous with the word "truth." In the first place, in ancient languages the root words for truth do not point to what is seen or known, but to what is spoken. It is something that is said, for example a proposition, which is said to be "true" or "not true." Truth is therefore something towards which science moves rather than being truth itself. In the temporal state, science "seeks after truth" and the antithesis between falsehood, mistake, illusion, inaccuracy and truth is basic to this search.

In the conception of science, the root idea of "to know" must be sharply maintained, and the question arises: Who is the subject of this knowledge and what is the object? Science is not the sum total of what one man knows, neither is it the aggregate of what three men know. The subject of science cannot be this man or that, but must be mankind at large, or if you please, the human consciousness. Yet already the content is so large that even the most richly-endowed mind can never know but a very small part of it. Again, science does not operate atomistically, as if the grand aggregate of individuals commissioned a few persons to satisfy the general thirst after knowledge, and as if these commissioners went to work after a mutually-agreed-upon plan. No, science works organically, that is, in the sense that the thirst for knowledge lies in human nature itself; that within certain bounds, human nature can obtain knowledge; that the impulse to devote oneself to this task, together with the gifts which enable one to work at it, become it is equally improbable that chance should produce such an organically inter-related result. The higher factor must here be at play, which at all time and among all peoples, maintains the unity of our race in the interests of life of our human consciousness; which impels people to obtain knowledge; which endows us with the faculties to know; which superintends this entire work; and as far as the results of this labor leads to knowledge, builds them up into one whole, after a hidden plan. Furthermore, this higher factor must be self-conscious, since the collective human spirit is brought to self-consciousness by science alone. This higher factor, who is to lead our human consciousness up to science, must himself know what he will have us to know. The idea of science implies, that from the manifold things I know, a connected knowledge is born, which would not be possible if there were no relation among the several parts of the object. The necessity of organic inter-relations, which was found to be indispensible in the subject, repeats itself in the object. The apparently accidental discovery or invention is as a rule, much more important to atomistic knowledge than to scientific investigation. As long as something is merely discovered, it is taken up into our knowledge but not into our science. Only when the inference and subsequent insight that the parts of the object are organically related prove themselves correct, is that distinction born between the special and the general which learns to recognize in the general the uniting factor of the special.

This is the more necessary because the subject of science is not a given individual in a given period of time, but thinking man in the course of centuries. If this organic relation were lacking in the object, thinking man in one age would have an entirely different object before him then in a following century or previously. The object would lack all consistency of character. Former knowledge would not stand in relation to our own, and the conception of science as a connected and as an ever self-developing phenomenon in our human life would fall away. But our impulse after science aims higher than this. As long as there is a Chinese Wall between one realm of the object and the other, that wall allows us no rest. Hence our ideal of science will in the end prove to be an illusion unless the object is grasped as existing organically.

There is an organic relation between subject and object. If there were no organic relation between everything that exists outside of us and ourselves, our consciousness included, the relation in the object would be wanting. There must be an organic relation between the object and our own persons. The relation between the object and our thinking would not be sufficient, since the thinking can not be taken apart from the thinking subject. Even when thinking itself is made the object of investigation, and generalization is made, it is separated from the individual subject, but remains bound to the general subject of our human nature. Thus for all science a three-fold organic relation between subject and object is necessary. Firstly, there must be an organic relation between that object and our nature. Secondly, there is the relation between that object and our consciousness; and thirdly, there is a relation between that object and our world of thought.

The first also lies pregnantly expressed in viewing man as a microcosm. The human soul stands in organic relation to the human body, and that body stands in every way organically related to the several kingdoms of nature around about us. For example, when chemically analyzed, the elements of our body appear to be the same as those of the world which surrounds us. The second can be expressed by saying that our consciousness stands in the desired organic relation to the subject of our science, in that it is possible for man to have an apprehension, a perception, and an impression of the existence and of the method of existence of the object. This organic relation has mistakenly been described in terms of mental "faculties." The capacity taken in the sense of "a faculty" is of its own nature always active, while in the case of the entering in of the object into our consciousness, we may be passive. If I examine a thing purposely, or see it involuntarily, in each case the entire self-same organic relation exists, with this difference only, that with intentional observation, our intellect and our will cooperate in this relation. Hence there can be no question of an active faculty which can operate independently of the intellect and of the will. There are lines of communication that can bring the object outside of us in relation to our ego. The nature of these relations depends of course entirely upon the nature of the object with which they are to bring us into communication. If the object is material these conductors must be partly material. If the object, on the other hand, is entirely immaterial, these relations must exhibit a directly spiritual nature. Compare for example, the perceptions of light and darkness, with the perceptions of true and false. In both cases it is self-evident that what is signalled along the several lines of communication to our consciousness, can only effect a result in our consciousness when this consciousness is fitted to take up into itself what was signalled. He who is born color-blind is not affected one way or another by the most beautiful exhibition of colors.

In many ways, the fact forces itself upon us, that there is also what we call "relation" in the object. The object does not appear to be simple, but complex, and numberless relations appear among its component parts. There is indeed a whole world of relations, which appear equally real and important as do the parts of the object that enter into relation to each other. We may compare these relations to the nerves that ramify through our body, or like telephone lines stretching across our cities. But this is not really so, since the nerves and lines of communication may be the vehicles for the working of relations, but they are not the relations themselves. The relations are not only entirirely immaterial, and therefore formless, but they are also void of entity in themselves. For this reason, they are grasped by thought alone, and all our thinking consist of the knowledge of these relations. Without other aids, therefore, science would enter into our consciousness in two ways only. First, as the science of the elements, and secondly, as the science of the relations which appear between these elements. An astronomer could obtain science of the starry heavens by looking at the stars with his eye, and obtain science of their mutual relations and of the relations between their parts by entering into those relations with his thoughts. Yet the activity of our consciousness with reference to the relations is not confirmed to this.

Our thinking does not define itself exclusively to playing the part of the observer of the relations (which is always more or less passive) but also carries in itself an active power. This active power roots in the fact, if we may put it so, that before we become aware of these relations outside of us, a setting for them is present in our own consciousness. This would not be so if these relations were accidental and if they were not organically related. But to be organically related is part of their very nature. It is for this reason that the object is not chaos, but cosmos; that a universality prevails in the special, and that there appear in these relations an order and a regularity which warrant their continuity and consistancy. There is a "system" in these relations. Our capacity of thought is so constructed as to enable it to see through these relations. If correctly understood, we may say that when human thought is completed it shall be *like* the completed organism of these relations. Therefore, when we study the relations, we merely think the thought over again, by which the Subject defined these relations when he called them into being. If there were no thought imbedded in the object, it could not be digestible to our thinking.

Yet it is not as if the cosmos exists only logically. This would amount to a cosmos which consists purely of relations. All we say, is that nothing exists without relations; that these relations are never accidental, but are always organic, flowing from a general principle; and that the cosmos, as a cosmos, in its collective elements exists logically and in this logical existence is suceptible to being taken up into our world of thought. The result of all science, both from our observation and from our study of the relations of what is being observed, is always certain before-hand. The science of the cosmos is only possible for us upon the supposition that in our thinking the logical germ of a world of thought is lodged, which if properly developed, will cover entirely the logical world of thought lodged in the cosmos. And this provides the possibility of our thinking showing itself actively. In this way does human science attain unto that high, dominant and prophetical character by which it not only liberates itself from the cosmos, but also understands it, enables its devotees to take active part in it, and partially to forsee its future development. Even more striking than this, by our abstract thinking, we constantly form conclusions, which presently are seen to agree entirely with actual relations. In this way object and subject stand over against each other as wholly allied, and the more deeply our human consciousness penetrates into the cosmos, the closer this alliance is seen to be, both as concerns the substance and morphology of the object, and the thoughts that lie expressed in the relations of the object. Further, since the object does not produce the subject, nor the subject the object, the power that binds the two organically together must of necessity be sought outside of each other. And however much we may speculate and ponder, no explanation can ever suggest itself to our sense of the all-sufficient ground for this admirable correspondence-affinity between subject and object, on which the possibility and development of science wholly rests, until at the hand of Holy Scripture we confess that the Author of the cosmos created man in the *cosmos* as *micro-cosmos* "after His image and likeness."

Thus understood, science presents itself to us as a necessary and ever-continued impulse in the human mind to reflect within itself the cosmos, plastically as to its elements, and to think it through logically as to its relations; always with the understanding that the human mind is capable of this by reason of its organic affinity for its object.

It is memory and language which enable the intellectual task to lap across the ages, and be divided among many thousands of thinkers, while amid all sorts of difficulties making often very slow progress. With the flight of time, neither science by representation nor science by conception can be retained with any permanency unless we have some means by which to retain these representations and conceptions. A representation expresses itself by art in the image, the conception by language in the word. Without language the human race falls atomistically apart, and it is only by language that the organic communion, in which members of the human race stand to each other, expresses itself. Since our consciousness has a two-fold manner of existence, that of representation and conception, the union of image and word will always be the most perfect means of communication between the consciousness of one and of the other. And communion can become so complete that a given content may be almost perfectly transmitted from the consciousness of one into that of another. It is to be further noticed that language by itself would only accomlish its task within the bounds of a very limited circle and for a brief period of time, if it had not received the means of perpetuation in writing and in printing. Not the spoken but only the written and printed word surmounts the difficulties of distance between places and times.

But even this does not exhibit the highest function of language for human life in general and for science in particular. Language does not derive its high significance from its assistance in retaining and collecting, nor as a means of communication, but much more from the fact that language makes the content of our own consciousness our property. Were it not for language, the human mind itself could not communicate with itself. It could not know itself. No certainty would be possible as to whether there was any real difference between myself and the external world.

It is the Christian position that taken apart from all disturbances by sin and curse, our human consciousness should of necessity, have entered more and more deeply into the entire cosmos, by representations as well as conception-forming thought. The cosmos would have been before us as an open book. And for as much as we ourselves are a part of that cosmos, we should have, with an ever-increasing clearness of consciousness, lived the life of that cosmos along with it, and by our life itself we should have ruled it. In the absence of disturbance, the multiformity of human personality would have been as harmonious, as now it works unharmoniously. That this disturbance, alas, did occur, from which subjectivism sprang as a cancer to poison our science, comes under consideration later. Only let it here be observed how entirely natural it is for thinkers who deny the disturbance by sin, to represent science to this day as an absolute power, and are thereby forced either to limit science to the exact sciences, or to interpret it as a philosophic system, after whose standards reality must be distorted.

In the first intention, there lies an honesty which deserves appreciation. It implies the confession that only that which can be weighed and measured sufficiently escapes subjectivism. But however honestly this theory may be intentioned, it is nevertheless untenable, for two reasons. First, it is impossible even for the most assiduous student of these exact sciences to confine themselves to *mere* weighing and *mere* measuring. Even for the sake of communicating their thoughts they must formulate conclusions and hypothetical propositions tainted by subjectivism. Secondly, the view is untenable because it tends to ignore the spiritual, and thus ends in pure materialism, or it ignores every organic relation between the material and the spiritual worlds, thereby giving up the hope of a science of the cosmos as a whole.

The second tendency has vigorously maintained the demand that science should lead to an organic knowledge of the entire cosmos, derived from one principle. Unfortunately however, this theory, which with a sinless development would have been entirely correct (and is still correct in an ideal sense), no longer meets the requirements of the actual state of things, partly because the investigating subjects stand inharmoniously opposed to one another, and partly because all sorts of anomalies have gained an entrance into the object. If the disturbance of the harmony and subject as well as in the object fails to be taken into account, and the effort is persisted in logically to explain the discord from one principle, one ends in speculation which does not impart an understanding of the cosmos but either imagines a cosmos which does not exist, or pantheistically destroys the boundary line, till finally the very difference between good and evil is made to disappear. The entire interpretation of science, applied to the cosmos as it presents itself to us now, being studied by the subject "Man" as he now exists, is in an absolute sense governed by the question of whether or not a disturbance has been brought in by sin, either in the object or in the subject of science.

The development of the spiritual sciences, possible only because at least some of the universe is nonmaterial, faces three difficulties.

In the first place all the psychic, taken in an ordinary sense, is amorphic, making weighing and measuring in the ordinary senses impossible. And since as psychosomatic beings we are naturally inclined to assimilate every object both plastically and logically, we certainly feel a want with a respect to this in the spiritual domain. This lack induces us all too easily to interpret this entire realm logically only, and so to promote a false intellectualism or a dangerous speculation.

The second difficulty under which the spiritual sciences labor is the instability of their object. Elements, plants and animals carry certain fixed marks which make classification fairly straight-forward. In the human interpreter there is asserted to its fullest extent that individuality which principle resists every effort to generalize, and so the way to the universal and necessary character of one's science is obstructed. Even common properties are endlessly modified, and the richer the individual as a personality the stronger his individuality, and the less he lends himself to comparison.

Thirdly, in most of the spiritual sciences one is dependent upon a self-communication of the object. A personality must reveal itself in order to be known. Many added difficulties arise including the fact that many people lack sufficient self-knowledge, together with the ability to impart this self-knowledge accurately. Again, much is repeated as self-knowledge which is only repetition of what others have said. Many do not want to reveal themselves and can make statements that mislead. Some people have good reasons for not communicating all the details. The same individuals' self-communication will be different from time to time. Finally, the maturity of the personality being studied may prevent sufficiently full expression.

It is not as if the *essence* of the object of the spiritual sciences contains deeper mysteries (for with the exact sciences, the essence is equally mysterious), but knowledge of the relations of the object of these sciences is so difficult to obtain because these relations are so uncertain in their manifestation and are therefore almost always bound to the self-communication of the object. Symbolism, mythology, personification, and also poetry, music and almost all the fine arts render us valuable service as interpretations of what is enacted in the spiritual realm, but by themselves they offer us no scientific knowledge. With all these expressions of art we must always reckon with the individuality of the artist who enchants our eye or ear. This individuality sometimes expresses itself very strongly, so that with all the products of art, independently of the sin and falsehood which have invaded this fallen cosmos, the above-mentioned objection of individuality returns.

The question therefore becomes: What renders the service in the spiritual sciences which the representation capacity in connection with the senses effects in things seen? Again and again it appears that there are all sorts of spiritual things which we know with far greater certainty than the facts which are brought to us by the observation of things seen. We nevertheless cease to be a man when the reality of spiritual things is not more certain to us than what by investigation we know of plants and animals. We maim our science when we deny it access to spiritual objects.

There is no other course therefore, than to construct the spiritual sciences from the subject itself; provided we do not overlook that the subject of science is not this inquirer or that, but *the* human consciousness in general. The two sciences differ, in that the element of the visible world enters into our consciousness by a different way than the element of the spiritual world. The elements of the visible world work upon our powers of representation through the senses, while in entire independence of our senses and of any middle link known to us, the elements of the spiritual world affect our subject spiritually, and thus to our apprehension appear to enter immediately into our consciousness. In both ways, however, our individual subject may never be taken independently of its organic relation to the general subject of the human race. Although the science of the spiritual object is derived through subjectivity in man, by far the larger part of the labor expended on spiritual studies has a certain objective character. The more objective side of these studies has a two-fold cause. First, there is the relation which exists between our soul and our body, and between the expression of our soul and the visible cosmos. Secondly, there is the necessity of examining our own psychical life not by itself, but in organic relation to the psychical life of the human race. In the subjective aspects of the spiritual sciences we begin to reach the motives of human action which hide behind the psychical exterior, and to interpret the mysterious power which, partly by and partly without these motives, causes hundreds of persons, and then whole nations to run a course, which if marked by retrogression, suggests the unwinding of a ball of yarn. And whenever we trace these motives, our own subjective psychical life is ever shown to be our starting point, and empiricism leaves us in the lurch. This is most forceably illustrated by philosophy in the narrower sense, which just because it tries logically to interpret the cosmos and the images we receive from it, always bears a strongly subjective character, and is never able to escape the significance of presuppositions. Subjective premises will dominate an entire study of spiritual science in a given circle, insofar as this, with the empirical data as building material, devotes itself architecturally to the erection of the building.

THE SPIRITUAL SCIENCES

If the cosmos, man included, consisted exclusively of ponderable things, the study of the cosmos would be much simpler than it is now, but there would be no subject to appropriate this knowledge. Hence science has no right to complain that the cosmos does not consist of mere matter. It is to this very fact that science owes its existence. Meanwhile we cannot overestimate the difficulty of obtaining a science, worthy of the name, of the spiritual side of the cosmos. This difficulty is threefold.

In the first place all the psychic, taken in the ordinary sense, is *amorphic*, from which it follows that the morphologic capacity of our consciousness, by which we form an image of the object and place it before us, must here remain inactive. Thus while, in the tracing of relations in all that is ponderable, our understanding finds a point of support in the representation of the elements among which these relations exist, here this point of support is altogether wanting. This does not imply that the object of these sciences is *unreal*; for even with the sciences of ponderable objects your understanding never penetrates to the essence. In your *representation* you see the form ($\mu o\rho\phi\acute{\eta}$) you follow the relations ($\dot{\alpha}\nu\alpha\phi o\rho\alpha\acute{\iota}$) with your *thinking*; but the essence ($o\dot{\upsilon}\sigma\acute{\iota}\alpha$) lies beyond your reach. This does not imply that the spiritual objects may not have something similar among themselves, to what in the non-spiritual we understand by $\mu o\rho\phi\acute{\eta}$; the *forma* in the world of thought rather suggests the contrary; but in either case these forms are a secret to us, and our consciousness is not able to take them up and communicate them to our *ego*. And since as somatic-psychic beings we are naturally inclined to assimilate every object both plastically and logically, we certainly feel a want with respect to this in the spiritual domain. This want induces us all too easily to interpret this entire realm logically only, and so to promote a false intellectualism or a dangerous speculation.

The second difficulty under which the spiritual sciences labor is the *instability* of their object. You can classify minerals, plants and animals, and though in these classifications you must ever be prepared for variations and anomalies, nevertheless certain fixed marks can be determined to distinguish class from class. But with the spiritual sciences, which constantly bring you in touch with man, this rule evades you. Even the classification according to sex frequently suffers shipwreck upon effeminate men and mannish women. In "man" only does there assert itself to its fullest extent that individuality which principle resists every effort to generalize, and thus obstructs the way to the universal and necessary character of your science. You find a certain number of phenomena in common, but even these common properties are endlessly modified. And the worst is that in proportion as an individual is a richer object, and thus would offer the more abundant material for observation, the development of his individuality is the stronger, and by so much the less does such an individual lend himself to comparison. From a sharply defined character there are almost no conclusions to be drawn.

And along with this amorphic and unstable characteristic a third difficulty is that in most of the spiritual sciences you are dependent upon the self-communication of your object. It is true, you can study man in his actions and habits. His face tells you something; his eye still more. But if it is your desire to obtain a somewhat more accurate knowledge of the spiritual phenomena in him, in order to become acquainted with him, there must be in him: (1) a certain knowledge of himself, and (2) the power and will to reveal himself to you. If, then, as a result of all such self-communication you desire to form some opinion on the spiritual phenomenon which you investigate, especially in connection with what has been said above, such self-communication must be made by a great number of persons and amid all sorts of circumstances. Moreover, many difficulties arise in connection with this self-communication of your object. (1) Most people lack sufficient self-knowledge. (2) So many people lack the ability to impart to you their self-knowledge. (3) Much is told as though it were the result of self-knowledge, which is in reality only the repetition of what others have said. (4) Many do not want to reveal themselves, or purposely make statements that mislead. (5) Self-knowledge is frequently connected with intimate considerations or facts which are not communicable. (6) With the same individual this self-communication will be wholly different at one time from another. And (7) a right understanding of what one tells you requires generally such a knowledge of his past, character, and manner of life as is only obtained from a very few persons. It is most natural, therefore, that in recent times the young child has been taken as the object of observation, for the reason that with the child these difficulties are materially lessened; but this is balanced again by the fact that, because of its immaturity, the child expresses so little.

Thus we find that the difficulty in the way of spiritual sciences does not lie in the mystery of the essence of their object. With the exact sciences the essence is equally mysterious. Neither does the difficulty of these sciences lie simply in the amorphic character of their object, or, if you please, in the lack of tangible elements. But the knowledge of the relations of the object of these sciences is so difficult to be obtained, because these relations are so uncertain in their manifestation and are therefore almost always bound to the self-communication of the object. It is noteworthy how slow the progress of these sciences is, especially when compared with the rapid progress of the exact sciences; and the more so since the effort has been made to apply to them the method of the natural sciences.

Symbolism, mythology, personification, and also poetry, music and almost all the fine arts render us invaluable service as interpretations of what is enacted within the spiritual realm, but by themselves they offer us no scientific knowledge. Symbolism is founded upon the analogy and the inner affinity, which exist between the visible and invisible creation. Hence, it is not only an imperfect help, of which we may avail ourselves since our forms of thought are borrowed from the visible, but it represents a reality which is confirmed in our own human personality by the inner and close union of our somatic-psychic existence. Without that analogy and that inner affinity there would be no unity of perception possible, nor unity of expression for our two-sided being as man. Your eye does not see; your *ego* sees, but through your eye; and this use of your eye could not effect the act of your seeing, if in the reflection of light in your eye there were no actual analogy to that which your *ego* does when you see something through your eye. And though this analogy may weaken when applied to the other parts of the cosmos, in proportion as their affinity to man becomes more limited, we cannot escape from the impression that this analogy is everywhere present. With the aid of this symbolical tendency mythology seeks to represent the spiritual powers as expressions of mysterious persons. And though with us the life of the imagination is subjected too greatly to the verification of our thinking, for us to appreciate such a representation, we constantly feel the need of finding in personification useful terms for our utterances and for the interpretation of our feelings. In fact, our entire language for the psychic world is founded upon this symbolism. Although in later days, without remembrance of this symbolism, many words have purposely been formed for psychical phenomena, the onomatopepoiemena excepted, all words used to express physical perception or phenomena are originally derived by the way of symbolism from the visible world. And where poetry, music, or whatever art comes in to cause us to see or hear, not merely the beautiful in the form, but also the interpretation of the psychic, it is again on the ground of a similar analogy between the visible and invisible, that they cause us to hear something in verse or in musical rhythm, or to see something by means of the chisel or the pencil which the visible and invisible part of the cosmos, and in the analogy founded on it, there lies an invaluable means of affecting the physical life and of bringing it to utterance; but however richly and beautifully the world of sounds may be able to interpret and inspire our inner life, it offers no building material for scientific knowledge. Moreover, with all these expressions of art you must always reckon with the individuality of the artist who enchants your eye or ear, which sometimes expresses itself very strongly, so that with all the products of art, independent of sin and falsehood, which have invaded this realm also, the above-mentioned objection of individuality returns.

If the empiricism of symbolism is of very limited service to us, the empiricism of the more general expressions of the psychic life is equally unhelpful. The method of tracing the expressions of the intellectual, ethic, social, juridic, aesthetic and religious life among the different nations through the course of time is justifiable, and it must be granted that the similarity and the similar process of these phenomena among different nations warrant certain conclusions concerning the character of these life-utterances; but by itself this historic-comparative study offers no sufficiently scientific knowledge of the psychical life itself. Because you know that water descends upon the mountains mostly in the form of snow; that there it forms glaciers; that these glaciers melt; and that first as foaming torrents, and then as a navigable stream, the water pushes forward to the ocean, your scientific knowledge of water is not yet complete. And really this historic-comparative study of the moral, social and religious life of the nations teaches us not much more. Hence though we would not question for a single moment the relative right and usefulness of these studies, we emphatically deny that these studies constitute the real prosecution of the spiritual sciences. You may excel in all these studies, and not know the least thing about your own soul, which subjectively forms the centre of all psychic investigation. And what is more serious still, in this way you run a great risk of, unknown to yourself, falsifying the object of your science, if not of denaturalizing it. Apply, for instance, this method to the science of law, and you must form the conclusion that existing law only is law. Since this existing law constantly modifies itself according to the ideas of law that are commonly accepted, all antithesis between lawful and unlawful becomes at last a floating conception, and law degenerates into an official stipulation of the temporarily predominating ideas concerning mutual relationships. Thus you deprive law of its eternal principles; you falsify the sense of law, which by nature still speaks in us; and your so-called study of law degenerates into a study of certain phenomena, which you mark with the stamp of law. For though it is asserted that the idea of law develops itself with an inner impulse in the process of these phenomena; yet this may never be taken naturalistically, in the form of a physiological process; and you should know the idea of law, which is entirely different from these phenomena, before you will be able critically to analyze the phenomenon of law. And thus we see in fact the simplest principles of law pass more and more into discredit, and the rise of two factions which, each in turn, call lawful what the other condemns as unlawful. This antithesis is especially prominent in its application to the conceptions of personal property and capital punishment. One wants violated law to be revenged on the murderer, while to the other he is simply an object of pity, as a victim of atavism. Every existing law (jus constitutum) declares, that property must be protected by law, but the anarchist declares that in the ideal law (jus constituendum) all property must be avenged as theft. Though, therefore, without hesitation we concede that the dominion of symbolism points to a strong analogy between things "seen" and "unseen"; and though we readily grant that the naturalistic method, by historic comparative study, is productive of rich results also for the spiritual sciences; we emphatically deny that the study of the spiritual sciences can be entirely bound to the method of the natural sciences.

The cause of this difference is that the science of things "seen" is built up (1) from the sensuous perception or observation of the elements by our senses, and (2) from the logical knowledge of the relations which exist among these *elements* by our thinking. This, however, is impossible with the spiritual sciences. In the object of this science the same distinction must be made between the real elements and their relations. But, fitted to bring us in connection with the elements of the things "seen," our senses refuse to render this service with reference to the elements of the things "unseen." Moreover, it is self-evident that the logical knowledge of the relations, which by itself would be insufficient, becomes floating, while the elements among which they exist are not known. The plastic capacity of our mind, which, by means of the senses, is able to take up into itself the elements of the things "seen," remains here inactive, and the logical capacity is insufficient by itself to form conceptions and judgments. If, nevertheless, the effort is made to treat these spiritual sciences after the method of things "seen," a double self-deception is committed: unknowingly one changes the object and unconsciously one chooses his point of support in something not included in this method. The object is changed when, as in Theology for instance, not God but *religion* is made the object of investigation, and *religion* only in its expressions. And something is chosen as point of departure which this method does not warrant, when the notion or the idea of religion is borrowed from one's own subject.

The question therefore is, what renders the service in the spiritual sciences, which the representation-capacity in connection with the senses effects in things "seen." Since the object of the spiritual sciences is itself spiritual, and therefore amorphic, our senses not only, but the representation-capacity as well, render here no service. If no other means is substituted, the spiritual object remains beyond the reach of our scientific research, and spiritual phenomena must either be interpreted materialistically as the product of material causes, or remain agnostically outside of our science, even as the present English use of the word *science* prescribes. This result, however, would directly conflict with what experience teaches. Again and again it appears that there are all sorts of spiritual things which we *know* with far greater certainty than the facts which are brought us by the observation of things "seen." The sense of right, the sense of love, the feeling of hatred, etc., appear again and again to have a much more real existence in our consciousness than many a member of our own body. And though the idealism of Fichte in its own one-sidedness may have outrun itself, you nevertheless cease to be man when the reality of spiritual things is not more certain to you than what by investigation you know of plant and animal. If we maintain the etymological root-idea of science, in the sense that what is *known* forms its content, you maim your science when you deny it access to spiritual objects.

There is no other course therefore than to construct the spiritual sciences *from the subject itself;* provided you do not overlook that the subject of science is not this inquirer or that, but *the* human consciousness in general. It was seen that with visible things all distinguishing knowledge would be inconceivable, if the archetypic receptivity for these objects were not present, microcosmically, in the human consciousness. And with reference to spiritual objects it may in a like sense be postulated, that the presence of such an archetypic receptivity for right, love, etc., is also found in our consciousness. Otherwise, these would simply have no existence for us. But with this receptivity by itself the task is not ended. An action must be exerted by the object of your science upon this receptivity. It is indifferent for the present whether this action comes to you mediately or immediately. We do not become aware of right, for instance, as a poetic product of our own spirit, but as a power which dominates us. We perceive the working of that power even when our feeling for right is not aroused, as in a concrete case by an occurrence outside of us. Entirely independently of the revelation, violation or application of right in given circumstances, we know that we must do right; and this sense cannot be in us, except that power of right, to which we feel ourselves subjected, moves and touches us in our inner being. This becomes *possible* since we possess the receptivity for right, but is only *established* when right itself, as a power which dominates us, works upon that receptivity, and by it enters into our consciousness. The question lying back of this, whether right itself exists as universal, or is simply an expression for what exists in God, need not detain us. It is enough as long as we but know that in the taking-up of the object of the spiritual sciences as well as in the perception of the object of the natural sciences, we must distinguish *in the object* between the *element* and its *relations,* and in our consciousness between the corresponding perception of the element and examination of its relations. Always with this difference in view, that in the world of matter the element works upon our consciousness through the senses, which provokes the action of the power of representation; while with the spiritual sciences the element does not work upon the senses, neither through the representation, but in keeping with its spiritual nature affects our consciousness subjectively, and finds a receptivity in our subject which renders this emotion possible. And this emotion may be constant, and thus result in a permanent *sense,* or it may be accidental, in which case it falls under the conception of *inspiration.* In the transmission of the object of the spiritual sciences into our consciousness the same process takes place as in the discovery of our consciousness to the object of the natural sciences. In each case we take up into ourselves the element and the relations *differently.* In each case the receptivity must be present in us for the elements and for the relations. And in each case it is our *thinking* that makes us know the relations, while the perception of the element comes to us from the object itself. But these two sciences differ, in that the element of the visible world enters into our consciousness by a different way than the element of the spiritual world; the elements of the visible world working upon our powers of representation through the senses, while in entire independence of our senses and of any middle link known to us, the elements of the spiritual world affect our subject spiritually, and thus to our apprehension appear to enter immediately into our consciousness.

Thus the science of the spiritual object is derived from the subjectivity in man; but always in such a way, that here also our individual subject may never be taken independently of its organic relation to the general subject of the human race. The individual investigator who seeks to construct the spiritual sciences exclusively from his own subjective perceptions, virtually destroys thereby the very conception of science, and he will have no place for Philology, History, Political and Social sciences, etc. And though it might seem that this would destroy the subjective character of by far the greater part of the investigations within the domain of the spiritual sciences, it is *not* so. All study of law, for instance, would be inconceivable by a scholar who did not have the sense of right, however imperfectly, in himself. The study of language is only possible because we know the relations between the soul, thought and sound, from our own subject. Statesmanship can only be studied, because by nature man is an active partner in all public affairs. The starting-point and the condition for the prosecution of these sciences consequently always lie in our own subjective sense. In the vestibule of Psychology the psychic phenomena of animal life receive ever greater attention, which study offers no mean contribution to the knowledge of simple perceptions; but the leading scientists unanimously protest against the conclusions drawn from this for the knowledge of the social life of animals, such as those for instance of Sir John Lubbock for the world of ants. If the possibility might be born at any time to determine by analogy that there are psychological and sociological relations in the world of animals, it could not affect our position. Even then it would not be the world of animals that interprets to us the world of man, but on the contrary it would still be our own subjective sense, from which by analogy a world is concluded analogous to ours; just as Theologians have set us the example with respect to the world of angels.

Neither should we be misled by the fact that the objective character predominates in by far the larger part of the labor expended upon spiritual studies. If it is true that with Psychology for instance the physico-psychic experiment, and the comparative study of psychic expression and ethnological-historic investigations offer very considerable contributions to this department of science, it must not be forgotten that all these preliminary studies are impelled and directed by the psychic sense itself, and that after these preliminary studies the real construction of Psychology only commences. The more objective side of these studies has a twofold cause. First the relation which exists in the entire domain of this study between our soul and our body, and between the expression of our soul and the visible cosmos. And secondly the necessity of examining our own psychical life not by itself, but in organic relation to the psychical life of our human race. Here, however, appearance should not deceive us. Whatever we observe physically in this respect, or observe in cosmic expressions of the psychical life, does not really belong as such to the psychical sciences. And where out of our own individual subject we try to find a bridge by which to reach the subjective life of humanity, that bridge is never anything but a bridge, and it is not the bridge, but the psychical world which we reach by it, that claims our attention.

Distinction, therefore, must be made between *pure* and *mixed* spiritual sciences. Language, for instance, is a *mixed* spiritual science, because everything that pertains to the modulation of sounds, and the influence exerted on them by the general build of the body, and especially by the organs of breathing, articulation, and of hearing, is *somatic;* and the real psychical study is only begun when in this body of language the logos as its psychic element is reached. Thus also in history the building of cities, the waging of war, etc., is the body of history, and its *psychical* study only begins when we seek to reach the motives of human action which hide behind this somatic exterior, and to interpret the mysterious power which, partly by and partly without these motives, caused hundreds of persons, and whole nations, to run a course which, if marked by retrogression, suggests, nevertheless, the unwinding of a ball of yarn. And whether you trace these motives, or whether you study the mysterious succession of generations, your own subjective-psychical life is ever shown to be your starting-point, and empiricism leaves you in the lurch. This is most forcibly illustrated by Philosophy in the narrower sense, which, just because it tries logically to interpret, if not the cosmos itself, at least the image received of it by us, ever bears a strongly subjective character, and with its coryphaei, least of all, is able to escape this individual stamp. The philosophical premises thus obtained by individual heroes among thinkers, according to the impulse of their own subjectivity, are then borrowed by the lesser gods (dii minores), in virtue of spiritual "elective affinity" (Wahlverwandtschaft), and equally in accordance with their subjective predilection. And these premises will dominate the entire study of spiritual sciences in given circles, as far as these, with the empiric data as building material, devote themselves architecturally to the erection of the building.

Let no one, therefore, be blinded by the appearance of objectivity, brought about by the exhibition of these empiric data. It is sheer self-deception to think that we can ever succeed in making the spiritual sciences fit the same last as the natural sciences. Even with the latter, simple empiricism can never suffice. Everything that is material and can consequently be counted, weighed and measured, no doubt offers us, at least as far as these relations are concerned, a universally compulsory certainty, which, if observation be correct, bears an absolutely objective character. As soon, however, as you venture one step farther in this physical domain, and from these empiric data try to obtain a construction by which to discover among these scattered data a unity of thought, the process of an idea, or the progression from a first phenomenon to a result, you have at once crossed over from the physical into the psychical, the universally compulsory certainty leaves you, and you glide back into subjective knowledge, since you are already within the domain of the spiritual sciences. Thus to make it still appear that these philosophical interpretations and constructions, such as, for instance, the Descendenz-theorie, are merely logical deductions from empiric data, is deception. And this deception continues itself within the domain of the spiritual sciences, since here, also, one thinks that he starts out from empiric data, when these empiric data at best can only serve as means to enrich your investigation and verify it, but are never able to reveal or to interpret to you the psychic self, which, after all, is the real object of these sciences. The result of this dangerous self-deception is, that in all these departments detail and preliminary studies greatly flourish, while for the greater part the real study of these sciences lies fallow. For instance, uncommon energy is spent in the study of the expressions and phenomena of religious life in different ages and among different peoples, by which to formulate them with utmost accuracy, while religion itself, which is the real object in hand, is neglected. In the same way the manifestations of the moral life of nations are studied in their several periods and localities, but certainty about the power which determines the norm of moral life, and knowledge of the means of causing moral life to nourish, are more and more lost,—an atrophy, which applies as well to the study of psychology, of history, or law, etc., and which can only be understood from a false desire to materialize the psychical, as if matter could be treated on an equal footing with the psychic. This desire, in itself, is readily understood, since an outwardly compulsory certainty in this domain would be still more desirable to many people than in the domain of the natural sciences; and it is even measurably just, since the empiric data, which with the spiritual sciences also are at our service, were formerly all too grossly neglected. But, as soon as it tries to exalt itself into a method, it meets an inexorable obstacle in the nature and character of the psychic; on the one hand, because the psychical image assumes no form for us except in its subjective individualization; and, on the other hand, because the psychic can never be grasped in any other way than by our own psychic sense.

CHAPTER II

SCIENCE IMPAIRED BY SIN

Science and Sin

The subjective character which is inseparable from all spiritual science, in itself would have nothing objectionable in it, if it had not been given a most dangerous exponent by *sin.* If there were no sin, nor any of its results, the subjectivity of A would merely be a variation of the subjectivity in B. In virtue of the organic affinity between the two, their subjectivity would not be mutually antagonistic, and the sense of one would harmoniously support and confirm the sense of the other. In the days of the Reformation, the impulse that impelled so many thousands to reform was preponderantly subjective. But the fact that in all these subjects a common conviction aimed at a common end, accounts for the irresistible force that was born from the cooperation of these many subjectivities. But, alas, such is not the case in the domain of science. It is all too often evident, that in this domain the natural harmony of subjective expression is hopelessly broken; and for the feeding of scepticism this want of harmony has no equal. By an investigation of self and of the cosmos you have obtained a well-founded scientific conviction, but when you state it, it meets with no response from those who, in their way, have investigated with equally painstaking efforts; and not only is the unity of science broken, but you are shaken in the assurance of your conviction. For when you spoke your conviction, you did not mean simply to give expression to the insight of your own *ego*, but to the universal human insight; which, indeed, it ought to be, if it were wholly accurate.

But of necessity we must accept this hard reality, and in every theory of knowledge which is not to deceive itself, the fact of sin must henceforth claim a more serious consideration. Naturally the terrible phenomenon of sin in its entirety can have no place in these introductory sections. This belongs in Theology to the section of sin (locus de peccato). But it is in place here to state definitely that sin works its fatal effects also in the domain of our science, and is by no means restricted to what is thelematic (i.e. to the sphere of volition). What the Holy Scripture calls, in Ephesians iv. 17, 18, the "vanity of the mind," the "having the understanding darkened, because of the ignorance that is in them," even precedes the being "alienated from the life of God because of the hardening of their heart." Even without entering too deeply into the theological construction of this phenomenon, it may fearlessly be stated, (1) that *falsehood* in every sense and form is now in the world. And since more than one spiritual science hangs almost exclusively upon personal communications, and since in consequence of "falsehood" all absolute warrant for the trustworthiness of these data be wanting, it is sufficiently evident how greatly the certainty of these sciences suffers loss in consequence of sin. This will be more fully shown in our study of the conception of "truth." For the present this single suggestion must suffice. (2) Alongside of this actual falsehood we have the unintentional *mistake,* in observation and in memory, as well as in the processes of thought. These mistakes may be reduced by manifold verifications to a minimum in the material sciences, but can never be absolutely avoided, while in the spiritual sciences they practise such usury that escape from their influence is impossible. (3) *Self-delusion* and *self-deception* are no less important factors in this process, which renders nothing so rare as a scientific self-knowledge, a knowledge of your own person and character in more than a hypothetical form. Since almost all deeper studies of the spiritual sciences start out from the subjective image which we reflect of ourselves in our own consciousness, it needs no further proof how injuriously with the students of these sciences this self-delusion and self-deception must affect their studies and the final results. (4) A fourth evil resides in our *imagination.* In a normal condition the self-consciousness would be able at once accurately to indicate the boundary line between what enters into our consciousness from the real world without, and what is wrought in our consciousness by our imagination. But this boundary line is not only uncertain because of sin, but in strongly impassioned natures it is sometimes absolutely undiscoverable, so that phantasy and reality frequently pass into one another. The difficulty does not consist merely in the uncertainty or in the destruction of this boundary line; the imagination itself is in an abnormal condition. In one it works too weakly, in another it is over-excited. When it is over-excited, it retains its imperfect images, subjects our minds to the dominion of these images, falsifies thereby our self-consciousness, so that the deliverance of our inner selves is lost in this imagery. This imaginary world will then assert its dominion over us, and weaken the susceptibility in us for knowledge of ourselves and of the cosmos. (5) Equally injurious are the influences which this abnormal element in the condition of other minds exerts upon us, since this evil, which by itself is already enough of a hindrance, is thereby given a coefficient. Not only are we subject to these influences from infancy, but our education frequently tends intentionally to give them domination over us. Language also adds its contribution. All kinds of untruths have entered into our every-day speech, and the names and words we use unconsciously mould our self-consciousness. The proverbs and common sayings (Schlagworter) which from our youth up we have adopted as a sort of axioms affect us no less strongly. "Truth defends itself" is what the ancients said, and theologians of the ethical color take up the refrain, but do not perceive that by this very thing our outlook upon history is blurred and our sense of duty weakened. Even in theological interests such an adage is bound to effect its fallacious influence, in causing the transcendence of God to be lost to our sense in a mere pantheistic consideration. Add to this the several ideas and current expressions approved by the spirit of the times and inculcated in us, in the face of the fact that they are fallacious, and it becomes clear that our mind, which of itself lies ensnared in all manner of deceptions, is threatened to be entirely misled. (6) The effects worked by sin *through the body* claim here an equal consideration. In consequence of sin there is really no one in a normal bodily condition. All sorts of wrong and sickly commotions bestir themselves in our body and work their effect in our spiritual dispositions. They make one to tend strongly to the material, and another too strongly to the acosmic. They will make A a pessimist, and B a light-hearted optimist. They also modify the judgment upon history, for instance, according to the influences which we see at work upon persons. (7) Stronger still, perhaps, is the influence of the sin-disorganized *relationships of life,*—an influence which makes itself especially felt with the pedagogic and the social sciences. He who has had his bringing-up in the midst of want and neglect will entertain entirely different views of jural relationships and social regulations from him who from his youth has been bathed in prosperity. Thus, also, your view of civil right would be altogether different, if you had grown up under a despotism, than if you had spent the years of early manhood under the excesses of anarchism. To which (8) this is yet to be added, that the different parts of the content of our consciousness affect each other, and no one exists atomistically in his consciousness. This entails the result that the inaccuracies and false representations which you have gleaned from one realm of life, affect injuriously again the similarly mixed ideas which you have made your own from another domain. And so this evil indefinitely multiplies. Especially the leading thought which we have formed in that realm of life that holds our chiefest interests, exercises a mighty dominion upon the whole content of our consciousness, viz. our religious or political views,—what used to be called one's life- and world-view, by which the fundamental lines lie marked out in our consciousness. If, then, we make a mistake, or a single inaccurate move, how can it fail but communicate itself disastrously to our entire scientific study?

All this refers merely to the *formal* working of sin upon our mind. But this is not all. Sin also works upon our consciousness through an endless variety of moral motives. "Everybody preaches for his own parish" (*chacun preche pour sa paroisse*) is the simple expression of the undeniable truth that our outlook upon things is also governed by numerous personal *interests*. An Englishman will look upon the history of the Dutch naval battles with the British fleet very differently from a Netherlandish historian; not because each purposely desires to falsify the truth, but because both are unconsciously governed by national interests. A merchant will naturally hold different views concerning free trade, fair trade and protection, from the manufacturer, simply because self-interests and trade-interests unconsciously affect his views. A Roman Catholic has an entirely different idea of the history of the Reformation from a Protestant's, not because he purposely violates the truth, but simply because without his knowing it his church interests lead him away from the right path. Thus our physicians will readily be inclined to think differently from the patients about the free practice of medicine; the jurist will judge the jury differently from the free citizen; a man of noble birth will maintain a different attitude toward democratic movements from that of a man of the people. These are all moral differences, which are governed by self-interests, and which sometimes work consciously and lead to the violation of conscience, but which generally govern the result of our studies unconsciously and unknown to us.

No word has yet been said of that third class of influences which are essentially sinful because they result from the injurious effect worked by sin immediately *upon our nature.* The Christian Church confesses this to be the *darkening of the understanding;* which does not mean that we have lost the capacity of thinking logically, for as far as the impulse of its law of life is concerned, the logica has *not* been impaired by sin. When this takes place, a condition of insanity ensues. It must be granted that sin has weakened the *energy* of thought, so that in all the fulness of its glories this wondrous gift manifests itself only now and then in a rare athlete; and it must be acknowledged that sin all too often makes us the victims of a false and apparently logical, but in reality very unlogical, reasoning; but man as man, or, if you please, the universal human consciousness, is always able to overcome this sluggishness and to correct these mistakes in reasoning. No, the darkening of the understanding consists in something else, and would be better understood if we called it the *darkening of our consciousness.* Over against sin stands love, the sympathy of existence, and even in our present sinful conditions the fact is noteworthy, that where this sympathy is active you understand much better and more accurately than where this sympathy is wanting. A friend of children understands the child and the child life. A lover of animals understands the life of the animal. In order to study nature in its material operations, you must love her. Without this inclination and this desire toward the object of your study, you do not advance an inch. Hence there is nothing problematic in the fact that the Holy Scripture presents man in his original state before he fell as having both by sympathy and affinity a knowledge of nature, which is entirely lost by us. And this is significant in every department of study. Sin is the opposite of love. It has robbed us, speaking generally, of all seeking sympathy, only to leave us this seeking love within some single domain, and that in a very defective form. But, taken as a whole, standing over against the cosmos as its object, our mind feels itself isolated; the object lies outside of it, and the bond of love is wanting by which to enter into and learn to understand it. This fatal effect of sin must naturally find its deeper reason in the fact that the life harmony between us and the object has been disturbed. What once existed organically, exists now consequently as foreign to each other, and this *estrangement* from the object of our knowledge is the greatest obstacle in the way to our knowledge of it.

But there is more. The disorganization which is the result of sin consists not merely in the break in the natural life-harmony between us and the cosmos, but also in a break in the life-harmony in our *own selves*. More than one string has been strung upon the instrument of our heart, and each string has more than one tone. And its condition is normal only when the different motives and tones of our heart harmoniously affect one another. But such is no longer the case. Disharmony rules in our innermost parts. The different senses, in the utterances of our inner selves, affect each other no longer in pure accord, but continually block the way before each other. Thus discord arises in our innermost selves. Everything has become disconnected. And since the one no longer supports the other, but antagonizes it, both the whole and its parts have lost their purity. Our sense of the good, the true, the beautiful, of what is right, of what is holy, has ceased to operate with accuracy. In themselves these senses are weakened, and in their effect upon each other they have become mixed. And since it is impossible, in the spiritual sciences, to take one forward step unless these senses serve us as guides, it readily appears how greatly science is obstructed by sin.

And finally, the chiefest harm is the ruin, worked by sin, in those data, which were at our command, for obtaining the knowledge of God, and thus for forming the conception of the whole. Without the sense of God in the heart no one shall ever attain unto a knowledge of God, and without love, or, if you please, a holy sympathy for God, that knowledge shall never be rich in content. Every effort to prove the existence of God by so-called evidences must fail and has failed. By this we do not mean that the knowledge of God must be mystic; for as soon as this knowledge of God is to be scientifically unfolded, it must be reproduced from our thinking consciousness. But as our science in no single instance can take one forward step, except a bridge is built between the subject and the object, it cannot do so here. If thus in our sense of self there is no sense of the existence of God, as if in our spiritual existence there is no bond which draws us to God, and causes us in love to go out unto him, all science is here impossible. If, now, experience shows that this sense has not worn away *entirely,* and that this impulse has not ceased *altogether,* but that, in virtue of its own motive, sin has weakened this sense to such an extent as to render it oftentimes unrecognizable, and has so falsified this impulse, that all kinds of religious emotions go hand in hand with hatred of God, it is plain that every scientific reproduction of the knowledge of God must fail, as long as this sense remains weakened and this impulse falsified in its direction. From which it follows at the same time that the knowledge of the cosmos as a whole, or, if you please, philosophy in a restricted sense, is equally bound to founder upon this obstruction wrought by sin. Suppose that you had succeeded in attaining an adequate knowledge of all the parts of the cosmos, the product of these results would not yet give you the adequate knowledge of the whole. The whole is always something different from the combination of its parts. First because of the entirely new questions which the combination of the whole presents: questions as to the origin and end of the whole; questions as to the categories which govern the object in its reflection in your consciousness; questions as to absolute being, and as to what *non*-cosmos is. In order to answer these questions, you must subject the whole cosmos to yourself, your own self included; in order to do this in your consciousness you must step out from the cosmos, and you must have a starting-point ($\delta\acute{o}\varsigma$ $\mu o\iota$ $\pi o\hat{v}$ $\sigma\tau\hat{\omega}$) in the *non*-cosmos; and this is altogether impossible as long as sin confines you with your consciousness to the cosmos.

From which it by no means follows, that you should sceptically doubt all science, but simply that it will not do to omit the fact of sin from your theory of knowledge. This would not be warranted if sin were only a thelematic conception and therefore purely ethic; but much less, now, since immediately as well as mediately, sin modifies so largely all those data with which you have to deal in the intellectual domain and in the building-up of your *science*. Ignorance wrought by sin is the most difficult obstacle in the way of all true science.

Truth

In a preceding section reference has already been made to the grave significance to scientific investigation of the conception which one forms of "truth." This significance can now be considered more closely in relation to the fact of sin. It will not do to say that seeking after truth is directed exclusively against the possibility of mistake. He who in good faith has made a mistake, has been *inaccurate* but not *untrue*. Falsehood is merely a milder expression for *the lie,* and the search after truth has no other end in view than escape from the fatal power of what Christ called the lie ($\tau\grave{o}$ $\psi\epsilon\hat{v}\delta o\varsigma$) This does not imply that "the mistake" does not stand equally related to sin. The former section tried to prove the contrary. But if the unconscious mistake stands in causal relation to sin, this relation is entirely different from what it is with the lie. The Holy Scripture teaches us to recognize an unholy principle in the lie, from which a caricature (Zerrbild) of all things is born, and the fatherhood of this lie is pointed out to us in Satan. In John viii. 44, we read: "The devil speaketh a lie—for he is a liar and the father thereof." This theological explanation need not detain us now, but it cannot be denied that a false representation of the real has made its way into almost every department of life; that with a closer investigation these several false representations appear to stand in an organic relation; and that a hidden impelling power is at work within this entire domain of the false and the untrue, which arouses our righteous indignation and bears a sinful character for our consciousness. The form of this spuriousness is not constant. It often happens that certain general ideas govern public opinion for a long time and then become discredited; that they maintain themselves a little longer with the less educated masses; and finally pass away altogether, so that he who still holds them is out of date. But with this shedding of its skin the serpent does not die. And Proteus-like, the false and untrue reappear in a new form, and the battle of life and death between truth and falsehood begins anew. Obviously, therefore, the lie is no mistake, nor a temporary dominating untruth, but a power, which affects injuriously the consciousness of man, and not merely puts into his hands phantasy for reality, and fiction for history, but intentionally brings into our mind a representation of existing things which proscribes reality, with the avowed aim of estranging us from it.

In this condition of affairs a holy interest is at stake in this struggle for *the truth.* This conflict does not aim at the correction of simple mistakes in the representation, neither does it combat prejudice, nor rectify inaccuracies; but it arrays itself against a power, which ever in a new form entangles our human consciousness in that which is false, makes us servants to falsehood, and blinds us to reality. Thus the saying of Christ, "I am the truth," has a deep significance; since he alone possessed such spiritual power of resistance that he was able to withdraw himself absolutely from the dominion of the false. The word "lie" itself confirms this interpretation. In our daily life this evil word is almost never used in circles where the lie is contraband; while on the other hand, in circles which, alas, admit the lie as a common weapon of defence, the contention for true or untrue is constantly in order with the reproachful epithet of "you lie." If you think of life in heaven, you perceive at once that every effort to establish truth falls away. Who would enter the arena in behalf of truth, in a place where the lie is not conceivable? Neither can truth have had a place among the conceptions which were originally common to man in the state of his innocence. As long as sin had not entered the heart, there could be no impulse to defend truth against the lie which had as yet no existence. In entire accordance with this the Scriptural narrative of the fall presents Satan as the first to whisper the lie, that what God had said was *not* true, and that moment marks the beginning of the conflict *for* the truth.

Hence it is none too strongly said, that the struggle for "truth" is legitimately only a result of sin. Science is entirely different from truth. If you imagine our human development without sin, the impulse to know and understand the cosmos, and by this knowledge to govern it, would have been the same; but there would have been no search after *truth,* simply because there could have been no danger of relying upon falsehood as a result of investigation. In our sinful condition, however, while the human consciousness is constantly ensnared in falsehood, from the very nature of the case science has the twofold calling, not only to investigate and understand the object, but also to banish the false representations of it.

But this is easier said than done, and as soon as you leave the material domain you see different men, who from their point of view are honest in their purposes, and whose talents for investigation are fairly equal, arrive at as many different and sometimes directly opposite results. This is less to be feared in the domain of pure matter, at least as long as one confines himself to the mere statement of what has been observed, and draws no inferences from his observations. As soon, however, as investigations reach the point where the reinforced eye and ear are no longer able to observe with absolute certainty, disputes may arise, though this has nothing to do with falsehood; and when, after all the applause that hailed Dr. Koch's preparation for tuberculosis, it was shown that this preparation not only failed of its purpose, but even caused injurious effects, he *had* to acknowledge it. When facts spoke, illusion was ended. It is entirely different, however, when one comes in contact with the *non*-material domain of life. The science of statistics, on which it was thought we could so safely build, is shown to be largely untrustworthy. And when we enter the domain of the real spiritual sciences, the most objective observation, such as the examination of documents, and the statement of a few tangible facts, are scarcely ended, but ideas everywhere separate, and there is no more objective certainty to compel universal homage, which can bring about a unity of settled result. This is not found in the domain of psychology; or of philosophy in the narrower sense; or of history; or of law; or in any spiritual domain whatever. Because here the subjective factor becomes preponderant; and this subjective factor is dependent upon the antithesis between falsehood and truth; so that both the insight into the facts and the structure which one builds upon this insight must differ, and at length become, first contrary and then contradictory.

The fatality of the antithesis between falsehood and truth consists in this, that every man from his point of view claims the truth for himself, and applies the epithet of "untrue" to everything that opposes this. Satan began by making God the liar and by presenting himself as the speaker of truth. And for our demonstration this applies more emphatically still to the custom among men; especially since in this section we speak exclusively of those persons who devote themselves to scientific research. Though we grant that in science also wilful mutilation of facts is not altogether wanting, it must be accepted, as a rule, that he who announces himself as a man of science is disposed to take things as they are, and to deal with them accordingly. Nobody writes a scientific thesis with the purpose of propagating falsehood; the purpose of all scientific labor is to champion the truth. And from this very fact it follows that where two scientific men arrive at directly opposite results, each will see the truth in his own result, and falsehood in the result of his opponent, and both will deem it their duty to fight in the defence of what seems to them the truth, and to struggle against what seems to them the lie. If this concerns a mere point of detail, it has no further results; but if this antithesis assumes a more universal and radical character, school will form itself against school, system against system, world-view against world-view, and two entirely different and mutually exclusive representations of the object, each in organic relation, will come at length to dominate whole series of subjects. From both sides it is said: "Truth is with us, and falsehood with you." And the notion that science can settle this dispute is of course entirely vain, for we speak of two all-embracing representations of the object, both of which have been obtained as the result of very serious scientific study.

If the objection be raised that science has cleared away whole series of fallacious representations, we repeat that this concerned the forms only in which the lie for a time lay concealed, but that that same lie, and therefore the same antithesis against truth, is bound to raise its head in new forms with indestructible power. All sorts of views, which for centuries have been considered dead, are seen to rise again resuscitated in our age. As far as principle is concerned and the hidden impulse of these antitheses, there is nothing new under the sun; and he who knows history and men, sees the representatives of long-antiquated world-views walk our streets to-day, and hears them lecture from the platform. The older and newer philosophers, the older and newer heresies, are as like each other, if you will pardon the homely allusion, as two drops of water. To believe that an absolute science in the above-given sense can ever decide the question between truth and falsehood is nothing but a criminal self-deception. He who affirms this, always takes science as it proceeds from his own subjective premises and as it appears to him, and therefore *eo ipso* stigmatizes every scientific development which goes out from other premises as pseudo-science, serviceable to the lie. The antithesis of principles among Theism, Pantheism, and Atheism dominates all the spiritual sciences in their higher parts, and as soon as the students of these sciences come to defend what is true and combat what is false, their struggle and its result are entirely governed by their subjective starting-point.

In connection with the fact of sin, from which the whole antithesis between truth and falsehood is born, this phenomenon presents itself in such a form that one recognizes the fact of sin, and that the other denies it or does not reckon with it. Thus what is normal to one is absolutely abnormal to the other. This establishes for each an entirely different standard. And where both go to work from such subjective standards, the science of each *must* become entirely different, and the unity of science is gone. The one cannot be forced to accept what the other holds as truth, and what according to his view he has found to be truth.

Thus, taken by itself, the triumph of Scepticism ought to result from this, and Pilate's exclamation, "What is truth," should be the motto of highest wisdom. But the process of history is a protest against this. However often Scepticism has lifted up its head, it has never been able to maintain a standing for itself, and with unbroken courage and indefatigable power of will thinking humanity has ever started out anew upon the search after truth. And this fact claims an explanation.

Wisdom

The threatening and of itself almost necessary dominion of Scepticism, stranded first upon the ever more or less problematical phenomenon which is called *Wisdom*. In order to appreciate the meaning of this phenomenon, the combination "philo-sophia" should not claim our first attention, since it identifies "wisdom" too greatly with "science," and the leading characteristic of "wisdom" is that it is *not* the result of discursive thought. An uneducated and even an illiterate man may convey in large measure the impression of being a *wise* man; while, on the other hand, scientifically developed persons often fall short in wisdom of sense. The etymology of the words, by which the conception of "wisdom" is expressed in different languages, makes this distinction between a scientific disposition and a disposition for wisdom to be clearly seen. Wisdom (sapientia) and science (scientia) are not the same. *Sapere* means to taste, to try, and in its metaphoric use points to a knowledge of things which expresses itself not theoretically, but practically, and works intuitively. The Greek word σόφος (wisdom), in connection with σαφής, σαπρός, and perhaps with ὀπός, belongs evidently to the same root, and points also to a radical-word which indicated the action of *smelling* or *tasting*. The Germanic word "wise" takes no account with the origin of this peculiar knowledge, but with its outcome. *Wisel* is the well-known name of the queen of the bees, who, taking the lead, by this superiority governs the entire swarm. Here also the *practical* element of knowledge appears in the foreground. He is wise who knows and sees how things must go, and who for this reason is followed by others. With the limited development of Semitic etymology, the Hebrew expression חכם is less clear, but from the description which the Chokmatic writings give us of this "wisdom," it appears the more convincingly that the Hebrew understood this wisdom to be something entirely different from what we call scientific development, and in this connection thought rather of a practical-intuitive understanding. The derivation of חכה, which means to *cleave to something,* would agree very well with this, as an indication of the spirit's sympathy with the object from which this Chokmatic knowledge is born. Phrases which are in common use with us, also, such as, for instance: "You have wisely left it alone," "When the wine is in the man, wisdom is in the can"; "He is a wise man"; or the Bible-text: "If any of you lack wisdom, let him ask of God"; all agree entirely with this etymological result. The root-idea always appears to be, that one possesses a certain natural understanding of the nature and process of things, and understands the art of accommodating himself to them in practical life. Wisdom has nothing to do, therefore, with intellectual abstraction, but clings immediately to the reality, proceeds from it and works out an effect upon it. But again, it is not artistic skill, nor what is called talent, for it is not the *action* which proceeds from the *insight* but the *insight* itself which stands in the foreground. Wisdom is the quiet possession of insight which imparts power, and is at the disposal of the subject, even when this subject is not called to action. Wisdom is also distinguished from artistic skill and talent, in that it bears an *universal* character. He who excels in a certain department of science is not *wise,* neither he *wise* who excels in a certain trade. Such an one-sided development of skill is rather opposed to the root-idea of wisdom. He who is wise, is *centrally* wise, i.e. he has a *general* disposition of mind which, whatever comes, enables him to have an accurate view of things, in conformity with which to choose and act with tact and with discretion. As the result, therefore, it may be stated that entirely apart from the development of science, there is in certain persons an aprioristic, not acquired, general *insight* which in its efficient, practical excellence shows itself in harmony with the reality of things.

But if among your acquaintances you meet with but few persons who have this insight to such an extent as to entitle them to the epithet of "wise folk," all the others are not *fools;* and yet only this antithetical conception of *foolishness* elucidates sufficiently the exact conception of *wisdom.* A *fool* and a *lunatic* are not the same. An *insane* man is he whose consciousness works in the wrong way, so that all normal insight has become impossible for him. A *fool,* on the other hand, is he whose consciousness works normally, but who himself stands so crookedly over against the reality of things, that he makes mistake upon mistake and constantly makes the wrong move on the chess-board of life. He acts foolishly who makes an evident mistake in his representation of reality, and who in consequence of his noticeable lack of accurate insight, chooses the very thing that will serve him a wrong end. He lacks the proper relation to the reality, and this accounts for his mistakes. Between these "wise folk" and these "fools" stands the great mass of humanity, who in all possible gradations form the transition from the wise to the foolish; while among these general masses is found what used to be called a *sound mind, common sense, le sens commun.* This implies something that does not scale the heights of *wisdom,* but which, nevertheless, maintains a relation to it and offers a general basis for it. We grant that, more especially since the close of the last century, this expression "common sense" has been used synonymously with that analogous "public opinion" in which the weakened form of Rationalism reflected itself, and that this spectre has repeatedly been evoked to banish idealism, to mock the faith, and to hush every nobler feeling; but this was simple abuse. Originally, "common sense" meant by no means the iteration of the program of a particular school, but, on the contrary, a certain accuracy of tact, by which, in utter disregard of the pretensions of the schools, public opinion followed a track which turned neither too far to the right nor to the left. This weakened wisdom, which generally directs the course of life, occasionally forsook public opinion, and this gave foolishness the upper hand, and mad counsels free courses; but, in the long run, common sense almost always gained the day. And in individual persons it is found, that if the particular "wise folk" be excluded, one class is inclined to foolishness, while another class remains subject to the influence of a weakened wisdom, and the latter are said to be the people of *common sense;* a term which does not so much express a personal gift (*charisma*), as the fact that they sail in safe channels.

If the phenomenon itself be thus sufficiently established, the question arises, how, culminating in *wisdom* and finding its antithesis in *folly,* this phenomenon of "common sense" is to be psychologically interpreted. It is not the fruit of early training, it is not the result of study, neither is it the effect of constant practice. Though it is granted that these three factors facilitate and strengthen the clear operations of this common sense and of this wisdom, the phenomenon itself does not find its origin in them. Two young men, brought up in the same social circle, of like educational advantages and of similar experience, will differ widely in point of wisdom; one will become a wise man, while with the other life will be a constant struggle. Thus we have to do with a certain capacity of the human mind, which is not introduced into it from without, but which is present in that mind as such, and abides there. The Dutch language has the beautiful word "be-*sef*–fen" (to sense), which etymologically is connected with the root of *sap*-ientia, and indicates a certain immediate affinity to that which exists outside of us. In this sense prudence and wisdom are innate; not an innate conception, but an insight which proceeds immediately from the affinity in which by nature we stand to the world about us, and to the world of higher things. Both point to a condition in which, if we may so express it, man *felt* Nature's pulse beat; in which he shared the life of every animate thing, and so perceived and understood it; and in which, moreover, he also apprehended the higher life not as something foreign to himself, but as "sensing" it in his own sense of existence. Or if we look ahead, both phenomena lie in the line, at whose end the seeing is reached, "the knowing as we are known." The energy of this intuition is now broken. With some it seems entirely lost, and these are called "fools." With some others it still works comparatively with great effect, for which reason they are called, preeminently, the *wise* folk. And between these extremes range the people of common sense; so called because in them something is still found of the old, sound, primitive force (Urkraft) of the human mind.

Now it is readily seen what a formidable dam wisdom and common sense prove against the destructive floods of Scepticism. If there were no other way open to knowledge than that which discursive thought provides, the subjective character which is inseparable from all higher science, the uncertainty which is the penalty of sin, and the impossibility between truth and falsehood to decide what shall be objectively compulsory would encourage Scepticism to strike ever deeper root. But since an entirely different way of knowledge is disclosed to us by *wisdom* and its allied *common sense,* which, independent of scientific investigation, has a starting-point of its own, this intuitive knowledge, founded on fixed perceptions given with our consciousness itself, offers a saving counterpoise to Scepticism. For now we have a certain insight, and on the ground of this insight a relative certainty, which has no connection with the discursive conflict between truth and falsehood, and which, being constantly confirmed in the fiery test of practical application in daily life, gives us a starting-point by which the conviction maintains itself in us that we are able to grasp the truth of things. And since this *wisdom* and *common sense* determined those very issues and principles of life, against which Scepticism directs its most critical and important attacks, we find in this phenomenon, so mysterious in itself, a saving strength which enables the human mind to effect its escape from the clutches of Scepticism. This wisdom can never supersede discursive thought, nor can it take the place of empiricism, but it has the general *universal* tendency to exclude follies from the processes of discursive thought, and in empirical investigation to promote the accuracy of our tact.

In answer to the objection that it is difficult to harmonize this interpretation of "wisdom" with the conception of σοφία in our word "philosophy" (φιλοσοφία) we observe that for a just criticism of this apparent objection we must go back to the original conception of "wisdom" as held by the Greeks, and to the most ancient meaning of the combination of φιλεῖν with this word. As for "wisdom," we refer first of all to the noteworthy sentence of Heraclitus: σοφίη ἀλη θέα λέγειν καὶ ποιεῖν κατὰ φύσιν ἐπαΐοντας, i.e. "Wisdom consists in knowing how to speak the truth, and how to live according to nature," in which the last words especially indicate that "wisdom" is taken as ripening from a natural instinct, while the verb "to live" (ποιεῖν) exhibits its practical character. With Thales only it was thought that "wisdom" also bore a somewhat theoretical character. See Plutarch's *Life of Solon,* 3, 9: "And, on the whole, it is likely that the *conception* of wisdom was at that time carried further by Solon alone, in speculation, than its significance in common use; but in the case of others the name 'wisdom' arose from its use in civil affairs." What Xenophon narrates concerning Socrates leads to the same conclusion. See Xen. *Mem.* III. 9, 4: "(Socrates) did not separate (i.e. distinguish between) wisdom and prudence," even in this sense that "Those who do not act rightly he considered neither wise nor prudent." Undoubtedly with Plato it is already "A possession of the truth in contemplation" (p. 414, *b*), and with Aristotle, "The science of things divine and human"; but this is not the original conception. With the oldest philosophers we do not find the mention of a philosophy which is the result of investigation. Their philosophy is rather an exposition of their insight into the relation of things, in the elaboration of which they deal more freely with their phantasy than with empiricism. Even in the word "theory" this ancient meaning of the wisdom-conception is still active. Etymologically, "theoria" refers to *intuition,* and as such it has nothing in common with the idea which we attach to the theoretical.

Faith

Even more effectually than "wisdom" Scepticism is counteracted by "faith" (πίστις). Faith in this connection is taken formally, and hence considered quite apart from all content. By "faith" here, then, we do not mean the "faith in Christ Jesus" in its saving efficacy for the sinner, nor yet the "faith in God" which is fundamental to all religion, but that formal function of the life of our soul which is fundamental to every fact in our human consciousness. The common antithesis between "faith and knowledge" places the content obtained by faith in contrast to the content obtained by knowledge. Thus we face two dissimilar magnitudes, which are susceptible neither of comparison nor of amalgamation. We encounter iron and clay, as Daniel pictures it; elements which refuse to intermingle. To take a position with reference also to this antithesis, it is necessary that we go back to the formal function of faith, and investigate whether this function does or does not exhibit an *universal* character. For if it does, this universal function of faith must also influence that particular function by which the scientific result is obtained, and the extent is traceable to which the function of faith is able to exert itself, as well as the point where its working stops. We purposely consider this function of faith, next to wisdom, as a similar reaction against Scepticism. All Scepticism originates from the impression that our certainty depends upon the result of our scientific research. Since, however, this result constantly appears to be governed by subjective influences, and is affected by the conflict between truth and falsehood which is the result of sin, there is no defence against Scepticism except in the subject itself. The defence against Scepticism which the subject provides, can prove no benefit to our science, except it is evident that this defence bears no individual-subjective character; but that in its real significance it belongs to the subject as such, and may therefore be called subjective in a general and communal sense. And faith exhibits this character.

In the explanation of this two difficulties present themselves, which we must not allow to overshadow us. The first difficulty is, that faith is a conception which has been introduced into our common speech, especially from the New Testament, and has received thereby a religious, and in a more restricted sense a soteriological, stamp. Thus understood, this conception has no place in our Erkenntniss-theorie, and the appearance is given that faith bears no universal character at all. The second difficulty is, that profane literature almost never uses the conception of faith technically, and hence attaches no definite meaning to it. The old philosophy, for instance, never deals with faith as with a special function of the soul. It appears, however, as if Pythagoras attached something more to this conception and that he classified it, as we learn in *Theol. Arithm.* X., p. 60, how the Pythagoreans "in their mystical explanations called it (i.e. $\pi i \sigma \tau \iota s$) at one time the world; at another, the heavens; still again, the universe; then again, fate and eternity; and, yet again, might, faith, necessity"; yet this appears to be the case in a very superficial sense only, since of this $\pi i \sigma \tau \iota s$ at once this more exact explanation is given in *Theol. Arithm.*, p. 61: "The number Ten indeed is called belief (or faith), since according to Philolaos by (the number) Ten, and its parts, which have to do primarily with realities, we have a clear idea of Belief." It may not be denied that Phillaos saw that in some instances faith stands on a line with $\dot{a} \nu \dot{a} \gamma \kappa \eta$ (necessity); but he makes no mention of a general application of this conception.

Neither of these two difficulties, however, should prevent us from making a more general application of this conception. Not the difficulty derived from the Holy Scriptures, since Heb. xi. 1 anticipates our wish to restore faith to its more general meaning. There we read that faith is "the assurance ($\dot{\upsilon} \pi \dot{o} \sigma \tau \alpha \sigma \iota s$) of things hoped for, the proving ($\ddot{\epsilon} \lambda \epsilon \gamma \chi o s$) of things not seen." Thus faith is here taken neither in an exclusively religious sense, much less in a soteriological significance, but very generally as an "assurance" and "proving" of objects which escape our perception, either because they do not exist ($\tau \dot{a} \ \dot{\epsilon} \lambda \pi \iota \zeta \dot{o} \mu \epsilon \nu \alpha$), or because they do not show themselves ($\tau \dot{a} \ \mu \dot{\eta} \ \beta \lambda \epsilon \pi \dot{o} \mu \epsilon \nu \alpha$). Far from excluding, therefore, a more general interpretation, the Scripture itself calls our attention to it. And as for the backwardness of profane literature in defining this conception more exactly, the above-quoted saying of the Pythagoreans shows that the idea of taking up faith as a link in a demonstration was not entirely foreign to the ancients; and this appears stronger still from what Plutarch writes (*Mor. 756, b*), "that in divine things no demonstration($\dot{a} \pi \dot{o} \delta \epsilon \iota \xi \iota s$) is to be obtained," and that it is not needed, "For the traditional and ancient faith is sufficient; than which it is not possible to express nor discover a clearer proof; but this is, in itself, a sort of underlying common foundation and support for piety,"—words which, although limited to the domain of religion, and rather used in connection with tradition, nevertheless betray a definite agreement with the teaching of Heb. xi. 1, and place faith as the ground of certainty over against "assurance."

Neither the etymology of $\pi i \sigma \tau \iota s$ and the words synonymous with it in other languages, nor the use of these words, prove any obstacle in the way of this general application. Faith with the root-idea of $\pi \epsilon i \theta \omega$ (to persuade), and in connection with the derivatives $\pi \iota \sigma \tau \dot{o} s$, $\pi \iota \sigma \tau \dot{o} \omega$, $\pi \epsilon \pi o i \theta \eta \sigma \iota s$, $\dot{a} \pi \epsilon \iota - \eta \theta \dot{\epsilon} \omega$, $\dot{a} \pi \epsilon \iota \theta \dot{\eta} s$, and $\dot{a} \pi \epsilon i \theta \epsilon \iota \alpha$, points etymologically to an action by which our consciousness is forced to surrender itself, and to hold something for true, to confide in something and to obey something. Here, then, we have nothing but a certain power which is exercised upon our consciousness, to which it is forced to subject itself. Upon our consciousness, which is first unstable, uncertain, and tossed about, a check is placed which puts an end to uncertainty. There is a restraint imposed on us from which we cannot escape. Or, as far as our consciousness itself desires this stability, this "underlying foundation and support'($\H\H\delta\rho\alpha$ $\kappa\alpha\iota$ $\beta\alpha\sigma\iota\varsigma$ $\upsilon\phi\epsilon\sigma\tau\H\omega\sigma\alpha$), as Plutarch expressed it, or, as Heb. xi. 1 states it, this "assurance" and this "proving" are offered us. Where the action of the $\pi\epsilon\iota\theta\epsilon\iota\nu$ (persuasion) is ended, certainty is obtained. In the middle voice $\pi\epsilon\iota\theta\epsilon\sigma\theta\alpha\iota$ (to be persuaded) expresses the function of the soul by which it establishes itself in that stability. And faith therefore may express this certainty itself, as well as the action by which I grasp it. The same root-idea lies in הֶאֱמִין. אָמֵן (amen) is that which stands fast and does not change. The Hiphil expresses that by which this certainty is born in us. And our *believing* comes from a different source, but it allows the self-same universal tendency. With the Latin *lubet,* allied to the Sanscrit *lubh,* which means to appropriate something to oneself, and which stands in immediate connection with the Dutch words *lieven* and *loven,* it points to a cleaving to something, to holding fast to something, and to being linked to it by an inner sympathy. Thus in *be-lieving* the relation is more prominent than in $\pi\iota\sigma\tau\iota\varsigma$ or in אֱמוּנָה, but that relation is taken as something not uncertain, but certain. He who cleaves to something holds himself fast to it, leans upon and trusts in it; while in this *believing* lies the fine secondary meaning, that this cleaving unto, this holding fast to, is accomplished by an inward impulse. And if the etymology of any of these expressions does not prevent a more general application of this word, the difficulty presented in the accepted use of these words is equally insignificant. Not only was this $\pi\iota\sigma\tau\iota\nu$ $\H\epsilon\chi\epsilon\iota\nu$ (to have faith), a current term in Greek, applied to every department of life, and the tendency of almost wider still (see, for instance, Deut. xxviii. 66, Judges xi. 20, etc.), but, what is more noteworthy, in our Christian society the use of the word "to believe" is limited so little to the religious and soteriological domain, that even more than "to have faith" the term "to believe" has become common property for every relation.

There is no objection, therefore, to the use of the term *faith* for that function of the soul ($\psi\upsilon\chi\H\eta$) by which it obtains certainty directly and immediately, without the aid of discursive demonstration. This places faith over against "demonstration"; but *not* of itself over against *knowing.* This would be so, if our knowledge and its content came to us exclusively by observation and demonstration, but, as we have tried to prove, this is not so. To know and *knowledge,* to know and *understanding,* are not the same. I *know* all those things the existence of which, together with some relations of this existence, is actual fact to me. No demonstration can ever establish with mathematical certainty the question that governs your whole life,—who it is that has begotten you; and yet under ordinary circumstances no one hesitates to declare, "I know that this man is my father." For though men may talk here of the theory of probabilities, it is not at all to the point. A proof proves only what it proves definitely and conclusively, and everything which in the end misses this conclusive character is not obtained by your demonstration but *from elsewhere;* and this *other* source of certainty is the very point in question. Or rather,—for even now we do not speak with sufficient emphasis,--this other source, which we call faith, is the *only* source of certainty, equally for what you prove definitely and conclusively by demonstration.

That this is not generally so understood can only be explained from the fact that, in the search after the means at our command by which to obtain knowledge, the investigation is abandoned before it is finished. The building is examined, and its foundation, and sometimes even the piles that are underneath, but the ground on which the lowest points of these piles rest is not explored. Or to state it in another way, let us say that the need is felt of a continuous line drawn from the outermost point in the periphery of the object to the centre of your *ego;* but when the *ego* is as nearly reached as possible, the distance which still separates us from it is not bridged; we simply vault the gulf. And this is not lawful, because it is illogical. Of necessity a chain must fall when a single link is wanting; for the two links which it ought to connect lose their point of union.

This comes out at once in the self-consciousness by which we say *I.* A child, in which self-consciousness has not yet awakened, speaks of itself in the third person. There is some thinking in the child, and a certain amount of knowledge, but it is not yet his possession. There is a property, but the owner is still anonymous. Meanwhile, this self-consciousness is an impenetrable mystery to us. To say that it originates through comparison is a vain attempt to soothe oneself with words, for the very subject to be compared is here in question. Neither can it be said that self-consciousness is identical with the nature of our soul, for then it ought also to be active in the child, and ought to stay with us under all circumstances of life, and that sort of insanity by which one thinks himself to be another would annul our human nature. Self-consciousness, therefore, is an entirely unaccountable phenomenon in the life of the soul, which reveals its activity only at a certain age, which sometimes may slumber, and may lose itself for years in insanity. It is a phenomenon that stays by us in the unconscious condition of our sleep, for in our dreams also it is ourselves who suffer anxiety and all things move themselves about our person. Neither is this self-consciousness an accidental something to that science which we seek to obtain. On this self-consciousness hangs the subject that investigates, and without that subject no investigation is conceivable. He with whom this self-consciousness is still wanting is, like the child, unable to separate himself from the object, and equally unable to draw conclusions from his inward perceptions. Thus *the starting-point* actually lies in this self-consciousness, and there must ever be a gap if this self-consciousness be not duly considered. From this it also follows, that without faith you miss the starting-point of all knowledge. The expression, "you must believe in yourself," has certainly been abused in humanistic circles to weaken both the denial of ourselves and our faith in God, but it is actually the case that he who does not begin *by believing in himself* cannot progress a single step. Northing but faith can ever give you certainty in your consciousness of the existence of your *ego;* and every proof to the *sum,* which you might endeavor to furnish by the exhibition of your *will,* or if need be by the revelation of your *ill will,* etc., will have no force of demonstration, except before all things else, on the ground of faith, the knowledge of your *ego* is established for yourself. In the *cogito ergo sum* the logical fault has indeed long since been shown. The *ego,* which is to be proved in the *sum,* is already assumed in the premise by the *cogito.*

But the indispensableness of faith goes much farther, and it may safely be said that with the so-called exact sciences there is no investigation, nor any conclusion conceivable except in so far as the observation in the investigation and the reasoning in the conclusion are grounded in faith. No play is intended here on the word "faith." Faith is taken by us in its most real sense. By faith you are sure of all those things of which you have a *firm conviction,* but which conviction is *not* the outcome of observation or demonstration. This may result from indolence by which you apply the much easier and ever ready faith, where the more arduous duty of observation and demonstration is demanded. But this is the abuse of faith, which should ever be reproved. In this abuse, however, the formal character of faith remains inviolate. Properly used or misused, faith is and always will be a means of becoming firmly convinced of a thing, and of making this conviction the starting-point of conduct, while for this conviction no empirical or demonstrative proof is offered or found. Faith can never be anything else but an immediate act of our consciousness, by which certainty is established in that consciousness on any point outside of observation or demonstration. "The ground on which your faith rests," and "the ulterior *ground* of your faith," are often spoken of, but in all such expressions faith itself is not meant, but only its content, and this does not concern us now. Fiath here is taken merely as the means or instrument by which to possess certainty, and as such it not only needs no demonstration, but allows none. And in that sense we referred to it in the first place, as certainty concerning our *ego* in our own self-consciousness, which precedes every act of thought or observation, and which can only be established in us by faith, or, if you please, is not acquired by us, but is a *received* good, of which no account can be given.

This is equally true of the starting-point of perception. All perception takes place through the senses, whether you allow them to act naturally, or whether you reinforce them by a technical apparatus. The case, however, is not that our senses perceive, for our *ego* perceives by means of those senses. The sick man who lies in bed with his eyes wide open, but whose mind is affected, perceives nothing; even though the images of his surroundings are reflected on the retina of his eyes. While you sleep, many sounds may vibrate in the air-waves of your room, but not waken you to hear and perceive them. To stop short with the senses is, therefore, both unscientific and superficial. The way of knowledge certainly leads through the senses, but it extends farther. It is also continued from the sense through the nerves and the brain, and back of these out of our sensorial avenues to that mysterious something which we call our consciousness, and, in the centrum of that consciousness, to what we call our *ego*. The students of the so-called exact sciences, who think that their as yet undemonstrated, immediate knowledge of the object rests exclusively upon the action of the senses, are thus entirely mistaken, and allow themselves a leap to which they have no right. If their *ego* is to obtain knowledge of the object, they must not stop with the action of the senses, but ask how the *ego* acquires certainty of the reality of the perception. By means of your senses, you receive sensations and impressions; but in your consciousness the result of this consists of forms, images, shapes, and figures, which are not dissimilar to those which loom up before your mind outside of perception,—in imagination, in dreams, or in moments of ecstasy. Your perception by means of your senses acquires value only when you know that your senses gave you movements in your sensorial nerve-life, which came from a real object, and in their changes and successions are caused by the state of this object. Actually it amounts to this: that your *ego believes* in your senses. If by faith the action of your senses is brought into the relation of certainty with your *ego,* then you can depend upon perception of faith and the certainty which it gives are so forcible that, as a rule, we grasp immediately the distinction between the products of dream, fancy and of perception. The action of faith becomes weaker when the condition of mind becomes abnormal, as in delirium of fever, in moments of anxiety, in hypochondria, or sudden insanity; then a feeling of uncertainty overtakes us as to what we perceive or think we perceive, which we know nothing of in a normal condition, when faith works regularly. It must be granted that wilful deception may tempt us to take for real what exists merely in appearance, but even these ever more or less humiliating experiences do not hinder us from resuming immediately our normal stand on reality, thanks to this faith. He who was deceived by the apparition of a ghost, which he afterward discovered to be unreal, will not be uncertain whether a runaway horse in the street is a real phenomenon or not, but will step out of the way of it. If, thus, it must be granted that this faith, by which our *ego* believes in our senses, can become abnormal by a perplexity of our mind, and in like manner can become the dupe of delusion, nevertheless this faith is, and always will be, a certainty-yielding process in our mind, which at once resumes its dominion.

This is even so true that we actually owe all our convictions of the reality of the object exclusively to faith. Without faith you can never go from your *ego* to the *non-ego;* there is no other bridge to be constructed from phenomena to noumena; and scientifically all the results of observation hang in air. The line from Kant to Fichte is the only line along which you may continue operations. It is true that perception is susceptible of verification: the perception of one sense by that of the other; the perception of to-day by that of to-morrow; the perception of A by that of B. But in the first place, this is no help whatever as long as faith provides no certainty concerning a single perception. You cannot verify x by x. And on the other hand, it is an undoubted fact that, with the exception perhaps of some weak-minded philosopher, every man, without thinking of verification or applying any verification whatever, is certain every moment of the day that his surroundings actually are as they appear; so that on the ground of this certainty he acts and works without the least hesitation. When you sit in your room and some one comes in and addresses you, you do not consider it your first duty to verify this fact, for in that very moment you are certain that this person stands before you and speaks to you; and you deal with this fact and act accordingly. All human intercourse is founded on this fact, as is also all observation, and consequently all scientific knowledge, which is built up on observation; and this fact falls away at once if faith does not work in you to make your *ego* believe in your senses.

This is so true, that the most exact science properly begins its scientific task in the higher sense only when observation is finished. To observe bacteria or microbes is by itself as little an act of science as the perception of horses and cows pasturing in the meadow. The only difference between the two is, that horses and cows in the meadow are perceptible with the naked eye, and bacteria and microbes can be observed only with the reinforced eye. Let no one, however, be misled. The reinforcement of the eye is partly the result of invention, and partly of scientific construction. But the bacteriologist, who uses a maximum microscope in his laboratory, did not make this himself, he bought it; and all he does is to see by means of his microscope. An aged person can no longer distinguish letters with his naked eye and buys glasses; but who will assert that he performs a scientific act, simply because with the aid of glasses he now reads what once he read without glasses. Technical skill is called into play in the use of the microscope; accuracy also; and a certain inventive instinct in the statement of what one observes. Scientific knowledge of the department in which one observes will also be a requisite. All this, however, does not deny that the observation itself bears no scientific character, and that the scientific task of the observer only begins when the result of the observation has been obtained. The farmer who, in his stables and fields, observes the data and phenomena of nature, exercises virtually the same function as the observer in his laboratory. To perceive is the common function of man, and perception in a full-grown man is not scientific study because an adult perceives more and better than a child. He who has a sharp and penetrating eye sees all sorts of things which a common observer does not see, but who has ever thought of calling the observation of a sharp-seeing man scientific? If then the observer in his laboratory sees with the reinforced eye what would not reveal itself in any other way, how can this put the stamp of science on his labor? If suddenly our eye should be so greatly strengthened as to equal the microscope in power of vision, then every one would see what *he* sees. His advantage consists simply in this, that his eye is reinforced. Reinforcement in the same way as the eye of the pilot on the bridge of a ship is reinforced, so that he discovers the approach of a coming ship at a great distance. Reinforcement in the same way as the eye of the Alpine huntsman, who through the spy-glass discovers from afar the wild goat on the glacier. Only with a difference of degree. But how can this difference of degree in the reinforcement of vision ever lend a scientific character to work in the laboratory, which no one ever grants to a sea-captain or chamois-hunter? Grant therefore that the preparation of the chemist is scientific, that his purpose lies in science, that presently he will go to work scientifically with what has been observed. Very well, if only you concede that his observation as such lacks all scientific character, and that a chemist who confined himself to observation would not be prosecuting science at all. All certainty indeed, as far as obtained by perception and observation alone, rests exclusively on the faith that that which we acquire by the senses deserves our confidence.

If such is the case with the self-consciousness of our ego, and with the certainty obtained by observation, it is equally so with demonstration or with the action of our reasoning understanding. Here also you can pursue no course, unless you have a point of departure. For this reason men have always recognized *axioms* as fixed principles introductory to demonstration. This word, however, is not happily chosen, since it suggests an opinion, or a meaning; but even in this less-happily chosen word you confess that the fundamental principles on which you build are not results of demonstration; indeed, that they are not capable of proof. All you can say of them is, that no one denies them; that every one, consciously or unconsciously, consents to them; so that you will meet no opposition if you start out from them. This by itself however is nothing more than an argumentum ad homines, and no proof whatever. Nothing remains, therefore, but to declare that these axioms are given with our self-consciousness itself; that they inhere in it; that they are inseparable from it; and that of themselves they bring their certainty with them. Since certainty is your highest aim, nothing more can be demanded than the entire certainty of these axioms. And what is this again but faith? To you they are sure, they are lifted above every question of doubt, they offer you certainty in the fullest sense, not because you can prove them, but because you unconditionally believe them. Thus faith is here also the mysterious bond which binds your *ego* to these axioms. It certainly has happened, and may happen again, that one will appear susceptible of proof; but at best this only shows that in connection with what we observed above about "wisdom" with our mind also has intuitive knowledge, and that this intuitive knowledge may readily be mistaken for the formal action of our faith. If one takes merely the identity-conception that A=A, the fact is still a fact that the conviction itself, which forms the starting-point for all demonstration, is not fixed by demonstration, but only and alone by faith.

This has by no means exhausted the significance of faith for the "way of knowledge." As faith provides us the starting-point for our observation and the axiomatic starting-point for every demonstration, it also offers us *the motive* for the construction of science. This motive lies in the codification of the general laws which govern the phenomena. Observation itself is no science yet in its higher sense. Science is born of observation only when from those phenomena, each of which by itself furnishes nothing more than a concrete and separate case, we have reached the universal law which governs all these phenomena in their changes. You admit that without certainty of the existence and of the validity of these laws, all scientific effort is futile. But how do you obtain the knowledge of these laws? Have you investigated beforehand *all* the phenomena that belong to one class, and do you now conclude, that because the same activity is seen to operate in all these phenomena in the same way, it should therefore be *the* law which, thus described, governs this class of phenomena? Of course not. It is not possible for you to do this. The very idea of such a general law even excludes such an all-embracing investigation. Just because it shall be a general law, it must have been valid in the ages when you were not yet born, and must be valid in the ages when you shall be no more. Moreover, while you live it must be valid everywhere, even in those places where you are not present, in which places, therefore, observation is impossible for you. Moreover, suppose that you had acquired your knowledge of this law in the aforementioned way, you would have lost your interest in it. For that which interests you in the knowledge of such a law, is the very fact that it enables you to state how this group of phenomena was conditioned before you were born, and how it shall be after you are gone. This law holds the key to the mystery, and it owes its attraction to this charm. But how did you acquire the knowledge of this law? You have observed a certain number of cases, which observation shows you a certain constant action; this constant action makes you surmise that this action will always be constant; you hear of others who have built like conclusions upon like observations; you apply a special test, and it appears that in this way you are able to call the same action into life; no case is known to you in which this action has not shown itself; no one contradicts your surmise; and every one who devotes his attention to what has attracted yours, arrives at the same conclusion: and, upon this ground, it is scientifically determined that in this group of phenomena such and such a law operates thus and so. Very well! But have you now *demonstrated* this law? Is the certainty which you have of the existence of this law, the result of demonstration? Your demonstration cannot extend farther than your observation, and your observation covered certainly not one billionth part of the cases which are concerned. Whether the *post hoc* in the cases observed is at the same time a *propter hoc,* can by no means always be empirically proved. This proof is only given when the genetic operation of the cause can be traced in its entire development. But no one hesitates to adopt a general conclusion, even where this genetic knowledge is wanting. That quinine counteracts intermittent fever is a generally accepted conclusion, even though no one has ever been able to explain genetically the action of quinine on the blood. In this case, however, no harm is done. But without knowing the genetic action of vaccine, the general conclusion was considered equally justifiable, that inoculation with this virus is a harmless preventive against smallpox, and, on the ground of this so-called scientifically discovered law vaccination has been enforced by public authority; while now, alas, in the end it appears how carelessly this conclusion was drawn. Hence extreme care is necessary, lest we proclaim as a general law what afterward appears to rest on defective observation. But even though we pass these cases by, and confine ourselves to those general laws which are no longer contradicted, the question ever returns, What foundation have you for your confidence that your conclusion is correct? You say: "I can show this at once and prove that it is so, since no one can call a phenomenon into being in which this law does not show itself." And again we say: Very well! The law of gravitation, etc., is as certain to us as to you; but we ask: *Where is your proof?* And to this question no answer can be given, except that here also *faith* enters in and makes you *believe* in the existence and in the absolute validity of such a law. Not that the formula is the result of your investigation. But the idea itself that there are such laws, and that when certain phenomena exhibit themselves, you are certain of the existence of such laws, does not result from your dem̃onstration, but is assumed in your demonstration and is the basis on which your demonstration rests, and in the end it appears the means by which your certainty is obtained. Without faith in the existence of the general in the special, in laws which govern this special, and in your right to build a general conclusion on a given number of observations, you would never come to acknowledge such a law. For one of the primordial principles in your logic reads: A particulari ad generale non valet conclusio, i.e. no conclusion from the special to the general, is valid. Just so, but all your observations deal with the special only. Hence you would never reach a general conclusion if faith did not give you both the idea of the general and the right to accept it as a fact.

Though this applies to *all* the sciences, it nevertheless creates no uneasiness in the man of science, because every student has the faith, in this universal sense, which is necessary for the self-consciousness of the *ego,* for securing the axiomatic starting-point and for the forming of general conclusions. This harmony may momentarily be disturbed by the report that some people still believe in the reality of *miracle;* but this alarming suggestion is readily dismissed. If miracles are real, they have no place in common science, for the very reason that they are miracles. Thus in scientific investigation faith is virtually taken as a quantity that can be neglected, because it is the same in all, and therefore makes no difference in the conclusion. This, of course, ought *not* to be so, and an ever stronger protest should be raised against this superficiality which is so unworthy of the name of science; but the false antithesis between faith and science is so generally current, that they who value science most, as a rule, prefer the removal of the last vestige of the leaven of faith.

But when we leave the domain of the natural, and enter the domain of the mixed and the spiritual sciences, what then; Here, also, faith ($\pi \iota \sigma \tau \iota \varsigma$) enters in as the indispensable factor, and in a way which is *not* the same with all. In the mixed and spiritual sciences we touch immediately upon the diversity of the subject, and constantly encounter what in a preceding section we explained as the fact of sin. Take history, for instance. With the exception of a small part belonging to your own times, all observation is at second, third and fourth hand. There is tradition. Is it trustworthy? A certificate bears a signature. Is it the name of the certifier? You need to consult a document; is this document genuine? In such cases doubt is not unnatural. A representation of events which you yourself have witnessed, is often made in public meetings, in the press, and in reviews, which you know is incorrect; this is often given by persons who were eye-witnesses as well as yourself; you have no right in every case to assume bad faith, and yet it is sometimes as clear to you as day. If, then, the difficulty is so great in establishing the truth of an event, the parties of which are still alive, the official records of which are at your service, and every particular of which is known to you, what then becomes of the history of bygone ages, of entirely different lands and countries, which comes to you from documents, the very language of which at times is doubtful? This concerns merely the attestation of facts; and this gives chronicles, but no history. History demands psychological explanations; the discovery of a leading motive in events; a connection among these events; and a conclusion that leads to prophetic insight into the future. Back of the facts, therefore, you must interpret the characters, the plans, and purposes of the actors; and back of those persons you must search out the general impulses by which often unconsciously many people were repelled. As long as this general motive is not found, there is no science in history. Moreover, history is likewise a *judge.* The past is no kaleidoscope which you turn before your eye. In history there is a struggle of what you deem holy and true against that which you despise and lament. Thus you must pass judgment. Your sympathy and antipathy are active. In history you spy the root-life of what lives in yourself and in your own surroundings and in your own times. If this is so, how then can there ever be a place in the ranks of the sciences for a science of history, if in your authentication of the past, in your effort to explain the past, and in your judgment of the past, you exclude *faith* and accept nothing but what has been obtained by the immediate observation of the senses or by logical demonstration?

What has been said of history applies, *mutatis mutandis,* in lesser or greater measure, to *all* the spiritual sciences, simply because in all these sciences the mystery of man presents itself, and you are as unable to bring the mystery of your own being, as that of your neighbor, within the reach of your senses or of your logic. As soon therefore as medical science leaves the domain of pure empiricism, and thus becomes scientific, it has to deal more or less with the same difficulties. Not only in Psychiatry alone, but in Physiology and in Pathology as well, does it come in contact with influences and processes, the explanation of which is not found in matter, but in the psyche. For this reason, even after the interesting studies of Professor Bornheim, Magnetism and Hypnotism have not yet been naturalized by the medical science.

Ordinary experience shows that in all contact with this invisible world, faith, and nothing but faith, forms the ground in the human personality of every act. When some one announces himself to us, and tells us who he is, we at once accept as true. We attach value to what he tells of himself, without having any proof of the truth or means of verification. Take away this mutual confidence from society, and conversation or intercourse is no longer possible. And so firmly and almost ineradicably is this confidence rooted in us, that even the constant experience of deception does not impair or take away this universal foundation of life. Experience makes us guarded and more careful; but as long as there is no reason for distrust, confidence remains the rule of society. This is accounted for by the fact that no one is able to disclose the inner life of a man except *that man himself.* What you call your observation is never anything else with man than the observation of his *life-expressions.* Since he has nine-tenths of these life-expressions entirely under his control, and is able to withhold or to falsify them, the knowledge of man obtained by observation is always extremely limited, and in itself uncertain. Not observation, but *revelation,* is the means by which knowledge of the human person must come to you. Hence, you know next to nothing of those individuals who are deaf-mute. And even the revelation which a person makes to you of himself is by itself of no use, unless you have in your person the allied data by which to interpret his revelation. There is certainly some verification by which one can judge of the self-revelation of another; but in the first place this verification is often of little use, and, again, it can only be applied in special cases. Hence in most cases the judge must depend upon the confessions of the accused and the explanations of witnesses, both of which obtain their force of evidence almost exclusively from faith. If such is the case in the acquisition of knowledge of your nearest surroundings, faith is still more strongly appealed to where it concerns persons who live at a distance from you, or who lived in former times. You only know what happens in Japan by what other people say; and though you may be entirely unable to verify these communications, you believe them *grosso modo,* and doubt not for a moment but that on reaching Japan you would find the conditions as stated. Your representation of many a part of Africa rests on the information of one man. This, however, does not make a sceptic of you. Yes, though time and time again you may be disappointed in your credulity, you do not abandon your ineradicable confidence, simply because this confidence cleaves to your nature and is indispensable to life itself. And this is also true with reference *to the past.* Even with reference to your past, you do not doubt for a moment that the woman whom you loved as mother *was* your mother, and that the man whom you addressed by the name of father *was* your father. You have not observed your conception and your birth. Equally unable are you to prove them. And yet when there is no special cause to make doubt *compulsory,* every child lives in the glad assurance of having its *real* father and mother. And herein lies the starting-point of the power and right of *tradition,* which, though frequently mixed up with mistake and falsehood, in itself forms the natural tie which binds our consciences to *the past,* and so liberates it from the limitations of the present.

All this but shows the utter untenability of the current representation that *science* establishes truth, which is equally binding upon all, exclusively on the ground of observation and demonstration, while *faith* is in order only in the realm of suppositions and of uncertainties. In every expression of his personality, as well as in the acquisition of scientific conviction, every man starts out from *faith.* In every realm *faith* is, and always will be, the last link by which the object of our knowledge is placed in connection with our knowing *ego.* Even in demonstration there is no certainty for you because of the proof, but simply because you are bound *to believe* in the force of the demonstration. That this is generally lost sight of, is because faith, which operates in our observation and demonstration, renders this service in the material sciences to all individuals equally and of itself. This prevents the rise of a difference of opinions. While in the spiritual sciences it has always been necessary to admit a certain unknown factor in the demonstration, and for the sake of this x to subtract something from the absolute character of the certainty obtained, which, however, has been disguised under the name of *evidence* or *moral certainty.* And for this reason it was very important to show that *faith* is the element in our mind by which we obtain certainty, not only in the spiritual, but equally in the material sciences. From which it follows that the lesser degree of certainty in the spiritual sciences is not explained by saying that in the spiritual sciences we have to deal with *faith,* which it is not necessary to do in the material sciences; but rather from the fact that in the spiritual sciences *faith* seems to operate differently in different persons. To obviate this difficulty the effort is now made to approach the spiritual sciences as much as possible from the visible world (physical and physicocratic psychology, etc.), but the knowledge of the psychical, which is the real object of these sciences, is not advanced thereby a single step. The cause of this *unlike* operation of faith in the domain of the spiritual sciences is twofold. On the one hand, the effect worked upon this faith by the disposition *of the subject;* and on the other hand, the fact that in spiritual science faith operates not merely formally, but also presents a *content.*

The first cause finds its explanation in the fact that in the spiritual sciences the unifying power of the object does *not* control the subjective differentiation. In the material sciences the subject is obliged to incline himself as far as possible from his psychical centre to the object, and this accounts for the fact that here all subjects present that side only, which is almost one and the same with all. As soon, however, as in aesthetic observation, as the subject resumes his active role, the subjective inequality and difference return at once, as is seen in the fine arts of painting and music. In the spiritual sciences the opposite takes place. Here the object is not physical, but psychical, and where the physical still claims considerable attention, as in the study of language, it is of secondary order, and the psychical remains of first importance. As in the street, and especially in a foreign city, most people appear alike, and their differences of nature and character are seen only in their home life and in their drawing-rooms, so, in viewing the material world, all spirits $(\psi\upsilon\chi\alpha\iota)$ show themselves one and the same; but in the psychic centrum their differences of nature come to light. The peculiar character of the spiritual sciences consists in this, that they look on the life of the psyche in its own home and in its own calling, and therefore in the domain of these sciences the result of *faith* is often so entirely different in one than in the other. The same phenomenon in language will make different impressions upon a Mongolian and upon a Romanic linguist; and a *High Churchman* will give an entirely different explanation of an event in English history from a partisan of the *Old Covenanters*. And if this subjective differentiation counts already for so much in Linguistics and in History, which have so strong a physical substratum in common, how much more powerful must be this influence of the subjective diversity, where psychology, morals, politics, economics, jurisprudence, etc., are in question. In these sciences almost everything depends upon the principles one starts out from, the meaning one attaches to words and the spiritual tendency by which one is governed. This subjective character of faith in these sciences is, therefore, no mistake, nor a defect, but a factor given of necessity in the nature of their object and their method. It is the essential condition (conditio sine qua non) by which alone these sciences can flourish.

The second cause of this unlike working of faith in the spiritual domain lies in the fact, that faith here not only renders the formal service of establishing the relation between the object and the self-conscious and thinking *ego,* but also becomes the immediate voucher of the *content.* This is not the case in the material sciences, but it is in daily life. Our walking, our climbing of stairs, our eating and drinking, are not preceded by scientific investigation, but are effected by faith. You run downstairs without inquiring whether your feet will reach the steps, or whether the steps are able to bear your weight. You eat bread without investigating whether it may contain poison, etc. But when the material world is the object of scientific investigation, everything is measured, weighed, counted, separated and examined, and faith renders the exclusively formal service of making us believe in our senses, in the reality of the phenomena, and in the axioms and laws of Logic by which we demonstrate. In the spiritual sciences, on the other hand, this is different. In Psychology it is faith, and faith alone, which directly guarantees to me the presence of my soul, of my *ego,* and of my sense of self. All the data by which I labor on psychical ground fall away immediately as soon as I consign faith to non-activity. And when I go out of myself, in order to communicate with other persons, in nine cases out of ten faith is the only means at command by which I can receive the revelation of their personality and attach a value to that revelation. Let it be emphatically repeated here, that only because my mother revealed to me who my father was, do I know this as a fact; and in almost every case this all-important circumstance that affects my whole existence cannot be certified except by *faith* in the content of this revelation. This presents no difficulty as long as it concerns *a content* which touches me alone; as soon, however, as *this content* acquires a general character, and tends to establish the laws of psychic life, in the domains of morals, politics, economics, pedagogy, jurisprudence and philosophy, we see all sorts of groups of individuals separate into schools, and nothing more is said of unity and common certainty.

Religion

That which in the given sense is true of all science of the creaturely, and by which in the end everything depends upon *faith*, is from the nature of the case still more eminently true of all scientific research which concerns itself with the matter of religion. Taking the conception of "religion" provisionally, without any more precise definition, this much is certain, that all religion assumes communion with something that transcends the cosmos, this cosmos being taken objectively as well as subjectively. Even when religion takes no higher flight than Ethics, it gropes about in that ethical world-order that it might find there a central ethical power which governs this whole domain, and before which every non-ethical phenomenon must vanish. As long as Ethics aims only at utility or eudemonism, it misses all religious character. Even with Kant this is the all-important point at which religion, however barren and abstract, enters into his ethical world. The ethical subject feels and recognizes a higher ethical will, to which his will must be subordinated. From which point of view, it follows of necessity that the whole world of phenomena is either reasoned out of existence as a mere semblance, or, as real, is subordinated to the ethical. But in whatever way it is interpreted, in any case the central power of the ethical world-order is made to be supreme, transcending all things else, and to it the subject not only subordinates himself, but also the object. With a somewhat higher religious development, however, this will not only suffice, but there can be no rest until, surpassing the thelematic, this subordination of subject and object to this central power has also been found for one's consciousness. The object of religion is not only placed outside of this object-subject, but the subject as well as the object, and the relation of both, must find their ground and explanation in this central power. The psyche addresses itself not merely to the general in the special, and to the permanent in the transient, but to the cause, the beginning, the constitution, and end of both. The extra-cosmic and hyper-cosmic character, however, of every central power, which in the higher sense shall be the object of religion, is the very reason that neither observation nor demonstration are of the least avail in establishing the tie between our subject and this central power, and that your reasoning understanding is as unable to foster as to exterminate religion.

This is different, of course, with Theology, which as a science concerns itself with the matter of religion; but the nature of this science, its method and its certainty, sustain the closest relation to the character of this central power, which is the impelling motive in all higher religion. As a physiological and physicocratic study can be for years made of the expressions of human life, without ever touching upon the study of the psyche, a lifetime can be spent in all sorts of interesting studies of religious ideas, culture-forms, and usages, without ever touching upon the study of religion. Since we now have a psychology without psyche, we also hear a great deal of a science of religion without religion. In which case all study remains phenomenal, but religion itself is not reached. Hence, in this domain also, everything addresses itself to faith. If the subject were to construe his religion out of himself, religion itself would be destroyed. Its characteristic is that the subject places not only the cosmos outside of him, but primarily himself in absolute dependence upon the central power whose superiority he acknowledges. Consequently he can never place himself above this central power; this, however, is just what he would do, if he placed this power under himself as object of his investigation, or construed it out of himself. Much less can he construe this central power from the cosmos; for if the moral sense demands that we subordinate all that is cosmical to our ethical life, *a fortiori* this cosmical can never be adequate to the central power which dominates our ethical world-order. By the study of phenomena, therefore, many definite ideas of religion may be derived from the subject and from the cosmos, but with all this there is nothing gained unless I have first grasped the heart of religion, of which the phenomenal is merely the outshining.

Thus, what in the preceding section we found to be the case with respect to our relation to other subjects, repeats itself here with still greater emphasis. No sense, no perception, and no knowledge is here possible for us, unless this central power reveals itself to us, affects us, and touches us inwardly in the centrum of our psyche. When we as man stand over against man, we are always able from our own subject to form our idea of the other subject, on the ground of *faith* in our common nature. But in religion this inference fails us. Except, therefore, this central power makes itself felt by us, and with entire independence reveals itself to us in a way which bends to the form of our sense and of our consciousness, it has no existence for us, and religion is inconceivable. For this reason all those systems which try to construe this central power ethically from the subject, or naturalistically from the object, fall short of religion and virtually deny it.

Against all such efforts the words of the Psalmist are ever in force: "In thy light shall we see light," and also in the words of Christ: "Neither doth any know the Father save the Son, and he to whomsoever the Son willeth to reveal *him*." Presently your demonstration may have a place in your theological studies of the knowledge that is revealed, and in your inferences derived from it for the subject and the cosmos; but observation or demonstration can never produce one single milligramme of religious gold. The entire gold-mine of religion lies in the self-revelation of this central power to the subject, and the subject has no other means than *faith* by which to appropriate to itself the gold from this mine. He who has no certainty in himself on the ground of this *faith*, about some point or other in religion, can never be made certain by demonstration or argument. In this way you may produce outward religiousness, but never religion in the heart.

It may even be asserted that faith obtains its absolute significance only in religion. In the cosmos you are supported by observation, in the knowledge of other persons by your own human consciousness and in the self-knowledge of your own person by the self-consciousness of your *ego*. But nothing supports you here. Especially not as the cosmos now is, and as your subject now exists. In that cosmos, as well as in your subject, all manner of things oppose your religious sense; and between you and the object of your worship there is always the fathomless abyss of the "transference into another genus" (μετάβασις εἰς ἀλλὸ γένος), the transmutation of that which is *not* God into God. This cannot be explained more fully now, because we must not anticipate the character of Theology. But enough has been said to show convincingly that without *faith* no forward step can be taken here, and that therefore there can be no science of religion unless, by *faith*, the inquiring subject holds communion with that which is the supreme element in the nature of all religion.

CHAPTER III

THE TWOFOLD DEVELOPMENT OF SCIENCE

Two Kinds of People

The certainty and unity of the scientific result, which, through the strong divergencies which exist in the thinking subject, and still more through the existence of the lie, almost fell victims to Scepticism, recover considerable strength through the influence of *wisdom* and the support of *faith*. Since, however, as soon as it performs its function in the domain of the spiritual sciences, *faith* passes again under the dominion of the subjective divergencies, it can indeed promote the *certainty* of the result in the conviction, but it proves, rather than a help, an obstacle in the way to the *unity* of this result. The degree of certainty of one's own conviction cannot be raised without causing the antithesis with the scientific result of others to become proportionately striking. This is true of every spiritual science, in so far as its object is psychic; but from the nature of the case this is most true of the science which has religion for the object of its investigation; because, here, the subjective-psychic must make a very important step, in order from one's own soul to reach the object of its worship.

And yet these darker spots in the orb of science would prove no obstacle in the way to the unity of its radiance, if these divergencies in the subject limited themselves to a *relative* difference. Since, as was seen at the beginning of our study, the subject of science is not the individual, but the general subject of human nature, the potentially higher might at length of itself draw the potentially lower up to and along with itself, and in spite of much resistance and hesitation bring the universal human consciousness to a clear insight, a firm conviction, and a certain knowledge. In every domain of the expression of human life the subjective powers are unequal; not only in that of science, but also in those of art, religion, the development of social life, and business. In the spiritual domain, i.e. as soon as the powers of the consciousness and of the will turn the scale, equality is no longer found. Here endless variety is the rule. But in this multiformity there operates a law, which makes a rule, and involuntarily causes the radically stronger and purer expressions to dominate the weaker. That which takes place in song, takes place in the entire spiritual domain: the stronger and purer voice strikes the keynote, and ends by getting the others in tune with it. In the domain of the sciences, also, experience shows that, after much resistance and trial, the man of stronger and purer thought prevails at length over the men of weaker and less pure thought, convinces them, and compels them to think as he thinks, or at least to yield to the result of his thinking. Many convictions are now the common property of the universal human consciousness, which once were only entertained by individual thinkers. And when we come into touch with the thinking consciousness of Buddhists, of the followers of Confucius, or of Mohammedans, we are in general so deeply conscious of their superiority, that it never occurs to us to ingratiate ourselves into their favor, but of itself and involuntarily, by our very contact with them, we make our conviction dominate them. When this does not succeed at once, this is exclusively because of their lesser susceptibility and backwardness; as soon, however, as they begin to develop and to approach maturity, they readily conform to us. According to the rule *"du choc des opinions jaillit la verite,"* i.e. "truth is formed from classing opinions," these provisional and necessary divergencies might be tolerated with equanimity, in the firm conviction that from this multiplicity unity will spring, were only the character of these divergencies among men exclusively relative and matters of degree.

But this naturally falls away when you encounter a difference *of principle,* and when you come to deal with two kinds of people, i.e. with those who part company because of a difference which does not find its origin within the circle of our human consciousness, but *outside* of it. And the Christian religion places before us just this supremely important fact. For it speaks of a regeneration ($\pi\alpha\lambda\iota\gamma\gamma\epsilon\nu\epsilon\sigma\acute{\iota}\alpha$), of a "being begotten anew" ($\grave{\alpha}\nu\alpha\gamma\acute{\epsilon}\nu\nu\eta\sigma\iota\varsigma$), followed by an enlightening ($\phi\omega\tau\iota\sigma\mu\acute{o}\varsigma$), which changes man in his very being; and that indeed by a change or transformation which is effected by a supernatural cause. The explanation of this fact belongs properly to Dogmatics. But since this fact exerts an absolutely dominating influence upon our view of science, it would be a culpable blindfolding of self if we passed it by in silence. This "regeneration" breaks humanity in two, and repeals the unity of the human consciousness. If this fact of "being begotten anew," coming in from without, establishes a radical change in *the being* of man, be it only potentially, and if this change exercises at the same time an influence upon his *consciousness,* then as far as it has or has not undergone this transformation, there is an abyss in the universal human consciousness across which no bridge can be laid. It is with this as with wild fruit trees, part of which you graft, while the rest you leave alone. From the moment of that grafting, if successful and the trees are properly pruned, the growth of the two kinds of trees is entirely different, and this difference is not merely relative and a matter of degree, but *specific.* It is not a better and tenderer growth in one tree producing a richer fruit, while the other tree thrives less prosperously, and consequently bears poorer fruit; but it is a difference *in kind.* However luxuriantly and abundantly the ungrafted tree may leaf and blossom, it will *never* bear the fruit which grows on the grafted tree. But however backward the grafted tree may be at first in its growth, the blossom which unfolds on its branches is *fruit blossom.* No tree grafts itself. The wild tree cannot change from its own kind into the kind of the grafted tree, unless a power which resides outside of the sphere of botany enters in and effects the renewal of the wild tree. This is no relative transition. A tree is not one-tenth cultivated and nine-tenths wild, so that by degrees it may become entirely cultivated; it is simply grafted or not grafted, and the entire result of its future growth depends on this fundamental difference. And though from the nature of the case this figure does not escape the weak side which every metaphor has, it will nevertheless serve its purpose. It illustrates the idea, that if in the orchard of humanity a similar operation or grafting takes place, by which the character of the life-process of our human nature is potentially changed, a differentiation between man and man takes place which divides us *into two kinds*. And if the sublimate, which from our being arrays itself in our consciousness, may be compared to the blossom in which the tree develops its hidden beauty, then it follows that the consciousness of the grafted and the consciousness of the *non*-grafted humanity *must* be as unlike as to kind, as the blossom of the wild, and that of the true, vine.

But the difficulty which we here encounter is, that every one grants this fact of grafting of trees, while in the world of men the parallel fact is *denied* by all who have *not* experienced it. This would be the case also with the trees, if they could think and speak. Without a doubt the wild vine would maintain itself to be the true vine, and look down upon that which announces itself as the true vine as the victim of imagination and presumption. The superiority of the cultivated branch would never be recognized by the wild branch; or, to quote the beautiful German words, the *Wildling* (weed) would ever claim to be *Edelreis* (noble plant). No, it is not strange that so far as they have not come into contact with this fact of palingenesis, thoughtful men should consider the assertion of it an illusion and a piece of fanaticism; and that rather than deal with it as fact, they should apply their powers to prove its inconceivableness. This would not be so, if by some tension of human power the palingenesis proceeded from the sphere of our human life; for then it would seem a thing to be desired, and all nobler efforts would be directed to it. But since palingenesis is effected by a power, the origin of which lies outside of our human reach, so that man is passive under it as a tree under grafting, the human mind is not quickened by it to action, and consequently must array itself in opposition to it. The dilemma is the more perplexing, since he who has been wrought upon by palingenesis can never convince of it him who has not been similarly wrought upon, because an action wrought upon us *from without* the human sphere, does not lend itself to analysis by our human consciousness; at least not so far as it concerns the common ground on which men with and without palingenesis can understand each other. They who are wrought upon by palingenesis can in no wise avoid, therefore, conveying the impression of being proud and of exalting themselves. The *Edelreis* everywhere offends the *Wildling*, not merely in that measure and sense in which a finely cultured, aesthetically developed person offends the uncouth parvenu; for with these the difference is a matter of degree, so that as a rule the parvenu envies the aristocrat, and so secretly recognizes his higher worth; but, and this is the fatality, the difference in hand is and always will be one of principle. The *Wildling* also grows and blooms, and as a rule its foliage is more luxuriant, while in its specific development the *Edelreis* is not seldom backward.

We speak none too emphatically, therefore, when we speak of two kinds of people. Both are human, but one is inwardly different from the other, and consequently feels a different content rising from his consciousness; thus they face the cosmos from different points of view, and are impelled by different impulses. And the fact that there are two kinds of *people* occasions of necessity the fact of two kinds of human *life* and *consciousness* of life, and of two kinds of *science;* for which reason the idea of the *unity of science,* taken in its absolute sense, implies the denial of the fact of palingenesis, and therefore from principle leads to the rejection of the Christian religion.

Two Kinds of Science

By two kinds of science we do not mean that two radically different representations of the cosmos can be simultaneously entertained side by side, with equal right. Truth is one, and so far as you understand it to be the object reflected in our human consciousness, science also can only be one. Thus if you understand science to be the systematized result of your perception, observation and thought, the difference in the result of your investigation may be a matter of degree but cannot be radical. If the result of A is contrary to the result of B, one or both have strayed from the path of science, but in no case can the two results, simultaneously and with equal right, be *true*. But our speaking of two kinds of science does not mean this. What we mean is, that both parts of humanity, that which has been wrought upon by palingenesis and that which lacks it, feel the impulse to investigate the object, and, by doing this in a scientific way, to obtain a scientific systemization of that which exists. The effort and activity of both bear the same character; they are both impelled by the same purpose; both devote their strength to the same kind of labor; and this kind of labor is in each case called the prosecution of science. But however much they may be doing the same thing formally, their activities run in opposite directions, because they have different starting-points; and because of the difference in their nature they apply themselves differently to this work, and view things in a different way. Because they themselves are differently constituted, they see a corresponding difference in the constitution of all things. They are not at work, therefore, on different parts of the same house, but each builds a house of his own. Not as if an existing plan, convention or deliberation here assigned the rule. This happens as little in one circle as in the other. Generation upon generation in all ages, in different lands, and among all classes of people, is at work on this house of science, without concert and without an architectural plan, and it is a mysterious power by which, from all this sporadic labor, a whole is perfected. Each one places his brick in the walls of this building, and always where it belongs, without himself knowing or planning it. But despite the absence of all architectural insight the building goes on, and the house is in process of erection, even though it may never be *entirely* completed. And *both* are doing it, they who have been wrought upon by palingenesis, as well as those who have remained unchanged. All this study, in the circle of the one as well as in that of the other, founds, builds and assists in the construction of a whole. But we emphatically assert that these two kinds of people devote their time and their strength to the erection of two different structures, each of which purposes to be a complete building of science. If, however, one of these two is asked, whether the building, on which he labors, will truly provide us what we need in the scientific realm, he will of course claim for himself the high and noble name of science, and withhold it from the other.

This cannot be otherwise, for if one acknowledged the other to be truly scientific, he would be obliged to adopt the other man's views. You cannot declare a thing to be scientific gold, and then reject it. You derive your right to reject a thing only from your conviction that that something is not true, while a conviction that it is true would compel you to accept it. These two streams of science, therefore, which run in separate river-beds, do not in the least destroy the principle of the unity of science. This cannot be done; it is absolutely inconceivable. We only affirm that formally both groups perform scientific labor, and that they recognize each other's scientific character, in the same way in which two armies facing each other are mutually able to appreciate military honor and military worth. But when they have arrived at their result they cannot conceal the fact that in many respects these results are contrary to each other, and are entirely different; and as far as this is the case, each group naturally contradicts whatever the other group asserts.

This would have revealed itself clearly and at once, at least in Christian lands, if from the beginning the development of each group had proceeded entirely within well-defined boundaries. But this was not the case, neither could it be. First, because there is a very broad realm of investigation in which the difference between the two groups exerts *no* influence. For in the present dispensation palingenesis works no change in the senses, nor in the plastic conception of visible things. The entire domain of the more primary observation, which limits itself to weights, measures and numbers, is common to both. The entire empiric investigation of the things that are perceptible to our senses (simple or reinforced) has nothing to do with the radical difference which separates the two groups. By this we do not mean, that the natural sciences as such and in their entirety, fall outside of this difference, but only that in these sciences the difference which separates the two groups exerts no influence on the *beginnings* of the investigation.

Whether a things weights two milligrams or three, can be absolutely ascertained by every one that can weigh. If it be mistakenly supposed that the natural sciences are entirely exhausted in this *first* and *lowest* part of their investigation, the entirely unjust conclusion may be reached, that these sciences, as such, fall outside of the difference. But inaccurate as this would be, it would be equally unfair, for the sake of accentuating the difference, to deny the absolute character of perception by the senses. Any one who in the realm of visible things has observed and formulated something with entire accuracy, whatever it be, has rendered service to *both* groups. To the validity of these formulas, which makes them binding upon all and for all time, the natural sciences owe their reputation of certainty, and, since we are deeply interested practically in the dominion over matter, also their honor and overestimation. For the more accurate statement of our idea we cannot fail to remark that, however rich these formulas and the dominion over nature which they place at our disposal may be in their practical results, they stand, nevertheless, and are so little scientific in their character, that formally they are to be equated with the knowledge of the farmer, who has learned how land must be tilled, and how cattle may be bred to advantage. Observation in the laboratory is certainly much finer, and the labor of thought much more exhaustive, and the skill of invention much more worthy of admiration, but this is a distinction in degree; the empiric knowledge of the farmer and the empiric knowledge of our naturalist in principle are one. If, however, it is important to reduce to its just equality the significance of that which, in the results of naturalistic studies, is absolutely certain, it should be gratefully acknowledged that in the elementary parts of these studies there is a *common* realm, in which the difference between view- and starting-point does not enforce itself.

Not only in the natural, but in the spiritual sciences also, a common realm presents itself. The mixed psychic-somatic nature of man accounts for this. Consequently, the object of the spiritual sciences inclines also, to a certain extent, to express itself in the somatic. Only think of the *logos,* which, being psychic in nature, creates a *body* for itself in *language.* Hence in the spiritual sciences the investigation is partly comprised of the statement of outwardly observable facts. Such is the case in *History,* the skeleton of which, if we may so express it, consists entirely of events and facts, the accurate narration of which must rest upon the investigation of all sorts of palpable documents. It is the same with the study of *Language,* whose first task it is to determine sounds, words and forms in their constituent parts and historic development, from all manner of information and observation obtained by eye and ear. This is the case with nearly every spiritual science, in part even with psychology itself, which has its physiological side. To a certain extent, all these investigations are in line with the lower natural sciences. To examine archives, to unearth monuments, to decipher what at first seemed unintelligible and translate it into your own language; to catch forms of language from the mouth of a people and to trace those forms in their development; and in like manner to espy the relation among certain actions of our senses and the psychic reactions which follow, etc., are altogether activities which in a sense bear an objective character, and are but little dominated by the influence of what is individual in the investigating subject. This should not be granted too absolutely, and the determination whether an objective document is genuine or not, or whether the contents of it must be translated thus or so, is in many cases not susceptible to such an absolute decision. But provided the study of the objective side of the spiritual sciences does not behave itself unseemly and contents itself within its boundaries, it claims our joyful recognition, that here also a broad realm of study opens itself, the results of which are benefits to both groups of thinkers, and thus also to the two kinds of science.

This must be emphasized, because it is in the interest of science at large, that mutual benefit be derived by both circles from what is contributed to the general stock of science. What has been well done by one need not be done again by you. It is at the same time important that, though not hesitating to part company as soon as principle demands it, the two kinds of science shall be as long as possible conscious of the fact that, formally at least, both are at work at a common task. It is with reference to this that to the two already mentioned common realms a third one should be added, which is no less important. The formal process of thought has *not* been attacked by sin, and for this reason palingenesis works no change in this mental task.

There is but one logic, and not two. If this simply implied, that logic properly so called as a subdivision of the philosophical or psychological sciences, does not need to be studied in a *twofold* way, the benefit would be small; the more because this is true to a certain extent only, and because all manner of differences and antitheses present themselves at once in the methodological investigation. But the influence of the fact aforementioned extends much farther, and contributes in two ways important service in maintaining a certain mutual contact between the two kinds of science. In the first place, from this fact it follows that the accuracy of one another's demonstrations can be critically examined and verified, in so far at least as the result strictly depends upon the deduction made. By keeping a sharp watch upon each other, mutual service is rendered in the discovery of logical faults in each other's demonstrations, and thus in a formal way each will continually watch over the other. And, on the other hand, they may compel each other to justify their points of view over against one another.

Let not this last be misunderstood. If, as we remarked, palingenesis occasions one group of men to exist differently from the other, every effort to understand each other will be futile in those points of the investigation in which this difference comes into play; and it will be impossible to settle the difference of insight. No polemics between these two kinds of science, on details which do not concern the statement of an objectively observable fact, or the somatic side of the psychical sciences, or, finally, a logical fault in argumentation, can ever serve any purpose. This is the reason why, as soon as it has allowed itself to be inveigled into details, and has undertaken to deal with things that are not palpable phenomena or logical mistakes, Apologetics has always failed to reach results, and has weakened rather than strengthened the reasoner. But just because, so soon as the lines have diverged but a little the divergency cannot be bridged over, it is so much the more important that sharp and constant attention be fixed upon the junction where the two lines begin to diverge. For though it is well known beforehand that even at this point of intersection no agreement can be reached; for then no divergence would follow; yet at this point of intersection it can be explained to each other what it is that compels us, from this point of intersection, to draw our line as we do. If we neglect to do this, pride and self-conceit will come into play, and our only concession to our scientific opponent will be the mockery of a laugh. Because he does not walk in our footsteps we dispute not only the accuracy of his results, but also formally deny the scientific character of his work. And this is not right. Every tendency that wants to maintain itself as a scientific tendency, must at least give an account of the reason why, from this point of intersection, it moves in one and not in the other direction.

And though nothing be accomplished by this, beyond the confession of the reason why one refuses to follow the tendency of the other, even this is an infinite gain. On the one hand it prevents the self-sufficiency which avoids all investigation into the deepest grounds, and lives by the theory that "the Will stands in place of reason." Thus we feel ourselves bound, not only to continue our studies formally in a severely scientific way, but also to give ourselves an increasingly clear account of the good and virtuous right by which we maintain the position originally taken, and by which we formally labor as we do. And since among congenial spirits one is so ready to accept, as already well defined, what is still wanting in the construction, the two tendencies render this mutual service; viz. that they necessitate the continuance of the investigation into the very soil in which the foundation lies. But, on the other hand also, this practice of giving each other an account at the point of intersection effects this very great gain, that as scientists we do not simply walk independently side by side, but that we remain together in logical fellowship, and together pay our homage to the claim of science as such. This prevents the useless plying of polemics touching points of detail, which so readily gives rise to bitterness of feeling, and concentrates the heat of battle against those issues of our consciousness which determine the entire process of the life of science. However plainly and candidly we may speak thus of a twofold science, and however much we may be persuaded that the scientific investigation can be *brought to a close* in no single department by all scientists together, yea, cannot be *continued* in concert, as soon as palingenesis makes a division between the investigators; we are equally emphatic in our confession, which we do not make in spite of ourselves, but with gladness, that in almost every department there is some task that is common to all, and, what is almost of greater importance still, a clear account can be given of both starting-points.

If this explains why these two kinds of science have remained for the most part interlaced, there is still another and no less important cause, which has prevented their clearer separation. It is the slow process which must ensue before any activity can develop itself from what potentially is given in palingenesis. If palingenesis operated immediately from the centrum of our inner life to the outermost circumference of our being and consciousness, the antithesis between the science which lives by it and that which denies it, would be at once absolute in every subject. But such is not the case. The illustration of the grafting is still in point. The cultivated shoot which is grafted into the wild tree is at first very small and weak; the wild tree, on the other hand, after being grafted, will persist in putting forth its branches; and it is only by the careful pruning away of wild shoots that the vitality from the roots is compelled to withdraw its services from the wild trunk and transfer it to the cultivated shoot. Later on this progress is secured, till at length the cultivated shoot obtains the entire upper hand and the wild tree scarcely puts out another branch; but this takes sometimes seven or more years. You observe a similar phenomenon in palingenesis, even to such an extent that if the development begun upon earth were not destined to reach completion in a higher life, the sufficient reason of the entire fact could scarcely be conceived, especially not in those cases where this palingenesis does not come until later life. But even when in the strength of youth palingenesis leads to repentance (transformation of the consciousness), and to conversion (change in life-expression), the growth of the wild tree is by no means yet cut off, neither is the shoot of the cultivated branch at once completed.

This is never claimed in the circles that make profession of this palingenesis. It has been questioned among themselves whether the entire triumph of the new element is possible on this side of the grave (Perfectionists), but that in any case a period of transition and conflict must precede this completeness has been the experience and common confession of all. If we call to mind the facts that those people who as a sect proclaim this Perfectionism, are theologically almost without any development, and soon prove that they reach their singular conclusions by a legal Pelagian interpretation of sin and a mystical interpretation of virtue, while the theologians in the church of Rome who defend this position consider such an early completion a very rare exception, it follows, that as far as it concerns our subject this Perfectionism claims no consideration. These sectarian zealots have nothing to do with science, and those who have been canonized are too few in number to exert an influence upon the progress of scientific development. Actually, therefore, we here deal with a process of palingenesis which operates continually, but which does not lead to an immediate cessation of the preceding development, nor to a sufficiently powerful unfolding at once of the new development; and as a necessary result the scientific account, given in the consciousness, cannot at once effect a radical and a clearly conscious separation.

Several causes, moreover, have assisted the long continuance of this intimate relation. First the fundamental conceptions, which have been the starting-points of the two groups of scientists, were for many centuries governed altogether by Special Revelation. Not only those who shared the palingenesis, but also those who remained without it, for a long time started out from the existence of God, the creation of the world, the creation of man as *sui generis*, the fall, etc. A few might have expressed some doubt concerning one thing and another; a very few might have ventured to deny them; but for many centuries the common consciousness rested in these fixed conceptions.

Properly, then, one cannot say that any reaction took place before the Humanists; and the forming of a common opinion upon the basis of Pantheism and Naturalism has really only begun since the last century. Since, now, those who lived by palingenesis found these old representations to conform entirely to their own consciousness, it is natural that they were not on the alert to build a scientific house of their own, as long as general science also lived by premises which properly belonged to palingenesis. Now, however, all this has entirely changed. They who stand outside the palingenesis have perceived, with increasing clearness, that these primordial conceptions as premises belonged not to them but to their opponents, and in a comparatively short time they have placed an entirely different range of premises over against them. Creation has made room for Evolution, and with surprising rapidity vast multitudes have made this transition from creation to evolution, because, in fact, they never have believed in creation, or because they had, at least, never assimilated the world of thoughts which this word Creation embraced. As natural as it has been, therefore, that in the domain of science both circles have been *one* thus far, it is equally natural that the unity of this company should not be irreparably broken. He who in building upon the foundation of creation thinks that he builds the same wall as another who starts from evolution, reminds one of Sisyphus. No sooner has the stone been carried up than relentlessly it rolls back again.

A second cause in point, lies in the fact that palingenesis does not primarily impel to scientific labor. It stands too high for this, and is of too noble an origin. Let us be sober, and awake from the intoxication of those who have become drunk on the wine of science. If you except a small aristocracy, the impulse to the greater part of scientific study lies in the ambition to dominate the material and visible world; to satisfy a certain intellectual tendency of the mind; to secure a position in life; to make a name and to harvest honors; and to look down with a sense of superiority upon those who are less broadly developed. Mention only the name of Jesus Christ, and you perceive at once how this entire scientific interest must relinquish its claim to occupy the first place in our estimate of life. Jesus never wrote a *Summa* like Thomas Aquinas, nor a *Kritik der reinen Vernunft* like Kant, but even in the circles of the naturalists his holy name sounds high above the names of all these coryphaei of science.

There is thus something else to make a man great, and this lies *outside* of science in its concrete and technical sense. There is a human development and expression of life which does not operate within the domain of science, but which, nevertheless, stands much higher. There is an adoration and a self-abasement before God, a love and a self-denial before our fellow-men, a growth in what is pure and heroic and formative of character, which far excels all beauty of science. Bound as it is to the consciousness-forms of our present existence, it is highly improbable that science will be of profit to us in our eternal existence; but this we know, that as certainly as there is a spark of holy love aglow in our hearts, this spark cannot be extinguished, and the breath of eternity alone can kindle it into the brightest flame. And experience teaches that the new life which springs from palingenesis, is much more inclined to move in this nobler direction than to thirst after science. This may become a defect, and has often degenerated into such, and thus has resulted in a dislike or disdain for science. The history of Mysticism has its tales to relate, and Methodism comes in for its share. But as long as there is no disdain of science, but merely a choice of the nobler interest, it is but natural that the life of palingenesis should prefer to seek its greatness in that which exalts so highly the name of Jesus, and feels itself less attracted to the things which brought Kant and Darwin their world-wide fame. Add to this fact that for most people the life of science depends upon the possibility of obtaining a professorship or a lectureship, and that in Europe they who have these positions to dispose of are, as a rule, inclined to exclude the sons of palingenesis from such appointments, and you see at once how relatively small the number among them must have been who were able to devote themselves, with all the energy of their lives, to the study of the sciences. And thus their strength was too small and their numbers too few to assume a position of their own, and to prosecute science independently from their own point of view.

One more remark will bring to a close the explanation of this phenomenon. One may have a scientific mind, and be able to make important contributions to the scientific result, and yet not choose the most fundamental principles of life as the subject of his study. There is a broad field of detail-study in which laurels can be won, without penetrating to the deep antitheses of the two world-views whose position over against each other becomes ever more and more clearly defined. In this class of studies success is won with less talent, with less power of thought, with less sacrifice of time and toil; one also works with greater certainty; more immediate results are attained; and more questions of an historical character are presented which can be solved within a more limited horizon. This accounts for the fact that of ten scientists, nine will prefer this class of studies. Theologians are the exception, but their position at the universities is uncommon. One tolerates in them what would not be tolerated in others, and a gulf between the theological and the other faculties is tacitly acquiesced in. If these faculties of theology were not an imperative necessity because of the churches, at most universities they would simply be abolished. With the reasonable exception of these, the ratio of one to nine, assumed above, between the men of detail-study and the men of the study of principles, is certainly a fair one; and thus when applied to the few sons of palingenesis who have devoted themselves to science and have been appointed to official positions, causes the number of the students of principles among them to be reduced to such a minimum, that an independent and a clearly defined attitude on their part has been fairly impossible.

Practically and academically the separation between these two kinds of science has thus far been made only in a few single points. The universities of Brussels and Louvain are examples of this. In Amsterdam and Freiburg, also, a life peculiar to itself has originated. And in America a certain division has begun. But these divisions bear too much a churchly or anti-churchly character, and for the greater "republic of letters" as a whole they are scarcely yet worthy of mention. Almost everywhere the two stems are still intertwined, and in almost every way the stem which grows from palingenesis is still altogether repressed and overshadowed by the stem of naturalism; naturalism being here taken as the expression of life, which, without palingenesis, flourishes as it originated. There was, indeed, a conservative period in university life, in which the old world-view still thought itself able, by an angry look or by persecution, to exorcise the coming storm; and a later period in which by all manner of half concessions and weak apologetics, it tried to repress the rise of the naturalistic tendency. But this Conservatism, which first tried compulsion and then persuasion, owed its origin least of all to palingenesis, and thus lacked a spiritual root. At present, therefore, it is rapidly passing away. Its apologetics lack force. It seeks so to comport itself that by the grace of Naturalism it may still be only *tolerated*; and it deems it no disgrace to skulk in a musty vault of the fornication in which once it bore command.

Neither the tardiness, however, of the establishment of this bifurcation of science, nor the futile effort of Conservatism to prolong its existence, can resist the continuous separation of these two kinds of science. The all-decisive question here is whether there are two points of departure. If this is *not* the case, the unity must be maintained by means of the stronger mastering the weaker; but if there *are* two points of departure, then the claim of two kinds of science in the indicated sense remains indisputably valid, entirely apart from the question whether both will succeed in developing themselves for any good result within a given time. This twofold point of departure is certainly given by palingenesis. This would not be true if the deepest foundations of our knowledge lay outside of us and not in us, or if the palingenesis operated outside of these principia of knowledge in the subject. Since, however, this is not the case, because, like sin, whose result it potentially destroys, palingenesis causes the subject to be different in his innermost self from what he was before; and because this disposition of the subject exercises an immediate influence upon scientific investigation and our scientific conviction; these two unlike magnitudes can have no like result, and from this difference between the two circles of subjects there follows of necessity difference between their science.

This bifurcation must extend as far as the influence of those subjective factors which palingenesis causes to be different in one than in the other. Hence all scientific research which has things *seen* only as object, or which is prosecuted simply by those subjective factors which have undergone *no* change, remains the same for both. Near the ground the tree of science is one for all. But no sooner has it reached a certain height, than two branches separate, in the same way as may be seen in a tree which is grafted on the right side, while on the left side there is allowed to grow a shoot from the wild root. In its lowest parts the tree is one, but at a given height it divides itself, and in this twofold development one branch grows side by side with the other. Which of these two is to be considered the *wild* development, is to be accounted as failing of its end and to be cut away, and which the *truer* development of the tree that shall bear fruit, cannot be decided by one for the other. The *negative* for the one determines here the *positive* for the other. This, however, is the same for both, and the choice of each is not governed by the results of discursive thought, but exclusively by the *deepest impulse* of the life-consciousness of each. If in that deepest impulse the one were like the other, the choice would be the same. That it is different, is simply because they are constitutionally *different.*

Meanwhile, it must not be concluded from this that in the circle of palingenesis scientific development must be uniform, in the sense that all, who in this circle devote themselves to science, must conform to *a given model* and arrive *at harmonious results.* Naturalistic science decorates itself with corn-flower and garden-rue, as symbols of the free character which it boasts, while the science of those who accept palingenesis is represented as festooned with autumn-leaves (feuillemorte), and as incapable of progress worthy of the name within the narrow limits to which it is confined. This entire representation, however, is but a play of the imagination, and in both circles a real scientific development takes place, which unfolds the beauty of truth only in the harmony of multiformity.

A fuller explanation may be considered important.

In the abstract every one concedes that the subjective assimilation of the truth concerning the object cannot be the same with all, because the investigating individuals are not as alike as drops of water, but as unlike as blades of grass and leaves on a tree. That a science should be free from the influence of the subjective factor is inconceivable, hence with the unlikeness of the individuals the influence of this factor must appear.

For this reason science in its absolute sense is the property of no single individual. The universal human consciousness in its richest unfoldings is and ever will be the subject of science, and individuals in their circle and age can never be anything but sharers of a small division of science in a given form and seen in a given light. The difference among these individuals is accordingly both a matter of degree and of kind. A matter of degree in so far as energy in investigation, critical perspicuity and power of thought are stronger in one than in the other. But a matter of kind also, in so far as temperament, personal inclination, position in life and the favorableness or unfavorableness of circumstances cause each individual investigator to become one-sided, and make him find his strength in that one-sidedness which renders the supplementation and the criticism of others a necessity. This accounts for the varieties of theories and schools which antagonize, and by this antagonism bless, each other. This is the reason why in each age and circle certain views prevail, and strike the keynote; and that all manner of personal influences are restricted by the power of public opinion. This piecemeal labor of every description would never advance science, if the object of science itself did not exist organically, and the investigating individuals in every land and age were not involuntarily and often unconsciously organically related. To annul this mutually supplementary, corrective and yet organically connected multiformity, would be the death of science. Not the military mechanism of the army, but the organic multiformity of social life is the type to which, in order to flourish, science must correspond.

Such being the case with naturalistic science, it would be different with the science which flourishes upon the root of palingenesis, only if palingenesis annulled the cause of this subjective pluriformity. This, however, is not at all the case. Palingenesis does *not* alter the differences of temperament, of personal disposition, of position in life, nor of concomitant circumstances which dominate the investigation. Neither does palingenesis take away the differences born from the distinction of national character and the process of time. Palingenesis may bring it about, that these differences assume another character, that in some forms they do *not* appear, and that they *do* appear in other forms unknown outside of it; but in every case with palingenesis also subjective divergence continues to exist in every way. The result indeed shows that in this domain, as well as in that of naturalistic science, different schools have formed themselves, and that even in the days of the Middle Ages there never was a question of uniformity. However much Rome has insisted upon uniformity, it has never been able to establish it, and in the end she has adopted the system of giving to each expression of the multiformity a place in the organic harmony of her great hierarchy.

No doubt the antitheses sometimes assume an entirely different character in the domain of palingenesis than in the domain of naturalistic science. No atheistic, materialistic, nor pessimistic system can flourish in its soil. Its schools, therefore, bear different names and divide themselves after different standards. But as after the entrance of the Christian religion into the world, the schools of Alexandria, of Antioch, of North Africa, of Constantinople, and of Rome, each bore a type of its own, so it has remained through all the ages, is now, and shall be to the end. Friction, fermentation and conflict are the hall-mark of every expression of life on higher ground in this present dispensation, and from this the science of the palingenesis also effects no escape.

Three objections may here be raised: (1) that this science is bound to the content of revelation; (2) that its liberty is impeded by the ecclesiastical *placet;* and (3) that its result is determined in advance. A brief remark is in place on each of these three objections.

Since the investigating subject is changed by palingenesis from what he was before, he will undoubtedly assume a different attitude towards the Revelation of God. He will no longer try, as in his naturalistic period, to denounce that Revelation as a vexatious hindrance, but will feel the need of it, will live in it, and profit by it. He will certainly thus reckon with that Revelation, but in no other way than that in which the naturalist is bound to and must reckon with the existing cosmos. This, however, would destroy the scientific character of his knowledge, only if this Revelation consisted of nothing but a list of conclusions, and if he were not allowed subjectively to assimilate these conclusions. This, however, is by no means the case. The Revelation offered us in the Word of God gives us gold in the mine, and imposes upon us the obligation of mining it; and what is mined is of such a nature, that the subject as soon as he has been changed by palingenesis, assimilates it in his own way, and brings it in relation to the deepest impulse and entire inner disposition of his being. That this assimilation does not take place by means of the understanding only, can raise no objection, since it has been shown that naturalistic science also can make no advances without faith. Moreover, naturalistic science, as well as that of palingenesis, has its bounds, beyond which it cannot go; its antinomies, which it cannot reconcile; and its mysteries, after which the interrogation point remains standing. If now knowledge is brought us by Revelation from across the boundaries, a reconciliation is offered for many antinomies, and many a new mystery is unveiled, it pleads in no respect against the scientific character of our science, that our reason is unable to analyze this new material and to place it in organic connection with the rest. It is not strange, therefore, that with reference to this Revelation, *faith* unfolds a broader activity than in the investigation of the cosmos, and harmonizes entirely with the aim and character of this Revelation: viz. to be of service first to the practical religious life, even of the simplest-minded people, and after that to science. But rather than protest against this, science ought to recognize the fact that she is called, (1) to investigate the nature and essence of this Revelation; (2) to analyze the material, which has been derived from it; and (3) to discover and indicate the way in which this material, as well as Revelation itself, enters into relation with the psychical life of man. The lack of unanimity on any of these three points, and that in all ages these three points, and everything connected with them, have been so differently judged, is readily explained. The tendencies of mysticism and pietism, of realism and spiritualism, of transcendentalism and immanence, of monism and dualism, of the organic and individualism have ever intruded themselves into these questions, and have crossed again those blended types, which are known by the name of Romanism, Lutheranism and Calvinism. Tendencies and types these, in which shortsightedness beholds merely ecclesiastical variegations, but which to the man of broader view, extend themselves across the entire domain of human life, science included. And though the science of the palingenesis may succeed as little as naturalistic science in scientifically bringing to a successful end the conflict between these different schools and tendencies on its own ground, it is still the task of science also within the realm of palingenesis constantly to test the assertions of these several tendencies, for the sake of enhancing the clearness of their self-consciousness.

This brings us of itself to the second objection: that *the liberty of this science is impeded by the ecclesiastical placet.* This also must be denied. There is no instituted church (ecclesia instituta) conceivable without a *placet;* and the position of an investigator, whose results antagonize this ecclesiastical *placet,* is thereby rendered false and untenable; but this does not impede the prosecution of science in the least. In the first place the church, as instituted church, never passes sentence upon that which has no bearing upon "saving faith." Even the church of Rome, which goes farthest in this respect, leaves the greater part of the object free. Again, this church *placet* is itself the result of a spiritual conflict, which was developed by contradictions, and in which the controversy was scientific on both sides. Hence it is every man's duty and calling constantly to test by scientific methods the grounds advanced from either side. And if, in the third place, an investigator becomes convinced that the *placet* of the church is an unjust inference from Revelation, he must try to prove this to his church, and if she will not allow him this privilege, he must leave her. This would not be possible if the church were a scientific institute, but no instituted church advances this claim. Hence in the realm of palingenesis one remains a man of science, even though he may lose his harmony with the church of his birth; and it is not science, but honesty and the sense of morality, which in such a case compels a man to break with his church. This, however, occurs but rarely, partly because the churches in general allow considerable latitude; partly because a false position does not seem untenable to many; but more especially, because the churchly types are not arbitrarily chosen, but of necessity have risen from the constellation of life. Since the scientific investigator, who is connected with such a church, stands for the most part under those same constellations, it is very natural that in most cases he will not come into any such conflict, but will arrive at the same conclusions as his church. Then, however, there is no compulsion; no bonds are employed; but the agreement is unconstrained and necessary. The danger would be more serious, if the whole church in the earth had only one form alike for all parts of the world, so that the *placet* would be everywhere the same; and indeed the existence of this danger of the loss of liberty could not entirely be denied during the Middle Ages, nor can it be denied to-day in those countries which are entirely uniform religiously. But since in the instituted church this unity is broken, so that now there are ten or more forms of church organizations, in which almost every possible type has come to an organization of its own, it is almost inconceivable that in the domain of palingenesis a scientific investigation would ever lead to a result which would not accord with the *placet* of one of these churches on the contested points. And if, in case a conflict cannot be avoided, one is impelled by love of truth and by a sense of honor to change his relations from one church to the other, it is as little of a hindrance to the liberty of the spiritual sciences, as when one is compelled by the results of investigation on political grounds to seek refuge from Russia in freer England or America.

Finally, concerning the last objection,—that in the domain of palingenesis there can be no science, because *its results are predetermined,*—let it be said that this is partly inaccurate, and that as far as it is accurate, it applies equally to naturalistic science. As it stands, this proposition is partly *untrue.* In general one understands by it, that in the ecclesiastical Creed or in the Holy Scriptures the results are already given. If a conflict arises between the result of our investigation and our ecclesiastical creed, it may render our ecclesiastical position untenable, but it cannot affect the maintenance of our scientific results. And as for the Holy Bible, it is ever the province and duty of science to verify what is inferred from it. Yet after the subtraction of these two factors, it is still entirely true that in the abstract the results of our investigation are beforehand certain, and that, if we reach other results, our former results are not valid and our investigation is faulty. This, however, is common both to the science of palingenesis and to naturalistic science. The actual nature of the cosmos conditions the results of all investigation, and so far as there is question of knowledge which we obtain by thinking, our thinking can never be aught than the *after*-thinking of what has been *before* thought by the Creator of all relations; even to such an extent that all our thinking, to the extent that it aims to be and is original, can never be anything but pure hallucination. Hence it is entirely true, that in the domain of palingenesis all results of investigation are bound to the nature of palingenesis, and determined by the real constitution of the spiritual world with which it brings us into relation; it is also true, that that which has been well investigated will prove to agree with what has been revealed to us in an accurate way from this spiritual world; nor may it be denied that in this realm also, all our thinking can only be the after-thinking of the thoughts of God; but it has all this in common with the other science, and all this is inherent in the nature of science. If the objection be raised that in the prosecution of science as directed by palingenesis, it is a matter of pre-assumption that there is a God, that a creation took place, that sin reigns, etc., we grant this readily, but in the same sense in which it is pre-assumed in all science that there is a human being, that that human being thinks, that it is possible for this human being to think mistakenly, etc., etc. He to whom these last-named things are not presuppositions, will not so much as put his hand to the plough in the field of science; and such is the case with him who does not know, with greater certainty than he knows his own existence, that God is his Creator, entirely apart from palingenesis. Facts such as are here named,—that there is a God, that a creation took place, that sin exists, etc.,—can never be established by scientific investigation; nor has this ever been attempted but some acuter mind was at hand to convict its predecessor of error. Only let it be remembered, that in this section we do by no means refer to Theology simply, or even especially. Science, as here considered, is science which has the entirety of things as its object; and only when we come to Theology may the special questions be answered, to which the entirely peculiar character of this holy science gives occasion.

The Process of Science

Our proposition that there are two kinds of science is, from the nature of the case, merely the accommodation to a linguistic usage. The two sciences must never be coordinated with each other. In fact, no one can be convinced that there is more than one science, and that which announces itself as science by the side of, or in opposition to, this can never be acknowledged as such in the absolute sense. As soon as the thinker of palingenesis has come to that point in the road where the thinker of naturalism parts company with him, the latter's science is no longer anything to the former but "science falsely so called." Similarly the naturalistic thinker is bound to contest the name of science for that which the student of the "wisdom of God" derives from his premises. That which lies outside of the realm of these different premises is common to both, but that which is governed, directly or indirectly, by these premises comes to stand entirely differently to the one from what it does to the other. Always in this sense, of course, that only one is right and in touch with actual reality, but is unable to convince the other of wrong. It will once be decided, but not until the final consummation of all things. For though it must be granted, that in what is called the moral and social "Banquerott der Wissenschaft," even now a test is often put in part to the twofold problem; and though it is equally clear that every investigator will come to know this decision at his death: yet this does not change the fact that, of necessity, the two kinds of science continue to spin their two threads, as long as the antithesis is maintained between naturalism and palingenesis; and it is this very antithesis which the *parousia* will bring to an end, or—this end will never come.

Hence, *formal* recognition only is possible from either side. The grateful acceptance of those results of investigation which lie outside of the point in question, is no recognition, but is merely a reaping of harvests from common fields. So far, on the other hand, as the antithesis between our human personality, as it manifests itself in sinful nature and is changed by palingenesis, governs the investigation and demonstration, we stand exclusively opposed to one another, and one must call *falsehood* what the other calls *truth*. Formally, one can concede, as we do without reservation, that from the view-point of the opponent, the scientific impulse *could* not lead to any other prosecution of science, even with the most honest intention; so that, though his results must be rejected, his formal labor and the honesty of his intention must claim our appreciation. That this appreciation is mostly withheld from us, is chiefly explained from the fact that, from the view-point of palingenesis, one can readily imagine himself at the view-point of unregenerated nature, while he who considers fallen nature normal, cannot even conceive the possibility of a palingenesis. For which reason, every scientific effort that goes out from the principle of palingenesis is either explained as fanaticism or is attributed to motives of ambition and selfishness.

Hence the urgent necessity to combat the false representation that that science which lives from the principle of palingenesis lacks all organic process, and consists merely in the schematic application of dogmas to the several problems that present themselves. This representation is antagonistic to the very conception of science, and is contradicted by experience. Very marked differences of insight prevail among the scholars of the science which operates from the principle of palingenesis, as well as among the others, and many institutions and schools form themselves. There is, therefore, no organic, multiform process of science among naturalists and a schematic, barren monotony with the men of palingenesis; but the calling of science to strive after an objective unity of result born from multiformity, in the face of all the disturbance of subjectivity, is common *to both.*

To both the general subject of science is, and always will be, the human mind at large and not the *ego* of the individual investigator. The rule is also common to both, that the human mind does not operate except through the subject of individual investigators, and that these, according to their differences of disposition, of age, and habits of life, can severally bring in but a very small and limited, a very subjectively tinted and one-sidedly represented, contribution to the final harvest of science. The many-sided variety gives rise to divers antitheses and contradictory representations, which for a time establish themselves in the institutions and schools, which are in process of time superseded by other antitheses, and from which again new institutions and schools are born. Thus there is continual friction and constant fermentation, and under it all goes on the process of an entirely free development, which is in no wise bound except by its point of departure, whether in unregenerate or in regenerate human nature. Let no one think, therefore, that Christian science, if we may so call the science which takes palingenesis as its point of departure, will all at once lead its investigators to entirely like and harmonious results. This is impossible, because with the regenerate also, the differences of subjective disposition, of manner of life, and of the age in which one lives, remain the same; and because Christian science would be *no* science, if it did not go through a process by which it advanced from less to more, and if it were not free in its investigation, with the exception of being bound by its point of departure. That which the prosecutor of Christian science takes as his point of departure is to him as little a result of science as to the naturalist; but he, as well as the naturalist, must obtain his results of science by investigation and demonstration.

Only let it be remembered, that not every subjective representation which announces itself as scientific is a link in the process of the development of science. The subjective element certainly bears on one side a necessary character, but also one which, all too often, is merely accidental or even sinful. In the spirit of humanity is a multiformity from which, for the sake of the full harmony, no single element can be spared; but there is also a false subjectivism which, instead of causing single tones to vibrate for the sake of the full accord, disturbs the accord by discord. To overcome this false subjectivism, and to silence these discords, is by no means the least important part of the task of science. However much this false subjectivism may exert itself in the domain of Christian science, as well as in that of naturalistic science, yet we may assert that with Christian science this parasite does not reach an equal development of strength. Palingenesis takes away from the human spirit much on which otherwise this parasite feeds, and the enlightening, which develops itself from regeneration, applies a saving bridle to this false subjectivism. But this parasite will never be wanting in the domain of Christian science, simply because palingenesis does not absolutely remove the after-workings of unregenerated nature. Hence it is also the calling of Christian science to resist this false subjectivism, but only by scientific combat.

As far, on the other hand, as this subjective element is of necessity connected with the multiformity of all human life, the differences born from this will reveal themselves in Christian science more strongly rather than more weakly, because palingenesis allows these subjective differences to fully assert themselves, and does not, like naturalism, kill them. From the earliest ages of the Christian religion, therefore, these antitheses in the domain of Christian science, and the tendencies born from them, have ever assumed a much firmer and more concrete form, especially where they ran parallel with the ecclesiastical distinctions. But in the realm of Christian science it will never do for these several tendencies to point to the ecclesiastical basis of operation, as the source from which they obtained their greater permanency. Every tendency is bound scientifically to defend its assertions in the face of those of other tendencies. One may even say that this scientific labor maintains the spiritual communion between those who are ecclesiastically separated and estranged from each other. And if this is objected to by the statement that the prosecutors of this science often assume the position over against one another, that *they* only possess truth in its absolute form, the threefold remark is in place: First, that in their realm the students of naturalistic science often do the same thing; that with them also one school often stands over against the other with the pretence of publishing absolute truth. Secondly, that we must distinguish between what the student of Christian science professes as a church-member, and what he offers as the result of his scientific investigation. But, in the third place, also, that idealism in science demands that every man of conviction shall firmly believe that, provided their development be normal, every other investigator must reach the same result as he. He who shrinks from this cannot affirm that he holds the result of his own investigation as true; he becomes a sceptic. He who in his own conception has not stepped out from his subjectivity in order to grasp the eternally true, has no conviction. And though it be entirely true that history plainly teaches, that the ripest and noblest conviction has never escaped the one-sidedness of one's own subjectivity, the inextinguishable impulse of our human nature never denies itself, but sees true in that which it has grasped for itself as truth.

Hence the result we reach is, that the effort which reveals itself in our nature to obtain a scientific knowledge of the cosmos by investigation and demonstration, is ever bound to the premises in our nature from which this effort starts out. That for this reason this effort leads to a common practice of science, as far as these premises remain equal, but must divide itself as soon as the fork is reached where the change effected in these premises by palingenesis begins to influence the investigation. That for this part of the investigation, therefore, two kinds of scientific study run parallel, one which is, and one which is not, governed by the fact of palingenesis. That they who study science under the influence of palingenesis, as well as they who leave it out of account, can only hold for true what rests on their own premises, and thus can appreciate each other's study only in a formal manner. That with Christian, as well as with naturalistic science, that only stands scientifically sure which, going out from its own premises, each has obtained as the result of scientific research. That consequently, in both studies of science, all sorts of antitheses, tendencies, and schools will reveal themselves, and that by this process alone science on both sides advances. And finally, that because the influence of the subjective element, occasioned by a difference of disposition, manner of life, spiritual tendency, and age, makes itself felt with both, every investigator deems his own result of science true in the broadest sense; thereby going out from the conviction that, provided he carries on his investigation well, every normal investigator will attain a like result with himself.

Both Sciences Universal

The proposition, that in virtue of the fact of palingenesis a science develops itself by the side of the *naturalistic*, which though formally allied to it, is differently disposed, and therefore different in its conclusions, and stands over against it as *Christian* science, must not be understood in a specifically theological, but in an absolutely *universal* sense. The difference between the two is not merely apparent in theological science, but in *all* the sciences, in so far as the fact of palingenesis governs the *whole* subject in *all* investigations, and hence also, the result of all these investigations as far as their data are not absolutely material. To support this proposition, however, two things must still be shown: first, that in both cases science is taken in the sense of *universal-human validity;* and, secondly, that palingenesis is not merely a subjective psychical, but a *universal* phenomenon, which involves both the investigating subject and the cosmos. Inasmuch, however, as we are writing a *theological* encyclopedia, we do not proceed here to the exposition of this, but reserve it for treatment under the development of the conception of Theology. At this point, therefore, a simple suggestion suffices. Concerning the first, the universally valid character is inseparable from all science; not in the sense that every individual agrees with you, but that the subject of your science is, and ever will be, the *universal human consciousness.* Well, then, the palingenesis, which does not operate within single persons atomistically, but organically upon our race, will produce this result: that the tree of humanity, our race, humanity as a whole, and thus also the *universal human consciousness*, shall be glorified and sanctified in the "body of Christ." He who remains outside of this till the end, *falls away from humanity.* Up to the time of this final solution, however, neither the naturalistic nor the Christian science have any universally conpulsive character outside of their own sphere. We encounter one another in open conflict, and a universally compulsory science, that shall be compulsory upon *all* men, is inconceivable. And concerning the second point, let the provisional remark suffice, that there is not merely a palingenesis of the human soul, but also a palingenesis of the body and of the cosmos. This accounts for the central character of the Resurrection of Christ, and for the far-reaching significance of the restoration of the cosmos, which in Matthew xix. 28 is indicated by this very word of *palingenesis.*

CHAPTER IV

DIVISION OF SCIENCE

Organic Division of Scientific Study

Before we can find a provisional answer, in the closing chapter of this division, to the question, whether Theology is or is not a necessary and an integral part of the organism of science, this organism itself must be somewhat closely examined. Only when the anatomy of this organism is known, can it be seen in what parts it consists, and whether among these parts a science in the spirit of what we call Theology occupies a place of its own. Of course, in the framing of this conclusion we must start out with a definition of Theology, which cannot be explained until the following division; but for the sake of clearness in the process of the argument, this hypothetical demonstration is here indispensable.

As far as the organism of science itself is concerned, we have purposely chosen as the title of this section the expression: The organic division *of scientific study.* If the organic division of science itself is viewed, apart from its relation to practice, nothing is obtained but an abstraction, which lies entirely outside of history and reality; and the question whether Theology is a science in this scientific organism can never be answered. For Theology is an historic-concrete complex, which, if brought over into the retort of abstractions, would at once slip through our fingers and volatilize.

As regards the organic character of science, three data must be taken into account: (1) the organic relation among the several parts *of the object of science;* (2) the organic relation among the different capacities of the *subject* and the data which lead to the knowledge of the object; and (3) the organic relation which in consequence of (1) and (2) must appear in the *result* of the scientific task. The object exists organically; the subject itself exists organically and stands organically related to the object; and consequently this organic character must be found again, as soon as the knowledge of the object has been attained by the subject with sufficient completeness and accuracy. The unity of these three reveals itself historically in the *scientific task,* which did not begin by making these distinctions clear for itself, but had its rise in the instinctive faith in this mutual relationship. The stimulus to undertake this scientific study is not given by an Academy of Sciences, but by our innate inclination to investigate. As a child breaks his toys and cuts them into pieces, in order to find out what they are and how they are constructed; or, as outside of his playhour he overwhelms you with questions; thus is man prompted by a natural impulse to investigate the cosmos. And, though with adults also this desire after knowledge may consist too largely of a playful inquiry, the needs of life add a nobler seriousness to this playful investigation and by it rule and continuity are imparted to the scientific task. If the practical need of physicians, lawyers, ministers of the Word, Academic professors, etc., did not continually press its claims, the very existence of universities would at once be jeopardized. If these were abolished, and with them the avenues to success were closed against those who desire to devote their lives to scientific pursuits, a small group only of competent persons would be able to allow itself the luxury of this pursuit. And if the number of scientists should thus be reduced, the study of science would likewise suffer from the gradual disappearance of the whole apparatus which is now at its service in libraries, laboratories, observatories, etc. The *vitae non scolae* is true also in the sense that only *life* gives the *school* its susceptibility to life.

The ideal representation that science would still be able to flourish when practised merely for its own sake, rests upon self-deception. This is best observed in the case of those special sciences whose study is not immediately born from the practical need of life, and whose development in consequence has been so greatly retarded. If there were no logic in this practical need of life, and if it were not connected with the organic motive of science itself, this dependence of the *school* upon *life* would be most fatal, and would obstruct the smooth progress of scientific investigation. This, however, is *not* so. The practical need of life is born from the relation in which the subject stands to the object, and from the necessary way in which the subject (humanity) develops itself organically from itself. It must be conceded that the claims which this practical need causes to be felt, are not always considered in the accurate order of succession, and that only after several fits and starts do they assume a more normal character; but the result also shows that science has made all these fluctuations with them, and only when the practical need of life has begun to express itself in clearer language, and, consequently, with clearer self-consciousness, has it assumed a more normal character. This would certainly have proved a difficulty, if the slow ripening of this clear insight the development of science itself; but it has created no disturbance, since both the development of these practical needs and the development of science have been governed by the self-same power, i.e. by the actual mode of existence and organic relation of object and subject. Every encyclopedical division of the sciences, which aims to be something more than a specimen of mental gymnastics, will therefore in the main always proceed from the practical division given historically in the academic faculties. Not as though this division were simply to be copied; for this division, which has already been modified so often, is always susceptible of further modification; but these future modifications also will not abstractly regulate themselves according to the demands of your scheme, but will be permanently governed by the demands of practical need; and only when your schematic insight has modified the form in which the practical need of life asserts itself, will this insight, through the medium of practical life, be able to influence effectually the process of discriminating the faculties.

But while criticism of the division of scientific study, as it is controlled by that of the faculties, is in every way lawful and obligatory, Encyclopedic science is nevertheless bound to set out from this historic division. It is not to dissect an imaginary organism of science, but it must take as its starting-point the body of science as it actually and historically presents itself; it must trace the thought which has determined the course of this study; and, reinforced with this leading thought, it must critically examine that which actually is. Encyclopedia is no speculative, but a positive, science; it finds the objective of its investigation in the actually given development of science. As long as this object had not sufficiently developed, the very thought of Encyclopedic science could not suggest itself. Its study only begins when the study of the sciences has acquired some form of permanency. Since historically Theology has called into life a faculty of its own and has presented itself in this faculty as a complex of studies; and since it is our exclusive aim to answer the question whether Theology takes a place of its own in the organism of the sciences; it would be futile to sketch the organism of science in the abstract. For in the case both of ourselves and of our opponents this sketch would of necessity be controlled by the sympathy or antipathy which each fosters for Theology. Hence that we may have ground beneath our feet, we should not lose ourselves in speculative abstractions, but must start out from the historic course which, under the influence of the practical needs of life, has been pursued by the study of the sciences.

Practically, now, we see that the theological faculty was the first to attain a more fixed form. Alongside of it, and following immediately in its wake, is the juridical faculty. Next to these two is the slow growth of the medical, as a third independent faculty. The so-called philosophical faculty finds its precursors in the Artistae; but it is a slow process by which these surmount the purely propaedeutic character which their study bore at first. The *facultas litteraria*, either in or out of connection with the faculty of natural philosophy, only gradually takes its place by the side of the above-named three. Clergymen, lawyers and physicians were everywhere needed, while a man of letters and a natural philosopher could find a place only in a few schools. To every one hundred young men, who studied in the first three faculties, there were scarcely five who found their career in the study of literature or natural philosophy. And for this reason the first three faculties were for a long time the principal faculties, and the study of the Artistae and Physicists were mere auxiliaries to them. Propaedeutics was the all-important interest, and not the independent study of Letters or of Natural Philosophy. From this it must also be explained, that at so many universities the study of Letters and of Natural Philosophy has always been combined in the same faculty. In Holland the untenability of this union has long since been recognized, and the Literary and Natural Philosophy faculties have each been allowed a separate existence; and the fact that elsewhere they still remain together is simply the result of the common propaedeutic character which was deemed to constitute their reason for being. The practical needs of life to broaden the knowledge of nature have for more than a century caused the independent character of the natural sciences convincingly to appear, and this very detachment of the study of natural philosophy has quickened the literary studies to a sense of their own independence. The difference of method especially, between the two kinds of sciences, was too pronounced to allow the auxiliary character of literary studies to be maintained. This last process of the emancipation of the literary faculty, however, is still so imperfect, that no common opinion has yet been obtained on the unity of matter, or, if you please, on the real object of this group of sciences. The philological, historical and philosophical studies still seek their organic unity. But in any case it seems an accepted fact, that the cyclus of studies will run its round in the circle of these five faculties. Although there seems to be a disposition abroad to let the Theological faculty become extinct, or to supersede it by a faculty of Philosophy, no serious desire is perceived to enlarge the number of faculties beyond the five, and it is scarcely conceivable that the practical needs of life will ever warrant the increase of this number. Neither the smaller or larger number of departments, nor the lesser or greater number of professors, but only the combination of studies demanded by a practical education, decides in the end the number and the division of the faculties.

Meanwhile it is by no means asserted that the prosecution of science, and in connection with it the university life, should aim exclusively at a practical education. On the contrary, the pursuit of science for its own sake is the ideal which must never be abandoned. We merely emphasize that the way to this ideal does not lead through sky and clouds, but through practical life. A science which loses itself in speculation and in abstraction never reaches its ideal, but ends in disaster; and the high ideal of science will be the more nearly realized in proportion as the thirst after and the need of this ideal shall express themselves more strongly in human life, so that the practical need of it shall be stimulated by life. As the transition from *unconscious* into *conscious* life advances, the impulse born of society increases of itself to account for every element and every relation, and, thanks to this impulse, the prosecution of science for its own sake carries the day.

In connection with this it is noteworthy that the three originally principal faculties were born of the necessity of warding off evil. This is seen in the strongest light in the case of the medical faculty, which still exhibits this negative character in name, and partly even in practice. It is not called the *somatic* faculty, to express the fact that the human body is the object of its study; nor the *hygienic* faculty, to express the fact that health is the object of its choice; but the *medical,* by which name the *diseased* body alone is designated as its real object. This accords with the attention which man bestows in real life upon his body. As long as one is well and feels no indisposition, he does not inquire into the location and the action of the organs in his body; and only when one feels pain and becomes ill does the painstaking care for the body begin. A like observation applies the *juridical* faculty. If there were no evil in the world there would be no public authority, and it is only for the sake of evil that the authority is instituted, that the judge pronounces judgment, and that the making of laws is demanded. Not for the sake of the study of law as such, but for the sake of rendering a well-ordered human intercourse possible in the midst of a sinful society, did jurisprudence undertake its work; and the juridical faculty came into being for the education of men who, as statesmen and judges, are leaders of public life. This also applies to the *theological* faculty, though not in so absolute a sense. Because it was found that salvation for the sinner, and a spiritual safeguard against the fatal effects of wickedness, were indispensable, both law and gospel were demanded. The purpose was *medical,* but in the Theological faculty it was psychic, as it was somatic in the so-called Medical faculty. For though it must be acknowledged that originally the aim of the Theological faculty was not exclusively soteriological, but that on the contrary it also tried to foster thetically the knowledge of God, yet the call for an educated clergy, and the concomitant prosperity of this faculty, are due in the first place to the fact that men were needed everywhere who would be able to act as physicians against sin and its results. Hence it is actually the struggle against evil in the *body,* in *society,* and in the *soul* which has created the impulse for these three groups of sciences, the need of men to combat this evil, and consequently the necessity for the rise of these three faculties. All three bear originally a militant character. This cannot be said of the Artistae, nor the faculties of Literature and Natural Philosophy which at a later period were formed from their circle. In the case of these studies *positive knowledge* was much more the immediate object in view, even though it must be granted that this knowledge was pursued only rarely for its own sake, and much more for the sake of *utility.* One studied natural philosophy and letters in order to become a jurist, physician, or theologian, or to obtain power over nature. But with this reservation it is evident that from the beginning these provisionally dependent faculties stood nearer to the scientific ideal, and formally occupied a higher point of view.

If it is asked what distinctions control this actual division of scientific labor, it is easily seen that the attention of the thoughtful mind had directed itself in turn to *man* and to *nature* that surrounds him; that, as far as his own being is concerned, man has occupied himself severally with his *somatic, psychic,* and *social* existence; and that even more than these four groups of sciences, he aimed distinctively at *the knowledge of God.* The accuracy of this division, which sprang from practical need, is apparent. The principium of division is the subject of science, i.e. *Man.* This leads to the coordination of *man* himself with *nature,* which he rules, and with his *God,* by whom he feels himself ruled. And this trilogy is crossed by another threefold division, which concerns "man" as such, even the distinction between *one* man and *many,* and alongside of this the antithesis between his *somatic* and *psychic* existence. Thus the subject was induced in the *Theological* faculty, to investigate the knowledge of God, and in the faculty of *natural philosophy* to pursue the knowledge of nature; to investigate the somatic existence of man in the *Medical,* his psychic existence in the *Philological* faculty, and finally in the *Juridical* faculty to embrace all those studies which bear upon human relationships. The boundary between these provinces of science is nowhere absolutely certain, and between each two faculties there is always some more or less disputed ground; but this cannot be otherwise, since the parts of the object of science are organically related, and the reflection of this object in the consciousness of the subject exhibits an equally organic character.

If science had begun with devising a scheme for the division of labor, these disputed frontier-fields of the faculties would have been carefully distributed. Since science, however, and the division of faculties both, are products of the organic process of life, it could not be otherwise than that uncertainty at the boundaries, which is the mark of all organic division, here also shows itself. Should the Medical faculty teach psychology for the sake of psychiatry and of the psychical influences upon the body? Does the philosophy of nature and of law belong to the Philological, or to the Psychical and Juridical faculty? Is the place for Church-law in the Theological faculty or in the Juridical faculty, which itself originated from it as the "Decretorum facultas," and which for many years it claimed in the title of *iuris utriusque doctor?* These questions, together with many others, have all been solved in a practical way such as is of course open to critical examination by self-conscious science in its Encyclopedia, but such as a closer investigation claims an ever-increasing respect for the accuracy that marks the decision of practice. The Encyclopedia of the sciences is safest, therefore, when it does not abandon this historic track marked out by practice. A speculative scheme, in which the organic-genetic relations of the sciences are fitted to another last, would have almost no other value than to evoke our admiration for the ingeniousness of the writer. Thus various titles of departments would be obtained, for which there are no departments of study. In our review of the history of Theologic Encyclopedia, it has been seen that, in the study of Theology also, such speculations have not been spared, and numerous departments for new and imaginary branches of study have been formed; but, meanwhile, practice has continued the even tenor of its way, and real study has been best served by this practical division. This would not be so, if the object and the subject of science, and also the development of life and of the consciousness of life, stood in no necessary relation to each other; but since this all-sided relation cannot be denied, and the process of science and the process of life almost always keep equal step, history offers us an important objective guarantee of accuracy. There is a power that directs the course of our life-process, and there is a power that directs the course of the process of science. This dominion does not rest in the hand of a single individual, but, for life and science both, is in the hand of a Spirit who stands above all individuals; and since in both realms (in that of life as well as in that of science) this power is exercised by one and the selfsame Spirit, the correct idea of the organism of science comes of itself to light in history, though it be only gradually and not without fits and starts.

The Five Faculties

In the preceding section the Theological faculty was numbered with the other four, in order to state the fact that it was born from the practical needs of life, and that it has stood behind none of the others in the manner of formation. Its right of primogeniture among these five can scarcely be disputed. But however important a weight this fact may add to the scale, it does by no means yet define the position which Theology is entitled to hold in the organism of science. The fact may not be overlooked, that at more than one university the faculty of Theology has practically been abolished; that at a number of universities it continues merely as the child of tradition; and that in this traditional prolongation of its life it has undergone, more than any other faculty, so violent a metamorphosis that at length the identity of the object of its study has been entirely lost. Not merely the need, therefore, of judicious criticism, but practice itself places a very grave interrogation mark after this heritage of history, and compels, with respect to Theology, a closer investigation into its certification of birth and its right to domicile. To do this, however, it is necessary that we first orient ourselves a little with reference to the other parts of the realm, in order to obtain a definite conception of the other four faculties.

Since for our investigation the *Philological* is the most important, we will consider that first. This faculty has not yet attained its self-consciousness. It would have done this much sooner, if the faculty of Natural Philosophy had been separated from it in Germany as timely as in Holland. Now, however, this unnatural conjunction has in many ways confused insight into the character of Philological study. Even when the studies of Philology and Natural Philosophy are separated, every difficulty is by no means yet surmounted, for then the antithesis is at once encountered between the studies of Philosophy and Philology in the narrower sense. It has more than once been proposed to allow Philosophy a faculty of its own and to give it the house in which Theology lies dying. The Philological faculty would then become exclusively the faculty of *letters,* and in an eminent sense engage itself with all those studies which the *littera scripta* gives rise to or renders possible. And from this point of view a third antithesis appears: viz. the antithesis between Historical studies and those of Philology proper. If indeed the criterium for the object of Philology lies in the *littera scripta,* then it both can and must investigate the historical documents and the historical expositions, as literary products, but the real content of History lies outside of its horizon. In this wise the faculty is more and more reduced, and at length its only remaining object is that *which is written* which condemns it as an independent faculty. However highly one may estimate its value, letters can never form a principal group in the organism of the object; and to a certain extent it is even contingent. The object existed long centuries before literary life manifested itself. Hence the name *Literary* faculty can in no case be taken as a starting-point. We owe this name to Humanism, which in this instance also did not forsake its superficial character. "Philological" is therefore in every way a richer and a more deeply significant name, because the Logos does not refer to the *letter*, but to that which the *letter* serves as body. For a long time the restricted meaning of *word* or of *language* was attached to the *logos* in "Philology," and consequently Philology was interpreted as standing outside of Philosophy and History. This, however, only showed how dimly it was understood that every faculty must have a principal group in the object of science as the object of its investigation. If word, and language still more, is a wider conception than that of *littera scripta*, yet language and word can never acquire the significance of being a principal group in the object of science. As a life-expression of man the life of language is coordinated with the expressions of the ethical, aesthetic and material life, and hence for each of these a separate faculty should have to be created. As long as only the expression of life is studied the object of science is not grasped. This is done only when life itself is reached, the expression of which is observed. This, in the case of the logos, is, in its general sense, *the life of the human consciousness.* It is this life which recapitulates itself in the logos, taken as *thought;* expresses itself in the logos, taken as *word;* and which for a very considerable part is at our disposal in the literary product. And thus we have laid our hand upon *a principal group* in the great object of science; for not only does man belong to this object, but is himself the most important factor in it, and it is in his wonderful consciousness that presently the whole cosmos reflects itself. If now in this sense the object of this faculty is understood to be *the conscious life of man,* the word *conscious* must of necessity be taken in its pregnant sense. Else *all* science could be brought under this faculty, even that of nature. But this danger is evaded if, on the other hand, full emphasis is placed upon the quality of *conscious* life, so that in this faculty our life is in question only from the side of our consciousness. By doing this we keep in the path first indicated by Boeck and extended so much farther by my esteemed colleague, Dr. J. Woltjer, in his Rectoral oration of 1891. If Boeck placed *thinking* too much in the foreground, Dr. Woltjer rightly perceived that from thinking we must go back to the *Logos* as reason in man; and it is therefore entirely in keeping with the relation established by him, that in Philology we interpret the word Logos as indicating that which is *conscious* in our life.

And thus the view-point is gained, from which the practice is justified, which has ever united philosophical and historical studies with that of Letters. Even if language and everything that is connected with language is the vehicle of human consciousness, the study of this vehicle does by no means end the study of that consciousness itself. That human consciousness also as such, according to its form and comprehensive content, must be made the object of investigation, and this necessitates the formal and material study of philosophy. Above all it should be taken into consideration that it is not the consciousness of a single individual, but the consciousness of man as such, and hence of humanity in its relation and continuous process, that is to be known; and this gives rise to the task of History. Hence it is the one Logos, taken as the consciousness of humanity, which provides the motive for Linguistic and Historic and Philosophic studies; so that no reasonable objection can be raised against the name of *Philological* faculty. "Logoi" was indeed the word used originally for an historical narrative, and this gave historians the name of Logographers. In this way the combination of Linguistic, Historic, and Philosophic studies does not lead to an aggregate, but to an organic unity, which in an excellent manner locates a principal group of the object of science in a *realm of its own.*

It is *man* in antithesis with *nature,* and in man his *logical,* in antithesis with his *bodily* manifestation, which determine the boundaries of this realm. The unity that lies in this may not be abandoned.

Meanwhile let it be observed, that the task of this faculty should not be extensively, but intensively interpreted. The object of its existence is not the study of *every* conceivable language, nor the investigation of *all* history, nor yet the systematizing of the *whole* content of the human consciousness. The Faculty, as such, must direct its attention to the consciousness of humanity taken as an organic unity, and thus must concentrate its power upon that in which *the process* of this human consciousness exhibits itself. It does not cast its plummet into a stagnant pool, but away out in the stream of human life. Its attention is not riveted by what vegetates in isolation, but by that which lives and associates with and operates within the life of humanity. For this reason the classical and richly developed languages from the old world and the new are so vastly more important to this Faculty, as such, than the defective languages of the more supine and undeveloped nations. It does not look upon Literature as an aggregate of everything that has been handed down in writing, but as an organic conception, which only embraces that which is excellent in form and content. History also is only that in which the human consciousness has developed strength to bring the human life to the fuller unfolding of its idea. And as material Philosophy, it merely offers that which has advanced the current of human thought, and has enabled its different tendencies to express themselves correctly. The proposal to overwhelm this Faculty with the study of conceivable languages and peoples and conceptions must therefore be declined. This deals the death-blow to this Faculty, makes it top-heavy, and causes it to lose all unity in its self-consciousness. In order to maintain itself as a faculty it must distinguish between main interests and side-issues, and maintain unity in multiformity, and keep its attention fixed upon that which in continuous process has ever more richly unfolded the consciousness of our human race, has enabled it to fuller action, and has brought it to clearer consciousness. We do not deny that other languages also, peoples and conceptions may be the object of scientific research, but this sort of study must annex itself to the work of this faculty, and not consume its strength. This self-limitation is not only necessary in order that it may handle its own material, but also that it may not lose its hold on life, and thus may keep itself from conflict with practical demands. Duty, therefore, demands that in the study of the human consciousness it should not swing away to the periphery, but that it shall take its station at the centrum, and never lose from sight the fact that the object of its investigation is the conscious life of our human race taken as an organic unity. With this in view it investigates *language* as the wondrous instrument given as vehicle to our consciousness; the richest development which language has proved capable of in the *Classical languages* of ancient and modern times; and the full-grown and ripe fruit which language has produced in classical *Literature.* Next to this study of language as vehicle and incorporation of our consciousness, follows the investigation into the activities of this consciousness in the life of humanity, i.e. the broad study of History. And then, at length, formal and material *Philosophy* follow; the first to investigate conscious life in its nature, and the laws which govern it; the second to answer the question, how the "World-Image" (Weltbild) has gradually formed itself at present. This order of succession certainly gives rise to objection, that formal philosophy should properly lead the van; nevertheless, we deem it necessary to maintain it, because formal as well as material philosophy assumes a preceding development of language, and hence also a preceding history.

The *Medical faculty* being of less importance for our investigation may therefore be more briefly considered. We for our part do not desire the name of *Medical* faculty to be changed into *Somatological* or *Philosomatical* faculty. We would not have the fact lost from sight that this science did not originate from the thirst after a knowledge of our body, but from the need of seeking healing for its diseases. For this implies the confession that our general human condition is neither sound nor normal, but is in conflict with a destructive force, against which help from a saving power must be sought and can be found. This, however, does not weaken the demand that the *medical* character of these studies should not too absolutely be maintained. Obstetrics in itself is no real medical study. Moreover, medical study has always assumed the knowledge of the healthy body. And Hygiene, which demands an ever broader place, is not merely medical-prophylactic, but in part stands in line with the doctrine of diet, dress, etc., as tending to the maintenance of the healthy body. On these grounds it seems undeniable, that the object of investigation for this faculty is the human body, or better still, man from his somatic side. Already for this reason the effort to take up the body of animals into this faculty should be protested against; and warnings should be sounded against entertaining too sanguine expectations from vivisection, and against the altogether too bold exploits which it adventures. In itself, veterinary surgery would never have become anything more than an empiric knowledge; and the insight it derives from the Medical faculty is a mercy which from our human life descends to suffering animals. But Darwinism should never tempt us in this faculty to coordinate man and animal under the conception of "living things." If the *human* body had not been subject to disease, there would never have been a medical science. Vegetation also has its diseases and invites medical treatment; but who will include the healing of plants in the Medical faculty? The *human body* must remain the exclusive object for the complex of medical studies. The pro-plastic forms also, or preformations which were created for this body in the vegetable and animal kingdom, must indeed be investigated with a view to this body, but the studies which this investigation provokes serve exclusively as *subsidiary helps,* and should not be permitted to destroy the boundary between the human body and these preformations. In the same way the boundary should be guarded which divides the somatic life of man from his psychical life. This psychical life is the heritage of the Philological and not of the Medical faculty. If this boundary be crossed, the Medical faculty *must* subordinate the psychical phenomena to the somatic life, and cannot rest until, under the pressure of its own object, it has interpreted this psychical life materialistically. But neither should it be forgotten that an uncertain and mingled region lies between the somatic and the psychic life. Both sides of human life stand in organic relation. The body affects the soul, and the soul the body. Hence, there is on one side a physico-psychical study which must trace the psychical phenomena on physical ground, and on the other side a psychico-physical study which determines the influence exercised by the soul upon the body. And this must serve as a rule, that Psychology derives its physical data from the Medical faculty; while on the other hand the Medical derives its psychological data from the Philological faculty. That the Theological faculty also comes into consideration here is not denied; but since it is the very purpose of this investigation to point out the place in the organism of science which belongs to the Theological faculty, we pass it by for the present. Only let the necessary observation be made, that it is contradictory to the peculiar character of the medical studies to leave the important decision concerning the imputability of guilt in the process of punishment to be accounted for by this faculty. Finally a last boundary must be drawn for the medical faculty on the side of the juridical faculty. For on that side also medical science steps constantly beyond the lines of its propriety. It demands, indeed, that public authority shall unconditionally adopt the results from medical and hygienic domains into civil ordinances, and shall execute what it prescribes. This absolute demand should be declined, first, because these results lack an absolute, and sometimes even a constant character; and in the second place, because it is not the task of medical, but of juridical science to investigate in how far the claims of the body should be conditioned by the higher claims of the psychic and social life.

Within these boundaries these medical studies naturally divide themselves, according to their object, into studies which investigate the healthy body; which trace the phenomena of disease; and which have for their purpose the cure of these abnormal phenomena. The study of the body as such, i.e. in its healthy state, divides itself equally naturally into the somatical and psychico-somatical, while the somatic studies divide again into anatomy and physiology. The sciences which have for their object the deviations from the normal, i.e. the sick body, are pathology and psychopathology. The studies, finally, which direct themselves to Therapeutics, divide into medical, surgical, and psychiatrical, to which Medicine and applied Medica join themselves. Only the place of Obstetrics is not easily pointed out, because a normal delivery, without pain, would not be a pathological phenomenon, and to this extent Obstetrics would not find its motive in the medical, but in the somatical character of these studies. As such it should belong as a technical department to Physiology. From the view-point of Revelation, however, delivery with pain is an abnormal phenomenon, and to this extent we see no difficulty in coordinating obstetrics after the old style with medical and surgical science. With the exception of these incidental questions it is readily seen, meanwhile, that as long as the Medical science confines itself to these independent studies, it still lacks *its higher unity,* and cannot be credited with having come to a clear self-consciousness. This would only be possible if it could grasp the deeper cause of the corruption from which all diseases originate; if, on the other hand, it could expose the relation between this cause and the reagents; and thus could crown its labor by the production of a *Medical Philosophy.*

The *Juridical* faculty claims a somewhat larger share of our attention, since it stands in a closer relation to that of Theology. In the object of science we found its province *in man,*—not in himself, but as taken *in his relation to other men.* This, however, must not be interpreted in the sense that man is merely a social being, and that therefore juridical study must lapse into sociology. The origin of this faculty is a protest against this. From the beginning it was a faculty for the study of *Sancta Justitia,* devoted to the education of those who were to administer the affairs of government and exercise the judicial function. Both these conceptions, of government and judicial power, were derived from the fundamental conception of the *Supreme Authority.* The folly of separating the powers of state had not yet been invented, and the intrinsic unity of all legislative, judicial, and governing power stood still firm in the common mind. Authority was exercised over men upon earth; this authority was not original with man, but was conferred of God upon the magistracy. Hence the way in which this authority was to be exercised by the magistracy was not left to the arbitrariness of despotism, but this authority fulfilled its end only when it operated in harmony with the order of human society ordained of God. The laws and regulations to which this authority bound its subjects and itself were obliged, therefore, to meet a fixed claim; and this claim had been established by God himself in the ordinances of his Creation, and had received its fuller interpretation in his special Revelation. Hence, though whatever the magistracy ordained as law was actually valid, as such, within the circle of their authority, and though as such it bound the conscience formally, the obligation that this enforced law should legitimate itself as law before a higher tribunal, and in other ways be corrected, could not be ignored. From this obligation the study of law in the higher sense is born; for profound and scientific study alone can obtain an insight into the nature of law in general, and into the special relations of law, as they should be in order to correspond to the relations which have been divinely ordained in creation and by history mutually between man and man or among groups of men.

The view, which formed the point of departure in this, was accurate in every way, viz., that there would have been no need of a magistracy, nor of the regulation of law, nor of a consequent study of law, if there had been no moral evil among men. In a sinless state, the correspondence of the social life to the demands of the holiest law would be spontaneous. Hence, when this faculty originated, it was still the common confession that sin alone was the cause that one man was clothed with compulsory authority over the other. In a sinless society every occasion for the appearance of such a compulsory authority would fall away, because every one would feel himself immediately and in all things bound by the authority of God. And so it has come to pass that the Juridical faculty, as well as the Medical and the Theological, has disclosed the tendency to oppose an existing evil. If the Theological faculty tended to militate against evil in the heart of man, and the Medical to overcome evil in the human body, in like manner the Juridical faculty has tended to resist evil in the realm of Justice. In connection with this, the Juridical faculty bore a *consecrated* character. It did not study human relations in its own self-sufficiency, but realized its calling to lead the authority imposed of God upon men into the path of Right ordained by Him. Meanwhile this almost sacred origin of the Juridical faculty does not prevent science from introducing the logical purpose of all science more prominently into the foreground of the Juridical domain, and from giving an account of the place which these studies also occupy in the organic unit of science. Viewed in this way, a proper, well-defined place in the object of general science should also be allotted to this study; and in this sense there is no objection against seeking this proper domain of the juridical science, this *provincia juris,* in the social relations of man. The great development of the sociological and economical *auxiliary departments* shows, that the study of law actually moves in this direction, while no one seriously thinks of separating all sociological and economical studies from this faculty and of classing them with the Philological faculty, or, as far as the material object of economical studies is concerned, with the natural philosophical.

It would be a serious matter, however, if for this reason the original juridical character of this faculty should be abandoned, and if gradually and by preference it should be allowed to merge into a *sociological* faculty. If there is apportioned to this faculty the study of all that originates the social life of man, makes it real, and belongs to its nature in its broad extent, then ethics would gradually claim a lodging with it, the life of science and art would come under its care, pedagogy would have to recognize its authority, and the technique also of agriculture, commerce, and of trade would partly come under its rule. It is necessary, therefore, to limit the object of this faculty by a more accurate definition, and that closer definition can be no other than that this faculty is concerned with human society only in so far as this calls out *the Jural Relationships.* Thus *authority* will ever be the characteristic of this faculty, since authority alone is able to verify these Jural Relationships as Law, to maintain them where they are normal, to modify them where they are abnormal, and, where they are still undeveloped, gradually to cause them to emerge. This is as valid for the Jural Relationships between the magistracy and their subjects as for the Jural Relationships of these subjects mutually, and of the nations at large. The sociological and economical studies in this faculty are not charged with tracing abstractly the organic relation among people at every point, nor yet with viewing from every side the relation between human social life and property; but it is their exclusive task to obtain such an insight into this twofold and very important relation as shall interpret the Jural Relationships it implies, and shall discover to the magistracy what in this domain it must and must not do.

In fact, the study of the Juridical faculty will always be governed by the principles professed with reference to *authority.* If authority is considered to have its rise from the State, and the State is looked on as the highest natural form of life in the organism of humanity, the tendency cannot fail to spring up to deepen the significance of the State continuously, and even to extend the lines of authoritative interference, which Plato pushed so far that even pedagogy and morals were almost entirely included in the sphere of the State. Indeed, more than one sociologist in the Juridical faculty is bent upon having his light shine more and more across the entire psychical life of man, in the religious, ethical, aesthetical, and hygienic sense. If sooner or later the chairs of this faculty are arranged and filled by a social-democratic government, this tendency will undoubtedly be developed. If, on the other hand, it is conceded that authority over man can rest nowhere originally but in God, and is only imposed by Him upon men with regard to *a particular sphere,* this impulse to continuous extension is curbed at once, and everything that does *not* belong to this particular sphere falls *outside* of the Juridical faculty. In the *moral* life, which is not included here, God himself is the *immediate* judge, who pronounces sentence in the conscience and various temporal judgments in the world, and who will utter final judgment in the last day; while public authority must appoint law only upon the earth, and must pronounce sentence as judge upon that alone which can be legally established and maintained in the *external* relations of life by *compulsion.* Hence ethics, as touching the relation of man *in foro interno,* will remain in the Theological and Philological faculty; pedagogy, as bearing upon the psychic life, belongs in the Philological faculty; hygiene remains with the Medical; the material side of property finds its study in the faculty of Natural Philosophy; while all that touches the real technics is treated by the *Artes* and not by the *Scientiae.* Thus the Juridical faculty stands in organic relation to all the others; it cannot forego the assistance of any; it must borrow data (Lehnsatze) from all; but it does not lose itself in these studies, while the object of its own science is the social life of man, not as abandoned to whim or accident, but as governed by an authority, and thus bound to a law, which is indeed framed by man, but which finds its deepest ground and hence its binding rule in Him who created this human social life, and who, in the interests of its outward relations, on account of sin, conferred authority *upon* man *over* man.

The science of Law, therefore, is not only to shed light upon the relation of the magistrate and the subject (public law and penal law), upon the relation of citizen to citizen (civil law, commercial law, etc.), and upon the relation of nation to nation (international law); but, before all this, it must develop the idea of Justice itself, so that it can be well understood at what view-point it takes its stand, and according to what rule the development of law must be guided. To accomplish this, it cannot rest content with the investigation of existing Jural institutions, their comparison with others, and a study of their historical origin. All this can never effect more than the knowledge of formal law; while Justice exhibits itself in its majesty only when it obtains its adamantine point of support in our psychical existence, and of necessity flows from what, to our deepest sense of life, is highest and holiest. The question whether one worships this highest and holiest in the living God, or whether it is sought in the pantheistic idea, or in the pressure of natural life, determines, really, the entire course of our further studies. But in any case the science of law must fix its point of departure, formulate its idea of justice, and make clear the vital principle of law. To do this it must borrow its data from Theology, Psychology, and Philosophy in the general sense, but by a proper *Philosophy of law* it must work out these borrowed *data* independently with a view to Justice, and unite them organically into one whole, in which the self-consciousness of Law expresses itself. The *Encyclopedia* of the science of law does not preclude the necessity of a separate study of the philosophy of law. For the object of Encyclopedia is not law itself, but the *science* of law, and though it is self-evident that there can be no exposition of the science of Law as an organic whole without due consideration of the questions what law is, what law is born from, and how we can learn to understand law, yet the answer of these does not rest with the Encyclopedia, but is accepted in the Encyclopedia as already determined; and this is only possible when in the organism of the Science of law the Encyclopedia also finds the Philosophy of law, with its results.

By this we do not detract in the least from the significance of the *historical* study of law. That historical study includes by no means merely the explanation of existing Jural institutions in their origin, but at the same time points out the forms which the character of our human nature, in connection with national and climatic differences, have given to law, and according to what process these forms have developed themselves one from the other. It also appears from these historical studies, that the development of law has been more normal in one direction, and that in definite circles the development of law has exhibited a classical superiority. What we contend is, that no criticism or even a mere judgment is possible, unless a critic is present subjectively in the investigator, and the authority which gives law its sanction determined in advance. Even where this criticism is rejected from principle, and in a pantheistic sense the distinction between right and wrong is actually abolished, in order to recognize law only in that which is in force as such as long as it maintains itself, there is a premise already in this, and back of this premise an entire system, that dominates our entire science of law. Even where one eliminates the Philosophy of law, the start is made insensibly, i.e. without a clear self-consciousness, from a point which the Philosophy of law alone can *scientifically* justify; and for this reason the omission of this study is at heart an *insincerity*.

Concerning the grouping of the several departments of study in this faculty, no one will longer defend the method of Kirchner of placing the fountain-studies, such as hermeneutics, criticism, and diplomatics in the foreground as the *exegetical* group. These are simply not juridical departments, but philological, and are here specially applied to documents of juridical contents. In this faculty also the grouping should derive its principle of division (*principium divisionis*) from its object, and hence this *principium* can only lie in the several elements, among which the Jural relationships are observed, i.e. government and subject, people and people, citizen and citizen. The fourth relation, God and Sovereignty, we purposely omit, because law also runs its course where this relation is not recognized or is even denied, and where the prerogative of Sovereignty is explained in other ways. From this, however, it follows that the three lines of relations which we have named form only the particular part in the juridical science, and that these three studies, which together form the particular part, must be preceded by a general part on *Law as such*. This general part should embrace the two departments: (1) the *philosophy* of Law; and (2) the *history* of Law; to which, for reasons fully developed above, *Encyclopedia* can be added (although, even as with the other faculties really a philosophical study), in an irregular way. Of course it is not denied that the three portions of the particular part have each a history of their own, but we are so fully convinced of the common fundamental trait which dominated these parts in every period and with every people, that Roman law, Germanic law, etc., are generally spoken of in an universal sense. Upon this general part follows the particular part, which falls into three: Public law, International law, Civil law, each with their auxiliary sciences. Public law divides itself again into public law in the narrower sense and Penal law, and to penal law the theory of procedure is added as a subdivision. Those which, on the other hand, are taken separately as political sciences, i.e. statistics, economics, politics, diplomatics, sociology, etc., are only auxiliary sciences which keep public law especially, but civil law also in part, from feeling their way at random, and help them to walk in the broad light of the knowledge of facts, conditions, and relations. The difference is that in olden times the unconscious life was stronger, and hence also the sense of law, since custom of itself determined all sorts of relations which now in our more conscious life are only obtained as the result of investigation. Of course material goods are here considered only in so far as they are subsumed under man, and thereby are brought under the conception of law, or at least can exercise an influence upon the decision of the relations of law. The relation between gold and silver, for instance, would of itself be entirely indifferent to the jurist, but it becomes of importance to him as soon as the question arises, in what way the government in its monetary system is to decide the relation between them. We cannot enter into further detail. To analyze more closely the several characteristics of civil law, commercial law, maritime law, etc., lies not in our province, and the fact that legal procedure, political science, etc., bear less a scientific than a technical character is self-evident. Our only purpose has been to explain that side of the science of law on which it lies organically linked in the organism of *general* science, and to indicate the partly sacred character which the Juridical science must maintain, for Justitia must remain *sancta* or cease to be Justitia, and for this reason it stands in immediate relation to the two great problems, of how authority from God comes to man, and whether or no it has been conferred upon man simply because of sin.

The faculty of *Natural Philosophy* can be considered more briefly. There is only one difference of opinion about the object of physical science. This arises from the fact that the mathematical and arithmetical sciences were formerly classed with Philosophy, while at present the tendency is stronger to class them with the physical sciences as the sciences of the relations of physical data. Those who hold these relations to be unreal, or at least explain them in the main as *subjective,* are obliged, for the sake of logical consequence, to prefer the custom of the old philosophy, and group these departments with the psychical studies. Since, however, the impression has become more universal that science in general and therefore each particular science, must seek its strength in the knowledge of the *relations* even more than in the knowledge of the *elements* among which these relations exist, it is not probable that with reference to the disposition of Mathematics and Arithmetic the subjective tendency will again gain the day. It is entirely true that our human consciousness is adjusted to measure and to number; else the most industrious effort would never bring us the conception of geometry or arithmetic. It is also entirely true that the laws which dominate the combination of measures and numbers, or, if you please, the Logica of measure and number, must find a point of connection in our human consciousness; else we should never be able to propound or solve an abstract problem in mathematics or arithmetic. This, however, does not take away the fact that it is the cosmos outside of us that first brings measure and number to our consciousness. On this ground there seems to be no objection to classing Mathematics, Algebra, and Arithmetic as three formal departments under the physical sciences. For the material departments, however, the principium of division here too lies in the object of physical science. This object ascends from the elements of nature to the cosmos, and in this ascent it follows the scale of the so-called natural kingdoms of our earth, and of that which has been observed in the cosmos physically outside of our earth. Hence those departments come first, which investigate the *elements* (matter as well as force), and which are to be embraced under *Physics* and *Chemistry*. Then come the sciences which investigate certain groups of elements in their organic relations, i.e. Mineralogy, Botany, and Zoology. After that come the studies which direct themselves to *our earth* as such, viz., Geology, Geography in its broadest extent, and Meterorology. And lastly follows Astronomy; and finally *Cosmology,* as embracing the whole.

Let no one imagine, however, that all these sciences as such belong to the so-called exact sciences. No one will be able to assert this of Cosmogony, and the evolution-theory of Darwin sufficiently shows that natural philosophy cannot afford to limit itself to the simple results of weight, number, and measure. The simple observation of what one hears, sees, tastes, and handles, even with the aid of instrumental reinforcement of our senses, and under proper verification, is never anything more than the primitive point of departure of all science and stands formally in line with common perception. Only by the discovery of the laws which exercise general rule in that which is particular does this science raise itself to its second stadium, and become able to exercise authority over matter. But though in this way it materially aids in establishing the dominion which was given man over all created things, and though physical science has contributed the valuable result that it has exalted the independent human consciousness and has set us free to so large an extent from the dominion of matter, it has by no means yet satisfied the highest scientific need. As long as it knows nothing beyond the several data and the law by which these data are governed, the thinking mind cannot rest. It searches also after the relations among the several kingdoms of nature, between our earth and the other parts of the cosmos, between all of nature outside of us and man, and finally after the origin of nature and of the tie which binds us to it, even in our body. These are the points of connection between the faculty of Natural Philosophy and the other faculties; and the fact that physical science inclines more and more to announce itself as the only true science, in order to coordinate man with the objects of zoology, and to explain the psychical life materialistically, shows how ill-advised it is to allow this physical science to make only practical advances, without attaining encyclopedically to self-consciousness and giving itself an account of the place which it occupies in the great organism of science. A scientific Encyclopedia, worthy of the name, is the very thing it altogether lacks; and only when it makes serious work of this can the question be answered, whether as a culminating department *Philosophy of nature* belongs to the faculty.

If now the outline of the four named faculties has been drawn fairly correctly, the question arises whether the *Theological faculty* joins itself to them in organic connection, with a proper object, and in good coordination. To make this clear it will not do to begin by making the conception of Theology fluid. All judgment concerning the Juridical faculty is rendered impossible so soon as you interpret it now as the *facultas juris,* or legal faculty, and again as the *facultas societatis,* or sociological faculty. Much less will a way of escape be discovered from the labyrinth on theological ground, if by Theology you understand, now, that which was originally understood by it, and again supersede this verified conception by an entirely different one, such as, for instance, the Science of Religion. The study of the nature of Theology is in order in the following division, so that in this chapter we can do no other than state the conception which we start out from, and after that review the Theological faculty, and in historical connection with this determine the place of Theology in the organism of science. Because of the importance of the subject we do this in a separate chapter.

CHAPTER V

THEOLOGY IN THE ORGANISM OF SCIENCE

Is there a Place for Theology in the Organism of Science?

The raising of this question intends no coquetry whatever with much-boasted "science." The theologian who, depressed by the small measure of respect cherished at present by public opinion for theological study, seeks favor with public opinion by loudly proclaiming that what he studies is science too, forfeits thereby his right to the honorable name of theologian. Suppose it were demonstrated that Theology is *no* science, but that, like the study of music, it is called to enrich our spiritual life, and the consciousness of that life, in an entirely different way, what would this detract from its importance? Does Mozart rank lower than Edison, because he did not work enchantments, like Edison, with the data of the exact sciences? The oft-repeated attempt to exclude Theology from the company of the sciences, and to coordinate it, as something mystical, rather with the world of sounds, was in itself entirely praiseworthy, and has commanded more respect from public opinion in general than the scholastic distinctions. If thus it should be shown that Theology has no place in the organism of science, it would not lower it in the least, even as, on the other hand, Theology would gain no merit whatever from the fact (if it be proved) that it has its rank among the sciences. In no case may Theology begin with renouncing its own self-respect. And those theologians who are evidently guilty of this, and who, being more or less ashamed of Theology, have tried, by borrowing the scientific brevet, to put it forth in new forms, have been punished for their cowardice. For the non-theological science has compelled them to cut out the heart of Theology, and to transform it into a department of study which shall fit into the framework of naturalistic science. Hence we definitely declare that our defence of the scientific character of Theology has nothing in common with this questionable effort. No Calvinist takes part in the renunciation of our character as theologians. And now to the point.

When treating of the historical development of the faculties it was shown that the general organism of science allows itself to be analyzed into its parts along plain and clearly discernible lines. Thinking man distinguishes in himself first between that which relates to his inner or *psychical,* and outward or *somatical,* existence. He distinguishes in the second place between his own *personal* existence and his social life *with others,* as far as this is not governed by the personal existence of the individuals. And in the third place he distinguishes between *human* life and the life *of nature.* This division comes of itself, is unsought, sees itself justified by the history of the faculties, and is in entire agreement with the needs of practical life. Now the question is whether, along with these four, there remains yet a fifth independent part or organ in the organism of science. And the answer lies at hand, that a final distinction still remains, even the distinction between man *and his God.* Thus in the complete object of science we have four antitheses and five independent parts: (1) God and his creation; (2) in that creation the rest of creation and man; (3) in man first the distinction between his material and spiritual existence, and, again, (4) the antithesis between unity and multiplicity. Or, if you please, five independent and yet organically connected objects present themselves to thinking man, viz.: (1) his God, (2) his psychical existence, (3) his somatical existence, (4) his existence as a member of humanity, and (5) nature outside of man. This division corresponds fully to the Theological faculty (object: God), the Philological (the human soul ψυχή), the Medical (the human body, σῶμα), the Juridical (the legal relationships among men), and Natural Philosophy (the cosmos outside of man). And this analysis of the entire organism into five parts causes the organic relation among the parts, at least in the case of the four faculties already outlined, to be clearly discerned, as well in the object itself as in the reflection of it in the subject, and develops the subdivisions organically in each of the four parts.

Nothing is gained, on the other hand, by the notion that Theology has religious feeling, subjective religion, the phenomena of piety, etc., for its object, and that for this reason it is not to be taken as Theology, but as the Science of Religion. It is impossible in an organic sense to coordinate man's psychical existence, man's somatical existence, man as subdivision of humanity, and nature outside of man, and then, as a fifth wheel to the wagon, man's religious feeling. For this religious feeling belongs to man's psychic existence, and the study of it as such tends to investigate the object *man.* Hence the religious feeling cannot be an independent part in the object to be investigated, distinguished from the other coordinated parts by an essential difference. This religious feeling is very important, and it is certainly right to investigate this phenomenon in the life of man and of his humanity; but this religious life is coordinate with his ethical, aesthetical, and intellectual life; and hence belongs to his psychical existence. In this way these studies come of themselves under the Philological faculty, and can never occasion the rise of a separate faculty of Theology.

One objection only can be raised. From the view-point of the Trichotomists it can be asserted that man does not consist of *body* and *soul,* but of *body, soul,* and *spirit,* and that it is therefore entirely rational, by the side of a faculty for the body, and a faculty for the soul, to place a third faculty, which has the spirit(πνεῦμα)of man for its object, and that this should be the Theological. Thus next to a Somatology and a Psychology, there should also be a Pneumatology as "Dritte im Bunde." This objection, however, cannot stand. The organism of science cannot be analyzed, or, if you please, divided, according to the measure of a distinction accepted only by a single school, but disputed by other schools, and finding no echo in the universal human sense. With all the Reformed we reject the Trichotomy, at least in so far as it assumes *three substances* in man. We are Dichotomists. Even if the distinction between soul and spirit (ψυχή and πνεῦμα) were able to maintain itself to a certain extent, body, soul, and spirit could never be coordinated. But the antithesis should be between *body* and *soul,* and within that soul the distinction between the psychical and the pneumatical should be sought. Even they who speak of a faculty of the Science of Religion are well aware that nothing can be done with the pneuma as such, wherefore they have thrown themselves upon *religion,* as being a very complicated expression of life and rich in phenomenal life. The pneumatical *per se* would not be capable of investigation to any considerable extent. Hence along this way there is no possibility of pointing out a proper ground in the object of general science for a science of Theology, and there can be no question of a Theological faculty. Both are possible only when you come to the antithesis of self-conscious man and *his God,* so that you find the object of your faculty *not* in religion, but *in God.*

But even this by itself will not suffice. Not so much because it will not answer to coordinate God with the incorporeal, with the *soul,* the *body politic,* or *nature.* For the distinction could well be made between the *creator* and *creation,* in the *creation* between *man* and *nature,* and in *man* between his *body* and *soul.* This would be no logical error.

But the difficulty is, that in science, as taken in this chapter, man is the thinking subject, and not God; that this thinking subject as such must stand above the object of science, and must be able to investigate it, and to grasp it with his understanding. And this he is well able to do with *nature*, with our *body, soul,* and *body politic,* but not with God, taken as an object of our human science. Thinking man, taken as *subject* over against God as *object,* is a logical contradiction in terms. It remains an incontestable truth (1 Cor. ii. 11) that "the things of God none knoweth, save the Spirit of God." Man himself would stand before us a closed mystery, if we were not man ourselves and thus able from ourselves to form our conclusions as to others. "For who among men knoweth the things of a man, save the spirit of the man, which is in him?" With man, accordingly, his phenomenal manifestation may always serve us; observation is possible; and the multiplicity of objects, through compariosn, may bring you to come clue. But with God taken as an object, all this forsakes us. In the most absolute sense, He is *univocus.* From yourself (at least so long as He has not Himself revealed to you the creation after His image) you can conclude nothing concerning Him; neither can you see or hear or perceive Him in any conceivable way. For which reason it is entirely logical that the naturalistic tendency in science has not hesitated to cancel Theology, and that the Free University at Brussels, and after her more than one university in America, have opened no faculty, or "Department," as it is called in America, for Theology. We can also understand that the Theologians who have broken with Special Revelation have refused to walk any longer in the old paths, have abandoned God ($\dot{o}$ $\theta\epsilon\dot{o}\varsigma$) as object of science, and have declared: We can investigate *religion,* but not *God.* And no fault could have been found with this, had they faced the consequence of this metamorphosis of the object, and after the demolition of the Theological faculty transferred their study of religion to the Philological faculty.

Something very different presents itself, on the other hand, when the old definition is readopted, that the science of Theology finds its object of investigation *in the revealed, ectypal knowledge of God;* which definition we hold ourselves, but which can be explained only in the following chapter. It is enough here to recall that, according to this representation, God alone knows Himself ("archetypal knowledge of God," cognito Dei archetypa), and that there is no created being that can know aught of Him, except He himself reveals something from His self-knowledge and self-consciousness in a form that falls within the comprehension of the creature ("ectypal knowledge of God, " cognitio Dei ectypa). Had this revelation, now, taken place in the form of complete analysis and synthesis, it would satisfy at once the most rigorous claims of our scientific wants, and would simply have to be inserted into the result of our other scientific work; just as in an historical sketch of an event, in which you yourself have played an important role, you simply insert and embody without further examination that which you yourself have planned and achieved, because you know your personal part in a way which does not provoke a closer investigation. Such, however, is not the character of this revelation, for it presents itself in such a form that all sorts of data are given, from which you are obliged to frame the result. Understood in this way, the complex of all that belongs to this revelation forms an object which, in its starting-point and end, is a unit (einheitlich); which invites investigation; and which by scientific effort must be transposed into a form that shall satisfy the claims of our human consciousness. Suppose that still more Egyptological discoveries were to be made, and, what is not impossible, that a number of inscriptions and communications were brought to light concerning a thus far lesser known Pharaoh; that momuments of his activity were unearthed; and that you were supplied with all sorts of letters, statistics, and records of his reign; all these discoveries would invite and enable you scientifically to explain the historical phenomenon of this prince. Then, however, the object of your investigation would still be Pharaoh himself, and not the knowledge of his person, simply because all these monuments and documents were not erected and written by him for the sake of giving you a specially intended representation of his person. But now imagine the other case. Suppose that an Eastern despot had purposed to hand down to succeeding generations, a particular representation of his person and work, which did not correspond to reality, and to this end had prepared numerous monuments and documents; then from these his real figure in history could not be known, but only that representation of himself which he had intended. And the object of your investigation would *not* be that despot himself, but "the knowledge of his person," such as he had purposed to hand down to posterity. And this is the case here. God has not unintentionally left behind Him traces of His works and revelations of His thoughts in monuments and documents, from which we are to search out who God is. But purposely, and fully conscious of what He was doing, the Lord our God has imparted a knowledge of His Being such as He desired that this knowledge should be. And He has done this in such a way that this revelation does not contain His absolute image, but conveys this knowledge in that particular form which alone can be of service to you. What we supposed in the case of the Asiatic despot to have sprung from the desire to have a different image of himself outlive him from that which he had exhibited in reality, takes place here by means of the third term of comparison (tertium comparationis). The image which is purposely exhibited here is different from the real Being, simply because it is only in that definite form, "according to the measure of man" (pro mensura hominis), that it can be taken up by us. We are therefore fully authorized to say that that which presents itself to us in these monuments and documents is not the knowledge of the real Being of God, which we are to search out from them, but, on the contrary, that in these monuments and documents lies an image of God, drawn by Himself, such as He desires us to receive. Hence, when we investigate these monuments and documents, the object which we search out is not the Divine Being, but that *ectypal knowledge of God,* which is posited in them by God Himself, and which corresponds entirely to the character of our human nature and our human consciousness. The investigation of those monuments and documents, and the search after the ectypal knowledge of God contained therein, is a scientific task in an equally rigorous sense as, in the supposed case, the historic expounding of the image of such a Pharaoh or Asiatic despot.

We admit, of course, that in this section it is only an hypothesis that the Lord our God has placed such monuments and documents at our disposal, that He has purposely hid in them an image of Himself, and that it is possible for us to obtain this ectypal knowledge from them. We only wanted to render it apparent, that with this hypothesis the necessity arises for a peculiar scientific work which does not indeed have God for its object,—a thing which cannot be,—but His *ectypal* knowledge; provided there exists a definite circle of phenomena from which, by investigation, this object can be known. And if, later on, it can be shown that what is here put as hypothesis is true, then in this way we have certainly found a Theology whose calling it is to do a scientific work, and which as such has a place in the organism of science. For this hypothesis itself implies that the phenomena from which this knowledge must be drawn, and this knowledge itself, must organically cohere with the object as well as with the subject of science: with the object, because these phenomena are given in the cosmos and in history; and with the subject, since it is only as *ectypal* that this knowledge corresponds to the measure of man. And this being so, the founding of a proper faculty for this scientific investigation is justified of itself. The object, indeed, which is sought in these phenomena cannot be brought under either of the four other heads. The phenomena which must be investigated form an entirely peculiar group. And the object itself is of such eminent importance, that not only the needs of practical life, but the incomplete character of all other science, alike render the study of Theology necessary.

One more objection, however, must be met. It might, indeed, be said that in an earlier section of this volume we designate *the cosmos* as the only object of science; that except we fall into Pantheism, God does *not* belong to the cosmos, but that as the ground of all being and cause of the cosmos, He must be sought *outside* of it; and hence He does not belong to it, and that therefore the search after God, i.e. Theology, cannot be classed with science. We answer, that this objection has no force when directed against our representation of the matter. To us, indeed, not the unknown *Essence* of God but the ectypal revelation (revelatio ectypa) which has been made *known,* is the object of Theology. This revelation does not lie *outside* of, but *in* the cosmos, and never presents itself to us in any but its cosmical form. Without the least modification, therefore, of our definition of the object of science, Theology, interpreted in this way, certainly obtains its proper place in the organism of science. And Theology extends no further than this. For though the assumption of a cosmos implies the confession of a ground of being for that cosmos, it is *not* science, and therefore not Theology, but only *the mysticism of our inner life,* which involves the data by which we personally know and experience that we stand in communion with that extracosmical ground of being.

The Influence of Palingenesis upon our View of Theology and its Relation to the Other Sciences

In the preceding sections the difference has repeatedly been shown between the conceptions which, according as you reckon with or without palingenesis, you must entertain of the task of the several faculties and their mutual relations. In this closing paragraph this difference is more definitely considered. There are two sorts of people, both of which claim to be the interpreters of our human race in its normal manifestation, and who, because thinking that their own apprehension is the scientific consciousness, cannot abandon the pretension that the result of *their* scientific work alone leads to the knowledge of the object; which knowledge is indeed not adequate, but as pure as lies within our reach. The difference between these two groups can briefly be designated by the word *Palingenesis,* in so far as this implies, first, the abnormal character of that which has *not* undergone this palingenesis, and, on the other hand, the gradual growth into normality again of what exhibits itself as fruit of this palingenesis. This accounts for the fact that he who not only stands outside of palingenesis but also rejects it as a play of the imagination, must consider everything as normal and can only view the divergencies or disturbances as necessary stages in the process of development. Hence such an one deems himself authorized to draw his conclusions from what exists—both from what exists outside of him and from what exists in himself,—and to make these conclusions compulsory for all. And from this point of view no other method is conceivable. He, on the other hand, who himself lives in the palingenesis, or who at least accepts it as a fact, has *eo ipso* an entirely different outlook upon himself and his surroundings. Palingenesis implies that all existing things are in ruins; that there is a means by which these ruins can be restored, yea, that in part they are already restored. He neither may nor can, therefore, draw compulsory conclusions from what exists outside of palingenesis; there can be no question with him of an evolution process; and for him the necessity of all science does not lie in what presents itself to him, but in the criticism of existing things by which he distinguishes the abnormal from the normal.

This applies to all the faculties, but becomes more important in proportion as the part of the object which a given faculty is to investigate stands higher. With the faculty of Natural Philosophy, therefore, this antithesis makes itself least felt; a little more with the Medical; more strongly with the Philological; almost overwhelmingly with the Juridical; but most strongly of all with the Theological faculty.

If I omit from my calculations the facts of palingenesis and sin, then *no* estrangement from God has taken place; then our understanding has *not* been darkened; and *no* disturbance has convulsed nature to cloud the transparency of God in the cosmos. And it is equally inconceivable that a restoring power should be operative in the world, in our heart and in our thought, or that there should be a revelation, in facts or in words, which does not coincide with the normal process of development. For in this case we have nothing but progress, continuous gain and clarifying of knowledge. And granted that there is a God and that a knowledge of this God seems possible, this knowledge of God stands infinitely higher in our nineteenth century than in the days of Abraham and Moses, of David and Isaiah, of Christ and his Apostles. Hence it is from no evil intent, at least not among men (of Satan we do not speak), but simply the necessary consequence of the lack of a personal experience of palingenesis, that, so far from acknowledging them, modern theological development *cannot* rest until it has dispossessed all religious phenomena of their uncommon character, and has included them in the scope of the normal development of our human consciousness. And it is but the consequence of principle, which is compulsory from this point of view, that the authority of the Holy Scriptures is attacked, and that the conflict against the Holy Scriptures *must* be continued until at length all that they offer us is reduced to the proportions of the *ordinary*.

And this gives rise to the question whether from this naturalistic point of view there can still be a theological science, and whether there is still room for a theological faculty. This question is not answered by a rehearsal of the gigantic labors of modern Theology in breaking down the so-called antiquated representations. Breaking down is not building up. And though it is indisputably the task of science to combat error, it is plain that this negative effort does not justify the existence of a faculty. Thus the question should be put as follows: When once the old building shall have been taken down entirely, so that without causing any more concern, antique Theology, properly catalogued, shall have been carefully put by in the museum of scientific antiquities, will there then still remain a work of a peculiar character like Theology which as such will justify the existence of a separate faculty? And this must be answered in the negative. It can be said superficially, that from this view-point also the five questions present themselves to the thinking mind—concerning his own spiritual and bodily existence, and his relation to his fellow-men, to nature and to his God; but—and this is the decisive point—from this point of view the very existence of God is questionable. One no doubt says there is a Bod, but another denies it. And among those also who acknowledge the existence of God, some hold that He can be known, while others dispute it. Suppose it were a question whether there are plants, should we be able to speak of a botanical science? So long as the existence of the object of a science remains uncertain, inquiry may take place; one may sound, feel his way and seek, but one cannot *investigate*. Science with a proper object, and a method derived from that object, is still wanting. Hence in no case can a complex of sciences be allowed to form an independent faculty, on the ground of its organic relation to life. As an escape from this dilemma an attempt has been made to substitute another object for this science, by placing the knowledge of *Religion* at its disposal instead of the knowledge of *God*. From now on it is to be called the Science of Religion. The existence of religion can in no case be denied. In religion we have to do with a notable phenomenon that has been observed at all times and among many nations. This phenomenon may be investigated and thus theological science be revivified. This, however, rests upon a misunderstanding. As a subjective phenomenon religion is one of the phenomena of man's spiritual existence, and as such it belongs to the Philological faculty, and more appropriately to history and philosophy. And as no one would think it proper to found a separate faculty for aesthetics or ethics, it is equally unreasonable to open a faculty for the religious life in man (or at least in many men). We do not deny that from this point of view also there may be a very earnest desire to learn what may be known of God in man and in nature; and to the study of religion or of the science of religion, to annex another study, which seeks after God, feels after Him, that it may find Him, tries to prove His existence and to establish knowledge concerning Him. But he who ignores the facts of the fall and palingenesis, must always reckon with the denial of God by so many thousands, for which reason he can never attain unto a positive knowledge, nor ever produce anything that falls outside of the scope of Philosophy. From this naturalistic point of view the five faculties must be reduced to four. The faculty of Theology, whose supposed object must still be sought, falls away. And everything that relates to religion, in its phenomena as well as in the postulates that produce these phenomena, as a department of study, goes to the Philological faculty. The so-called history of religions is classed with history, more appropriately with the science of countries and nations. Religion as a psychological phenomenon is relegated to the psychological sciences. And finally the assumptions to which religion leads find their place in speculative philosophy, which here finds a point of support for its favorite monistic conclusions.

This whole matter assumes an entirely different phase, however, when palingenesis is taken as the starting-point. For then it ceases to be a problem whether there is a God; that the knowledge of God can be obtained is certain; and in the revelation which corresponds to this palingenesis there is presented of itself an *objectum sui generis,* which cannot be subserved under any of the other faculties; this impels the human mind to a very serious scientific investigation, which is of the utmost importance to practical life. Then every necessary claim, for the emergence of Theology as a proper department of science, is fully met; and its right to a special faculty is entirely indisputable. He who knows from personal experience that there is such a palingenesis, and conceives something of the important change wrought by this fact in our entire sensibility, cannot remain in the suspense of this vague impression, but feels impelled to explain it to his consciousness, and to give himself an intelligent account of all the consequences which flow from it and which are bound to affect his entire world- and life-view. And since this fact does not stand by itself in him, but corresponds to similar facts in the spiritual existence of others, and to analogous facts in the cosmos and in history, the demand of the human spirit is absolute, that these facts, *in* him as well as *outside* of him, must be investigated and placed in relation and in order. And this no other science *can* do; hence a special science *must* be found to do this; since the object to be investigated bears an entirely independent character. The further exposition of this will be the task of the following chapters. But at this point let us briefly consider the relation which, from the view-point of palingenesis, must exist between the Theological faculty and the other faculties.

All prosecution of science which starts out from naturalistic premises denies the subjective fact of palingenesis, as well as the objective fact of a special revelation, which immediately corresponds to this. Even though the inconsistency is committed of maintaining from this point of view a Theological faculty, no influence worth the mention can ever be exerted by this faculty upon the other faculties. Religion, which *as a phenomenon* is the object to be investigated by this faculty, is and remains an expression of the life of the emotions, which, however strong its hold may be upon life, either remains unexplained, or allows itself to be classed in the common scope. Alongside of the ethical and aesthetical life, there is also a religious life; but the study of that religious life imposes no claims upon the studies of the other sciences, nor does it exercise an influence upon their methods.

This, of course, is altogether different, when in palingenesis we recognize a critical and a restorative fact, which both subjectively and objectively places all things, along with their origin and issue, before us in an entirely different light. In the Holy Scriptures palingenesis is a *general* conception, which is applied to the *subject* of science (*vide* Tit. iii. 5), as well as to the *object* of science (*vide* Matt. xix. 28). It assumes a first genesis, which by a departure of the process of life from its principle has led to death, and now it declares that a repetition of the genesis takes place, but this time as a springing up again of that which went down, and that in this restoration the method of genesis repeats itself, viz. the development from a germ. This is applied to man in all his inward life, but will sometime be applied as well to man's somatical existence, as to the whole cosmos outside of him, as far as this also has shared in the false process. Hence palingenesis is now operative in the human mind; and, analogous to this, palingenesis will hereafter appear in the somatical and cosmical life. This palingenesis is introduced spiritually by an act of God's Spirit in the spiritual life of humanity (inspiration in its broadest sense), and somatically by an act of the power of God in the natural life of the world (miracles in their widest interpretation). From which it follows that all study of science, where the investigator occupies the view-point of palingenesis, must reckon with the four phenomena: (1) of personal regeneration; and (2) of its corresponding inspiration; (3) of the final restoration of all things; and (4) of its corresponding manifestation of God's power in miracles (*Niphleoth*). These four phenomena have no existence to the scientist who starts out from naturalistic premises. On the contrary, *his* principle and starting-point compel him to cancel these phenomena, or, where this is not possible, to explain them naturalistically. He, on the other hand, who has personally been taken up into this powerful, all-dominating activity of palingenesis, finds his starting-point in these very phenomena, and mistrusts every result of investigation which does not entirely correspond to them. If now this palingenesis applied only to the religious life, one could say that the faculty of Theology alone is bound to deal with it. But this is *not at all* the case. Palingenesis is a universal conception which dominates your whole person, and all of life about you; moreover, palingenesis is a power that exerts an influence not merely in your religious, but equally in your ethical, aesthetical, and intellectual life. A Jurist, a Physician, a Philologian, and a Physicist, who have personally come under the action of this palingenesis, experience its influence as well as the Theologian, and not only in their emotional but in their intellectual life. This, indeed, has been too much overlooked in earlier periods; wherefore the consequences of palingenesis have been looked for in Theology alone, and thus the mischievous demand has been imposed upon the other sciences that they should subject themselves to the utterances of Theology in those points also which did not pertain to its object of investigation. The Reformed alone have established the rule with reference to the magistracy, that it should not ask the Church to interpret God's ordinances regarding the duties of its life, but that the magistrates should study them out independently for themselves from nature and from the word of God. In this way homage was paid to the principle that every one who shares this palingenesis should exercise independent judgment in all his own affairs. If this principle, which is the only true one, were applied to all the sciences, it would readily be seen that Theology is by no means called upon to arbitrate in every domain of science; while, on the other hand, also, it would be seen that a twofold study must develop itself of all the sciences,—one, by those who *must* deny palingenesis, and the other by those who *must* reckon with it.

This, however, does not take away the fact, that the other sciences must leave Theology the task of investigating palingenesis. For this is its appointed task. Theology alone is called to do this. If there were no palingenesis, there would be no other than a natural knowledge of God, which belongs in the Philological faculty to the philosophical, and more especially to the psychological and ontological, sciences. Since, on the contrary, palingenesis has come in as an universal phenomenon, dominating all things, a faculty of its own had to be created for Theology, and it is the task of Theology to take the four above-mentioned phenomena as the object of its independent investigation. It must examine: (1) inspiration, as the introductory fact to psychical palingenesis; (2) the psychical palingenesis itself; (3) the manifestation that operates introductory to the cosmical palingenesis; and (4) the cosmical palingenesis. Later on it will be shown why this entire study must be drawn from the Holy Scriptures as the principium of Theology, and how it owes its unity just to this common principium. For the present, let it suffice that we simply assume this as a fact, and conclude from it that the investigation here to be instituted forms a special, well-defined ground, and that the other faculties must leave *this* investigation to Theology. And as, in virtue of the mutual relations of the sciences, one adopts its borrowed data (Lehnsätze) from the other whenever it is necessary, so that the Juridical science, for instance, does not compose a psychology for itself, and does not teach a physics of its own in economics, but borrows as much material as it requires from the philological and physical sciences; so also is the relation here. No one of the other faculties can institute an investigation of its own palingenesis, but must borrow its data for this from Theology. And as to their own ground of investigations, they operate from the consciousness of palingenesis, as far as this refers to their own department; and they cannot rest until with their own method they have brought the insight and the knowledge of their own object into harmony with the study of palingenesis.

DIVISION III

THEOLOGY

CHAPTER I

THE CONCEPTION OF THEOLOGY

The Name

In the answer to what we are to understand by Theology, even *the name* is in our time too superficially explained. The reason is that men are in some perplexity about the name. Having broken away from old-time Theology, and having displaced it by something else, the old name is merely kept to maintain in a moral and formal sense an hereditary right to the heritage of Sacrosanct Theology. This is only arbitrary, unless one can prove, genetically at least, his relation to old-time Theology. If this cannot be done, it does not infringe the right to abandon what has become unfit for use, and to replace it by a new complex of studies entirely differently understood, but in that case the old name should be discarded. For then the name becomes a false label, and its retention would be dishonest. Our going back to the name of Theology is therefore no antiquarian predilection, but is demanded by the method that must guide us in defining the conception of Theology. The effort more and more put forth in the second half of this century, either in the psychologic-empiric line of Schleiermacher, or in the speculative track of Hegel, or in both, to form a certain idea of the departments taught in the Theological faculty, to translate this idea into a conception, and to take this conception as the definition of Theology, is a method which can stand no testing, because in this way the certainty that the object of this science remains the same is altogether wanting. In his *Cratylus* Plato does not say in vain: "To teach a thing rightly it is necessary first to define its name." Even in itself, therefore, a study of the name of Theology is demanded; but this is much more necessary now since a genealogical proof must be furnished by those who claim hereditary right, and this hereditary right to the Theological inheritance must be disputed with more than one contestant.

For the right understanding of the name *Theology* the *etymology* and the *usage* of the word claim our attention. With respect to the etymology three questions arise: In what sense is *-logia* to be interpreted? In what sense θεός? And in this connection is θεός to be taken actively or passively? The addition of *-logia* occurs, just as the allied terms, in the sense of *speaking about something,* as well as in the sense of *thinking about something.* Λογεῖον was in Athens what we call the platform, and θεολογεῖον was the place on the stage from which they spoke who represented the gods as *speaking.* The conception of *speaking,* therefore, and not of *thinking,* stands here clearly in the foreground. In ὀστεολογία, φυσιολογία, and other combinations, on the other hand, *-logia* has the sense of tracing, investigating. In itself, therefore, θεολογία could indicate etymologically the action of a θεολόγος, i.e. of one who *speaks* about God, as well as the *thinking* about God. The only thing that serves as a more precise indication here is the age of the word and the object to which *-λογία* is coupled. The root of λέγειν (to speak) with Homer almost always means "to gather," with or without choice. Only later on it obtains the sense of speaking. And only later still, in its last development, the *utterance* of the thought is put in the background, in order to cause the *thought* itself to appear in the front. Since now the word θεολογία occurs already in Plato, the first understanding of λογία has the choice; a choice which is confirmed by Plato's own words. In his *de Re*

Publ. Lib. II., p. 379*a*, he writes: "We, O Adimantos, are at this moment no poets (ποιηταί), but speak as founders of a city (οἰκισταὶ πόλεως), and as such we should understand the forms (τύποι) in which the poets must tell their legend." The question is then asked, "What should be the forms (types) of Theology?" upon which the answer follows that the gods must be proclaimed as they are, whether they are spoken of in "epics, in lyrics, or in tragedy" (ἐν ἔπεσι, ἐν μελεσιν or τραγῳδία). This statement admits of no doubt. In this place at least -λογία is used in the sense of *speaking*. And with reference to its composition with θεο-, it is evident that the idea of *investigating* the being of God must have originated much later than the necessity of *speaking* about the gods. Hence our first conclusion is that -λογία in this combination was originally used in the sense of *speaking*. The second question, what θεο- in this combination means, the gods in general or the only true God, can likewise be answered by the above citation from Plato. Plato himself interchanges 'theology' with a speaking of the *gods* in epics, in lyrics, or in tragedy. Concerning the third question, however, whether in this combination θεο- is object or subject, we must grant the possibility of *both*. In θεοδόσιος,, θεομηνία, θεοκρατία, θεοκρισία, θεογαμία, θεοπραξία, θεοπροπία, etc., a god is meant who gives, who is angry, who rules, judges, marries, acts, speaks, and thus θεο- is the *subject*. On the other hand, in θεοσέβεια, θεομιμησία, θεοκλύτησις, θεολατρεία, etc., it is a god who is feared, imitated, invoked, and honored, hence θεο- is the *object*. Θεολογία, therefore, can mean etymologically the speaking of God, as well as the speaking *about* God. Or if you take θεολογία in the later sense of knowledge, then it indicates a knowledge which God Himself has, as well as a knowledge which we have of God. Finally, in the last-mentioned sense θεολόγος seems to be older than θεολογεῖν, and it appears that θεολογεῖν as well as θεολογία are derived from it. The result therefore is that Theology etymologically is no combination of θεός and λόγος, but means originally a speaking of or about a god or gods; and that only with the further development of the word *logos*, which at first indicated a collected mass, then a word, and only later reason or thought, θεολόγος, θεολογεῖν, and θεολογία also were conceived as a knowledge of or concerning a god or the gods.

Since the etymology admits so many possibilities, the more accurate knowledge of the term "Theologia" should be gleaned from the usage of the word. With Lucian and Plutarch θεολόγος occurs in the general sense of one who treats of the gods, and Augustine declares in *de Civ. Dei*, XVIII., c. 14: "During the same period of time arose the *poets*, who were also called *theologians*, because they made hymns about the gods." With Aristotle θεολογεῖν indicates, to be a theologian, or to act as a theologian. Ἐπιστήμη θεολογική means with Aristotle (*Metaph.* X. 6) a knowledge concerning the divine; while with Plato, "theology" occurs as a speaking about the gods, and with Aristotle in the plural number, "Theologies" were investigations into divine things (*Metereol.* 2. 1). Thus far in all these combinations the general conception was implied of engaging oneself with the matter of the gods or deity, either in consultation with tradition, or in reflection for the sake of a more accurate understanding. With the name "Theology," this general conception has been adopted by Christian writers, modified according to the requirements of their point of view, and carried out upon a large scale. He who reads the exhaustive explanation of Suicer, *Thes. graec.*, under the words θεολόγος, θεολογία, and θεολογεῖν perceives at once how greatly the use of these words was increased and how much more deeply the thinking consciousness entered into the sense of these words, than with the classical writers. That the apostle John was early called the Theologian (ὁ θεολόγος), even in the title of the Apocalypse, cannot properly be explained from his reference to the *Logos* in the prologue to his Gospel and in his first Epistle; but indicates that John was esteemed to be more versed in the divine mysteries than any other apostle. This readily accounts for the fact that he is indicated as such in the title of the Apocalypse and not in the title of his Gospel. In a like sense all the writers of the Old and New Testaments, but more especially the prophets and apostles, are called *theologians*. Thus Athanasius says, *Oratio de incarnatione Verbi*, I., p. 62, ταῦτα δὲ καὶ παρὰ τῶν αὐτοῦ τοῦ Σωτῆρος θεολόγων ἀνδρῶν πιστεύσθαι τις δύναται, ἐντυγχάνων τοῖς ἐκείνων γράμμασιν ; i.e. one thing and another concerning the Saviour you can also confirm by an appeal to the theologians if you turn to their writings. But shortly after this follows the significance of theological investigations of ecclesiastical questions. Thus Gregory of Nazianzus was called "the Theologian," not to place him on a level with John, as though to him also divine mysteries had been revealed, but because in the treatment of dogma he always ascended to God, and thus, as Gregory the Presbyter writes, reached the height of dogma (ὕψος δογμά-των). (See Suicer, I., p. 1360.)

If thus the word "theologos" itself admitted of a twofold meaning, that of "a speaker in the name of God," and that of "a thinker who in his thinking ascends to God," the word "theologein" was still more pliable. This also signified at first to speak in the name of God; for instance, περὶ τούτων τῶν δογμάτων θεολογεῖ Ἡσαίας, i.e. concerning these things Isaiah speaks as commanded by God. Secondly, to explain any point theologically; for instance, Λόγον εἶπεν ἵνα τὴν τελείαν ὕπαρξίν σοι τοῦ Ἰησοῦ θεολογήσῃ, i.e. he names Christ the Logos, in order to explain the absolute relation of Jesus to the very essence of God, — a use of this word which already with Justin Martyr obtained more general currency to indicate an investigation which was instituted *with a certain dignity* of form. Thus, for instance, in his *Dial. c. Tr.* (ed. von Otto, Jenae, 1876, I. 400 B), "Do you inquire in the spirit of theological discussion why one 'a' was added to the name of Abraham, and ask with an air of importance why one 'r' was added to the name of Sarah?" (Διὰ τὶ μὲν ἐν ἄλφα πρώτῳ προσετέθη τῷ Ἀβραὰμ ὀνόματι, θεολογεῖς, καὶ διὰ τὶ ἐν ῥῶ τῷ Σάρρας ὀνόματι, ὁμοίως κομπολογεῖς); where from the coupling of κομπολογεῖν and θεολογεῖν it clearly appears, that in both cases a dignity, a gravity, and a rhetoric are implied, which did not correspond to the unimportance of the question. But besides these two meanings, which run parallel with those of "theologos," the great Fathers of the Christological conflict also used, in the footsteps of Justin, the word "theologein" in the sense of proclaiming one to be God, of announcing one as God. Justin Martyr wrote in his *Dial c. Tryph.* (ed. von Otto, Jenae, 1876, I., p. 104 C), with the Messianic prophecy in Psalm xlv. 6 *sq.* in mind, "If, therefore, you say that the Holy Spirit calls any other God (θεολογεῖν) and Lord (κυριολογεῖν) except the Father of all the Universe and his Christ," — which manner of speech, both by the sense and by the addition of κυριολογεῖν, leaves no doubt but that θεολογεῖν is taken in the sense of calling one God. Thus also we read in Athanasius (Tom. I., p. 1030): Ἐν ἅπασιν οἷς δοξάζεται ὁ πατὴρ θεολογούμενος, ἐν αὐτοῖς δοξάζεται καὶ ὁ υἱὸς καὶ τὸ πνεῦμα τὸ ἅγιον, i.e. "In all points in which the Father is glorified by being spoken of as God, the same also takes place with the Son and with the Holy Ghost." For the sake of still greater clearness, the word θεόν is even added, θεολογεῖν τινα θεόν, as for instance, in Philostorgius, *Hist. Eccl. XIV.*, p. 103, τὸ βιβλίον θεολογεῖ θεὸν τὸν δημιουργὸν ἀπάντων, i.e. This book, the gospel of John, calls the author of all things *God.* Thus also Caesarius, *Quest.* 22, p. 44, says of the Christ, "also when he is incarnate, nevertheless ὑπὸ τῶν προφητῶν θεολογεῖται, i.e. is he called God by the prophets; the Latin *praedicare Deum.*" And finally there was developed from this the more general significance of *deifying something or making it to be God.* For instance, οὐ πάντα κατὰ φύσιν γίνεται, ἵνα μὴ θεολογηθῇ ἡ φύσις (Chrysostom, V., p. 891), i.e. "It is by Divine appointment that all things do not happen in accordance with nature, lest nature be taken for God."

In this way only can we understand the history of the word "theology" in Patristic literature. If a theologian is one who speaks in the name of God, and *theologein* the act itself of speaking in the name of God, then we understand how "Theology" could mean *the Old and the New Testament:* Τῆς παλαίας θεολογίας καὶ τῆς νέας θεολογίας τὴν ξυμφωνίαν ὁρῶν, θαυμάσεται τὴν ἀλήθειαν, i.e. "Seeing the harmony of the Old and New Testament, one marvels at the truth" (Theodor. *Therap.* See Suicer, I., p. 1359). For the word of God comes to us in these two Testaments. If in the second place the word *theologein* means to explain a point so fully as to trace it back to God, then it is clear how "Theology" could mean: reduction to the mystery of the essence of God. Thus says Theodoret (*Quaest. in Genes.* I., p. 3), τί δήποτε μὴ προτέταχε τῆς τῶν ὅλων δη-)μιουργίας θεολογίαν; i.e. "Why did not Moses preface the creation-narrative with an introduction on the mystery of the essence of God?" If, in the third place, "theologein" was used in the sense of "to declare some one God," then it follows also that "Theology" could signify: the divine appellation. Thus says Pachymeres in his note on Dionysius Areopagita (Suicer, I., p. 300), τὰ κοινῶς τῇ θείᾳ φύσει ἁρμοζόντα ὀνόματα ἡνωμένην ἐπιγράφει θεολογίαν, i.e. the names which in general belong to the divine nature, he calls *theologia unita*. And since in the bitter conflict against the Arians everything hinged on the point of proclaiming Christ as God, "Theology" in this sense became almost synonymous with the Deity of Christ. Thus Gregory of Nyssa speaks of a κηρύσσειν τὸ μυστήριον τῆς θεολογίας, with his eye on John i. 1, which thus means to say, "to announce the mystery of the Deity of Christ." This Theologia was then placed over against οἰκονομία as the appellation for his *human* nature. Thus in Theodoret, *Comm. in Heb.* iv. 14, p. 414: we ought to know τίνα μὲν τῆς θεολογίας, τίνα δὲ 'τῆς οἰκονομίας ὀνόματα, i.e. what names belong to his divine, and what to his human, nature. In connection with this, "Theology" was also used in the sense of the "mystery of the Trinity." The knowledge of God, which as such was the characteristic of Christianity, was contained just in this trinitarian mystery. Thus Athanasius, *de Definitionibus*, Tom. II., p. 44: Ἐπὶ τῆς θεολογίας μίαν φύσιν ὁμολογοῦμεν τῆς ἁγίας Τριάδος, τρεῖς δ' ὑποστάσεις, i.e. "Of the mystery of the Divine Being we confess that in the Holy Trinity there is only one nature, but a threefold hypostasis." Photius, *Epist.* XXXIV., p. 95, ὥσπερ ἐπὶ τῆς θεολογίας τὸ τρεῖς ὁμολογεῖν οὐσίας πολύθεον, i.e. even as it is Polytheistic to confess three substances in the mystery of the Trinity. Theophylact, *Comm. in Math.*, c. xxviii., p. 185, εἰπὼν ὅτι δεῖ βαπτί-ζειν εἰς τὸ ὄνομα τῆς 'τριάδος τὴν θεολογίαν ἡμῖν παρέδωκεν, i.e. by the command to baptize in the name of the Trinity, Christ has revealed to us the mystery of the Divine Being. And in like sense Gregory Nazianzen uses the word when in *Oration* I., p. 16, he writes, τρία ἔστι περὶ θεολογίας ἀρρωστήματα, i.e. there are three weaknesses with reference to the interpretation of the Divine mystery.

Thus the development of the term *Theology* is not doubtful. First the word was adopted from the pagan usage to indicate a speaking of the things that pertain to the gods or God, whether materially, as declarations of divine affairs, or simply formally, as a speaking with dignity and with a certain unction. In the conflict about the divine nature of Christ the still living Grecian language-consciousness began to use the term θεολογεῖν actively in the sense of calling one God, and thereby θεολογία obtained gradually the significance of the confession of the Deity of Christ. Since the Christological conflict speedily assumed a Trinitarian character, and the confession of the Trinity hinged upon the acknowledgment of the Deity of Christ, Theology began gradually to be interpreted in the sense of the mystery of the Divine Essence as Trinitarian. And finally, by Theology there began to be understood that which is revealed to us concerning this mystery, since to this extent only we can deal with this mystery. At the point of history when the supremacy of the Church was transferred from the East to the West, and the living word θεολογία was lost in the dead barbarism *Theologia*, this Latin term was understood to mean the revealed knowledge of the mystery of the Threefold Being of God, and by no means a prosecution of Theological departments of study.

Theological Modality of the Conception of Theology

Thomas Aquinas (*Summa Theol.* I. 9, i., art. 7) already protested against the abuse of making the nature of Theology to consist, not in the knowledge of God, but in the knowledge of an entirely different object of investigation; and thus against those who assigned, not God, but "another subject for this science, for example, either things and signs, or the works of redemption, or else the whole Christ, that is, both head and members"; for, says he, "all these are treated in this science, *but according to their order with respect to God"* ("aliter assignaverunt huius scientiae *subjectum,* sc. vel res, et signa, vel opera reparationis, vel totum Christum, id est, caput et membra," . . . "de omnibus istis tractatur in ista scientia, *sed secundum ordinem ad Deum"*). So far as this protest directs itself against the soteriological or Christological interpretation of the science of Theology, it is equally pertinent to almost all definitions which in the course of this century have been given of the conception of Theology. What he says, on the other hand, of Theology as a study of the *Signa et Res,* refers in part to Peter Lombard's *Sententiae,* but principally to Augustine, who, in his *Libri IV. de doctrina Christiana,* had followed the division into *Signa et Res,*—a division which Thomas does not reject, but which in his view does not define the "subject of Theology," or what we would call the *object* of Theology.

The important interest defended by Thomas in this protest, a protest to which all earlier Reformed theologians have lent their influence, lies in the requirement that the conception of Theology must not only be construed abstractly *logically,* but also *theologically.* Augustine already tried to do this, though he rarely used the word *Theology* to indicate the conception intended by us. What in the Western Church also was called Theology, he called *Doctrina de Deo* or *Christian Doctrine;* and however strange it may seem, by the word *Theology* Augustine understands the pagan rather than the Christian conceptions of the Divine. This appears prominently in his *De Civitate Dei,* in which he (Lib. VI., c. 5 *sq.,* ed. Bened. Bass. Ven., 1797, pp. 179-255) discusses the system of Varro, as though there were three kinds of Theology: mythology (theologia *fabulosa*), which lived in tradition and in the theatre; natural theology (theologia *naturalis*), which is found in the writings of the philosophers; and State religion (theologia *civilis*), which was maintained by official public worship. And it is noteworthy that while continually quoting this threefold description of Theology, Augustine nowhere places theologia Christiana, or vera, over against it, but always speaks of *Doctrina* Christiana. Once only, in caput 8 (p. 203), does he take theologia in its general sense, but still not to express doctrina Christiana, but that after which the doctrina Christiana seeks. In refuting the physiological representations of the philosophers he says: "But all these things, they say, have certain physical, i.e. natural, interpretations, showing their natural meaning; as though in this disputation we were seeking physics and not theology, which is the account, not of nature, but of God." From this we see, that by "Theology" Augustine did not understand the study of our science, nor that science itself; by him this was called *doctrina;* but much more the knowledge of God, as the aim of theological study.

Thus with Augustine already this deeper conception of Theology bore a decidedly *theological* character. This is seen in his *Libri IV. de doctrina Christiana,* where he goes back to God, as Himself the Wisdom (Sapientia), and calls Christ, as the Word of God (Verbum Dei), the first way to God (prima ad Deum via), and then by the side of the intellectual method of attaining the knowledge of God, he also emphasizes the way of contemplation (via contemplationis) and the *seeing of God.* Thomas Aquinas also occupies this point of view in the main, and in his footsteps also Calvin. Thomas' chief work bears, indeed, the title of Summa *theologica,* but in his introduction he systematically treats of the *sacra doctrina,* which really is not Theology itself, but *circa theologiam versatur.* Only rarely does the word *theologia* occur with him, as, for instance, when in P. i. i. Qu. art. 7, ed. Neap., 1762, I., p. 12 , he says: "But in this science discourse is chiefly made about God, for it is called Theology, as being discourse about God" ("Sed in hac scientia fit sermo principaliter de Deo; dicitur enim theologia, *quasi sermo de Deo"*). Here, however, he gives us least of all a definition, but derives an argument from the etymology of the word to maintain "God" ($\dot{o}$ $\theta\epsilon\dot{o}s$) as the object of the 'sacred doctrine.' The real conception which he attaches to Theology is therefore much more clearly seen from what he says concerning faith, hope and love as the three *virtues theologicae* (see I., secundae, qu. 62, art. i. *sq.*). Let it be noted also that he did not write as the title of his work: Summa theolo*giae,* but Summa theolo*gica.* De Moor, in his *Comm. in Marck.*, Tom. I., p. 9, quotes these words of Thomas: "Theology is taught by God, teaches of God, and leads to God" ("Theologia a Deo docetur, Deum docet et ad Deum ducit"); since, however, he does not name the place where he found this citation, it is not to be verified. In like manner Calvin does not give to his dogmatics the title of Epitome Theologiae, but of *Institutio religionis Christianae*, and translates the word *theologia*, which he almost everywhere avoids, by *notitia Dei* (cf. Lib. I., c. i., i. *sq.*). The indexes are not trustworthy with reference to this. The index to Thomas as well as to Calvin's *Institutes* gives a meaning to the word *Theology* in which the word *Theology* itself was used neither by Thomas nor by Calvin.

This distinction, now, which maintained itself for a long time between theological science as sacred learning or instruction (*sacra doctrina, institutio*), etc., and Theology itself as *knowledge of God (notitia Dei)*, was not trivial; but tended to interpret the conception of Theology *theologically*, as this theological conception is more precisely analyzed into the theologia archetypa and ectypa. And this must be maintained. The field of knowledge disclosed to us in Theology cannot logically be coordinated with the other fields that are investigated by our understanding. As soon as this is done, Theology is already robbed of its peculiar character, and cannot be interpreted except as a part of metaphysics, or as a science whose object of investigation is the empirical phenomenon of religion, or, more precisely, the *Christian* religion. If, on the other hand, Theology is a knowledge which, instead of dealing with created things, illumines our minds with respect to the Creator, and the "origin and end of all things," it follows that this knowledge must be of a *different* nature, and must come to us in *another* way. The *normae* that are valid for our knowledge elsewhere have no use here; the way of knowledge must here be another one, and the character itself of this knowledge must differ from all other science. As within the boundaries of the infinite you must follow a different way to the knowledge for the spiritual than for the natural sciences, the way to the knowledge of that which transcends the finite and lies beyond its boundary cannot coincide with the Erkenntnisstheorie of the finite. Hence we have no warrant for making a logical division and saying: Science investigates nature, man, and God, and the science which does the latter is Theology, simply because the coordination of nature, God and man is false. He who views these three as coordinates, starts out logically from the denial of God as God. This was entirely correctly perceived by the Greek Fathers, and in the steps of Augustine by the Western Fathers, in consequence of which, even though without sufficient clearness of insight, they refused to place *Theo*logy in line with the other -logies or -nomies, and demanded a *theological* interpretation of the conception of Theology. The force of this theological interpretation was still felt in the second half of the eighteenth century, whenever the dogmatici described Dogmatics not as a subdivision of Theology or as one of the departments of theological study, but as *the* theologia propria, to which exegesis, church history, church polity, etc., were added as auxiliary studies. They had already lost the conception of Theology to such an extent that, though not theoretically, they practically applied the name of Theology to the human study which was devoted to this revealed knowledge of God; but from their limitation of this name to Dogmatics it was evident that they took this to be the study that leads to the right understanding of the real knowledge of God. They were not concerned about all kinds of learning, but about God Himself, and that alone which could bring us a closer knowledge of that God could claim in the more precise sense the name of Theology. It is indeed true, as is shown by the history of Encyclopedia, that the Encyclopedists gradually began to understand by Theology the complex of the several departments of theological study; but no one will contend that in doing this they contributed to an organic interpretation of the conception of Theology. Of Schleiermacher only it can really be said that, seeing the unskilfulness of the earlier Encyclopedists, he seriously tried to bring Theology, not as a knowledge of God, but taken as a theological science, to a unity of interpretation. It is too bad that he went to work at this so unhistorically; that he paid almost no attention to the development of the conception of Theology in former ages: and still more is it a pity that, mistaken in the idea of the object, he could not attain to an organic interpretation, and advanced no further than to explain it as an aggregate, united by the tendency of these several studies to aid in preparation for the sacred office. By this he cut off the *theological* understanding from the conception of Theology; and they who have come after him have no doubt superseded his aggregate by an organic conception, and his exceedingly limited object by a broader object, but have not removed the breach between what Theology was originally and what has since been understood by it. The rule continued to be derived exclusively from Logica by which to define the conception of Theology, and thus it was impossible to regain the theological conception of this science. This does by no means imply that repristination of the former conception would suffice. The very contrary will appear from our further exposition. All we intend to say, is that here also no progress is possible, unless we continue our work along the line of those threads that were spun for us in the past.

And in looking back upon this past we find that in the conception of Theology a characteristic *theological modality* exhibits itself almost constantly; by which we mean that the peculiar character of Theology has exerted an influence also upon the forming of this conception. How far this influence extended can only be shown in the following sections; but in order to place the significance of those sections in the desired light, it was specially necessary to refer to this point.

The Idea of Theology

He who is called to the fifth story of a large building, and finds an elevator, which without any effort on his part brings him in a moment where he wants to be, will not climb the hundred or more steps on foot. Applied to our knowledge, this implies that common, slow investigation, with its inductions and deductions, is merely the stairs with its hundred steps by which we climb the heights of knowledge, while the *attainment of* knowledge is ever the aim in view. From which it follows that if that same height of knowledge can be reached by a shorter or less laborious way, the former stairs become worthless. This is true horizontally as well as vertically. Since now there are railways to all corners of Europe, no one travels any longer by stage-coach. Though there may be a peculiar pleasure attached to that slow rate of progress, or rather to creeping along the way of knowledge, it is, nevertheless, somewhat morbid to abandon for the sake of this lower pleasure the much higher delight of the *knowledge* of the truth. Lessing's proverb has led us astray on this point, and therefore the brief indication of the only true point of view was necessary. What surprises still await us of locomotion by electricity or through the air are not easily foretold; but this is certain, that every more rapid communication antiquates the less rapid. This compels us in Theology, also, to distinguish between the conception and the idea of Theology. The *conception* is bound to the way of knowledge which we travel. The *idea*, on the other hand, views the end, independently of the question of the way by which this end shall be reached. This was the distinction in view in the formerly generally current division of Theology into a theologia *unionis, visionis* and *stadii*. This supplied three conceptions, which found their unity in the idea of Theology. The theologia unionis was that highest knowledge of God, which Christ possessed in His human nature, by virtue of the union of *this* nature with the Divine nature. The theologia visionis, also called *patriae*, was the appellation of the knowledge of God which once the elect will obtain in the state of heavenly blessedness. And the theologia *stadii*, also called *studii*, or *viatorum*, expressed that knowledge of God which is acquired here upon earth by those who are known of the Lord. That which was common to them all, and which united these three conceptions, was the general idea of the *knowledge* of God. The aim of Theology, therefore, did not lie in the theological investigation, neither in all sorts of studies and learning, but exclusively in *knowing God*. All study and learning served only as scaffolds for erecting the palace of our knowledge; but as soon as the building was finished that scaffolding lost all its meaning, even became a hindrance, and had to be cleared away. And this was more clearly perceived in olden times, than by most theologians after Schleiermacher. The idea of Theology can be none other than the *knowledge of God,* and all activity impelled by Theology must in the last instance be bent upon the *knowledge of God.* This is not said in a metaphorical, but in a very exact sense. And this must be maintained as the idea of Theology, when you come to consider also the science of Theology, as it is studied and taught by the Theological faculty. By a different notion of the idea, and by lowering your ideal, you degrade theological science itself. According to its idea, Theology does not at first demonstrate that there is a God; but it springs out of the overwhelming impression which, as the only absolutely existing One, God Himself makes upon the human consciousness, and finds its motive in the admiration which of itself powerfully quickens the thirst to know God. Though Theology may be permitted to seek after proofs for the existence of God, by which it may open the eyes of those half-blind, it cannot itself start out from doubt, nor can it spent itself in the investigation of religious phenomena, or in the speculative development of the idea of the absolute. It may do all this when it is convenient and as a dialectic auxiliary, but all this is only secondary; at most, a temporary bridge, by which itself to reach the other side or bring others there, but its purpose, wading the mountain stream, remains to come to the mountain itself, and in the sweat of its brow to climb the mountain path, until at length the highest peak is reached, the top itself, where the panorama, the knowledge of God, unveils itself. Only when thus interpreted does Theology regain its necessary character, and otherwise it lapses into an accidental dilettantism. Thus only it regains its value, and, apart from every conception of utility or eudemonistic purpose, it recovers an absolute significance in itself. Thus in its very idea it advances beyond the boundary of our present existence, and extends itself into the eternal and the infinite.

The older Theologians derived this more accurate insight into the nature of Theology and this necessary distinction between the idea and the several conceptions of the one Theology from the Holy Scriptures. In the Scriptures "the knowledge of God" is clearly stated as the *forma* of "eternal life," and of that knowledge of God several degrees are indicated. The distinction is evident at once between the knowledge of God disclosed to man before he sinned, and that modified knowledge of God given to the sinner. There was a knowledge of God for Him who said: "Neither doth any know the Father, save the Son, and he to whomsoever the Son willeth to reveal him"; and a knowledge of God for those who could not attain this save by that Son. And finally in the Scriptures a very significant distinction is made between the knowledge of God of those who have been "enlightened" and of those who still "walk in darkness"; between the knowledge of God, already obtained here by those who have been enlightened, and that which shall sometime be their portion in the realm of glory. Hence a rich difference of form was found in the Scriptures, but still the same idea was common to all these forms, which idea was and is: *to know God,* and to know Him as *men.* For in the Scriptures a knowledge of God in the world of angels is also spoken of, which is not entirely lost even in fallen angels, so that "the devils also believe that there is one God"; but since this knowledge assumes another subject, we need not here take it into account. This treatise deals exclusively with *human* Theology (Theologia *humana*), and for the sake of clearness we leave the other distinctions alone, in order now to study the distinctions between our knowledge of God here and in heaven (Theologia *stadii* and *patriae*).

The classical proof-text for this is 1 Cor. xiii. 8-13, where the holy apostle definitely declares, that the gnosis which we now have "shall be done away," since now it is only a knowing "in part"; that in this matter of our knowledge of God there is a "perfect" contrasted to that which is now "in part"; that when that which is "perfect" is come, a seeing of "face to face" shall come into being; and that this seeing shall be a "knowing even as also I have been known." Elsewhere also, in Matt. v. 8, in 1 John iii. 2, in Psalm xvii. 15, etc., a knowledge of God is mentioned, which shall consist in a *seeing of God;* but for brevity's sake we confine ourselves to the utterance in 1 Cor. xiii. Two things are here included. First, a sharp dividing-line is drawn between the knowledge of God which is acquired on earth, and that other knowledge of God which is in prospect on the other side of the grave. But secondly, the relation is indicated which is sustained between these two forms of knowledge. Knowledge does not disappear in order to make room for sight. It is not a *knowing* here and a *seeing* of God there. No, it *is* a knowing both here and there; but with this difference, that here it is "in part" and there it shall be "perfect." The seeing, on the other hand, is, here as well as there, the means by which to obtain that knowledge; here a seeing "through a glass darkly," there a seeing "face to face." The holy apostle treats even more exhaustively the relation between Theology here and in heaven by indicating the analogy of the child that becomes a man. The child and the man have both a certain knowledge, but the knowledge of the child dissolves in that of the man. By becoming a man he himself brings the putting away of that which belonged to the child. Thus the unity between the two forms of our knowledge of God is most firmly maintained, and both conceptions of knowledge emphasized as finding their higher unity in the idea of Theology, which is and always will be: *the knowledge of God.* That Paul speaks very expressly here of the *knowledge of God,* and not of "the knowledge of divine things" in general, appears clealry from the $\kappa\alpha\theta\grave{\omega}\varsigma$ $\dot{\epsilon}\pi\epsilon\gamma\nu\acute{\omega}\sigma\theta\eta\nu$ vs. 12. "Knowing even as also I am known" cannot mean anything save knowing Him by whom I am known.

The objection also that this future *seeing* of God is merely mystical or contemplative, and that therefore it has nothing to do with our logical consciousness, but falls outside of Theology, is set aside by 1 Cor. xiii. The logical is not a temporal form of our human consciousness, fundamentally fictitious, and therefore bound to pass away. But God Himself is logical, for in Him also knowledge is assumed, and between our knowledge here and that which shall be ours in eternity, there is no essential, but only a proportional, difference: now in part, then perfect. Similarly the difference betwtween the two modes of knowledge is merely that of the immediate and mediate. Then our knowledge will turn immediately on God Himself, while now we only observe the image of God *in a glass,* in which it is reflected. Thus the continuity of our knowledge of God is not broken by the passing away of present things. When the knowledge "in part" shall have passed away, the identity of our consciousness shall continue. That same *ego,* which now can only faintly discern the image of God *in a glass,* shall presently be conscious of the fact that it knows that selfsame God whose image it first saw "darkly," and will recognize in the Divine face those very features which formerly it observed in the glass imperfectly and indirectly. From this, at least, we see that the so-called *scientific* investigation shall sometime fall away; that it bears no *absolute* character; and that it derives its temporal necessity merely from the condition brought about by sin, and its possibility logically from "common grace" and theologically from the "particular grace" of divine illumination. And if this is so, it follows of itself that scientific investigation can never be Theology, and is only an accidental activity amid present conditions and within given boundaries, impelled by the thirst after Theology, or rather by the thirst after the knowledge of God. Hence the higher idea of *the knowledge of God* determines Theological science and not Theological science the idea of Theology. There can, and there will hereafter, be a rich Theology without the aid of a Theological science; while on the other hand when Theological science withdraws itself from the knowledge of God, it loses all sufficient reason, and can lead no other than a nominal existence.

The naming of the animals by the original man in paradise presents a partial analogy. In the domain of zoology, also, the real end in view is not scientific study, but knowledge of the animal. In our present condition this knowledge cannot be acquired except by empirical investigation and the drawing of conclusions from the data obtained. But if we knew and understood the animal at once, this empirical investigation and this drawing of conclusions would be purposeless, and hence dispensable. And something like this is told us in the story of paradise. There was here really a knowledge of the animal by the "seeing of face to face." To Adam the animals were no enigma as to us, but were known and understood by him; and therefore he could give them a name according to their nature. Had this capacity remained intact in us, zoology of course would have assumed an entirely different form; and not in a lesser but in a much higher sense it would still have been zoology. For the knowledge of animals in paradisaical man was not analogous to the vague perception which we now have immediately of the world of sounds or of moral phenomena, but it was logical; as is evident from the fact that it led to the giving of the name. And in this sense it presents an analogy for Theology in its two different phases. Just as now in zoology scientific study is indispensable if we would obtain a logical knowledge of the animal, in our present dispensation Theological study is equally indispensable to obtain the logical knowledge of God. But as in paradise knowledge of animals was at the disposal of man without this study, in the dispensation of glory man will similarly attain a much more complete and yet logical knowledge of God, without theological study. This is equally applicable to *theologia paradisi* and *theologia unionis,* but this we pass by because for the sake of clearness we are considering only the antithesis between our knowledge of God "in a glass" here and "face to face" in glory.

If it is now plain that the theological idea lies in the impulse of our human consciousness *to know God,* entirely independently of the way in which this knowledge is to be acquired, our object has been gained. The idea of Theology as such is imperishable, but according to the demands of our condition, it leads us by different ways to our ideal. The way which we must travel is that of *theological study,* and the science which is born from this study can with entire propriety be called *Theology,* provided this is not done in an exclusive sense, and this science admits no other motive than *to know* or *learn to know God.* Every *conception* of Theology which is not subordinated to the *idea* of Theology must fail.

The Dependent Character of Theology

If the idea of Theology lies in *the knowledge of God,* an entirely peculiar character flows from this for all Theology, which distinguishes it from all other knowledge or investigations of science. For in all other investigations the investigating subject places himself *above* the object to be investigated, is the *active* agent in the investigation, and directs his course in obedience to his *own* free judgment. And this is both possible and proper with created things, because among all these *man* ranks first. But when the thirst for knowledge directs itself to Him to whom man and all creation owe their origin, existence, and consciousness, the circumstances are materially changed. Then man stands no longer *above,* but *beneath* the object of his investigation, and over against this object he finds himself in a position of entire *dependence.* Our earlier Theologians explained this by distinguishing between archetypal Theology (Theologia archetypa) and ectypal Theology (Theologia ectypa)—a distinction which as it was finally defended could not be maintained, but which contains an element of truth that should not be abandoned. For the real thought fundamental to this distinction between archetypal and ectypal Theology is that all personal life remains a closed mystery to us as long as he whose life This does not himself disclose it to us. And this thought must be maintained. We purposely limit ourselves to personal life in order to exclude the zoological question, even though we readily grant that in animals also a similar mystery presents itself; but this mystery need not detain us now, because the *knowledge of man* presents already the entirely sufficient analogy for the *knowledge of God.* With man also the rule applies to each individual that you *cannot* know him in his personal existence, except he himself disclose the mystery of his inner being.

And yet as far as man is concerned, appearance might readily deceive us. We quickly form an idea about the persons we meet in daily life, and some of us can form a fairly accurate idea of a man at the very moment of meeting. Let us observe however: first, that being human ourselves we have a means in our own existence by which measurably at least to understand a fellow-creature. Were we not ourselves man, we would not understand what man is; as it reads in 1 Cor. ii. 11: "For who among men knoweth the things of a man, save the spirit of the man, which is in him?" In the second place, this knowledge which we owe to our mutual relationship, is strengthened by the fact, that as a rule we associate with fellow-citizens, congenial spirits, and those to whom we are united by a certain community of lot. Hence not only our common humanity, but the fact also that the modality of existence is largely common to us all, makes it easy from ourselves to form conclusions concerning others. How important this factor is, we perceive at once when we cross the boundaries of our native land, and especially when we come among other races and into entirely different countries. A Russ or Finn understands very little of the real inner nature of the Red man, and what does a Frenchman understand of the inner nature of a Lapp or Finn? In the third place, let it be noted that however much there may be something personal in every man, characters divide themselves into certain classes, which are recognized by certain combinations of phenomena, so that he who knows one or more of these kinds readily understands a great deal of a person, as soon as he perceives to what class he belongs. Fourthly, man is no spirit but a spiritual being, and exists simultaneously psychically *and somatically,* so that a great deal of his inner life manifests itself without the person being conscious of it; often indeed against his will and purpose. The look of the eye, feature and color of face, carriage and manners, composure or restlessness in the whole appearance, etc., betray much of what goes on in man. To which may be added, in the fifth place, that in conversation or in writing a man may say to us or to others, something of himself from which very important data may be gathered directly or by inference concerning the mystery of his person. No doubt there are "closed characters," and also "characters that falsify themselves," which you can never fathom, but as a rule you can obtain considerable knowledge of a man, even when he does not purposely disclose to you the mystery of his person.

If, now, on the other hand, you turn from the knowledge *of man* to the knowledge *of God,* you perceive at once that almost nothing of these five means of help is at your disposal. Standing before God you do not find an analogy in your own being to His Being, because He is God and you are man. The closer knowledge of your fellow-man which you acquire from your sharing his modality of existence falls entirely away, since the distance between you and the Eternal Being discovers itself the more overwhelmingly as your existence specifies itself. The division into kinds is of equally little service, because there is but one God, of whom therefore no conclusion can be drawn from the species to the individual. Unintentional somatic unveiling is equally impossible with God, since asomatic and only spiritual existence characterizes Him as God. And finally, the casual dropping of a remark does not occur with respect to the Eternal Being, since the casual and unconscious doing of a thing is not predicable of God.

The difficulty which the biographer encounters when he undertakes to sketch the development of a character that belongs to another age, land and surroundings, and of which almost no personal utterances are handed down in writing, repeats itself with the Theologian, only in an absolute measure. His aim and purpose is to acquire knowledge of a Being which is essentially distinguished from himself and from all other creatures; a Being which, by no amount of investigation, he can compel to give knowledge of itself; which as such falls entirely outside of his reach; and over against which he stands absolutely agnostically, in accordance with the true element of Spencer's Agnosticism.

Let it not be said, that an infinite number of things are manifest and knowable of God, in the works of creation, in history, and in the experiences of our own inner life; for all this leads to a certain knowledge of God, only when God has begun to reveal Himself to me as a God, who exists and exists as God. Even though for the moment we do not reckon with the darkening of sin, all that is called "natural revelation" would not impart to us the least knowledge of God, if it were not willed by God, and as such make an intentional *revelation,* i.e. a disclosure in part of His Divine mystery. Suppose that on the fixed stars there lived a race of beings, of an entirely different type from what we have ever known; the simple report of what they had done would never advance our knowledge of them, as long as the idea, not to say every conception, of their kind of being were wanting. From the nature of the case this is much more forceful with reference to the knowledge of God, and the contemplation of visible things would avail us absolutely nothing, if the sense that there is a God, and of what a God is, were not imparted to us in an entirely different way.

In this sense we speak of a *dependent* character for Theology. When an absolute stranger falls into the hands of the police, which is no infrequent occurrence anywhere, and steadfastly refuses to utter a single syllable, the police face an enigma which they cannot solve. They are entirely dependent upon the will of that stranger either to reveal or not to reveal knowledge of himself. And this is true in an absolute sense of the Theologian over against his God. He *cannot* investigate God. There is nothing to analyze. There are no phenomena from which to draw conclusions. Only when that wondrous God will speak, can he listen. And thus the Theologian is absolutely *dependent* upon the pleasure of God, either to impart or not to impart knowledge of Himself. Even verification is here absolutely excluded. When a man reveals something of himself to me, I can verify this, and if necessary pass criticism upon it. But when the Theologian stands in the presence of God, and God gives him some explanation of His existence as God, every idea of testing this self-communication of God by something else is absurd; hence, in the absence of such a touchstone, there can be no verification, and consequently no room for criticism. This dependent character, therefore, is not something accidental, but essential to Theology. As soon as this character is lost, there is no more Theology, even though an investigation of an entirely different kind still adorns itself with the theological name. In his entire Theology the Theologian must stand in the presence of God as his God, and as soon as for a single instant he looks away from the living God, in order to engage himself with an idea about God over which he will sit as judge, he is lost in phraseology, because the object of his knowledge has already vanished from his view. As you cannot kneel in prayer before your God as worshipper, in any other way except as dependent upon Him, so also as Theologian you can receive no knowledge of God when you refuse to *receive* your knowledge of Him in absolute dependence upon Him.

This deep sense of dependence has ever induced our real theologians, in the days of their power, to place all our knowledge of God as *ectypal* Theology, in absolute dependence upon the *self-knowledge* of God, which they called *archetypal* Theology. As the ectype is absolutely dependent upon the archetype, is governed and formed by it, thus, they would say, all our knowledge of God is absolutely governed by the knowledge which God has of Himself. Thus they taught that we of ourselves can never enter into the holy place of the Lord, to examine it and gather knowledge concerning it, but that it behooves us to take our stand on this side of the veil, and to wait for what God Himself will communicate to us from this holy place and from behind this veil. This revelation or communication, which is *imparted* to our knowledge, we may consider, analyze, systematize and cast into the form of our consciousness; but in all these operations all active investigation after what is God's remains excluded, all knowledge remains *received* knowledge, and it is not God Himself, but the *knowledge* He has revealed to us concerning Himself which constitutes the material for theological investigation. Hence *ectypal* Theology.

The objection raised against this division and appellation cannot stand. It has been said, that in this way we can also speak of an ectypal zoology, botany, etc. For these parts of His creation are also known to God before they are known to us; and all our knowledge of the world of animals and plants, etc., is either in harmony with the knowledge God has of them and then true, or in antagonism with it and then false. This distinction between archetypal and ectypal knowledge is valid in every department, and therefore may not be claimed as something characteristic of Theology. But this objection is altogether inaccurate. For instance, I can order a sketch to be made of a gable-roof, which upon examination is seen to agree entirely with the original drawing of the architect; but does that prove that this last sketch has been copied from the original drawing? No, only if this sketch had not been made from the gable, but immediately from the original drawing, would it have been ectypal; but not now. It is not true, therefore, that our botanical and zoological knowledge can be called ectypal. It would be this, if we did not draw this knowledge from the world of animals and plants, but copied it apart of these realities from the decree of creation, as far as it referred to animals and plants. We will not stop to consider the question whether our knowledge of the world of angels, of the soul, of the other side of the grave, of the future, etc., is not ectypal; this question is in order in the section on the *ambitus* (circle) of Theology. It is enough if the essential difference is clear between a knowledge which is the result of the active investigation of an object, and that wholly different knowledge which we must first passively receive and then actively investigate. And with the old Theologians we maintain the ectypal character of the knowledge of God, since no man can investigate God Himself, and all the knowledge which we shall have of God can only be a copy of the knowledge God has of Himself, and is pleased to communicate to us.

Besides the strictly *dependent* character of Theology, there lies in this *ectypal* characteristic two suggestions, which must be emphasized. First, that there is no *involuntary* revelation. This refutes the idea that God may be more or less unconscious of Himself, or that He could be seen by us in His works, without His willing or knowing it. Since this ectypal Theology has its rise only from the fact that archetypal Theology imprints itself in it, there is nothing in the ectype which was not first in the archetype. Everything, therefore, from without that mingles itself with the ectype and does not come to it from the archetype, is contraband and must be excluded. A child may watch his father without his perceiving it or wanting to be watched; a precocious child can sometimes know his father better than he can know himself; but nothing of all this can ever take place with reference to God, because all this springs from the imperfection of the father or from the superiority of his child, and the very idea of God excludes every possibility both of incompleteness in God and of superiority in His creature. All representations of this sort, therefore, which have crept more and more into Theology, must be banished as impious, since they start out essentially from the exaltation of man above God. The second point, which must be emphasized in the ectypal character of our knowledge of God, is the *truth* of our knowledge of God. If the ectypal originates by the imprint of the archetypal, the ectypal image is no phantasy, no imagination, but an image *in truth.* Just as we saw in the antithesis between Theology here and hereafter, that our knowledge of God on earth shall be done away, and rise again in a higher form of a knowledge "face to face"; but always such, that the *truth* of our knowledge "in part" shall be the more fully exhibited by the completer knowledge in heaven. Our given knowledge of God derives from this its absolute character, not as to its degree of completeness, but with reference to its connection with its object, i.e. with God. God who is, has knowledge of Himself; and from this self-knowledge God has taken the knowledge given to us. This excludes not only doubt, but also the dilution of subjectivism, as if our formulated statement of the knowledge of God in our confession were unimportant, and *without loss of truth* could be exchanged for every other confession or placed on a line with it.

Meanwhile we should guard against anthropomorphism in our representations of this archetypal knowledge of God. As human beings, we do *not* know ourselves at the beginning of our lives; gradually we obtain a certain consciousness of our own person, and we frame a certain representation of our personal existence and of our inner being. In intimate intercourse we can impart this representation of ourselves to others. And in this way it is also possible to speak of a certain archetypal and ectypal knowledge of our person. But if this were applied similarly to God, we would incur a very serious error. We cannot conceive of a gradually increasing self-consciousness in God, and consequently of an existence of God that preceded His *consciousness.* Consciousness in God covers His entire existence, and the word "eternal" is predicable of both in an intensive sense. Hence with God there can be no self-knowledge which has been formed in a human way by observation, analysis, inference, etc. The self-knowledge in God is *sui generis,* and therefore Divine. If this condemns the admission of all anthropomorphism in the archetypal knowledge, this mode of representation is equally inadmissable in our communication of this knowledge to man. When we communicate something concerning ourselves to another, it is man who imparts something to man, and thereby deals with analogies that are mutually present, and with similar representations which render the understanding of our communications possible. All this, however, falls away when God approaches man. Then it is not God revealing knowledge of Himself *to a God,* but God imparting His self-knowledge *to man.* Moreover, in our communications with others concerning ourselves, we are bound to the form of thought, and must take the capacity for knowledge as it is; but there is no such limitation with God, who Himself created the creature to whom He has determined to impart this self-knowledge, and thus was able to adapt this capacity for knowledge to His revelation. And, finally, it should be remembered that we can mutually come close *to* each other's heart, but can never penetrate each other's inner selves; while the door to the secret and innermost recesses of our being is open to God.

It was entirely correct, therefore, when in olden times it was additionally stated that ectypal Theology reveals to us the self-knowledge of God according to our *human capacity;* and that the necessity was felt in the eighteenth century (see De Moor, *Comm. in Marck.,* Vol. I., p. 29) of limiting archetypal Theology to that self-knowledge of God, *quam creaturae manifestare decreverat,* i.e. *"which he had decreed to reveal to the creature."* In itself this was correctly viewed; in order to preserve the image of the type, the ectypal must be equal in extent and form to the archetypal. And yet this further explanation has not made the matter itself more clear, but more confusing,–both mechanically and intellectually. In the self-knowledge of God there are not ten parts, six of which he has decided to reveal unto us; but, though only "as in a glass darkly," the *whole* image has been reflected to us in Revelation. Neither will it do to interpret the revelation of God's self-knowledge as a merely intellectual communication, independent of Creation and the Incarnation; for this would cut in Revelation itself the main artery of religion.

Rather, therefore, than lose ourselves in this intellectualistic abstraction, we adopt the names of Archetypal and Ectypal Theology in the originally fuller sense, i.e. as standing in immediate relation to the creation of man after the image of God. As man stands as ectype over against God, the archetype, man's knowledge of God can therefore be only ectypal. This is what we meant when we called Theology a *dependent* knowledge–a knowledge which is not the result of an activity on our part, but the result of an action which goes out from God to us; and in its wider sense this action is God's self-revelation to His creature.

Ectypal Theology the Fruit of Revelation

The ectype does not arise unless there is a material that can receive the impression of the archetype, and the act of impressing it on this material has taken place. And though in the preceding section it was maintained that the ectypal knowledge of God did not arise from our observation of God but from self-communication on the part of God, and consequently bears a *dependent* character, we do not assert, that for the acquisition of this knowledge of God the nature and disposition of the subject are indifferent. On the contrary, all revelation assumes (1) one who reveals Himself; (2) one to whom he reveals Himself; and (3) the possibility of the required relation between these two. In revelation, therefore, *man* (and more especially *sinful man*), who is to receive it, must be taken into account. If, as was done formerly, we exclusively consider Him who reveals Himself and that which He reveals, this revelation lies outside of man; the actual perception and assimilation are wanting; and the whole end of revelation is lost. In the second place, it will not do to interpret revelation as an announcement or communication of the one subject to the other subject, without taking due account of the fact *that the subject God created the subject man,* and that God wholly maintains and governs man from moment to moment; the result of which is, that He does not follow a way of communication that happens accidentally to be present, but that He Himself lays out the way of communication in keeping with His purpose. In the third place, it must be kept in view that the revelation of God is not an act of a single moment, but *a continuous process,* which extends itself across the ages, and in this extension does not purposelessly swing back and forth, but propels itself according to the motive contained in its idea, according to the nature of its successive content, and according to the nature of the bed which its stream must form for itself. In the fouth place, this revelation may not be interpreted as an atomistical self-communication of God *to the several individuals,* but must be taken as a revelation to man in his generations, i.e. to the organic unity of humanity, and only in this organic unity to the single man. And finally, in the fifth place, account must be kept of *the special character* which this revelation had to assume, both with regard to the act of revelation and its content, and the forming of its channel in the human spirit, in order, in spite of the obstruction of sin, to accomplish its original plan and to realize the purpose implied in its tendency. Though it is thus unquestionably true that in our sinful state we could never attain to a true Theology, i.e. a true knowledge of God, unless the form of revelation were *soteriological,* it is nevertheless necessary that in our representation of revelation also the fact be emphasized that the soteriological element is ever accidental, bears merely an intervenient character, and remains dependent upon the fundamental conception of revelation which is given in creation itself, and which teleologically looks forward to a state of things in which there shall be no more sin, so that every soteriological act shall belong to a never-returning past.

The first proposition therefore reads: *God reveals Himself for His own sake, and not in behalf of man.*

This only true starting-point for the real study of Revelation has been too much lost from view, not only in recent times, but even in the more prosperous periods of sound Theology. Even in the treatment of the *dogma* of "the necessity of sacred Scripture," the fact of sin was always taken as the point of departure, and thus the starting-point for Revelation was found in the soteriological necessity of causing light to arise in our darkness. A revelation before sin was, to be sure, recognized, but it was never successfully placed in relation to revelation in the theological sense; and this was especially noticeable in the mechanical placing side by side of natural and revealed Theology. To repair this omission is therefore a necessity. Every interpretation of Revelation as given for *man's* sake, deforms it. You either reduce Revelation to the Creation, or cause it to occur only after the Creation. If you accept the latter view, you make it intellectualistic, and it can only consist, as the Socinian conceived, of an outward mechanical communication of certain data, commandments, and statutes. Thus, however, true revelation, which is rooted in religion itself, is destroyed. If for this reason you favor the other horn of the dilemma, viz. that Revelation goes back to Creation itself, then the motive for this Revelation *cannot* be found in man; simply because man was not yet in existence, and therefore could be no motive. For though it be asserted that, as the apostle Peter says, man was foreknown in the Divine decree before the creation, and that therefore Revelation could well point to this foreknown man, the argument is not valid. For in the decree a motive must have existed for the foreknowledge of man himself; and if it be allowed that this motive at least could lie only in God, it follows that Revelation also, even if it found its motive in man, merely tended to make man what he should be for the sake of God, so that in this way also Revelation finds its final end in *God,* and *not* in man.

But even this might grant too much. With a little thought one readily sees that Revelation is not merely founded in Creation, but that all creation itself is revelation. If we avoid the Origenistic and pantheistic error that the cosmos is coexistent with God; the pagan representation that God Himself labors under some higher necessity; and the Schleiermachian construction that God and the world were correlate, at least in the idea;

and if, consequently, we stand firm in the sublime confession: "*I believe in God the Father Almighty, Creator of heaven and earth,*" the motive for Creation cannot be looked for in anything *outside* of God, but only and alone *in God Himself.* Not in an eternal law (lex aeterna), a fate ($\mu o \hat{\imath} \rho a$) or necessity($\dot{a} \nu a \gamma \kappa \dot{\eta}$), nor in some need of God nature, nor in the creature that was not yet created. He who does not worship God as self-sufficient and sovereign, misconceives and profanes His Being. Creation neither can nor may be conceived as anything but a sovereign act of God, for His own glorification. God cannot be glorified by anything that comes to Him from without. By His own perfections alone can He be glorified. Hence creation itself is primarily nothing else than a revelation of the power of God; and of the God *Almighty,* who as such is *the Creator* of heaven and earth.

If this is true of creation, and of the self-revelation of God which was effected in the creation, this must be true of *all* revelation, simply because the cosmos, and every creature in the cosmos, and all that is creaturely, are given in the creation. If you deny this, you make an essential distinction between all further revelation and the revelation in creation; you place it as a second revelation mechanically alongside of the first; and lapse again into the irreligious, intellectualistic interpretation of revelation. If, on the other hand, further revelation is not taken except in organic relation to the revelation given in creation, and thus is postulated by it, the motive of creation becomes of itself the motive of *its* manifestation; and all later revelation must likewise be granted to have been given us, not for our sake, but in the last instance for God's own sake. For though it is self-evident that the manner of operation of this revelation in every concrete case adapts itself to the disposition of the creature, and in this creature reaches its temporal end, yet in the last instance it only completes its course when in this operation upon or enriching of this creature it glorifies its Creator. When this revelation, therefore, leads to the creaturely knowledge of God, i.e. ectypal Theology, this knowledge of God is not given primarily for our benefit, but because God in His sovereignty takes pleasure *in being known of His creature;* which truth is thus formulated in Holy Scripture,—that God doeth all things *for His Name's sake;* sometimes with the additional words: *not for your sakes, O Israel.*

From this the second proposition follows of itself, that *Divine Revelation assumes a creature capable of transposing this Revelation into subjective knowledge of God.*

Revelation by itself would not be able to realize its aim. Imagine that there were no reasonable creatures, and that the creation consisted of nothing but entirely unconscious creatures, incapable of consciousness, the perfections of God revealed in His creation could not be evident to any one but God Himself. This, however, would be a contradiction in terms. He who is Himself the Author of revelation, knows the entire content of His revelation before He reveals it. Hence nothing can become known to Him by His revelation, which at first He did not know. This is possible in part with us. When by the grace of God a poet first carries a poetical creation in his mind, and afterwards reveals it in his poem, many things become known to him in this poem which at first were hid from him. This is accounted for by the fact that this poet was inspired in his poetic creation by a higher power, so that he himself did not know all the obscure contents of his imagination. With God, on the other hand, such cannot be the case, simply because God cannot be inspired by one higher than Himself, and because there is nothing in His Being which He does not see with fullest clearness of vision. This implies that there can be no mystery for God, either in His Essence, counsel, or plan of creation; and hence nothing can become revealed or known to God by creation. By creation the contents of His virtues are in nothing enriched; in no particular do they become more glorious to Himself; hence there would be *no* revelation in creation or in any later activity of God, if there were no creature to whom all this could become the revelation of a mystery. For though we grant that God Himself sees and hears the beautiful in His creation; we deny that this display in creation is a greater joy to God than the view of His perfections in Himself. Every effort to seek a necessary ground in this sense for the creation of the cosmos results in cancelling the self-sufficiency of the Eternal Being, and in making God, by His creation, come to the knowledge and possession of His own divine riches; and by a little deeper thought this of itself leads back again to the theory of the world's coexistence with God.

The proposition of an *unintentional* revelation is equally untenable. This often happens with us, because the revelation of our person or of our disposition is not always under our control. Not only unintentionally, but sometimes against our intention and in spite of our purpose to the contrary, all sorts of things are constantly heard and seen of us, which it was by no means our desire to reveal. But this again you cannot apply to the Eternal Being, without lapsing into the anthropopathic representation of His existence. Such unintentional discovery of self to others results from a lack of power or insight, and from a consequent dependence upon many human data. Thus the omnipotence and absolute independence of God would be impaired, if in Him you assumed this unconscious, unintentional, and in so far accidental, revelation. His revelation postulates both the will and the purpose to reveal Himself, and this is inconceivable, unless there is at the same time a conscious being outside of God, which is able to appropriate what is revealed, and for which this revelation is intended. Though a star is praised for sparkling, which it does without knowing it, and a flower for the aroma that flows from its cup without this cup perceiving it, and though, in a similar strain, we praise the native simplicity of a beautiful character that radiates without effort and conscious aim, yet with no such conception can we approach the Lord our God, for He has nothing that He does not owe to Himself, and in no single particular is He a mystery to Himself. In Him whose is the highest and the most complete consciousness, there is no room for the conditions of semi- or total-unconsciousness. What the *Confessio Belgica* states in Art. 12, that all created things are "for the service of man, to the end that man may serve his God," applies also to the realm of revelation, since man is the creature, by whom whatever is creaturely on earth becomes the instrument of revelation of the attributes of God.

Our second proposition, however, implies more than this. The conscious creature is not only indispensable in order that revelation can be *revelation,* but that which is revealed must also be transposed by man into subjective *knowledge* of God and of His perfections. That which God reveals is conscious knowledge of Himself, *before* He reveals it. He is not a Light from which effulgence radiates, while He Himself does not *know* that light. His self-knowledge is absolute, and the impulse to reveal His perfections arises from His knowledge of them. And therefore this revelation of His perfections does not reach its aim nor point of rest until God *is known.* Hence, without ever giving themselves to intellectualism, the Holy Scriptures always put this *knowledge of God* in the foreground, and stand in prospect a "knowing of God as we are known." If Mozart had been a completely self-conscious musician, he would not have been able to develop his compositions otherwise than with the will and aim of finding performers and hearers who would not only hear his compositions and perform them, *but would also understand them.* And in like manner revelation flows from the archetypal knowledge of God and strives to become ectypal knowledge of God in man. Thus revelation itself is properly no Theology, but flows from the auto-Theology in God Himself and has Theology, i.e. knowledge of God in man, for its result.

This leads to our third proposition, viz. that man, *in order to do this, must be adapted by nature, relation and process to interpret what has been revealed as a revelation of God and to reduce it to subjective knowledge of God.*

It was the aim of propositions one and two to show that man did not come into being indifferent as to the manner how, and only afterwards revelation was added to him as an auxiliary, and was therefore adapted to his need; but that, on the contrary, revelation finds its end in God, and our human race was in its creation entirely adapted to this revelation. In this third proposition examine this original and necessary relation between revelation on the one side and the nature, relation and development process of our race on the other. And we point at once to the twofold office of man in revelation. He is not only to appropriate that which has been revealed, but he is himself a link in that revelation.

This is exhibited most strongly in his logos, since by his logos he appropriates revelation to himself, and in his logos reflectively (abbildlich) reveals something of the eternal logos. If the cosmos is the theatre of revelation, in this theatre man is both actor and spectator. This should not be taken in the sense that, in what is revealed in him, he adds one single drop to the ocean of cosmical revelation, but rather, that man himself is the richest instrument in which and by which God reveals Himself. And he is this not so much on account of his body and his general psychical organization, but chiefly on account of that deepest and most hidden part of his being, in which the creaturely reaches its finest and noblest formation. And if, without lapsing into trichotomy, we may call this finest element in our human being the *pneumatical*, we define it as being both the choicest jewel in the diadem of revelation and the instrument by which man transmutes all revelation into *knowledge of God*. Both are expressed in the creation of man after the *image of God*. On one hand, one's image is his completest revelation, and on the other hand, from just that creation after God's image originates that higher consciousness of man, by which in him also the logos operates. This is what the older Theology called innate or concreate Theology (theologia innata or concreata), and to which the doctrine of *faith* must be immediately related.

To make this clear we must go back a moment to the first man, who, in so far as he represented our entire race, was no individual, and in whose case we do not yet need to reckon with the relation in which we stand to other men. It is evident that, when thus taken, Adam possessed in himself, apart from the cosmos, everything that was necessary to have *knowledge of God*.

Undoubtedly many things concerning God were manifest to him in the cosmos also; without sin a great deal of God would have become manifest to him from his fellow-men; and through the process of his development, in connection with the cosmos, he would have obtained an ever richer revelation of God. But apart from all this acquired knowledge of God, he had in himself the capacity to draw knowledge of God from what had been revealed, as well as a rich revelation from which to draw that knowledge. Our older theologians called these two together the "concreate knowledge of God"; and correctly so, because here there was no logical activity which led to this knowledge of God, but this knowledge of God coincided with man's own self-knowledge. This knowledge of God was given *eo ipso* in his own self-consciousness; it was not given as discursive knowledge, but as the immediate content of self-consciousness. Even in our present degenerate condition, when much of ourselves can only be learned by observation, there is always a background of self-knowledge and of knowledge of our own existence, which is given immediately with our self-consciousness. Before the fall, when no darkening had yet taken place, this immediate self-knowledge must have been much more potent and clear. And thus it could not be otherwise but in this clear and immediate self-knowledge there was, without any further action of the logos in us, an equally immediate knowledge of God, the consciousness of which, from that very *image itself,* accompanied him who had been created in the image of God. Thus the first man lived in an innate knowledge of God, which was not yet understood, and much less expressed in words, just as our human heart in its first unfoldings has a knowledge of ideals, which, however, we are unable to explain or give a form to. Calvin called this the seed of religion (semen religionis), by which he indicated that this innate knowledge of God is an ineradicable property of human nature, a spiritual eye in us, the lens of which may be dimmed, but always so that the lens, and consequently the eye, remains.

In connection with this, now, stands *faith*, that wonderful πίστις, the right understanding of which has been more and more lost by the exclusively soteriological conception of our times. Of course as a consequence of the fall faith also was modified, and became faith in the Saviour of the world. But the form which anything has received as a consequence of sin can never be its proper or original form; and it is equally absurd to look upon saving faith as a new spiritual sense implanted for the first time by regeneration. Nothing can ever be added to man by regeneration which does not essentially belong to human nature. Hence regeneration cannot put anything around us as a cloak, or place anything on our head as a crown. If faith is to be a human reality in the regeneration, it must be an attitude (habitus) of our human nature as such; consequently it must have been present in the first man; and it must still be discernible in the sinner. To prove the latter is not difficult, provided it is acknowledged that ethical powers (sensu neutro) operate in the sinner also, even though in him they appear exclusively in the privative, i.e. sinful form. Taken this way, the pistic element is present in all that is called man; only in the sinner this pistic element assumes the privative form, and becomes unfaith ($\dot{a}\pi\iota\sigma\tau\dot{\iota}a$). If sin is not merely the absence of good (carentia boni), but positive privation (actuosa privatio), $\dot{a}\pi\iota\sigma\tau\dot{\iota}a$ also is not only the absence of faith (absentia fidei), but the positive privation of faith (actuosa fidei privatio), and as such sin. By overlooking this distinction our earlier theologians came to‚ speak of the innate knowledge of God (cognitio Dei innata) as an attitude (habitus), which properly invited criticism. Cognitio can be no habitus. But while they expressed themselves incorrectly, they were not mistaken in the matter itself; they simply failed to distinguish between concrete theology (concreata), and faith which is inseparable from human nature. Faith indeed is in our human consciousness the deepest fundamental law that governs every form of distinction, by which alone all higher "Differentiation" becomes established in our consciousness. It is the daring breaking of our unity into a duality; placing of another ego over against our own ego; and the courage to face that distinction because our own ego finds its point of support and of rest only in that other ego. This general better knowledge of faith renders it possible to speak of faith in every domain; and also shows that faith originates primordially from the fact that our ego places God over against itself as the eternal and infinite Being, and that it dares to do this, because in this only it finds its eternal point of support. Since we did not manufacture this faith ourselves, but God created it in our human nature, this faith is but the opening of our spiritual eye and the consequent perception of another Being, excelling us in everything, *that manifests itself in our own being.* Thus it does not originate after the Cartesian style from an imprinted idea of God, but from the manifestation of God in our own being to that spiritual eye which has been formed in order, as soon as it opens, to perceive Him and in ecstasy of admiration to be bound to Him. By faith we perceive that an eternal Being manifests Himself in us, in order to place Himself over against our ego, in the same way in which we discover the presence of light by our eye; but *what* this eternal Being is and what it demands of us, is not told us by faith, but by the innate knowledge of God, presently enriched by the acquired.

The discovery, the perception of a mightier Ego, which is above and distinct from our own ego, is therefore the starting-point of all religion and of all knowledge of God. If we were not created after God's image, this manifestation would affect us strangely and cause us fear; but since in virtue of our creation there is an affinity between our own ego and that other Ego revealing itself to us, the manifestation of that mighty Ego affects us pleasantly, it fascinates and satisfies us with a feeling of infinite rest. *It appeals to us.* And as all revelation finds its completion only in this, this appeal becomes at length *a speaking to us.* There is fellowship between that peace-bringing Being, that reveals itself to us, and our own ego. He is the heavenly Friend, who does not merely reveal himself as a silent presence, but who, asking for *our* word in prayer, addresses us in the highest utterances of spirit, i.e. in the transparent word, and only in thus speaking to us becomes our God, unto whom goes out the worship of our hearts. In this way only does man *know* his God; not with a knowledge of Him or concerning Him, but in such a way that with the deepest utterance of the soul he *knows* his God personally; not yet with the full vision, but with something already of the seeing of face to face lost by sin, and only to be perfected in the full unfolding of our nature. Thus there is a revelation of God *about* us and *within* us, and the latter culminates in the personal knowledge of the living God, as a God who dwells among and associates with us, and allows us to associate with Him. He who understands it differently from this separates Revelation *from religion,* and degrades it to an intellectualistic communication of certain facts or statutes. For the fact must not be abandoned that religion germinates only when it attains unto that which is written of Enoch, viz. *that he walked with God.* Neither knowledge nor pious feeling by themselves can ever be called religion. Only when your God and you have met each other and associate and walk together, does religion *live* in your heart.

But even this does not fully construe the conception of innate *theology.* The distinction between the seed of religion and faith, both of which are increated in our human nature, explains how from the side of God a revelation takes place in us, and how our ego is disposed to observe this revelation in us, but this by itself does not give us any theology yet, i.e. knowledge of God. Even though revelation in us on the one hand, and the working of our faith on the other hand, have so far advanced that at length we have perceived God in us and consequently *know* God, we have as yet no knowledge *of* God, and hence no theology. I may know a number of persons in the world whom I have met, whose existence has been discovered to me, and of whom I have received general impressions, while yet I have no knowledge of them. That I may have knowledge *of* him whom I have met, the logical action must first take place. When I have met some one and thus know him, I inquire about him, or seek an interview with him, that I may obtain knowledge *of* his person. And such is the case here. Though God *works* and *manifests Himself* in our being, and though I have the power of faith to perceive this inworking and this manifestation, this produces nothing in me beyond perceptions, impressions and feelings; while I am left to the mysticism of my emotions. If from this mysticism I want to advance to *knowledge,* and transform revelation into theology, the logical action must enter in between; perception must pass over into *thought;* impression must sublimate itself into a *conception;* and thus the seed of religion must unfold the flower-bud in the *word;* viz. the word of adoration. Hence this logical action also was included in innate theology; simply because otherwise it could have been no theo*logy.* This, however, should not be taken in the sense that Adam was created with some sort of a catechism in his head; for logical *action* presumes subjective *action* of the human mind. If, therefore, we should speak with entire accuracy, we should say that there was no increated theology in Adam, but that he was so created, that, in his awakening to self-consciousness, he arrived of necessity at this original theology from the data that were present in him. In a literal sense respiration was not increated in Adam, for the first inhalation only came when the creation was completed, while before the creation was ended he could not draw breath. Breathing is an action of the person which comes only when the person exists. Since all the conditions for breathing are given in our nature, and every person born in this nature breathes of himself and from necessity, no one hesitates to acknowledge that respiration is inborn with us all. It were mere prudery, therefore, to object to the expression of innate or concreate theology; for though theo*logy* is the result of a logical action in the subject, with Adam this logical action took place immediately and from necessity; and it was by this alone that the receiving of an oral revelation was already possible in paradise. For it is plain that the entire representation which the Scriptures gives us of the intercourse with God in paradise, of the fall and subsequent promise, becomes unintelligible and falls away, if we assume in Adam exclusively the sense of the eternal, and deny him all conscious knowledge of God.

Language itself decides the case. Speech without language is inconceivable, and he who in contradiction to the Scriptures declares that the first man could utter at most a few vague sounds, but was not in possession of language, wholly denies thereby the Christian doctrine of creation and the fall, and consequently of the Salvation in Christ. If, on the other hand the original man, to speak with Heraclitus, possessed a language by xvxvx, the very possession of that language assumes a logical action which is immediate, regular and pure equally with our respiration. And if from the nature of the case this logical action was originally limited with reference to its content to what man perceived in himself, and, in his inner perceptions, the perception of God stood majestically in the foreground, it is evident that the first natural action of the human consciousness could have been no other than the necessary translating into knowedge of God of the inner sensibilities and perception effected in him by God Himself. And on this ground we hold that innate or concreate theology presumes three factors: (1) the inworking and manifestation of God Himself in Adam's inner being; (2) faith, by which the subject perceives and grasps this inworking and manifestation; and (3) the logical action, by which of himself and of necessity he reduces this content in his heart to *knowledge of God,* in the form of thought and word.

From this it does not follow that one of these three factors should fall outside of Revelation. With none of these three factors do we overstep the boundary of *creation,* and all creation as such belongs to the domain of revelation. This does not need to be shown of the first factor. The action of God in our being is of itself revelation. But this same thing is true also of the second factor: faith. For what is faith but the sympathetic drawing of the image (Abbild) to the original (Urbild); and what is there revealed in this faith but that God has created us after Himself, for Himself, and to Himself? And concerning the third factor, viz. the *knowledge* which is the result of the logical action, what expresses itself in this but the reflective (abbildliche) working in us of that Logos, which is in God and itself is God? The whole man, therefore, in his existence, in his relation to God, in his communion with, and his knowledge of, God, is originally but *one* rich revelation of God *to man.* At a later period revelation may also come to him from without; but it begins by being *in* him, as an immediate result of his creation.

This innate or connate theology was destined to be enriched by acquired (acquisita) theology. Not in the sense of addition, as though this increated knowledge would gradually increase by such and such a per cent. Innate theology was rather a completed whole by itself. It constituted all that knowledge of God, which was to be obtained from the immediate communion of God with the *individual soul.* It completed that knowledge of God, whose principium lies in the mystery of the emotions. But since the creation did not consist of that single soul but of a human race, and of a cosmos as the basis of this entire human race, a revelation of God was also necessary in that cosmos and in that organic unit of humanity; and since the individual soul stands in organic relation to humanity and to the cosmos, its knowledge of God had to include both these other spheres of revelation. Even though you conceive a development *apart* from sin, acquired theology would of itself have been joined to innate theology, as soon as man entered into conscious relation to the cosmos and humanity as an organic unit. Not for the sake of filling out what was incomplete, but of enriching the knowledge complete in itself with the revelation in both these other spheres. Thus, for instance, to enlarge upon this with a single word, the idea of God's Omnipotence, Wisdom, etc., would never have entered into the consciousness of the soul from the cosmos nor from the universal human life. These ideas lie in innate theology, and are given in the idea of *God* as such. Nevertheless the significance and tendency of these ideas are only clearly seen "since the creation of the world, being perceived through the things that are made." And as to the acquired theology which comes to the individual soul from its relation to the organic unity of humanity, it is evident at once that the Divine is too potent and overwhelming to reveal itself in one human soul. Only in the combination of the whole race of man does this revelation reach its creaturely completeness. Which could *not* be so if one man were merely a repetition of another, but which leads to that completeness since every individual is a specific variation. Herein also lies the ground for the social character of all religion. The knowledge of God is a common possession, all the riches of which can only be enjoyed in the communion of our race. Not, indeed, as if even outside of religion man is a social being, so that of necessity his religion also is of a social character, for this would reverse the case; but because humanity is adapted to reveal God, and from that revelation to attain unto His knowledge, does one complement another, and only by the organic unity, and by the individual in communion with that unity, can the knowledge of God be obtained in a completer and clearer sense.

For this reason reference was made not merely to our *nature*, and to the *relation* we sustain to one another, but also to the *process* or *course* run of necessity by human development. Without sin Adam would not have remained what he was, but he and his race would have developed themselves into a higher condition. The process as known in reality may be dominated by sin, but even with a sinless existence there would have been a process of development; and this element must be reckoned with in *theologia acquisita.* Of course we cannot enter into the particulars of a supposed possibility cut off by sin. This were to lose ourselves in fiction. But in general it may be affirmed, (1) that even without sin human existence would have been a successive existence in time, and consequently an existence in the form of a process; (2) that the entire human race was not in existence at once, but could only come successively to life; and (3) as is seen from the paradise narrative itself, the study of the cosmos would have borne a successive character. Hence in this process there would have been progress, and not simple repetition. Difference of relation to the Eternal Being would have resulted from the difference of conditions. The relations among these several conditions would have been organic. Hence in this process of human development there would of itself have appeared a process of development of the knowledge of God. Yea, this process itself, as history foreordained and ruled by God from step to step, would in turn have become a revelation *sui generis.* In this development of the human race the logical consciousness in man would likewise have obtained a development of its own. Thus parallel to the process of history there would have run a history of man as a logical being. In proportion as revelation enriched itself, the instrument would thus have become more potent by which man transmuted the treasures of this revelation into The*ology.* We do not say that this would have taken place in the form of our present science. In our human existence everything is so intimately connected, that the modification which our entire existence experienced by sin and by sin-restraining grace, both "common" and "particular," impresses its stamp upon our science also. Abstraction, which at present is absolutely indispensable to our science, would certainly not have exercised so strong an influence without sin as it does now. But in whatever form common human consciousness might have developed itself without sin, Theology, i.e. the knowledge of God, would have occupied a sphere of its own in the world of thought, and would by no means have been restricted to the secret reverie of individuals upon the sensations of their inmost soul. All revelation proceeds from the *Logos* (John i. 1-8), and therefore cannot rest content as long as it is not grasped and reflected back by the logical consciousness of individuals and of the whole of humanity, i.e. by the "logos in humanity." In this way knowledge of God would have proceeded immediately from revelation, and in virtue of the organic relation and development of our race this knowledge of God *eo ipso* would have assumed a scientific form, even if by another effort of the mind than that from which at present the science of Theology is born. Theology as a science would then have proceeded immediatley and of necessity from Theology as the personal and universal knowledge of God, and it would never have entered the mind of any one to understand by the name of Theology anything but that God-knowledge itself. Scientific Theology also would rigorously have maintained its character as knowledge of God. The three above-mentioned factors—revelation, faith and the logical action—are and ever will be with acquired Theology also, which develops of itself into scientific Theology, the three constituent elements of ectypal Theology. Without *revelation* nothing is known; without *faith* there is no apprehension nor appropriation of that revelation; and without the logical action, that which has been perceived cannot be transmuted into subjective knowledge of God.

We, however, may not rest content with this supposition of a sinless development. The development is a sinful one, and all closer insight into the nature of Theology must therefore deal with this fact. And yet we do not deem the exposition superfluous of the relation which would have arisen in the case of a sinless development. It is rather a significant fault that in later theological studies this has been too much neglected. We understand what darkness is only from the antithesis of light. Pathology assumes the knowledge of the normal body. And so too the sinful development of our race and of its world of thought, in relation to intervenient grace, can never be understood except we first leave sin *out* of account. He only who has before his eyes the straight line understands the crooked line. To note a deviation, I must know where the right path runs. And the negative or privative character of sin makes this also necessary with the study of Theology. By the too exclusively soteriological interpretation of Theology we have become unaccustomed to this; while the theologians, who avoided this danger, weakened the fact of sin, and so lost more or less the whole antithesis. Formerly, however, in the days when Theology was still taken *theologically,* this distinction was rigorously maintained; and every one who, as theologian, aims again at *Theology* in its real sense, must return with us to this distinction.

But neither in this discussion of the Revelation of God *to the sinner,* any more than in the first part of this section in our explanation of the Revelation of God *to man,* will we describe the content and form of that Revelation itself. For so far as the *form* of this revelation is in order in Encyclopedia, it falls to be treated in the chapter on the *Principium of Theology.* Since now, however, we have only just begun to develop the conception of Theology from its idea and history, we cannot concern ourselves with that content and form, but must confine ourselves here to its *general character.*

In view of this our fourth proposition reads, *that the revelation of God to the sinner* remains the same as the revelation of God to man without sin, only with this twofold necessary difference, that formally the disorder in the sinner must be neutralized, and materially the knowledge of God must be extended so as to include the knowledge of God's relation to the sinner.

In this connection we need not concern ourselves with the fact that it is *grace* that speaks in the so-called soteriological Revelation. This belongs properly to Dogmatics and not to Encyclopedia. In passing, however, we suggest that the possibility is conceivable, that after man had become a *sinner,* God might have continued to reveal Himself as before. The result of this would not have been, as is commonly asserted, that the natural knowledge of God alone would have survived; for, as will be shown later on, this natural knowledge of God also is a fruit of grace, and more particularly of *"common grace."* Imagine that *all* grace had been withdrawn, so that sin would have been able to develop its deepest energies in the sinner all at once, without any check or opposition, nothing would have remained but spiritual darkness, and all "knowledge of God" would have turned into its opposite. Hence to obtain a clear insight into the modification suffered by the original revelation on account of sin, we must go back to this hypothesis and put the question, in what condition the three factors of the knowledge of God—revelation, faith and the logical action of the human mind—would exhibit themselves under this constellation.

Revelation, taken as limited to man and interpreted as the inworking and manifestation of God in man's hidden being, does not cease with sin; nothing can annihilate the omnipresence of God, not even sin; nor can man's dependence as image upon the archetype be destroyed, neither can the mystical contact of the infinite and the finite in the human soul be abolished. Thus revelation is continued in the heart of man. That which in his hellish terror drove Judas to despair and suicide, was but the perception of this fearful manifestation of God in the deepest centre of his person. Only this revelation, which was originally sympathetic, turns into its opposite and becomes antipathetic. It becomes the revelation of God who sends out His wrath and punishes the sinner. Even in hell the sinner continues to carry in himself this inworking of God's omnipresence. Because as sinner also he remains forever *man* and *must* remain such, he can never escape from that revelation. "If I make my bed in hell, behold, Thou art there."

The same is true of the second factor, πίστις. Faith also belongs to human nature, consequently the sinner can never rid himself of it; it also turns into its opposite and becomes unfaith (ἀπιστία); which must not be understood as a mere want or defect of faith, but always as an active deprivation (actuosa privatio). The energy which by nature operates in faith remains the same, but turns itself away from God and with all the passion at its command attaches itself *to something else.* This is accounted for by the fact that revelation can no longer reach its highest point in the sinner, viz. the personal manifestation of God to the sinner. So that it is limited to the internal operations of God in His anger, and thus to perceptions in the subject of an awful power that terrifies him. This perception can affect faith in two ways: the sinner to whom God can no longer appear personally can either attribute this inworking to some powerful, terrible creature, and for that reason direct his faith to this *monstrous* creature itself; or, against this terrifying power in his inmost soul he can seek protection elsewhere, and thus centre his faith upon a creature that is *sympathetic* to him. After he has become a sinner, man still continues to seek after a *something* to which to cleave with his faith; even though, in Diabolism, Satan himself became this to him.

And finally the third factor, *the logical action* by which that which faith receives by revelation is raised to subjective knowledge, remains also operative in the sinner, and, cases of idiocy and lunacy excepted, maintains itself in him. The sinner also is impelled to reflect in his consciousness the perceptions which by means of faith he has grasped as real, and placed in relation to an author. Though the stimulus of the logical activity generally operates less strongly in the sinner, since it is the tendency of sin to slacken all activity yet this is by no means the case with all individuals, and so far as faith has turned into unfaith it can strongly stimulate this activity from sheer enmity against God. Even then, this logical activity does not lead to the knowledge of God, but simply to the erroneous effort to explain the potent and terrible perceptions, actually received in one's being by the inworking of God, in such a way that God is denied by the intellect, and all such inworking is either explained away or explained from the creature. That which is written of Satan: "The devils also believe and tremble," expresses the condition of the sinner under the perception of the inworking of God in his soul; only with this difference, that the *demons,* as non-somatic, cannot deceive themselves with reference to the reality of the existence of God, and can work no eclipse of His existence by the substitution of a creature, which is the very thing that man as sinner can do; at least so long as he is upon earth, and especially in connection with the restraint of sin by common grace.

In case, therefore, that *revelation* had not been modified on the part of God, by way of accommodation to the sinner, *revelation* would have worked nothing in man beyond the sense of the presence of a terrible power that makes him tremble; *faith* would have turned into unfaith toward God, and would have attached itself to an antipathetic or sympathetic creature; and the *logical activity* would have sought an explanation of that perception, but would never have achieved any knowledge of God. There would have been *no* Theology; and nothing could have been done on the part of the sinner to create light in this darkness. This light could only come from the side of God.

This implies, as the facts of history show, that there was in fact a modification introduced in the original plan of revelation and of the construction from this revelation of a knowledge of God. It was changed, but not by the addition of something new and foreign. This would have worked magically; it would have stood mechanically by the side of man, and would have been incapable of assimilation. That which is to be knowable to man and is to be known by man must correspond to the disposition of human nature. That which does not approach us in a human perceptible form has no existence for us, that which is not adjusted to our subjective logos can never become the content of our knowledge. Hence revelation to the sinner must continue to exhibit that same type to which man is adjusted in his creation. This first, and in the second place there must occur such a modification in revelation as will make it correspond to the modification which took place in man. The nature of the change worked in man by sin governs the change which must follow in revelation. This also affords no room for arbitrariness or whim. The fundamenal type remains what it is in original revelation, and modification in this type must entirely agree with the modification occasioned by sin. In the third place, it must not be lost from view that immediate restraint of the deadly operation of sin was necessary, in order that such a modified revelation might still be of use. If sin had once worked its absolute effect, there could be no more help against it by revelation. All they who have once received the hellish character, lie in a darkness which no ray of light can penetrate. And in that case all contact with the light of revelation but leads to sin against the Holy Ghost. All "special" revelation, as it is commonly though not altogether correctly called, postulates *common grace,* i.e. that act of God by which *negatively* He curbs the operations of Satan, death, and sin, and by which *positively* He creates an intermediate state for this cosmos, as well as for our human race, which is and continues to be deeply and radically sinful, but in which sin cannot work out its end $(\tau \acute{\epsilon} \lambda o s)$. In the covenant with Noah especially, which embraced the whole earth and all that has life upon it, this "common grace" assumed a more definite form; and human life, as we know it, is not life in paradise, nor life as it would be if sin had been allowed to work out its final effects, but life in which evil truly predominates and works its corruption, but always in such a way that what is human as such is not destroyed. The wheel of sin is certainly revolving, but *the brakes are on.* This is what our churches confessed when they spoke of sparks (scintillae) or remnants (rudera) which still remained of the image of God, which did not mean that they have remained of themselves, as though sin would not have extinguished those sparks or destroyed those remnants had it been able to do so; but that by "common grace" God has restrained and curbed for a time the destructive power of sin. In virtue of the Noachic covenant this restraint continues to be applied till the Parousia. Then the brake is taken from the wheel and those sparks also go out into entire darkness.

The so-called "special" revelation, therefore, does not adapt itself to the sinner, as he would have been, if sin had worked in him its destruction to the end. Such a sinner would have become satanic, and consequently have passed beyond all possibility of salvation. But special revelation is intended for the sinner who stands in common grace. This is not said in order to postulate in the sinner anything positive, that could ever produce regeneration. Even while standing in common grace the sinner is "dead in trespasses and sin," and in regeneration is absolutely passive; only under common grace palingenesis is still *possible,* while it has become an entire impossibility in the angel absolutely fallen and will be impossible in man when he shall have become absolutely satanic. This refutes the representation that the sinner is a "stock or block," and what we maintain is but the antithesis of the Reformed against the Lutheran representation, in which it was objected to on our part, that every point of connection for grace was wanting in the sinner. Re-creation may never be interpreted as an absolute creation.

With reference now to the modifications which of necessity must occur in the fundamental type of revelation, it is evident that these must take place in each of the three factors which lead to the knowledge of God.

Since God in *revelation* could no longer *appear* to be the spiritual vision of man, after it had been darkened by sin, that self-manifestation had to be transferred from the mystery of soul-life to the *outer* world, with the incarnation as its central point, which is by no means the necessary complement of the normal human development, but was demanded only and alone by sin. From this it follows of itself that the method of revelation became inverted. If it began originally in the mystical nature of the individual, that so it might grow into a common revelation to our race, this was no longer possible after the fall. All knowledge, which as a connected whole directs itself from the external to the internal, is bound to the method of first establishing itself in the common consciousness, and from this only can it enter the consciousness of the individuals. And *formally* it is by these two data that special Revelation is entirely governed; while its *material* modification could consist in nothing else than that God should no longer reveal Himself to the sinner antipathetically in His anger, but sympathetically, i.e. in His pitying grace.

So much for revelation itself. On the other hand, the modification effected in the second factor—*faith*—bears an entirely different character. The faith life of the sinner is turned away from God in ἀπιστία, and attaches itself to something creaturely, in which it seeks support against God. If, now, this turning of faith into its opposite stood as a psychical phenomenon by itself, this faith could only again be made right. But such is not the case. That faith turned into its opposite took place in connection with the entire change occasioned in the psychical existence of man, and extended not only to the outward act but even to the root. Recovery of the original working of faith is, therefore, only possible by palingenesis, i.e. by bending right again, from the root up, the direction of his psychical life. Potentially, in order from the potential to become actual. In the second place this faith, which was originally directed only to the manifestation of God in the soul, was now to be directed to the manifestation of God in the flesh, and thus become faith in Christ. And in the third place this faith, which originally could turn to unfaith, was now to obtain such a character, that, once grasping God in Christ, it should hold fast *forever*, and so far as its fundamental tendency is concerned, would not again turn back.

It is not so easy to lay hand on the change, necessitated by sin in the entire scheme of revelation, with reference to the third factor: *the logical action.* Here, confusion has sprung from the almost exclusively soteriological interpretation of the knowledge of God. It was thought that Revelation was exclusively intended to save the elect; consequently Revelation could not be understood except as directed to the individual person; and this has prevented every collective view of special Revelation as a whole. In this way one becomes at once involved in the insoluble antinomy, that in order to be saved the first fallen man in paradise must already have had this Revelation in a state of sufficient *completeness,* and that therefore all that came afterward was really superfluous, since that which was sufficient to save Adam ought also to suffice for Isaiah, Augustine and Luther. From this point of view an historical, progressive and an ever increasingly rich revelation is inconceivable. Already in its first form it must be complete; and what is added at a later date is superfluous luxury. If meanwhile you face the fact, that this Revelation has a *history,* and in part still progresses, and that from this long process a broadly ramified and organic whole is born, you incur the other danger, that in this Revelation the saving germ is distinguished from that which has grown around it; in which way a retreat is suggested from the clearly conscious to the less clearly conscious; which opens the door to boundless arbitrariness; and ends in a return to mysticism, and in viewing all logical action as accidental. Which evil is still more aggravated by the consideration that the humblest-minded people should have the full offer of salvation, and that even children, who die before they have awakened to any consciousness, should not be excluded. And this obliges you to conceive the germ to be *so small* that even the simplest mind can grasp it, and to place the degree of consciousness *so low,* yea, even below zero, as not to exclude the infant that dies at its very birth. Thus you see that this exclusively soteriological interpretation of special Revelation tends directly to its destruction; for from the nature of the case nothing whatever remains of an external revelation as the means of salvation for the young dying child. Hence it is no help to you, that along with the logical action you point to divine illumination. This may be added to it, but soteriologically can never be the essential condition. And the fact is well known, that this soteriological interpretation of revelation as a revelation of salvation has of necessity led many minds to seek refuge again in the tents of mysticism; and to deem themselves accordingly authorized to try to their heart's content their anatomical skill upon the Holy Scriptures as upon a corpus vile.

From this difficulty there is no escape, until special Revelation is no longer viewed as directed soteriologically to individual man. Revelation goes out to *humanity* taken as a whole. Since humanity unfolds itself *historically,* this Revelation also bears an *historic* character. Since this humanity exists organically, having a centrum of action, this Revelation also had to be *organic,* with a centrum of its own. And as individuals partake of this human life only in relation to humanity as a whole, so also in relation to this whole alone is Revelation of any significance to individual man. By this we do not deny the soteriological aim of special Revelation, but merely assert that salvation of the individual soul is not its rule. Its standard is and will be theological; its first aim is *theodicy*. Surely whosoever believes on Christ shall be saved; this is possible first and only because God has sent His Son; but the aim, and therefore also end, of all this is, to make us see how God has loved *His* world, and that therefore the creation of this comsos, even in the face of sin, has been no *failure*. Hence Revelation taken as a whole aims at three things: (1) the actual triumph over sin, guilt and death,–a triumph which for the sake of Theology could not be limited to God's plan or counsel, but was bound to go out into the cosmical reality; (2) the clear reflection of the manifold wisdom of God in the logical consciousness of man; and (3) such a dioramic procedure, that at every given moment of its career it offers all that is necessary for the salvation of the contemporaneous generation and of all persons in that generation. Passing by the first and third for a moment, we consider the second alone as touching directly upon the *logical action*. The realization of the triumph over sin, guilt and death belongs in revelation to life itself; the salvation of individuals does not depend in principle upon the logical action, which is the point in hand, the main point is what we called, in the second place, the reflection of the wisdom of God in the logical consciousness of humanity. The subject of this action is not the individual person, but the general Ego of believing humanity–a limitation in which the additional term of "believing" is no contradiction, if only it is understood how wrong it is to suppose that the real stem of humanity shall be lost, and that merely an aggregate of elect individuals shall be saved. On the contrary, it should be confessed that in hell there is only an aggregate of lost individuals, who were cut off from the stem of humanity, while humanity as an *organic whole* is saved, and as such forms the "body of Christ." By "believing humanity," therefore, we understand the human race as an organic whole, so far as it *lives,* i.e. so far as unbelief has turned again to faith or shall turn.

In the general consciousness of humanity thus taken, the content, according to the original disposition of our creation, should be formed by individual accretion. Bud by bud unfolds, and thus only is the foliage of the bush gradually adorned with flowers. Without sin the logical action, which translates the content of faith into a clear conception, and thus into *knowledge* of God, would have gone out from the individuals, and from these single rills the stream would have been formed. Here, also, the way would have led from within outward. This, however, was cut off by sin. As soon as sin had entered in, revelation had to work from without inward, since sin had fast bolted the door which gave access to the manifestation of God in the soul. No sooner had sin gained an entrance than Adam discerned and perceived the presence of the Lord approaching him *from without* in the cool of the day. And thus the problem arises, in what way the logical action, which is to transmute the content of faith into knowledge of God, can come from without, in order now inversely, from the general consciousness, to reach the consciousness of the individual. And from the nature of the case there is no simple solution for this very complicated problem, but a very complex one, which can only be fully explained in the chapter on the *principium* of Theology. The lines alone can here be indicated, whose combination and crossing offer the figure for this solution.

In the first place, then, let us observe that the general subject of the essential ego of restored humanity can be no abstraction, simply because an abstraction is incapable of any logical action. Agreeably to this the Scripture teaches that this general subject is *the Christ*. As we commonly say that there is a thinking head in an association, group, or party, or that he who forms a school is the essentially thinking head for all his school, so in a much more rigorous sense is Christ the thinking subject of our restored humanity, in whose common consciousness "the manifold wisdom of God" is to reflect itself. The Church confesses this by honoring him as *prophet,* and Paul expresses it by saying that Christ is first given us as *wisdom* (1 Cor. i. 30). Even though it is the Holy Spirit who executes the logical action, it is Christ himself who said: "He shall receive of mine, and shall show it unto you." He is not only the light and the life and the way, but He is also *the truth*. And Christ *can* be this, because he is himself the Logos, as the Evangelist emphasizes so strongly, and because the logos in man exhibits the image of this Logos of God. If now there were no causal relation between these two, Christ would be inconceivable as subject of the new humanity. Since, however, our logos is reflectively (abbildlich) the counterpart of the divine Logos, and since this Logos is in consequence, also independently of sin, "the Light of the world," thus supporting and animating the logical existence of man, it is in every way conceivable that this Logos should approach individual man from without, for the sake of executing for him and in his stead the logical action, for which he himself had become disabled, and thus by *indoctrination* in the literal sense to bring him back again to that logical action.

This was implied in the saying of the older theologians, that the Logos had revealed himself to us in a twofold way, viz. in the reality of *being* by *incarnation*, and in the world of our *consciousness* by what, for brevity's sake, we will call *inscripturation*, without emphasizing for the present the scriptural part. There was a revelation of the Logos, they said, in the *flesh,* and a revelation of the Logos in *the word,* or if you please, in *being* and *thought.* And because both these revelations were revelations of the one Logos, they were organically united in him, and together formed one whole. If the incarnation were nothing but a physical fact, without a logical content, this fact could not be taken up into our consciousness as far as its content is concerned. And, on the other hand, if the revelation *by the word* had no background in reality, and no central motive in the incarnation, it were nothing but an abstraction. Since, however, the subject of the incarnation is one with the subject of the revealed word, there is not merely harmony between the two, but organic relation; and this organic relation is most strongly evident when the incarnate Logos utters even as man the oracles of God. To be sure the Logos is not bound to the organ of his own human nature for revelation by the word; as organic head of the new humanity he can also speak through the organ of other human persons; so Peter affirms of the prophets (1 Pet. i. 11, what the spirit of Christ which was in them did signify) and Jesus himself declares of the apostles; yet the coincidence of the two lines, that of the incarnation ($\dot{\epsilon}\nu\sigma\dot{\alpha}\rho\kappa\omega\sigma\iota\varsigma$) and of the words ($\lambda\alpha\lambda\dot{\iota}\alpha$) in Christ's own manifestation, lends an entirely unique majesty to his word, which does not appear to this extent either before or after him.

Thus, if it is true of sinless humanity that the "knowledge of God" could gradually ripen in individual persons and from the few enter into the general human consciousness, it is the opposite of this that takes place with sinful, and therefore to be restored, humanity. Christ, as the Head of the Body, is the general subject of restored humanity; and the knowledge of God is not only complete in him, but from him it descends to individual believers. It is the same difference that is found in the domain of ethics between the dispensations of paradise and Golgotha. In paradise ethical life is first personal, and then common, and is intended to progress toward perfection. In Christ, on the other hand, holiness is centrally given for his entire mystical body, from him to communicate itself to his members; while in Christ also an ethical perfection is offered to us which is no more to be acquired, but is now finished. And the same is true of the knowledge of God. This also is first in Christ as our common head and *centrum,* and descends from him to individual believers ("Neither knoweth any man the Father save the Son, and he to whomsoever the Son will reveal him." Matt. xi. 27); and again this knowledge of God in Christ is perfect ("As the Father knoweth me, even so know I the Father." John x. 15). Our older theologians expressed this entirely exceptional position of Christ as our *prophet* by attributing to him the *Theologia Unionis,* i.e. that "knowledge of God" which resulted from what he himself described by saying: I and the Father are one. The Christological explanation of this is not in order here, but in Dogmatics. But to show the significance of this fact to special revelation, we here indicate these three points: (1) that the *theologia unionis* is not taken as an adequate divine self-knowledge, but always as *a human knowledge of God,* i.e. a knowledge as complete as the measure of human capacity will allow, but nevertheless ever bound to this measure. Our eye can only take in light to a limited degree of intensity; stronger light does not lighten us, but blinds our eye, and that degree of light only which is adjusted to our eye gives us entire clearness. In the same way a knowledge of God which exceeds our human limitations would throw no light into our darkness, but cause us to see *still less*. (2) Let it be observed that this knowledge of God as the fruit of Christ's union with the Father was not the result of a dialectical analysis, but was intuitive, and therefore was not acceptable "to the wise and the learned," but intelligible to babes. It is not said, therefore, that Christ is our knowledge ($\gamma\nu\tilde{\omega}\sigma\iota\varsigma$), much less that he is our understanding ($\sigma\acute{u}\nu\epsilon\sigma\iota\varsigma$), but that he is our wisdom ($\sigma o\phi\acute{\iota}a$). Christ does not argue, he *declares;* he does not demonstrate, he *shows* and *illustrates;* he does not analyze, but with enrapturing symbolism *unveils* the truth. The statement that Christ "increased in wisdom" cannot detain us here; in this instance we merely deal with Christ after his baptism, when the "hear him" had been proclaimed of him. And the objection that Christ consulted the Holy Scriptures of Israel has no weight with those who confess, with the apostle Peter, that Christ is also the subject of prophecy. But in whatever way this may be taken, the result remains the same. The Son, who was in the bosom of the Father, has declared Him unto us, and this implies what we postulated: (1) that the knowledge of God of restored humanity was first in its *general* subject, i.e. in Christ; and (2) that in this general subject it was *perfect*.

If this is *the beginning* of the logical action by which regenerated humanity turns into knowledge the content of revelation received by faith, it is at once evident that this does not end the logical action. First, there is still wanting the logical action of the individual, by which he comes to a personal knowledge of God; and, in the second place, the central and complete knowledge of God, which the whole body of Christ possesses in Him who has been given it of God for wisdom, must be radiated from all the combining articulations of regenerated humanity, and must become "understanding" in its dialectical consciousness.

With reference to the first it is necessary that the organ or instrument for this logical action in the sinner shall regain the power which it has lost by sin. Although we are not deprived by sin of the power of thought, and though our law of thought is not broken, the pivot of our thought has become displaced, and thereby our activity of thought, applied to divine things, has a wrong effect. This is restored by divine illumination, which does not imply that he who has thus been enlightened is to think more acutely. Greater or lesser acuteness of thought depends upon personal conditions which are entirely different. Paul is a more acute thinker than James, and in acuteness of thought Aristotle and Kant excel by far the majority of Christians. If I put a sharp knife in a mowing-machine, but place it too high, so that it cannot touch the grass, all action of the machine is in vain; and with a duller knife, which touches the grass, I will produce ten times as much effect. And such is the case here. As long as the divine illumination remains wanting, the logical instrument in the sinner is out of relation to divine things. It does not touch them, and therefore its action is in vain. The instrument of the logical action is not repaired mechanically; this postulates the palingenesis of our person, which is only effected by the Holy Spirit in the regenerate. When, however, this divine illumination has once become actual, at least in its beginnings, our consciousness is able to appropriate to itself logically also the content taken up by faith. Not in the sense that every believer is able to think out in a clear way the entire content of revelation. This is only done by all believers together. After these many centuries, this task is still by no means completed. Personally this enlightening simply means that, according to the peculiarities of his person, according to his needs and the measure of his gifts, every believer understands everything that is necessary for confession. Under the influence of divine illumination, this logical action therefore does not direct itself to the entire field of revelation, but to its central content, while the knowledge which extends itself also to a part at least of the periphery is only the possession of a very few. Moreover, this logical action does by no means effect a clear understanding with all, but gives each the insight suited to the peculiar susceptibility of his person, which is entirely different with a humble day-laborer from what it is with the scholar. But as a result so much knowledge of God in each case is obtained as corresponds to the clearness of each consciousness.

Next to this individual insight into the content of revelation, no less attention should be paid to the logical action which brings the content of revelation to clearness in that *general* understanding, which in turn serves and enriches personal knowledge. The foundation for this is laid by apostolic revelation, which affords us a more varied and distinguishing look into the wisdom of Christ. This does not imply that the apostles offered us anything that falls under the conception of scientific Theology. He who makes this assertion totally underestimates their authority. But in their writings the lines are indicated along which the logical activity of the so-called scientific Theology must conduct itself through all ages. Thus they indicate what the content of revelation is, as well as the relation in which this content as a whole stands to the past, to the antithetical powers, and to personal faith and practice. This apostolic knowledge is, therefore, the *complement* of revelation itself, since this revelation would be incomplete if it did not itself produce the roots from which the understanding must develop itself. This development can only follow when it finds its point of departure in revelation itself. Even then this development is not left to abstract and independent thought, but remains dependent upon the inworking and guidance of the Holy Spirit. The human logos, as weakened by sin, can certainly deal with the content of this revelation, as has been the case in all ages; but as soon as this movement has reached out after something more than a mere superficiality, it has become at once antithetical, has placed itself in opposition to revelation, and has sought, and still seeks, logically to destroy it. Hence the development we referred to can only come from that circle in which the *divine illumination* operates, and the logical action of the circle outside of this can only serve to stimulate the action of those who have been enlightened and to make them careful of mistakes. Since in the circle of the "enlightened" the Holy Spirit operates not merely in individuals, but also in groups and in the whole circle, it is actually the Holy Spirit who, as "the teacher of the Church," interprets the content of revelation, and so enriches and purifies the knowledge of God; not, however, by the suppression of logical action, but by stimulating and by employing it as its instrument. The necessary outcome of this is that this working is not perfect; that it propels itself by all sorts of vibrations between truth and error; that it only gradually obtains more firmness, and finally results in the dogma of the Church.

But even this does not end the task of the logical action. The understanding of Revelation must be taken up into the general understanding, from which of itself the need arises of giving an organic place in the unit of our knowledge to that knowledge of God lodged in the regenerate, and which under the guidance of the Holy Spirit the Church, in deadly conflict, has formulated into dogma. Our knowledge of the cosmos and of revelation must not merely be brought into practical harmony for the sake of the life of faith, but in the human consciousness as such it must also become an organic whole, and thus Theology rise as a *science:* first, in the *scholastic* sense, so long as it serves no other purpose than the justification of the content of Theology at the tribunal of thought; after that, *polyhistorically,* when it swarms upon every sort of flower-bed that stands in less or more relation to Theology; and finally, in the *organic* sense, when it places its subjective action, as well as its given object, in their relation to our world of thought and the world of other objects. Thus only can that which is at first potential knowledge unfold itself to a complete and actual science.

But in this process, from start to finish, it is ever and always Theology in its proper sense, i.e. the knowledge of God divinely given, that is taken up *into* our consciousness, and is reflected *from* our consciousness (personal as well as general). Hence nothing is significant to Theology, because nothing belongs to it organically, but that which interprets this "knowledge of God" in its origin, content, significance, working and tendency.

By way of recapitulation, therefore, we arrive at what was stated in our fourth proposition, viz. that ectypal Theology, as revealed by God Himself, is the same in all its stages; and that special revelation, i.e. revelation to the sinner, is only modified to the extent that now it can also be known what God is willing to be *to the sinner.* That, further, this development of revelation goes hand in hand with an accommodation to the lost condition of the sinner, so that now revelation does not work from within outward, but makes its approach from the outer world to the inner life of man, and that the logical action goes out from the *central* ego of Christ, and thus only benefits the individual subject in the personal believer. And that finally, for the sake of the assimilation of this knowledge of God by the sinner, his unbelief must be changed to a faith in Christ, which is only possible through, at least a potential, palingenesis of his whole being.

And thus we reach the point which renders the forming of the *conception* of Theology as *science,* possible, and which will be considered in the following section.

Conception of Theology as Science

Like every other science, the science of Theology can be spoken of in a twofold sense, viz. either with reference to the intellectual labor expended upon Theology, or with reference to the results of that labor. In the latter sense, Theology as science also remains the *knowledge of God;* for though its result is not an increase in the knowledge of God, and can only lead to a clearer insight into the revealed knowledge of God, yet every gain in clearness of insight magnifies the worth of that knowledge. The microscope adds nothing to the wing of the butterfly, but enables me to obtain a richer knowledge of that wing. And while the science of Theology adds no new knowledge of God to the knowledge revealed to us, scientific Theology renders my fuller assimilation of its content possible.

Whether this scientific insight into the knowledge of God is possible and necessary, depends upon the stage of development which has been reached by the human consciousness. In fact, in the sense in which we now interpret the domain of theological studies as one organic whole, the science of Theology has only been born in our century. Even down to the middle of the last century, while there was a Theology, as Dogmatics, with which other studies were connected, yet the necessity was not felt of moulding these into one organic whole, and still less the impulse to conjoin this unit of Theology organically with the other sciences into one architectural whole of science. This was not accidental, but the immediate consequence of the general spirit of the times. This same phenomenon presented itself not only in the domain of Theology, but in the domain of every other science. The Encyclopedia of Theology had already made considerable advances, while all encyclopedical insight into the psychical and medical sciences was still entirely wanting, and in the philological and juridical sciences it had scarcely yet begun. Impelled by its own exceptional position, as well as by the alarming attitude the other sciences assumed against it, Theology was the first to give itself an account of its place and of its calling. For the greater part of the last century, however, this attempt bore an apologetic character; and only when, by and after Kant, the question about the essence and the method of our knowledge, and consequently of the nature of science in general, pressed itself forcefully to the front, in our human consciousness, was there gradually adopted the organic interpretation of Theology as a whole and as one of the sciences in the great unit of the sciences, which is now dominant in the Theological faculty, and is being more widely recognized by the other faculties. Formerly a science of Theology in that sense was *not necessary,* because the human consciousness in general did not feel the need of such an interpretation; neither was it *possible,* because the data for such a construction of Theology, and of all the other sciences, cannot be borrowed from the *knowledge of God,* but from Logic in the higher sense.

Hence the conception, which was formed of Theology in the academic sense, has certainly been modified. Theology, taken in the subjective sense, was understood to be our human insight into the revealed knowledge of God, and this insight was graded as the subject chanced to be a layman, a scholar, or more especially a theologian; but even in this highest sense Theology was limited to Dogmatics, generally with Ethics included. This learned insight into the revealed knowledge of God was for the most part explained after the scheme of Aristotle or Peter Ramus, and defended against all objections. This study alone was called Theology, besides which some theologians would study Church History and other similar branches; but the relation of all these to real Theology was merely mechanical. At present, however, the name of Theology covers the entire realm of these studies; there is no rest until a starting-point for Theology has been found in the unit of science; and, in this connection, the effort is also made to understand organically the essence of Theology itself.

It is evident that this has given rise to a serious danger of falsifying the nature of Theology. As what used to count as the whole of Theology has been classed as a mere part, the tendency was bound to exhibit itself to seek the heart of Theology no longer in its principal factor, but in its auxiliary departments; and similarly when the articulation of Theology to the organism of science is traced, of necessity its Nature can no longer be explained simply from its own principle alone, but also from the general principle of science. Both these dangers have shown themselves and have brought their veil with them; even to such a measure that in the conceptions of Theology, as severally formed in our times, scarcely a trace of the original significance remains. This compels us to hold fast, tooth and nail, to the original meaning; and therefore, starting out from the idea of Theology, we have made a transition from the *idea* to the *conception* of Theology, in which the conception of the *knowledge of God* remains the principal part.

The way in which the several departments of theological study are organically related to this *knowledge of God* can only be *shown* when we come to consider the organism of Theology; here, however, this organic relation is merely *assumed,* so that we do not even say *which* departments of study do and which do not find a place in this organic unit. At present we only speak of a certain group of studies which together have announced themselves as a theological science, and are recognized as such at the great majority of universities. This group of departments offers a scientific treatment of all sorts of material, which, however widely they may differ, must nevertheless be bound together by a common motive. This motive neither can nor may be anything else but the idea of Theology itself, and hence must be contained *in the knowledge of God revealed to us.* If for a moment, therefore, we dismiss from our thoughts the division of departments, and thus picture to ourselves the theological science *as one whole,* "this revealed knowledge of God," and this alone, is its object of investigation. This investigation would be superfluous if this knowledge of God were revealed to us in a dialectic, discursive form. Then, indeed, the human mind would be released from all necessity for assimilating this knowledge of God. But such is not the case. The knowledge of God is revealed to us in a veiled form, just such as was necessary in order that it might be valid for every age and people, for every time of life, grade of development, and condition. Not the dialectically acute Greek, but the mystic-symbolic man from the East, was chosen as the instrument to reveal to us this knowledge of God. Hence a considerable distance still separates this knowledge of God, as it has been revealed, from the world of the entirely clarified human consciousness, and the consciousness of man has yet to perform a giant's task, before it has appropriated the treasures of that Revelation with transparent purity and has reflected it from itself.

This labor, therefore, is nevertheless not scientific labor in its *entire* extent. There are lower grades in the development of our consciousness, which, though they do not bear the scientific stamp, are yet productive of early fruit. The assimilation of the revealed knowledge of God by our human consciousness has gone through all these grades. There is a labor of thought devoted to this knowledge of God, which has had for its exclusively practical purpose the persuasion of him who stands afar off to confess Christ. There is a labor of thought expended upon this Revelation with no other purpose than to defend it against opposition and heresy. This knowledge of God has been reflected upon by the human consciousness in the personal application of it to one's own condition and experience of soul. Human power of thought has entered upon this knowledge of God in preparation for preaching and catechizing. No less in the formulation of dogma has human power of intellect labored in the sweat of its brow. And all that national acumen and the spirit of a given age, or the sense of a peculiar confession, could produce in rich variation has been applied with indefatigable diligence and indomitable perseverance to cause the beauty of this "knowledge of God" to glisten to its utmost in the prism of our human thought. But all this, however excellent and rich, is not yet what we understand by Theology as *science*. Of this we can speak only when our intellect does not perform mere menial service for other purposes, but when in our consciousness itself awakens the sense of its higher calling, viz. to transmute the mechanic relation between itself and its object into an organic one. Of course, this does not imply that science should exist merely for the sake of knowledge, and that in entire self-sufficiency it should lose itself in abstractions. On the contrary, science also, as a sphere of the Logos, is called as a creature of God to serve its Creator, and its high and practical purpose in our behalf is, that it should emancipate us, afford us an independent position in the face of threatening powers, and that thus it should advance our human existence to higher estates. This, however, can only be more fully explained when we come to consider concretely the place of Theology in the whole organism of science. For the forming of the conception of Theology, it is sufficient if it is seen that the *science* of Theology can flourish as a plant by itself only when our human consciousness takes the reins in its own hands and becomes aware of its sacred calling to melt the ore of this "revealed knowledge of God" into shining gold, in order, apart from every incidental aim, as soon as this task is done, to place the fruit of its labor at the disposal of the higher aim to which *its* labor especially must be directed.

But because this science engages itself with *theologia,* i.e. the knowledge of God, as its object, it could not claim the name of *Theology,* if it were not included in the plan of Revelation and in the nature of this knowledge of God that the Logos in this higher sense should be one of the means to enrich our subjective insight into this ectypal knowledge of God. For which reason we mentioned the fact, in our discussion of Revelation, that it is also the calling of the logical activity to introduce this knowledge of God into the general subject of re-created humanity. Christ is no doubt this general subject in its central sense, on which account, as shown above, "wisdom" is given in Him; but this is still entirely different from the "understanding" of the general subject of humanity in the general human consciousness. Only when from the central subject (Christ) this "wisdom" has entered into individual believers and into circles of believers of different times is it possible that, from these individual and social insights into the wisdom of God, a different kind of insight can gradually be formed as "understanding," which cannot rest until it has become adequate to the content of the wisdom which was in the central human consciousness, i.e. in Christ. But even if for a moment we imagine the unattainable ideal that the content of each were adequate, yet the nature of each would be entirely different; what was "wisdom" in Christ as the central subject would have become "understanding" and "science" in the general subject of regenerated humanity; and it is the science of Theology alone that can lead to "understanding" in this given sense. As in every domain science, by the establishing of the general human consciousness, unveils the possibility of single persons and individual groups, broadening their insight and clarifying it, such is also the case here. The more the science of Theology succeeds in giving theology to the general subject of regenerated humanity, and thus in bringing this general subject to the knowledge of God, the more clearly does it open the way to the churches and to believers to attain, at least so far as the intellect is concerned, to a fuller knowledge of God, and thus to a better theology. Even as science it adds its contribution to the subjective assimilation of the knowledge of God within its appointed sphere, and so derives its right to claim for itself the name of *Theology.* Thus it presents itself to us as a logical activity, which transfers ectypal knowledge of God from Revelation, as "understanding," into the general subject of (regenerated) humanity.

Meanwhile this qualification of *regenerated* humanity demands a fuller explanation. God does not love individual persons, but *the world*. His election does not abandon the human race to perdition, merely to save individuals, and to unite these as atoms to an aggregate under Christ; but He saves *humanity*, He redeems *our race* and if all of our race are not saved, it is because they who are lost are cut off from the tree of humanity. There is no organism in hell, but an aggregate. In the realm of glory, on the other hand, there is no aggregate but the "body of Christ," and hence an organic whole. This organic whole is no new "body," but the original organism of humanity, as it was created under Adam as its central unity. Therefore the Scripture teaches that Christ is the second Adam, i.e. that Christ in His way now occupies the same place in the human race which was originally occupied by Adam. Hence it is not something else or something new, but it is the original human race, it is humanity, which, reconciled and regenerated, is to accomplish the logical task of taking up subjectively into its consciousness this revealed ectypal Theology, and to reflect it from that consciousness. Whatever a man may be, as long as he does not share the life and thought of this regenerated humanity, he cannot share this task. "The natural man receiveth not the things of the Spirit of God: for they are foolishness unto him: neither can he know them, because they are spiritually discerned" (1 Cor. ii. 14). Our *consciousness* is connected with our *being*. Without palingenesis there is no adaptation of our consciousness conceivable, which would enable it to assimilate or reflect ectypal Theology, and it is only by the "enlightening," as the result of palingenesis, that our consciousness receives the susceptibility for this. As in the general subject of humanity the spirit of man $(\tau\grave{o} \ \pi\nu\epsilon\hat{v}\mu\alpha)$ is the real agent, so in the general subject of regenerated humanity, or in the body of Christ, the spirit $(\pi\nu\epsilon\hat{v}\mu\alpha)$ in this body, i.e. the Holy Spirit, is the inner animator. And therefore the science of Theology is a task which must be accomplished, under the leading of the Holy Spirit, by regenerated humanity, and by those from among its ranks who, being partakers of palingenesis, and enriched by "enlightening," have also in their natural disposition those special talents which are necessary for this intellectual task.

That the science of Theology is thereby not isolated nor cut off from the common root of all science, can only be explained when we consider the organism of Theology. Here we affirm that in every domain palingenesis revivifies the original man as "a creature of God," and for no single moment abandons what was given in the nature of man. Sin tries to turn the excellencies of this nature into their opposites, but this fatal effect of sin has been restrained by common grace; and where particular grace renders this restraint potentially complete, and at the same time potentially recovers original purity, from the nature of the case the action of the Spirit in the sphere of palingenesis remains identical with the action of the Logos in human nature, and joins itself to the common grace, which has called all science into being, at every point of investigation.

The science of Theology, therefore, is nothing but a specialization of what is given in the idea of Theology. It is not all Theology, neither may all subjective assimilation of ectypic knowledge of God be appropriated by it. Among the different assimilations of this knowledge of God, Theology as a *science* occupies a place of its own, which is defined by its nature as an organic member in the unit of sciences. And thus we come to this conception of Theology, viz. that it is that science which has the revealed knowledge of God as the object of its investigation, and raises it to "understanding." Or in broader terms, the science of Theology is that logical action of the general subject of regenerated humanity by which, in the light of the Holy Spirit, it takes up the revealed knowledge of God into its consciousness and from thence reflects it. If, on the other hand, the science of Theology is not taken in its active sense, but as a product, then Theology is the scientific insight of the regenerated human consciousness into the revealed knowledge of God.

This conception diverges entirely from what the several schools at present understand by Theology as a science; and this compels us, in defence of our definition, to investigate first the several *degenerations* of Theology as *knowledge of God,* and then the several *falsifications* of the conception of Theology as *science.*

Degenerations of Theology as "Knowledge of God"

The idea and significance of Theology has been corrupted in two respects: on the one hand with reference to Theology as "knowledge of God," and on the other with reference to Theology as "science." This section treats of the first kind of degeneration, and the following of the falsification of Theology as science.

With reference to the degeneration of Theology, taken in the sense of "knowledge of God," we must begin with Natural Theology (theologia naturalis), since only in view of this natural knowledge of God can there be any question of Theology with those who reject special revelation (revelatio specialis). It is common in our times to seek the tie which unites the higher life of the pagan nations to our own, in *religion.* A general conception of religion is then placed in the foreground. It is deemed that in this general sense religion is present in almost all these nations. Affinity is observed among their several religions, but also a gradual difference. In all this it is thought that a process is perceptible, and it is by means of this many-sided process that the Christian religion is brought into relation to these lower forms. We do not take this way, because religion and knowledge of God are *not* the same, and it is in the latter that Theology finds its only point of departure. Religion can be interpreted as a sense, a service, or an obligation, but in none of these is it identical with the "knowledge of God." This is most strongly emphasized by the *pious agnostic* who claims himself to be religious, and yet on principle excludes all knowledge of God. The loss from sight of this specific difference between religion and Theology accounts for the fact, that even in the science of Theology religion has been put in the place of its original object.

This compels us to seek the tie that binds us to pagan nations, not in the phenomenal side of their religious life-expressions, but, along with Scripture, in *natural Theology;* which at the same time offers this advantage, not to be despised, that we need not confine ourselves to the national forms of ritual, but can also deal with the theology which, outside of these rituals, can be observed in their mysteries and in their poets and philosophers. It is well said, that even the most repulsive idolatry stands in organic relation to the purest revelation. There is a generic unity, which in former times was too greatly lost from sight, and is still overlooked too much, especially by Methodism; overlooked also in the work of missions. The purest confession of truth finds ultimately its starting-point in the seed of religion (semen religionis), which, thanks to common grace, is still present in the fallen sinner; and, on the other hand, there is no form of idolatry so low, or so corrupted, but has sprung from this same *semen religionis.* Without natural Theology there is no *Abba, Father,* conceivable, any more than a Moloch ritual. In so far, then, we agree in principle with the present day Science of Religion (Religionswissenschaft). On the other hand, we place ourselves in direct opposition to it, as soon as it tries to fill in the interval between this *Abba, Father,* and the Moloch ritual with the undulations of a gradually advancing process. There is here no transition nor gradual development, but an antithesis between the positive and negative working of a selfsame power. With natural Theology it is the same as it is with faith and ethics. Ethical life knows only one normal development, viz. that to *holiness;* but over against this positive stands the negative development along the line of *sin.* Sin is an "actual deprivation," and not merely a want (carentia), and therefore it is virtue turned into its opposite, and such by the negative working of all the glorious power which by nature belongs to the ethical life. Likewise unbelief, as shown above, is no want of faith, but an actuosa privatio fidei, i.e. the power of faith turned into its opposite. And in the same way idolatry also is no outcome of the imagination, nor of factors in the human consciousness that gradually develop themselves, but of an actuosa privatio of the natural knowledge of God. In the idolater both the motive and the content of this natural theology are turned into their opposites. It is the same wheel, turning itself on the same pivot, but in a reverse or averse direction. The Christian Religion and Paganism do not stand related to each other as the higher and lower forms of development of the same thing; but the Christian religion is the highest form of development natural theology was capable of along the positive line; while all paganism is a development of that selfsame natural theology in the negative direction. Christendom and Paganism stand to each other as the *plus* and *minus* forms of the same series.

From this it appears that natural theology is not taken by us in that worn-out sense in which, at the close of the seventeenth century, a barren scheme of individual truths was framed, which was made to stand as natural theology alongside of the supernatural. Natural theology is with us no scheme, but the knowledge of God itself, which still remains in the sinner and is still within his reach, entirely in harmony with the sense of Rom. i. 19 *sq.* and Rom. ii. 14 *sq.* Sin, indeed, is an absolute darkening power, and were not its effect temporarily checked, nothing but absolute darkness would have remained in and about man; but *common grace* has restrained its workings to a very considerable degree; also in order that the sinner might be without excuse. In consequence of this common grace there remain the *rudera* or sparks of light in the sinner, and the curse upon nature has not yet come in such measure but that "invisible things" are clearly seen, because understood by the things that are made (Rom. i. 20). Hence the condition of man and his world are not such as they would have been if sin had at once accomplished its end; but, thanks to common grace, both are of such a character that knowledge of God is still possible, either by way of tradition, or as the result of personal insight, such as has been found in generous measures in the midst of paganism, in its mysteries as well as with its poets and philosophers. But, and this is the point, instead of clinging fast to this, the sinner in general has played a wilful game with this fruit of common grace, and consequently his "foolish heart" has become entirely "foolishness" and "darkness." And only as result of this abuse which the sinner has made of natural theology, God at last has "given him over," as Paul reiterates it three times in Rom. i. God has *let go His hold* upon him; and in consequence of this desertion of God the curse of self-degradation and of brutishness has come upon paganism, and now constitutes its real mark.

Hence two mistakes have here been made, and two errors are to be guarded against. Our older theologians have too greatly ignored paganism, and have explained it too exclusively from a demoniacal motive, and thereby have not allowed the organic relation to show itself sufficiently, which unmistakably exists between true and false theology, as the normal and abnormal working of one and the same impelling principle; while, on the other hand, it is the error of our times to abandon the antithesis of true and false, to identify the two, and to prefer the form of the process of development to this organic relation. If formerly they failed *per defectum,* we now fail *per excessum.* And true insight into the organic relation between *true* Theology and Paganism is only obtained when the antithesis is fully recognized between the positive and negative development of common grace. There is here also an antithesis between *true* and *degenerate* development, which the more they progress, the farther they separate from each other,—an antithesis which is in no single particular a lesser one than that between good and evil, as both expressions of the one ethical principle implanted in us all.

We do not deny that a process has taken place; only this process is twofold. As at the fork in the road where good and evil separate a twofold process begins, of which one leads to an ever richer revelation of that which is holy, and the other to an ever sadder exhibition of that which is demoniacal in sin, such also is here the case. From the times of Abraham the lines of true and false theology separate. Not as though this antithesis did not exist before; but because at this point the two manifestations assume each an historic form of its own. And from this point we have on the one hand a development of true theology, which reaches potentially its acme in Christ, and on the other hand also a deterioration of *false* theology, which in a negative sense must likewise run its course to the end. In another volume this will be more fully explained. Here we can only locate the point of view where one must stand, in order that the organic relation between our own confession and that of Paganism may fully exhibit itself again, and at the same time the danger be avoided of weakening the distinction between these two to a relative difference.

To preclude the possible objection, that the theology of Greek philosophy stands higher and approaches nearer to the truth than the Animistic and Fetishistic forms of paganism, we observe: first, that it should not be considered proper to link the theological representations of a negro tribe to those of a people so highly cultured as that which gave being to Greek philosophy. The hypothesis that all nations have begun with Animism, and have gradually mounted the several rounds of the scale, is entirely unsupported. Our second observation is, that dissimilar magnitudes cannot be compared, and hence the cultus-forms of any people cannot be compared to the theological teachings (theologumena) of philosophers. For comparison the cultus-forms of paganism must be contrasted with the practical religion of these philosophers, and their theological teachings with the ideas concerning the infinite and its workings which are fundamental to the cultus-forms of the nations of lower standing, or of the Greeks. By which comparison it appears at once that the philosophers had *no* cultus-forms, and obtained them only when in Neo-Platonism, Gnosticism, etc., they had adopted elements from the Christian religion. This shows that Natural Theology operated in them more as an intellectual power than as a devotional impulse,—a fact which of itself leads to our third observation, viz. that however high, from an intellectual point of view, the theological teachings of Greek philosophy may stand, in the main they exhibit a much stronger deterioration of the true knowledge of God, inasmuch as they destroyed the feeling of dependence, in place of which, in Stoicism, they substituted human self-sufficiency. In the negro, who trembles as he kneels before his Fetish, there is more of the fear of God than in the proud philosopher, who reasons about the gods (or about $\tau\grave{o}$ $\theta\epsilon\hat{\iota}o\nu$) as about powers, of which he will determine what they are. In the negro there is still a considerable degree of vitality of the seed of religion, while in the self-sufficient philosopher it is dead. He reasons; in however imperfect a way, the negro worships.

As Christian Ethics not only deals with the positive development of good, but reckons as well with the negative development of evil, Christian theology also is not to confine itself to the study of true theology, but must also deal with false theology in paganism; and this it must do not merely for the sake of making obvious the monstrosity of pagan representations,—this, indeed, would not be a proper interpretation of its task,—but rather that it may show that this paganism also is born of natural theology, and discover the law which this false development has obeyed. There is no single datum in idolatry, which is inherent in it, but has sprung from natural theology. Of course this does not underestimate the inworking of tradition from paradise, nor the influence exerted by Israel. When the antithesis between true and false theology is sharply seen, the true must have preceded the false, and idolatry can be nothing else than *deterioration;* which implies of itself that, as with all *deterioration,* some elements of the originally pure development still cooperate. And with reference to the inworking of special revelation, it should not be lost from sight, that from the days of Abraham, the people of revelation have ever been in touch with the surrounding nations, and that extensive journeys, for the sake of finding out what other nations taught concerning Divine things, suited entirely the spirit of the ancients. With this purpose in view the passes of the Himalaya were crossed from China to the Ganges. Add to this the great significance and calling of the empire of Solomon, and the fact that the prophets appeared long before the Greek philosophers, and it betrays little historical sense, when *a priori* all effect of Israel upon paganism and pagan philosophy is denied. But this after-effect of tradition, as well as that possible inworking of Israel, are accidental. They are not inherent in the contrary process of natural theology in its deterioration. Hence this process itself must be investigated, not for the sake of paying homage to the theology of paganism as such, but to show that the religious life of these pagan nations was founded upon some theology, which as such was not invented, but is the necessary result of the sinful development of natural theology.

Islam occupies here a somewhat separate position. Just as with Gnosticism and Manichaeism, we here deal with a unit of theological representations which has special revelation back of it, and partly included in it. This presents three factors for our consideration. First, the contrary development of natural theology, which here also forms the pagan background. Secondly, the contrary development of supranatural theology, which had an entirely peculiar career. And, thirdly, the syncretistic element, which united these deteriorations into one. Islam is not merely pagan, nor is it merely heretical, but both together, and hence it occupies an entirely peculiar place among the deteriorations of true theology, in which it now stands alone, simply because Manichaeism, Gnosticism, etc., as religious societies, have passed away. On the other hand, Islam, as such, is allied to those theological representations that have become current again, especially since the beginning of this century, and which have embroidered the flowers of Christian revelations upon the tapestry of a radically pagan philosophy. With this difference, however, that these philosophic deteriorations have not established religious communions, but have invaded the Church of Christ.

Falsifications of the Conception of Theology

The falsifications of Theology as *science* bear an entirely different character. By these we do not refer to the heretical divergencies, such as Protestants assert of Romanism, and Rome in turn affirms of Protestantism. With every heretical divergence both sides occupy the same point of view as to natural theology; from both sides it is confessed that their theology is derived from special Revelation; and the difference arises only from the diverging views of this special Revelation. In speculative and empiric theology, on the other hand, one is met by falsification, which, from *principle,* denies all special Revelation, and thus in reality takes counsel with natural theology. Both forfeit thereby the right to the name of theology, because in this way speculative theology really ends in *Philosophy,* and empiric theology disappears in *Naturalism.* Natural Theology can exhibit itself as a regnant power only when human nature receives the beams of its light in their purity and reflects them equally completely. At present, however, the glass has been impaired by a hundred cracks, and the receiving and reflecting have become unequal, and the image that was to reflect itself is hindered in its clear reflection and thereby rendered untrue. And for this reason you cannot depend upon natural theology as it works in fallen man; and its imperfect lines and forms bring you, through the broken image, in touch with the reality of the infinite, only when an *accidens* enables you to recover this defective ideal for yourself, and natural theology receives this *accidens* only in special revelation. Speculative and empiric theology are correct, therefore, in their reaction against methodistic superficiality, which actually annuls natural theology, and accepts special revelation by faith as something entirely independent by itself. While, on the contrary, it is only by the natural knowledge of God, by the *semen religionis,* that a special revelation is possible for us, that our consciousness can unite itself to it, and that certainty can be born of its reality in our sense. Yea, to speak still stronger, we may say that special theology is merely *temporal,* and natural theology *eternal.* This is not stated more boldly than the Scriptures justify, when they explain the mutual relation between the special priesthood of the Aaronic ceremonial and the natural priesthood of Melchizedek. Melchizedek appears as one standing entirely *outside* of the special revelation; he is a priest-king, who has natural theology only, together with a weakened tradition of the once blessed paradise. Aaron, therefore, on whom shone the full light of special revelation, stands far above him in knowledge of God, in loftiness of religion, and in purity of priestly ritual. With a little less thought one would have been tempted to place Aaron's priesthood far above that of Melchizedek, in order to find the ideal high-priesthood of Christ in Aaron, and not in the order of Melchizedek. And yet revelation, in both Old and New Testaments, teaches the very contrary. Aaron's ceremonial bears merely a temporal character; Melchizedek's office is eternal; and Aaron disappears in Christ, in order that in Christ Melchizedek may reappear. Thus Aaron's service merely fulfilled the vocation of rendering the service of Melchizedek possible again, and enabling it to resume its original significance. And this is the point of view which dominates also the relation between "natural theology" and "particular grace." Undoubtedly the content of special revelation is much richer than the meagre content which natural theology now offers fallen man; and it is also evident that without its *accidens* in special revelation this natural theology is no help to you whatever. Aaron's service was much richer than that of Melchizedek, and without the Aaronic ordination Melchizedek's offering missed every atoning merit. But this does not take away the fact, that natural theology always remains the originally real one, and that special revelation can never be anything else than accidental. Hence, when it comes to a state of purity, when sin shall have been eradicated so that its very memory shall no longer work its after-effects in the creation of God, then all the riches of special revelation shall merely have served the end of bringing natural theology back again to its original lustre, yea, of causing it to glow with a brightness which far excels its original lustre. In the prophetic domain of the knowledge of God, also, Aaron disappears, and Melchizedek returns with all the glory of the original creation. This is the deep significance of the oath sworn by the Lord in Psalm cx., concerning the priest after the order of Melchizedek. Jesus Himself spoke of a future in which His disciples would no more ask Him anything, because the Father Himself loved them. And in the perspective of 1 Cor. xv., when God shall be "all in all," the entire special revelation has receded; the object for which it was given has been obtained; and with reference also to the knowledge of God, the "all in all" expresses nothing else than what once existed in paradise.

Though this deeper truth was not recognized by Schleiermacher, the spiritual father of subjective empiricism, and by Hegel, the master thinker, who founded the school of recent speculative theology, they perceived it, nevertheless, sufficiently clearly to vindicate the primordial authority of natural theology. Calvin saw deeper than both, when he compared ectypal theology, as thanks to common grace it still exists in and for the sinner, to a book the writing of which had become blurred, so that it could only be deciphered with a glass, i.e. with the help of special revelation. In this figure the thought lies expressed, that the theology which reflects itself as such in our nature, is ever the real theology, which, however, must be augmented and be explained, and which without this assistance remains illegible; but which, even during and after this help, always remains the true divine writing. So also it is foretold in prophecy, when Jeremiah declared that there was a time coming in which the outward special revelation would be ended, and every one would bear again in his heart the divine writing, and all should know the Lord from the least unto the oldest. This, too, is only the representation that the outward special revelation merely serves *for a time,* and that it has no other tendency than to lift natural theology from its degeneracy. Natural theology is and always will be the natural pair of *legs* on which we must walk, while special revelation is the pair of *crutches,* which render help, as long as the weakened or broken legs refuse us their service. This indeed can be frankly acknowledged, even though it is certain, that as long as our legs cannot carry us we can only walk by means of the crutches, so that during this abnormal condition our legs do not enable us to walk truly in the ways of the Lord, but only our crutches, i.e. not natural theology, but only special revelation. This last point has been less denied than entirely abolished by Schleiermacher, as well as by Hegel, and in so far we deny that the subjective-empiric and the speculative schools, which they called into life, are able to offer us any real and actual theology. But this does not destroy the fact that the motive which impelled them contained an inward truth. After the Reformation orthodoxy withdrew itself all too quickly from general human life. It became too greatly an isolated phenomenon, which, however beautiful in itself, was too much disconnected; and when it undertook to distil a kind of compendium from the so-called natural theology, and in all its poverty to place this by the side of the rich display of special revelation, it belittled this natural theology to such an extent, that rationalism could not fail of its opportunity to show itself and to administer reproof; while orthodoxy, removed from its basis, was bound to turn into inwardly thin supranaturalism with its external supports. Thus there was no longer a scientific theology worthy of the name. All that remained was, on the one hand, a mysticism without clearness, and on the other hand a barren framework of propositions and facts, without the glow of life or of reality. This was observed with great sharpness of vision by Schleiermacher, as well as by Hegel, and both endeavored to find again, in the reality of life, a δός μοι ποῦ στῶ (starting-point) for religion, and thus also for theology. They did this each in his own way: Schleiermacher by withdrawing himself into human nature, as religious and social in character; and Hegel, on the other hand, by extending the world of human thought so broadly, that theology also found a place in it. From subjectivity, i.e. from mysticism, Schleiermacher came to theological thought, Hegel, from the thought of man, hence from intellectualism, to religion. Thus together they grasped natural reality by the two hands which this reality presents for religion. Natural theology includes two elements: first, ectypal knowledge of God as founded in the human consciousness, and secondly, the pistic capacity of man to grasp this ectypal knowledge with his inner consciousness. Hegel made the ectypal knowledge of God to appear in the foreground of human consciousness; Schleiermacher, on the other hand, started out from the pistic capacity increated in the inner nature of man. Hence it is not surprising in the least, that both formed a school of their own, and that only by their initiative theology revived again as a science. They indeed abandoned the isolation to which theology had fled. Each in his way restored religion and theology to a proper place of honor in human life and in the world of thought. By their work the "unheimisch" feeling of confusion in the face of reality was taken away from the theologian; he had again a standing. The thirst after reality could again be quenched. And that even orthodox theologians, whose earnest effort it was to maintain by far the greater part of the content of special revelation, sought refuge in the two schools need not surprise us, for the reason that the strength of each lay not so much in their positive data, as in their formal view, which to a certain extent was also adapted, if needs be, to cover an orthodox cargo. With respect to this formal part, Schleiermacher and Hegel even supplemented each other. If in Schleiermacher's subjective school theology was threatened to be sacrificed to religion, and in Hegel's speculative tendency to be glorified as the sole substance of religion, it was evident that those who were more seriously minded foresaw the future of theology in the synthesis of both elements. There were two sides to natural theology, and only in the combination of Schleiermacher and Hegel could natural theology again obtain a hearing in its entirety.

But this whole effort has ended in nothing but bitter disappointment. Not, as already said, as though in these two schools men began at once to cast the content of the special revelation overboard. On the contrary, Schleiermacher and Hegel both did not rest content with the meagre data of natural theology, but made it a point of honor to demand the exalted view-point of the Christian religion for its own sake, and, so far as they were able, to vindicate it. What good was this, however, when they were bent on explaining, at any cost, this ideal view-point of the Christian religion from the normal data? They no doubt acknowledged the considerable interval between this ideal religion and the imperfect religious expression outside of the Christian domain, but they refused to attribute this to the supernatural, and thus to what seemed to them the abnormal action of the living God. The interval between the highest and the lowest was not to be taken any longer as an antithesis, but was to be changed into a process, by which gradually the highest sprang from the lowest. Thus each in his way found the magic formula of the process. From Theism they glided off into Pantheism. For thus only was it possible to maintain the high honor of the Christian religion, and at the same time to place this exalted religion in organic relation to the reality of our human existence. And this was the thing that avenged itself. For from the meagre data of natural theology they were not able to operate along straight lines, and thus even these fundamental data were *falsified*. This became especially apparent in the school of Hegel, when in their way his younger followers tried to systematize religion, and soon rendered it evident that, instead of vindication, the result, which in this school they reached by strict consequence, was the entire undermining of historic Christianity and of all positive religious data. What Hegel thought he had found was not religion, but philosophic theology, and this theology was no true "knowledge of God," but a general human sense, in which the immanent Spirit (der immanente Geist) gradually *received* knowledge of himself. This did *not* find archetypal knowledge in God, but in man, and ectypal knowledge in the incomprehensible God. Hence it was the perversion of all Theology, and the inversion of the conception of religion itself, and both dissolved in a philosophic system.

Though at first the subjective-empiric school of Schleiermacher appeared less dangerous, and though it did not lead to those repulsive consequences in which the young Hegelians lost themselves, yet even this did not escape its Nemesis, and with fatal necessity tends more and more to Naturalism. It did not come to religion from the sphere of thought, but sought its connecting point *in human nature*. Man, not as individual, but taken as an integral part of the organism of humanity, presented himself as a subject with certain emotions and perceptions, and bearing a religious character; from these perceptions and emotions, by virtue of the "social instinct" (Sociale Trieb), which is peculiar to man as an organic being, sprang a certain desire after religious communion (Verein); and since man inclines to take up his emotions and perceptions into his consciousness, there was gradually born of this selfsame subjective mysticism a world of religious representations. Only with these ethical premises at his disposal, does Schleiermacher come to the phenomenon of the Christian Church, which, both by way of comparison and in principle, seems to satisfy the highest aspirations these premises inspire. Faithful to his naturalistic interpretation he concedes that it is the vocation of the Church to remain the leader of this ethic-social process in humanity. This requires elucidation of insight. And so he arrives at an interpretation of theology which is nothing but an aggregate of disparate sciences, which find their bond of union *ad hoc* in the phenomenon of the Church.

We readily grant that Schleiermacher did not mean this naturalistically. His purpose was to save the ideal life of humanity. But we maintain, that this whole interpretation sprang from the naturalistic root, and is chargeable with the naturalistic tendency, which became more strongly evident in his followers. Of the three data which he deals with,—human nature, God and thought,—he takes human nature alone to be autonomic. All that he teaches of God is not merely bound in its form of expression to the data of our nature, but the content also is the mere reflection of subjective perceptions; man is and remains the subject, that is, thinks and speaks, and in his presence God obtains no autonomic position. The reality even of the existence of God appears to the very end to be dependent upon the reality which vindicates itself in the subject man. The same is true with reference to the factor of *thought*. With Schleiermacher, thought is the result of being, not in the absolute sense, but of being in man and of that which springs from this being of man. Actually, therefore, human nature alone and its phenomena are real for Schleiermacher; from this nature only you come to God as to its projection; and thought exercises so little independent power, that the unconscious senses, feelings and perceptions not only govern our entire thought, but even repress it, and already prepare the primacy of the will of later date. With this, however, Schleiermacher as a theologian had passed the handle entirely out of his hands. It is self-evident, that the autonomic study of human nature held the mastery also over the future of theology. If that physiological and psychological study should lead to materialistic results, the whole of Schleiermacher's religion would fall away. Or, where the result was less disappointing, yet so far as the method is concerned, the physiological factor was bound to dominate entirely the psychological factor, and this would also include everything that relates to religion under the power of the naturalistic view. In this wise the Christian religion was bound to be reduced to the product of all preceding religious development; that preceding religious development could at length be nothing more than the necessary development of a psychological peculiarity; that psychological peculiarity, in turn, must be the result of the fundamental data in our human nature; that human nature could be nothing else than the product of the unbroken development of organic nature; that organic nature could not differ essentially from the inorganic nature; so that finally, everything that is high and holy in the Christian domain has been brought under the power of the evolution theory, and the theologian has to be informed by the naturalist where to look for the origin of the object of his science.

Thus, in both schools, everything that had so far been known by the name of theology was in principle destroyed. There were no longer two, God and man, the former of whom has imparted knowledge of Himself to the latter; there was, in fact, nothing else but man, in whom alone, according to the speculative school, "the Ever-Immanent Spirit" (der ewigimmanente Geist) came to consciousness of himself; and who according to the subjective-empiric school, experienced subjective perceptions, from which he formed for himself subjective representations of a religious character. Neither in one school nor in the other was there any more question of an extrahuman God, no room for a theology which should be able to introduce actual knowledge of that God into the general human consciousness. The abandonment of the name *Theology,* and the substitution in its room of the name of *Science of Religion,* was nothing but the honest consequence of the fundamentally atheistic point of view which was held. Is atheistic too strong a word in this connection? It is, when by atheism we understand the denial of the spirit and perceptions of the infinite; but not, when we interpret it as the refusal longer to recognize the living God, who has made Himself known to us as God. Though both schools held to the name of God, they both afterward denied that we have the right to reckon with the reality of the living God, as a personal, self-conscious Being, who from that self-consciousness reveals Himself to us. And from that time on, the object that engaged the investigator in this domain was no longer the reality *God,* but *religion.* With reference to the eternal Being everything had become problematic; the religious phenomenon was the only certain thing. There revealed itself in human nature and in history a mighty factor, which was known by the name of religion. It was possible to trace and to study the historic and ethnologic development of this factor; psychologically, also, an explanation of this religious phenomenon could be sought; and in this perhaps at length sufficient ground could be found to assume a general agent as cause of this phenomenon; but no venture could be made outside of this phenomenal circle. The νούμενον remained problematic.

That nevertheless most students shrank from the immediate adoption of this radical transition, had a threefold cause,—the historic form of our theological faculties, the existence of the Christian Church, and the exalted character of the Christian religion. By far the larger number of theologians of name do not reach their destination except in the theological faculty. That faculty, as an historic institute, is bound to the *theological* name, and more particularly still to Christian Theology. The revolution which has taken place on theologic ground must of necessity either modernize these faculties entirely, or perhaps occasion their disappearance, and the transfer of their chairs to other faculties. But this is not done at once. Every academic institute is conservative. And since one cannot wait for this, and meanwhile is not willing to abandon the influence of the chair, one adapts himself to the inevitable, and continues to call himself a theologian, and to speak of theological study, even though in the main he has broken with theology, in the historically valid sense of the word. The second reason, why the name of theology has been maintained, lies *in the Christian Church.* For her sake the Ministers of the Word must be educated. If it were not for her, there would be no question after pupils for this faculty. Dilettant theologians are becoming ever more scarce. And thus one had still to adapt himself to practical needs in these departments. From a scientific point of view the study of other religions might promise richer harvests; but almost no one would frequent the lecture-rooms where exegetical readings were given from the holy books of other religions. And thus the scientific standard had to be abandoned, and for the sake of practical needs the old theological tracks are still continued. This is indeed an unenviable position, in which self-respect is regained in part only by the consideration of the third cause mentioned above, that is, the relative excellency of the Christian religion. Even when, after the fashion of botanists, we treat religion as a flora of poorer and richer types, it is but natural that fuller study should be devoted to the religious plant of higher development; and, as such, homage is paid to the Christian religion. Not generally any longer as *the* highest, for Buddhism, and even Islam, are placed by its side; and much less as the highest conceivable, for in ethics Christ is thought to be far excelled, and it is maintained that further development is not at all impossible. But in general the Christian religion still counts as one of the higher developments; especially as that development, which is of greatest interest to us historically, and which, so far as the lower classes of people are concerned, is even yet the only one that claims our general notice. And thus it comes to pass, that this faculty is still called theological, and is still regulated with a view to the training of Ministers of the Word for the Christian Church, and, though the other religions are reviewed, the Christian religion is still the main study pursued. This is done, in antagonism with principle, for the sake of secondary considerations; and it is for this reason that the ancient name of *Theology* is still borne, though now as a misnomer, and that the only fitting name for what is really meant, that of "science of Religion" (Religionwissenschaft), remains still banished from the official curriculum.

In order to restore harmony to a certain extent between name and matter, it has been tried in more or less conservative circles, to define Theology as "the science of the Christian religion"; which, however much better it may sound than Schleiermacher's prudish and unnatural definition, is nevertheless equally unable to stand the test of criticism. Is there likewise a science of English history? Of French philosophy? Of Greek art? Of course not. The science of *history* devotes a chapter to England's national past; the *history* of philosophy devotes a separate investigation to that which has been pondered and reflected upon by French thinkers; and the *history* of aesthetics engages itself especially with Greek art; but no one will undertake to represent these parts of a broader object as a proper object for an independent science. Hence, in the religious domain also, there is no separate science of Parseeism, of Buddhism, of Israelitism, of Christianity, or of Islam. He who takes one of these phenomena as such an object of investigation, may not take it outside of its relation to correlated phenomena, and can take no stand except in a science which embraces these correlated phenomena as a whole. It is unscientific, therefore, to speak of a "science of the Christian religion." If I confess a Revelation, which has *no* correlates and which is a phenomenon of an entirely *singular* kind, it may well be the object of an *independent* science. But if one views the Christian religion as one of several religions, even though it is comparatively the highest of all religious developments known to us, he is as unable to create an independent science of the Christian religion as the botanist is to speak of a special science of the cedar. If, on the other hand, with other more or less orthodox theologians, we assert that the Christian religion is distinguished from all other religious phenomena by a special specific revelation, its distinguishing element is not in the *religion,* but in the *revelation* of Christianity, and hence this revelation must be the object of this science.

This was felt by Hodge, the champion of scientific orthodoxy in America, and therefore he tried to escape from the dilemma by choosing *the facts of the Bible* as the object of his theology. His intention was good, for in the main he was correct in saying that the Holy Scriptures offer us no scientific theology, but contain the *facts and truths,* "which theology has to collect, authenticate, arrange and exhibit in their internal relation to each other" (*Syst. Theology,* I., p. 1). And yet we may not rest content even with Hodge's definition. For in this way the conception of "ectypal Theology" is lost, and from all sorts of facts we are to conclude what must follow from them with respect to the Being of God. His combination of "facts and truths" overthrows his own system. He declares that the theologian must *authenticate* these truths. But then, of course, they are no *truths,* and only become such, when I authenticate them. His idea was, of course, to save theology as a *positive* science, and to do this in a better way than they who took the "Christian religion" as the *given object;* but it can scarcely be denied that he succumbed to the temptation of placing Theology formally in a line with the other sciences. All the other sciences have the data of nature and of history for their object, and Theology, in like manner, has the data of this supernatural history. There were two spheres, two worlds, which have become object of a proper science each. That the distinction between God as creator and all the rest as His creature draws the deep boundary-line between theology and all other science, could not be established in this way. The authentication of his "facts" brought him logically back again under the power of naturalistic science. And though as a man of faith he bravely resisted this, his demonstration lacked logical necessity.

Our result is that, though still called by the name of theology, the entire subsequent development of theological study has actually substituted an utterly different object, has cut the historic tie that binds it to original theology, and has accomplished little else than the union of the subdivisions of psychology and of historic ethnology into a new department of science, which does not lead to the knowledge of God, but aims at the knowledge of *religion* as a phenomenon in the life of humanity. Along this way also the return was made to natural theology, and whatever was still valid as "Christian revelation" was cited to legitimatize itself before the tribunal of natural theology. The harmony between the results of these modern investigations, and those derived in former ages from natural theology in India and elsewhere, could therefore arouse no surprise in the least. This only should be added, that the exchange of *theologia naturalis* for *religio naturalis* accounts for the loss with us of what the Vedanta still maintains, viz. the divine reality, which corresponds to the impressions and perceptions of the religiously disposed mind.

Deformations of Theology

If the effort to obtain Divine knowledge from natural theology, *without* the help of special revelation, was bound, after the fall, to effect the entire deterioration of the knowledge of God; and if, on the ther hand, the effort to substitute *religion* as object of investigation for the "knowledge of God" was bound to *falsify* the conception of theology; the evil worked within the theological domain by what we call its *deformations,* the results of schism and heresy, is of an entirely different character. The difference is still clearly evident between what is called Protestant, Romish and Greek or Eastern Theology; and though on Protestant ground the antithesis between the Lutheran and Reformed type of doctrine is less significant than before, it is self-deception to suppose that it has become extinct; while, on the other hand also, the variegations of the mystic-apocalyptic and the pietistic-methodistic mode of teaching still maintain themselves in ever wider Protestant circles. The illusion that the former confessional differences have had their day, in order gradually to make room for a general Protestant sense, scarcely held itself intact for a quarter of a century. It was evident all too soon, that this indifference to confessional standards sprang from an unhistoric tendency and was fed by an exceedingly serious hypertrophy of the philosophic element. Almost everywhere, therefore, we see the revival of confessional standards in theology, the moment it escapes from the arms of philosophy, and, for the sake of defending its position, is bent upon the recovery of its independence. This, however, makes it necessary, just as our fathers did before us, to deal with the *deformations* of Theology.

This conception of *deformation* excludes, on our side, two untenable points of view: first, the *sceptical,* which attributes no higher worth to Protestant Theology than to the Romish or Eastern, and evermore tends to place these in a line; and secondly, the *absolute,* which counts out every other theology but its own as worthless, and frankly declares them to have originated with the Evil One.

The *sceptical* point of view falls short in faith, decision and courage of conviction.

Here, in reality, one takes truth as something that lies beyond human reach; hence one's own confession also is valued no higher than as an effort to express truth, which from the nature of the case has met with ill success. One feels his way in the dark, and hence must readily concede others the right of doing the same. Their confession and yours contain equally little or much of worth, just as you please. They are variations of the same theme. Each of these variations enrich and complement, and you stand personally higher, just in proportion as being less narrow in the attachment to your own confession, you have an open eye and ear to rejoice in all expressions of life. This is not meant to be taken eclectically, for since you have no favorite flower, you gather no bouquet from the several confessions, but simply walk among the several flower-beds to enjoy whatever is beautiful in this confessional garden. All this lacks seriousness of purpose. From this view-point every form of confession becomes an article of luxury. Confessional life aims no longer at truth, but serves as a kind of poetry. In the life of his emotions one experiences certain pious perceptions; one also seeks a certain mystical communion with the hidden world of the infinite; and in so far as one accepts the reality of the world, he is seriously minded; but he has no faith in what he himself expresses or in what he hears others say concerning it. It does not become us, it is said, to do anything but stammer. No significance, therefore, should be attached to the sounds, forms, or words which we speak, as though these expressed the higher reality. At most these sounds have the worth of a musical character. They give utterance to our better feelings, and presently aid to revive them again. But for this very reason the song which another sings from *his* heart is equally beautiful. There is no more *truth* to be confessed. All that remains is a pious, aesthetic enjoyment of what has been stammered by man in all manner of ways concerning the truth. A Calvinistic prayer, which drinks in encouragement for higher life from the fountain of eternal election, impresses, from this point of view, equally strongly as the *Ave verum corpus* of the Romish worshipper, as he kneels before the uplifted host.

This sceptical point of view, therefore, should not be confounded with the mystical antithesis, which opposes all dogma, all confessions and also all special revelation. This mystic antithesis springs from the tendency to let being triumph over consciousness, and, while it apparently antagonizes barren intellectualism, in reality it opposes every modification which by virtue of religion must be brought about in our world of thought. It is said that our so-called modern ethical tendency sets no store by conceptions; but from the nature of the case this is not so. No one can get along without thought; without a life of consciousness no human life is conceivable; every one goes out from certain general conceptions; and, voluntarily or otherwise, in those who live in higher spheres those general conceptions form a system, i.e. they stand in a certain relation to each other. As an actual fact, therefore, the conflict against "barren intellectualism" banishes all influence of revelation or even of religion from the development of our world of thought; while eventually the world of thought, which from natural reason has become common property, is permitted to assert itself as unassailable and self-evident. With these men it is ever the old conflict between the primacy of the consciousness and of the will, while our entire higher life is subsumed by them under the will. With the deformations of theology, however, we need not take this into account; since all such efforts end in an entire falsification of the conception of theology, and as such belong to our former paragraph. The sceptics, on the other hand, whom we here speak of, occupy the selfsame view-point with us of special revelation; with us they feel the need of holding dogma in honor, and readily agree that no church can get along without confessional standards; only, to all these confessions together they attribute nothing but a relative value. *The truth is not contained in one confession, nor in all the confessions taken together;* to push propaganda, therefore, of one confession above another is entirely void of motive. Going from one church to another, except for the sake of marriage or of national interests, has no significance. And the poor martyrs who faced death for the sake of their convictions, died like naive victims of a confessional mistake.

If thus in this confessional scepticism the energy of conviction is wanting, the confessional *absolutists,* on the other hand, sin through the excess of conviction, when they anathematize everything that falls outside of their own confession. This ground was *not* held by the Reformers and the learned divines who theologically expounded the confession of the Reformers. Even Calvin is clearly conscious that he builds on the theology of Augustine and Thomas Aquinas; and he who reads the original Lutheran and Reformed dogmatists, perceives at once that they make constant use of what has been contributed by Romish theologians. But in the subsequent period this usage has become extinct. Every church withdraws itself within its own walls; and finally it seems that there is no theology for the dogmatist, but that which rests upon his own confession. Hence, not only in the case of every antithesis, is one equally firm in cleaving to his own conviction, and in rejecting whatever opposes it; but also every suggestion is banished that, at least in that which is *not* antithetic, some theologic depth, development and truth may lodge with the opponent. The Romish theologians carry this confessional absolutism to the farthest extreme. With the Lutheran theologians this absolutism is quickly carried into practice, even at the expense of Reformed theology. The Reformed theologians alone have longest reacted against this confessional absolutism. If the confessional sceptic knows little besides irenics, and if in his eyes all controversy is folly, the absolutist, on the other hand, is averse to all irenics, and controversy or polemics is his only point of contact with the confessions of the other churches, which he considers simply false.

But it is readily seen that neither this sceptical nor this absolutist point of view is in harmony with the claim of theology. Not the *sceptical,* for if theology is "the knowledge of God," and if, consequently, theology as a science can have no other object than to introduce that revealed knowledge of God as clearly as possible into our human consciousness, *personal conviction* must ever be the starting-point of all theology. Taken generically, theology is, and always will be, *knowledge,* and for this reason there can be no theology where the conviction *that one knows* is wanting. Confessional indifferentism is in irreconcilable conflict with this, for many things may lie in the farthest circumference of each one's conviction which are not attached to his personal consciousness; but these do not belong to our confession. But that which one *confesses,* one must mean; of this we must be *certain;* if necessary, the greatest sacrifice must be made for this; if needs be, the sacrifice of life. That now this confessional conviction in the Lutheran Church is different from that in the Eastern, and in the Reformed than in the Church of Rome, certainly does not depend upon our personal preference. This difference is connected, rather, with our position in life and genealogy. No objection should ever be raised on that account, however, against the reality of our conviction, since the entire world of our representations, those of the non-religious kind also, are determined by the circle from which we spring and the age in which we live; the Pelagian only, may encounter some difficulty here, because *he* does not believe in a divine plan, which determines our whole position; but, for the rest, no conviction ever strikes deeper root than when it has been prepared atavistically in us. He, therefore, who has in this way obtained his conviction as one with his life, does not ascribe its possession to his own excellencies, but renders thanks for it to the grace of God. A true theologian, therefore, will and must hold for real and true the theology which he embraces, and to the further development of which he devotes his life, and should not hesitate to consider all other theology to be *deformation.* A Lutheran theologian, who is not firmly convinced of the truth of his own confession and who has no courage to denounce all theology which is opposed to it as deformation, has lost his way. The same is true of the Romish theologian. And we as Reformed theologians stand equally firm in our unshakable conviction that the track, along which we move, runs the most accurately, and that every other track leads to lesser or greater deformation.

But though from his own point of view no single theologian should shrink from this qualification of *deformation,* this conception of deformation contains, on the other hand, an element of *appreciation,* and therefore a sentence against confessional *absolutism.* Deformation passes judgment on the imperfection of the form, but honors the essence.

Whether this deformation is the outcome of schism, and consequent onesidedness, by the contraction of the energy of truth at one single point; or whether it has found its origin in heresy, i.e. in the adoption into one's confession of elements that are foreign to the truth, can make no difference. In either case you acknowledge that there is a "knowledge of God," and that that which calls itself theology is truly possessed of the theologic character. It is still commonly accepted in the confessions that there is an ectypal knowledge of God, that in the natural way this cannot lead the sinner to saving results, and that there is a *special revelation* to supply this want. The canonical books also of the Old and New Testaments are honored by all these churches together as the Divine documentation of this revelation. Difference only begins with the addition to these Scriptures of the apocrypha, of tradition, of papal inspiration, of the mystic inspiration by the internal light (lumen internum), etc. Thus from either side we are abundantly able to show how the deformation originated with the other; and this is the point of attack; yet this does not destroy what is common in all confessions and theologies.

And if this opens the way to the appreciation and use of what has been prepared also by theologians of other confessions, in what is common to us all, it leads at the same time to still another consideration. Even Rome does not deny that *charismata* are also at work outside of her church; and where in this way even Rome maintains a unity, our Protestant principle includes the open recognition of the correlation of the other churches with ours. No single confessional group claims to be *all* the church. We rather confess that the unity of the body of Christ extends far beyond our confessional boundaries. The theological gifts that operate outside of our circle may supply what we lack, and self-sufficient narrow-mindedness alone will refuse such benefit. With us irenics go ever hand in hand with polemics. Firmly and unshakably we stand in our confession, that the track along which we move is the most accurate known to us, and in virtue of this conviction we do not hesitate a moment to mark the divergence of the tracks of others as *deformation.* Against all such deformity we direct our polemics. But we are equally conscious of the fact that *we alone* do not constitute the Church of Christ in the earth; that there is a conviction of truth which operates also outside of our circle; and that in despite of all such deformation divine gifts continue to foster a theologic life worthy of the name. Hence our irenics.

To us, therefore, there is no theology *as such,* which, exalting itself above all special theologies, is *the* theology in the absolute sense. Such a theology would effect at once a new confession and call into life a new church organization; simply because one can hold no different conviction as theologian than as church member. But this would reverse the order of things. The Church does not spring from theology, but theology has its *rise* in the life of the Church. And if the objection is raised, that in this way theology is robbed of its character of universal validity and thus becomes unscientific, we answer: (1) that for universal validity the acceptance of all individuals is not demanded; but only of those who are receptive to the truth of a matter and are well informed of it; (2) that every convinced theologian in the presence of his opponent also appeals from the mind that has been ill-informed (male informatum) to the mind that is to be better informed (melius informandum). The fact that unity of conviction, which is fairly common with the material sciences and rare with the spiritual sciences, is altogether wanting with the highest, viz. theology, is no plea against theology, since it merely shows that, as it touches that which is most tender, it of necessity stands highest, and consequently has most to endure from the ruin worked by sin in our spiritual life.

On this ground we maintain the *confessional* character of theology, since otherwise either the unity of our theological thinking is lost, or the integrity of our theological conviction. To us who are members of the Reformed Churches the most exactly defined object of theology is, the knowledge of God, as given in the Reformed or purified confession.

The Relation of Theology to its Object

Thus far the course of thought has run smoothly. Knowledge of God is the crown of all that can be known. Knowledge of God is inconceivable, except it is imparted to us by God Himself. This knowledge, given us by nature in our creation, has been veiled *from* and darkened *in* us by the results of sin. Consequently it now comes to us in the form of a *special revelation,* and we have received the *divine illumination,* by which we can assimilate the content of that revelation. And *science* is called in, to introduce this knowledge of God, thus revealed, into human thought. Just here, however, a very serious misinterpretation is possible, which must needs be prevented. It can be represented that it is only science that places the revealed knowledge of God within the reach of the pious. In which case it is science that investigates the *special revelation;* the results of this investigation are gradually more fully established; that which is established is brought to the knowledge of all; and thus the knowledge of God is made universal. This entirely intellectualistic way excludes, meanwhile, the spiritual experience of the Church in its entirety, as well as of individual believers. Taken in this way, scientifically theological study must have preceded all faith, and the knowledge of God would only have come within our reach after theology had as good as finished its task. This, however, is inconceivable, since theology is born of the Church, and not the Church of theology. Reflection does not create life, but *suo jure* life is first, after which reflection speaks its word concerning it. And thus spiritual life became manifest in the Church of Christ, and as the result of Revelation practical spiritual knowledge of God had been the rich possession of thousands upon thousands, long before the idea of a scientific theology was suggested. It cannot even be said that scientific theology presented the forms of thought which led to the formulations of dogma. Those formulations were much more the product of the conflict for truth which took place in the life of the Church, and therefore they have borne much more an ecclesiastical than a scientific character. The knowledge of God, held by the Church, did not remain naively mystical, until science analyzed this mysticism. But sharp and clear thinking was done in the Church as such, long before the science of theology as such had won a place for itself. The Church has not lived *un*consciously, but *consciously,* and so far as the personal life of believers is concerned, no urgency for a closer scientific explanation has ever been observed.

Much less can it be said that scientific theology is called to add more certainty to the confession of the Church and to demonstrate its truth. The desire to have theology perform this service, so entirely foreign to it, has not originated in times of spiritual prosperity and healthful activity of faith, but was always the bitter fruit of the weakening of faith, and consequently was ever incapable of checking the decline of the life of the Church. The Church that has leaned on theology, instead of presenting its arm to theology for its support, has always lost the remnant of higher courage which reminded it of better days, and has always degraded itself to a dependency upon the school. No, the need of scientific theology does not spring from the need of the soul, but always finds its motive in our human thought. There is a world of thought which binds man to man, and which, notwithstanding the change of individuals, passes on from generation to generation. Only a few, however, live in that world of thought with such clear consciousness as to feel themselves at home there. But they also who do not enter in so deeply, derive general representations from this world of thought which are the common property of all and thereby render the mutual correspondence among minds possible. And this world of thought cannot resist the impulse to take *all* things up into itself, and therefore also this knowledge of God; and of this impulse theology as a science is born. This *seems* to be otherwise, when we observe that the practical purpose of the first theological studies was to defend themselves apologetically, or to train preachers for the Church; but appearance must not mislead us. The actual need, expressed in these attempts, was to seek a point of support for one's propaganda in the world of thought that was common to Jews and heathen. It was soon learned that with one's preaching pure and simple no gains were made. Hence the need was felt of something of a more transparent character, to supply which the content of the faith was gradually interpreted in the language of our thinking consciousness. In proportion as the significance of this effort after clearer consciousness was more sharply seen, the sense also gradually awakened of a vocation, which, independent of necessity and defence, should cause the content of the revealed knowledge of God to shine likewise in this world of thought. By obedience to this, that content was not brought closer to our heart, but was presented with more clearness to our consciousness. The distance was lessened between our general conceptions and the content of that revelation. The confession of that content became more transparent and accurate, and though this scientific theology was unable to add one grain to the content of this knowledge of God, it has unquestionably heightened the pleasure of our possession. The Church, therefore, has not hesitated to profit by it; and though there is no single pearl in her confession which she owes theology as such, since all her pearls are gathered from the depths of spiritual life, it is equally certain that she would not have been able to string these pearls so beautifully in her confession, had not the light of theology illumined her spiritual labor. From clearer consciousness to go back to mystic darkness, is obscurantism; and since theology has also made the scientific torch to burn, no church that wants to avoid being wilfully "blind" can afford to act as though this torch had never been lighted, but must duly take it into account. In this wise, moreover, theological science is no abstraction. On the contrary, it springs of necessity from the life of the Church, upon which it exerts an influence in all the stages of its development. What we protest against is, that theology should be thought to exist *merely* for the sake of rendering this auxiliary service, and that the Church by itself should be considered not to be able to do without it. Spiritually the Church has prospered long centuries without it, and in so far can never be dependent on it. But on the other hand, again, theology should not be explained from utility. That it did originate, is accounted for by the nobility of our human thought, which *can*not rest, so long as there is still a single domain within reach which it has not annexed to itself. Thinking man, converted to God, has felt himself called to cause the honor of God's truth to shine also in the world of our representations and conceptions. If that which God causes us to perceive of Himself were limited to a mystic esthesia, we might philosophize about this phenomenon, but we would never be able to analyze this perception theologically. Since, however, at sundry times and in diverse manners God has *spoken* unto the fathers, and thus *light upon God* has arisen in our consciousness, that revelation itself has impelled a scientific investigation, and Christendom would have done violence to the impulse of its consciousness if it had lived *without theology*.

Theology, therefore, like every other science, aims at as complete and accurate a knowledge of its object as possible. It too is born from the thirst after insight and clearness, and cannot rest so long as there is still a possibility of making the insight into its object more clear. Theology should not be denied this ideal character of all science, and therefore its motive should ever be sought in knowing God, and not in knowing religion or Christianity. Religion and Christendom by themselves are excellent and important subjects, but as such they do not cover a necessary department in our consciousness. But this is entirely different with respect to the Eternal Being. In every human consciousness of higher development, or at least in the general consciousness of humanity, there is a vacant space, which can only be filled by the knowledge of the Eternal One. If, therefore, as was shown above, theology is to find its object only in the *revealed, ectypal knowledge of God,* this should never be taken in the sense of scholastic learning. The motive for all theology is and ever will be the knowledge of the Eternal Being, not now in the interest of the needs of our heart, and not, as a rule, for the practical purposes of life, but solely in the interest of the world of our thought. More than this it *cannot* give. As a science, it is and always will be *intellectual work,* and can never be *anything else.* Only as far as the revealed knowledge of God has a *logical* content, is theology able to master it. Outside of the domain of our thinking it is powerless; but when the matter concerns this thinking, it is indisputably the province of theology to do it.

But if in this way we concentrate its calling upon the critical examination of the self-revelation of the Eternal Being to us sinners, we do not mean that it is merely to explain from this revelation what relates exclusively to God and to His Nature. It must be strictly *theological*, so that from the beginning to the end of its epic God Himself is the *hero;* but as was observed by the older theologians, one can treat of God both in the direct and oblique cases (de Deo in casu recto et obliquo). Not only, therefore, that which in revelation deals with the being of God, but also His attributes, activities, and creations, so far as these contribute to the knowledge of God, should be taken up in the investigation; nature, therefore, as well, and history, i.e. from the *theological* side; and man likewise, provided he is taken as created after the image of God, and thus interpreted *theologically*. And as knowledge of a powerful thinker is deemed incomplete for his biography, unless you include his ideas concerning the significance of man, the great problems of life, and the development which awaits us in the future, it is self-evident, that it belongs to the knowledge of God, to investigate what He declares concerning man, His relation to the children of men, and His counsel which shall stand. The emphasis, which we put upon theology, as *theology*, tends by no means to impoverish it; we take it that its content is thereby greatly enriched; we only claim that whatever shall belong to its content must be governed by the one and the same leading thought, which leading thought is *the knowledge of God.* This provides at the same time a standard, as shall be shown later on, by which to bring perspective into the Scripture; provided we avoid the errors of distinguishing between Scripture and the Word of God, and of concentrating the significance of the Scripture upon the religious-ethical. The knowledge of God alone teaches you to distinguish between eminent, common, and less important interests in the Scripture. Only that which you have made your own *theologically,* you possess as part of revelation; while that which to your sense is not connected with the knowledge of the Eternal Being, lies still outside of it.

Even this, however, does not *entirely* determine the relation of theology to its object. All this concerns exclusively the content of Revelation, and does not yet reckon with the revealed knowledge of God as such. Thus far a dogmatic-ethical study might develop itself, but this would not provide room for a theology in the broader unfolding of all its departments of study. Only with the organic construction of theology as a scientific unity can it be shown more accurately of every department, in what relation it stands to the knowledge of God, and what place, therefore, belongs to such a department in the theologic unit. To this, then, we refer; but it is necessary here to indicate, in broad outline, from whence theology derives these many departments of study. It will not suffice to say, that they have appeared *de facto,* neither will it be enough to emphasize the significance of these departments as preparation for the preaching of the Word. To be capable of being scientifically interpreted, the unit of science must spring from the root of its object, or, at least, its object must be its motive. This object here is: *the revealed knowledge of God,* or the *theologia ectypa revelata.* From this it follows, that we are not simply to deal with the content of revelation, but also that this revelation as such must be investigated; that the activity must be traced, which has gone out from this revelation; and that the relation must be traced between revelation and our psychic data, in order to make action from our side possible with that revelation. He who is to make a scientific examination of a mineral spring, is not permitted to rest content with an analysis of its ferruginous quality, but is bound to inquire into the history of this spring, to watch the action of its waters, and to experiment as to how its content is best applied. Apply this to the revealed knowledge of God, and you perceive at once, that the theological science cannot deem its task completed, when it has analyzed the content of revelation, but the revelation itself and the action that went out from it, together with the method demanded by its application, must be studied in their relation to each other. With the strictest maintenance, therefore, of the *theologic* character of our science, nothing prevents a view of the relations of the several departments of study. For instance, what is church history but the broad narrative of the *effects* which the ectypal knowledge of God has exerted in the life of nations? Meanwhile we content ourselves with the simple indication if it here. This relation can only fully be explained in the closing sections of this volume.

Sacred Theology

Before we enter upon the study of the principium of Theology, we insert here a brief explanation of the ancient epithet of *Sacred* before *Theology*. Not that *we* should insist on this title, or that to our idea this title implies any special merit, but because the purpose of its omission is the *secularization* of theology, and for this reason it has an essential significance as an effort to destroy the distinguishing character of theology. The habit of speaking of *Sacred* Theology has the indorsement of the ages. At the Reformation the churches found it in this form, and they felt themselves bound to reverence and maintain it. The first mention of the omission of this title appears, after the conflict had begun against a *principium proprium* for theology; and the dislike which the effort to restore this ancient title to theology creates in many people, is identical with the dislike which is shown by those same people for every representation of a *special revelation*. As the omission of *Sancta* was no accident, our effort is equally intentional, to renew the use of that name in our Reformed circles. By inserting *Sancta* before *Theologia* we desire it to be clearly understood, that we take no part in the secularization of Theology, but maintain that it has a sphere of its own.

The Church of Christ has borrowed from the Holy Scriptures this word *sacred* as a prefix to whatever stands in immediate relation to the *special revelation*. This prefix is constantly used in the Old as well as in the New Testament. The spot of ground at the burning bush is called *holy* ground, because there the holiness of the Lord revealed itself to Moses. The קְהַל in Israel, or the congregation of the people, is called *holy*. In Exod. xvi. 23 it speaks of "the *holy* sabbath unto the Lord." The people itself is called an "holy people," and its members are called "holy men" (Exod. xxii. 31). In a still more pregnant sense the altar is called "holy" and "whatsoever touches the altar" (Exod. xxix. 37), which refers to places and buildings, as well as to persons, their garments, tools and acts. Jerusalem itself is called the "holy city" (Neh. xi. 1). Holy, therefore, is the definite epithet not only for what is in heaven, with all the hosts of angels, but equally for that which on earth is chosen of God for His service. Thus the Psalmist speaks of "the saints that are in the earth." "God's faithfulness is in the assembly of the holy ones." Thus the Proverbs speak of the knowledge the people of God received by higher light, as "the knowledge of the holy" (A. V. ix. 10 and xxx. 3); and, in short, without a closer study of the idea of קָדוֹשׁ, it may be said that in the Old Testament this title of "holy" is attached to everything that transmits the special revelation, flows forth from it, or stands in immediate relation to it.

That it will not do to explain this prefix, "holy," simply from the symbolic and typical character of the Old Dispensation, appears from the entirely similar use of "holy" in the writings of the New Covenant. Here also we find Jerusalem spoken of as the "holy city" (Math. iv. 5; xxvii. 53 and Rev. xi. 2; xxi. 2 and xxii. 19). Christ also speaks of "the holy angels" (Luke ix. 26). Christ himself is called "that *holy one* that shall be born of Mary." The men of God of the Old Covenant are spoken of as the "*holy* prophets." The members of the Church of the New Covenant, from the Jews as well as from the heathen, bear the almost fixed name of "the saints," so that οἱ ἅγιοι was provisionally the technical name for those who subsequently were called "the Christians." In an entirely similar sense the books of the Old Covenant are spoken of as the "Holy Scriptures." The kiss, with which the partakers of the ἀγάπαι greeted each other, receives the name of "holy kiss." Children born of believing parents receive the same honorary title. Like the prophets of the Old Covenant, the apostles and prophets of the New Dispensation are called "*holy* apostles and prophets." Believers on the Lord are called a "holy people," a "holy priesthood." Their prayers come up before God as "the prayers of the *saints*"; the martyr's blood is "the blood of the *saints*"; and the Gospel itself is announced as "the *holy* Gospel."

In connection with this use of language the Church of Christ has introduced this epithet of "holy" into her public utterances; and not only the Romish Church, but the churches of the Reformation as well, spoke of the "holy church," of the "holy prophets," the "holy apostles," the "holy Scriptures," the "holy Gospel," the "holy sacraments," "holy Baptism," "holy Communion," and thus likewise of "sacred Theology" and the "sacred ministry." This use of language was constant, and, at least in this limited sense, met with no opposition. This only manifested itself when the Romish church applied this epithet of "holy" distinctively to individual persons of a higher religious standing. This opposition, however, was not unanimous nor logical. Even where the so-called Romish saints were passed by, it remained invariably the custom to speak of "Saint Augustine," "Saint Thomas," etc. These were inconsequences, however, to which men were led by the accustomed sound, and which represented in the case of no writer in the days of the Reformation any intentional principle; in addition to which it is observed that the Reformed theologians offended less in this respect than many a Lutheran.

This does not mean that by this reformatory correction the use of the ancient Christian church was restored in all its purity. Originally, indeed, the name of holy ($\check{\alpha}\gamma\iota o\varsigma$) was a general distinction, to discriminate between what was within and what without. *Everything* that had entered holy ground was considered *holy;* everything outside was spoken of as "lying in wickedness"; but in the Scriptures of the New Testament no such distinction occurs between a lower and higher holiness within the bounds of the Church. The error of the Romish Church lies in the application of this title to this non-Scriptural distinction. While in the Holy Scriptures *all* confessors of Christ are called *saints,* the Romish Church deprived the people at large of this title, and reserved it for a special class of Christians, either for the clergy in general, or for those under higher vows, or for those who, as church fathers and teachers, held a special position; or finally, in its narrowest sense, for those who were canonized. The Reformation opposed this non-Scriptural distinction, but lacked courage to restore the name of *saint* in its original significance to *all* believers. Spiritualistic apocalyptic circles tended toward this; from the side of Protestantism also, in addresses, etc., the whole congregation were again called "a holy communion" (eine heilige Gemeinde); poets frequently followed this use of language; but the Reformation has not restored the name of *saint* as a general term for every Christian. It preferred rather to abandon the name in its general sense, than by the use of it to encourage the Romish misuse.

From this, however, it is evident that there was no superficial work done in the days of the Reformation, and that the representation that by speaking of "holy Scripture," "holy Gospel," "holy Baptism," etc., they merely imitated Rome, rests on a misunderstanding. The reformers did most careful work. There were cases in which the epithet "holy" was purposely dropped; but others also in which this prefix was purposely kept; and to this last category belongs the word "*Sacred*" before *Theology.* If it is asked what was meant to have this qualification of theology, no special reason seems to have been given. As in the Proverbs "the knowledge of the holy" was spoken of, it was thought proper that that knowledge and science, whose principium lies in the Holy Scriptures, should be distinguished from all other knowledge; and thus it may be said, that in the sixteenth century *Sancta theologia* chiefly indicated the antithesis between that which came to us from profane literature and from the Holy Scriptures.

At present, however, this general indication will not suffice. The significance of this epithet for the object, the subject, and the method of theology should be more accurately analyzed. And with reference to the *object,* the *principium proprium* of theology stands certainly in the foreground. What we understand by this "proper principle" of theology, we will endeavor to explain in the following chapter; here it is merely remarked that the ectypal knowledge of God, in which the science of theology finds its object, does not come to us in the same way, from the same fountain and by the same light, as our other sciences. There is a difference here, which in its deepest root reduces itself to a straightforward antithesis, which places two principles of knowing (principia cognoscendi) over against each other. The particular principium of theology characterizes itself by the entrance of an immediate, divine action, which breaks through what is sinful and false, in order in the midst of these false and sinful conditions to reveal unto us, by a light of its own, what is true and holy in antithesis to what is sinful and false. The heathen antithesis between *profane* and *sacred* has no application here. That was simply the pride of the initiated that expressed itself at the expense of the uninitiated. The *odi profanum vulgus et arceo* is refuted and censured by the character of everything that is holy in the Scriptures, and we might wish that our theologians would never have employed the word *profane* as an antithesis. In Scripture the antithesis is between the *special source* and the *natural,* which is more sharply emphasized by the antithesis between what is *wicked, foolish* and *satanic,* and what is true, holy and divine. But however much this proper principium of theology, far from underestimating the natural principium, rather takes it up in itself, as the next chapter will show, the antithesis between the normal and abnormal, the general and special, and between that which is bound by sin and that which surmounts sin, of these "two sources of knowledge," can never be destroyed. To emphasize *this* antithesis, the word "sacred" was used in simple imitation of the Scripture, and in this entirely Scriptural sense our science was called *Sacred Theology.*

If thus the principal motive for the use of this word "sacred" lies in the peculiar character of the *object* of the science of theology, a second motive was added in consequence of the peculiar quality which in the investigation of this object was claimed as a necessity in the *subject.* This was on the ground of 1 Cor. ii. 14, that "the natural man receiveth not the things of the Spirit of God, for they are foolishness unto him"; and also because he who stands outside of palingenesis "cannot see the kingdom of God." Hence, there was not simply an antithesis to be considered between the *object* of this and of all other sciences; but a similar antithesis also presented itself in the *subject,* that was to take this theology up into itself and presently to reproduce it. Not every one can engage in this work, but only they who are *spiritually minded.* No intellectual relation is possible in the domain of this science, between those to whom this theology is "foolishness," and the others to whom it is the "wisdom of God." They only, who by virtue of palingenesis are partakers of *spiritual illumination,* have their eyes opened to see the object to be investigated. The others do not see it, or see it wrongly. By reason of the lack of affinity between subject and object, every deeper penetration into the object is impossible. The rule that "in thy light we see light" finds here its special application. No blind man can be our guide in the domain of optics. Though it is entirely true, therefore, that in the *science* of Theology the *ego* of the general human consciousness is the general subject, yet this *ego* is here incapable of its task, unless the darkening worked by sin in his consciousness is gradually withdrawn.

This leads, in the third place, to the conviction that the science of theology is not governed by the general human mind, such as it now operates in our fallen race, but only to that extent in which this universal human mind has been animated by the *Holy Ghost,* i.e. also to a difference *in method.* Only later on can this point be fully explained. At present let it be said that that same Holy Spirit, who offers us the Holy Scriptures and the Church as the result of His activity, is the real Doctor ecclesiae, who enables us to grasp the truth from the Scriptures, and from our consciousness to reflect the same in scientific analysis. As it advances in the course of centuries, there is coherence and steadiness of progress in the science of theology, and a decided unity of effort, even though individual theologians are not conscious of it or able to determine its course. But while this unity of effort in the course of centuries is determined in the other sciences partly by the inherent Logic, and by natural events keeping pace with it, theology derives this determination of its process from a Logic which presents itself in light pneumatically only, in connection with events which flow from the dealings of Christ with His Church. Hence, this leading of the Holy Spirit as subject of theology makes itself felt in a threefold way. First, through the Church, which has the formulation of dogma in hand, and with it the choice of the course to be taken, and which effects this formulation of dogma officially, i.e. as the instrument of the Holy Spirit. That in this the Church is not an infallible organ, and the reason for it, will be explained later on. We here content ourselves with pointing to this mingling of ecclesiastical power in the development of theology, as one of the actions of the Holy Ghost. Secondly, this action of the Holy Spirit presents itself in the logical development of those tendencies opposed to the truth, which, without any fault or purpose of its own, the Church has had to resist successively, and which only subsequently prove themselves to have been the means of revealing truth in its logical relation. Not from the Church, but rather from without comes the frequent impetus, which stimulates and necessitates spiritual thought, and yet the thinking born from this is not aphoristic, but logical and organically coherent. And in the third place this action of the Holy Spirit is evident from the productiveness of theology in times when the operations of the Spirit in the Church are powerful, and from the poverty and meagreness which are seen in contrast, as soon as those operations of the Spirit withdraw themselves from the Church. Subjectively this can be expressed by saying that theology has flourished only at the times when theologians have continued in prayer, and in prayer have sought the communion of the Holy Spirit, and that on the other hand it loses its leaf and begins its winter sleep when ambition for learning silences prayer in the breast of theologians.

In this sense, both with reference to its *object,* and to the extent in which it concerns its *subject,* and its *method* as well (in virtue of the leading of the Holy Spirit as *Doctor ecclesiae*), the peculiar character of theology demands that its peculiarity shall be characterized also by its title of *Sacred* Theology.

CHAPTER II

THE FUNDAMENTAL, REGULATIVE, AND DISTINCTIVE PRINCIPLE
OF THEOLOGY, OR PRINCIPIUM THEOLOGIAE

What is here to be understood by Principium

When theology abandoned its proper and original character, it also ceased to speak of a principium of its own; and gradually we have become so estranged from the earlier theological life, that it is scarcely any longer understood what our old theologians meant by the *principium theologiae.* This *principium* of theology is not infrequently taken as synonymous with *fons theologiae,* i.e. with the fountain from, which the science of theology draws its knowledge. Why is this wrong? When I speak of the fountains of a science, I understand thereby a certain group out of the sum of phenomena, from which a separate whole of science is distilled by me. For the Zoologist these fountains lie in the animal world, for the Botanist in the world of plants, for the Historian in many-sided tradition, etc. But however much in each of these domains of science the fountains may differ, the principium of knowing (cognoscendi), from which knowledge comes to us with these several groups of phenomena, is ever one and the same. It is, in a word, the natural man who *by his reason* draws this knowledge from his object, and that object is *subjected* to him as the thinking subject. If now I proceed in like manner on theological ground, formaliter at least, then my principium of knowing remains here entirely the same that it is for the botanist or zoologist, and the difference consists only in the difference of the object. Whether I seek that object in God Himself, or in the Christian religion, or in religious phenomena makes no fundamental difference. With all these it is still the thinking man who subjects these objects to himself, and by virtue of his general principium of knowing draws knowledge from them. For, and I speak reverently, even when I posit God Himself as the object of theology, this God is then placed on trial by the theologian, and it is the theologian who does not cast himself down in worship before Him, saying, "Speak, Lord, for thy servant heareth," but of his own right (suo jure) investigates Him. The result, indeed, has shown that he who has taken *this* attitude, has either entirely revolutionarily reversed the order of things and placed himself as critic above his God, or has falsified the object of theology and substituted for it religious phenomena; a method which seemed more innocent, but which actually led to a like result, since from this standpoint "knowledge of God" remained wanting, and want of knowledge of God is little else than intellectual atheism.

The propounding of a special principium in the theological sphere (even though we grant that this was not always done correctly), viewed in itself, was little else than the necessary result of the peculiar character of theology. If the object of theology had stood coordinate with the objects of the other sciences, then together with those sciences theology would have been obliged to employ a common principium of knowing. But, since, on the other hand, the object of theology excluded every idea of coordination, and thinking man, who asked after the knowledge of God, stood in a radically different relation to that God than to the several kingdoms of created things, there *had* to be a difference in the principium of knowing. With every other object it was the thinking subject that *took knowledge;* here it was the object itself that *gave knowledge.* And this antithesis is least of all set aside by the remark, that the flower also provides the botanist with knowledge concerning itself. This replaces a *real* manner of speech by a *metaphorical* one. The flower indeed does nothing, and the whole plant, on which the flower blooms, is passive. Even though it is maintained that the flower exhibits color and form, this is by no means yet the knowledge of the flower, but merely so many data, from which this knowledge is gathered by the botanist. Hence our speaking, with reference to theology, of a special principium of knowing of its own, is the result of the entirely peculiar position, in which here the knowing subject stands over against God as the object to be known. Theology, taken in its original and only real meaning, as *"knowledge* of God," or as "the *science* of the knowledge of God," cannot go to work like the other sciences, but must take a *way of its own;* which not merely in its bends and turns, but in its entire extent, is to be distinguished from the ordinary way of obtaining knowledge (via cognitionis), and therefore assumes a principium of knowing of its own as its point of departure.

Even if the fact of sin were left out of account, and the *special revelation* were not considered, formaliter a principium of its own must still be claimed for theology. This claim may be more sharply accentuated by these two facts, but it may never be represented as though the necessity of a source of its own were only born formaliter from sin. This necessity does not merely lie in the abnormal, but in the normal as well, and must ever find its ground in this fact, that God is *God,* and that consequently the Eternal Being cannot become the object of creaturely knowledge, as coordinate with the creature. Let it be supposed that the development of our race had taken place without sin; man would nevertheless have known the things that may be known of God, from the world of his heart and the world round about him, but *not* as the fruit of empiricism and the conclusions based thereon. From the finite no conclusion can be drawn to the infinite, neither can a Divine reality be known from external or internal phenomena, unless that real God *reveals* Himself in my consciousness to my ego; reveals Himself as *God;* and thereby moves and impels me to see in these finite phenomena a brightness of *His* glory. Formaliter, neither observation nor reasoning would ever have rendered service here as the principium of knowing. Without sin, this self-revelation of the Divine Ego to my personal ego would never have been, even in part, the fruit of Theophany, or of incarnation, but would have taken place normally in my personal being, and in such a way that even then the way by which knowledge is obtained would have divided itself into two, one leading to the knowledge of those objects which, being *passive,* I subject to myself, the other leading to the knowledge of that one Object, to which I myself am passively subjected. That "faith" assumes its peculiar office here, and that, as belonging to our human nature, it may turn into unfaith, but can never fall away, has been remarked before. In this place it is enough to note the distinction, that formaliter the thinking subject can obtain his knowledge from a twofold principium: either from himself, by going to work *actively,* or, if he must remain passive, not from himself but from a principium, the impulse of which proceeds from the object, *in casu* from God, and only thus operates in him.

From this it already appears that the proposition of the old theology,–Principium theologiae est Sacra Scriptura, i.e. the Sacred Scripture is the Principium of Theology,–has nothing in common with the representation of a few remaining supranaturalists, who still grant that the Scripture spreads light upon much that otherwise would be dark to us. The very word *principium* indeed, which may never be mistaken for fons or phenomenon, claims, that by nature this principium stands in organic connection with the real nature of theology. But, as was observed above, the peculiar character of theology, and therefore also the special nature of its principium, is accentuated still more by sin. Under its power it continued not merely a fact that the thinking subject stood *passively* over against God as object; but in addition to this, the normal means, for receiving in the passive sense this knowledge of God, could no longer operate accurately, and therefore failed of the desired effect. By nature man could not *take* knowledge of God *actively,* and as sinner he could no longer let himself even *passively* be *given* this knowledge of God by God. This modification in man and in his relation to God could issue only in one or the other result, viz. that either the sinner should live on without "knowledge of God," or that from the side of God there should proceed an activity to impart this knowledge to *sinful* man, in keeping with his *need* as sinner. The latter then, however, took place outside of the life that sprang of itself from the creation principium and the knowledge connected with it; it was a special principle (proprium quid), which only stepped in between provisionally, and was destined to disappear again, as soon as the normal development of our race had reached its final end. In this way this self-revelation of God to the sinner was also *materialiter* an action from a special principium in God; from this principium in God this action went out to the world and, to the sinner; and as soon as man thus operated upon began to give an account to himself of the common phenomena of, and of this abnormal process in, his life, from the nature of the case the principium of all the rest would lie in creation, while the principium of this entirely special action is found in a *re-creative* act of God. It made no difference that, along with this action, existing elements from creation were employed. Such elements were then assimilated by the active principium and rendered serviceable to it, just like the chisel in the hands of the sculptor, or as a board sawn from a tree, which serves for the hull of a ship. If in theology, therefore, as such *formaliter,* there lay the claim that it springs out of a principium of knowing of its own, this principium of Theology is distinguished, by and in consequence of sin, from the principium of knowing in the domain of the other sciences *materialiter* also, and hence concerns both the formal and the material principium.

In part it may even be maintained, that the principium of being (essendi) is also included here. That self-revelation of God to the sinner is possible even without a preceding regeneration, is shown in the case of Balaam; but this exception does not make the rule; the general rule is, that regeneration precedes spiritual illumination. The "enlightened" of Heb. vi. 4 do not stand in the same line with the "enlightened" of Eph. i. 18. The latter only are "spiritual" and "have received the things of the Spirit of God." This regeneration is not an element in knowing (cognoscere), but in being (esse), and if account is taken of the fact that the whole revelation of God, though directed by the Logos, nevertheless proceeds through an entire series of events and wonders, and finally culminates in the essential incarnation and all it carries with it, then it is evident that the distinction between theology and the other sciences not only formally touches the principium of faith, and materially the "good word of God" ($\kappa\alpha\lambda\grave{o}\nu$ $\theta\epsilon o\hat{u}$ $\dot{\rho}\hat{\eta}\mu\alpha$), but also penetrates into our real being (esse). This explains the fact that the Theosophists, and in part the Mystics in the tracks of the former, have sought to obtain the knowledge of God along this way of being (via essendi). And this difference in the real being (esse) must indeed be taken into account, at least so far as it concerns its modality. He who neglects to do this, annuls regeneration, and thereby undermines all faith in miracles. Meanwhile it must not be lost from sight that the distinction in the essential forms no fundamental antithesis. Sin is no essence (esse), but a modality of it ($\tau\acute{o}$ esse); and consequently regeneration, which annuls and conquers sin, can create no other essence, but can merely re-establish from its perverted modality the original real being (esse) into its ideal modality. He who deems that this touches the essentia itself, and not its modus simply, becomes a Manichaean. And if it be said that we must take account of "the powers of the world to come," etc., we answer, that from the beginning there has been an organic connection between the creature in his present and eternal condition. Even with the most radical metamorphosis there could never be a change of the essence. If, then, it is beyond doubt, that, on account of regeneration and miracles, real being (esse) must also be considered, no two principles of being stand over against each other; in the realm of nature, as well as in the realm of grace, it is and remains the original principium of being, even though this principium operates in the two in different ways. Very properly, therefore, Theosophy has been dismissed, and the full emphasis has been put on Theology as such.

This has made it customary to seek the proper principium of theology immediately in the Holy Scripture, by which was meant of course simply the material principium of knowing (principium cognoscendi materiale). The knowledge of God, which God Himself had communicated by numerous facts and revelations, and which under his guidance was embodied in the Holy Scripture, was the gold which theology was to delve from the mine of the Holy Scripture. Meanwhile this could not be intended otherwise than as an abbreviated manner of speech. A principium is a living agent, hence a principium of knowledge must be an agent from which of necessity knowledge flows. And this of course the Bible as such is not. The principium of knowledge existed before knowledge had emerged from this principium, and consequently before the first page of Scripture was written. When, nevertheless, the Sacred Scripture is called the sole principium of theology (principium unicum theologiae), then the Scripture here is taken as a plant, whose germ has sprouted and budded, and has unfolded those buds. It is not, therefore, the naked principium, but the principium together with what it has brought forth. Speaking more accurately, we should say that the material principium is *the self-revelation of God to the sinner*, from which principium the data have come forth in the Holy Scriptures, from which theology must be built up. Since, however, theology can only *begin* when Revelation is *completed*, we may readily proceed from the ultimate cause (principium remotum) to the proximate (proximum), and say that theology sprang from the completed revelation, i.e. from the Scriptures, as the proximate cause, while that revelation itself originated from the ultimate cause of the self-revelation of God.

It is unfortunate, however, that in olden time so little attention was paid to the formal principium. For now it seemed altogether as though the still darkened understanding was to investigate the Scripture as its object, in an entirely similar way to that in which this same understanding threw itself on plant and animal as its object. At first this compelled the understanding to adapt and accommodate itself to the authority of the Holy Scripture, which then still maintained a high position. But, in the long run, roles were to be exchanged, and the neglect of the formal principium was to bring about a revision of the Scripture in the sense of our darkened understanding, as has now actually taken place. For if faith was considered under Soteriology, and in connection with faith the "illumination," what help was this, as long as theology itself was abandoned to the rational subject, in which rational subject, from the hour of his creation, no proper and separate principium of knowing God had been allowed to assert itself?

Different Representations concerning the
Operation of this Principium

In the first section of this chapter, it has been shown that the possession of a special principium of knowing is indispensable to theology, for the reason that God is never a *passive* phenomonen, so that all knowledge of God must ever be the fruit of self-revelation on His side. Hence it is the distinct nature of the object of theology which renders a special principium of knowing necessary. This is essentially agreed upon, without distinction, by all who still hold fast to theology in its original sense. Not by those who, though they have adopted an entirely *different* object for their science, still call themselves theologians; but by the theologians of all churches and tendencies, who, in whatever else they may differ from each other, are still agreed in this, that theology is bent upon the knowledge of the living God, and that from God Himself alone this knowledge can come to us. Among all these, there is no difference of view concerning this ultimate cause (principium remotum).

It is different, on the other hand, when it is further investigated *in what way* this principium of God's self-revelation has operated or still operates. The confession is still almost universal that this self-revelation lies at our disposal in the Holy Scripture; but while one group affirms: In the Holy Scripture *and nothing else,* another group asserts that the apocryphal books as well, and tradition, yea, the papal inspiration also, claim our attention; those who are mystically inclined tend to supersede the Scriptures by personal inspiration; and minds that wander off yet farther point you to a Word of God in nature, in history, in the conscience, or in the ideal disposition of your heart. Two things must be carefully distinguished. There is, on the one hand, the question whether by sin the self-revelation of God is compelled to take a temporary side-road, in order, when sin shall have been entirely overcome, to resume again its original way, or whether in the sinner, also, the internal address of God is still heard in sufficiently clear accents. This touches the relation of natural theology to specially revealed theology, and can pass into the question whether natural theology is not sufficient for the sinner; a matter which in turn is connected with the doctrine *of sin.* If the reality of sin is finally denied, by dissolving its antithetic character and by viewing it as a stage in a continuous process of development, then it is evident that there is no longer any question of the darkening of our knowledge of God by sin. This, however, is not the point that is in order in this section. Here we assume, therefore, that the reality of sin is acknowledged, that the darkening of our knowledge of God by sin is confessed, so that without a *special revelation* no sufficient knowledge of God for the sinner is deemed obtainable. If this is accepted, then we come to face an entirely different question: viz. how this *special revelation* is to be conceived.

The most general conception under which these representations can be grasped is that of *inspiration,* i.e. of an inworking of the Spirit of God upon the mind and heart of the sinner, by which God makes Himself known to him, and communicates His will or His thoughts. For the present we pass by the quantitive element in this inspiration; we take it now only qualitatively; in which case it is clear that fundamentally it is one and the same conception, whether I speak of theopneusty in the prophets and apostles, of an internal light in the mysticism of the emotions, or of a papal infallibility. The prophet, the mystic, and the bishop of Rome are all sinners, and of each of these three it is affirmed not that they conceive or imagine something concerning God of themselves, but that there has gone out or goes out upon them an operation of the Holy Spirit, which *eo ipso,* as wrought by God, bears the divine mark of genuineness. In the application only do these inspiration, internal light and infallibility differ. The most general conception of this inspiration is that of the mysticus. He is the individualist; takes, therefore, every sinner by himself; and now thinks that God, being desirous to reveal Himself to sinners, could scarcely do this in any other way than by communicating Himself separately to every sinner, and thus make Himself known by each. This representation is both the most primitive and simple. Entirely aphoristically God makes Himself known first to A and then to B. That they should know of each other is not necessary. Every one spiritually sick sits as it were in a cell of his own, and in this separated cell receives the visit of the heavenly Physician. Thus it goes on from year to year, and from age to age. This inspiration repeats itself in land upon land. In the main it is always the same, and can only vary according to age, sex, nationality, needs of the soul, etc. With all these variations the type of this inspiration remains unchangeable. It is ever God Almighty turning Himself to the *individual* sinner, and making Himself known in His eternal mercies. The truth of this mysticism lies naturally in the high estimate of the personal element in religion, and in preaching that not only every individual person must come to his God, but also, *that God must reveal Himself to every individual,* so that the *secret walk with God* may be found by every one for his own soul. As a fundamental principle of theology (principium theologicum), on the other hand, this representation of the internal light (lumen internum) is of no use whatever, simply because it rests on fiction. If it were true, if the Lord our God did give to each one personally not merely a disposition, an emotion, a perception, but a real *knowledge* of God, then he who has been thus mystically inspired should be able to speak just like the prophets of old, and the witness of one should confirm the witness of another. Such, however, is not the case. You never receive from these mystics a clear communication of what has been revealed in this way to enrich our knowledge of God. For the most part they even avoid clear language, and hide themselves behind indefinite expressions of feeling and sounds without rational sense. And where they go a little further and come to the communication of definite representations, you always notice one of two things: either they borrow the content of their communications from the Holy Scriptures, or fall back entirely into natural theology, and treat you to philosophemes well known from other quarters. From this it appears that the pretended communication of knowledge of God, which they claim to receive, is the fruit of self-deception. The Holy Spirit simply does *not* work along this individual way, at least not now, after the Scriptures are completed. What the Holy Spirit personally does, is to direct faith to the revealed knowledge of God, to explain and apply this revealed knowledge of God to the heart according to its particular need, and also to quicken in the soul a lively sense of truth; but along this individual way He does not impart an *increase of content.*

With a clear understanding of this, the best known mystics have modified this monotonous-individual conception of inspiration. This conception was not interesting enough, therefore they have inclined to perpetuate the prophets' mantle. Not every child of God has received such an inspiration, but only a few. As in former times among the twelve tribes there were no twelve prophets of influence at once, but generally a single "man of God" appeared in a given period, so the work of God is carried on now. Hence there are present-day prophets; not many, but a few; now here, then there. These men of God receive special inspirations, which do not tend so much to enrich our knowledge of God, but rather serve to make prophecies concerning coming disasters, to establish the claim that all God's people shall subject themselves to such a mystical prophet, and to regulate life and religion according to his orders. This, then, is no longer the theory of an individual, internal light in every child of God, but the representation that prophetic inspiration, as an extraordinary instrument, was not merely temporal and local, but is ever continuous. With this conception the Holy Scriptures are always assumed as existent; from those Scriptures material is drawn; and only the temporal and local application of what was revealed in those Scriptures is vindicated for the mystical fanatic. The tendency reveals itself indeed again and again to soar paracletically above the revelation of the Scriptures, and Montanistically to wander off; but this is almost always the sure sign of approaching dissolution. As soon as the break with the Scripture is entire, the spiritual authority of what was mystically inspired is ended.

They who seek the proximate cause (principium proximum) exclusively in the Holy Scriptures, do not deny the mystical inworkings of the Holy Spirit upon individuals, but maintain that this mystical inworking as such never leads to knowledge of God, and therefore can only be added by way of explanation and application to the knowledge of God obtained elsewhere. With this they do not deny, that an inspiration which brings knowledge of God is possible, but they assert that this is not general but exceptional, and is not primarily for the benefit of individuals but *organically* for the good of the whole. It remains to them therefore an open question, whether God the Lord could have followed the mystic individual way of communicating the knowledge of Himself; but it is certain that God did not take this way, and that His not taking this atomistic way is in close harmony with the entire method of knowledge in our human race. Our race does not know by adding together what is known by A + B + C, but knows organically. There is a process in this knowledge. This knowledge developing itself in process is the common property of all, and each one takes part in this treasure according to the measure of his susceptibility. This organic conception of our human knowledge lies, therefore, in the very creation of our race, and it does not surprise us that God the Lord has also revealed His divine knowledge for the sinner in an organic way. Hence inspiration is no inshining of God's Spirit in the human spirit that endlessly repeats itself, but an action from the side of God which is limited to a definite period and bound to definite conditions. That which is revealed of the knowledge of God within this given period of time and in connection with those conditions forms *one whole;* not by the addition of one revelation to the other, but in virtue of the fact that the one rich thought of God develops itself ever more richly from *one* germ. And since now this process has been ended, so that this revealed knowledge of God has been brought within the reach of our race, there *can* of course be no more real inspiration, and the individual and organic working of the Holy Spirit which follows after, can have no other tendency than to lead and to enlighten the church in the spiritual labor which it must expend upon this revelation. This organic interpretation, then, brings with it that whatever you confess concerning the Holy Scriptures is only valid when they are completed, so that during the ages which intervened between Paradise and Patmos, the self-revelation of God to His people bore in part a different character. From this point of view distinction is made between the first period in which the tree begins its growth, and that other period, when year by year the tree casts its fruit into your lap. Thus inspiration appears as a *temporal* activity, which effects a result, organic in nature, and of an organic significance for our entire race. It has had a beginning, and also *an ending;* and the benefit we derive is no longer a continuous inspiration, but *the fruit of the finished inspiration.* Not as though this fruit is simply cast at the sinner's feet, for him to do with as he pleases. On the contrary, there are operations of the Holy Spirit, by which He renders the use of this fruit possible for the sinner. Illumination, the witness of the Holy Spirit, the sacred office, the leadership of the Church, etc., all exert an influence on this. In the sphere of the new life all these operations of the Holy Spirit are no longer abnormal, but *normal,* and therefore may never be placed in a line with the ever *abnormal inspiration.* Inspiration, therefore, is here taken in connection with all sorts of other operations of the Holy Spirit, as an abnormal, temporal, organic process, the fruit of which lies before us in the Holy Scripture. The desire to draw the boundary lines sharply here between the normal and the abnormal, expressed itself most clearly in the rejection of the apocrypha.

The third point of view, that of the Romish Church, does *not* differ essentially from this. Rome also rejects the mystic-atomistic character of inspiration, and interprets it organically. Rome also affirms a difference, though in a *weaker* form, between the first growth and the later life of this plant. The abnormal character of inspiration is equally certain to Rome as to us. About the authority, therefore, of the Holy Scripture, you will not readily come in controversy with Rome. But the point of view held by Rome differs entirely from ours, when Rome does not bring special inspiration to a close with Patmos, but continues it till the present day in the Church, even in the bishop of Rome *e cathedra loquente.* This exerts a twofold influence. First, as far as it *adds* to the content of the Holy Scriptures, and again, in so much as the Church absolutely *interprets* the Scripture. Since the prophets and apostles are no more among the living, but the Church always is, it is evident that neither prophets nor apostles can exercise any compulsory authority in the Church, while by its official interpretation the Church has it always in her power to interpret the utterances of prophets and apostles as she likes. It should be observed, not only that from this view-point inspiration is always continuous, but also that the inspiration of the past becomes of secondary significance, compared to the inspiration of later times. And this is what Rome has come to, by weakening the difference between the normal and the abnormal. The operations of the Holy Spirit in the sphere of the new life through the ordained ministry and the councils of ecclesiastics are placed on one line with the inspiration of Moses, David or Isaiah; the apocrypha share the authority of the canonical books; and on the other side, the applying and expository operations of the Holy Spirit are withdrawn from the individual life and concentrated in that which is official.

We pass by the small differences from each of these three points of view which occur in Greek, Lutheran, and Baptist Theology. In this section it was our only purpose, where the ultimate cause (principium remotum) is fixed, to distinguish the conceptions which had been formed of the manner in which the Divine energy, in revealing itself to sinners, had reached its result. This process has been represented either as mystic-atomistic or as organic. The first has been done by all fanatics, the latter by all churches. But though all the churches have agreed in the organic interpretation of Revelation, they have separated in this: namely, one group has conceived inspiration not merely as organic, but temporal as well, and consequently as completed; while Rome still thinks that inspiration is continuous in the organism of the Church.

The Relation between this Principium
and our Consciousness

For the present, we leave the further study of the different conceptions that are formed of the working of this principium, in order to go back to the more weighty question of the connection between this principium and our consciousness—a question the answer to which lies for us in the qualification of this connection as *immediate.* There is no third something, that guarantees to our consciousness the reality of this principium. The working of this principium upon our consciousness is direct. This is really self-evident, since every principium finds its peculiar character in this, that it is itself *ground,* and therefore allows no ground *under* itself; but in the case of the principium of theology ideas have been so confused, that a separate study of it cannot be omitted. For the sake of clearness we start from the ultimate cause, i.e. *from special inspiration. God from His own mind breathes* (inspirat) *into the mind of man,* more particularly into *the mind of sinful man, and that, too, in a special manner.* This, and nothing else, is the principium, from which knowledge of God comes to us sinners, and from which also theology as a science draws its vital power. That besides this inspiration there is also manifestation, and that both inspiration and manifestation are related to what, thanks to common grace, has remained in and about us of natural theology, is neither denied by this nor lost from sight, and will appear later on. To prevent misunderstanding, however, the principium must here be taken as simply as possible; and then this principium lies in God, in so far as He from his Divine consciousness inspires something into the consciousness of the sinner. Imagine this act of God away; say that it does not exist; deny this agency, which goes out from God; and no theology remains. All that remains is poetry, conjecture, supposition; but you have no more theology. It will not do to say "est Deus in nobis, agitante calescimus illo," for this is nothing but an emotion in your feelings, a vibration of a Divine power in your inner life, a something that can very well take place, repeat itself and continue, without effecting any knowledge of God in you.

For this very reason this *inspiration of God into the human mind,* as often as it takes place, is sufficient unto itself. Who on earth can know what takes place between God and my heart, but myself; and how can I know that that which works in me goes out from God to me, except God Himself gives me the certainty of conviction concerning this? The sense of this stands entirely in line with every other primordial sense, such as with the sense of our ego, of our existence, of our life, of our calling, of our continuance, of our laws of thought, etc. All that God gives me in the natural way, to constitute my sense as a human being, I not merely receive from Him, but by Him alone is it guaranteed to me. When this sense of certainty becomes weak, I become sceptical, I lose my higher energy of life, and end in madness, and no human reasoning can restore to me the lost certainty of my human starting-point. The only difference here is, that the general principles of my consciousness are common to me with almost all men, while with the *inspiration of God into the mind of the sinner,* one has it and the other has it not, so that these two stand over against each other. He who has it not, must deny it; and he who has it, is often shocked by the contradiction of him who has it not. This, however, is not the case with inspiration only. In many other domains one knows an inner impulse, which is foreign to another. Think of the poet, the virtuoso, the hero, and the adventurer. The want of general consent is no proof of want of foundation, and often works the effect, that conviction becomes the more firmly founded. Contradiction *can* weaken, but it can also strengthen. The question only is, whether there is sufficient ground for the fact of its being present in one and absent in the other. Therefore, the Reformed theologians have ever considered theology also to rest upon the election. If one reasons that all men are entitled to the same thing, and that every sinner has the right to equal gifts of grace, then the fact "that all men have not faith" (2 Thess. iii. 2) is an "offence" to us; and this weakens our sense of what God works upon and in our soul. Hence there is nothing to be done about it, that one man is more deeply sensible of this than another, and that even this sense of God's inspiration appears much more clearly in one age than in another. Human supports avail nothing here. When the fogs are too dense, the sun cannot penetrate to us in its full splendor; as soon as they lift or lessen, the light of itself shines again more brightly in our eyes; and the law remains intact: *in thy light shall we see light.* The conflict concerning the reality of inspiration may safely, therefore, be ended. Because it is primordial, it *cannot* be demonstrated; and because it is sufficient unto itself and admits of no proof, it cannot be harmed by counterproof. And it was seen by our fathers entirely correctly, in so far as they founded their confession of the Scripture ultimately upon no other testimony than the *witness of the Holy Spirit.* All that you add to this may serve as a support to the side-wall, but is never, either wholly or in part, the foundation for the building. If, therefore, our knowledge of God is only derived from the self-communication of God, i.e. is the fruit of inspiration, then God as inspirer (Deus inspirans) must be the principium, the first agent in our knowledge of God; and the finding of a something *back* of this principium, from which it should follow or flow, is simply inconceivable.

The objection, indeed, may be raised, that in this way two principles, entirely separated from each other, operate in our consciousness: on one side God as Creator (Deus creans), and on the other God as inspirer (Deus inspirans), and more particularly in a special manner (modo speciali). And this we readily grant. This *is,* indeed, unnatural, and, in a sense, does violence to our consciousness. A twofold source of knowledge in our consciousness is not in accord with the original demand of our consciousness; and he who lives and thinks strongly, can never cease from the effort to make those two one, or to cause one of those two to disappear. Indeed, this duality of principium is no slight obstacle in the way of the assurance of faith, with reference to the special principium. Almost all doubt arises from this dualism. Furthermore, the result *must* be, that finally this duality shall fall away again, and that the unity of principium shall be restored in our consciousness. Such, indeed, it shall be in the state of glory. In the *status gloriae* there shall be "no more temple in the city," but also no more Bible in the oratory. A Bible in the oratory is a sign that you yourself are still a sinner in a sinful world. Sinner or no sinner, therefore, is the question which here, too, is decisive; in him who is still sinless or who is no longer a sinner, no conflict, no duality in his consciousness can operate from the side of his God; and in him, therefore, no second principium of Divine knowledge can be added to the original natural principium. But if you reckon *with* sin, then, of course, it is not sufficient that you recognize the incompleteness of our human conditions; or acknowledge that a great distance still separates your ideal of love and holiness from your actual nature; neither is it sufficient that you heap all sorts of reproaches upon yourself, and whet the sword against sin. All this does not touch the *principium of the knowledge of God.* This is only touched, when you yourself know that a *breach* has taken place; and that sin has so broken you, that the channels, through which the knowledge of God flowed to you in virtue of your creation, have been stopped up and otherwise injured, and that thus it is an assured fact to you, that from this *natural* principium, however good in itself, because once broken and injured, no real knowledge of God *can* any more come to you. Then only will your consciousness be disposed to look upon a second, a different, a temporarily auxiliary, principium as natural; and with this disposition only will your consciousness be able to grasp the guarantee of the Divine witness in this witness itself. On the other hand, it is equally true that this deep sense of sin, by which you learn to know your state as *broken* before God, does not come to you from the *natural* principium, but only from this *special* principium. There is an interaction here. The more powerful your conviction of sin is, the more readily you grasp the special principium, as suited to your condition; and also, the more decided you are in your acceptance of the knowledge of God from this special principium, the deeper the sense of being a *sinner before God* will strike root in you. Later on it will be shown, how this *witness of the Holy Spirit* in its structure is also ethical in its nature. Here, however, let it be said, that this witness of the Holy *Spirit* always roots in the conviction of sin, and in degree of certainty runs parallel with the certainty of your sense of guilt.

What is said above would not lightly rouse contradiction, if this *inspiration of God into the mind of the sinner* took place individually. Even those who stand outside of this inspiration would then acknowledge that they can deny the reality of it for themselves, but not for others. But, and this is the difficulty, this principium does *not* work in this way. To speak plainly, there is no inspiration which goes out directly from God to the soul's consciousness of every one of the elect separately, and offers the same content to all, one by one; on the contrary, there is one central revelation given for all, and it is from this central revelation that every elect one is to draw for himself his knowledge of God. Public charity may provide each poor man a sum of money with which to buy provisions for himself, or may spread in a hall a common table from which all poor people may be fed. And thus it might be conceived that God should give to every sinner whom He chose a special light in the soul, an individual inspiration in his consciousness, and that every one should have enough of this for himself. This is what the mystics of every sort affirm. But such has not been the will of God. God the Lord has spread one table for His entire Church, has given one organically connected revelation for all, and it is from this one revelation designed for all, and which neither repeats nor continues itself, that the churches of all places and times, and in those churches every child of God, has to draw his knowledge of the Eternal Being. And the witness of this one central revelation which neither repeats nor continues itself, lies for us in the Holy Scripture. Not, of course, as though that Bible, by itself, were sufficient to give, to every one who reads it, the true knowledge of God. We positively reject such a mechanical explanation; and by their teaching of the witness of the Holy Spirit as absolutely indispensable for all *conviction* concerning the Scripture, by their requirement of illumination for the *right understanding* of the Scripture, and by their high esteem of the ministry of the Word for the *application* of the Scripture, our fathers have sufficiently shown that such a mechanical explanation cannot be ascribed to them. That they nevertheless took the Holy Scripture, and nothing else, as principium of the knowledge of God, yea, as the *sole* principium, had its ground in the circumstance that in the witness of the Holy Spirit, in the enlightening and in the application by the ministry of the Word, there is a recognition of what happens to or in the subject, in order that what has been revealed may be appropriated by him; but by these the knowledge of God itself is not increased nor changed. That knowledge of God as such does not come to the sinner from a mystical inworking of the Holy Spirit, neither from the illumination of the regenerate, nor from what the preacher adds to the Scripture, but simply from what he takes from the Scripture. Viewed from whatever point, the Holy Scripture always remains the real principium which brings about the knowledge of God. How this expression principium, applied to the Holy Scripture, is to be understood, can only be explained later on; it is enough that here we translate the individualistic-mystical conception of inspiration into the organically general one. When we viewed inspiration in relation to individual man, we said: In the sinner, so far as pertains to the knowledge of God, the *natural* principium has been maimed, so that no more new or sufficient knowledge of God comes to man through this channel. This is remedied by a second principium which as *principium speciale* is provisionally added to the first. This principium also is, if you please, God Himself, or goes out from God. He it is who inspires knowledge of Himself in a special manner into the mind of the sinner (in mentem hominis peccatoris modo speciali sui cognitionem inspirat); and consequently He alone can give assurance concerning His revelation. It concerns here a principium in the proper sense under or back of which therefore there can lie none other. Applying this to the central Revelation, we now say: Our human race, once fallen in sin, can have no more supply of pure or sufficient knowledge of God from the *natural* principium. Consequently God effects an *auxiliary* revelation for our human race, which, from a *special* principium of its own and under the necessary conditions, places a knowledge of God within the reach of the sinner which is suited to his condition. It took many centuries to accomplish this central Revelation, until it reached its completion. The description of this action of God, i.e. the providing of this central Revelation for our human race, is contained in the Holy Scripture. He who would know this central Revelation, must seek it therefore in the Holy Scripture. And in *that* sense the question, where the *special* principium with the central Revelation to our race as its fruit is now to be found, must be answered without hesitation as follows: In the *Holy Scripture* and in the Holy Scripture *alone.*

If, however, this is taken as if the knowledge of God hidden in the Bible, but not the Bible itself, has come to the sinner from God, then a link in the chain is cracked, and the chain breaks. For then indeed the Bible as such is nothing but an accidental, human annotation, and we have first to decide which parts of it do or do not hold firm. As criterium for this we have *no* individual inspiration; if we had, the whole conception of a central-organic revelation would again fall away. Hence we have no other criterium at our disposal than our *natural* principium. And thus the outcome of it *must* be, that from this untenable view-point you not only ravel out the Scripture by historic criticism, but also annul the content of the central Revelation and reduce it to the *natural* principium, in order finally to deny every *special* principium, and after the completed round of the circle to return to the *nothing* with which you began. Thus indeed it has actually taken place. Having stripped the whole Scripture of its leaves, having peeled and shelled it, we come back, after a struggle of eighteen centuries, by way of Origen, to the Greek philosophers, and the choice remains: Aristotle or Plato. This could not be otherwise, as soon as once the Scripture was placed outside the Revelation, and it was for the sake of protection against this that our fathers emphasized so strongly the Divine authorship of the Scripture as such. Even as your person, by an optical process, photographs itself and produces its own image upon the collodion plate, so it is likewise the Revelation itself which has given its own image in the Holy Scripture. The Scripture as the document of the central Revelation is therefore organically connected with that Revelation itself. The ice in which, in summer, cold is condensed and conserved for you, is organically one with the cold which it brings you. It was cold which caused the water to congeal, and from the ice the cool breath is refreshingly wafted to you. Therefore in olden times it was ever emphasized that the *content* and *form* of the Holy Scripture were most intimately and organically connected, and that not merely its content but also *its form* sprang from the *principium speciale,* i.e. from that special action which has gone out from God to our sinful race, in order to discover Himself to the sinner. The *distinction* of course between these two actions of the Holy Spirit must ever be kept in view; even more sharply than our fathers were accustomed to do this. For by their summary exposition they gave some occasion for the idea, that it were almost indifferent whether in earlier ages a real revelation had ever taken place, so long as we but had the Scripture. With a too high estimate of the chart which was drawn of the country, the country itself at times seemed a superfluity. In this way spiritual intellectualism was fed, and oftentimes the reality of history was sacrificed to a barren abstraction. The representation of a Bible dictated word for word did not originate from it, but was materially advanced by it: an error which of course cannot be overcome, except first the inspiration that operated in the revelation itself be separately considered, and then a proper representation be given of the inspiration that operated in and with the compilation of the canon of the Holy Scripture. But however strongly we emphasize that the real inspiration of the Scripture must be carefully distinguished from the inspiration of the revelation as entirely dissimilar, yet this may never be taken as though the one action of the Spirit stood in no organic relation to the other. Both, indeed, are expressions of the one will of God, to grant to our race, lost in sin, a central Revelation, and to bring this central Revelation within the reach of all ages and people.

For the simple believer it is, therefore, by no means necessary to consider this distinction, provided he makes no dogma of his own thoughtless representation, and with this dogma, formulated on his own authority, resists the accurate representation. *How* the central Revelation has come, concerns the believer only in so far as it must be to him the fruit of the *grace of God*—of God, and of that God in His *grace*. It is quite enough if the Holy Scripture is but the Word of God's grace, by which he may live and die. The Heidelberg Catechism requires, therefore, no theory concerning the Scripture, but merely asks that one *believe,* and believe in such a way, "that one hold for truth *all* that God has revealed to us in his word" (answer 21). The Scripture, and all the historic content of which that Scripture bears witness, is therefore not something by itself, which inserts itself with a certain independence between our consciousness and God, as the principium *of revelation;* but is as the wave of ether, upon which the beam of light from the source of light moves itself directly to our eye. To him who does not feel that, at the moment when he opens the Holy Scripture, God comes by and in it and touches his very soul, the Scripture is not yet the Word of God, or has ceased to be this; or it is this in his *spiritual* moments, but *not* at other times, as when the veil lies again on his heart, while again it is truly such when the veil is taken away. With the Holy Scripture it can never be a God *afar off,* and the Scripture a something God sends from afar. The telephone rather supplies an illustration that interprets this reality. God is, indeed, a God afar off; but He approaches you by and in the Scripture; unveils His presence to you; and speaks to you as though you were standing right by Him, and He drew you close beneath His wings. The action on God's side is not ended when the Scripture is completed for all nations. The revealing activity is then, indeed, completed and decided to the end, in so far as the central instrument is concerned, and, nothing will ever be added to it; but this is not all. This central instrument of revelation is not placed in the midst of the world, in order that God may now look on and see what man will do with it. On the contrary, now follows that entirely distinct action of preserving the Scripture, of interpreting and of applying the Scripture, and—still more specially—of bringing the Scripture to individual souls, of preparing those souls for its reception, and bringing them in contact with it, and thus finally, by what our Reformed Theologians called *providentia specialissima,* of rendering this Scripture a special revelation for this and that given person. The confession of all those who have possessed the Scripture most fully and enjoyed it most richly, has ever been that it was God who brought *them* to the Scripture and the *Scripture* to them; that He opened their eyes, so that they might understand the Scripture; and that only by the light which shone on them from the Scripture, light had appeared in their own person and the life round about them.

At no single point of the way is there place, therefore, for a support derived from demonstration or reasoning. There is no man that seeks, and seeking finds the Scripture, and with its help turns himself to his God. But rather from beginning to end it is one ceaselessly continued action which goes out from God to man, and operates upon him, even as the light of the sun operates upon the grain of corn that lies hidden in the ground, and draws it to the surface, and causes it to grow into a stalk. In God, therefore, is the principium from which this entire action proceeds. This principium of grace in God brings it to pass that a central Revelation is established in and for our sinful race. That same principium is the agent by which the image of that Revelation is reflected in the Scripture. And it is again that same principium of grace, the motive power of which goes out to the soul of the sinner, that by the Scripture it may bind him personally to that Revelation, and by that Revelation back again to his God. From this it follows of itself that with each one personally you must distinguish between his experimental (netto) and purely intellectual (bruto) faith in the Scripture, i.e. between that in the Scripture which has been personally assured to his heart by the living God, and all the rest, which still lies outside of the life of his soul, and only bears a holy character for the sake of its connection with the first, though it is as yet unknown to him. The proportions of these experimental and intellectual faiths will be different with every individual according to the depth of his inner life and the flight of his wings. It will be constantly modified with each person whose life of faith advances, so that the experimental and intellectual faith will proportionately decrease and increase. But however this purely intellectual (bruto) faith may diminish, it is not conceivable that there has ever been one single believer to whom the entire Scripture has been the possession of his heart. This may even be maintained of those who have literally covered the entire Bible, and have served the Church of God with an exposition of its entire contents. Just because the Divine character of the Scripture rests for us *exclusively* on faith, the richest exposition can never *constitute* anything for us a Word of God. The distinction must clearly be maintained. What God Himself does not bear witness to in your soul personally (not mystic-absolutely, but through the Scriptures) can never be known and confessed by you as Divine. Finite reasoning can never obtain the infinite as its result. If God then withdraws Himself, if in the soul of men He bear no more witness to the truth of His Word, men *can* no longer believe, and no apologetics, however brilliant, will ever be able to restore the blessing of faith in the Scripture. *Faith*, quickened by God Himself, is invincible; *pseudo-faith,* which rests merely upon reasoning, is devoid of all spiritual reality, so that it bursts like a soap-bubble as soon as the thread of your reasoning breaks.

The relation between the principium of Theology and our consciousness can therefore be nothing else than *immediate.* Not immediate in the sense that God could not be pleased to make use of all kinds of transmissions, arrangements and processes, by which to reach man's inmost soul; but such that at no single point of the line the *natural* principium can come in between to fill up the void, which might remain open in the going out of the principium *of grace* to our heart. The *principium gratiae* operates from the side of God right through the periods of Revelation, the Scripture, the mystical union, etc., till our heart has been reached and touched; and our heart gives itself captive, not because critically it allows and approves the approach of God; but because it can offer *no* resistance, and *must* give itself captive to the operation which goes out from God.

All faith in the Scripture quickened by God, and in God quickened by the Scripture, which does not bear this immediate character, and would borrow its assurance from any course of reasoning, is therefore absurd. For you must accept one of two things, either that each one personally must reason this out for himself, or that only a few are able to do this, so that the others must depend upon these few. The first is impossible, for the simple reason that not one-tenth per cent. of the children of men are capable of entering upon the required investigation; and the second is equally impossible, since then you would substitute faith on human authority in the place of faith in God. Moreover, faith is not a demand that belongs to the more advanced periods of life, but it must be exercised from youth up; how, then, would you have faith be born as the result of a study, of which the best are not capable until the years of mid-life? It should be observed, how in this way the faith of one would continually be shocked by the mistakes in the investigation of another. What would it profit you, if you had reached a sufficient and satisfactory result for yourself? Tomorrow a book appears with new objections, and then everything with you must remain unsettled, so long as you cannot successfully unnerve *all* those new objections. Scarcely, however, has this been accomplished, when still another advances new difficulties, and thus you are engulfed in an endless whirl between doubt and faith. Worse still: after a study of more than twelve centuries spent on the Scriptures, there is yet no faintest outlook that these studies will ever lead to a satisfactory result. The conflict concerning the Holy Scriptures will most likely be continued till the final return of the Lord. How, then, can faith ever rest on the result of these studies as foundation, when its presence has been a necessity from the beginning, and when in those early times, in which there was no question for these studies, faith was most vital and powerful? For no single moment, therefore, may we entertain the admission that argument may be the ground of conviction. This would be a "passing into another kind," which is logically condemned. Faith gives highest assurance, where in our own consciousness it rests immediately on the testimony of God; but without this support, everything that announces itself as faith is merely a weaker form of opinion based on probability, which capitulates the moment a surer knowledge supersedes your defective evidence.

And as regards the objection, that all this is very excellent, provided it does not include the Scriptures, and no other thought is entertained than of the mystical communion with the eternal Being, simple reference to what was explained previously would suffice; but even without this reference, we might say that, as a matter of *fact*, such faith has only shown itself where it concerned the Holy Scriptures. In other circles many different emotions have likewise been experienced, brilliant exhibitions of ethical heroism have been seen, and many sorts of religious expressions observed, both aesthetic and otherwise; but here we treat of the "Knowledge of God" (Cognitio Dei) and of the principia from which this *knowledge* of God flows. And that faith, which leads individuals and whole circles to conscious worship, not of the "unknown God" at Athens, but of the *known* Father who is in heaven, is not found, except where the *Scriptures* have been the Divine instrument, in God's hand, of that knowledge.

Relation between this Principium and the Natural Principium

The acknowledgment of the Holy Scriptures as the principium of theology gives rise to an antithesis between *this* principium and the common principium of our knowledge. From this antithesis a certain relation between the two is born, and this relation also must be investigated. We speak here only of theology in the narrower sense as knowledge of *God* (cognitio Dei), and in so far we might limit ourselves to the relation between natural and revealed theology (theologia naturalis and revelata), which is virtually the contents of this section. But this we will not do. First, because the formal action of our thinking is also involved, and secondly, because with natural theology one thinks more of *the content*, while here we are interested almost exclusively with the principium from which this content flows.

As stated above, the *natural* principium not only may not be ignored, but is even permanent and lasting, while the *special* principium falls away as soon as its task is ended. Only with this reservation can we speak of a twofold principium. A twofold principium of knowledge is thinkable with reference to different objects, as, for instance, God and the cosmos; but not, as in this case, with reference to God alone. In both cases indeed, in *natural* and in *revealed* theology, we speak of *knowledge of God,* of knowledge, therefore, of the same God, and of knowledge of the same God to be obtained by the same subject, i.e. man, or more correctly, humanity. No doubt a temporary inability in man may render the knowledge of God no more sufficiently *possible* for him in the normal way, and thus it *must* be supplied in an abnormal way; but this does not modify the fundamental plan, and the outcome must ever be, that the *knowledge of God* is imparted to humanity in the normal, and hence in only *one way.* At present nature stands temporarily over against grace; but in the end, in glorified nature, there will be no more question of grace. All that the Holy Scripture teaches concerning the knowledge of God in its consummation, aims, indeed, at a condition in which the abnormality of the ordinance of redemption falls entirely away, and whatever was grounded in creation returns, but carried up to its end $(\tau \acute{\epsilon} \lambda o \varsigma)$. In part it even seems as though Christ then effaces Himself, in order that it may be "God all in all." Even as Christ before His death pointed His disciples away from Himself to the Father, saying: "I say not unto you, that I will pray the Father for you; for the Father himself loveth you."

This implies at the same time, that the eternally enduring knowledge of God, possessed by the redeemed, shall not be after the nature of the *special,* but according to the nature of the *natural* principium. However rich the dispensation of grace may be, it ever remains *a bandage* applied to the injured part of the body, and is never that *vital part* itself. When a wound of the throat prevents the taking of food in the common way, it may be brought into the stomach artificially. The purpose of this, however, is always *to save life,* by the vitality thus saved to bring on healing, so that finally food may again enter the stomach in the normal way *through the throat.* The scaffolding placed before a dilapidated gable may be the only enclosure about the house for a long time, and may render it quite invisible, but the purpose in view is, that presently the scaffold shall disappear, and the house itself be seen again, and remain in its normal condition. In a similar sense it must be confessed of the original principium of knowledge, that by sin it has become temporarily insufficient and has been rendered incapable; that consequently the temporary aid of *another* principium has become indispensable; but that the tendency of this can be no other than to restore the *natural* principium, i.e. the principium grounded in our nature to its normal activity; and as soon as this has been realized, to dismiss the *special* principium, which renders merely a temporary service. Let no misunderstanding, however, enter here. We by no means assert that the purpose of extraordinary revelation is to restore us to the knowledge of God which Adam had. All knowledge we possess in this earthly dispensation *shall pass away,* and in place of this defective knowledge there is to come the "seeing face to face." Even now the form of our consciousness differs by day and by night; ecstasy and vision affect us differently from common fancy and sober reasoning. But this effects no change in our psychic constitution. Even if you imagine sin never to have entered, so that no ruin of our nature had taken place, and there would consequently have been no question of a *special* revelation, the knowledge, nevertheless, which Adam had as connate, would sometime have passed into the "seeing face to face." The butterfly exhibits an entirely different form from the caterpillar, and yet that butterfly came forth from the natural conditions of the caterpillar, without any assistance in the transition from an abnormal something. Call the knowledge which Adam had in paradise the caterpillar, and the "knowing face to face" the beautiful butterfly, and you perceive how this higher and to be completed knowledge belongs, nevertheless, to the sphere of the *natural* and *not* to the sphere of the *special* principium.

This, however, has been heretofore too much overlooked by orthodox theology. Losing itself almost entirely in the content of the *special* revelation, it has taken this too much for the essential one, and has scarcely been able to represent it otherwise than that this *special* revelation is to be permanent. The insight, that of course the Scripture ceases its use to us with our dying, that after death no sacrament is any more conceivable, and that in the realm of glory the Christological period, if we may so express it, shall disappear, in order that the triune God may again be "all in all" has not been given its place even dogmatically. Rome, by the action of the church on earth in behalf of the dead, had concentrated eschatology entirely into the period preceding the Judgment-day; the Reformation neglected eschatology sorely; what from the side of modern orthodoxy has been supplied in our times to make us think of a church with a soteriologic ministry beyond the grave, has occasioned mere confusion; when the state of the blest was considered, it was more a mystical fanaticism than the sober putting of the question of the *consciousness* of the redeemed: it is not strange, therefore, that the question, from what "principium of knowledge" the redeemed will think, was not even formulated. Light on the subject, however, was not wanting. "Prophecies, tongues, knowledge," everything that constitutes our riches here, will disappear, according to the word of the apostle. *Special* revelation is called a "glass," which renders temporary aid, to receive for us the image and reflect it back again; but that glass also shall sometime belong to the past. And then there comes an entirely different knowing, *even as we are known,* which includes of itself, that this knowledge will come to us entirely by the data provided in creation. Not of course so as to lose anything of what was revealed in the rich revelation of the mercy of God in an uncommon way, but, and herein lies the mystery, in order to take up this rich gain into our *normal* existence; which mystery finds its explanation in the dogma de Christo. It is revealed to us, that the Mediator shall make surrender of the kingdom to God, even the Father, but in such a way, that He Himself remains eternally the Head of His mystical body (corpus mysticum). The Christ will *not* disappear, in order that Adam may again take his place as head of our race. On the contrary, Adam *never* resumes the place of honor lost by sin; but the mystery is this,—that Christ shall sometime be no longer the interposed Mediator, but the *natural* Head of the human race in glory. This, however, may not detain us now. But the suggestion of the dogmatic relation between the question in hand in this section, and the questions of eschatology and Christology, was necessary. And provisionally our purpose is accomplished, if it is clear, why the whole dispensation of special grace passes away, and how in consequence the special principium of knowledge, from which theology draws its life, is destined sometime to disappear into the natural principium.

This, however, does not explain the mutual relation of the two, though this indeed is most necessary, if we hope to escape the false representations abroad, especially concerning natural theology (theologia naturalis). If at first the Reformation fostered more accurate ideas, soon the temptation appeared too strong, to place *natural* theology as a separate theology *alongside* of special theology (theologia specialis). The two were then placed mechanically side by side. To natural theology we owed the knowledge of God's Being, of the Divine attributes, of His works, providence, moral law, the last judgment, etc., and although special theology made us know a great deal of *sin and grace,* in fact it enriched the real knowledge of God only with the knowledge of His "Grace" and of His "Threefold Being"; at least, in so far as real clearness is concerned; for the fundamental feature of this mystery too was soon thought to be also found among the Heathen. With this division it became apparent, that the real *Theology* as knowledge of God gave the lion's share to *natural* theology, and that the theology *of grace,* while it occupied itself with many and exalted mysteries, in reality abandoned the foundation of all knowledge of God, and therefore the heart of the matter, to its twin sister. This furnished natural theology the occasion to unfold its wings ever more broadly; to expand itself and lessen the importance of special theology; until finally it has succeeded in stepping forth as a monarch and in contesting all right of utterance to special theology. And this could not be otherwise, and will repeat itself again and again, so long as the error is committed of representing special theology as sufficient in itself, and of making natural theology do service as Martha by the side of Mary. It is, therefore, of the greatest importance, to see clearly, that *special* theology may not be considered a moment without *natural* theology, and that on the other hand natural theology of itself is unable to supply *any* pure knowledge of God.

That special revelation (revelatio specialis) is not conceivable without the hypothesis of natural theology, is simply because *grace* never creates one single new reality. This does not even take place in miracles. In no miracle does anything originate which is to be added as a new element to the existing cosmos. The very possibility of this is inconceivable and would destroy the organic character of the cosmos. In regeneration no new component part, which in creation lay outside of our being, is added to man. And even in the incarnation it is no new "Divine-human nature," which as something new (novum quid) is added to what exists, but our own human nature that becomes the revelation of that same God, who stood over against Adam in the creation. That in heaven no new reality has originated, needs no assertion. But since neither in heaven nor on earth any new reality is created by grace, how can *special revelation* stand on a root of its own? If you go outside of reality, then, it is a fiction with which you cannot deal. If, on the other hand, as the Church confesses, it lays hold upon the reality of heaven and earth, then it can be no other than the existing reality, and in order to be true, it cannot borrow its strength from any but that existing reality. All that the Scriptures teach, therefore, concerning "the making of all things new," the "new creature" and the works in Christ," views at no time anything but new relations, new methods of existence, new forms, and never puts us face to face with a newly originated element. As far as the substance is concerned, God remains unchangeable, the being of man is now what it was before the fall, and the cosmos is indeed impaired, but always the identical world of Gen. i. 1. In man also no new capacities are created, for even faith (as was shown above) roots in our nature, as created by God in Paradise. In what domain then can the reality be found, in which a *special grace*, outside of natural life, could soar on wings of its own? Where would be the spot to offer it a resting-place for the sole of its foot? This entire representation, therefore, as though *grace* had produced a knowledge of God of its own, which as competitor runs by the side of natural theology, must be most decidedly rejected. There can be no such *special* theology; it is simply unthinkable. When Calvin, therefore, speaks of the "seed of religion" which is present in every sinner, and our *Confessio Belgica* teaches in Art. 2, "that we know God by two means, Nature and the Scriptures," this may not be taken in the sense of the later rationalistic supranaturalists, for there lies in it only the simple confession, that *without the basis* of *natural* theology there is no *special* theology. "God has given to all," says Calvin, "some apprehension of his existence, the memory of which he frequently and insensibly renews" (*Inst. Rel. Chr.* I. 3. i.). "So that the sense of the Divinity can never be entirely lost" (*Ibidem*). And it is upon the canvas of this natural knowledge of God itself that the special revelation is embroidered. He expresses it so accurately and beautifully: "the Scripture, collecting in our minds the otherwise confused notions of Deity, dispels the darkness, and gives us a clear view of the true God" (*Inst.* I. 6. i.). It is, therefore, beside the truth when the separate mention of Nature and the Scripture in the Reformed confessions is taken as an indication of our principium of knowledge, by way of juxtaposition or coordination. Later dogmatici may have taught this, but it is not in accord with the spirit of Calvin or of the Reformed type of doctrine. His metaphor, that the Bible is a pair of spectacles which enables us to read the Divine writing in nature, may be insufficient as an explanation of the problem in hand; in any case it cuts off absolutely every representation that the idea of natural and special theology as two concurrent magnitudes is derived from Calvin.

If we might choose another metaphor to explain the relation between the two, entirely in the spirit of Calvin but more fully, the figure of the grafted tree pleases us most. He who grafts, plants no new tree, but applies himself to one that exists. That tree is alive, it draws its sap from the roots, but this vital sap is wild, in consequence of which the tree can bear no fruit that is desired. And now the grafter comes, and inserts a nobler graft, and thereby brings it to pass that this vital sap of the wild tree is changed, so that the desired fruit now ripens on the branches. This new graft does not stand by the side of the wild tree, but is *in* it; and if the grafting is a success, it may equally well be said that the true graft lives by the old tree, as that the uncultivated tree is of use solely because of the new graft. And such, indeed, is the case here. The wild tree is the sinner, in whose nature works the *natural* principium of the knowledge of God as an inborn impelling power. If you leave this natural principium to itself, you will never have anything else than *wild wood,* and the fruit of knowledge does not come. But when the Lord our God introduces from without, and thus from *another* principium, a shoot of a true plant, even the principle of a pure knowledge into this wild tree, i.e. into this natural man, then there is not a man *by the side* of a man, no knowledge *by the side* of a knowledge, but the wild energy remains active in this human nature, i.e. *incomplete* knowledge; while the ingrafted new principium brings it to pass, that this impelling power is changed and produces the fruit of *true* knowledge. The *special knowledge* is, indeed, a new and proper principium, but this principium joins itself to the vital powers of our nature with its natural principium; compels this principium to let its life-sap flow through another channel; and in this way cultivates ripe fruit of knowledge from what otherwise would have produced only wood fit for fire.

If now we investigate the meaning of this figure, entirely clear by itself, it appears at once that the grafting of true upon wild wood is only possible because both, however different in quality, are one, nevertheless, in disposition of nature. Grafting succeeds the better in proportion to the closeness of correspondence between the two kinds of wood, and if all relationship were wanting between wild and true wood, grafting would simply be impossible. For the subject in hand, this means that *natural* and *special* theology possess *a higher unity,* are *allied* to one another, and, by virtue of this unity and relationship, are capable of *affecting* each other. This higher unity lies (1) in God, (2) in man, and (3) in the purpose for which the life of grace, and consequently the special knowledge, comes forward. *In God,* because the principium of *natural,* as well as of *special,* knowledge lies in Him; because He remains the object of both kinds of knowledge; and because the revelation of His grace is revelation of grace in Him who created natural life for the glory of His name. Secondly, *in man,* since it is the same *ego* that draws knowledge from both principia; since in this *ego* it is one and the same *consciousness* in which this knowledge of God is taken up; and since it is no other kind of man, but the very man who fell, who as sinner needs the knowledge of this grace. And, finally, in the purpose of *the special knowledge,* which consists not in a cutting off of our natural life, but in the restoration of that same life, which is ours by nature, into a normal state guaranteed against a new fall. Special revelation does not begin, therefore, by ignoring what has already been effected by natural revelation, but unites itself to this in so positive a sense, that without these sparks (scintillae) or remnants (rudera) it were itself unthinkable; and for this reason Reformed Theology has ever resisted the Lutheran representation as though the sinner were merely "a stock or block." If the "seed of religion" did not operate in the sinner, he would not be susceptible to special revelation. Whatever still remains in the sinner of this seed of religion and the knowledge of God connected with this, is, therefore, adopted by special revelation, as the indispensable instrument by which it operates. Without this, it neither reaches nor touches man, remains an abstraction, and misses its *form* of existence. How can there be a sense of sin without the sense of God, or susceptibility for grace without the consciousness of guilt? The Holy Bible is, therefore, neither a law-book nor a catechism, but the documentation of a part of *human life,* and in that human life of a *divine process.* Of the Apocalyptic vision only, it can be said that it misses this quality in part; but because of this very antithesis with the Apocalypse, one perceives at once the real human character of all the other parts of the revelation-life. Nowhere in the Scriptures do you find, therefore, an attempt to divide into certain compartments what is severally supplied by *natural* and *special* knowledge; but, throughout, you find the special revelation grafted upon the natural. Natural knowledge is not only assumed by the special, but only in this does it fully assert itself. Knowledge is the pinnacle which is not placed on the ground alongside of the steeple, but is supported by the body of the steeple and is lifted up on high. You may not say, therefore: This is my *natural* revelation, in addition to which comes the *special*. For as a result, you obtain but *one* "knowledge of God," the content of which has flowed to you from *both* sources, whose waters have mingled themselves.

And if for this reason an exhibition of the *special* knowledge without the *natural* is inconceivable, the representation is equally absurd that the *natural* knowledge of God, without enrichment by the *special,* could ever effect a satisfying result. The outcome has shown that this natural knowledge, as soon as it threw off the bridle of paradise tradition, led the masses to idolatry and brutalization, and the finer minds to false philosophies and equally false morals. Paul indicates one of these two phases by the remark, that there was first a condition in which the natural knowledge of God allowed "that which may be known of God" (Rom. i. 19) to be manifest, but that this was followed by the period in which God gave the sinner up παρέδωκε Not to speak now of that first period, it is clear that at least *after that* the natural knowledge of God could lead to no result; not even in philosophy, of which the same apostle testifies that the "wisdom of the world is made foolish" (1 Cor. i, 20). Hence it is only by the *special* knowledge that the *natural* knowledge becomes serviceable. By the light of the Scripture the sinner becomes able to give himself an account of the "seed of religion" in his heart and of the "divine things" visible in the cosmos; but, where this light hides itself even upon the Areopagus I advance no farther than to the Unknown God.

If therefore this entire juxtaposition, as though a *special* knowledge of God stood side by side with a *natural* knowledge of God, falls away, the way is cleared thereby to view more accurately the relation between the two principia of this knowledge thus distinguished. Both principia are one in God, and the beam of this light is only broken when the soundness of our human heart is broken by sin. The knowledge-bringing impulse goes out from God to us; the active element, the first mover (primum movens) as the ultimate cause (principium remotissimum), lies in the Divine Being. This impulse of self-communication to man attains its end completely in creation by the whole instrumentation for the *natural* knowledge. And where, after sin, this Divine impulse encounters an evil cataract, which prevents the entrance of light, this impulse seeks and finds another and more sure way by *special revelation.* Hence it is the same God, and in that God the same impulse, by which both principia appear in action. That in the origin of all things, or, more particularly, in God's eternal counsel, both these stood in this unity before God, cannot detain us here, since this belongs to the domain of dogmatics; but here it must be indicated that the *natural* principium lays the foundation of all knowledge, and that the *special* principium either fails of its purpose or must adapt itself entirely to the provisions that are original in the creation. Even the miracles, whose character cannot be considered closely here, link no new element into the sum of things, but, so far as their origin is concerned, they are entirely identical with the wondrous power which became manifest in the creation itself. The same is true of the several means, which God has employed, to introduce the special revelation into our human consciousness. In the interests of this also you see no new or other capacities appear in man; but merely the application in a peculiar manner of what was given in the creation. Before the fall God speaks with Adam, God causes a deep sleep to come upon Adam, and, by an encroaching act of God, Eve enters upon existence. God has entrance to our heart by nature, and not first by grace; He is able to rule the human spirit by His Spirit; and able to communicate to man what He will. The communication of the test-commandment is an immediate communication of a conscious thought, which could not rise from Adam's own consciousness. Actually, therefore, in special revelation no single means is used which was not already present by nature in or about man. No new structure is provided for human consciousness. All that has taken place is, that God the Lord has restored a few broken strings of the instrument, tuned these restored strings in a different way, and by this immediate modification He has evoked such a tone from the instrument as, being without significance to sinless man, had become indispensable to the sinner. Hence there would have been no question of a second principium, if there were not this act of God, by which He has accommodated Himself to the sinner. It is with this, as it is with you, when for the sake of making yourself understood by a member of the family who has become deaf, you no longer choose his ear as a vehicle for your thoughts, but make him read with his eyes the words from your lips. Thus, when we became deaf to God, He has employed *a different means* by which to make Himself knowable to us; and in so far as with a deaf person the hearing of sound and the reading of lips might be called a different "principium of knowledge," there is here also the mention of such different principles, but only in so far. There has gone out an act from God to reveal Himself to the sinner, however deaf this one had become; for this God has availed Himself of the means that were present in the creation, but which were now applied in a different way; and it is by this abnormal act of God, brought about by the modified application of present means, that special revelation was established; and in this, i.e. in this *abnormal* act of God, brought about by means applied in a *different* way, lies the special principium for the knowledge of God as All-Merciful to sinners. When croup prevents the breathing in of air, the heroic operation in the throat is sometimes undertaken, in order in this way to obtain a new opening for the supply of fresh air; but they are still the same lungs for which the air is intended, and it is the same atmosphere from which the air is drawn; only another entrance has been unlocked *temporarily,* and in so far a *different* principium of respiration has been established. In this sense it can be said, that the normal entrance, which in creation God had unlocked for Himself to our heart, had become inaccessible by sin, and that for this reason, by an act of heroic grace, God has temporarily opened for Himself another entrance to our heart, to reveal Himself as the same God to the same creature, only now with the aid of a *different* principium of revelation.

In God, who is and always will be Himself the principium of all being (essentia) and all knowing (cognitio), nothing else is conceivable than the unity of principium. But when from His eternal *being* our *becoming* is born, there is majesty in this eternal being to maintain His divine identity over against every abnormal process in our *becoming;* and this takes place by the appearance of the special principium, which actually is nothing else but the maintenance of God's holiness over against our sin, of God's truth over against our falsehood, and of God's counsel over against the demoniacal design of Satan.

Is the Natural *Principium able to summon the* Special *Principium before its Tribunal?*

Having freed ourselves, in the preceding section, of all dualism, which is so often inserted between the two principia of Divine knowledge, we now face the no less important question, whether the *natural* principium, either formally or materially, is to sit in judgment upon the *special* principium. This is the frequent claim. They who oppose us, and do not recognize another principium alongside of the natural data, continually demand, that we demonstrate the reality and the reliability of the *special* principium at the bar of human reason. And to a certain extent this demand is fair, at least over against Methodism, and, in fact, over against every dualistic tendency, which, in the sense we disapprove, places special revelation as a new unit alongside of the natural principium, as though the latter were under sentence of death, and the special principium could furnish the guarantee of eternal permanency. Over against every representation of this character our conviction remains dominant that our life, as originally given in the Creation, is the substratum of our real existence; that as such it is and remains for us the real; and that, therefore, whatever special revelation may supply, must be taken up into this and, for us personally, can only thus obtain its reality. From this, however, it does *not* follow that the natural principium should be qualified to judge the special revelation. If special revelation assumes that in consequence of sin the normal activity of the natural principium is disturbed, this implies of itself that the natural principium has lost its competency to judge. He who considers it possessed of this competency declares thereby *eo ipso* that it is still normal, and thus removes all *sufficient reason* for a special revelation. You must either deny it the right of judgment, or, if you grant it this right, the object disappears upon which judgment shall be passed. The psychiater, who treats the maniac, cannot render his method of treatment dependent upon the judgment of his patient. Equally little can you attribute this right of judgment over the special principium to the natural principium, if you consider the character of a *principium*. As soon as you grant that special revelation falls under the judgment of your natural principium, it is hereby denied *eo ipso* that it has proceeded from a principium of its own. No other judgment except death unqualified ("la mort sans phrase") is here possible for the special principium, simply because a judgment, derived from the natural principium deeming itself normal, cannot posit a second principium. A principium in its own sphere is exclusive. In order to subject the principium of theology to the judgment of another principium, you must first confess that it is no real principium. For a thing is either no principium, or it must be autonomous and sufficient unto itself.

This is of the more force, in this instance, insomuch as the natural principium, taking its stand in judgment over against us, presents itself as unimpaired, and pretends to be normal. If it recognized the reality of another principium, it would at the same time imply the confession, that it itself has become disabled, and is consequently in need of the corrective or of the supplement of another principium. Hence this question also has a moral side. If self-knowledge, quickened by the inshining of a higher light, leads to the recognition that the natural principium has become imperfect, then it is most natural (1) to grant the necessity of a corrective principium, and at the same time (2) to recognize that our darkened natural principium is incompetent to pass judgment. If, on the other hand, I stand in the high-spirited conviction that the natural principium is in good order, that nothing is wanting in it, and that consequently it has the right of supremacy, then it follows that every corrective must seem insulting, upon all of which alike I must pass the sentence of death, and that I cannot rest until each corrective lies executed under the dissecting knife of criticism. The outcome, indeed, has shown that this standpoint has never been taken and maintained with any degree of consistency, without the whole of special revelation being always and inexorably declared to be the product of delusion or of self-deception. Grace has been granted only to those component parts of this revelation which allowed themselves to be brought over to the natural principium. Every effort to defend the good right of your position is therefore entirely vain, over against a man of thought, who holds the natural principium to be unimpaired, and who has not himself come under the overwhelming power of the special principium. Being as he is, he can do nothing else than dispute your special revelation every right of existence; to move him to a different judgment you should not reason with him, but change him in his consciousness; and since this is the fruit of regeneration, it does not lie with you, but with God.

From this, again, it does not follow that you may now accept everything that comes into your mind, and that thus you may be unreasonable *with yourself.* Reformed Theology has always antagonized this caprice, and in imitation of the *Cur Deus homo?* of Anselm it has, with reference also to special revelation, first of all instituted an investigation into the *necessitas Sacrae Scripturae.* He who, thanks to the inshining of higher light, has perceived the darkening of the natural principium, and has given himself captive to the special principium, cannot on this account abandon his reason, but is bound to try to understand these two facts in their mutual relation and in relation to the reality in which he finds himself. This is both demanded and rendered possible by what we found in the last section concerning the relation of the special principium to our creaturely capacities; even in the sense, that one *is* able to see for himself the reasonableness of his conviction and confession; is able to prove this to those who start out from similar premises; and can place them before the opponent in such a light that, with the assumption of our premises, he can accept our conclusions.

The argument may even then be continued concerning those premises themselves, more particularly with reference to the question, whether our reason is in a condition of soundness or of darkening; but suppose that the unsoundness or abnormality of our reason be granted on both sides, this would by no means *compel* the opponent to accept the special principium which we defend. From the coincidence of the facts, that one of your children is lost and that I have found a lost child, it does not in the least follow, that the child I have found is your child. Even though it were frankly granted that something is lacking in our reason, that our reason by itself is insufficient,–yes, that it calls for a complement,–the conclusion can never be logically drawn from this that the Sacra Scriptura, or, better still, the special principium lying back of this, either is or offers this complement. Even though you compel the opponent to recognize, that your special principium fits into the imperfection of your natural principium as a piece of china into a broken dish, this would not prove the reality of this natural principium. For it could still be answered, that the defect would surely be supplemented, if indeed a revelation, such as you pretend, were at our disposal; but that this is the very thing in which you are mistaken; that your special principium, with its supposed fruit in the Sacra Scriptura, is nothing but the shadow cast upon the wall by the existing defect; is the product of your own imagination; the minus balance of your account changed into plus. In a word, there would always be defence ready against the proof that this special principium is real, and this proof is not possible of any principium. Could this be furnished, it would *eo ipso* cease to be a *principium.*

But this will not be reached. For though you succeed in showing that your reason founders upon antinomies, that it finds itself shut up within limits which cannot be made to agree with the impulse after knowledge that works in it, and that it leaves the higher aspirations of our nature unsatisfied, this has no compelling force with him who has an interest in not accepting your special principium. For he can make good his escape by the way of agnosticism, which accepts the incomplete character of our knowledge as an iron necessity; or make the side-leap to the pantheistic process, which calculates that from the incomplete the complete of itself will gradually come forth. Moreover, though he evade you in this manner, you may not question the honesty of your opponent. From your own point of view you acknowledge that he who stands outside of spiritual illumination does not perceive, and cannot perceive, the real condition of his own being, nor of his reason. In a religious-ethical sense you may indeed say, that the impulse of his opposition is enmity against God; but this does not make him dishonest as a man of science, within the domain of logic. He takes his premises, as they actually present themselves to him, and so far acknowledges with you, that in the natural principium there is something that does not satisfy us; but he disputes that, for the present at least, it *needs* to satisfy us, and more still, that the satisfaction, of which you boast, is anything more than appearance.

Hence the dispute can advance no farther than the acknowledgment of antinomies in our consciousness and the insufficiency of our reason to satisfy entirely our thirst after knowledge. But where the recognition of this leads *you* to the conclusion of the *necessity of the Sacred Scripture,* the rationalist either stops with the recognition of this disharmony, or glides over into other theories, which allow him to limit himself to the natural principium. And rather than call in the aid of another principium with you, he will cast himself into the arms of materialism, which releases him at once from the search after an infinite world, which then does not exist. All the trouble, therefore, that men have given themselves to make advance, by logical argument, from the acknowledgment of the insufficiency of our reason as a starting-point, has been a vain expenditure of strength. The so-called Doctrine of Principles (Principienlehre) may have served to strengthen in his conviction one who has confessed the special principium; and to shield prevailing tradition from passing too rapidly into oblivion; it has never provided force of proof against the opponent. He who is not born of water and the Spirit, cannot see the kingdom of God, and the human mind is sufficiently inventive so to modify its tactics, whenever you imagine that you have gained your point, that your proof is bound to lose its force. It is a little different, of course, when you touch the strings of the emotions, or appeal to the "seed of religion"; but then you enter upon another domain, and cease to draw conclusions from logical premises.

The same is true in part of the apologetic attempt to refute objections raised against the content of our Christian confession, and more particularly against the Holy Scripture as the principium of theology. Polemics will never be able to attain satisfactory results with reference to these points, simply because the spheres of conceptions and convictions, from which the argument proceeds on the two sides, are too widely apart: the result of which is that scarcely a single concrete point can be broached, which does not involve the whole subject of anthropology and the entire "Erkenntniss-theorie." In order, therefore, to make any gain, the general data that present themselves with such a concrete point should first be settled, one by one, before the real point in question can be handled. This makes every debate of that sort *constrained.* Scarcely has a single step been ventured in the way of such a controversy before it is felt on both sides that the acknowledgment of a different opinion on this *one* point would unsettle one's entire life- and world-view. If the naturalist grants the break of the chain of natural causes in one point, by acknowledging that a psychic or physical miracle has taken place, his entire system is overthrown; and, in like manner, if the Christian theologian acknowledges in one cardinal point the assertions of historical criticism with reference to the Holy Scripture, he thereby loses his grasp upon the whole principium by which his theology lives. By this we do not assert that, with reference to the Holy Scripture, there are not many remarks that have been made on logical incongruities, either in the economy of the Scripture itself, or between it and cosmic and historic reality outside of it, which, unless our confession is to lose its reasonable character, claim an answer from our side; but though these remarks might compel us to make confession in our turn of a partial agnosticism, or to subject the dogma of inspiration to revision, to us the special principium will never lose thereby its characteristic supremacy; just as on the other hand the most triumphant solution of the objections raised against it never could, and never can move him, who does *not* confess this principium, to accept it. The acceptance of this principium in the end cannot rest upon anything save the witness of the *Holy Spirit,* even as the acceptance of the natural principium has never rested upon anything save the witness of *our spirit,* i.e. of our self-consciousness. If this testimonium of our self-consciousness fails us, then we become sceptics or insane; and, in like manner, if the witness of the Holy Spirit is *not* present in us, or is at least inactive in us, we *cannot* reckon with a special principium.

The effort, therefore, put forth by theology in the days of the Reformation to derive from the Scripture itself proofs for its divine character, is devoid of all force with the opponent. Not because of the objection, that you reason in a circle, by seeking from the Scripture itself what the Scripture is. Our earlier theologians answered this correctly by saying, that this argument was not meant *authoritative,* but *ratiocinative;* that the glitter of the sapphire could only be proven by the sapphire; and that in like manner the divine majesty of the Holy Scripture could only shine out from that Scripture. But however accurate this statement was, what avail is it, if you show the most beautiful sapphire to one blind, or to one of "that worst kind of blind people who refuse to see"? One needs, therefore, but examine the series of these proofs for a moment, and it is at once perceived how utterly devoid of force they are over against him who merely accepts the natural principium. The *miracles* and *the fulfilment of prophecy,* indeed, have been pointed to, as if these had some power of proof for him who denies the very possibility of miracle and emasculates all concretely fulfilled prophecy as being "prophecy after the event" (vaticinium ex eventu). The divine character of the Doctrina Scripturae was cited, as though criticism had not already then been exercised against it, and, as it was claimed, its insufficiency been shown. The majestic style of the Scriptures was referred to, the consensus of its books, the effectiveness of its entire content, as though even then the arms were not already being welded by which each of these attributes of the Scripture would be disputed, or attributed to it only in common with other writings. And when outside of the Scripture the blood of the martyrs was mentioned, the consensus of the Church, and the "natural and human character (conditio) of the writers themselves," arguments were produced which were so easily applied to other sacred books that all their force evaporated. Whatever may be the worth of these arguments for those who are within the walls (intra muros) to combat doubt, outside of these walls (ad extra) they are of no value. Our acutest dialectici, such as Maccovius for instance, have clearly seen this in their day. His reference to Hagar in the wilderness shows this. "Hagar," he writes, "at first did not see the well near by; but after her eyes were opened, then at last she saw the well" (antea non vidit puteum in proximo; sed postquam oculi ipsi adaperti sunt, tum demum vidit puteum) (Joh. Maccov. II., *Theologic. quaestionum*, p. 4 in *Macc. redivivus*, Franeq, 1654),–an analogy by which he tries to show, that the marks of its divine origin are truly in the Scripture; but that no one can see them as long as the veil still hangs before his eyes. This is only taken away by the "enlightening" "by which the Holy Spirit discovers to us those inner relations of the Scripture, which had hitherto been concealed" (quo ostendit Spiritus Sanctus eas rationes Scripturae insitas, quae antea ei occultae erant) (*Ibidem*).

Hence our conclusion can be no other, than that whosoever confesses the Holy Scripture to be the principium of theology, both for himself and his fellow-confessors must certainly be able to give an account of the way in which this auxiliary principium is related to the permanent natural principium, in order that his confession may remain rational; but that this ratiocination can neither for himself be the ground on which his confession stands, nor ever compel the opponent to come to this confession. The witness of the Holy Spirit is and ever will be the only power which can carry into our consciousness the certainty concerning the special principium. Moreover, in the footsteps of our old theologians, it must be observed that it is also the witness of God as Creator (Testimonium Dei Creatoris) that can alone give us certainty for the natural principium. When God refrains from giving this certainty to our self-consciousness, we lapse into insanity, generally after the course has been run of the several stadii of scepticism. It is indeed true, that with respect to this natural principium, as a rule, we make no mention of the "witness of God as Creator," but this is explained from the fact, that it coincides with our self-consciousness, and that further account of the origin of this self-consciousness is rarely taken. It is simply the *first truth* from which departure is made. The special principium, on the other hand, enters into this self-consciousness as a sense of a *different kind,* and is thereby of itself reduced to its deeper origin in God. But however strongly this may appear with men of higher development, who, after they have lived for a long time by the natural principium only, now perceive the light in their consciousness from that other source as well, this is much less the case, and sometimes not at all, with common believers, who, regenerated in their youth, have never experienced this transition in their consciousness. In the case of such, immediate *faith* has been given equally naturally and as fully with their self-consciousness, as immediate *knowledge* for the natural principium is given with the awakening of our natural self-consciousness. For man as creature there can never be any other principium of knowledge but his Creator, naturaliter, as well as by the way of grace. What the Psalmist declares, only "in thy light shall we see light," remains the absolute ground of explanation for *all* human knowledge.

Universality of this Principium

One who, himself of a sound mind, should have to live on some isolated island among insane people, would run a great risk of becoming himself insane; and in such a condition a very strong mind only could maintain the reality of its consciousness. Just because we do not exist atomically, but are bound together with others organically, also in our consciousness, in order to remain firm our own sense cannot afford to lose the support of a similar sense in others. The same applies to the special principium. With this also, as a rule, the communion in our own consciousness can be strong and permanent only when this communion finds a support in the similar conviction of others. This rule, however, does not always hold. As one sane person, because of a strong mind, might be able in entire isolation to maintain his self-consciousness, it is possible for one person to experience the inworking of the special principium, and live by it, even though in his entire surroundings there should operate nothing but the natural principium. At first, indeed, this *had* to be so, in order that the working of this special principium might become manifest. It could not begin its work except in single persons. As a rule those individuals were men of strong minds, and to support their isolated faith the Lord gave them signs, mostly in the material world, which kept them from falling away from the power which had taken hold of them. Heroism of spirit is here called into play. When Christ, forsaken of all, even of His disciples, battled alone in Gethsemane, this struggle in loneliness became so fearful, that angels came to break His isolation, in order to support Him. So long, then, as revelation is still in process of completion, we see again and again the manifestation of extraordinary powers, by which the maintenance of faith is rendered possible, and these signs only disappear when Revelation has reached its completion, and the special principium finds a circle, in which faith can assume such a communal character, that the conviction of one supports that of the other.

If thus, like the natural principium, the working of the special principium requires a broad circle in which to exert itself organically, this circle becomes still more indispensable when a scientific account is given of what this special principium is and offers. Science demands *universality*. Not in the sense, of course, that nothing is established scientifically in the natural world until every individual has agreed to it, but in the sense that all men of sound understanding can readily be brought to perceive the truth of it. The same applies to the special principium. The law of universality must prevail here also, and must always be well understood by those who live by this principium. These only are taken into account, just as in natural science we reckon with those alone who are men of sound sense, i.e. who live by the natural principium. *All these,* then, must be able, if they follow your demonstration, to perceive the correctness of it. This accounts for the fact that in later ages only the question arose of a *science* of theology. Before that time there was a theology as knowledge of God; even measurably in a dogmatic sense; but as yet no theological *science.* This could only originate when the Revelation was completed, and liberated from the restrictions peculiar to Israel. Then there arose that universal circle among all nations, that circle of confessors in their general human character, who live by this special principium.

This communal character, which, along with every other principium, is common to the special principium, received no sufficient recognition in the conflict of the Reformation. From our side, the line of personal faith was ever drawn too tightly; while Rome, from her side, substituted the institutional Church too largely for the organic communion. Each of the two parties defended thereby an element of truth, but it was done by both in an insufficient and one-sided manner. Very properly did our Reformers maintain the personal character of faith, which does not reach its full unfolding, until it places our inner life in direct communion with the Eternal Being; but they lost sight of the fact that this is the fullest development of the faith, not its beginning, and that in its maturity it cannot flourish as it should, except in the communion of saints. Rome, on the other hand, defended very rightly the common feature, which marks faith, but committed a double mistake,—first, that it did not allow the personal character of faith to assert itself, and made it amount to nothing more than communion with God through the intermediation of the Church, and secondly, that it substituted the ecclesiastical institution for organic communion. This might, perhaps, have been more clearly seen if in their dogmatic exposition our Reformers had added, at once, to their distinction between the Church as a visible body and at the same time invisible, the more careful distinction between the visible Church as composed of believers (ecclesia visibilis in fidelibus) and the visible church as an institution (ecclesia visibilis in instituto). They did this, indeed, in their ecclesiastical law; observing thereby that the Church of Christ may be visible in a city or village, because of the believers who live there, even while no Church organization is established by these believers, and that the ecclesia instituta only originates by this organization. But in their dogmatics they referred almost exclusively to the general antithesis between visible and invisible, and thereby could not fail to convey the impression, that by visible Church they merely understood the Church as an institution. Since Rome outdid this, and wholly identified the visible Church with the Church as an institution, the problem could not be solved; since the Church as an institution was certainly subjected to the rule of the Word of God; and therefore our Reformers observed correctly, that the institute must borrow its guarantee from the Scripture, and not the Scripture its proof from the institute. Transfer this difference to the life of the world, and it will at once be understood. In society at large the natural principium is in force and the institute is the government, which, to be sure, is in the community, but is ever sharply distinguished from it. Can the assertion now be made that the truth of this natural principium is to be determined by the State? Of course not; simply because the State, so far as it is constituted by man, is an outcome of the natural principium. Undoubtedly, therefore, this natural principium can support the State, but not lean upon the State. On the other hand, by general conceptions, and public opinion derived from these, this natural principium finds its point of support in human society. And this is the case here. The Church is to the special principium what the State is to the natural principium. The Church as an institute, founded by man, is built after the rule of the special principium, as this speaks to us from the Holy Scripture. Hence the churchly institute can borrow support from the special principium, but not the special principium from the churchly institute. But what is true on the other hand—and this is the position which we defend—is, that faith in this special principium is supported and maintained by the churchly community, i.e. by the *non*-instituted but organically present communion mutual among believers.

It is unhistorical, therefore, to imagine that every person, taking the Bible in hand from his own impulse, should formulate the truth from it for himself. This is simply absurd, for actual experience shows that one either grows up in, or in later life enters, a circle in which confessions of the truth already exist; and that, in vital communion with this circle, clearness is reached in his consciousness of what was potentially given in regeneration, but which only from this communion can draw the life-sap needed for its development. As one tree of the forest protects another against the violence of the storm, so in the communion of saints does one protect the other against the storm-wind of doubt.

This fellowship of believers, carefully distinguished from instituted Churches, exhibits its universal human character in the fact that it continues its life in successive generations and extends itself to all peoples and nations. So far as the first is concerned, it has a history back of it which extends across many centuries, and by its confession it ever preserves communion with the past. Not merely in the sense in which a nation holds its ancestors in sacred memory, for in national life the dead are gone. He who dies loses his nationality, and belongs no more to his people. This fellowship of believers, on the other hand, knows that its departed ancestors still live and always stand in organic connection with it. Moreover, while a people changes its public opinion from age to age, in this ecclesiastical fellowship the same world of thought remains constant for all time. Hence the tie to the special principium is not maintained by those alone who are now alive with us and subscribe to the same confession as ourselves, but much more by those millions upon millions who now rejoice before the throne. And so far as the second is concerned, the outcome shows that the Christian religion, originating in Asia, passed over from the Semitic to the Indo-Germanic race, presently conquered the Northern Coast of Africa and the entire south of Europe, and never allowed itself to be nationalized. Christ had *humanized* his confession, by breaking down every partition wall ($\mu\epsilon\sigma\acute{o}\tau o\iota\chi o\nu$); and this universal human character stands in immediate connection with the possession of a special principium of knowledge. That which is national may give tradition, but cannot provide a special principium for our consciousness. It is seen, therefore, that every effort, applied outside of this principium, has merely led to national forms of religion; and even Buddhism—which, by the chameleon character of its pantheism, lent itself to stealthy invasions among many nations—remains in principle, nevertheless, an Indian world of thought. Islam alone—and this is worthy of notice—still exhibits, to a certain extent, an oecumenic character, which is attributable to the fact that Mohammedanism is grafted upon the special principium, such as it flourished, thanks to the Scripture, in the Christian life-circle. Even thus Islam has never taken root in the finer branches of the human tree. Islam is and remains Arabic, and outside of Arabia has gained an entrance only among those nations, which either have taken no part in the general human development, or have stood at a much lower level. Even the accession of Persia to Islam is attended with the disappearance of this nation, once so great, from the world stage.

If thus we leave out of account for a moment the working of this special principium *before* Golgotha, we face the fact that for almost twenty centuries a separate human life has developed itself in our human race; principally in the nobler branches of the human tree and among the more finely organized nations; and that the development of this separate life has not taken place with isolated nations such as China and India, but even now in five parts of the world, and chiefly in *that* current of our human life which has carried the hegemony, and caused the development of our human race to ascend to its present heights. We see that this separate life has been characterized everywhere by the action, in addition to that of the natural principium, of *another* principium of knowledge, and that wherever the Christian religion has withdrawn, as in West-Asia and North-Africa, all human life has sunk back again to a much lower level. We see that in this broad life-circle, which has extended itself across many ages and among many people, there has arisen a special world of thought; modified universal conceptions have begun to prevail; and in this genuinely human circle the human consciousness has assumed an entirely peculiar form. In this way have originated that *universal* life and that *universal* thought, which have certainly clashed with the other circle, that rejected the special principium, but which have possessed, nevertheless, entirely sufficient consistency to invite and to render possible scientific construction upon the foundation of that principle which, in this circle, is universal. It will not do, therefore, to represent this special principium as an idiosyncrasy of a few enthusiasts. The melancholy decline of all mystic fanaticism shows what the profound difference is between the parasite, that springs from fanatic imagination, and the cedar, that has struck its roots in the fertile soil of this real principle. This special principium is as universally human as the natural principium, with this difference only, that it is not given to each individual, but is organically grafted upon the tree of humanity. The life-circle, indeed, which finds its centrum in Christ as the bearer of the new life-principle, is not a branch of our race that is set apart; but this body of Christ *is the real trunk of our human race,* and what is not incorporated into this body, falls away from that trunk as a useless branch. He is, and remains, the second Adam.

Moreover, the peoples and nations that have stood or still stand outside of this life-circle, involuntarily bear witness to the insufficiency of the natural principium in its present working. When in Deut. xviii. inspiration is announced by God as the peculiar working of the special principium, He says: "I will raise them up a prophet from among their brethren, like unto thee; and I will put my words in his mouth, and he shall speak unto them all that I shall command him." An important thought, however, precedes the announcement of this rich inspiration, which in all its fullness is given in Christ as "Prophet." In the tenth verse, reference is made to divination and necromancy, which were common among the nations, and toward which Israel betrayed strong tendencies; and now they are told that the satisfaction of the need which spoke in this desire was not to be sought in the way of this enchantment, but that God alone is able to grant them the aspirations of their hearts. This impulse after necromancy, taken in its deepest significance, can be no other than the desire to find, in addition to the natural principium, *another* principium of knowledge for all those profound questions of life upon which the natural principium can cast no light. From this it appears, that the insufficiency of the natural principium declares itself in the universal human sense, so long as this still expresses itself in an unconstrained and natural way. The appearance, therefore, of another principium of knowledge in the Christian religion does not enter the present state of things as something foreign, but fits on it as a new spire upon a steeple, the former spire of which has fallen into ruin. We grant that afterwards, in philosophy, the natural principium has tried to show the superfluousness of such an auxiliary-principium. However, we must not fail to observe that these efforts of the philosophic spirit, so long as they were religiously colored, never occasioned in the religious world anything but endless confusion of speech; that they have never resulted in the founding of a religious life-circle of universal significance; and that these systems, drawn from the natural principium, have more and more abandoned eternal concerns in order in materialism to deny their existence, or in agnosticism to postulate the special principium. It is noteworthy, therefore, that since the apostasy, which began in the latter part of the last century, a broad life-circle has been formed in Europe and America, which has abandoned the special principium, in order, in Spiritualism, to revive the ancient effort after necromancy. This Spiritualism now counts its followers by the millions, and its main desire is to obtain an answer to the questions which force themselves upon our human mind, in another way than that which comes from the natural principium. While in other circles, where this Spiritualism has gained no entrance, the effort is certainly manifest, to obtain knowledge from the mysticism of the emotions, of what "common sense" has left uncertain. Every philosophical tendency, which, for the sake of defending itself against intellectualism, seeks another source of knowledge, pleads at heart for the necessity of a special principium. Pure intellectualists alone maintain to this day the sufficiency of the principium of rational knowledge; and this is even in opposition to Kant, who, in his "practische Vernunft," placed a second something dualistically over against the "reine Vernunft." But the barrenness of such intellectualism is sufficiently evident.

We refuse, therefore, to allow the charge, that the special principium, as an invention of fanaticism, floats like a drop of oil upon the waters of our human life, and we maintain, on the contrary, that the need of such an auxiliary principium is *universally human;* that in its organic working this principium bears an *universally human* character; and that in the final result towards which it directs itself, it has an *universally human* significance.

This Principium and the Holy Scripture

That the sphere of the special principium is wider than the compass of the Holy Scripture, needs no separate demonstration. Even though you firmly maintain that here you deal with a principium of knowing, it is here as impossible as elsewhere to ignore the principium of being (essendi). It is for this reason that in special revelation also *fact* and *word* run parallel and stand in connection with each other. There is not simply an inspiration that kindles light in our consciousness, but there is also a manifestation in *miracles* which operates upon the reality of being; and both flow naturally from that same principium in God, by which He works re-creatively in His deranged creation. The representation as though a way of life could have been disclosed for us by a book descended from heaven or by a Bible dictated from heaven, rests upon an intellectualistic abstraction, which interprets altogether incorrectly the relation between *being* and *thought,* between *fact* and *word.* If it is entirely true, that God created by speaking, so that the creatural *being* originated by the *word,* it must not be forgotten that this word went out from Him who carries the $\tau\grave{o}$ $esse$ in Himself. In the creation therefore there is no question of an abstract word, but of a word that carries in itself the full reality of life; and that the Scripture-word does not meet this requirement, appears from the fact, that without concomitants it is inert, even as the most glittering diamond without inshining light and admiring eyes differs in no particular from a dull piece of carbon. Protest therefore has ever been entered from the side of the Reformed against Luther's effort to place Word and Sacrament on a line, as though an active power lay concealed in the Scripture as such. Even though Luther's representation of an "eingepredigter" Christ allows defence to a certain extent, the Bible, as book, may never be accredited with a kind of sacramental power. By itself the Bible is nothing but a carrier and vehicle, or, if you please, the instrument prepared by God, by which to attain His spiritual purpose, but always through the ever-present working of the Holy Spirit.

If thus we take the sphere of action which belongs to this special principium in its entire compass, we find that it embraces everything that has taken place from the side of God, either immediately or mediately, and that has not proceeded from the natural principium, i.e. the whole plan of redemption; everything that has tended to realize this plan; all the special leadings, signs, and wonders; and in this connection the entire inspiration and the formation of the Scripture; and also all palingenesis, all illumination, all revelation of the Church of Christ; while from this same principium there shall yet come forth the palingenesis of heaven and earth, until the kingdom of glory is begun. The Bible, therefore, instead of being identical with this principium so far as its activity is concerned, is itself a product of this activity. Neither can it be said, that the Bible at least is identical with the fruit of the principium of knowledge, as such, for this also invites two objections: First, that many histories are contained in the Bible, so that it resembles in nothing a text- or law-book; and secondly, that this principium of knowing (cognoscendi) has produced by no means the Scripture only, but from it proceeds even now the working of the Holy Ghost, which maintains, applies and vitalizes the knowledge of God, partly by illumination in the consciousness of individuals, and partly by the work of the sacred ministry.

To understand the just relation between this special principium in God and the Holy Scripture, a more accurate definition is demanded, and this is only obtained by a double distinction. First, by the distinction between that which concerns our race as an organic unit and the knowledge of God in the single individual; and secondly, by the distinction between the content of the material of our knowledge and the way in which our knowledge takes this material up into itself. Both these distinctions demand a brief explanation. The Romish dogmaticians were properly observed, that the Holy Scripture could not be the instrument of salvation in the absolute sense, for the reason that many centuries elapsed before it was completed, and that there were nevertheless not a few who in the meantime, and without Scripture, were saved. This admits no rejoinder. It is simply true. But this objection loses its force at once, when we consider the great *mystery*. In Rom. xvi. 25; in Ephes. i. 9, iii. 9; Col. i. 26; 1 Tim. iii. 9; Tit. i. 2; and 1 Pet. i. 20, this mystery is referred to again and again as the key which unlocks for us insight into the course of revelation. This involves no secondary point, but a main point, and this main point, as we read in Col. i. 26, amounts to this: that there is the "mystery which hath been hid from all ages and generations," which eighteen centuries ago has been revealed to the saints of God, "to whom God was pleased to make known what is the riches of the glory of this mystery among the Gentiles, which is Christ in you, the hope of glory." By this falls away every conception as though revelation after the fall had progressed aphoristically or atomistically; and we get the conception of a revelation which goes through its definite stages, and thus moves along towards its final goal; which goal has been reached only when the whole earth unlocks itself for the reception of this revelation, and this directs itself, not to single persons, nor yet to a single nation, but to our *human race* as a whole. If thus letter or greater parts of the Holy Scripture, and finally even the whole Old Testament may have rendered provisional service in Israel, the Holy Scripture as such obtains its full significance only when special grace directs itself to our *race as an organic whole* and causes the *Catholic Church* to appear in humanity. The holy apostle Paul expresses this most pertinently, when of the Old Testament he declares in Rom. xv. 4, "For whatsoever things were written aforetime were written for our learning"; a thought which he repeats in 1 Cor. ix. 10 and in 1 Cor. x. 11, and in the latter especially emphasizes very strongly. There he does not only say that "all these things are written for our *admonition,*" but even prefaces this by saying that all these things happened unto Israel, "by way of *example.*" Entirely therefore from the question, how God saved individual persons in the times when the revelation had not yet been placed in the centrum of our human race, the fact must be held fast, that the Holy Scripture was intended to discharge its full task from that moment only when our race, taken as a whole, in its heart and centre, was apprehended with a view to salvation. Only when the saving hand was extended to the cosmos, and God "so loved *the world* that He gave His only begotten Son," had the moment come, when the Holy Scripture also would attain its entirely exceptional significance. All that lies back of this is merely preparation, and now for the first time, when in Christ the divine *esse* has been brought into our race, in the Holy Scripture also the divine *word* goes out not to one nation, but to all nations, and to those nations as an organic unity, as *cosmos.* All true understanding of the significânce of the Holy Scripture also is given *to the world,* cannot tolerate it. It is the one *Logos* which in Christ by incarnation, and in the Scripture by inscripturation goes out to humanity at large, as it is being saved by God and shall hereafter shine in glory. If thus the question is put what goes out to our human race as such from the special principium as matter of Divine knowledge, the answer reads: The Scripture and nothing but the Scripture; and in this sense the Scripture is identical in its working with the principium.

The second distinction, referred to above, between the material of the knowledge of God which is imparted to us and the way in which that material becomes our own, is no less important. After the unveiling of the mystery, indicated by the former distinction, it lies in the nature of the case that the individual obtains no part in this salvation except as member of the organic whole. Noah, Moses and Samuel received separate revelations, simply because humanity as such did not yet possess its revelation. But when once humanity as a whole had received its revelation, and this was completed, the need for all separate revelation fell away; and all mysticism, which even after this still pretends to receive separate personal revelation, frustrates thereby the organic ministration of the Lord. He who has lived, lives, or shall live, after our race in its unity has received its Christ and its Scripture, has no other way at his disposal, by which to come to the knowledge of God, except in union with this central revelation; and in so far as the life-stream of the Christ propels itself in the Church, and the Scripture is borne by her as "the pillar and ground of the truth," the Church of Christ (provided it be not taken as institute) is the only means of salvation. There is no salvation outside of her. But however firmly the organic relation both of our race and of revelation must be maintained, it is not asserted that the Holy Scripture by itself is enough for the individual. This is *not* the case at all, and he who thinks that the Holy Spirit really gave the Scripture, but low leaves its appropriation to our natural reason, is wofully mistaken. On the contrary, the Holy Spirit, who gave the Scriptures, is Himself the perpetual author (auctor perpetuus) of all appropriation of their contents *by* and of all application *to* the individual. It is the Holy Spirit who, by illumination, enables the human consciousness to take up into itself the substance of the Scripture; in the course of ages leads our human consciousness to ever richer insights into its content; and who, while this process continues, imparts to the elect of God, as they reach the years of discretion, that personal application of the Word, which, after the Divine counsel, is both intended and indispensable for them. Only, however many-sided and incisive this constant working of the Holy Spirit may be, it brings no new content (and herein lies the nerve of this second distinction), no increased supply of material, no enlargement of the substance of the knowledge of God. A believer of the nineteenth century knows much more than a believer of the tenth or third century could know, but that additional knowledge is ever dug from the selfsame gold mine; and that former generations stood behind in wealth of knowledge, can only be explained by the fact, that in those times the working of the mine was not so far advanced. This, of course, does not imply that the former generations fell short in knowledge of God, but simply, that the development of the human consciousness in those times did not make such demands on our knowledge of God. A child can be equally rich in his God as the full-grown man, but because the consciousness of the adult is more richly unfolded, he holds the knowledge of God likewise in a more richly unfolded form. With the fuller development of the consciousness of humanity the increase of insight into the contents of the Scriptures keeps equal step. But however far this increase of knowledge may proceed in the future, it will never be able to draw its material from any other source than from the Holy Scripture. And it is for this reason, that for the several nations also, and for the individuals among these nations, the rule remains valid that the *substance* of the knowledge of God, which comes to us from the special principium, is *identical with the Holy Scripture.*

This would not be so if the Holy Scripture were merely a collection of inspired utterances concerning the Being of God, His attributes, His will and counsel of grace. Then, indeed, by the side of the realm of the Scripture there would also lie the realm of *facts,* both of the leadings of the Lord and of His miracles, and the knowledge of these facts could only come to us by tradition. But this is not the character of the Holy Scripture; and it is to be deplored that the Methodistic tendency in particular has degraded it so much to such a volume of inspired utterances. The Holy Scripture offers us a photograph of the entire sphere of life, in which the action of God from the special principium has appeared, with His activity out of the natural principium as its natural and indispensable background. The logical revelation, which directs itself immediately to our consciousness, does not stand independently by the side of this photograph, neither is it woven through it, but belongs to it, and constitutes a part of it. More than or anything else than this photograph could not be offered us, simply because facts that lie in the past cannot be alive except in the memory or in the imagination. For though there is also a real after-effect of past events in the actual conditions in which we live, which is, moreover, the no less real activity which uninterruptedly goes forth from Christ out of heaven upon His Church, yet the presentation of this double, real activity and correct insight into it is possible only by a thorough study of the photograph offered us in the Holy Scripture. Not as though we would deny that the rich past, which lies back of the completion of the Holy Scriptures, does contain an innumerable multitude of facts which you do *not* find in this photograph, but for this the answer from John xx. 30 is ever conclusive: that many other signs therefore did Jesus, but these are written, that ye may believe that Jesus is the Christ, the Son of God; and that believing ye may have life in His name. Not a hundredth part of course is told us of what happened or was spoken in former times, but here also there was light and shadow, there was perspective, and even as you take the fruit from the tree, but not the leaves which presently wither, so also the ripened fruit of Revelation is offered us in the Holy Scripture, while all that aided that fruit to ripen has disappeared in the shade and sunk away in forgetfulness. This is incomprehensible to him who thinks that the Scripture originated by way of accident, but agrees entirely with the nature of the case for him who believes that the origin of the Scripture was determined and foreseen in the counsel of God, and that the distinction between the fruit that was to be plucked and the leaf that was to wither was given in the facts themselves in keeping with this purpose of the Holy Scripture. Hence the reason that we reject tradition, in which Rome seeks a complement for the Holy Scripture, is not because we deny that there is an abundance of material for a very interesting tradition, nor yet alone because we foster a just doubt concerning the reliability of this tradition, but rather because such a complement by tradition is *antagonistic* to the entire conception of the Scripture. In that case the Holy Scripture would attain no higher value than of being itself *a part of tradition.* Then it no longer would form a completed whole, an organic unity. Suppose that after a while letters were to be found of Thomas or of Philip, or a gospel according to Andrew, you would be bound to let these parts be added to your Bible. The Bible would then become an incomplete, contingent fragment of a whole, and would need to postulate its complement from elsewhere; and so the theologic, and therefore the organic and teleologic, view of the Holy Scripture would pass away in the historic-accidental. Since this view is in direct conflict with the view given concerning the Old Testament in Rom. xv. 4, etc., upon Scriptural ground this preposterous view of the Holy Scripture may not be tolerated for a single moment, but the confession must be maintained that so far as the substance of the knowledge of God is concerned, which is given to humanity as such, the Holy Bible itself is the proximate and sole cause (principium proximum et unicum) for our knowledge of God.

The Special Principium and the Written Word

The indispensableness of the Holy Scripture, therefore, rests: (1) upon the necessity that a special principium should be actively introduced, inasmuch as the working of the natural principium is weakened or broken; and (2) upon the necessity that this special principium should not direct itself atomistically to the individual, but organically to the human race. From these two considerations it follows that an auxiliary-principium is needed, and that a revelation must be given to humanity as such (i.e $\tau\hat{\omega}$ $\kappa\acute{o}\sigma\mu\omega$) but it does not follow directly from this that "this special Word of God to the world" should assume the form of the *written* word. It is necessary, therefore, that we inquire into the peculiar character of the *written* word, and ask ourselves why the special Revelation of God to the world needed *this* form.

To this we reply with emphasis, that in comparison with the spoken word the *written* word is entitled to claim the four characteristics of *durability, catholicity, fixedness* and *purity,*—four attributes, the first two of which impart something of the Divine stamp to our human word, and the last two of which form a corrective against the imperfection of our sinful condition.

Writing by itself is nothing but an auxiliary. If the power of our memory were not limited, and if our capacity for communication were universal, the need of writing would never have been known. The sense of shortness of memory and our limited ability of communicating our thoughts personally, strengthened by the need of guarding that which has been spoken or agreed upon from being misrepresented, has, through a series of gradations, called into life, first, pictographic writing, then idiographic writing, then phonographic writing, after that syllabic writing, and finally, alphabetic writing. Hence writing bears almost entirely a conventional and arbitrary character. Only as pure idiographs did it escape from the conventional, and then only upon the condition of being delineation instead of writing. Writing, in the real sense of the word, tries to photograph the somatic part of our human language, in order that by seeing these photographed signs one person may understand psychically what has gone on psychically in another person, or has gone out from his lips. Writing tries to do the same thing that phonograph does, but by attaching a meaning, not to sound, but to root-forms. When we have our picture taken, it is our own face that, with the aid of the light, draws its upon the collodion plate. If, now, it were possible for our human voice to delineate itself immediately in all its inflexions upon paper, we should have absolute and organic writing. Since, however, thus far this is not possible, we must content ourselves with conventional writing, which is not produced by the voice itself, but by our thinking mind. It is our thinking mind which watches the sound and the inflexion of the voice in connection with the movement of the visible organs of speech, and now indicates either the voice-action itself or the content of that voice-action, by signs, in such a way that when another sees these signs he is able to reproduce that same inflexion of voice and impart to it the same content. The question whether, with a sinless development, writing would have run the same course cannot possibly be answered; but it is evident that then also something similar would have taken its place. For then also memory would have been limited in its power, and the need of communication would have originated with the sense of distance. Only for the realm of glory the question can arise whether, in that exalted state of the life of our spirits, and with its finer organisms, all such auxiliaries will not fall away. By itself, therefore, it cannot be said that writing is a need which has only come as a consequence of sin; even though it is certain, as will appear from the last two of the four characteristics mentioned above, that the need of writing has been *intensified* in every way by sin.

With reference to the first of these characteristics, it is readily seen, that writing first of all relieves the spoken word of its transitoriness. "The word that is heard passes away, the letter that is written remains." (Verba volant, littera scripta manet.) Our voice creates words, but lacks the ability to hold them fast. One word drives the other on. The spoken word, therefore, bears the character of the transitory and the unchangeable, which are the marks of our mortality. It comes in order to go, and lacks the ability to maintain itself. It is a πάντα ῥεῖ καὶ οὐδὲν μένει (everything flows and nothing remains) in the most mournful sense. And even when, by the phonograph, it is secured that the flowing word congeals and is presently liquefied, it gives us at most a repetition of what was spoken or sung, and no more. But this very imperfection is met by the mighty invention of human writing. By writing, in its present state of perfection, the word or thought spoken is lifted above transitoriness. It is taken out of the stream of time and cast upon the shore, there to take on a stable form, and after many ages to do the same service still which it performed immediately upon its first appearing. The correspondence, which is discovered by a fellah in a forgotten nook of Egypt and presents us with the interchange of thought between the then Eastern princes and the court of Egypt, speaks now as accurately as three thousand years ago; and if, after the fall into sin, the bitter emotions of his soul could have been written down by Adam, our hearts could sympathize to the last minutiae with what went on in Adam so many thousand years ago. Writing, indeed, is human thought set free from the process of time. By writing, human thought approaches the eternal, the enduring, and, to a certain extent, impresses upon itself a Divine stamp. It is noteworthy, therefore, how in the Holy Scripture the durability and permanence of the thoughts of God are expressed by the figure of the Book of Life, the Book of the Seven Seals, etc. Nor is this all. Not only, thanks to writing, does human thought approach in a measure the eternal, but also by writing only, on the other hand, does it meet the demand raised by the unity of our human race. The whole human race does not live upon the earth at once. It appears on earth in a succession of generations, one of which comes and the other passes away. If the means, therefore, are wanting to perpetuate the thought of one generation for the others, then thinking becomes aphoristic, and the unity of the human consciousness in our whole race is not established. Tradition might lend some aid so long as those thoughts are few and bear a little-complicated character, and the restricted form of poetry might offer assistance so long as those thoughts preferred the form of images; but in the course of centuries no question of unity for our human consciousness could have been permanent, if Aristotle had had to entrust his word to memory, or Plato his thesaurus of ideas to memoriter poetry. Thus, writing alone has created the possibility of collecting human thought, of congealing it, of handing it down from age to age, and of maintaining the unity of our human consciousness in the continuity of the generations. If, now, the special revelation from God is not destined for the one generation to which a certain part of the revelation was given, but for the *world*, and hence for the generations of all ages until the end is come, it is evident that it was necessary for this special revelation to take the form of writing. Only by this written form could it be a revelation to our race *as a whole*.

In connection with this stands the second characteristic which we mentioned; viz. *writing is catholic*, i. e. universal, in the sense that, bound by neither place nor nation it overcomes the limitation of the local. Even the most stentorian voice does not carry a single spoken word beyond the distance of one kilometer, and a more extended expression of thought cannot reach across one-tenth part of this; but so soon as the word has been committed to writing, no distance can resist or break its power. The written word travels around the world. He who speaks, may communicate his thoughts to ten thousand persons at most; he who writes, to ten millions and more. In the mystery of writing lies, thus, the wonderful power of overcoming at the same time the two mighty limitations of our human existence, those of *time* and *place*. An important statement by Gladstone, spoken in the English Parliament after sundown, is printed before the sun rises again, and in a million copies spread among the masses, in Europe and America. Dislocation, no less than *time*, is a mighty factor that resists the unit-life of our race. In olden times, when this dislocation was not modified in its fatal effects by quicker means of communication, the sense of the sodality of the nations, and in connection with this the ideas of a common humanity, were in consequence very little alive; and it is only by these quickened means of communication, which greatly augment the effect of the written word, that now a feeling of international communion has mastered the nations, and a sense of organic unity permeates all the articulations of our human race. If now, as was shown before, the mystery of Revelation consists in this: that our race, even as it was created of one blood, shall sometime shine in the realm of glory as one body under Christ as its head, then it needs no further proof that this catholic characteristic of writing agrees entirely with the catholic character of the whole Revelation and the catholic character of the Church. As writing sets thought free from every local restriction, special Revelation in like manner, released from all local and national restrictions, seeks the human race in the whole world as one organic whole. God has loved not individuals nor nations, but the *world*. Only by writing, therefore, can special Revelation attain its end; and in proportion as the development of human consciousness has made higher demands, printing and afterward more rapid communication have augmented this dispersing power of writing. Writing, therefore, is the means of perpetuating thought and at the same time of dispersing it, i.e. of making it universal in the highest sense, and of bringing it within the reach of all. Writing lends wings to thought. It neutralizes distance of time and place, and thereby puts upon thought the stamp of the eternity and of omnipresence. So far as human thought can formally approach the divine, it owes to writing alone this higher nobility. For this reason, therefore, when *divine* thoughts take pleasure in the garment of *human* words, *the Scripture* is the only form in which they can rest.

But this does not exhibit in full the excellency of the Scripture as such, and therefore we mentioned the two other characteristics of *fixedness* and *purity,* which protect the word of thought against the dangers that threaten from the results of sin. With respect to tradition we have to contend not merely with the limitation of the human memory, by which so much becomes lost, broken, and impaired, but almost more still with its *multiformity* and *untrustworthiness;* and it is against these two dangers that the spoken word is shielded in the *fixedness* and *accuracy* of the written or printed word.

Every religious sense from its very nature is in need of *fixedness.* As long as the divine reflects itself only in the changing stream of the human, it fails to take hold of us, simply because this trait of changeableness and movability is in conflict with the idea of the divinely majestic. The *quod ubique, quod semper* may have been pushed too far by Rome, on the ground of hierarchical by-views, but in the realm of religion *antiquity* is of so much more value than the *new* and constantly changing idea, simply because the old makes the impression of fixedness and of being grounded in itself. So far now as the sinful mind of man chafes against the divine revelation, he will always be bound to break this fixedness. Hence the injurious multiformity in tradition. A little liberty, which each successive transmitter allows himself, brings it to pass that in the course of two or three centuries tradition is wrenched entirely away from the grooves of its fixedness. This may occur unconsciously or without ill intent, but in every case it breaks the working power of the transmitted revelation. This is seen in the unwritten tradition, which from paradise spread among all nations, becoming almost irrecognizable; this is seen in the traditions committed to writing at a later date in the apocryphal gospels; this is seen in the different authority of tradition in the Eastern and Western churches. It is this same infatuation against the fixedness of the truth, which now appears again in the opposition against every confessional tie, and no less in the loud protest against the written character of revelation, and this in a time which otherwise emphasizes so strongly the written for the entire *Cultur.* On the other hand, it is seen in the holy books, which every more highly developed form of religion has created for itself, in India, China, among the Persians and Islam, etc., how the pious sense which, from the ever changing, seeks after a basis of fixedness, applies writing, as soon as found, as a means of resistance against the destructive power of what is individual and multiform in tradition. What Paul wrote to the church at Phil. iii. 16, "whereunto we have already attained, by that same *rule* let us walk," is unchangeably the fundamental trait of all religion, which does not end in individual wisdom or fanaticism, but organically works in upon our human life as such. And since writing only, and in a more telling sense, the press, is able to guarantee to the Divine thoughts which are revealed to us that *fixed* form, it is not by chance, but of necessity, that special Revelation did not come to us by way of oral tradition, but in the form of *the Scripture.*

This brings with it the *purity,* which likewise can be guaranteed by writing only, among sinful men, and this only in a limited sense. Since Divine revelation directs itself against the mind and inclination of the sinner, sinful tendency could not be wanting, to represent that revelation differently from what it was given. Not merely did forgetfulness and individualism threaten the purity of tradition, but the direct effort also wilfully to modify what was revealed according to one's own idea and need; which psychologically is done the sooner, if one knows the revelation only from tradition, and thus thinks himself entitled to mistrust its certainty. One begins by asking whether the revelation might not have been different, and ends in the belief that it *was* different. If printing in its present completeness had been in existence from the times of the beginning of revelation, it would have been the surest safeguard against such falsification. If what was spoken at the time had been taken down by stenography and been circulated at once in thousands of copies by the press, we would have been so much more certain than now of the authenticity of what is handed down. Since, however, printing, as a strengthened form of writing, did not exist at that time, handwriting alone could guard against falsification. And though we must grant that this safeguard is far from being absolute, yet it is certain that the written tradition has a preference above the oral, which defies all comparison, and thus, in order to come down to us in the least possibly falsified form, the Divine revelation had to be *written.*

To him who thinks that the Revelation came from God, but that the writing was invented by man, the relation between that Revelation and its written form is of course purely accidental. He, on the other hand, who understands and confesses that writing indeed is a human invention, but one which God has thought out for us and in His own time has caused us to find, will arrive at the same conclusion with ourselves, that also in His high counsel the Divine revelation is adapted to writing, and writing to the revelation. We do not hesitate to assert that human writing has reached its highest destiny in the Scripture, even as the art of printing can attain no higher end than to spread the Word of God among all peoples and nations, and among those nations to put it within the reach of every individual. To this still another and no less important spiritual benefit attaches itself, in so far as printing (and writing in part) liberates men from men and binds them to God. So long as the revelation is handed down by oral tradition only, the great multitude was and ever remained dependent upon a priestly order to hierarchy to impart to them the knowledge of this revelation. Hence there ever stood a man between us and God. For which reason it is entirely natural that the Roman hierarchy opposes rather than favors the spread of the printed Bible. And it behooves us, in the very opposite sense, to confess, that the Divine revelation, in order to reach immediately those who were called to life, *had* to assume the form of writing, and that only by *printed* writing could it enter upon its fullest mission of power.

Inspiration. Its Relation to the Principium Essendi

If we have not failed entirely in our endeavor to apprehend the special principium in its fullest significance, and if thereby we intend to maintain the confession of the theology of the sixteenth century, that the only principium of theology is the Holy Scripture, the question now arises,—by what action the Holy Scripture came forth from this principium in such a way that at length the principium and the product of this principium (i.e. the Holy Scripture) could be interchanged. Theologically taken, this action lies in *inspiration,* and therefore in this section we proceed to the study of this majestic act of God, to which we owe the Holy Scripture. It is not enough for Encyclopedia to declare apodictically that the Holy Bible *is* the principium of theology. Such a declaration is sufficient, when one writes an Encyclopedia of a science whose principium is self-evident. A medical Encyclopedia does not need to give an account in the first place of the fact that pathological conditions appear in the human body, nor of the fact that in nature there are reagents against these conditions. But for theological Encyclopedia the matter stands differently. It has to investigate a matter as its object, whose principium is not given normally in the creation, but has abnormally entered into what was created. The right understanding, therefore, of this science demands an explanation of this principium, its action and its product, in their mutual connection. This *principium* is the energy in God by which, notwithstanding the ruin worked in the cosmos by sin, He carries out His will with reference to that cosmos; and more properly as a *principium of knowledge* it is that energy in God, by which He introduces His theodicy into the human consciousness of the sinner. The product of this principium, which is placed objectively before the human consciousness, is *the Holy Scripture.* And finally the action by which this product comes forth from this Divine energy is *inspiration.* Hence this inspiration also must be explained.

It should, however, not be lost from view, that this inspiration is no isolated fact, which stands by itself. He who takes it in this sense arrives at some sort of Koran, but not at the Holy Scripture. In that case the principium of knowing (cognoscendi) is taken entirely apart from the principium of being (essendi), and causes the appearance of an exclusively intellectual product which is outside of reality. We then would have an inspiration which dictated intellectually, and could not communicate to us anything but a doctrine and a law. Entirely different, on the other hand, is the action of this Divine energy, which, in spite of sin, carries out the plan of the Lord in and by the cosmos. Since indeed sin is not merely intellectual in its character, but has corrupted the whole nature of man and brought the curse and disorder even upon nature outside of man, this Divine energy could not overcome the opposition of sin, except it directed itself to the whole reality of our human existence, including nature round about us. Hence this Divine energy constituted in part the principium essendi, and from it comes miracles, — nor miracle taken as an isolated phenomenon, which appears without causal connection with the existing world; but miracle, as the overcoming, penetrating working of the Divine energy, by which God breaks all opposition, and in the face of disorder brings His cosmos to realize that end which was determined upon in His counsel. It is from the deeper basis of God's will, on which the whole cosmos rests, that this mysterious power works in the cosmos; breaks the bands of sin and disorder, which hold the cosmos in their embrace; and centrally from man so influences the entire life of the cosmos, and at length it *must* realize the glory intended for it by God, in order in that glory to render unto God what was the end of the entire creation of the cosmos. Every interpretation of the miracle as a magical incident without connection with the palingenesis of the whole cosmos, which Jesus refers to in Matt. xix. 28, and therefore without relation to the entire metamorphosis which awaits the cosmos after the last judgment, does not enhance the glory of God, but debases the Recreator of heaven and earth to a juggler $(\gamma \acute{o} \eta s)$. This entire recreative action of the Divine energy is one continuous miracle, which shows itself in the radical renewal of the life of man by regeneration, in the radical renewal of the life of humanity by the new Head which it receives in Christ, and which finally shall bring to pass a similar radical renewal of life in nature. And because these three do not run loosely side by side, but are bound together organically, so that the mystery of regeneration, incarnation and of the final restitution forms one whole, this wondrous energy of re-creation exhibits itself in a broad *history,* in which what used to be interpreted as incidental miracles, *could* not be wanting. Because our *soul* is organically connected with our *body,* and this *body* unites us organically to nature, a palingenesis, which should limit itself to the psychic domain, without at the same time working an effect upon the body and upon the cosmos, is simply unthinkable. The fuller explanation of this belongs from the nature of the case to dogmatics. Here it is sufficient that the attention is directed to the significance, which the recreative Divine energy, also in so far as it appears as the principium of being (essendi), has for the life of our consciousness, and therefore for the principium of knowing (cognoscendi). The tie that binds thought to being and being to thought operates also here. There is not a revelation by the dictation of a doctrine and law, and by its side a revelation by what is called miracle; but the revelation in the world of reality and the revelation in the world of thought are interwoven. The thought explains the reality (as, for instance, prophecy the Messiah), and again from the reality the thought receives its content (for instance, in the gospels). The preparation of the consciousness for the thought (illuminatio) proceeds from the reality of the palingenesis, and again in faith (as the act of the consciousness) the reality of the new life finds its utterance. In a like sense inspiration does not lie isolated by the side of the Divine energy in history, but is organically united to it and forms a part of it. If in the meantime it is demanded, that theology as science indicate its principium, it has to deal from the nature of the case as such with the *principium of knowing* only, and cannot reckon with the reality, and therefore with the *principium of being,* except so far as the facts and events have been transformed beforehand *into a thought,* i.e. have become a *narrative.* It is in the glass of our human consciousness that reality reflects its image; by the human *word* this image becomes fixed; and it is from this word that the image of the reality is called up in the individual consciousness of him who *hears* or *reads* this word. A *reality,* such as the recreative Divine energy has woven through the past as a golden thread, was not intended only for the few persons who were then alive, and whom it affected by an immediate impression, but was of central and permanent significance to humanity. It could not be satisfied with simply having happened; it only effected its purpose when, transformed into an idea, it obtained permanence, and even as the Divine *word,* that accompanied it, and in the unity which joined this *word* to the facts of history, it could be extended from generation to generation. If now our human consciousness had stood *above* these facts and these Divine utterances, the common communication by human tradition would have been enough. But since our human consciousness stood *beneath* them, and, left to itself, was *bound* to misunderstand them, and was thus incapable of interpreting the correct sense of them, it was necessary for the Divine energy to provide not only these facts and utterances, but also the image of this reality so as to insure re-creation likewise in the world of our consciousness. This provision was brought about by the Divine energy from the special principium in inspiration in a twofold way: (1) by means of the word in the past transforming the Divine *doing* into *thought,* and thus introducing it into the consciousness of those who were then alive; and (2) by bringing to us this entire past, together with these Divine utterances, as one rich idea, in the Holy Scripture.

Thus inspiration is not added to this wondrous working of the Divine energy, but flows, and is inseparable, from it. It does not come from the principium of creation, but from that of re-creation. Though, indeed, it finds an analogy in the communion of paradisiacal man with his Creator, and its connecting-point in the capacity of paradisiacal man for that communion, inspiration, in the narrower sense, may never be confounded with this communion. Inspiration, as it here appears, is not the working of the general "consciousness of the divinity" (Gottesbewusstsein). It does not rise from the *seed of religion*. It may not be confounded with the utterance of the mystically disposed mind. Neither may it be placed on a line of equality with the way in which God will reveal Himself to the blessed in the realm of glory. Appearing as an abnormal factor in the work of re-creation, it bears a specific character, belongs to the category of the miraculous, and is consequently of a transient nature. As soon as the object for which it appears has been attained, it loses its reason for being, and ceases to exist. Though it must be granted that the illumination, and very much more, was indispensable, in order that the fruit of inspiration might ripen to the full; yea, though from everything it appears that the Holy Spirit ever continues to this day more fully to explain the rich content of the fruit of inspiration in the confession of believers and in the development of theology; yet in principle all these operations of the Spirit are to be distinguished from inspiration in its proper sense. In the counsel of God before the creation of the world, there was a provision for the carrying out of His plan concerning the cosmos, in spite of the outbreak of sin. In that counsel of God, all things were predestined in organic relation, which to end were to be done by the Divine energy, and this, indeed, severally: on the one hand, what was to be done centrally in and for our entire race, and, on the other hand, what was to be done in order that this central means might realize its purpose with the individual elect. Inspiration directs itself to this central means; the individual is left to illumination. This central means is to be taken in this threefold way: First, as *an idea in Divine completeness,* lying predestined in the counsel of God; secondly, as from that counsel it entered into the reality of this cosmos and was ever more fully executed; and thirdly, as it was offered to the human consciousness, as tradition under the Divine guarantee, and by inspiration as the *human idea.*

Hence the thought, that it comes to an end, is not foreign, but lies in the nature of inspiration. This is *not* arbitrary, but flows from the fact that our human race forms an organism, and that, therefore, here, as with all organisms, distinction *must* be made between that which *centrally* directs itself to all and that which *individually* limits itself to single persons. And if this distinction is noted, then it follows from this with equal force, that that which centrally goes out to all *must* appear in that objective form in which it could continue from age to age and spread from nation to nation. That which is individual in its character may remain subjective-mystic in its form, but not that which is intended to be centrally of force for all times and nations. In order to exist objectively for all, this revelation of necessity had to be *completed.* As long as it was not finished, it missed its objective character, since it still remained attached to the persons and the life-sphere in which it had its rise. Only when it is completed, does it become independent of those persons and of that special life-circle, and obtain its absolute character. An ever-continuous inspiration is therefore only conceivable, when one mistakenly understands by it mystical inworking upon the individual, and thus takes the work of re-creation atomistically. Then, however, inspiration fails of all specific character and loses itself in the general "est Deus in nobis, agitante calescimus illo (Lo, God is in our soul, we kindle when He stirs us);" while re-creation is then imagined as coming from phantasy, and is no longer suitable for humanity, which only exists organically. In all organic development there are two periods,—the first, which brings the organism to its measure or limit, and the second, which allows it, once come to its measure, to do its functional work. The plant, animal and man first grow, till the state of maturity has been reached, and then that growth ceases. An organic action which restlessly continues in the same way, is a contradiction in terms. Considered, therefore, from this point of view, it lies entirely in the organic character of revelation, that it passes through two periods, the first of which brings it to its complete measure, and the second of which allows it, having reached its measure, to perform its work. And this is what we face in the difference between inspiration and illumination. Inspiration *completed* the revelation, and, appearing in this completed form, the Revelation now performs its work.

This first period (that in which Revelation attained its measure by inspiration, and which lasted so many centuries) does not flow by itself from the principium of knowledge. If you think that revelation consisted merely in a communication by inspiration of doctrine and law, nothing would have prevented its being finished in a short time. Since, on the other hand, revelation did not merely make its appearance intellectually, but in life itself, and therefore dramatically, the inspiration, which only at the end of this drama could complete its action, was *eo ipso* linked to that process of time which was necessary for this drama. This would not have been so if the special principium had merely been a principium of knowing, but *must* be so since simultaneously it took in life. The long duration of the first period of Revelation has nothing, therefore, to surprise us; but this long duration should never tempt us to allow that first period to pass unmarked into the second. However many the ages were that passed by before the incarnation, that incarnation came at one moment of time. The new drama which began with this incarnation is relatively of short duration; and when this drama with its apostolic postlude is ended, the Revelation acquires at once its oecumenic working, and thereby shows, that its first period of its *becoming,* is now completed. Thus inspiration obtains a sphere of its own, in which it appears; a definite course which it has to run; a boundary of its own, which it cannot stride across. As the fruit of its completion, a new condition enters in, which shows itself in the oecumenic appearance of the Church, and this condition not only does not demand the continuance of inspiration, but excludes it. Not, of course, as if a sudden transition took place which may be indicated to the very day and hour. Such transitions are not known in spiritual things. But if the exact moment escapes our observation in which a child ceases its growth and begins its life as an adult, there is, nevertheless, a moment, known to God, in which that growth performed its last act. In like manner, we may assert that these two periods of revelation lie, indeed, separated from each other by a point of transition known to God, even though we can only approximately indicate the beginning of the second period.

Inspiration in Connection with Miracles

So far as the special principium in God directs itself as principium of knowledge to the consciousness of the sinner, it brings about *inspiration* (with its concomitant illumination); on the other hand, as principium of being (essendi), the spiritual and material acts of re-creation commonly called *miracles* (נִפְלָאוֹת and τέρατα). Since, however, the world of *thought* and the world of *being* do not lie side by side as two separate existences, but are organically connected, inspiration *formally* has in common with the wonderful (פֶּלֶא) that which to us constitutes the characteristic of *the miracle.* Consequently the *formal* side of the miracle need not be considered here.

Very unjustly at the mention of miracles one thinks almost exclusively of those in the *material* domain, and almost without a thought passes by the *spiritual* miracles. This of course is absurd. The *creation* (if we may so call it) of a mind, such as shone forth in the holy apostle John, or such as in the secular world sparkled in a Plato, is, if we make comparison, far more majestic than even the creation of a comet in the heavens; and in the same way the *re-creation* of a person inimical to God into a child of God is a profounder work of art than the healing of a leper or the feeding of the five thousand. That nevertheless the material miracle captivates us more, is exclusively accounted for by the fact, that the spiritual miracle is gradually observed after it is ended, and only in its effects, while the material miracle, as a phenomenon, is immediately visible to the spectator. In order not to be misled by this one-sided appearing in the foreground of the material miracle, it is necessary that we first explain the connection between the spiritual and the material miracle. The undeniable fact, which in this connection appears most prominently, is, that from the days of paradise till now the spiritual miracle of palingenesis is ever unceasingly continued, and occurs in every land and among all people, while the sphere of the material miracle is limited and confined to time and place. The question of psychico-physical processes, which are often spoken of as miracles, is here passed by. Whether the study of hypnotism will succeed in lifting the veil which still withholds from our sight the working of soul upon soul, and of the soul upon the body, time will tell; but in any case it appears that in this domain, under definite circumstances, there are forces at work which find their *causa causans* in our nature, and therefore do not belong to the category of the miracle. With reference to the real miracle, on the other hand, the Holy Scripture reveals to us that there is a palingenesis, not only of things *invisible* but also of things *seen.* The Scripture nowhere separates the soul from the body, nor the body from the cosmos. Psyche, body and world form together one organic whole. The body belongs to the real existence of man as truly as his psyche, and for human existence the cosmos is an inseparable postulate. To the stae of innocence, i.e. to that existence of man, which was the immediate product of creation, there belonged not only a holy soul, but also a sound body and a glorious paradise. In the state of sin the unholiness of the psyche entails therefore the corruption of the body, and likewise brings the curse upon the cosmos. Even as this organic connection of these three elements appears both in the original creation and in the state of sin, it continues to work its effect also in the re-creation. Here also the effect begins with the psyche in regeneration, but will continue to operate to the end in the palingenesis of the body, and this body will see itself placed in a re-created cosmos delivered from the curse. If now regeneration consisted in a sudden cutting loose of our psyche from every connection with sin, so that it were transformed at once into an absolutely holy psyche, not merely potentially, but actually, the palingenesis of the body would enter in at once, and if this took place simultaneously in all respects, the palingenesis of the cosmos would immediately follow. This, however, is *not* so. Since our race does not enter life at one moment, but in the course of many centuries, and exists, not individualistically as an aggregate of atoms, but in organic unity, the transition from potentia to actus cannot take place except gradually and in the course of many centuries; and since each man has no cosmos of his own, but all men together have only one and the same cosmos, our ancestors (see Heb. xi. 40) *could* not be perfect without us, i.e. without us they could not attain unto the end of their palingenesis, and therefore the apostle Paul does by no means expect his crown at present, nor yet immediately after his death, but only at the last day, and then simultaneously with all them also that love the appearing of Christ (2 Tim. iv. 8).

The very order, which is founded in the nature of our race, brings it to pass, that the re-creation of the body and of the cosmos tarries till the end. If thus the miracle as such, in that special sense in which we here consider it, had not appeared until the parousia, the saving power would have brought about none other but a *spiritual* effect. There would have been regeneration, i.e. palingenesis of the psyche; but no more. A power would have become manifest capable of breaking psychically the dominion of *sin;* but that the same power would be able to abolish the *misery,* which is the result of sin, would have been promised in the word, but would never have been manifested in the deed, and as an unknown *x* would have been a stone of offence upon which faith would have stumbled. The entire domain of the Christian hope would have remained lying outside of us as incapable of assimilation. This is only prevented by the fact, that already in this present dispensation, by way of model or sample, the power of palingenesis is shown within the domain of matter. In that sense they are called "signs." As such we are shown that there is a power able to check every result of sin in the material world. Hence the rebuke of the elements, the feeding without labor, the healing of the sick, the raising of the dead, etc.; altogether manifestations of power, which were not exhausted in the effort at that given moment to save those individuals, for this all *ratio sufficiens* was wanting; but which once having taken place, were perpetuated by the tradition of the Scripture for all people and every generation, in order to furnish a permanent foundation to the hope of all generations. For this purpose they could not create a *new* reality (Lazarus indeed dies again), but tended merely to prove the possibility of redemption in facts; and this they had to do under two conditions: (1) that successively they should overcome every effect of sin in our human misery; and (2) that they should be a model, a proof, a σημεῖον, and therefore be limited to one period of time and to one circle. Otherwise it would have become a real palingenesis, and they would have forfeited their character of *signs*. There were hundreds in and about Jerusalem whom Jesus might have raised from the dead. That Lazarus should be raised is no peculiar favor to him; for after once having died in peace, who would ever wish to return to this life in sin? but it was to glorify God, i.e. to exhibit that power of God which is also able to abolish death. This is what must be shown in order that both psychically and physically salvation shall be fully revealed. Thus only does *hope* receive its indispensable support. And in this way also by these *signs* is regeneration immediately bound into one whole with the palingenesis of the body and of the cosmos as object of faith. What Paul writes of the experiences in the wilderness: "All these things happened unto them by way of example; and they were written for our admonition" (1 Cor. x. 11), is true of all this kind of miracles, of which with equal authority we may say: "Now all these things happened by way of example; and they were written for our admonition."

The destructive and rebuking miracles are entirely in line with this. With the parousia belongs *the judgment*. The *misery*, which as the result of sin now weighs us down, is yet by no means the consummation of the ruin. If now that same power of God, by which the palingenesis of soul, body and of cosmos shall hereafter be established, will simultaneously, and as result of the judgment, bring about the destruction as well of soul, body and cosmos in hell, then it follows that the *signs* of salvation must run parallel with the *signs* of the destruction, which merely form the shadow alongside of the light.

If both these kinds of miracles, however strongly contrasted with each other, bear one and the same character at heart, it is entirely different with the real miracles, which do not take place as ensamples (τυπικῶς) but invade the world of reality. Only think of the birth of Isaac, of the birth of Christ, of his resurrection, of the outpouring of the Holy Spirit, etc. The motive of these miracles, which form an entire class by themselves, lies elsewhere, even in this, that the re-creation of our race could not be wrought simply by the individual regeneration and illumination of the several elect, but must take place in the centrum of the organism of humanity. And since this organism in its centrum also does not exist psychically only, but at the same time physically, the re-creation of this centrum could not be effected, except by the working being both psychical and physical, which is most vividly felt in the mystery of the incarnation. The incarnation is the centrum of this entire central action, and all miracles which belong to this category tend to inaugurate this incarnation, or are immediate results of it, like the resurrection. All clearness in our view of the miracles must be lost, if one neglects to distinguish between this category of the real-central miracles and the category of the typical miracles in the periphery; or if it be lost from sight, that both these real as well as these typical miracles stand in immediate connection with the all-embracing miracle that shall sometime make an end of this existing order of things.

If, now, it is asked to what category inspiration belongs, it is evident at once that inspiration bears no typical, but a real, character, and belongs not to the periphery but to the centrum. Itself psychical by nature, it *must*, meanwhile, reveal its working in the physical domain as well: (1) because the persons whom it chose as its instruments existed physically also; (2) because it sought its physical crystallization in the Scripture; and (3) because its content embraced the physical also, and, therefore, often could not do the manifestation. Nevertheless the psychical remains its fundamental tone, and as the incarnation brought life into the centrum of human *being*, inspiration brings the knowledge of God into human *knowledge*, i.e. into the central consciousness of our human race. From this special principium in God the saving power is extended centrally to our race, both by the ways of *being* and of *thought*, by incarnation and inspiration.

From this it appears that *formally* the miracle bears the characteristic of proceeding forth from the *special*, and *not* from the natural principium, in God. The miracle is no isolated fact, but a mighty movement of life, which, whether really or typically or, perhaps, in the parousia teleologically, goes out from God into this cosmos, groaning under sin and the curse; and that centrally as well as peripherally, in order organically to recreate that cosmos and to lead it upward to its final consummation. Are we now justified in saying that miracle antagonizes nature, violates natural law, or transcends nature? We take it, that all these representations are deistic and take no account of the ethical element. If you take the cosmos as a product wrought by God, which henceforth stands outside of Him, has become disordered, and now is being restored by Him from without, with such a mechanical-deistical representation you must make mention of something that is *against* or *above* nature; but at the penalty of never understanding miracle. This is the way the watchmaker does, who makes the watch and winds it, and, when it is out of order, repairs it with his instruments; but such is not the method pursued in the *re-creation*. God does not stand deistically over against the world, but by immanent power He bears and holds it in existence. That which you call natural power or natural law is nothing but the *immanent* power of God and the *will* of God immanently upholding this power, while both of these depend upon His transcendent counsel. It will not do, therefore, to represent it as though the world once created miscarried against the expectation of God, and as though, after that, God were bent upon the invention of means by which to make good the loss He had suffered. He who reasons like this is no theologian; i.e. he does not go to work theologically, but starts out from the human representation, viz. that as we are accustomed to manufacture something, and after we see it fail try to repair it, so he carries this representation over upon God. And so you derive the archetype from man and make God's doing ectypal; and this is not justifiable in any circumstance, since thereby you deny the creatorship in God. Our Reformed theologians, therefore, have always placed the counsel of God in the foreground, and from the same counsel from which the re-creation was to dawn they have explained the issue of creation itself. Even the infra-lapsarian Reformed theologians readily acknowledged that the re-creation existed ideally, i.e. already completely in the counsel of God, before the creation itself took place. What they called the appointment of a Mediator (constitutio mediatoris) preceded the first actual revelation of sin. Hence there is no twofold counsel, so that on the one hand the decree of creation stands by itself, to which, at a later period, the decree of salvation is mechanically added; but in the deepest root of the consciousness of God both are one. Interpreted to our human consciousness, this means to say, that the creation took place in such a way, that in itself it carried the possibility of re-creation; or, to state it more concretely still, man is not first created as a unity that cannot be broken, then by sin and death disjointed into parts of soul and corpse, and now, by an act of power mechanically applied from without, restored to unity; but in the creation of man itself lay both the possibility of this break and the possibility of the reunion of our nature. Without sin, soul and body would never have been disjoined by death; yet in the creation of man in two parts (dichotomy) lay the possibility of this breach. But, in like manner, if our body had merely a mechanical use in actuality, and did not develop organically from a potentia or germ, reunion of what was once torn apart would have been impossible. Just because, in the creation, this potential-organical was characteristic of our body, the redemption also of the body is possible and its reunion with the separated soul.

Thus one needs merely to return to the counsel of God, which lies back of creation and re-creation, and embraces both in unity, in order once for all to escape from the mechanical representation of a Divine interference in an independently existing nature. Sin and misery will, without doubt, continue to bear the character of a disturbance, and consequently all re-creation the character of providence and restoration, but both creation and re-creation flow forth from the selfsame counsel of God. This is most clearly apparent from the fact, that re-creation is by no means merely the healing of the breach or the repairing of what was broken and disturbed. Spiritually, regeneration does by no means restore the sinner to the state of original righteousness (justitia originalis). He who has been regenerated stands both *lower,* so far as he still carries the tendrils of sin inwoven in his heart, and *higher,* so far as potentially he can no more fall. Likewise physically, the resurrection of our body does by no means return to us an Adamic body, but a glorified body. Neither will the parousia bring back to us the old paradise, but a new earth under a new heaven. Hence the matter stands thus, that in the counsel of God there were two ways marked out, by which to lead soul, body and world to their organic consummation in the state of glory: one *apart* from sin, by gradual development, and the other, *through* sin, by a potentially absolute re-creation; and that, furthe.more, in creation everything was disposed to both these possibilities. If *nature* is taken in its concrete appearance, it is no longer what it was in the creation, but its ordinance is disturbed; and if this disturbed ordinance is accepted as its real and permanent one, then indeed, its re-creation, *in* us as well as *about* us, must appear to us as a violence brought upon it, for the sake of destroying the violence which we inflicted upon it by sin. If, on the other hand, you take nature as it appears in creation itself, and with its foundations lies in the counsel of God, then its original ordinance demands that this disturbance be reacted against, and it be brought to realize its end ($\tau\acute{\epsilon}\lambda o\varsigma$) and for this purpose the action goes out from the selfsame counsel of God, from which its ordinance came forth. In God and in His counsel there is but one principium, and if we distinguish between a special principium or one of grace, which presently works in upon the natural principium, we only do this in view of the twofold providence, which must have been given, in the one decree of creation, just because the cosmos was ethically founded. That the working of these two principia form a twofold sphere for our consciousness, cannot be avoided, because the higher consciousness, which reduces both to unity, will only be our portion in the state of glory. This antithesis, however, is not present with God for a moment. He indeed works all miracles from the deeper lying powers, which were fundamental to the creation itself, without at a single point placing a second creation by the side of the first. Wherever the Scripture speaks of a *renewal,* it is never meant that a new *power* should originate, or a new *state of being* should arise, but simply that a new shoot springs from the root of creation itself, that of this new shoot a graft is entered upon the old tree, and that in this way the entire plant is renewed and completed. Creation and re-creation, nature and grace, separate, so far as the concrete appearance in the practical application is concerned, but both in the counsel of God and in the potentialities of being they have one root. The miracle, therefore, in its concrete form is not from nature, but from the root from which nature sprang. It is not mechanically added to nature, but is organically united to it. This is the reason why, after the parousia, all action of the principium of grace flows back into the natural principium, brings this to its consummation, and thus, as such, itself disappears.

Inspiration According to the Self-Testimony of the Scripture

The naive catechetical method of proving the inspiration of the Holy Scripture from 2 Tim. iii. 16 or 2 Pet. i. 21, cannot be laid to the charge of our Reformed theologians. They did not hesitate to expose the inconclusiveness of such circle-reasoning. They appeal indeed to this and similar utterances, when it concerned the question, what interpretation of inspiration the Holy Scripture itself gives us. And that was right. As the botanist cannot learn to know the nature of life of the plant except from the plant itself, the theologian also has no other way at command, by which to learn to understand the nature of inspiration, except the interrogating of the Scripture itself. Meanwhile, there is this difference between a plant and the Scripture, that the plant does *not* speak concerning itself, and the Scripture *does.* In the Scripture dominates a *conscious* life. In the Scripture the Scripture itself is spoken about. Hence, two ways present themselves to us by which to obtain an insight into the matter: (1) that we, as with every other object which one investigates, watch for ourselves, where in the Scripture the track of inspiration becomes visible; but likewise (2) that we interrogate those, who in the Scripture declare themselves concerning the Scripture. And, of course, we must begin with the latter. Inspiration is a specific phenomenon, strange to us, but which was not strange to those holy persons, called of God, who were themselves its organs. From them, in the first place, we must learn what they taught concerning inspiration. In them the spirit, which animates the entire Scripture, consciously expresses itself. Not with equal clearness in all. Here also we find a gradual difference. In the absolute sense it can be said of the Christ only, that the self-consciousness of the Scripture expressed itself completely in Him. When Christ was on earth the entire Scripture of the Old Testament was already in existence; which renders it of the utmost importance to us to know what character Jesus attributed to the inspiration of the Old Covenant. If it appears that Christ attributed absolute authority to the Old Covenant, as an organic whole, then the matter is settled for every one who worships Him as his Lord and his God, and confesses that He *can* not err. This proof, however, from the nature of the case, is without force to him who does not thus believe in his Savior, and for him there *is* no demonstration possible. He who stands outside of the palingenesis cannot entertain any other demonstration but that which is derived from nature and reason in their actual form; and how would you ever be able from these to reach your conclusions concerning the reality of that which does not pretend to spring either from nature or from reason? Hence they only, who stand in conscious life-contact with the life-sphere of Christ can accept the force of demonstration, which lies in the testimony concerning the Scripture by Jesus, as its highest organ. Even then, however, it must be clearly held in view, that the reports of the Gospels concerning what Jesus said about the Old Testament, appear at this point of our argument as *reports* only, and not as testimony already authenticated. The value to be attached to this tradition concerning the utterances of Jesus, springs (while taken as yet outside of faith in inspiration) not from the bare communication of these utterances, but (1) from their multiformity; (2) from the stamp of originality which these utterances bear; (3) from their being interwoven with the events described; and (4) from their agreement with the utterances of Jesus' disciples, whose epistles have come to us. If such reports of Jesus' ideas about the Scripture were very rare, if they appeared for their own purposes only, or if it was their aim to formulate a certain theory of inspiration, then (always reckoning without faith in the Scriptures) they would not possess such a historic value to us; but since there is no trace of such a design, and no insertion of a system is thought of, and only the use is shown which Jesus made of the Scripture amid the most varied circumstances and with all sorts of applications, from these reports it is historically certain, for him also who does not reckon with inspiration, that Jesus judged the Scripture thus, and not otherwise.

This value, moreover, rises in importance by the fact, that that which Jesus appears to have thought about the Old Testament, agrees with the conception which, before his appearing, was prevalent concerning the Old Covenant. He introduces no new way of viewing it, but seals the conception that was current, and characterizes himself only by the original, i.e. not borrowed, application of the dominant manner of view. It was but natural, therefore, that the theory of accommodation became current a century ago, and that on the ground of these accommodations all value was disputed to these utterances of Jesus. But by accepting the possibility of accommodation with Christ, He *eo ipso* is already forsaken as *the* Christ; which is the more apparent, when one hears how the inspiration-theory, which was current at the time and which still forms an essential part of the confession of *all* Christian Churches, was execrated as being unworthy of God, antagonistic to the character of the *spiritual,* and as barren and mechanical. At present, therefore, the opponents of this theory themselves acknowledge that they would do violence to their consciences and commit sin, if for the sake of the masses they carried themselves as though they put faith in this theory. This they deem themselves not warranted in doing. How, then, will you accept such a *sinful* accommodation of what is unworthy of God and in conflict with the character of *spiritual* life, in Him whom you worship as the incarnate Word? The accommodation-theory, still tenable in days when the diverging theologians themselves accommodated, and considered it no *evil* but *duty,* became untenable with the Christ from the moment when all such accommodation was rejected as *moral weakness.* He who perseveres, nevertheless, in his application of this theory to what Jesus said concerning the Scripture, attacks not the Scripture, but the Deity of Jesus and even His moral character. Even in the pretence that Jesus accommodated in *good faith,* while this would be *bad faith* for us, does not help matters. If Jesus did *not* know that the conception which He accepted was untrue, there was no accommodation; if Jesus did know this, then all such accommodation, *in spite of better knowledge,* was sin also in Him.

To come to the point, we emphasize in the first place, that Jesus looked upon the several writings of the Old Testament as forming *one organic whole.* To him they did not constitute a collection of products of Hebrew literature, but He valued them as a holy unity of a peculiar sort.

For this we refer in the first place to John x. 34, 35: *the Scripture cannot be broken.* This utterance is of threefold importance. First, the whole Old Testament, from which Psalm lxxxii. 6 is here quoted, is entitled by the singular $\gamma\rho\alpha\phi\acute{\eta}$, by the article $\acute{\eta}$ is indicated as a whole of a peculiar sort, and to this whole an absolute character is attributed by the "cannot be broken." Secondly, it is out of the question that by $\acute{\eta}$ $\gamma\rho\alpha\phi\acute{\eta}$ can have been meant not Scripture, but spiritual revelation, because the "word of God" in what immediately precedes is clearly distinguished from the $\gamma\rho\alpha\phi\acute{\eta}$. And thirdly, it is impossible that $\gamma\rho\alpha\phi\acute{\eta}$ should indicate the quotation in hand, and not the Old Testament, since a conclusion *a generali ad particulare* follows, and just in this form: The Scripture cannot be broken; this saying from Psalm lxxxii. 6 occurs in the Scripture; hence Psalm lxxxii. 6 also cannot be broken. Which, moreover, is confirmed by the expression "in your Law." He who quotes from the Psalms, and then declares that it is found in the Law, shows that he uses the name *Law* for the entire Old Testament, and thus views this Testament as one organic whole.

This unity appears likewise from Matt. xxi. 42, where Jesus asks: "Did ye never read in the Scriptures?" and then quotes Psalm cxviii. 22, 23. No citation, therefore, from two different books, but a citation from one book, that of the Psalms, even two verses from the same Psalm. This shows that "the Scriptures" here does not refer to the Psalms, but to the whole Old Testament, in which the Psalms occur, and likewise that Jesus comprehends this Old Testament under the name of $\gamma\rho\alpha\phi\alpha\acute{\iota}$ as a unity, and by the article $\alpha\acute{\iota}$ isolates it from all other $\gamma\rho\alpha\phi\alpha\acute{\iota}$. The same we find in Matt. xxii. 29, in the words: "Ye do err, not knowing the Scriptures, nor the power of God." Here, also, $\alpha\acute{\iota}$ $\gamma\rho\alpha\phi\alpha\acute{\iota}$ appears absolutely as the designation of the entire Holy Scripture then in existence. Keeping no count with those Scriptures is indicated as the cause of their erring, and the Scripture, i.e. the Old Testament, is here coordinated with "the power of God." In like manner we read in Matt. xxvi. 54: "How then should the Scriptures be fulfilled, that thus it must be?" Here also the Scriptures of the Old Testament appear as one whole, which is called $\alpha\acute{\iota}$ $\gamma\rho\alpha\phi\alpha\acute{\iota}$, and it is a Scripture, such as offers the program of what was to come, and gives that program with such authority, that the fulfilment of it *could* not fail. This program was not contained in this word or that, but in the whole Scripture, which here appears as organically one. Compare with this the similar utterance in Mark xiv. 49: "But this is done that the Scriptures might be fulfilled." That at another time Jesus indicated the same unity by *the law,* appears from John x. 34, and appears likewise from John xv. 25, where the Lord quotes from Psalms xxxv. and lxix., and declares concerning this, that that is written "in their law." And if proof is called for, that Jesus viewed this unit not only as organically one, but represented to Himself the groups also in this unit as organically related, then look in John vi. 45, where He quotes from Isaiah liv. and from Jeremiah xxxi., and affirms, not that this occurs as such in Isaiah and Jeremiah, but *in the prophets* This subdivision also of the Scripture, which is called ' the prophets,' is thus indicated by the article as one organic whole, which as such offers us the program of the future.

In the second place, it appears that Jesus recognized of the Scriptures of the Old Testament in the sense of a single whole of authoritative writing, that a word, or a fragment of it was authoritative, and that as γραφή, or γεγραμμένον, or γέγραπται it possessed that high condition, that men could make their appeal to it. The use of these expressions does not point to a *citation* but to an *authority* in the sense in which Pilate exclaimed: "What I have written I have written," which he did not say as author but as governor, clothed with discretionary authority. Neither the γέγραπται nor the γεγραμμένον can be thought without a subject from whom it goes forth, and this subject must have authority to determine something, simply because he *writes.* If now γέγραπται, as in this instance, is used in an entirely absolute sense, and without the least indication of this subject, it implies that this subject is the *absolute* subject in that circle. In the state γέγραπται expresses that something is *law;* and in the spiritual domain γέγραπται indicates that here God speaks, prophesies, or commands. Since in this sense Jesus again and again uses all sorts of utterances from the Old Testament as decisive arguments in His reasoning, it appears that Jesus viewed the Old Testament as having gone forth from this absolute subject, and therefore as being of imperial authority. That Jesus really uses the Scripture of the Old Testament in this way, as "judge of the cause" (iudex litis) appears, for instance, from Mark xii. 10: "And have ye not read even this Scripture?" and then there follows a citation from Psalm cxviii. By Scripture here the Old Testament is not meant; but to this definite utterance from Psalm cxviii. 23 the character is attributed of being a Scripture. Likewise in Luke iv. 21, where, after having read a portion from Isaiah lxi., He said to the people in the synagogue at Nazareth, "To-day hath this Scripture been fulfilled in your ears," by Scripture He does not refer to the Book, but to this particular utterance, and honors this utterance itself as γραφή.Whether, in John vii. 38, γραφή refers to the entire Scripture or to a given text, cannot be determined; but we meet with a similar use of Scripture in John xiii. 18, where, in view of the coming betrayal by Judas, Jesus says: "That the Scripture may be fulfilled," and then adds: "He that eateth my bread lifted up his heel against me." Even though it does not read here ἡ γραφὴ αὕτη, it is very clear that here again the utterance itself is called γραφή, otherwise it would need to read, ἡ γραφὴ ἥτις λέγει. Then γραφή would refer to the Scripture; but not now; now it must refer to the text quoted. Of γέγραπται or of γεγραμμένον this needs no separate proof, since these expressions admit of no doubt. When, in Matt. iv. 4 and the following verses, Jesus places each time His "it is written" over against the temptation, it implies of itself that Jesus not merely quotes, but appeals to an authority which puts an end to all contradiction. Without this supposition the appeal to Deut. viii. 3, etc., has no meaning. When such an appeal is introduced, not by saying: *Thus spake Moses,* but by the formula *"It is written,"* it admits no other interpretation than that, according to the judgment of Jesus, this word derived its Divine authority from the fact *that it is written;* in the same way in which an article of law has authority among us, *because it is in the law.* To attribute a weaker significance to this is simply *il*logical and subverts the truth. Even though one may refuse to attribute such an authority to the Old Testament Scripture, it may never be asserted that Jesus did *not* attribute this to them; at least so long as it is not affirmed that none of these utterances of Jesus are original with Him; which even the most stringent criticism has not as yet asserted.

But Jesus goes farther. It is not simply that He attributes such an authority to this and other utterances of the Old Testament, but in these utterances He attributes that authority even *to single words.* This we learn from His argument with the Sadducees concerning the resurrection from the dead, Matt. xxii. 32. From the fact that God, centuries after the death of the patriarchs, still reveals Himself as the God of Abraham,

Isaac, and Jacob, Jesus concludes that these three patriarchs were still in existence, since God could not call Himself *their God* if they were no more alive. This demonstration would have no ground if by a little addition or modification in the construction, "I am the God of thy father," were intended in the preterite. Then God would have *been* their God. This expression, in its very form, is nevertheless so authoritative for Jesus, that from this form of the saying He concludes the resurrection of the dead. Jesus extends this authority even to a letter, when, in Luke xvi. 17, He says that it is easier for heaven and earth to pass away, than for *one tittle of the law to fail;* which, as appears from the preceding verse, does not refer to the ten commandments, nor even to the laws adduced, but to the law and the prophets, i.e. to the entire Scripture. This *tittle,* which referred to the apostrophized *iod,* was the smallest letter in the apographa, and the saying that even no *tittle* shall fail, vindicates the authority even to the letter. In Matt. xxii. 41, the strength of Jesus' argument hangs on the single word *Lord.* "The Lord said *unto my Lord;*" yea, even more precisely, on the single *iod.* The emphasis falls on the "*my* Lord." In John x. 35 the entire argument falls to the ground, except the one word "gods" have absolute authority. In the same way it can be shown, in a number of Jesus' arguments from the Scripture, that in the main they do not rest upon the general contents, but often upon a single word or a single letter. The theory therefore of a general *tendency* in the spiritual domain, which in the Old Testament should merely have an *advisory* authority, finds no support in Jesus.

The same result is reached when notice is taken of Jesus' judgment concerning the *contents* of Old Testament Scripture. Without the spur of any necessity, entirely voluntarily, in Luke xvi. 29 Jesus puts the words upon Abraham's lips to the rich man: "They have Moses and the prophets; let them hear them." This is said in answer to the prayer that some one might be sent to earth in the name of God to proclaim the will of God. This is denied by the remark, that in the earth they already are in possession of a Divine authority, even the Old Testament. The "hear them" here has the same significance as the "hear him" at the baptism of Jesus; it means, to subject oneself to Divine authority. Jesus appears to attribute entirely the same character to the content of the Old Testament as often as He refers to the fact that the Scripture "must be fulfilled," and "cannot be broken." All that men have thought out or invented can be corrected by the result, can be seen from the outcome to have been mistakenly surmised, and is therefore susceptible to *being broken.* The only thing not susceptible to this is the program God Himself has given, and given in a definite form. The *need,* the *must,* which Jesus again and again applies to His passion, and applies to particulars, is only in place with the supposition of such a program for His passion given by God. Not to see this is to be *unwise,* and shows that one is "slow of heart to believe," Luke xxiv. 25. It needs scarcely a reminder that this *need of fulfilment* is by no means exhausted in a general sense, as though there were merely a certain necessity and, in a certain sense, a typical parallelism between that which befell the faithful of the past and of the present, but that Jesus applies His rule with equal decision to that which is apparently accidental. Thus in Luke xxii. 37, when He says: "I say unto you, that this which is written must be fulfilled in me, And he was reckoned with transgressors: for that which concerneth me hath fulfilment," here, indeed, Jesus points to a concrete and very special $\gamma \epsilon \gamma \rho \alpha \mu \mu \acute{\epsilon} \nu o \nu$, which except in a very rare instance did not intensify the bitterness of the martyr's death. The simultaneous crucifixion with Jesus of two malefactors lacks, therefore, all inward necessity. And yet of this very definite $\gamma \epsilon \gamma \rho \alpha \mu \mu \acute{\epsilon} \nu o \nu$ Jesus purposely declares that it *must* be fulfilled in Him, and as a motive of thought He adds, that what has been prophesied concerning Him cannot rest before it has accomplished its end. In Matt. xxvi. 54 Jesus declares that He does not exercise His omnipotence, nor invoke the legions of angels to save Him from His passion, since the prophecy of the Old Testament *forbids* Him doing this. Beyond all doubt it is certain that the prophetic program *must* be carried out, and in case He were to oppose it, "how then should the Scriptures be fulfilled, that thus it must be?" Thus Jesus acknowledges that in prophecy there lies before us a copy of the counsel of God concerning Him, and for this reason the realization of this program could not remain wanting. Jesus expresses this same thought even more strongly in John xiii. 18, where He characterizes the betrayal by Judas not only as unavoidable that the Scripture may be fulfilled, that he who ate bread with Him should lift up his heel against Him, but even adds: "From henceforth I tell you before it come to pass, that, when it is come to pass, ye may believe that I am he," and thus imposed upon them His insight, that this prophecy referred to Him, as Divine authority.

This, however, may not be taken as though in the Old Testament Jesus had merely seen a mosaic from which He took a separate Scripture according to the occasion. On the contrary, the Old Testament is one whole to Him, which as a whole refers to Him. "Ye search the Scriptures," said He (John 5:39) to the Scribes, "because ye think that in them ye have eternal life; *and they are they which bear witness of me.*" As a whole the Scripture points thus concentrically to Him. Hence His citation of two utterances of the Old Testament in one dictum, as for instance in Matt. ix. 13, from Hosea vi. 6 and from Micah vi. 8; which is only explicable from the point of view that back of the secondary authors (auctorés secundarii) of each book you recognize one first author (auctor primarius), in whose plan and utterance of thought lies the organic unity of the several Scriptures. The secondary author is sometimes named, but only with the quotations of those utterances which did not come forth *from* them, but which were directed *to* them, as for instance in Matt. xiii. 14, where we read: "And unto them is fulfilled the prophecy of Isaiah," and then follows Isaiah vi. 9, "concerning those who seeing do not perceive," which was spoken by God *to* Isaiah in the vision of his call. We find the same in Matt. xv. 7, 8, where Jesus says: "Ye hypocrites, well did Isaiah prophecy of you, saying: This people honoreth me with their lips, etc.," in which the "Me" itself indicates that Isaiah did not speak these words, but God. That this conception embraced not merely the prophetical, but likewise the historical, books appears from the constant reference to what occurs in the Old Testament concerning Noah, Abel, Abraham, Sodom, Lot, the queen of Sheba, Solomon, Jonah, etc., all of which are historic references which show that the reality of these events was a certainty to Jesus, even as they were a certainty to those to whom He spake. If it be true, therefore, that in no given instance Jesus utters an express declaration concerning inspiration, it appears sufficiently clearly, that He considered the Scriptures of the Old Covenant to be the result of a Divine act of revelation, the original and real subject of which was "God" or "the Spirit."

But there is more; it can be shown that Jesus Himself has given utterance to *the idea of inspiration,* and, on the other hand, that He, by no single word, has opposed the ideas which at that time existed concerning inspiration. The idea of inspiration is, that God by His Spirit enters into the spirit of man, and introduces into his spirit, i.e. into his consciousness, a concrete thought, which this man could not derive from himself nor from other men. This very idea we find even put antithetically, in Matt. xvi. 17, where Jesus says to Peter that his confession of Him as the Christ, the Son of the living God, is no product of what he himself has thought or other people had whispered in his ear; flesh and blood taken here as the human, in antithesis to God, have *not* imparted this knowledge to him; it has come to him by *revelation,* even from *the Father who is in heaven.* That this idea of inspiration did not limit itself to the quickening of a certain disposition or perception, but in the conception of Jesus implied also the inspiration of conscious thoughts, appears sufficiently clearly from Luke xii. 12, where Jesus says: "For the Holy Spirit shall teach you in that very hour what ye ought to say." This does not prove that Jesus explains the Old Testament to have originated in this same way, but it shows that there was nothing strange to Jesus in the idea of such an inspiration, that He considered it by no means unworthy of God, and that He raised its reality above all doubt. And if we connect with this the fact, that the contemporaries of Jesus explained the Scriptures of the Old Covenant from such an inspiration, and that Jesus nowhere contradicted this representation, but rather confirmed it by His use of the Old Testament, then no one has the right to combat, by an appeal to Jesus, such an inspiration of the Old Testament as one less worthy of God. From the above it rather appears that Jesus viewed the Old Testament in the same way as His contemporaries and as the Christian Church has done throughout all ages in all its official confessions, and views it to this day. By which we do not mean to say that the later outworking of this conception may not become open to severe criticism, but from it, nevertheless, the result may and must be drawn that to appeal to the Old Testament as to a decisive Divine authority, as is still done this day by those who hold fast to the Scripture, finds not merely a support in the example of Jesus, but became prevalent in the Christian Churches by His example and upon the authority of His name, and by His example is ever yet maintained in the face of all dissolving criticism; not as the result of scientific investigation, but as the fruit of a higher inworking in the spiritual consciousness.

The objection to this, derived from Matt. v. 21-45, scarcely needs a refutation. In this pericope, the Lord declares very emphatically that the ancients have said thus and so, and that He puts *His sayings* over against these. But this does not form an antithesis between Jesus and the Old Testament; on the contrary by His *accurate* exegesis He but maintains the Old Testament over against the *false* exegeses of the Sanhedrin of His day. In this connection Jesus speaks nowhere of a *Scripture,* but of an oral tradition, and of sayings; and in this oral tradition of the ancients the commandment had either been limited to its letter, or weakened by addition, or falsified by an incorrect antithesis, and what was a Divine dispensation had been made to be a fixed rule. Against this Jesus ranges Himself with the *spiritual* interpretation of the law. That a man must not look upon a woman to desire her was the simple application of the tenth commandment to the seventh, in connection with Job xxxi. 1 and Psalm cxix. 37. Likewise, the love of an enemy is not put by Jesus as something new above or against the Old Testament, but the narrow and pregnant meaning given by the Sanhedrin to the expression *neighbor* is combated by Jesus in the spirit of Proverbs xxv. 21. It is, indeed, entirely inconceivable how the absurd idea that Jesus here placed Himself in opposition to the Old Testament, could be entertained for a single moment, by those who have studied the connection. Just before this pericope, in this same address of our Lord, it is said that he who had broken one of these least commandments stood guilty; and that He was come, not to destroy the Scripture of the Old Covenant, but to fulfil these by "His doctrines, life and passion." The warning, *not* to think that Jesus draws the sword against the Old Testament, is expressly added here.

In closing let it be noted, that for three years Jesus had been most narrowly watched by the Sanhedrin, and every word He spoke had been carefully sifted. At that time there were two holy things in Israel: their Scripture and their temple. Of these two Jesus gave up the temple, of which He said that not one stone would be left upon the other; while, on the contrary, of the Scripture He declared, that no jot or tittle of it shall pass till all shall be fulfiled. Concerning His speech against the temple. Of these two Jesus gave Him, though the form of the charge was unjust. If He had uttered a single word against the Scripture of the Old Testament, He would certainly have been similarly accused. With reference to this, however, you observe no charge, not even a weak reproach, and from this it may be inferred, that in this matter of the Scripture His enemies had no fault to find with Him.

The Testimony of the Apostles

The self-testimony of the Scripture lies so much concentrically in Jesus, that only in connection with His judgment has the testimony of the apostles any real value. His disciples were His followers. If with reference to the Old Testament Jesus had paid homage to a method of viewing it which diverged from the then current one, the disciples would not have followed the common conception, but the diverging conception of Jesus. If, from their ministry, it appears that they themselves adhered to the current conception, it may be inferred from this that they were at no time warned against it by Jesus, that He had rather confirmed it, and Himself had not departed from it. The testimony of the apostles, therefore, has this value, that it throws further light upon Jesus' own conception, and confirms the result of the former section.

Of the apostles, also, it is not difficult to show that they were familiar with the idea of inspiration and that they held it. This appears most strongly from Acts ii. 4: "And they were all filled with the Holy Spirit, and began to speak with other tongues, as the Spirit gave them utterance." Now ἀποφθέγγεσθαι is to utter an audible sound. Without solving the question whether by "other tongues" languages of other peoples are to be understood, or sounds of an entirely peculiar sort, in either case the apostles brought forth sounds which were not produced from their own consciousness, but were the product of an action which went out upon them from the Holy Ghost. This is inspiration in the fullest sense of the word. Thus we read in Acts vii. 29: "And the Spirit said unto Philip, Go near, and join thyself to this chariot." It does not say that this thought arose in him, but that a speaking took place; and where it is our point to know the conception which was current in the apostolic circle, we must, of course, be careful to note their way of expressing themselves. Of the Jews, it is said in Rom. iii. 2, "That they were entrusted with the oracles of God." Πιστευθῆναι implies that to you, as ruler, or manager, or steward, something is committed which does not belong to you, has not been produced by you, but is the property of another subject and over which you are placed in a position of responsibility. Of the grain which he himself has raised, the farmer cannot say that it is committed to him; this is only true of the grain which was raised by another, and is stored in his barn. Hence, the apostolic representation is not that thoughts, but that "utterances" (λόγια) were given to them for safe-keeping and care, which were not original with themselves, but had another as subject, author and owner. And that other subject is named, for they are called "the oracles of God." In 1 Cor. vii. 40, after having given a rule for matrimony, the apostle says, "and I think that I also have the Spirit of God." There is, therefore, no question here of a moral excellence, nor yet of more holiness, but of an insight into the will of God. God alone can decide the question of marriage; the only question for us is to know the will of God, and, by his statement, Paul claims to possess that knowledge, on the ground that he, as well as the writers of the Old Testament and other apostles, had received the Holy Ghost. That this exegesis is correct, appears from 1 Thess. iv. 9; cf. verse 2. In verse 2, he had said: "For ye know *what charges* we gave you," and after an instruction in the principles of these charges, he follows it up with these words, in verse 8: "Therefore he that rejecteth, rejecteth not man, but God, who giveth his Holy Spirit unto you." Thus he assumes that his ordinances are the clear expression of God's will; that for this reason they are divinely authoritative; and he explains this from the fact that a work of the Holy Spirit has taken place in them or on behalf of the church. Of Moses, it is written in Heb. viii. 5, that he was admonished of God when he was about to make the tabernacle: "See that thou make all things according to the pattern that was shewed thee in the mount." To him, therefore, had come an utterance from the *oracle,* for such is the meaning of κεχρημάτισται, according to the conception which was then current in the apostolic circle; something that did not come up from himself, but was given him from without; it referred to a very concrete affair, to wit: that the plan for the tabernacle was not to be designed by himself, but had been brought to him from outside. In James v. 10, we read that the prophets "spake in the name of the Lord,"which implies that what was spoken by them was not binding in virtue of the authority of their own person or insight, but was spoken by them in the name of Christ Himself; which either assumes a fanatical presumption, or, since the apostle does *not* mean this, can only be explained by the idea of inspiration. In Rev. xxii. 17-20, it is said that Christ bears witness to that which, by exclusively Divine authority, *is written* in the Apocalypse (to the words of the prophecy of this book), so that adding to or taking away from the things written in this book involves the penalty of eternal loss. According to 1 Pet. i. 12, the preaching of the apostles is done "by the Holy

Ghost sent forth from heaven": even as it was "the Spirit of Christ" who in the prophets did signify beforehand (προμαρτυρόμενον). Even though the ἐν πνεύματι point to a different modality from the προμαρτυρόμενον, both expressions, nevertheless, in their connection refer to one and the same idea of inspiration, which receives its more general description in 2 Pet. i. 21, by the authentic declaration that prophecy did not find its origin in the "will" of the prophets themselves, but in the fact, that they, as "men of God" spoke that which entered into their consciousness while "they were being moved by the Holy Ghost;" a representation which was evidently applied by them, even though in modified form, to the entire Scripture of the Old Testament, as appears from the "all Scripture is theopneustic," in 2 Tim. iii. 16. The fact, therefore, that the apostles held the idea of inspiration, and applied it to the Old Testament, admits of no difference of opinion.

In the second place, it must also be noted that the apostles, also, did not look upon the Old Testament as a collection of literary documents, but as one codex, which was organically constructed and clothed with Divine authority. That unity lies already expressed in the πᾶσα γραφή of 2 Tim. iii. 16, which does not mean the *whole* Scripture but *every* Scripture, and hence does not emphasize the unity only, but simultaneously the *organic* unity. The same thought lies in 1 Pet. i. 12: "To whom it was revealed, that not unto themselves, but unto you, did they minister these things." First, all the prophets are here taken under one head, and to their collective labor the character is attributed, not of its being a work of their own, over which they have the right of disposal, but of its being a labor which they have performed with another purpose, which lay outside of them, and which was determined by God. According to Heb. i. 1, it is not human insight, but God Himself, which spake to the fathers when they were spoken to by the prophets, and however much this took place "by divers portions and in divers manners," it all belonged together, formed one whole, and together constituted God's testimony to the fathers. The apostolic manner of quoting confirms this. They also do not quote by the name of the author, but as γραφή and γέγραπται ·In Rom. iv. 17, proof is furnished by "as it is written"; in Rom. x. 11, the phrase, "for the Scripture says," is conclusive. By the words, "according as it is written," in Rom. xi. 8, all contradiction is cut off. This shows, indeed, that according to the apostolic representation, the entire Old Testament forms one whole, which is organically connected, and the content of which is authoritative, *because* it appears in this codex. Even the prayer of Elijah is quoted in Rom. xi. 2, as "What the Scripture saith," after which the answer of God to his prayer is mentioned as ὁ χρηματισμός (the Divine response), and thus distinguished from the excitement of his own spirit. Especially characteristic in this respect is the extensive quotation in Rom. iii. 10-18, which is referred to as one continuous argument, and yet is constructed from no less than six different chapters; viz. Ps. xiv. 1-3, Ps. v. 9, Ps. cxl. 3, Ps. x. 7, Isaiah lix. 7, and Ps. xxxvi. 1. These parts are introduced by a γέγραπται, "it is written," and explained by the "what things soever the law saith, it speaketh to them that are under the law." Γέγραπται as the perfect tense, especially in a quotation composed of so many parts, is even stronger that xvxvxv, because it is equivalent to what we call a law: "law enacted is sacred" (lex *lata*, lex *sancta* est) Γέγραπται implies not only that it occurs or is found in the Scripture, but that as an expression of truth it bears the Divine seal. In the same way, after a quotation from the Psalms and Isaiah, the "what things soever the law saith" convincingly indicates that no importance is attached to Isaiah nor to David, but simply to the fact that it occurs in the holy codex. In these quotations the apostles do not confine themselves for support to the authority of pericopes or extended passages, but base their argument equally well upon a single word from the Old Testament; one may almost say upon a single letter. In Gal. iii. 16, the entire argument rests upon the singular "seed"; if in the original one letter had been written differently, and the plural had appeared, the entire apostolic argument would have lost its force. The same you find in 1 Pet. iii. 5, 6, where the exhortation rests upon the fact that Sarah called her husband "lord." In the apostolic circle, no such quotations could have been made, if the conviction had not been prevalent that inspiration extended even to the word and to the form of the word; which connection between form and content, Paul also confirms for himself, when in 1 Cor. ii. 13, he declares: "Which things also we speak, not in the words which man's wisdom teaches, but which the Spirit teaches; comparing spiritual things with spiritual." In this statement, indeed, the "human" and the "pneumatic" cannot stand over against each other as the intellectual and the mystical. He also bears witness instrumentally through his *mind;* his speaking, also, is the expression of intelligence, mostly calculated to address the *understanding* rather than the emotions. The "pneumatica," therefore, cannot intend anything else but the fountain from which the impulse for his utterances proceeds, and that fountain, he says, does not lie in man, but in the Spirit, and thus in a power which affects him from without.

In the third place it must be conceded, that in the apostolic circle also the Old Testament was considered as the predestined *transcript* of God's counsel, of which the instrumental author has, often unconsciously, produced the record, and which, as being a higher origin, has Divine authority. This appears clearly in Acts ii. 24, 25, where Peter says: "It was not possible that He should be holden of death." And why does he deem this impossible? Because Jesus was the Son of God? Undoubtedly for this also; of this, however, Peter makes no mention, but states as the only reason that it was thus written in Ps. xvi.: "Neither wilt thou give thy Holy One to see corruption." Hence the "impossibility" rests upon the fact that the opposite to this was written in the Old Testament; an argument which suits only with the supposition that the Old Testament furnishes us with the program of what *must* happen according to God's counsel and will. To that counsel and to that foreknowledge of God he refers us definitely in what immediately precedes: "Him being delivered up by the determinate counsel and foreknowledge of God." Of a similar tendency is what we read in Acts i. 16, where Peter says: "It was needful that the Scripture should be fulfilled, which the Holy Ghost spake before by the mouth of David." The thought here quoted is not from David, but from the Holy Ghost, even though the Holy Ghost made use of *the mouth of David* by which to utter it, and because the Holy Ghost took this thought from the counsel of God, it *had* to be fulfilled. In Matt. xiii. 34, 35, the apostle Matthew inserts the observation, that Jesus *had* to speak in parables, "that it might be fulfilled which was spoken by the prophet." In a similar way the apostle John inserts his "that the Scripture might be fulfilled" in John xix. 24, and elsewhere. And all these expressions of "must needs be," "it is necessary," "was not possible," "that the Scripture might be fulfilled," etc., have no meaning unless it was believed in the apostolic circle as an undoubted fact, that the Old Testament presents us the Divine program of things to come, with such certainty as to render it entirely trustworthy. Hence there is no hesitancy in announcing God the Holy Spirit as the speaking subject in the Old Testament. Acts vii. 6, "And God spake on this wise"; Rom. ii. 4, "But what saith the answer of God unto him?" Heb. i. 6, "When he bringeth in the firstborn into the world, he saith"; Heb. i. 13, "But of which of the angels hath he said at any time"; Acts i. 16, "the Scripture. . . which the Holy Ghost spake before by the mouth of David"; Heb. x. 15, "And the Holy Ghost also beareth witness to us; for after he hath said . . . saith the Lord": expressions which are used not only when it concerns a saying of God (dictum Dei), but also when God is spoken of in the third person, as for instance Heb. iii. 7, "Wherefore, even as the Holy Ghost saith, To-day if ye shall hear his voice," or with the mention of facts, as in Heb. ix. 8, "the Holy Ghost this signifying, that the way into the holy place hath not yet been made manifest."

The stringing together of quotations from different books, such as appears in Acts i. 20, Rom. xi. 8, 26, xv. 9, 1 Tim. v. 18, etc., shows equally clearly, that in the estimation of the apostles the human authors fall entirely in the background. Such quoting is only conceivable and warranted by the supposition that all these sayings, however truly they have come to us by several writers, are actually from one and the same author; exactly in the same way in which one quotes from the works of the same writer or from the articles of the same lawgiver. That this was indeed the apostolic apprehension appears more clearly still from the fact, which they state: that the words of the Old Testament often contain more than the writers themselves understood. In Rom. iv. 23 it is said of the words from Gen. xv. 6, that "it was reckoned unto him for righteousness," did not refer to Abraham only, as the writer must have intended, but also to us. In Rom. xv. 3, Ps. lxix. 9 is quoted, and what David exclaimed in a Psalm, which cannot stand before the ethical judgment of many, is cited as coming from the Messianic subject; and yet this quotation furnishes the apostle the occasion for the general statement, "that whatsoever things were written aforetime were written for our learning, that through patience and through comfort of the Scriptures we might have hope." This, of course, could not have been the intention of the instrumental authors. David sang when his heart was full, Jeremiah prophesied when the fire burned in his bones. Thus this intention is thought of as in the "mind of the first author," and it is only by divine direction, that the Scriptures are thus predestined to realize their given purpose in the Church of all the ages. This is applied not only to moral and doctrinal *dicta*, but also to the historical parts. "Do ye not hear the Old Testament ($\tau\grave{o}\nu$ $\nu\acute{o}\mu o\nu$)?" Paul asks in Gal. iv. 22; "For it is written, that Abraham had two sons"; and of this he says: "Which things contain an allegory," i.e. a meaning was hidden in all this, which was neither foreseen nor intended by him who wrote these words. The same appears in Heb. v. 11, 12, where the exposition of the priesthood after the order of Melchizedek is introduced, an exposition in which numerous deductions are made from the common historic narrative, which were *not* intended by the writer of Genesis. The understanding of this deeper sense is called in verse 11 "hard of interpretation"; it does not lie at hand, and deeper insight only discovers it. And yet, this deeper insight is no play of magic with the word. One may readily acquire it if only one is not dull of hearing. If one is but mature, he is able of himself to enjoy this strong meat, for they "by reason of use have their senses exercised." It is therefore a mysterious meaning not included in it by the writer, but by the Holy Spirit, which now from behind is revealed by that same Holy Spirit to those who are perfect. A no less broadly prepared example of this is given in 1 Cor. x. 1-18, where a spiritual-typical significance is attached to the crossing of the Red Sea and to the events in the wilderness, which *could not* have been intended by the writer of the narrative. That meaning was beyond him, and directed itself from the mind of the primary author to us "upon whom the ends of the ages are come." Now only, because the antitypical has come, can the typical be understood.

It can scarcely be denied, therefore, that in the apostolic circle, the conviction was prevalent that, without controversy, the Old Testament had come into existence as a *sacred codex* by Divine inspiration, and must be viewed as clothed by Divine authority. This shows that Jesus, who knew this conviction, did not contradict it, but put His seal upon it in His intercourse with His disciples. The apostolic use of the Old Testament tends to give us a better knowledge of Jesus' judgment concerning this codex, and, so far as in Jesus the self-testimony of the Scripture expresses itself most clearly and correctly, to make us know how the Scripture itself desires us to esteem it. The different objections that have been raised against this apostolic use of the Old Testament, particularly upon the ground of Gal. iv. 21-24 and 1 Cor. x. 1-13, cannot here be examined. The question, indeed, *what* use the apostles have made of the Old Testament, is not critical but historic. The critical examination, therefore, of these objections is not in place in Encyclopedia, but in the disciplina canonica. One objection, however, may be considered here, because it really sheds light upon the use made by the apostles of the Holy Scripture of the Old Testament. Their quotations are by no means always a literal translation of the original. This would create no surprise if they had not understood Hebrew, but it does with a man like Paul, who was well versed in the original text. The fact that they wrote in Greek to Greek-speaking churches is, from the nature of the case, no sufficient explanation. This, no doubt, explains why as a rule they followed the Greek translation which they knew was in use among their readers, but states no ground for their own departure from the original, nor yet for their following of that translation in places where it was incorrect.

They who think that the writers of the apostolic circle wrote without assistance (suo Marte), can scarcely come to any other conclusion than that this mode of procedure was faulty and rested upon mistake, either voluntary or involuntary, but in no case pardonable. The matter assumes an entirely different aspect, however, when one starts out from the position that these writers themselves were inspired in a way analogous to the writers whose text they quoted. He who cites the language of another must quote literally, but a writer who quotes himself is bound to the actual content only, and not to the form of what he wrote, except in the face of a third party. If, therefore, it is the same Holy Spirit who spoke through the prophets and inspired the apostles, it is the same primary author (auctor primarius) who, by the apostles, *quotes himself,* and is therefore entirely justified in repeating his original meaning in application to the case for which the quotation is made, in a somewhat modified form, agreeably to the current translation. Suppose an oration you have delivered has been translated into English, and that you appear before an American audience which knows your position only from that English translation, will it not be natural, in so far as your original meaning comports with that translation, to quote from what your audience knows? Any one would; and to do so is logical. And, therefore, from this point of view, there is nothing strange in it that in the apostolic circle the *auctor primarius* quotes from his own words agreeably to the accepted translated text. No one else could do this but the *author himself,* since he is both authorized and competent to guard against false interpretations of his original meaning.

The citation from Psalm xl. 6 in Heb. x. 5 may still further explain this. The translation which is here given is undoubtedly borrowed from the LXX., and it is equally certain that the translation of the LXX. is faulty and corrupted in the copies, either by the change of ὠτία, or, as others assert, by that of στόμα into σῶμα. אָזְנַיִם is not σῶμα, but ὠτία or ὦτα. Must it be said, that the reading σῶμα indicates another thought? Most assuredly, if one translates אָזְנַיִם כָּרִיתָ לִּי as given in the Dutch version: "Mine ears hast thou pierced," in the sense in which the willing slave was pinned through the ear to the doorpost of his lord. This translation, however, is absolutely untenable, simply because this never *could* or *can* be said of the אָזְנַיִם (ears) in the dual. The only correct translation is: Mine ears hast thou digged, in the sense of *opened,* i.e. Thou hast prepared me for the service of obedience. For this thought the expression "a body hast thou prepared me" would do just as well, after the rule of the "whole for the part." If my thumb is hurt, I can use three forms of expression: my *thumb* is wounded, my *finger* is wounded, or my *hand* is hurt. For the preparation of the ear can be put: the preparation of the body; provided both are taken in the sense that this, physico-symbolically, points to spiritual obedience, which is also to be accomplished in outward things. That in Heb. x. 5, body is taken in this sense appears from verse 9, where the exegesis from Ps. xl. 7 is used: "Lo, I come to do thy will," i.e. to obey. And that it is intended as the actual explanation of the "a body hast thou prepared me," appears from the additional words: "He taketh away the first (the burnt offerings and offerings for sin) that He may establish the second (the complete sacrifice of obedience)." The atoning act of Christ's sacrifice lay not in the crucifixion of His body by itself, but in His *will* to obey; as it is expressly stated in verse 10: by which will (not by which body) we have been sanctified. The question whether the following, "through the offering of the body of Jesus Christ," does not refer back to the body in verse 5, can never be answered with certainty. Even if this inference is accepted, it can never follow from this that in verse 5 the incarnation, i.e. the providing of the body for His self-sacrifice, is meant. Rather the contrary; for the exegesis which, as we saw, makes verse 9 follow immediately upon verse 8, affirms the opposite. The undeniable fault in the translation, or at least in the copies, lent itself easily to express, nevertheless, the original meaning of the first author in Ps. xl. 6, and this accounts for the fact that in a Greek copy this Greek reading does not need to be changed necessarily to the letter according to the Hebrew requirement, but can be taken as being equal in sense and thought to the original. This would have been indeed unlawful in common quotation by *another,* but offers not the least difficulty since the *auctor primarius* of Ps. xl. and Heb. x. is *one and the same.* An observation, from which at the same time it appears how, in the apostolic circle, they did not represent to themselves the authority, carrying and ever accompanying the entire Scripture. It presented itself differently to them than to us. For us this inspiration belongs to the past; it is an ended matter; we ourselves stand outside of it. In the same way the Sanhedrin were under the impression that inspiration had died out for as many as four centuries. In the apostolic circle, on the other hand, by Jesus' promise that the Holy Ghost would resume his working, they were prepared to entertain a different view, and after the day of Pentecost they actually lived in another reality. They perceived that this same wondrous power, which had worked in former times and the product of which was the Scripture, had resumed its action, even though in a different way. By this the apostolic circle lived in the Scripture as in a part of its own life. This broke the barrenness of the mechanical contact, and caused the organic contact to resume its liberating process; and it is in this way that subjectively, from the side of the apostles, their liberty in the use of Scripture is explained, as we explained it objectively from the identity of the author in the quotation and in what was quoted.

Significance of this Result for the Old Testament

The period in which the opponents of the Christian confession exegetically misrepresented the Scriptures, in such a way that at length they were said to contain *their* opinions, is irrevocably past. In controversies of a sectarian character, such dogmatic exegesis may still be resorted to; in the conflict for or against the Christ as the Son of God, this weapon is worn out. Negation has destroyed the gain of this untrue position, and now feels itself sufficiently strong to continue the undermining of orthodox Christendom without the assistance of the authority of the Scripture. This we consider no loss, since it has rendered the position clear and free. The first result is, that one begins by granting that orthodoxy is correct in a most important point, which formerly was combated and derided. Only remember what material was gathered by the waning rationalistic-supranaturalistic period, by which to prove, in an amusingly learned way, that in the Holy Scripture Christ appeared nowhere as a Divine person, and that there was as little mention in the Scripture of a vicarious sacrifice made for sinners. This was altogether a churchly dogma, but no representation of Scripture; and thus the hopeless task was undertaken to exegete all such mysteries out of the Scripture. The authority of Christ or of the apostles stood too high at the time, in public estimation, to be put aside or to be defied. In order to obtain a hearing for one's "free" ideas, it was necessary, at the time, to press the argument that the churchly representation was forced upon Christ and His apostles, but that, on a more accurate exegesis, it appeared to be foreign to the Scripture. Whatever of protest was entered against this, from the side of the orthodox, was commonly said to have neither rhyme nor reason. It was soon treated with ridicule; and in some inconceivable way the opinion became prevalent that, in all honesty, Jesus and His apostles had fostered those very same ideas, which eighteen centuries later, in a jaded period of enervated theological thought, were sold off as the newest sample of religious wisdom. If you pass from the period of negation of that time to view its present phase, you observe that this breastwork, cast up with so much exertion, is entirely deserted, and that literally no one defends any longer the representation which was then generally accepted. On the contrary, opponents and supporters of orthodoxy are now fairly well agreed that, in that earlier conflict, upon exegetical ground, the orthodox exegetes were right, and that the Scripture, as it lies before us, really preaches those mysteries then so sharply antagonized.

This has not been granted, of course, with the purpose of accepting those mysteries.

This recognition was arrived at only after men had become well assured that nothing was to be derived from it in the interest of the truth of those mysteries. Now it was said that the Scripture itself must be abandoned, and that these mysteries had not been promulgated by the Christ, but were attributed to Him by Scripture documents of later composition. A *da capo,* indeed, of the ancient assertion; only with this difference, that in the earlier period battle was given in the domain of the Scripture, and now it was turned against that Scripture itself. And when this failed of providing a conception of the Christ which divested him of all supernatural elements, they have now even wrested themselves sufficiently free from his moral authority, boldly to declare that a certain circle or conceptions belonged indeed to Jesus, which nevertheless have ceased to be true to us. But even this implies for us a twofold gain. First, the gain that, now we may see what the tendency of the earlier exegetical attack on Christendom was, and that in the main the exegesis of the orthodox was correct. And secondly, there is the gain that it is no longer denied that Jesus and His apostles entertained conceptions concerning several mysteries, which exhibit a clear relationship to the orthodox confession—a fact which is particularly granted with respect to the conception of Jesus and His apostles concerning the Old Covenant. Aside from the question whether the further development of the dogma of inspiration does not diverge from that conception in more than one particular, and in so far stands in need of correction, no one at present will deny that in the circle of Jesus and His apostles there was a current conception, gainsaid by none, which assigned to the Old Testament, as a Holy Book, a normative authority. Even those who think that the portrait of Jesus, as the New Testament delineates it, allows us only with difficulty to form an idea of the figure of the Rabbi of Nazareth which lurks behind it, confess that Jesus cannot be represented in any other way than as having adopted at this point the current opinion of pious Israelites of His times. Even the accommodation theory has long since been abandoned. But after the frank confession that Jesus shared that conception, this fact is emptied of its significance by the simple statement that Jesus' opinion on this point has no value,—that He Himself, no less than His contemporaries, has simply been mistaken. Hence the confession of the fact has only become possible at the price of respect for Jesus' person. As long as this respect was retained, the fact could not be granted. Since this respect has been lost, the confession is freely made.

This reveals at the same time the weighty consideration which this confession puts in the scale for him who finds this respect for Christ as the Son of God in the depths of his soul, and to whom, therefore, Jesus shines in the full glory of the divine mystery. Can He have been—mistaken, mistaken—with respect to holiest things, in what must be to us the ground and source of our faith! Mistaken also, therefore, in assigning, on the basis of the Scripture, a high Messianic character to Himself! But the very idea is incompatible with the confession of Jesus' Divine nature. Erring in what is holy is no mere failure in intellect, but betrays a state of ruin of one's whole inner being. In the sinner, therefore, a mistake is natural, but not in one who is holy. Hence, here you face a dilemma, from the stress of which there is no escape. One of two things must follow: either, if in the centrum of what is holy Jesus took His stand upon a *lying conception,* then He Himself had *no instinct for the truth,* was not God manifest in the flesh, and could not even have been the purely sinless man; or, if He was "the Christ, the Son of the living God," in all things like ourselves, sin excepted, then whatever He sealed as true in the centrum of what was holy must also be true to him who thus believes in his Saviour. Nothing can here be put in between. As long as the effort was prosecuted to prove that Jesus shared the view of the Scripture of the Old Testament held by the more liberal tendency at the beginning of this century, inspiration could be abandoned without the loss of one's Christ. Since, on the other hand, this effort has suffered total shipwreck, and since it is, and must be, historically acknowledged that Christ viewed the Scripture in about the same way in which the Church of all ages has done this in her symbols, the conflict against this view of the Scripture has become directly a *conflict against the Christ Himself.* He who breaks in principle with that ancient view of the Scripture cuts the cord of faith, which bound him to that Christ as his Lord and his God. And he who cannot refrain from kneeling low before his Saviour *cannot* break with the ground of faith in the Scripture, as Jesus Himself has sealed it.

The tendency, which becomes more and more manifest, to withdraw oneself from the Scripture into an individualistic mysticism and from the Christ to go back to the Holy Spirit, cannot be maintained for one moment by a worshipper of Christ in the face of the fact that Jesus acknowledged the Scripture. For, even though we take them as historical witnesses merely, the Scriptures of the New Testament afford abundant proof that Christ knew this mysticism of the Holy Spirit and honored it, but even in the Gospel of John, in which this mysticism is most often mentioned, almost more strongly than in the Synoptics, you find the conviction of Jesus expressed that He is bound to the Scriptures; bound not only for His conceptions, but bound for His person, for the program of His life and passion, and for the future of glory which awaits Him. Hence the desire to remain orthodox in one's Christology, and so far as the way of knowledge is concerned to withdraw oneself into mystical territory, in order to be able to make concessions in the domain of the Scripture-question, is the fruit of lack of thought, a measuring with two measures, and self-contradiction. The question is more serious than is surmised by this well-meaning orthodoxy. The conflict, which is begun in order to rob us of the Scripture, as Holy Scripture, can have no other tendency than to rob us of the Christ. If the Holy Scripture *qua talis* falls, then Jesus was a man and nothing more, who was mistaken in the centrum of what was holy, and who consequently can neither escape from the fellowship of sin, nor yet in what is holiest and tenderest be your absolute guide.

It is not true that on this point there could be error in Jesus, without detriment to His person and His character as authority in what is holy. In history entirely innocent inaccuracies are certainly possible, which, so far from doing harm, rather bring to light the free utterance of life above notarial mannerism. But of this character, Jesus' error could have been least of all. For three reasons. In the first place, because, if the historical-critical school is right, there is not merely a dispute about the author and the origin of several books, but in the Old Testament you frequently encounter *deceit* and *falsehood*. There are not only several representations of facts and events which are fictitious, but many pretensions, also, to Divine revelation which are feigned, and the intrusion of writings under other names which are nothing but "prophecies after the event," but which nevertheless present themselves as authentic prophecy. Whether this *deceit* and this *falsehood* is the personal work of one individual or the result of tradition, makes no difference; falsehood does not cease to be *falsehood* if it is generated gradually in the course of time. And however much one may talk of "pious fraud," even that can only be represented as free from deceit when the rule is adopted that the end sanctifies the means. Grant that you may make no scientific claims on Jesus, which fall outside of the scope of His person and time, may this ever authorize one to deny Him also the instinct for truth? And yet He must have been entirely devoid of this instinct, if He could have taken such a structure of fictitious and designedly untrue representations as the ground of that truth, which He confessed and for which He died.

In the second place, such error could not have been innocently made for the reason stated above, viz. that Jesus accepted the entire program of His life at the hand of the Scripture. The Old Testament Scripture had a meaning for Jesus which it could have had for no other, either before or after Him. From the fatal standpoint of an error no other conclusion can be formed than that in the program of the 'Ebed Jahvah, of the Messiah, and of the man of sorrows Jesus wrongly saw the plan of His own existence, public appearance, passion and glory, and that He labored under an illusion when, on the ground of the Scripture, He conformed Himself to this. His great life-work, then, is no result of a Divine impulse, but a role in a drama which He found projected by some one else, and of which He imagined Himself to be the chief actor. Thus if this error is granted, it entails with it a condemnation of Jesus' whole interpretation of His task. Not only His interpretation of the Scripture, but His entire position in history has then been one mistake. He then has walked in a dream. A beautiful dream wrought into His phantasy by the Old Testament. By this, however, His life and sacrifice forfeit the serious character of being a moral reality sprung from God.

And the third reason, why the idea of an *innocent* mistake cannot be entertained, is evident from the very conflict of our times. At first the Old Testament was antagonized by means of the New, in order on ethical grounds to exhibit the lower standard of the Old. The religious and ethical representations of the Old Testament must be repelled, in order that Christ and the New Testament might find an entrance as the principium of what was higher and holier. Now one does not hesitate on the ground of his own religious and moral sense to apply his criticism to Christ and the New Testament. But even if we pass this second suggestion by, it is alleged that in the centrum of the religious and moral life there yawns an abyss between the Old Testament and the Christ. Notwithstanding all this the attempt is being made to make it appear as though it had merely been an innocent mistake in Christ that for eighteen centuries by precept and example He has bound His followers and confessors to the authority of that Old Testament. But is it not absurd to qualify in the Founder of your religion, as Jesus is called, as of no importance a mistake which for ages has led millions upon millions astray, and still continues to do this? We may safely prophesy that after not many days the stress of the dilemma, which we here face, will be realized and generally acknowledged. Either Jesus' view of the Scripture is the true one, and then we should kneel in His presence; or Jesus' view of the Scripture is one enormous mistake, in which case the Rabbi of Nazareth can no longer be the absolute guide along the way of faith.

We accept this dilemma the sooner since it determines most definitely our point of departure. There are two kinds of people, thus we wrote, in or outside of the circle of palingenesis, and connected therewith there are two kinds of consciousness, subjectively with or without illumination, and objectively with or without Holy Scripture. Applied to the above-named dilemma, this affirms: That if by palingenesis you stand vitally related to the Christ as "the head of the body," the relation between your consciousness and the Holy Scripture is born from this of itself. But if that relation of the palingenesis does not bind you to the Christ of God as head of the body of the new humanity, you cannot kneel before Him in worship, neither can the Scripture be to you a Holy Scripture. The scientific form, in which your confession of the Scripture will cast itself, we do not consider here. No one, able to think and to ponder, has ever come either to palingenesis, to faith in the Christ as the Son of God, or to the acceptance of the Scripture, as the result of scientific investigation. Faith is of *a different kind,* and can never be plucked as fruit from the branches of science. Faith in, as well as the rejection of, the Christ and the Scripture, i.e. of a Logos embodied in the flesh and embodied in writing ($\dot{\epsilon}\nu\sigma\alpha\rho\kappa\acute{\omega}\mu\epsilon\nu o\varsigma$ and $\ddot{\epsilon}\gamma\gamma\rho\alpha\phi o\varsigma$), springs from the root of our spiritual existence. Hence it can*not* be that by nature every one accepts the Christ and the Holy Scripture. The antithesis cannot remain wanting between those who believe and reject. It lies in the very nature of every intervenient process, which does not find its rise in the natural principium of the creation, but in a special principium that is bent upon *re*creation. The very nature of special grace brings with it that by one it *must* be accepted, but also by another be rejected. Faith *can*not belong to all. As soon as *rejection* stands no longer over against *faith,* special grace has reached its end, and by the parousia passes over into the then *glorified* natural principium. This was not felt for many years, because faith on the Scripture floated on tradition only, and became thereby unspiritual. The apostasy from the Christ and from the Scripture is therefore nothing else than the falling away from this traditional position, which for a long time had no more spiritual root. Now only, thanks to the simultaneous conflict against Christ and the Scripture, the great dictum, that Christ is set for the rising up but also for the falling of many (Luke ii. 34), also for those who are *outside* of Israel, begins to be realized as truth.

The Inspiration of the New Testament

The Scripture of the New Testament is not so directly covered by the authority of Christ and His apostles as that of the Old Covenant. The *Law* and the *Prophets* formed a Scripture which already existed, and concerning which, therefore, Jesus' verdict and use can give a final explanation; but the New Testament did not yet exist, and therefore could not be subjected to judgment in the circle of Jesus. The absolute and immediate authority which the Bishop of Rome claims as vicar of Christ and head of the Church lacks the Divine seal, which it needs in order to impress the Divine stamp upon the Scripture of the New Testament. The absolute authority necessary for such a sealing, outside of us, is here wanting. Our fixed point of departure, therefore, does not lie in the *New*, but in the *Old*, Testament. The Old Testament is to us the fixed point of support, and the New cannot legitimate itself other than as the complement and crown of the Old, postulated by the Old, assumed and prophesied by Christ, actually come, and by the continuity of faith accepted in the Church of Christ, A certain parallel with the standing of the authority of the Old Testament before Jesus' appearance is here not to be denied. Even though Jesus' decisive witness concerning the Scripture then in existence lays for us the firmest objective foundation on which its authority rests, it may nevertheless not be lost from sight that respect for this authority did not originate first by means of Jesus' coming, but was already prevalent before He was manifest in the flesh. Christ had merely to connect Himself with what existed, and put His seal to an authority that was universally recognized. The authority of the Scripture of the Old Covenant arose of itself even as that of the New Testament. It was, as Jesus found it, the result of organic factors which had worked in upon the people of God in the Old Dispensation; an authority which only gradually had been firmly established, and did not maintain itself in an absolute sense, except through conflict and strife, over against the pretension of the Apocrypha and other influential writings, but at length prevailed universally within a sharply bounded domain. As a parallel to the rise of the authority of the New Testament this is the value to us, because it shows that such an authority *can* establish itself gradually by psychical factors and in organic connection with the life of the people of God, and in such a way that the Christ ratifies it afterwards as an entirely lawful and valid authority. From this the possibility also is evident that in a proper way, without outward legitimation, such an authority may be imposed as of itself, and that afterwards it can appear to have been entirely lawfully established. Thus there is nothing strange in it, that in a similarly unmarked way the Scripture of the New Testament gradually acquired the authority which it has since exercised. From the psychological point of view the process of the rise of this authority, both with the New and with the Old Testament, is one. The description of this process is the task of the science of Canonics, and therefore lies outside of our scope. But the inner necessity needs to be indicated with which the *Old* called for the *New* Testament, and how this necessity has been *universally* realized.

We begin with the latter. Consider then how difficult it must have been at first for the pious mind, to add to the Holy Scripture, consisting as it then did of the Old Testament, new part, with the claim of equal authority. An absolute boundary line separated the Old Testament from every other writing. Even the conflict with the Apocrypha had ceased. And now the idea arises, of placing all sorts of other writings, which lack every mark of antiquity, and are of very recent date, on a line with this Holy Scripture, even with respect to authority, and yet this idea meets with no opposition, but enters as of itself; and while at the same time all sorts of other writings are circulated, one sees in the main very soon a boundary line drawn between what commends itself as clothed with that authority, and what does not. What are one hundred years in such a process of spiritual development? And not much more than one century has passed after Jesus' ascension, before a complement for the Old Testament has formed itself, begins to run by its side, finds recognition, and comes into sacred use. And this went on so unobservedly and of itself, that although all sorts of controversies arose concerning the question, whether this or that book should be adopted, yet of a fundamental controversy against the idea itself, of adding a New Testament to the Old, there is absolutely *no* trace discoverable. Reaction against this idea as such proceeded, and very reasonably, from the side of the Jews alone, but was not even suggested in the circle of the Christians. They were as controversial then as we are now, and there is no difference, however small, dogmatic, ethic, or ecclesiastic, but has been fought for and against from the beginning. But no trace of any significance appears anywhere of opposition to the idea itself, that a new Scripture should be added to the Old. Hyperspiritualism may have reacted against *all* Scripture, New as well as Old; but that cannot claim our attention here: we speak simply of those, who, while loyally subject to the authority of the Old Testament, faced the question whether or no a second Scripture, clothed with equal authority, should be added to the accepted canon. Psychologically one would have expected a negative answer to this question from more than one side. Imagine what it would mean to you if to your Bible, as it now consists of Old and New Testaments, a third volume was to be added, clothed with equal authority of later origin, and you perceive at once that reaction against this effort, yea, fierce opposition almost, could not be wainting. And yet such was the case faced by the church at large at that time. Both *what* was to be added to the Old Testament, and *that* anything should be added, was entirely new to them. That, nevertheless, all opposition of any essential character and significant influence against this idea as such remained wanting, shows indeed that the minds and hearts must have been predisposed to the reception of a second Scripture; that the enlightening, when this Scripture arose, bound the minds and hearts to it; and that the appearance of the New Testament, so far from sowing unrest in the mind, rather produced that natural rest which is enjoyed when what was incomplete in itself obtains its natural complement. And this sense was so general that not only the orthodox but also the heterodox tendency, as far as it moved in the bed of the Christian Church, supported the rise of this new Scripture. Even though many efforts went out from the side of the heterodox to exclude this or that writing, to modify or replace it by another, yet in this very effort the general consciousness voiced itself, that an authoritative Scripture of the New Testament was a necessity. Even though the authority was questioned of certain books, or of a part of it, the heretic and the orthodox confessor were unanimous in the conviction that the Old Scripture called for a New.

There was indeed some reaction, but this was aimed exclusively against the manner how, and not against the matter itself. By that reaction against the manner of execution, the matter itself was rather strengthened. The adoption of the ἀντιλεγόμενα was reacted against; reaction took place for the sake of introducing other writings, which did not belong to the canon; to modify the text of universally acknowledged writings, agreeably to all sorts of heterodoxy: but this threefold reaction is but a proof that the conflict was waged with reference to certain products of the first Christian literature, but very definitely not with reference to the acceptance of a *new Holy Scripture.* That such a man as Paul alone wrote perhaps ten times as much as is contained from his hand in the New Testament, lies in the very nature of the case. Is it reasonable to suppose that one of the apostles never wrote anything? How large, then, the literary product must have been about one hundred years after Jesus' birth. But no proposal was made to add the whole of this literary inheritance, not even all the apostolic writings, as the complement to the Old Testament. There was room for choice, there was room for sifting. This will do; that, not. And in this lies the recognition of the distinction between what should and what should not be received as authoritative. This certainly was not effected mechanically nor conventionally nor scholastically. Whatever in the end compiled this Scripture canonically, it was not simply human sharp-sightedness, but rather Divine providence. Even so, however, it appears from the threefold reaction, mentioned above, that with clear consciousness a second Holy Scripture as such was in view, and that the assignment of such high authority to this or that book was contested, but not the reality of such an authority as such. It is evident that this occasioned a period of uncertainty; but let it be observed that this uncertainty concerned the whole New Testament only for a very short time, and, sooner than could be expected, reduced itself to a very small part of it. In that limited sense, however, this uncertainty *could* not remain wanting, for the very reason that such a canonical authority could only be the outflow of the finally unanimous and ever spontaneous recognition of the churches. A recognition which was greatly impeded by the distances between the farthest outlying churches in the West and in the East; which experienced still more impediment from the absence of a regular communication; and which, in the midst of the confusion brought about by persecution and by heterodoxy, could only be established as by miracle. And yet the result is that persecution had scarcely ceased, and the ecclesiastical bond been regulated, and heterodoxy been repressed, when on every hand you find the churches in the possession of a second Holy Scripture, and the authority of the New Testament standing in nothing behind that of the Old.

This would be inexplicable, if the Old Testament had announced itself as exclusive and in itself complete, and had not, rather, itself called for a New Testament as its complement. The prophetic character of the Old Covenant bars out this exclusive point of view. Everything in the Old Testament *will* be nothing but anticipatory, and calls for the "age to come"(עוֹלָם הַבָּא). In the estimation of all who revered its authority, the entire Old Scripture postulated a reality which was to come, the shadow of which alone was given in the old dispensation. The glimmerings were there, the light itself still tarried. One read the prologue; the drama itself was to follow. The pedestal was finished for the monument about to be erected, but the figure itself was still to be placed upon it. There was a protasis, but the apodosis of fulfilment was yet to come. When this end, this complementing reality, came, the same problem arose as of old. This apodosis, this plerosis, came not in one moment of time, immediately to be ended and closed by the parousia, but this manifestation was also to be perpetuated, as has been the case now nearly twenty centuries. The same *necessity of the Scripture,* which existed for the manifestation of the prophetic dispensation, was here repeated. What took place only once, and was to project its energy for centuries together and to all the ends of the earth, must pass over into tradition, and this tradition must clothe itself in the only conceivable form of human trustworthiness, viz. that of the Scriptura. This necessity would have fallen away if the indwelling of the Holy Spirit in the mystical body of Christ had worked actual holiness and infallibility at once. Then, indeed, oral tradition would have been guaranteed against involuntary and wilful falsification. Since, however, this is not so, and they who are regenerated must struggle till their death with the after-throes of sin, and since in the Church of Christ many hypocrites are continually numbered with the children of palingenesis, the oral tradition was in imminent danger of being falsified. The necessitas *scripturae,* therefore, to perpetuate the manifestation which took place eighteen centuries ago was undeniable. Thus, the content of the Old Testament called for the complementing manifestation in *Christ,* and the Scripture of the Old Testament for its written complement in the *New.*

This holds the more because the manifestation, however much it may be plerosis with respect to the prophetical dispensation of the Old Testament, bears in itself, in its turn, an incomplete and therefore a prophetical character. Potentially the Divine reality is seen in the manifestation of Christ, but this will find its actual consummation only in the parousia, when the palingenesis shall have worked its effect in the universal cosmical sense. Hence, the second manifestation in Christ calls for a third manifestation in the parousia. Of this, Paul says, 1 Cor. xv. 24: "Then cometh the end, when he shall deliver up the kingdom to God, even the Father." In the new dispensation, therefore, there is not only the manifestation of what was prophesied in Israel, but the prophecy, as well, of a manifestation which only comes after this. An ethical "It is finished" has been heard from Golgotha, but the final "It is come to pass" (Rev. xxi. 6) will only be proclaimed after the Parousia. There is also a program, therefore, of what lies between the first coming of Christ and His return, and an apocalypse of what shall be the end; and as the tradition of what had taken place called for the support of writing, from the nature of the case this support was much more necessary for the tradition of what was program-like.

Agreeably to this, we find that Christ Himself postulates such a second Holy Scripture. This already appears from the charge given by Christ to John on Patmos: "What thou seest, write($\gamma\rho\acute{a}\psi\text{ov}$) in a book, and send it unto the Seven Churches" (Rev. i. 11), in connection with the strong sense in which the meaning of $\gamma\epsilon\gamma\rho\alpha\mu\mu\acute{e}\text{vov}$ appears in the entire Apocalypse. But since this $\gamma\rho\acute{a}\psi\text{ov}$ comes in too abruptly-mechanically, occurs in an $\dot{a}\nu\tau\iota\lambda\epsilon\gamma\acute{o}\mu\epsilon\text{vov}$, and refers merely to one single book, we point rather to the position to which Jesus exalts the apostolate. With respect to this, we see that Christ indeed took measures to assure the durability of His work, by which to realize the end of His mission. No trace is found with Jesus of a spiritualistic-mystical *laisseraller*. He institutes the apostolate, attaches to it a definite authority, and commissions this apostolate with a definite task. With respect to our present subject, this task is twofold: (1) the appearing as witnesses of the manifestation which they had seen; and (2) the proclaiming of things to come. This double task was imposed upon them, not merely with respect to those who were then alive, before whom they should stand and preach by word of mouth, but with reference to "all nations," in those nations to all believers, and for those believers "to the end of the world." Now put this together, and how could the apostles bring this witness to all nations and through all ages, except either by not dying, or, since they died even very early, by the instrumentality of writing?

That Christ gave a call to the apostolate not merely to bring the Gospel to those who were then alive, but to be until the end his authoritative witnesses to all believers, is already observable from John xvii. 20, where Jesus prays, not only for the apostles themselves, "but for them also that believe on him through their word." That this refers to all believers among all nations and of all ages lies in the nature of the case, since the intercession of Christ applies to all his people; but it appears, moreover, very clearly from the connection. There follows, indeed, a double "that" (*iva*): (1) that they may all be one, and (2) that the world may believe that thou didst send me. It is self-evident that the unity of believers cannot refer merely to the immediate converts of that time, and in the same way that the cosmos of all ages must receive this witness. Now look at verse 14, where Jesus declares that He has given this Logos as a word of God first to the apostles, and that it is that Logos which, by the apostolate, is to be brought within the reach of the world of all ages, and it follows from this that in the mind of Jesus this apostolic witness must remain available in a fixed form after their death. Entirely in the same sense, therefore, in which in Matt. xxviii. 19 he extends the significance of the apostolate to all the nations and till the end of the world. That the apostles themselves saw the exceptional significance of the apostolate is shown among other things by John in his First Epistle, i. 1-3, in which he declares of himself and of his fellow-apostles: (1) that *they* received the manifestation so realistically that he even says: "and our hands have handled;" and (2) that they were called to preach this manifestation; and (3) that the fruit of this preaching must be the adoption of converts into the fellowship of the apostolate, because by *this* fellowship only could they enter into the mystical union with God and His Christ. We even see Paul taking measures, as long as the Scriptura still tarries, to fill in the gap, when to Timothy he writes: "And the things which thou hast heard from him among many witnesses, the same commit thou to faithful men, who shall be able to teach others also" (2 Tim. ii. 2). The conception lies expressed very clearly in this that the apostolate bring something to the world that is to remain for all time the fixed and reliable tradition.

This significance of the apostolate extends itself even farther, when notice is taken of those utterances of Jesus contained in John xiv. 25, 26; xv. 26, 27; xvi. 12, etc. In John xvi. 12-15, the difference is clearly anticipated, which later on was to assert itself between the gospel $\tau\grave{o}$ $\epsilon\grave{v}a\gamma\gamma\acute{e}\lambda\iota\text{ov}$) and the apostolate ($\acute{o}$ $\dot{a}\pi\acute{o}\sigma\tau\text{o}\lambda\text{os}$ The task of the apostles was to be twofold: (1) as witnesses of what they had seen and heard, they were to embody the record of the life and work of Jesus upon the earth in a well-guaranteed tradition; but (2) also, to reveal to the world what, *after His ascension,* Jesus would testify and make known unto them. Not as though this revelation after Jesus' ascension should advance, in a Montanistic sense, beyond Jesus, for of this Jesus Himself declares, "I have yet many things to say unto you," and the only reason why as yet He did *not* reveal them was "that the apostles were not yet able to bear it." This later revelation, indeed, will proceed in a different way, and come to them by the Holy Ghost, i.e. by way of inspiration, but this will not render the character of this later revelation different in kind; for the Lord declares emphatically that the Holy Ghost will take from the things that are His, "What things soever he shall hear, these shall he speak," and thus only be able "to declare unto you the things that are to come." This excludes, therefore, the representation that this working of the Holy Spirit should consist in mystical leadings. Definite material is here spoken of, which is present in the consciousness of the Mediator; which purposely He does not as yet impart to His apostles; and which, after His ascension, the Holy Ghost will borrow as content from the Mediator-consciousness (He shall take of mine), in order by inspiration to communicate it to the apostles. This is so strongly emphasized that Jesus repeats the selfsame thought three times: (1) in the thirteenth verse, "He shall not speak from himself, but what things soever he shall hear, these shall he speak"; (2) in the fourteenth verse, "He shall glorify me: for he shall take of mine"; and (3) in the fifteenth verse, "therefore said I, that he taketh of mine, and shall declare it unto you." Evidently no mystical sensations are here spoken of which were to be quickened by the Holy Spirit, but *thoughts* and *purposes* are referred to which were present in the consciousness of the Mediator, and which are indicated by the "of mine." Of these *thoughts,* it is said, "He will guide you into all the truth"; and of these *purposes,* "He will declare unto you the things that are to come." And in both cases it applies to a definite content, which is obtained by *hearing,* and after that is transmitted by *declaring.* From which it likewise follows that no reference is made here to what Jesus spake after His resurrection, but exclusively to that which only later on should enter into their consciousness by inspiration. On the other hand, John xiv. 25, 26, views what we call the gospel (τὸ εὐαγγέλιον). Here is mention, not of what was still to be revealed, but of what had been revealed unto them, and by a failing memory might escape them. Against this the Holy Spirit shall watch, since "He shall teach you all things, and bring to your remembrance all that I [Christ] said unto you," a process of inspiration, as will be seen later, of an entirely different character, referring to the past, even as the inspiration of John xvi. 12, to the things that are to come. And if the question is raised how this double tradition, which the apostolate was to bequeath to the Church of all ages, would find an entrance and belief, John xv. 26, 27 gives answer; for their witness would be accompanied and supported by the *witness* of the Holy Spirit in the heart of believers.

With the holy apostle Paul, however, an exception took place. With him there could be no remembrance by the Holy Ghost, because he had not followed Jesus. Therefore, Paul declares that the exalted Mediator had also revealed the Gospel to him. This, indeed, is the only meaning that can be attached to his statement in 1 Cor. xi. 23, "For I received of the Lord that which also I delivered unto you," which testimony he repeats in 1 Cor. xv. 3 almost literally, where testimony he repeats in 1 Cor. xv. 3 almost literally, where he treats of the resurrection of the Lord. This is likewise referred to by what he says in 1 Cor. vii. 12, "But to the rest say I, not the Lord," which, from the nature of the case, may not be taken as though his advice following should possess *no* Divine authority, but as indicating that in His revelation of His earthly appearance the Christ had given him no direction concerning this, so that with reference to this the apostle speaks, not from the remembrance, but from the revelation of the Holy Ghost; which representation, with the apostolic Scripture before one's eyes, may not be dismissed as being far-fetched. With so many words, indeed, Paul testifies in Gal. i. 11, 12, "For I make known to you, brethren, as touching the gospel which was preached by me, that it is not after man. For neither did I receive it from man, nor was I taught it, but it came to me through revelation of Jesus

Christ." For the matter in hand, however, this makes no difference. With Paul, also, there is a difference between what is revealed to him of the past, and what is given him by inspiration concerning the *thoughts* and *events,* the knowledge of which was given by Jesus to His Church after His ascension, through the Holy Spirit.

The inspiration itself of the apostles will be considered in a separate paragraph. For the purpose in hand it is sufficient to have shown: (1) that the Old Testament postulated a second revelation, which could only come later; (2) that this second revelation also was destined for all nations and every age, and on this ground called for documentation; (3) that up to the time of Jesus' ascension *a part* only of this second revelation had come, while another part still tarried, and that the end can only come with the parousia; (4) that Jesus instituted His apostolate as a definite company (*koivwvia*), and imposed upon this apostolate the task of being His witnesses until the end of the world; (5) that Jesus, in order that they might accomplish this task, promised and granted them a double inspiration of the Holy Ghost; first that of remembrance ($\dot{v}\pi\acute{o}\mu\nu\eta\sigma\iota s$) and secondly that of guidance ($\dot{o}\delta\acute{\eta}\gamma\eta\sigma\iota s$) and of declaring ($\dot{a}\nu a\gamma\gamma\epsilon\lambda\acute{\iota}a$) and (6) that since Christ honored the Old Testament as an authoritative Scripture for the confirmation and documentation of the revelation which *preceded* His advent, the idea was given *of itself* to have a similar Scripture do service for the confirmation and documentation of this second revelation.

The result, indeed, puts the seal upon this. Such a second Scripture *did* arise of itself. This second Scripture legitimized itself as a New Testament to supplement the Old Testament within a relatively short time, and has fused with it into one whole in the consciousness of the Church. There is no question here of a mechanical compulsion. The apostles had no thought of preparing a book which, under the seal of their name and common authority, was to be handed down to posterity. The tie braided itself entirely organically between this new Scripture and the ever broader circle of believers. It was the Holy Spirit Himself who on one side caused the component parts of this Scripture to originate, and on the other side secured the choice of these documents in the churches. The hesitancy, which arose with reference to a number of these documents, shows with what unanimity the others obtained an immediate entrance, and how conscientiously the work was undertaken. The idea that such a second Scripture must come encountered no opposition, but was alive in the heart as an idea and a presumption, before it showed itself above the horizon. Orthodox and heterodox united in this Scripture-idea, and the result was, that in proportion to the measure in which the oral tradition changed color and the spread of the church threatened its unity, the significance of this *second* Scripture was more and more felt, until at length there was a complete documentation, not only of the shadows (*okiai*) but also of the fulfilment ($\pi\lambda\acute{\eta}\rho\omega\sigma\iota s$), which was acknowledged by the churches in all parts of the earth as clothed with Divine authority. This acknowledgment implied that the authority assigned to the New Testament was understood in the same sense as the authority attached by Christ to the Old Testament. To the sense of faith both soon formed one organic whole. Whatever dominion the Old Testament had, that was the dominion that was attributed to the New Testament. And though it is entirely true, in the strict sense, that 2 Tim. iii. 16, and similar utterances, were written with exclusive reference to the Old Testament, yet the Church was entirely right when it applied this as a matter *of fact* to the New Testament as well, since indeed, after the organic fusion of both, one and the same life flowed through both parts of the Scripture, and in both the Divine Word was communicated unto us. No mistake was made even when they went farther; and in the treatment of the organic life of the Scripture, utterances from the Psalms were also applied to the New Testament. It was indeed well known that originally such utterances could refer merely to what was then written; but it was understood that the same physiological law for one and the same life is valid in all its stages, and that for this reason the explanation of what had already appeared on this plant of the Scripture applied also to the branches which sprang from it at a later period.

This physiological *unity* of the organic life of the Scripture demands that attention shall likewise be paid to the instrumental diversity by which it came into being. The unity lies in the *auctor primarius,* but this can only be fully known when the needed light is thrown upon the rich multiformity in the *auctores secundarii.* Let attention, therefore, now be centred upon that instrumental side of inspiration.

Unity and Multiplicity

The Holy Scripture offers itself to faith as *a unity,* and it is that unity which our old theologians called its *essentia,* i.e. that which makes it Scripture. This unity becomes apparent when Jesus simply quotes it with an "It is written," and when, by His authority likewise, *the Holy Scripture* becomes the name by which it is called. In this sense *the* Scripture is *the* Word of God, and every distinction, by which we have only a Word of God *in* the Scripture, is a denial of its essentia or being.

This representation of its unity is not only *right* but of *highest* right for faith, and if it did not give rise to such terrible abuse, it might serve, if necessary, as the sole sufficient one in the realm of faith. Since, however, this representation tempts one so readily to quote every sentence which occurs in the Scripture, in whatever place, as forming by itself a Divine saying, and thus to destroy the organic character of revelation, it is the mission of the church to keep alive also the sense of the multiformity of the Holy Scripture. Even though it is entirely true that Jesus briefly quotes with an "It is written," and does this also when a word is quoted which in the Old Testament does not occur immediately as a saying of the Lord, yet with Jesus such an "It is written" betrays always a spiritual significance. A word of Satan is not an "It is written," neither is every saying of men, nor even every utterance of God's ambassadors. Hence, in order to be able to quote Scripture authoritatively, the guidance of the Holy Spirit is necessary, to impart the spiritual tact of distinguishing the gold from the ore. One needs only to turn to the book of Job in order to perceive how much spiritual maturity is required to know what may or may not be quoted from among the numerous utterances of Satan, of Job, of his three friends and of Elihu, and an "it is written." Everything that grows on and in the stalk is by no means wheat, and especially with finer plants it always takes the eye of the *connoisseur* to distinguish fruit from what is *no* fruit. Upon the *multiplicity,* therefore, in the case of the Holy Scripture, emphasis must also be put, not from the desire to exalt the human factor, but to keep the gold vein of the Divine factor pure; and this will do no harm, provided its organic unity, and not its multiformity, is chosen as the starting-point from which to arrive at its unity. In all organic life unity in the germ is first, from which multiplicity spreads itself. By fastening leaf, blossom and branch to each other you never form a living plant. He who, in the case of the Scripture, thus begins with the multiplicity of the human factor, and tries in this way to reach out after its unity will never find it, simply because he began with its denial in principle.

It was not mistakenly, therefore, that a predestined Bible was spoken of in Reformed circles, by which was understood that the *preconceived form* of the Holy Scripture had been given already from eternity in the counsel of God, in which at the same time all events, means and persons, by which that preconceived form would be realized in our actual life, were predestined. Hence in the course of ages all sorts of events take place, and persons appear who do not know of each other, and in the midst of these events these several persons are induced, without the knowledge of a higher purpose, to commit to writing certain facts, thoughts and perceptions. These persons also write other documents, and other persons among their contemporaries write as well as they. But, nevertheless, all those other writings are lost, or are put aside, while those special documents, which were destined and ordered of God to compose His Holy Scripture, are not merely saved, but are made honorable, are compiled, and gradually attain that authority which He had ordained for these Scriptures. Thus, according to a plan, known to God alone, a structure is gradually raised on which in the course of many ages different persons have labored without agreement, and without ever having seen the whole. No one of the children of men had conceived the plan, to compile such a Scripture; not one had added his contribution with premeditation, nor exhorted others to supplement his contribution with theirs. Thus the plan of the Holy Scripture was hidden, back of human consciousness, in the consciousness of God, and He it is, who in His time has so created each of these writers, so endowed, led and impelled them, that they have contributed what He wanted, and what after His plan and direction was to constitute His Scripture. The *conception,* therefore, has not gone out of men, but out of God; and it was in connection with this conception, that in every document and by every writer in the course of the ages there should be contributed that very thing, of such a *content* and in such a *form,* as had been aimed at and willed by God. There is no chance, and hence this composition and compilation of human writings are not accidental, but predetermined. And this whole has thus been ordained, and in virtue of this fore-ordination has thus been executed, as it had to be, in order to respond to the spiritual needs and wants of the Church of God in every age and among every nation. For, of course, in the strict sense it may be said that every writing is predestined, and this we readily grant; but when our Reformed circles spoke of a "predestined Bible" they intended to convey thereby the idea of a *medium of grace,* which was taken up as a link in the counsel of God for the salvation of His elect. In the accomplishment of *this* purpose lay the justification of the Scripture, and the result has fully shown that this wondrous book contains within itself the mystery of being suited to every nation, new to every age, profound for the scholar and rich in comforts for the meek. By this Scripture the world has been changed, and thanks to its power a moral authority has been established among the nations, of which it was correctly prophesied by Kant, that though it might be destroyed in part, it can never be superseded by another equally immutable authority. In this universality this Scripture works an effect which is beyond calculation, and its influence is not capable of analysis. There it lies in the midst of the Church and of the nations. A certain mystical tie unites the life of the soul to it, as a phenomenon. It makes thereby an impression, and by that impression it fashions spirits. It does this in very different ways, and no theory is able to trace or to interpret the working of that impression. Its light and its glow radiate solemnly, and the result is that the coldness of human hearts retreats and the darkness is driven back. Such is its majesty, and it is by that majesty, that as one mighty γέγραπται, as one overpowering word of God, it masters our sense of self. In that unity it shines as *the Holy Scripture.*

He who believes in God cannot represent it otherwise than that there must be a *Word of God,* one coherent utterance of His Divine thought. Not in that anthropomorphic sense in which we men string word to word, but, in such a sense as becomes the Eternal One, who is not subject to a succession of moments, in the rich and full unity of the conception. And in that sense the Holy Scripture speaks of the *Logos of God,* which is something entirely different from his spoken words (ῥήματα) and which in itself indicates merely the psyche of the thought, independent of its somatic slothing in language and sound. If man is created after the Image of God, and thus disposed to communion with the Eternal, then this *Word of God* also must be able to be grasped by man; and even after his fall into sin, this Word of God must go out to him, though now in a way suited to his condition. This takes place now, since man has received *being* and *consciousness,* in two ways. In the way of the *esse* by the *incarnation* of the Logos, and in the way of consciousness as this selfsame Logos becomes embodied in the Scripture. Both are the spoken Word (Λόγος προφορικός) but in the one case it is the Word "become flesh" (σάρξ γενόμενος), in the other "written"(ἔγγραφος), and these two cover each other. Christ is the whole Scripture, and the Scripture brings the τό esse of the Christ to our consciousness. Care, however, must be taken to guard against the mistake, that our consciousness can only be wrought upon by the spoken word. Very certainly this takes place with spoken words, and the Holy Scripture emphasizes the fact that God the Lord, who gave us language and in language our human word, Himself made use of those words by which directly to address us. Sinai bears witness to this. But besides through the *ear,* our consciousness is also affected through the *eye,* both by real revelation in events and by symbolical shadow and manifestation; and it is by these three means, first, the spoken word, secondly, the common or extraordinary inworking in the real world, and third, the shadows, types and figures, that God the Lord has brought to pass, that His thought Logos, His divine Word, has been conveyed to sinners. Only when in this wise these *spoken words, signs* and *shadows* are taken together and joined in their organic relation, can the rich revelation of the Word of God be viewed in its unity. Not merely the spoken words, but also the signs, and not merely these two, but likewise the shadows, in the relation in which God Himself has revealed them, together give us the *Word of God*. He only who places himself under the full impression of this majestic whole, can and may say, that *the* Word of God has been revealed to him. For this reason the Logos of God is both violated and maimed, when it is sought in the spoken words only, and when consequently one speaks of the *words* of God in the Scripture. The Scripture as a whole, as it lies before us as a unit, offers us the organic whole of this threefold revelation of God, and he only who takes up in himself *that whole,* has in himself the image of the full revelation of God, and consequently possesses *the Word of God*. That God's Word is not *in* the Scripture, but that the Scripture itself is the photograph of God's Word, does not refer therefore to its formal inspiration, but simply states, that you cannot miss any part of that Scripture without marring the picture, the photograph, the etching, the copy, which holds before our eyes the full image of God's word. To this unity faith stretches forth its hands. From this unity of conception flows the Divine authority, to which the child of God gives itself captive. How this unity hides in that wondrous book remains a mystery which refuses all explanation. Only when you stand before it, at the proper distance, and with the faith eye of 'he connoisseur you gaze upon its multiplicity of tints and lines, the full image discovers itself stereoscopically to you. Then you see it. Then you can no longer *not* see it. The eye of your soul has caught it. In all its glory it speaks to you.

But, of course, the *multiplicity* of that appearance does not cease to exist on account of that *unity*. The Holy Scripture is not abstractly transcendent. It is this in some apocalyptical parts, but by no means when taken as a whole. And as a protest must be entered against every effort to take the revelation of God's consciousness to man as being simply immanent, as though it consisted merely of the unnoticed influences upon our inner being, equally strong must our protest be against the effort to interpret the Holy Scripture as a transcendent phenomenon standing outside of our human reality. Here also, the parallel maintains itself between the incarnate and the written Logos. As in the Mediator the Divine nature weds itself to the human, and appears before us in *its* form and figure, so also the Divine factor of the Holy Scripture clothes itself in the garment of our form of thought, and holds itself to our human reality. This is what our old theologians meant by their combination of the first and secondary authors, but it is something that goes yet farther; for even when, on Sinai, God with His own finger engraves in human words His law upon the tables of stone, the revelation remains not absolutely transcendent, but makes use here, also, of the human as instrument. All the shadows and types bear the same mixed character. All of sacred history rests upon the same entwining of both factors. And even in miracles, the Divine factor remains never purely transcendent, but in order to reveal Himself, ever enters into human reality. Hence, in all parts of the rich scenery interpreted to you by the Word of God, it is ever the transcendent, Divine facotr, which exhibits itself to your eye in human form or in a human reality. If, now, in order to be the bearer of the Divine factor, that human form or that human reality were carried up to its perfection, no contradiction would be born from this in the appearance; but this is not so. As the Logos has not appeared *in the form of glory,* but in the form of a servant, joining Himself to the reality of our nature, as this had come to be through the results of sin, so also, for the revelation of His Logos, God the Lord accepts *our* consciousness, our human life *as it is*. The drama He enacts is a tragedy, quickening a higher tendency in the midst of our human misery. The forms, or types, are marred by want and sin. The "shadows" remain humanly imperfect, far beneath their ideal content. The "spoken words," however much aglow with the Holy Ghost, remain bound to the limitation of our language, disturbed as it is by anomalies. As a product of writing, the Holy Scripture also bears on its forehead the mark of the form of a servant. This, then deceives our vision. This produces a result like what occurs in the case of many paintings of the latest French school, in which, at first sight, one sees, indeed, bubbles and daubs of paint, and even tints and lines, but not *the image*; and only after repeated attempts a view is finally obtained, so that those daubs and bubbles disappear, the tints and lines become active, and the image stands out before us. This was the case with Christ Himself. How many an intelligent Jew has seen the Christ, but has *failed* to discover in Him the Son of God. Somatically, by merely gazing upon the multiplicity of the features of the phenomenon, this was not possible. No chemical investigation, however accurate, could have discovered any difference between the flesh and blood of Christ and ours. He had a face like our face, an eye like our eye; and he only who took his stand at the proper distance, and who himself had received light in the eye of his soul, was able at length to see the shining out of the Divine nature in that Rabbi of Nazareth. Hence, from the attention bestowed upon the human phenomenal in the Holy Scripture, you must never promise yourself the impression of faith. This rather leads many away from the unity, and as such it stands in the way of faith. And however much it is your duty to study that *multiplicity* and *particularity* in the Scripture (both materially and formally), yet from that multiplicity you must ever come back to the view *of the unity of the conception,* if there is, indeed, to be such a thing for you as a Holy Scripture. The Scripture does not exist otherwise than after the "divers portions and divers manners" of Heb. i. 1, but in this diversity the principal thing is ever the *word of God.*

So far, therefore, as the representation of the secondary authors (auctores secundarii) as amanuenses of the Holy Spirit, or also as an *instrument* played upon by the Holy Ghost, exclusively tended to point to that unity of conception, there is nothing to be said against it. In that sense, one can even say that the Holy Scripture has been given us from heaven. If, on the other hand, one goes farther, and for the sake of maintaining that unity of conception closes the eye to the many-sidedness and multiformity of the Scripture, and the organic way in which it gradually came into existence as a sum-total of many factors, then nothing remains but a mechanical lifelessness, which destroys the vital, organic unity. This was certainly not intended by our older theologians. They, indeed, pointed, and sometimes even with much detail, to the differing origin of the books, to the difference of style and content, to the difference of character of the authors and of the vicissitudes of their lives, and also to the different tendency of the parts of the Scripture. But yet it can scarcely be denied that they had established themselves too firmly in the idea of a logical theory of inspiration, to allow the animated organism of the Scripture to fully assert itself. This obliges us, just because we join ourselves as closely as possible to the historic Theology of the Reformation, in order to prevent misunderstanding to explain in some detail this very different and multiform character of *the multiplicity* in the Scripture, first, as it concerns the instruments of inspiration, and then as it concerns inspiration itself.

The Instruments of Inspiration

Every revelation, which is not involuntary but voluntary and intended, assumes a consciousness in God from which it goes out, and a consciousness in man toward which it directs itself. It assumes, in the second place, a content which can take on the form of the conscious. And finally it assumes an instrument or vehicle by which it is brought from the consciousness of him who will reveal himself, into the consciousness of him for whom the revelation is intended. All revelation, therefore, falls away if the consciousness in God be not taken as its starting-point, and becomes weakened when, though not entirely pantheistically but in a pantheistic manner, one grants that perceptions arise in us, but denies that the fruit of those revelations in our consciousness was beforehand known and intended by God. In the second place, the essential character of revelation is undermined when, in a mystical sense, it is left to be choked in the world of our emotions, rather than made to come to its sublimate in our consciousness. And, thirdly, revelation becomes darkened and clouded when one studies exclusively its *point of departure* in God and its *point of arrival* in man, without a due consideration also of the conducting wire or line along which it directed itself to us. By our creation after God's image, we are authorized to take, with reference to this matter, the transmission from the consciousness of one man to that of another as an analogy, and in that case it is certainly true that this transmission is accomplished most readily and most often by the vehicle *of language*; but by no means by this alone. In all sorts of ways also are we able, without ever speaking a word, to convey something from our consciousness to the consciousness of others. First, there is that entire series of communications which is calculated upon the eye as the vehicle; all object lessons, pictures, the look of the eye, the changes of the facial expression, the movements of the body, the pointing to something, the doing of a symbolical or illustrative act, etc. To this is added, in the second place, the strong impression of a deed, of a repeated action, of the example. And, finally, in the third place, there enters here for our consideration, that varied hypnotizing influence by which one is able to subject the psychic life of the other to his will. But however broad our repertory may be for this purpose, it nevertheless remains a limited one, because we have no power over the person himself; neither have we the disposition of his lot. With God, on the other hand, there is no such limitation. He can influence man by all the means that are present in his human composition and in his surrounding world. Hence, for the communication of His revelation, first of all He has the disposal of all the means that are at our service; but also, in the second place, the human body and mind, and all increated capacities and powers, and the conditions in which one may be placed. None of these means may be taken as standing dualistically outside of God and over against Him. God Himself formed our consciousness, and preserves it in existence from moment to moment. All our nervous life is in His hand and is His creature. Our imagination is a capacity quickened in us by Him. Our language is language wrought in us by Him. He gave us the susceptibility for impressions by our sense of sight. The mystical influence, which is shown by biology or hypnosis, of soul upon soul, has been thought out by Him and realized in us. To which is added, moreover, that as our Creator He formed our personality and our disposition, approaches us in the root and centrum of our inner being, and can involve our life in all those events and experiences whose impression in us He will use for His ends. Thus, in the fullest sense of the word, He has *the whole of man* at His disposal and *the world* in which He has placed man. This leads of itself to the distinction between the *subjective* and *objective* instruments of inspiration, and to the distinction between those means which of themselves are present in man or in the world round about him, and those which He purposely *causes to originate or institutes* for this end.

Among these subjective and present means of inspiration, we name *internal address, external address* and the *impulse*.

By *internal address* we understand that God speaks to man, without making use of his organ of hearing, in the same way in which, outside of our organs of speech and of hearing, we hold a dialogue with ourselves. This is an ἐντὸς λαλεῖν (a speaking within), by which God the Lord inworks directly upon our psychic consciousness, and there causes such thoughts or perceptions to arise as He wills. As a rule we are not able to do this immediately from man to man. We generally employ in this an action which goes out from our own consciousness to our nerves, thence to our organs of speech, thence to the air, by the repercussion of the air upon the auditory nerves of the other, and only along this way enters into his consciousness. But already in magnetic sleep we have an example of a transmission from consciousness to consciousness, which does not stand in need of this middle-link of speech and hearing; and in the dialogue which we hold with ourselves from moment to moment, we perceive again and again that our organs of speech do not operate, neither, indeed, our organs of hearing, and that nevertheless successive changes of thought take place in us. And since God has access to our consciousness, not simply from without, but also from within, He *cannot* be bound to organs of speech and hearing; hence by this *internal address* we must understand that He brings thoughts directly into our consciousness, as coming to us from Him, which we understand as a dialogue of God and our soul. In this sense Jesus constantly affirms, "As I hear, I judge" (John v. 30), which cannot be interpreted otherwise than as a constant internal address of God in His inner being. With Adam, also, such internal address must be assumed before the fall, so that only after the fall we read that he heard God, as though His voice walked in the garden upon the wind of the day; and entirely natural description of the perception of God's voice, now no longer within him, but outside of him; not as *internal address,* but as *external address.* It is self-evident that by sin the susceptibility for this internal address was blunted, but this does not take it away, that also after sin, in still the same way, but now from the special principium, the Lord was able to reveal His thoughts and thus also His words in man, viz. in the prophets. This internal address takes account, of course, of the observation of conceptions that are present in our memory, and of the language in which we express these thoughts and conceptions. There is something in this that offends, if one takes it that the forming of our conceptions and of our words is arbitrary and the fruit of conclusions ($\theta\acute{\epsilon}\sigma\iota\varsigma$); but it has nothing strange in it, when one perceives that the forming of conceptions and of words is the fruit of our natural disposition ($\phi\acute{\upsilon}\sigma\iota\varsigma$) and is thus necessary, and has been appointed, therefore, for us by God Himself. Moreover, we leave it entirely undecided whether, in this internal address, God forms these thoughts and words in our consciousness, or whether He merely occasions such an urgency in our consciousness as interprets itself to our conception in those given words and thoughts. We read, to be sure, in Deut. xviii. 18, "I will put my words in his mouth," an expression which, in comparison with Exod. iv. 15 (where it is said to Moses: "Thou shalt speak unto him and put the words in his mouth," i.e. of Aaron), makes one almost think of a *whispering in the ear,* even as Christ promises His apostles that "it shall be given you in that hour what ye shall speak" (Matt. x. 19); but by no means prevents our accepting with this figure of speech also that the inworking has taken place in the centrum itself of the human consciousness, and from thence extended itself to the organs of speech. This, however, by no means excludes the speaking through the organ of speech of a human being without having the action go out to his organ of speech. It is well known how, in magnetic sleep, one person is able to accomplish this with the other. With those who were possessed similar phenomena occur. In our dreams also our organs of speech sometimes utter words which at least do not rise from our normal consciousness. And the strongest proof for this lies in the speaking with the glossolaly, by which the mouth uttered words which were entirely foreign to the thought-sphere of the speaker. Analogous to this is the speaking that has sometimes been taught to birds, and which from the side of God occurs in the significant speaking of the ass of Balaam. All these analogies show that the organs of speech of one can enter the service of the consciousness of another; as, for instance, when one who knows no Latin and has no understanding of medicine has been magnetized, and dictates a prescription which not he but his magnetizer has thought out.

The *external address* bears another character, and is even said to be (Num. xii. 8) "mouth to mouth," or also (Exod. xxxiii. 11) to take place "face to face." Here the emphasis falls not upon what man speaks after the suggestion of God, but upon what he *hears,* even in such a way that the bystanders also can *hear* it. This is most clearly seen in Exod. xix. 9, where the Lord says to Moses: "That the people may hear when I speak with thee." This direct address appears equally clearly in the speaking from Sinai to the people, of which we read in Deut. v. 26: "For who is there of all flesh that hath heard *the voice of the living God* speaking out of the midst of the fire, as we have?" An entirely unique fact, spoken of with emphasis no less than four times. With the call of Samuel the selfsame phenomenon appears. Samuel heard the sound of a voice, which he first took to be Eli's voice, and which only afterwards by the direction of Eli was recognized by him as the voice of the Lord (1 Sam. iii. 8, 9). What we likewise read of the voice of the Lord at the baptism of Jesus, and from the cloud at His transfiguration, falls under the same category even as the speaking of God to Adam after the fall, when he heard the voice of the Lord walking in the garden upon the wind of the day. With respect to this *external address* Num. vii. 89 is especially noteworthy, where the very place is indicated from which the voice went forth. There we read: "Then he (Moses) heard the Voice speaking unto him *from above the mercy-seat* that was upon the ark of the testimony, *from between the two cherubim*; and he spake unto him." The distinction between this *external address* and the *internal address* allied to it, exists principally in this, that with the *internal address* the voice of the Lord is observed as coming up from within, while with the *external address* a perception arises that the sounds *come from without.* At the foot of Sinai the people hear the voice coming down to them from above. Moses hears the voice come to him from between the cherubim. Samuel observes the voice from the side of Eli's chamber. At the baptism of Jesus the bystanders heard the voice *from heaven.* According to 2 Pet. i. 17, Peter heard the voice on Tabor "from the excellent glory," etc. Of course the addresses of Jesus on the way to Damascus and on the Island of Patmos do not lie in the same line. After His ascension, Jesus bears somatically, also, our human nature. The question with regard to His speaking from heaven, therefore, is simply whether Jesus descended in order to speak with Paul from the ordinary distance, or whether this speaking took place in a way similar to what is indicated to us by the telephone. With the speaking of God in the address, on the other hand, the somatic remains wanting; hence, also, the organs of speech by which to form the words. The question, therefore, here remains whether indeed this sound of a voice was produced by the vibration of the air-waves, or whether in the tympanum of the hearer a sensation was occasioned similar to what we occasion by the inflection of our voice. "He that planted the ear, shall he not hear? He that formed the eye, shall he not see?" (Ps. xciv. 9). In like manner, is not God, who has established for us so wondrous a relation of voice, organs of speech, waves of air, tympanum, auditory nerve and consciousness, Himself able to use each of these, His creatures, and apply them in like manner as He appointed and maintains them for us from moment to moment by His omnipresent omnipotence? There is no room here for choice, since the more subjective interpretation is equally intricate, or, if you please, equally divinely-natural, as the more objective. Neither does the occurrence on the way to Damascus, when the bystanders about Paul did not hear what he heard, offer any explanation; simply because the speaking of the glorified Christ rests upon the somatic basis, which is *not* present with God, and the telephone even now shows how one can hear what the other does not observe. Whether, therefore, the *address* was accomplished by God's working on the air-waves, or merely upon the tympanum, the same effect wrought by us when we use our organs of speech, cannot be decided; if only we hold fast to the fact that the person addressed heard words in his own language, in the same way as though he were spoken to by his neighbor.

Merely for the sake of completeness we add in the third place the *impulse.* By itself the impulse is nothing else than the "being moved" ($\phi\acute{\epsilon}\rho\epsilon\sigma\theta\alpha\iota$) of 2 Pet. i. 21, in entire agreement with the "moving" פַעַם of Judg. xiii. 25. This "moving" indicates merely that the one moved has received a push, a touch which has driven him out from his repose, in the full sense "an impulse urging the mind." "And the spirit of God *came upon* Saul" (וַתִּצְלַח), in 1 Sam. xi. 6, has precisely the same meaning. The most forcible example of this impulse, however, occurs in Jer. vi. 11 and Jer. xx. 9, collato 7; in both of which Jeremiah testifies that he experienced in his heart an impulse so overpowering that, try as he might, he was not able to offer resistance to it until it became to him "as a burning fire shut up in his bones." This impulse we number among the subjectively present means, for the reason that the poet and artist in general speak of similar experiences. In the "Deus est in nobis, agitante calescimus illo," an allied sensation announces itself, which is even experienced by the writer of prose, when, as the French call it, he moves *en veine*. Such an impulse also forms the background of heroism. The hero feels in himself an impulse to action which he cannot explain, either from the world about him or from his world within. To him as well as to the artist this impulse is a mystery. The question whether such an impulse from the world of mysteries is not connected with the basis of genius in such select spirits, need not detain us here. Nothing prevents us from allowing that such a basis was also present in the whole personality of Jeremiah. He even knew himself to be prepared for his calling from his mother's womb. But even if this impulse in connection with inspiration is nothing else than the use of what is present in the subject, and the application of that for which he had the susceptibility, this impulse here bears nevertheless a peculiar stamp, insomuch as it always occurs as an impulse of the Holy Ghost. This is a closer definition, which certainly concedes the fact that God the Lord can cause such an impulse to come to us in the centrum of our psychical life; but now employs it for a definite purpose, limits it to the sphere of the holy, and places it in connection with the entire plan of Revelation, which He is in the act of giving. The "clothing" (לָבַשׁ), however closely allied to the "moving" (פָּעַם), may not be placed on a line with the impulse. The former indicates the sensation, by which he who was apprehended feels himself enveloped and overcome as by an unknown power. It refers to a sensation, which, far from being an incitement to action, rather impedes and paralyzes. The פָּעַם makes active, the לָבַשׁ passive.

The second class of subjective means of inspiration includes the tardemah, "sleep" (תַּרְדֵּמָה), the chalom, "dream" (חֲלוֹם), and the chazon, "vision" (חָזוֹן).

The *Tardemah*, which occurs with Adam in Gen. ii. 21, Abraham in Gen. xv. 12, and Saul in 1 Sam. xxvi. 12, is mentioned as a deep sleep, which falls upon a person from without. "Fall" (נפל) is the constant word with which this "sleep" is contrued, and while at one time it says that the Lord *caused* such a sleep *to fall*, at another time it says (1 Sam. xxvi. 12) that this *deep sleep from the Lord had fallen upon them*. The same word occurs in Job iv. 13 and xxxiii. 15 to indicate a very deep sleep, which *falleth upon men, in slumberings upon the bed,* but as shown by the connection in both cases, as a prelude to a Divine revelation; while in Isaiah xxix. 10 such sleep is mentioned in an unfavorable sense, by way of a figure, to express a spirit of entire dulness and insensibility which should be poured out upon the people. This last, therefore, is a sleep in a metaphorical sense, for which reason it reads "the spirit of deep sleep," and consequently "pour" (נסך), and not "fall" (נפל), is used as verb. In all other places, on the other hand, the Tardemah is taken in its *real* sense, and occurs again and again as an absolute anaesthesis, which is effected by God upon the person, in order in this entirely passive state to cause an entirely other world to reveal itself to his inner consciousness, or as was the case with Adam, to operate upon him in a violent way. The narcotic sleep offers itself as analogy to this, and especially in the case of the violent operation which Adam underwent, one thinks naturally of the condition produced by chloroform or of the first effects of strychnine. But though it appears from these analogies that human nature is susceptible to such a state of absolute insensibility, the action which took place remains nevertheless an effect of what God directly wrought, and so far as the nature of the psychical life during this sleep is concerned, it is an action of a different sort. It makes the impression of an entire liberation of the psyche from the connection which through the body it has with its surrounding world: a leading back of the psychic life into its centrum, and in that centrum a disclosure to the psyche of a mysterious world, in which God comes to it and speaks to it. A form of revelation particularly noteworthy, because evidently this Tardemah does not enter into *this* life, but isolates the person, to whom the revelation comes, from *this* life, and then deals with him according to the law which applies to another than this earthly existence.

The "dream" bears a different stamp. In the first place, here sleep or slumber maintains its common character; and, secondly, revelation-dreams exhibit almost always the form of our common dreams, in so far as these dreams also an isolated drama is seen by the *ego* of the dreamer. The world of dreams is still a mystery to us. No one can tell whether in sleep one dreams only when on awakening one remembers it, or whether one always dreams when asleep but that as a rule in awaking one has no remembrance of it. Our dreams bear very different characters. In the common dream all connection is wanting with the actual condition, consisting in the fact that we lie in bed; but with the nightmare one dreams mostly of exciting experiences which overtake us while we lie there. In what is more slumber than sleep we dream that we lie awake and are not able to get asleep. He who saw us slumber knows that we slept, but to us no transition took place from our day into our night consciousness. The content of our dreams generally is made up from images and remembrances which lie in orderly arrangement in our mind, but now appear ofttimes before us in entirely different combinations. Generally the outlines of the images in our dreams are vague, but often they are so sharply drawn, especially in the nightmare, that what we see we could readily reproduce in a drawing. There are dreams which as mere play of the imagination pass away; but there are also dreams which work lasting effects, which discover one to himself, and dreams which are not free from guilt. Holy and demoniacal influences often work side by side in our dreams. Whether indeed this wondrous world of our dreams simply shows the aimless movement of the images in us, or whether these dreams are the result of the activity of our spirits in our sleep, and constitute a component part of the spirit's activity, remains an absolute secret to us. This, however, may be said, that our dreams cannot be verified by us, that they are not consciously produced by us, but that they leave the impression of a drama shown to us by some one outside of ourselves, in which we ourselves are concerned, without knowing how, and by which an outside power leads us involuntarily into scenes which arise without our aid.

It must not be said, however, that the *dream* in revelation is nothing else than a common dream, in which, simply, other images appear. Not in the ordinary sense, but undoubtedly in a pregnant sense (sensu praegnanti), it is said in 1 Sam. xxviii. 6: "And when Saul inquired of the Lord, the Lord answered him not, neither by dreams, nor by Urim, nor by prophets." Three distinct revelation-forms are here mentioned in which Saul might have received an answer, and of these three the dream is one. And it is noteworthy that next to false prophets the pseudo-dreamers also are separately mentioned as "the dreamers of dreams" in Deut. xiii. 1, 3. Hence he who dreamed such a dream did by no means at his awakening entertain the opinion that it had been a common dream, which he could safely pass by and forget; but he lived under the impression that something had been shown or told him which was possessed of symbolic or actual reality. The difference, therefore, between these two kinds of dreams was clearly perceived. This much, indeed, may be said, that in the scale of the means of revelation "the dream" does not stand high. The "dream" is, indeed, the common means of revelation for those who stand outside of the sacred precincts, such as Abimelech, Pharaoh, Nebuchadnezzar. The false prophets imitated nothing so easily as the dream (see Jer. xxiii. 32); and according as the revelation becomes richer and clearer, the dream becomes rarer. Neither with Moses, nor with the Christ, nor with the apostles do we find the dream mentioned as a revelation-form. When this dream was real, it consisted in this, that in the dream God appeared and gave His charge. When it was half-symbolic, as at Bethel, then the appearance of God took place in a given surrounding. And if it was purely symbolical, as with Pharaoh, then it needed the interpretation (פִּתְרוֹן),   and was in itself unintelligible and incomplete. Revelation, therefore, by the symbolical dream consists of two parts: the dream itself and its interpretation, *both* of which bear a supernatural character. Every effort to explain the interpretation as a simple application of the rules of symbolism is vain, from the fact that in the case of both Joseph and Daniel the interpretation of the dream is not given by those who were versed in symbolism, but they were unable to do this, and it is given only by men who stood outside of this peculiar science, and who frankly declared that this interpretation was no fruit of their ingenuity, but of Divine suggestion. The peculiar character of the revelation-dream, therefore, consisted in this, that the person to whom it came saw, indeed, the scene or drama in a similar way as with so-called common dreams, in his night-consciousness; but what he saw and heard was *no* product of the hidden workings in his own psychical life, but of an act of God in him. That, nevertheless, the drama in these dreams was generally formed from remembrances and images that were present in the memory and in the imagination of the dreamer, does not conflict with this in the least, As with *internal address* and *external address* the conceptions and words maintain the connection with the subjective nature of the person addressed, it is self-evident that a similar connection existed in the dream between what was present in the subjective imagination as constitutive element, and what God showed him. Only thus was it rational.

The *vision* bears almost the same character as the dream, with this difference, however, that the dream occurs when one *sleeps,* while the vision appears on the horizon of our inner consciousness when one is *awake.* As little as the dream, however, is vision a phenomenon foreign to our nature, which occurs exclusively in the economy of What is exceptional, therefore, by no means lies in the vision, but in this, that God the Lord makes use of the visionary capacity of our psyche, by which to introduce something into our consciousness. It must be granted that the dream is more common than the vision, but this is no proof that the visionary does not belong to our nature. No one, indeed, will exclude from our human nature a thirst and talent for art, even though this aesthetic power, with most people, never passes the *potential* stages; and such is the case with the visionary capacity. Whether or not it will discover its existence depends upon the inner and outward disposition of the person. In the East the chance for this is better than in the West. The Semitic race developed this capacity more strongly than the Indo-Germanic. By one temperament its development is favored; by another weakened. In times of excitement and general commotion, it is more usual than in days of quiet and rest. He who is aesthetically disposed becomes more readily visionary than the intellectualist. Sensitive nerves court the vision more than what have been called nerves of iron. Psychically diseased conditions are more favorable to the visionary than the healthy and normal; and often before dying a peculiar visionary condition appears to set in, which is exceedingly worthy of note. Vivid *imagination* forms the transition between the common wakeful consciousness and real vision, which operates in a threefold form. It is strongest when one becomes agitated by a phantom, especially when this is occasioned by an evil conscience. Macbeth sees everywhere the image of Duncan, the king he murdered, and in his inquiry whether that image is real, he is unable to distinguish appearance from reality. Of an entirely different nature is what is called "absent-mindedness," i.e. a life in another world than the real, either as the result of much study and thought, or of the reading of history or novels. This is carried so far by some people, that the very members of their family affect them strangely at times, and they imagine themselves to be in the company of their novel heroes. Finally the third form is the vision of the artist, in whose spirit looms the image, which from his spiritual view he will paint on the canvas or chisel in marble. But these are not visions in the real sense, since the horizon of our inner view here still remains subject to the verification of our consciousness. And this is the very thing lost with vision. Images and forms then rise before us, which force themselves upon us as an outside power, repress the autonomous activity of our imagination, and bring us outside of ourselves. Then one is awake, and sits, stands, walks, or rides, and meanwhile loses himself, and sees sometimes close at hand sharply outlined images in colors and in forms, which, even when the vision departs, leave him a sharp and clear impression, so startlingly vivid that he can scarcely make himself believe it was not reality. Hyperesthesis can introduce such illusory conditions, and can even assume the form of monomania and be a precursor of insanity. In the "Fixed Idea" (Zwangvorstellung), also, a visionary image may obtrude itself upon us against our will. And finally we observe, that vision occurs in rest, in action, in dialogue, and even with the adoption of the person in the drama of the vision. But in whatever form it occurs, it is always characteristic of the vision that the person who sees it ceases to be master of his own consciousness and in his own imagination, and is nothing but a spectator, while another power is active within him.

With this general discrimination of that which is visual, it is not in the least surprising that in the Holy Scripture the vision is also attributed to false prophets (Is. xxviii. 7, Jer. xiv 14, Ezek. xii. 24, etc.), and that outside of Scripture even, in history, the visionary plays such an important role. When, therefore, in the Holy Scripture the vision (חָזוֹן and מַחֲזֶה,, Gen. xv. 1) appears as a fixed form, especially of prophetical revelation, it must not be taken as though there were anything uncommon in this vision; but it should be understood in the sense that God the Lord made use of the capacity for visions in man in order to reveal to us His will and His counsel. At best it may still be remarked that the revelation vision often appears with a certain connexity and continuity. Not some strange vision now, and again one some years after, but the vision is constantly repeated in definite series, even introduced by a vision of a call, by which all the visions become together the successive acts of one mighty drama. Thus construed, the visionary phenomena are certainly subjected to a governing power, while the visions themselves have nothing uncommon about them. That which is uncommon consist exclusively in this, that God the Lord announces Himself in the vision, that it is He that shows what is seen, and that the visionary person knows that he is dealing with God.

Of the content of the vision, it may be said that the same remarks apply to it as apply to that of the "dream." The content is generally composed from the data which were present in the imagination or in the memory of the visionary person; but from these data a new drama is composed, and in this way all sorts of mysteries of the counsel of God are shown. The difference, however, between the prophetic and apocalyptic vision is apparent. In the first the vision joins itself to the historic reality, in the midst of which the prophet lives, while in the Apocalypse the drama arises from the hidden world and moves towards him. For which reason the forms and images in the prophetic vision are mostly known and common, while in the apocalyptic vision the images are monstrous, or appear in a wondrous manner, and sternly set themselves against every effort to reduce them to a figure intelligible to us. Recall, for instance, the cherubim in Ezekiel, or the appearance of Christ to John on Patmos, as sketched in Rev. i. 13-16. The content, however, of such a vision is not always dramatically realistic, so that it contains both speech and action. There are also visions that are purely *symbolical* (such as the well-known visions of the olive tree, the flying scroll, etc., of Zechariah), which, just like the symbolical dream, miss their aim unless an interpretation accompanies them. Wherefore, both in Zechariah and in the Apocalypse of John we find this symbolic vision constantly followed by its *interpretation.*

The *ecstasy* needs no separate treatment here; later, in connection with prophetical inspiration, it will come in its own order. Ecstasy is distinguished from vision in degree of intensity, but not in kind. As soon as the action of the visionary power communicates itself to the motory nerves, and consequently withdraws the muscular action from the will of the person, ecstatic conditions follow, which according to the intensity of the action exerted, are weak in impulse or overwhelming in their pressure. A single word is needed here concerning מַרְאָה (Mar'ah, vision), which does not stand on a line with מַחֲזֶה (Mach'zeh, vision). The mar'ah is to be distinguished from the chazon, in so far that the *mar'ah* seldom plays any part in the sphere of psychic-visions, and rather indicates *the seeing of a reality which reveals itself. Chazah* is a gazing at something that requires effort, and in so far indicates the psychical weariness which the seeing of visions occasioned, while *Ra'ah* of itself indicates nothing more than the perception of what passes before us. When a *Mar'eh* appears, the seeing of this form or image is called the *Mar'ah.* Special mention of this *Mar'ah* occurs with Moses. After him no prophet arose (Deut. xxxiv. 10) "whom the Lord knew face to face"; and since this "face to face" is chosen by the holy apostle, by which to express the *immediate* knowledge of the blessed, with Moses also it must be taken to mean *a seeing of the reality of heavenly things.* In

Numbers xii. 6-8 it is said in so many words, that the Lord reveals Himself to other prophets in a vision or in a dream, but "my servant Moses is not so." With him the Lord speaks "mouth to mouth, even apparently (וּמַרְאֶה), and not in dark speeches; and the similitude (תְמוּנָה) of the Lord shall he behold." We need not enter here upon a study of the character of this appearing of Jehovah, but we may say that this is no seeing in the visionary condition, but rather the falling away of the curtain behind which heavenly realities withdraw themselves from our gaze. This was a temporary return of the relation in which sinless man in paradise saw his God. Not continuously, but only in those moments in which it pleased the Lord to reveal Himself to Moses "with open face." A form of revelation which, of course, had nothing in common with the Christophany or Angelophany.

In this pregnant sense the *Vision* forms of itself the transition from the subjective to the *objective* means of revelation. Distinction can here again be made to a certain extent between such mediums of revelation (media revelationis) as were present in the ordinary course of life, and those others which in a supernatural way proceed from the special principium; even though it is self-evident that it is by no means always possible for us to draw the boundary-line sharply between the two. In itself, the birth of a person is a common event; but when such a person is set apart and anointed from the womb to a holy calling, in this very birth already mingles the working of the special principium. These objective *means of revelation* must claim our attention here, because they also were made ancillary to inspiration. This appears most forcibly in the case of the Christophany and Angelophany, which is never silent, but always tends at the same time to reveal to man what was hidden in God. This applies also to the signs אוֹתוֹת) in the widest sense, because all these, the ordinary as well as the extraordinary, the permanent as well as the transient, *uttered audible speech,* or tended to support a given revelation, to explain or to confirm it. The field for this should therefore be taken as broadly as possible. The whole appearing of Israel and its historic experiences must here be brought to mind: all the difficulties between Israel and its neighbors; the national conditions which the Lord called into life in and about Israel; the covenant with His people; the persons which the Lord raised up in Israel and put in the foreground; the natural phenomena which Israel observed; the diseases that were plagues to the people; the tabernacle and temple-service,–in short, everything comprised in the rich, full life that developed itself in Israel. To this is added as a second factor, but woven into the first, that series of extraordinary actions, appearances and events which we are mistakenly wont to view exclusively as miracles. It was under the broad and overwhelming impression of this past, of this nation as a whole, and of these events, that he grew up who was called to extend the revelation, and was trained for that revelation; which education was still more definitely accentuated by personal surroundings and experiences.

But besides this general service which the objective phenomena rendered, both the ordinary and the extraordinary, they tended at the same time, by inspiration, to reveal the thoughts of God to the agents of His revelation. This applies especially to the whole utterance of nature, in so far as the veil, which by sin was put upon nature and upon our eyes, was largely lifted in that higher life-circle of Israel, so that the language of nature concerning "the glory of the Lord, which filleth the whole earth," was again both seen and heard. It will not do to view the revelation of the power of God in nature as an outcome of mechanical inspiration. It was established organically, in connection with what the messengers of God both saw and observed in nature. This revelation assumes a different character, when the "rainbow," the "starry heavens," and the "sand of the seashore" are employed, not as natural phenomena, but in their symbolical significance with respect to a definite thought of God. Only then does that which is common in itself become a *sign;* as, for instance, when Jesus points His disciples to the golden cornfields, and speaks of "the fields, that are white for the harvest." The speech, which in this sense goes forth from the common phenomena of nature, can thus be strengthened by the extraordinary intensity of their manifestations; as, for instance, the thunder in Ps. xxix. has become the voice of the Lord—the lightning-bolt, more intensively violent in Ps. xviii., the mighty storm-wind of Habakkuk iii., or these three together upon Horeb. This significance can also be emphasized by their strikingly noticeable succession, as in 1 Kings xix. 10-12. Striking events, like that meeting with Melchizedek upon Abraham's return from war with the mountainous tribes, may give, as here appears, an entire series of thoughts from the revelation of God. What is common in itself can become a sign, simply because prophesied beforehand (for instance, 1 Sam. x. 7). And, finally, all sorts of things that were common in themselves can obtain a significance by their combinations or positions, such as the tabernacle, together with all the things that belonged to the sacred cultus; the memorial stones in Jordan; the boards which Isaiah put up in the market-place; the scrolls of the law and Tephilloth, and even the iron pan of Ezekiel. With all these things and phenomena, common in themselves, the "sign" originates; either because God attaches a definite significance to them, or because they derive that significance from history or from attending circumstances. And it is not so much these things themselves, but much more the significance, original or given to them, which, understood by faith or indicated by a special inworking of the Holy Spirit, rendered service as an instrument to reveal and to inspire the thought of God.

This applied in still stronger measure to those extraordinary phenomena and events which are called "wonders" מוֹפֵת, or, in narrower sense, are spoken of as wonderful works (Niphleoth). The root from which these spring has been spoken of in connection with our study of the special principium, and the effort to explain them subjectively may be said to have been abandoned. If it is entirely true that they mostly fell to the share of believers, and that unbelievers sometimes did not see what believers saw very clearly, this affords not the least ground to subjectivize the miracles as such, after the intention of the Holy Scripture. Together with those single wonders, which one observed and another not, there are a number of others, which revealed themselves with an overwhelming impression to all that were present. Just remember the exodus from Egypt and the miracles in the wilderness. Again, it may not be forgotten that the simple presence of a fact is not enough to cause it to be perceived. As often as our mind is abstracted, and our intention refuses its action, it occurs that something is said or done in our presence which escapes our notice. Of this, therefore, nothing more need be said. All these meditation-theories have had their day, and nothing remains except the absolute denial of the miracle on one hand, and on the other hand the frank confession of its reality. Meanwhile, in the matter of inspiration, we are less concerned about the reality of the miracle, or the general revelation of God's power, which it reveals, than about the sense, thought, or significance which hides in these "wonderful works." In those miracles and signs there also lies a language, and in the matter of inspiration that language claims our attention. This peculiar *language* lies in all the phenomena and events which are extraordinary; and therefore no distinction need here be made between the Theophanies, the miracles in nature, the miracles of healing and of destruction, etc. In all these miracles a thought of God lies expressed, and in the matter of inspiration that thought of God is the principal interest. For this reason, however, the reality should not be looked upon for a moment as accidental or indifferent. Without that reality even thought misses its ground in God, and it is by this very union and combination of τὸ ὄν with the mind that thought receives its *ratification,* and comes to us, not as an idea suggested by ourselves, but as a communication from God to us. The principal thought in all *miracles* now is the thought of redemption. When the existing order of things distresses us, and turns us pessimistic, and places nature with its curse over against us and above us, as a power against which all resistance is vain, the miracle proclaims that the power is *not* the highest, that the heavens of brass above us *can* be opened, and that there is still another reality, entirely different from this order of things, which does not clash with our moral aspirations, but is in harmony with them. The world, such as it became by the curse, and now is, under the tempering of that curse by *common grace,* offends the only fixed point which the sinner retains in his moral consciousness, viz. his sense of right. Wrong triumphs again and again, while innocence suffers. Between the hidden life and outward conditions there is no harmony, such as our sense of right postulates. It is this problem which presented itself with great force in Israel, and for which no solution is given except in the miracles. The miracles voice a palingenesis which, first in the psychical and after that in the physical world, shall hereafter dissolve all dissonance in entire harmony. Every miracle is a real prophecy of the parousia and of the *restitution of all things* which it introduces. The miracle is the basis of the *hope,* in that entirely peculiar significance which in Scripture it has along with *faith* and *love.* It shows that something different *is* possible, and prophesies that such it shall sometime *be.* It is an utterance of that free, divine art, by which the supreme artist, whose work of creation is broken, announces the entire restoration of his original work of art, even in its ideal completion. Hence there can be no question of a "violation of the order of nature." This assumes that this order of nature has obtained an independent existence outside of God, and that at times God interferes with this independent order of things. Every such representation is deistic at heart, and in fact denies the immanent and omnipresent omnipotence by which God supports the whole cosmos from moment to moment, and every order in that cosmos. The miracle, therefore, may not be interpreted as being anything else than an utterance of the special principium, taken as *principium essendi.* An utterance which, preformative and preparative, and thereby at the same time annunciatory, views and ends in the parousia. The Niphleoth, therefore, include the spiritual as well as the material miracles. They react savingly against *sin* as well as against the *misery* which flows from sin.

Hence the miracles are no disconnected phenomena, but stand in connection with each other, and, as was shown above, they form one organic whole, the centre of which is Christ as the "Wonderful" and its circumference His people. The great central miracle, therefore, is the Incarnation, which in turn lies foreshadowed in the Christophanies. With those Christophanies the manifestation consisted in this, that, as in paradise God had created the body of Adam, He likewise here provided a human body, which presently returned to nothing, and merely served to render the appearance *as of a man* possible. In the plains of Mamre Abraham does not perceive at first that he is dealing with anything else than a common human occurrence. Even where angel appearances are spoken of, we may not represent angels as winged beings. Angels have no bodies; they are spirits; and they appear with wings only in the symbolic representation of the vision. In real appearances they always stand before us in the form of a man. All this, however, was altogether outside our nature. It gave us to see what was *like* unto our nature, not what was *of* our nature. Thus Christ is *the* "Wonderful" (Is. ix. 6), and in connection with this there arranges itself about His person the whole miracle-cyclus of His baptism, the temptation in the wilderness, the transfiguration upon Tabor, the voice in the temple, the angel in Gethsemane, the signs at the cross, the resurrection and the ascension, in order to be succeeded by the second miracle-cyclus of the parousia. In like manner we see that entire series of Niphleoth, or mighty works, going out from Christ and becoming established by Him in the sphere of the elements, in the vegetable kingdom, in the animal kingdom, and among men—a series of miracles, the afterglow of which still gleams in the miracles of the apostles. Peter, indeed, testifies (Acts iii. 16) that the authorship of the healing of the cripple lay in Christ.

In this organic connection the one group of miracles appears before us which is immediately connected *with Christ.* To this is joined a second group of miracles which does not point to the Christ, but to the appearance and the maintenance of *His people.* The fixed point in this group is the miraculous birth of Isaac, placed in the foreground as the great "wonder" by Paul in Rom. iv. 17 sq. What lies behind this merely serves to prepare the ground, and render the appearance of God's people possible. Only by the calling of Abraham and the birth of Isaac, when he and Sarah had become physically incapable of procreation, is this people born upon this prepared ground, and come to its incarnation. This was the great mystery. After this follows in the second place the miracle-cyclus of Egypt, of the wilderness, and of the taking of Canaan. Then the miracles which group themselves about Elijah and Elisha in conflict with the worship of Baal. And finally the group of miracles which, outside of Canaan, is seen in the midst of the heathen, when the great conflict between Israel and the nations was temporarily ended with the apparent destruction of Israel, as with its Golgotha.

Of course it extends beyond the lines of our task to work out more fully this concentric exposition of miracles. We merely wanted to show that in this entire phenomenon of miracles there lies one continuous manifestation of the great predominant thought of Redemption. This manifestation by itself was not enough to cause the thought that expressed itself in it to be understood and to be transmitted. To the "handling with hands" $\psi\eta\lambda\alpha\phi\hat{\alpha}\nu$ of 1 John i. 1 is added the "seeing" ($\theta\epsilon\omega\rho\epsilon\hat{\imath}\nu$), and it is only by that seeing that insight is obtained into the meaning and significance of the miracle. So much, however, is evident that the sight of these several miracles, or the reading of the narrative, counts among the means used by God in the revelation of Himself to the holy men of old. This is true in a twofold way: First, in so far as the miracles occasioned a deep impression of God's presence and of His overwhelming omnipotence, by which the ban, put upon believers by the superior power of the cosmos, was broken, and they were set free and faith was wakened. And secondly, because in each miracle by itself and in the mutual connection of all these wonderful works one grand, ever-varied thought of God expressed itself, the language of which only needed to be understood in order to have one's spiritual consciousness enriched. It should be noted, however, that the holy men of God separated that God who manifests Himself in His miracles, so little from the God who created and maintains the cosmos, that in their perception the glory of the Lord in creation and in nature constantly identified itself with that other glory which He revealed to and in His people. The last four Psalms show this most plainly: First, in Ps. cxlvii. 1-11 the glory of God in nature is sung, in verses 12-14 the glory of God's people appears, in verses 15-18 the power of God over nature is again exalted, and finally we read, "He sheweth his word unto Jacob, his statutes and his judgments unto Israel. *He hath not dealt so with any nation.*" Thus to the singer the Niphleoth of the natural and special principium form one grand whole, while the antithesis is not lost for a moment. In the same way, in Ps. cxlviii. all that lives not only, but every creature that exists, is poetically called upon to praise Jehovah, while the manifestation of the special principium asserts itself in the end, when it reads: "And he hath lifted up the horn of his people, the praise of all his saints; even of the children of Israel, a people near unto him. Hallelujah." And comparing Ps. cxlix. with cl. it is seen that in Ps. cxlix. the glory of the Lord among His people is the theme of the Hallelujah, while in Ps. cl. it is His greatness as creator and preserver of everything. Doubtless the singers and prophets of Israel owed this majestic conception of nature, which is entirely peculiar to Israel, to the prayer (Ps. cxix. 18), Open thou mine eyes, that I may behold, etc.; only by the working of the special principium were they enabled to see the greatness of the Lord in the utterances of the natural principium; but with this result that they by no means viewed the miracles as standing isolated by themselves, but always with the Niphleoth in the realm of nature for their background.

Thus we see that apart from real inspiration itself, all sorts of subjective as well as objective mediums of inspiration were employed by God, by which either to prepare His servants for inspiration, to impart it unto them, or to enrich, ratify, or explain its content.

83. *The Factors of Inspiration*

In the study of the factors of inspiration proper we begin with a sharp distinction between inspiration as a means of revelation and inspiration of the Holy Scripture. If, for instance, I take the fiftieth Psalm, the questions may be asked how, in what way, and on what occasion the singer was inspired with the content of this song, and what the relation is between what he himself sang and what God sang in and through him; but these are entirely different from the question by what action of the Holy Spirit this ancient song, in just this form, was adopted into the holy codex, by which it became a word of God to His whole church. For the present, however, this latter question as to the special inspiration of the Holy Scripture may be passed by. It can only be considered when the inspiration of revelation has been explained more fully. The thought cannot be entertained that a prophet like Amos, as an inspired person, may never have spoken or written anything more than those nine chapters we now have as oracles of God in his name. In length these nine chapters are scarcely equal to one short sermon. The assertion, therefore, is none too strong, that he spoke under prophetic inspiration at least twenty times as much, while whatever has been lost has nothing to do with the inspiration of the Holy Scripture. With these nine short chapters only *can* there be a question of this. The two kinds of inspiration, therefore, must be kept apart, and we must consider first what came first, viz. inspiration as the means employed of God, by which to cause His revelation-organs to speak, sing, or write what He desired and purposed. It cannot be denied that in the Holy Scripture, even for the greater part, utterances occur from the revelation-organs which make the impression of being the utterance of their subjective consciousness, but back of which a higher motive appears to have been active, flowing from another consciousness standing above them. In Psalm xxii., for instance, a speaker is evidently present who moans from the depths of his own sorrows, but before the song is ended the impression is received that an altogether different "man of sorrows" addresses you. Nothing derogatory is here implied to the more objective medium of inspiration treated in the former section, by which foreign words and scenes affected the ear and eye of the men of God. But in the Holy Scripture these objective means of revelation are not the rule, and the greater part of the content of the Scripture presents itself as having come forth subjectively from the human author, while nevertheless in his subjective utterance there worked a higher inspiring $\pi\nu\varepsilon\hat{v}\mu\alpha$ and it is properly this action of the Holy Spirit which here introduces inspiration as means of revelation *in its narrowest sense.* For this reason inspiration bears one character in lyric poetry, and another with the prophets, and still another with the Chokma, with Christ and with the apostles, so that each of these kinds of inspiration must separately be considered. But these lyrical, prophetical, chokmatic inspirations, etc., have something *in common,* and this must first be explained.

Inspiration rests upon the antithesis between the Spirit of God and the spirit of man, and indicates that the Spirit of God enlists into His service the spirit of man, disposes of it, and uses it as His conscious or unconscious organ. In this the human spirit is either more active or passive, in proportion as it has greater or lesser affinity to what God will reveal by it. If that affinity is entire, as is the case in some apostolic epistles, the action of the human spirit will seem to be the sole factor, and inspiration will scarcely be observed; while, on the other hand, where this affinity is very limited, as is the case with the most of Ezekiel's visions, the human spirit appears as little more than a phonograph, which serves to catch the action of the Spirit of God. This inspiration lies grounded in the nature of our human spirit. This is no isolated potency, but one that is pervasive. Our spirit can be affected by other spirits, and this can be done in two ways: either by entering in by the periphery, in order thence to approach the centrum of our spirit; or by entering into that centrum, in order thence to extend itself to the periphery. A great orator approaches his hearers in the periphery of their consciousness, and thence penetrates to the roots of their sense of self; while, on the other hand, the biologist or hypnotizer finds a means in the nervous system by which to penetrate at once to the centrum of the human spirit, and is able from thence to reach the periphery in such a way that the mesmerized subjects think and speak *as he wills.* Such a central inworking upon the human spirit goes out from the Spirit of God, and by inversion from Satan. Our spirit in our innermost being is not independent, but dependent, and, even without inspiration (taken in its narrower sense of means of revelation as *Theopneustic*), workings and inspirations from the spiritual world go out to the centrum of the life of our soul, which affect us for good or for evil. The poetical impulse, the inner promptings in every department of art, heroism, enthusiasm, animation in speech and writing, the stimulus of genius, premonition, and in connection with this the entire chapter of divination and all that it entails, show incontestably that our consciousness is not a boat propelled solely by the oar-stroke of our own exertions, but that it may likewise carry a sail which may be filled by winds over which we have no control.

Passing by Satanic inspiration, which will be discussed later in connection with the energumens, this general inspiration finds its ground first of all in the *omnipresent immanence of God.* ("In him we live and move and have our being.") There is not merely an "of him" and a "through him," but also an "in him." He is the fountain of all good, not in the sense that now and then we fill our life-jar with waters from that fountain, and afterward live of ourselves, but in the sense that, like plants, we flourish by the side of that fountain, because the root of our life is constantly refreshed by waters from that fountain. This relation of God is defined, in the second place, more closely by our creation *after the image of God.* If one may say so, there is a general inspiration of God in all nature. It is lasting and limited in animal instinct, and in a measure even in wine and in the stimulating agents of several medicines. When a dog jumps in the water to save a child, there is an inspiration of God in that animal; and when thunder distresses us, and fresh mountain air makes breathing an exhilaration, there is inspiration of a higher power. But with man, this inspiration assumes a special form by virtue of the affinity between God's Spirit and ours. God is Spirit. This is, according to Christ, $\tau\grave{o}$ $\mathring{o}\nu\tau\omega\varsigma$ $\mathring{o}\nu$ of His being, and consequently with us also the deepest point of our human life lies in our pneumatical existence. In so far as our nature is created after the image of God in original righteousness, this excellency could be lost and our nature become depraved; but not our creation after God's image so far as it pertains to its essence (quod ad substantiam). Our human nature is unassailable. The capability of having consciousness, which is the distinguishing mark of the pneumatical, has not been lost, and in this lies man's openness to inspiration (*Inspirationsfahigkeit*). Hence, inspiration can work in the unconverted as well, as was the case with Balaam and Caiaphas, and though it generally occurs in connection with conversion, it is by no means dependent upon this. The creation of man as a pneumatic being opens the possibility of communion between his spirit and the Spirit of God, by which the thoughts of God can be carried into his thoughts. To which is to be added, in the third place, that man is created, not as one who is always the same, but as a self-developing being, and that it is his end ($\tau\acute{e}\lambda os$) that God shall be in him and he in God, so that God shall be his temple (Rev. xxi. 22), and he a temple of God (Eph. ii. 21). This, likewise, offers the means by which the influence of the Spirit of God upon his spirit can be supremely dominant.

Care, however, should be taken against a confusion of terms, lest by an exchange with its metonymy inspiration itself escape from our grasp. Inspiration is not the same as communion. This, indeed, places the *ego* of man over against the *ego* of God, and makes them wed or enter into covenant, but ever in such a way that the *ego* of man accepts the communion, enters upon it, and lives in accordance with it,—a unity, but one which rests upon a duality. Neither may we confuse the ideas of inspiration and *mystical union*. This, indeed, rests upon the necessary and natural union between the head and members of one organism and the body of Christ, and is not grounded in the consciousness, but in the essentia. The mystical union makes us one plant with Christ. Neither, again, may inspiration be confused with *regeneration* and with its consequent enlightening. To illustrate: inspiration is the use of the telephone, in order to communicate a thought, while regeneration is the act which repairs the telephone when out of order. With such a man as Isaiah, regeneration was the means to save him unto life eternal, and inspiration to make him of service to the Church of God. Every effort, therefore, to interpret inspiration from an ethical basis, and to understand it as a natural fruit of sanctification, abnormal condition of the nature of man, but lies in his nature as a pneumatic being, which as such is open to the central inworking of the Spirit of God.

Hence, with inspiration we deal with three factors: (1) with the spirit that inspires (spiritus inspirans), (2) with the spirit of man that is inspired (spiritus hominis cui inspiratur), and (3) with the content of what is inspired.

In God who inspires, inspiration assumes *thought* and *will*. He who pantheistically denies consciousness in God or merely darkens it, abandons every idea of inspiration. For this very reason God is ever revealed unto us in the Holy Scripture as *the light,* and this light in God is pictured as the brightness from which the light of self-consciousness is ignited in our spirit. "In thy light shall we see light." Nothing, therefore, can be present in our consciousness but God knows it. "For there is not a word in my tongue, but, lo, O Lord, thou knowest it altogether." That this does not refer to our words merely, appears sufficiently clearly from the statement, that "the righteous God trieth the heart and reins" (Ps. vii. 9); for by that word "reins" the deepest root is indicated in the subsoil of our conscious soul-life. The most complete transparency of pure, clear consciousness is likewise a characteristic of the being of God, by which His theistic existence stands or falls. The ethical representation must, therefore, be dismissed, that inspiration gives rise to certain perceptions in us, which only afterwards produce thoughts in our human consciousness. At heart, this is nothing but the pantheistic representation of a deep (βυθός) out of which the thought separates itself in us only. If it is asked whether consciousness in God is anthropomorphic, and whether our world of thought is not limited by and bound to the finite, we readily reply: that the question contains some truth. The apostle himself acknowledges that our knowledge is a knowledge "in part," and that all our *gnosis* will sometime pass away, in order to make room for a higher "seeing." He, however, who infers from this, that for this reason there is *no* consciousness in God, contradicts the apostle's assertion that even to us a still higher form of consciousness is coming. If consciousness could assume one form only, even the finite form of our consciousness by day, the conclusion would certainly be correct. But this is not true, since consciousness has many forms, one by day and one by night, one without and one in ecstasy, one now and one in the realm of glory, which proves it to be entirely natural that consciousness in God has its own Divine form. Neither does this end the question. That Divine consciousness has affinity to our human consciousness. "We shall know, *even as we are known.*" If it is self-evident, that our future consciousness must stand in the genetic connection of identity with our present consciousness, this of itself provides the bridge which connects the divine consciousness with ours. Even among men, the consciousness of a child differs from the consciousness of a man, and yet the greater can enter the consciousness of the child. Consciousness differs with each and all, but true love is able to place itself in another's place; yea, in another's consciousness. With reference to its formal side, susceptibility for learning foreign languages sufficiently shows that consciousness is possessed of very great pliability, and is by no means frozen solidly in its form. If these are features in us of the image of God, we may safely conclude, that in the consciousness of God (1) there is affinity to our consciousness; and (2) the possibility is found of entering into the form of the consciousness of another. This becomes a certainty, when you remember, that God Himself has fixed the form of our consciousness, and has first thought it in this way before He created it. Our form of consciousness, therefore, is not a strange something to God, for He knew it before He enriched us with it. And though we grant unconditionally that the thoughts of God may not be assumed as clothed in our forms, we maintain that God is able to cast them into our consciousness-form, and hence is also able to think them in our form.

Next to this clear consciousness of thought, inspiration assumes in God who inspires *the will* to inspire this or that thought. This element of the will was neglected in former times, but in the face of the pantheistic representation of involuntary communication it now deserves a special emphasis. A twofold inspiration goes out from us: one is voluntary, the other involuntary. Voluntary when *purposely* we try to exert a certain influence; involuntary when our act or person exerts an influence *independently* of our will. This is so, because our self-consciousness is exceedingly limited, so that we observe a very small part only of the working that goes out from us. With God, however, this is not so. He is not like the star that sparkles without knowing it, but is transparent to Himself to the deepest depths of His Being and the utmost circumference of His action. Here, therefore, is no door that stands open for every passer-by to look in at will, but a door which on each occasion is opened. Inspiration of itself, therefore, presupposes in God the will and the purpose, from His Divine consciousness, to introduce into the consciousness of man this or that thought, transposed and interpreted into our form of thought, and thus to reveal it among men.

The second factor that claims our attention is *the spirit that is inspired;* viz. the spirit of man. The nature of this human consciousness may differ materially, and this difference may arise from its disposition as well as from its content. With reference to the disposition there can be affinity, neutrality, or opposition. In the case of the venerable Simeon in the Temple, there was a strong affinity of mind and inclination to the inspiration that was given him. The disposition of Jeremiah in Chapter xx. of his oracles bears witness to a strong opposition against inspiration; while in Chokmatic poetry the disposition of the singer does *not* appear, and thus remains neutral. Of course, with affinity and sympathy the subjective expression is far more strongly apparent; with an antipathetic disposition more violence must be done to the man of God; and with a neutral disposition neither the subject nor the feelings of the subject come to light. With a sympathetic disposition and a neutral mind both, it is possible that the revelation-organ itself should not observe that inspiration takes place, as is seen in many a Psalm and in the prophecy of Caiaphas, John xi. 50 and 52. The strongest possible expression for inspiration is the "Now this he said not of himself." Connected with this appears also the difference between aphoristic, more continuous, and altogether continuous inspiration. We catch inspired words from the lips of Zechariah and Simeon, with whom it is restricted to one single inspiration; we read of prophets and apostles, with whom repeated inspiration frequently bore an official character; and in Christ, of whom it is written that the Spirit not merely descended upon Him, but also remained upon Him, we see an inspiration in His human consciousness, which *ever continues,*—"As I hear, I judge" (John

But the *content* at hand in their consciousness must likewise be taken into account. By consciousness in this connection we do not merely understand the action of *thinking,* but also, sensation, perception, and observation in the general sense. With a man of genius from the upper strata of society, like an Isaiah, the content of this consciousness was, of course, much richer than with Amos, who had lived in the country among herdsmen; and, on the contrary, poorer with James, who originally was a fisherman, than with Paul, who had attended the schools of learning. If, in such a consciousness, the conceptions and representations are already present which are necessary for the oracle as its component elements, the oracle needs merely to effect the new combination. If, on the other hand, they are wanting, the material of imagery for the symbolical manifestation must be borrowed from the content of the imagination. Though, thus, the so-called $\sigma\upsilon\nu\text{-}\tau\acute{\eta}\rho\eta\sigma\iota\varsigma$ (i.e. our memory, our store of things) is in the first place the all-important factor, the imagination is needful as well, and not merely for the images in its portfolio, if we may so express ourselves, as for what, perhaps, the imagination is capable of doing with those images. Even outside of inspiration, with writers of note, you will see that series of images in the foreground which are in harmony with their inner nature; and in proportion as the writer lives either by apprehension or by conception, the images will lie loosely among his words or they will dominate his style. The many-sided content of the consciousness must not be estimated by what lies ready for use at a given moment, but also by its almost forgotten treasures. All that has ever gone through our memory has left its impression behind, and we often discover that there has been stored in our consciousness the memory of conditions, persons, names and conceptions, which, except for some impulse from without, would never have recurred again to our mind. And finally, to this content of our consciousness must be added all that which, outside of us, has been chronicled and committed to writing or image, and thus lies in reach to enrich our consciousness, The significance of this ready material in the consciousness, or of whatever else our consciousness has at its disposal, becomes plain at once, if we but recognize the organ of revelation to be a messenger who has something to communicate, on the part of God and in His name, to His Church. If, for instance, a superior officer in the army has to employ a captured farm-hand to send tidings to an inferior officer who has command in some distant town, the entire communication must be committed to writing, or, if the man is clever, be explained to him clearly and in detail. If, on the other hand, the officer sends an adjutant who saw the battle from beginning to end, and knows the position of the entire army, a hasty word in passing whispered in his ear is sufficient, and quick as lightning the adjutant rides to obey the given order.

It must not be imagined, however, that in the case of inspiration God the Lord is limited by this affinity of disposition, or by this content of the consciousness. Most of the apocalyptical visions rather prove the contrary. We have simply intended to indicate that, as a rule, that affinity and that content of the consciousness are employed by God as elements in inspiration. This is true even theologically; not as if God, for the sake of the success of Revelation, selected the most suitable persons from among those who were accessible, but rather that He Himself caused these men to be born for this purpose, predestined them for it, and caused them to spend their youth amid such circumstances and surroundings, that in His own time they stood in readiness as suitable instruments. As Jeremiah declares that to him it was said: "Before I formed thee in the belly I knew thee: and before thou camest forth out of the womb I sanctified thee. I have appointed thee a prophet unto the nations" (Jer. i. 5). This constitutes the fundamental thought which dominates the appearance of the revelation-organs from first to last. The words, "I know thee by name," in Ex. xxxiii. 12, indicate the same thing. And what is said of the ideal prophet in Isa. xlix. 1, 2, 5, by virtue of the comprehensive character of predestination, applies to all. This predestination cannot be limited to these men personally, for it embraces the whole sphere of life from which they sprang and in which they appeared. Such inspiration would simply have been inconceivable in England or among any of our Western nations. *Our* consciousness stands too greatly in need of sharp conceptions, visible outlines and rigid analysis. Since the world of thought that discovers itself to us in inspiration lies at first concentrated in its centrum, from whence it only gradually proceeds, there could be no question here of sharply drawn lines as the result of rigid analysis. The lines of the acanthus leaf cannot be admired so long as this leaf still hides in the bud. Inspiration, therefore, demanded a human consciousness that was more concentrically constituted, and this you find in the East, where dialectic analysis is scarcely known, while intuition is so much more penetrative, for which reason it describes its content rather in images than in conceptions. Moreover, intuitive consciousness lends itself more easily to that passiveness which, in a measure, is needful with all inspiration. The Western mind reacts more strongly and quickly against impressions received; the Oriental has that passive receptivity by which he surrenders himself to perceptions and drifts along with their current. He is more deeply inspired by nature, and therefore more susceptible to the Divine influence πάσχειν ὑπὸ τοῦ θεοῦ which is the characteristic of all inspiration. While we are more ready *to speak*, the Oriental is more inclined *to listen;* he does not know what conversation is, in our sense of the word, and that very inclination to listen aids his predisposition to inspiration. To this we may add, that among the nations of the East, Israel possessed these peculiarities in that modified form which prevented one-sidedness. It was Eastern, but formed the frontier against the West. The intuitiveness of the Israelitish consciousness, therefore, did not easily turn into an extravagant fancifulness, neither was it lost in a deep revery. The Jew possesses all needful qualities to secure a position of influence for himself in the Western world. Within himself he carried two worlds, and this rendered Israel more capable than any other people of receiving inspiration and of reproducing it intelligibly to the Western world. Paul, the dialectician, and Zachariah, the seer of visions, were both from Israel. In connection with this, the Jew in the East had that peculiarity, which still marks the French of to-day, of being inflamed by an idea, which is no result of logical thought, but springs from national life. The promise given to Abraham in Ur of the Chaldees becomes the pole-star to Israel's life as a nation. That one animating thought elevates Abraham above Lot, and presently Jacob above Esau, maintains Israel's independence in Egypt, appears again and again during the period of the Judges, finds at length its embodiment in the idea of the King, finds its acme in the expectation of the Messiah, and preserves Israel in Babylon under Antiochus Epiphanes, under Herod, and in its periods of deformation. From the nature of the case, such an idea animating an entire people is a valuable preparation for inspiration. It accustoms the whole nation to live under a higher inspiration. It has its disadvantages; life in an imaginary world may tempt to sin, as it did Tamar, and feeds falsehood especially, which is one of Israel's characteristic sins, but this is *the defect of its quality*, and does not affect its excellence in the least.

If such was the general soil prepared in Israel for inspiration, there was added to this in the second place that particular factor, which intensified and specialized this predisposition in individual persons. This took place *in their creation*, this creation being taken in connection with their genealogical origin, and going back, therefore, into the generations. But with all the emphasis this genealogical connection deserves, there is, nevertheless, the individual creation of the person, the moulding of his disposition, the tuning of the harpstrings of his heart, the endowment of him with charismata and talents, and the quickening in him of what in lesser measure was common to all his people. An election, if you please, not to salvation, but to service, to the task of an holy vocation, together with the fitting out of the elect one with every requisite for that service. The bow is provided, and also the arrows in the quiver. What lies hidden in the natural disposition is brought out by the leadings of Providence in education and surroundings,—Moses at Pharaoh's court, David as the shepherd lad, Peter and John the fishermen on the waters of Gennesareth. The casting of the net, the watching of the water's ripple, the quiet waiting of an almost inexhaustible patience for higher power to send fish into the net, and the constant readiness with fresh courage and hope of blessing to begin anew, constitute a choice preparation of the spirit for that restful and soulful abiding for the work of grace, in which it is known that God alone brings souls into His nets. To these leadings of Providence is added, as a rule, the *leadings of grace,* which God the Lord imparted to His chosen organs of revelation. By this grace most of them were personally regenerated, and thus themselves established in the salvation, the inspiration of which fell to their share. In an uncommon way this increased the affinity between their own spirit and the Spirit of God, as well as between the content of their consciousness and the content of their inspiration. Not in the sense, as stated above, that inspiration itself might be explained from this ethical affinity. He who affirms this virtually places the inspiration of prophets and apostles in line with the animation of poets and preachers. A virtuoso on the organ will work charms, if need be, from a poor instrument; but only when the organ is worthy of him will his talent be shown in all its power: but who will say that for this reason his playing proceeds from the excellence of the organ? No, the excellence is his who plays, and the organ merely serves as instrument. In the same way, the ethical excellence of the organs of revelation must certainly be taken into account, but it may not be said that this ethical excellence gave birth to inspiration. God alone is He who inspires, and even Isaiah or John are never anything but choice instruments, animated and tuned by God, who plays on them His inspiration. The difference of disposition in these instruments, however, determines the difference of intensity of inspiration. As "a virtuoso on the violin" can only exhibit a part of his art on a violin of two strings, and only on the full-stringed instrument can bring all his powers into play, so the holy playing of inspiration that sounds in our ears, is entirely different, far richer, and infinitely more intensive, when God makes use of a David or a Paul than when Nahum comes from the woods or James' epistle is unrolled before us. There are certainly degrees of inspiration. Habakkuk affects one more mightily than Haggai. And with the same organs of revelation inspiration is at one time much richer and fuller than at another time, which undoubtedly depends again upon the mood of the singer or writer. But however necessary the close study of these degrees may be, and however often we may be permitted to connect them with the subjective disposition of the instrument used, nevertheless, to derive inspiration itself from this, can never be allowed. All these differences may modify, specialize, and graduate the effect of inspiration, but inspiration itself does not proceed from the consciousness of man, but always from the consciousness and the will of God. All efforts to explain inspiration ethically is a passing into another genus, and is a leap from the ethical into the abstract life of our consciousness.

Finally, there may be added the ready help which every later inspiration found in that which had gone before, as well as in the progress of the revelation of salvation, to which it ran parallel. The content of inspiration is not aphoristic. The one rather builds upon the other. In its beginnings, therefore, inspiration is mostly concentric and deep, and only gradually passes over into detail and moves upon the surface. As a rule, at least, the person to be inspired knew what had formerly been inspired to others, and with these earlier inspirations his own inspiration formed a concatenation of ideas. It connected itself with these. It found in them a thread which it spun to greater length. It is no inspiration now in China, then again in Rome, presently in India or in Elam, but an inspiration which uses men from one and the same milieu of life, and which historically exhibits a certain continuity. For which reason the very images perpetuate themselves with a certain continuity, and certain forms and ways of speech pass on from one to the other. Just bring to mind the *Root,* the *Shepherd* and the "sheep of his pasture." If on account of this, numerous factors were present in the consciousness of the person about to be inspired for the use of Him who inspires, the same applies to the actual dispensation of grace in Israel. There is not merely a disclosing of the holy world above to the consciousness, but the creation as well of a reality in Israel, which bears a holy character. This has its beginning already in the wondrous birth of Isaac. This reality establishes itself in the people, accentuates itself in the tribe of Judah and in the house of David; in its usages and institutions; in its holy ceremonials, and in the types which point to the full reality to be realized by the Incarnation. From the nature of the case, this reality also exerted an influence, moulded and fashioned the more finely disposed spirits in Israel, and enriched the consciousness of those who were to be inspired with those ideas and representations and images, which were fit in every way to do service in inspiration. It made the language, in which Jehovah was to interpret His Divine thoughts, altogether a richer vehicle for inspiration.

The third factor which claims our attention in inspiration is *that which is inspired:*—Id quod inspiratur. This content of inspiration is not accidental. It does not consist of magic sentences, nor yet of enigmatical communications concerning secret powers or incidental events. The whole content of what is inspired is taken from the counsel of God, and is dominated by the supreme thought of how the profaned majesty of God, both in man and in the cosmos, may again come to its theodicy. We have purposely taken pains to state the case in these definite terms, because the limitation of that content to the salvation of man's physical life both is irrational and is contradicted by the Holy Scripture. The latter needs no explanation, and so far as the first is concerned, it would be irrational to intend exclusively the salvation of our psychical life, since the conditions of our somatical life are equally disabled. Irrational, to fix the eye upon the salvation of man alone, since man is an organic part of the cosmos. And it would be equally irrational to find the end of inspiration in man, since either the confession of God must be abandoned, or all things must find their end *in Him.* At this very point the effort falls away to seek the content of what was inspired exclusively in what is ethical-religious. This ethical-religious does not exist in isolation. In the case of the individual person it touches his body and circumstances as well; in the case of a people, its earthly existence, its history, and its future. Separation, therefore, is here impossible. Even as you cannot find a man except in his body, you cannot expect to find what is inspired except it is alike physchical, somatical and cosmical. However, it may and must be granted that the of what is inspired does not lend itself to this cosmical, except in so far as it stands in central connection with the work of the Holy Spirit. Not because the rest is indifferent, but because inspiration has a purpose of its own; viz. to introduce into the consciousness of the Church of God that world of thought which belongs to palingenesis. What lies outside of this is not received by the Church as such, but by the members of the Church, as "men and citizens," in a natural way. And the question, whether the nature of this content joins itself to what God who inspires finds on hand in the person whom He inspires is answered as follows: that the restoration of what was profaned of necessity joins itself to the condition of the profaned, and that the organs of revelation, whose own condition was that of depravity, and who themselves lived in this desecrated cosmos, found, both in themselves and in that cosmos, the canvas stretched on which the floral designs of grace were to be embroidered.

The Forms of Inspiration

Man received in his creation more than one string to the harp of his soul, and according to the nature of the objects that hold his attention his mood changes, he strikes a different key, and his mental action assumes new phases. The lyrical world differs in principle from the epical; the dramatic impulse far exceeds both in creative power; while, on the other hand, poetical inspiration accentuates itself least in didactic poetry. Thus the human mind is disposed by nature to a *multiformity* of expression, which sustains connection with the multiformity of material that engages our attention. And since there is a wide difference in the material that constitutes the content of Revelation, it is entirely natural that the inspiration of the Holy Spirit has made use of that *multiformity* of our spiritual expression, and thus assumes at one time a lyric character, at another time an epical, sometimes even a dramatic, but especially also one that is didactic. To some extent one may even say that in these aesthetic variegations certain fundamental forms are given for inspiration, and if need be the entire content of the Scripture might be divided after these four fundamental types. Since, however, outside of the Scripture also these four fundamental types continually overlap each other and give rise to mixed forms, it is more advisable to borrow the division of these types from the content of the Scripture itself. This we do when we distinguish between *lyric, chokmatic, prophetic and apostolic* inspiration, among which the inspiration of the Christ stands as *univocal,* and to which is added the later *graphic* inspiration in the narrower sense.

Let each of these types be separately considered.

Lyric inspiration comes first, because lyric itself, to some extent, bears an inspired character, and so offers us the most beautiful analogy to holy inspiration, and really supplies the only trustworthy key for the correct interpretation of the lyrical parts of the Scripture. Real lyric, worthy of the name, is not the passionate cry which describes in song the concrete, personal experience of sorrow or of joy, but appears only when, in the recital of concrete and personal experience, the note is heard of that which stirs the deeper depths of the hidden life of the universal human emotions, and for this reason is able to evoke a response from other hearts. In his *Aesthetik,* ii., p. 568 (3d Ausg. Lpz. 1885), Carriere states it thus: "That which is entirely individual in lyric poetry obtains the consecration of art only by being represented as it answers to the nature of man, and by striking the chord of something universally human, whereby it is reechoed in the of others." Even this statement is not sufficiently full; for when, by his personal emotions, the lyric poet has descended to the depths where his own life mingles with the waters of human experience, he has not reached the deepest bottom of this ocean. That which is common in the emotional life of humanity is not grounded in itself, but derives its powers of life from the immanence of God, whose Divine heart is the source of the vital breath that stirs and beats this ocean. Von Hartmann (*Philosophie des Schonen,* ii., p. 736) very properly observes that there is "*a mode of feeling which transcends the purely anthropological,*" which, from his Pantheistic point of view, he explains more closely as "an extension of self-feeling (Selbstgefuhl) unto a form of universal sympathy (Allgefuhl), the outreach of this sympathy (Weltschmerz) toward the world-ground, i.e. its expansion into the intuition of the Divine (Gottesschmerz)." Reverse this, and say that his concrete feeling is governed by the universal human feeling, and that, so far as it affects him, this universal human feeling is governed by the vital emotions in God, and the pathway of lyric inspiration is cleared. In every lyric poet you find first a considerable commotion of feeling, occasioned by his own joy or sorrow, or by the weal or woe of that which he loves. Secondly, that sense of solidarity, by which in his personal emotions he discerns the wave-beat of the human heart. And finally, there works in him a dominant power, which, in this universal human emotion-life, effects order, reconciliation, or victory. However subjective the lyric may be, it always loses the personal subject in the general subject, and in this general subject the Divine subject appears dominant. Since we may speak to this extent of a certain Divine inspiration in the case of all higher lyric, it is readily seen how naturally lyric lent itself as a vehicle for holy inspiration, and required but the employment in a special way of the Holy Spirit, to effect the lyric inspiration of the Psalmist.

The lyric poet does not merely sing for the sake of singing, but from the thirst for deliverance. Under the weight of unspeakable joy or of consuming sorrow he is near being overcome. And now the spirit arouses itself within him, not to shake himself free from this feeling of sorrow or joy, but, *luctor et emergo,* to raise the head above those waves of the ocean of his feeling, and either pour oil upon the seething waters, that shall quiet their violence, or bring those waves into harmony with the wave-beat of his own life, and thus effect reconciliation, or, finally, with power from on high to break that wave-beat. This is always done in two stages. First, by his descent from the personal into the solidary-human. He aptly remarks: I am not alone in these sorrows; there are "companions in misery" (consortes doloris); hence that sorrow must have deeper causes. And secondly, from this "companionship in misery" he reaches out after the living God, who does not stand as a personified Fate over against this necessity, but with Sovereign Authority bears rule over it. It is evident, that God the Lord has led His lyric singers personally into bitter sorrows, and again has made them leap for joy with personal gladness. But it also appears, in the second place, that these experiences of deep sorrow and high-strung gladness almost never came to them in concrete-individual, and, therefore, to a certain extent, accidental circumstances, but that almost always their lot in life was interwoven with the lot of their people, and thus from the start bore a solidary character. David views even his sicknesses as standing in connection with the combat he wages for God and His people. However, you observe, in the third place, that in and through the utterance of personal feeling, once and again a higher and a more general subject, and, if you please, another *ego,* supplants the *ego* of the singer, and often ends by God Himself in the Messiah testifying through the mouth of the singer. This makes a confusing impression on him who does not understand lyric, and is the cause of many an error in exegesis. But this phenomenon, which at first sight seems somewhat strange, becomes entirely clear when in this instance also you allow the antithesis to be duly emphasized between sinful and sanctified humanity, between humanity in its state of depravity and humanity in the palingenesis. The lyric poet who stands outside of the palingenesis cannot descend deeper than the emotional life of fallen humanity, and if from thence he presses on to God, he can do nothing more than was done by Von Hartmann, who, being depressed by sorrow, through the world-sorrow (Weltschmerz) reached the supposed God-sorrow (Gottesschmerz), and thus falsified the entire world of the emotions. Such, however, was not the case with the singers of Israel. From their personal joy and grief, they did not descend to the general human feeling, but to the emotion-life of humanity in the palingenesis, i.e. of God's people. And when in God they sought the reconciliation between this higher life of the palingenesis and actual conditions, their God appeared to them in the form of the Messiah, that other subject, who sang and spake through them, and caused them simultaneously to experience the reconciliation and the victory over sorrow and sin. In the imprecatory Psalms, especially, this is most strongly apparent. Applied to our human relations in general, the imprecatory Psalm is, of course, a most grievous offence to our feelings, and entirely beneath the nobility of lyric. If, on the other hand, you place the lyric singer of the imprecatory Psalms under the absolute antithesis between that which chooses for and against God; if you separate him from his temporal-concrete surroundings, and transfer him to the absolute-eternal, in which everything that sides with God lives and has our love, and everything that chooses eternally against God bears the mark of death and rouses our hatred, then the rule, "Do not I hate them, O Lord, that hate thee?" becomes the only applicable standard, and whatever departs from this rule falls short of love for God. When Jesus speaks of the man who should have a millstone hanged about his neck, that he may be drowned in the depths of the sea, the same fundamental tone which sounds in all the imprecatory Psalms is sounded also by Him. As unholy and repulsive as the imprecatory Psalms are in the lips of those who apply them to our relative universal human life, they are solemnly true and holy when you take your stand in the absolute palingenesis, where God's honor is the keynote of the harmony of the human heart. This is naturally denied by all those who refuse to believe in an eternal condemnation of those who continue in their enmity against the Almighty; but he who in unison with the Scripture speaks of "a going into everlasting pain," from this absolute point of view cannot resent the imprecatory Psalm, provided it is taken as a lyric.

(2) *Chokmatic inspiration* certainly belongs to didactic poetry, but forms, nevertheless, a class by itself, which, outside of the domain of poetry, can make its appearance in prose. Under Chokmatic inspiration, the parables, too, are classed, and other sayings of Christ which are not handed down to us at least in a fixed form. When the question is asked in what particular didactic poetry distinguishes itself from non-didactic, aesthetici say that the didacticus first thinks, and then looks for the image in which to clothe his thoughts, while the non-didactic lyricist, epicist, or dramatist feels the initiative arise from phantasy, and only derives the form from the ideal image. In itself, inspiration is much less strong with the didacticus, and there are didactic poets with whom poetical inspiration is altogether wanting. With this kind of poetry, inspiration is not in the feeling, neither in the imagination, or in the heroic impulse, but exclusively in the sway of the consciousness. Not as a result of his discursive thought, but by an impulse of his perception, the real didacticus is impelled to song. By this immediate perception he understands what he sees the other does not understand, and this he communicates to him in song. Subsidiarily to this, is added that the didacticus, since he does not speak as one who is learned, but sings as one who is wise, is, at the same time, in sympathy with symbolism which unites the spiritual with the material world, and therefore expresses himself in the form of nature-illustrations and parables. In the Chokmah, this universal human phenomenon obtained a character of its own. Even as the prophet, the "wise man" was an isolated phenomenon in Israel. Similarly to didactic poetry, this Chokmah confines itself mostly to the domain of the life of nature and to the natural relationships of life. That life of nature and of man, in its rich unfolding, is the realization of a thought of God. It is not accidental, but develops itself after the Divine ordinances, which, even as the existence of life, are the outflow of a Chokmah in God. Nature does not observe this, but man perceives it because, created after God's image, he is himself an embodiment of that thought of God, and is therefore himself a *microcosmos*. In his perception lies a reflected image of this Chokmah, which by nature is *Wisdom,* and not *science,* but which only by analysis and synthesis can become science. The purer and clearer that glass of his perception is, the purer and clearer will the image of that Chokmah reflect itself in him. For this reason, Adam was created, not merely in justice and holiness, but also in original

wisdom. By sin, however, this perception became clouded. There was a twofold cause for this. First, it reacts no longer accurately, and again, because nature itself and man's life in nature have become entangled in much conflict and confusion. For this reason, this natural Chokmah does no longer give what it ought to give; it works most effectively with simple folk, to whom only separate problems present themselves, but it refuses its service to the more richly developed mind, which faces *all* problems at once, and thus necessitates it by way of analysis to seek refuge in close thought. Palingenesis meanwhile presents the possibility of resuscitating again this original wisdom in fallen man, and, at the same time, of giving him an insight into the order and harmony which hide behind the conflicts of our sinful life, and are active to provide the cleansing of them. This does not happen to everybody, not even though the enlightening has entered in, but it takes place with those individuals whom God has chosen and inspired for this purpose, and these are the real, specific, *wise men,* and what they produce is called the Chokmah. In this, therefore, we deal with an activity of the Holy Spirit, which directs itself to this original sense-of-life, to this practical consciousness of nature and life, and clarifies this, so that the wise man discerns again the wisdom which is apparent in God's creation and in life, is affected by it, and proclaims it in parable or song. This Chokmah, however, does not appear to him as arising from his subjective consciousness, but as addressing him from another subject, such as Wisdom, which must not be taken as a personification, but as the pure word in God (see 1 Cor. i. 30), that to him coincides with the image of the Messiah. This does not imply that for this reason the solution of all problems, as for instance the problem of the incongruity in the suffering servant of God, stands clear and plain before his eyes. On the contrary, there are conflicts, which cannot be explained on chokmatic ground, but the impression of the Chokmah is, nevertheless, so overwhelming that the interrogation mark after these problems bears in itself the prophecy that it shall sometime disappear. Hence the "wise man" stands over against the "scorner," the "fool," and the "ungodly," who think after their fashion to have found a solution in cynicism, but have abandoned God and faith in his wisdom. To the wise man, on the other hand, *the fear of the Lord* is the beginning of wisdom. God must not be wiped out for the reason that we are not able to indicate harmony between Him and the world; but from Him every departure must be made, even though by doing this we should lose the world. This assertion may not methodistically be applied to discursive thought. It only applies to that Wisdom of which it is asked in Job xxxviii. 36, "Who hath put wisdom in the inward parts? or who hath given understanding to the mind?" The entire action, by which this wisdom is quickened, follows along the inward way, and does not come from without. For which very reason it could become a vehicle of inspiration. This also applies to its form, which is almost always symbolical, entirely apart from the question whether it is more commonly lyrical, epic, or dramatic. Its form is and remains that of the Proverb מָשָׁל, the utterance of a thought in its material analogy. In the "riddle" (חִידָה) and "enigma" (מְלִיצָה) which words indicate entwining and intertwisting, the symbolical character may be less clearly apparent; in both forms, however, lies the same symbolical tendency. The phenomena are significant of something, they are reminders of a thought, which comes from God, and can be understood by us; not by these phenomena themselves, but by the affinity of our spirit to Him who speaks in them. And since this Wisdom does not consist of thoughts loosely strung together, but forms one organic whole, and needs the light of grace, by which to solve the problems of sorrow and of sin, this Wisdom at length concentrates itself in Christ Jesus, whom finally the apostle places over against the foolishness ($\mu\omega\rho\iota\alpha$) of the world as the incarnated Wisdom (Chokmah or $\sigma\omega\phi\iota\alpha$)

(3) So far as its result is concerned, *Prophetic inspiration* is distinguished from the lyric and chokmatic chiefly by the fact that in general it exhibits a conscious dualism of subject, whereby the subject of the prophet has merely an instrumental significance, while the higher subject speaks the word. That other higher subject appears sometimes in lyrics (Ps. ii. *et al.*) and in the Chokmah (Prov. viii. *et al.*), but where it does this

appearance bears no dualistic character, and at least never becomes antithetic as in prophecy (Jer. xx., Ezek. iii., *et al.*). In the lyric and in the Chokmah there is "Konsonanz" of subjects, never "Dissonanz." In prophecy, on the other hand, duality of subject is the starting-point for the understanding of its working, and is even present where it is not expressly announced. Nothing can be inferred concerning this from the word נָבִיא. The etymology of the word is too uncertain for this. Who indeed will prove whether we must go back to נבי, נבע, נבא which would be identical with ϕa-, in $\phi \eta \mu \ell$, or to נבִיא? Or also whether the form נבוא is a passive or intransitive katil-form, and whether, if *effundere,* to pour out, is the primary meaning of this root, we must think of a *poured-out* person, or of a person who causes his words to *flow out* like water across the fields? One can offer conjectures, but to infer anything from the etymology as to the meaning of the word is at present simply impossible. The synonyms also, רֹאֶה and חֹזֶה, merely indicate that the prophet is some one who is given to seeing visions. From the description of some of these visions, as for instance the vision of the calls, from the phenomena that accompanied them, and from the form in which the prophet usually expressed himself, it can be very definitely shown, on the other hand, that, as subject, he felt himself taken hold of by a higher subject, and was compelled to speak not his own thoughts, but the thoughts of this higher subject. The frequent repetition of the "Thus saith" (אָמַר יְהוָֹה) proves this. In Jeremiah's spiritual struggle (Jer. xx. 7 *sq.*) this antithesis reaches its climax. In 2 Sam. vii. 3 Nathan first declares as his own feeling that David will build the temple, while in verses 4, 5 he receives the prophetical charge to announce to David the very opposite. In Isa. xxxviii. 1-5 we read the twofold "Thus saith," first, that Hezekiah will succumb to his sickness, and then that he will again be restored. The fundamental type is given in Deut. xviii. 18 as follows: "I, Jehovah, will put my words in his mouth, and he shall speak unto them all that I shall command him." We find this all-prevailing fundamental thought still more sharply brought out by Ezekiel in Chap. ii. 8: "But thou, son of man, hear what I say unto thee; open thy mouth, and *eat that I give thee.*" And in Chap. iii. 1, 2: "Son of man, *eat that thou findest,* eat this roll, and go and speak. So I opened my mouth, *and he caused me to eat that roll.*" To eat is to take up and assimilate in my blood a material or food which originated outside of me. This, therefore, is a most definite indication that the subject from whose consciousness the prophecy originated is not the subject of the prophet, but the subject Jehovah. Whichever way this is turned, the chief distinction in prophecy is always that the subject of the prophet merely serves as instrument.

From this, however, it must not be inferred that the character or disposition of this instrumental subject was a matter of indifference. The same musician who at one time plays the flute, the other time a cornet, and at still another time a trumpet, produces each time entirely different tones. This depends altogether upon the instrument he plays and the condition of the instrument. In the same way this personal character and present disposition of the prophet will give tone to his prophecy to such an extent that with Isaiah the result is entirely different from what it is with Hosea, and with Jeremiah from what it is with Micah. Only do not lose from sight that this noticeable difference in prophecy, which is the result of the great difference between prophet and prophet, was also determined by the higher subject. As the player chooses his instrument according to the composition he wants to be heard, Jehovah chose His prophetical instrument. God the Lord, moreover, did what the play cannot do: He prepared His instrument Himself, and tuned it to the prophecy which by this instrument He was to give to Israel, and by Israel to the Church of all ages. If thus without reservation we must recognize the personal stamp which a prophet puts upon his prophecy, it may never be inferred that the *fons prophetiae* is to be sought in him, and that the *primoprimae* issues of thought should not come from the consciousness of God. We may even enter more fully into this, and confess that it was the preparation, education, and further development of a prophet and his lot in life generally that it brought it about that in his consciousness all those elements were available which God the Lord should need for His prophecy. It may indeed be assumed that the ethnological and political knowledge of the kingdoms with whom Israel came in contact, and from which so many judgments proceeded, was present in the synteresis of the prophets. The capacity to gather thoughts and unite them into an opinion may likewise have been active in this, it did not go to work from its own spontaneity, but was passively directed by another subject, in whose service it was employed.

Even this doesnot end our study of the anthropological basis of prophecy. Ecstasy, which is so strongly apparent on the heights of prophecy, is no uncommon phenomenon. We know as yet so very little of the nature and working of physhical powers. Biology, magnetic sleep, clairvoyance, hypnotism, trance, insanity, telepathy, as Stead called his invention, are altogether phenomena which have appeared from of old in all sorts of forms, and which science has too grossly neglected. Evidently these workings are less common in quiet, peaceful times, and show themselves with more intensity when public restlessness destroys the equilibrium. This accounts for the fact that at present they are prominently coming again to the front. *This* at least is evident, that our psyche, over against its consciousness, as well as with reference to its body, can become so strongly excited that common relations give place to those that are entirely uncommon. Whole series of stations lie between common enthusiasm and wild insanity, by which in its course this action assumes a more or less concrete, but ever modified, form. And so far as insanity has no direclty physical causes, it carries wholly the impression of being a tension between the psyche and its consciousness, which is not merely acute, but becomes chronic, or even permanent. Ecstasy is commonly represented as being the outcome of the mastery of an idea, a thought, or a phantom over the psyche, and by means of the sensibilities over the body, to such an extent that for the moment the common working of the senses and of the other spiritual powers is suspended, and psyche and soma are used entirely as instruments of this mania, idea, or visionary image. If we combine these ecstatic phenomena with the biological, i.e. with the power which the psyche of one can obtain over the psyche of another, and grant that the power which other men can exert upon us can be exerted upon us much more strongly by God, we must conclude that in prophecy also God the Lord made use of factors which He Himself had prepared in our human nature. With this difference, however, that in this instance He makes use Himself of what at other times He places at the disposal of biologians. A complete analogy to prophecy would be given in this, especially if Stead's ideas about his so-called *thought,* which rests upon the system of telepathy, were found to be true. He asserts to have reached this result telepathically, – that at a distance of ten or twenty miles, without any means of communication whatsoever, one man wrote down literally what the other man thought. This may lack excitement and passion, but by no means excludes ecstasy; it is well known that besides a passionate, there is also an entirely restful, ecstasy, which, for the time being, petrifies a man, or causes him to lie motionless as in deep sleep.

If we inquire what the prophets themselves relate concerning their experience in such prophetic periods, a real difference may be observed. At one time the seizure is violent, at another time one scarcely receives the impression that a seizure has taken place. When that seizure comes they receive the impression of a לבֹשׁ׳, i.e. as though they are put into a strait-jacket by the Spirit. This admits of no other explanation, except that they lost the normal working of their senses and the common use of their limbs. There is an *Iad Iah'wah* which takes hold of them; which indicates that the pressure came not gradually, but suddenly, upon them. Sometimes a "fall" is the result of this; they fell forward, not because they wanted to kneel down, but because their muscles were paralyzed, and, filled with terror, they fell to the ground. Meanwhile they perceived a glow from within which put them as on fire, as Jeremiah declares that it became a fire in his bones which he could not resist. Ezekiel testifies (iii. 14), "I went in bitterness, in the heat of my spirit, and the hand of the Lord was strong upon me." At the close of the ecstasy the prophet felt himself worn-out and faint, and pathologically affected to such a degree that he said he

232

was ill. In that condition he saw visions, heard speaking and saw whole dramas played; and when presently he is again so far restored to himself that he can speak, the continuity of his consciousness is by no means broken. He knows what happened with him, and tells what he saw and heard. By itself there is nothing strange in all this. That which is distinctively prophetic does not consist of these physcical phenomena. These were common with pseudo-prophets. But these phenomena, which were commonly produced by pathological physchical conditions, or by superior powers of otehr persons, by the influence of mighty events, or by demoniacal influences, in prophecy *were worked by God* that He might use them for His revelation.

This dualistic character of prophecy, coupled with the repression of the human subject, prompts us to explain prophecy as being *epical,* even if at times this epical utterance receives a lyrical tint. In the epos the *ego* of the singer recedes to the background, and the powerful development of events, by which he is overwhelmed, is put wholly to the front. An epos teaches almost nothing about the poet himself. To such an extent is his personality repressed in the epos. The second characteristic of the epos is, that the singer not merely communicates what he has seen and heard, but also pushes aside the veil, and makes you see what mysterious powers from the unseen world were active back of all this, and that the things seen are in reality but the effect worked by these mysterious factors. To this extent the epos corresponds entirely to the content of prophecy, and only in the third point does the epos differ from prophecy. In the epos the poet deals merely with *tradition,* subjects it to his own mind, lifts himself above it, and exhibits his sovereign power by pouring over into the word, i.e. in the *epos,* what has *happened*, but at the same time, and this is the triumph of the epos, explains it and makes it understood. And the epical poet differs from the prophet in this very thing; the epicus rules as artist, while passively the prophet undergoes inspiration from a higher subject. We may grant that the epical poet also invokes a higher inspiration, as is shown in the "Jerusalem Delivered;" and the "breathe into my bosom" (tu spira al petto mio) is certainly a strong expression, but with Tasso it is followed immediately by the statement: "and forgive if I mingle fiction with truth—if I adorn my pages in part with other thoughts than your own," which were inconceivable with the passivity of the prophet.

If it is asked, where lies the mighty fact, which appears epically in the epos or *Word* of prophecy, we answer, that prophecy takes this drama *from the counsel of God.* While Chokmatic inspiration discovers the ordinances of God that lie hidden in creation, and lyric interprets to us the world of our human heart, in prophecy there is epically proclaimed the ordinance of God with reference to history, the problem of the world's development. This history, this development, must follow the course marked out by God in His counsel, and to some extent it amounts to the same thing, whether this course is seen in the facts or is read from God's counsel. The program lies in the counsel of God, in history the performance of the exalted drama. Meanwhile there is this noteworthy difference between the two, that in the days of the prophets especially, the drama had been worked out only in a very small part, while in God's counsel the complete program lay in readiness. And secondly, even so far as it realized God's counsel, history could never be understood in its mystical meaning without the knowledge of God's counsel. It is noteworthy that the cômpilers of the books of the Canon classed Joshua, Judges, Samuel and Kings with the prophets as *the former prophets,* and that the later prophets join themselves to these, as *the later.* If dioramatically we transfer the Oracles of what we call the prophets to beyond the last judgment in the realm of glory, and add Joshua to Kings inclusive, these together give us both parts of the drama, viz. (1) what was already performed, and (2) what was to follow; while the comparison, for instance, of Kings with Chronicles makes the epical excellence of the former to appear clearly above the latter.

The drama then begins from the moment God's people are settled in the Holy Land. What lies behind this is not history, but preparation. The Thorah gives the Toledoth. With Israel in Canaan the starting-point is given for the all-governing drama. What lies back of that is a description of the situation by way of prologue. With Joshua the drama begins, and ends only when the new humanity shall enter upon the possession of the new earth, under the new heaven. In this drama the prophet stands midway. As a Semite he knew but two tenses, the *factum* and *fiens,* a perfect and an imperfect. The prophetical narrative presents that part of the programme which *is* performed. It does this epically, i.e. with the disclosure of the Divine agencies employed; while that which is to come is not seen by the prophet in reality, but in vision. Always in such a way, however, that to him a review of the whole is possible. He therefore is not outside of it, but stands himself in its midst. In his own heart he has passed through the struggle between this Divine drama of redemption and the roar of the nations, whose history must end in self-dissolution. He is conscious of the fact that that spirit of the world combats the Spirit of God, not only outside of, but also within, the boundaries of Israel. Thus by virtue of his own impulse he pronounces the Holy Spirits criticism upon the unholy spirit of the world, and is filled with holy enthusiasm in seeing in vision, that that Spirit of God and His counsel shall sometime gloriously triumph. Thus there is an organic connection between what was, and is and is to come; a connection between one prophet and another; a connection also with the same prophet between the series of visions that fall to his share; and this states the need of the vision of the call, in which God revealed to him, that he himself was called to cooperate in the realizing of the Divine counsel and in the further unveiling of the drama. It is as foolish therefore to deny the element of prediction in prophecy, as it is irrational to make real prophecy consist of single aphoristical predictions. Undoubtedly *in the main* prophecy offers the unveiling of *that which is to come* provided it is viewed from the point where the prophet stood and lived, so that very often he himself is active in the process which reflects itself in his Oracle.

The apocalyptic vision only forms an exception to this, which exception, however, accentuates the more sharply the indicated character of common prophecy. The Apocalypse does not move from the prophet to the horizon, but leaves between him and the horizon nothing but a vacuum, in order suddenly to cause a vision to appear on that horizon, which is to him surprising and strange. A veil is pushed aside, which mostly consists of this, that "the heavens were opened," and when the veil is lifted, a scene reveals itself to the eyes of the seer which moves from the heavens toward him. Hence, the Apocalypse unveils the end, and is by its very nature eschatological, even when its meaning is merely symbolic. It rests upon the assumption that the end is not born from the means, but that, on the contrary, the end is first determined, and that this end postulates the means by which to realize it. Hence, it is far more severely theological than common prophecy, since it takes no pains to join itself to human history, but abruptly shows itself on the horizon. God's counsel is what is really essential. From that counsel God shows immediately this or the other part, and for this reason the forms and images of apocalyptic vision are described with so great difficulty. The purpose in hand is to show the seer a different reality from that in which he actually lives, a reality which surely is analogous to his own life, but as under the antithesis of the butterfly and the caterpillar. How could the form of the butterfly be made more or less clear in outlines borrowed from the caterpillar, to one who knows a caterpillar but not a butterfly? This is the problem which every apocalyptical vision faces. The forms and images, therefore, are composed of what the prophet knows, but are arranged in such different combinations and connections as to produce a drama that is entirely abnormal. The appearance of Christ in His glory on Patmos is truly the brilliancy of the butterfly, but sketched in forms borrowed from the caterpillar. From this, however, the apocalyptic vision derives its artistic composition. This does not imply that the aesthetic element is wanting in common prophecy; but in this no *tableaux* are exhibited which, in order to be exhibited, must first be arranged. With the apocalyptic vision, however, this is indispensable. On the prophetic horizon, which at first is vacant, it must show its form or drama in such a way that, however strange it may be to him, the prophet, nevertheless, is able to receive and communicate it. It is Divine art, therefore, which makes the composition correspond to its purpose, and this accounts for the fact that the artistic Unity, in the symmetry and proportion of parts, in symbolism, and in numbers, is seen so vividly in the Apocalypse. This is not artificial, but spontaneous art. By counting it over, the fact has been revealed that the allegro in Mozart's Jupiter Symphony is divided into two parts of 120 and 193 bars; that the adagio of Beethoven's B-major symphony separates itself into two parts of 40 and 64 bars. Naumann has found similar results in the master-productions by Bach. The proportion of the golden division always prevails in highest productions of art. No one, however, will assert that Bach, Mozart, or Beethoven computed this division of bars. This artistic proportion sprang spontaneously from their artistic genius. In the same way the unity of plan (Gliederung) in the Apocalypse must be understood, just because in vision the action of the seer is least and the action on the part of God is greatest.

The exhibition and announcement of things to come, i.e. the predictive character, belongs not merely to the Apocalypse, but to common prophecy as well. "Before it came to pass I shewed it thee: lest thou shouldest say, Mine idol hath done them." "I have declared the former things from of old; yea, they went forth out of my mouth, and I shewed them; suddenly I did them, and they came to pass" (Isa. xlviii. 3-5, *passim*). Entirely in the same sense in which Jesus said to His disciples, "And now I have told you before it come to pass, that, when it is come to pass, ye may believe" (John xiv. 29; comp. xiii. 19 and xvi. 4). However strongly it must be emphasized, therefore, that in the person of the prophet, in his disposition, education, surroundings, position in life, and in his preparation in the school of the prophets, a number of data are present which claim our notice in connection with his prophecies, all this, however, is no more than the preparation of the soil, and the seed from which presently the fruit ripens comes always *from above.* Even when seemingly he merely exhorts or reproves, this preaching of repentance or reproof is always the coming into our reality of what is ideal and higher, as the root from which a holier future is to bloom.

(4) *The Inspiration of Christ.*—Since inspiration has been interpreted too exclusively as Scripture-inspiration, too little attention has ever been paid to the inspiration of the Christ. The representation, however, that the Christ knew all things without inspiration spontaneously (sponte sua), is virtually the denial of the incarnation of the Word. The consciousness of God and the Mediatorial consciousness of the Christ are not one, but two, and the transfer of Divine thoughts from the consciousness of God into the consciousness of the Christ is not merely inspiration, but inspiration in its highest form. The old theologians indicated this by saying, that even the Christ possessed no archetypal, but ectypal theology, and he obtained this *via unionis,* i.e. in virtue of the union of the Divine and human nature. In this there is merely systematized what Christ Himself said: (John xiv. 10) "The words that I say unto you, I speak not of myself"; (John vii. 16) "My teaching is not mine, but his that sent me"; (John xiv. 24) "The word which ye hear is not mine, but the Father's who sent me"; (John v. 30) "As I hear, I judge"; (John viii. 26) "The things which I have heard from him these speak I unto the world"; and (John xii. 49) "The Father which sent me, he hath given me a commandment, what I should say, and what I should speak." This in itself is the natural outcome of His real adoption of human nature; but the necessity for this, moreover, was the greater, on account of His assuming that nature in all its weakness, with the single exception of sin (Heb. iv. 15), which at this stage indicates that in Jesus no falsehood was arrayed against the truth, which, as with the common prophets, had first to be repressed. But in Christ there was an increase in *wisdom,* a gradual becoming enriched more and more with the world that lived in the consciousness of God. This was effected by the reading of the Scriptures, by the seeing of things visible in creation, by His life in Israel, as well as by prophetical

inspiration. In that sense, the Holy Spirit to Him also was *given*. In connection with His preaching we are told, "For he whom God hath sent speaketh the words of God: for he giveth not the Spirit by measure" (John iii. 34), an utterance which, as seen from the connection, may not be interpreted ethically, which would have no sense, but refers to inspiration. This "not by measure" is also evident in this, that all kinds of inspiration, the lyric, chokmatic and epical-prophetical, unite themselves in Jesus, while everything that is connected with the suppression of vital energy, the will, or mistaken thoughts in the case of the prophets, in the case of Jesus falls away. Even in inspiration, He could *never* be passive without becoming *active* at the same time. That the form of vision never takes place with Jesus, but all inspiration in Him comes in clear concept (notione clara), has a different cause. Before His incarnation, the Christ has seen the heavenly reality which to prophecy had to be shown in visions: "I speak the things which I have seen with my Father" (John viii. 38); "and bear witness of that we have seen" (John iii. 11). One may even say that the sight of this heavenly reality was also granted Him after His incarnation: "And no man hath ascended into heaven, but he that descended out of heaven, even the Son of Man, *which is in heaven*" (John iii. 13). This very absence, in the case of the Christ, of all instrumental means, which were indispensable with the prophets because of sin, together with the absence of all individual limitation ("for he had not taken on man, but man's nature," non hominem sed *naturam* humanam assumpserat), gives that absolute character of the teaching "as one having authority" to what He spake as the fruit of the inspiration, in virtue of the Divine union, the impression of which to this day, in the reading of His Word, takes hold of one so overwhelmingly. Entirely in harmony with this, the Scripture indicates that inspiration had in Him its centrum. He is *the* prophet; who spake in the Old Covenant by the prophets; after His ascension bears witness by His apostles; and who is still our prophet through the Word. (See Deut. xviii. 18; 1 Pet. i. 11, "The spirit of Christ which was in them testified beforehand"; John xvi. 13).

(5) *The Inspiration of the Apostles.*—He who derives his conception of inspiration exclusively from the inspiration of the prophets, is bound to conclude that there is no question of inspiration in the case of the apostles. In the case of the apostles, indeed, inspiration bears an entirely different character from that of the lyric, chokmatic, or prophetical organs of the Old Covenant. This difference sprang from a threefold cause. First from the fact that the Holy Spirit had now been poured out and had taken up His abode in the Church of God. This difference is most succinctly stated by the antithesis of inshining (irradiatio) and indwelling (inhabitatio). Secondly, from the fact that with the apostles inspiration adapted itself to their *official* function. And thirdly, from the fact that they came *after* the Incarnation, which the seers of the Old Covenant anticipated. As soon therefore as, on Patmos, inspiration deals no longer with the reality which appeared in the Christ, but refers to things to come, inspiration resumes with them its prophetical character, viz. in its apocalyptical form. The revelation that came to Peter was equally vision-like. And so far as Paul had not belonged to the circle of Jesus' disciples, an entirely separate calling, tradition and ecstasy were given him, which were needful to him and adapted to his isolated position. With these exceptions, there is nothing that suggests inspiration in the oral and written preaching of the apostles, as given in the Acts and in their Epistles. They speak as though they speak of themselves, they write as though they write of themselves. In all probability the same phenomenon showed itself in the hundred or more of their addresses and epistles, of which no reports have come to us. The "cloke and the parchments left at Troas," as an incident, stands by no means by itself. Almost the entire contents of apostolic literature bears the same ordinary character. If from outside sources nothing were known of the inspiration of the prophets, the simple phrase "Thus saith the Lord" already shows that there is at least the pretence of inspiration. With apostolic literature, on the other hand, the suggestion of inspiration scarcely presents itself. In 1 Cor. vii. 10, coll. 12, we even read of an antithesis between "I give charge," and "Yea, not I, but the Lord," but this refers to the difference between what

Paul knew from the special revelation given to himself (1 Cor. xi. 23, "For I received of the Lord"), and by apostolic inspiration, as he expressly adds at the close of this same chapter: "And I think that I also have the Spirit of God" (1 Cor. vii. 40). That inspiration, however, took place with the apostles, appears meanwhile from Matt. x. 19, 20; John xvi. 12-14, 14-26, etc.; from Acts xv. 28, "For it seemed good to the Holy Ghost, and to us"; from 1 Cor. ii. 10-12, "But unto us God revealed them through the Spirit," and this Holy Spirit alone could reveal to them the deep things of God. Paul, as well as the other apostles, had not received the spirit of the world, but the spirit which is of God, and the effect of this is that he knew the things that were freely given by God. The same appears from 2 Cor. iii. 3, where on the tables of the heart an *epistle of Christ* is said to be written, not with ink, but "with the spirit of the living God," and instrumentally this was effected by the apostles: "ministered by us." In Eph. iii. 5 it is stated that the mystery, which had been hidden from former generations, "hath now been revealed unto his holy apostles in the Spirit." In Rev. i. 10 John declares even, "I was in the Spirit." Paul does not hesitate to say that what they had heard of him is not a "word of men, but as it is in truth, the word of God" (1 Thess. ii. 13).

Evidently with them this inspiration was the working of the Holy Spirit dwelling in them, and this indwelling demands full emphasis. In the first place they had received inworkings of the Holy Spirit before the Day of Pentecost, and, in breathing on them, Jesus had officially communicated to them the *gift* of the Holy Ghost. Before Pentecost moreover they had been regenerated, for Jesus had prayed, not that Peter might have faith, but that the faith which he had might not fail. Nevertheless Jesus repeatedly declares that only when the Holy Spirit shall have been sent them from the Father, shall real apostolical inspiration begin, as it did on Pentecost in the sermon of Peter. In the Old Covenant the Holy Spirit stands truly "in the midst of them" (Isa. lxiii. 2); but He is not yet the formative principle (principium formans) for the circle. That circle was still national, and not yet oecumenical. It only became such on the Pentecostal Day, when the Church appeared, liberated from the wrappings of Israel's national life, as an independent organism, having the Holy Spirit as its πνεῦμα. Neither this mystery nor this difference can be more fully explained here. For our purpose it is enough, if the difference is made clear, that *after* Pentecost there was the indwelling of the Holy Spirit, while *before* that day there were merely radiations and inworkings as from without. From the nature of the case this was bound to give to inspiration an entirely modified form. Now it came no more as from without, but from within, and that same Holy Spirit, who, in us, prays for us with unutterable groanings, was able in like manner to use, guide, and enlighten the consciousness of the apostles, without any break taking place in them as of a duality; yea, without their own perception of it. To this is added, as we observed, in the second place, that the impulse for the working of this inspiration lay in their official function itself. Dualistic action of the Holy Spirit is thereby not excluded with them, as when, for instance, the Spirit says to Peter: "Behold, three men seek thee" (Acts x. 19), or when the Holy Spirit did not suffer Paul to go into Bithynia (Acts xvi. 7), etc. As a rule, however, such a break did *not* occur, and their official calling itself formed the basis on which inspiration took place. The prophets' appearance was also official, but in a different sense. Their prophecy itself was their office, hence this office was very aphoristic and without a cosmical basis. But the apostles had to discharge the regular duties of a *fixed* office, which found its bed in life itself. This office was continued until death, and inspiration was merely given them, to direct their service in this office. They do not speak or write because the Spirit stimulates them to speak, or impels them irresistibly to write, but because this was demanded on them by their office. Thus inspiration flowed into their everyday activity. This involves in the third place the different point of view, occupied by prophets and apostles, with reference to the centrum of all revelation; viz. the Christ and His truth. It is the antithesis of *imagination* and *memory,* poetry and remembrance. With the prophets, who came before the incarnation, the centrum of revelation could assume no other form than the dioramatic figures of their representation, while theapostles, who came after the Christ, testified of what they had heard and seen and handled of the Word of life. What was vague with the prophets, with them was concrete. Not the *poetical,* but the *remembering* spirit strikes with them the keynote. Since the inspiration of the Holy Spirit ever joins itself to what is present in its organ and adapts itself to this, it is evident that the inspiration, which with the prophet worked upon the poetical side of his consciousness, was with the apostle first of all a "remembrance" (John xiv. 26). Their spiritual activity, however, did not limit itself to this. They had to proclaim the message, and for this they were endowed with the remembrance. In the second place they were to announce things to come, and for this they were given the apocalyptic vision. But in the third place they had to give the apostolic reflection concerning the "word oflife"; and for this the Holy Spirit led them into the deep things of God (1 Cor. ii. 10-12). And here we do not speak of any apostolic dogmatics, or of a Pauline Theology. He who does this destroys the essential difference between the apostle as "the first teacher of the whole Church" and the common ministers of the Word. The apostolate may not be thought to be continued either in the papistical or Irvingite sense, nor can it be made common in an ethical way with the ministry of the Word. According to John xvii. 20, 1 John i. 3, etc., the apostolate is *univoca.* Only by their preaching does the Christ appear to the consciousness of humanity, in order successively to be assimilated and reproduced by this human consciousness in dogma and theology. The apostles have dug the gold from themine, and from this gold the Church has forged the artistic ornaments.

Every effort, therefore, to make the inspiration of the apostles identical with their enlightening must be resisted. For this places them virtually on a plane with every regenerated child of God, that shares the enlightening with them. This would be proper, if the enlightening were already absolute in the earth. This, however, it is not. No less than sanctification enlightenment remains in fact most imperfect till our death, however potentially it may be complete. The apostles never claimed that they had outgrown sin. Romans vii., which describes Paul's spiritual state as an apostle, sufficiently proves the contrary. Galatians ii. also shows an entirely different state of things. With so much of *unholiness* still present in them, how could their enlightening have been complete? Their partial enlightening would never have been a sufficient cause for the absolute authority of their claims. This is only covered by the inspiration, which ever accompanied them, both in the remembrance and in the revelation of the mystery.

A single remark should be added concerning the charismata, and more particularly about the "speaking with tongues," since the apostles themselves thus spoke. It is evident at once that this speaking of tongues was essentially different from the apostolic inspiration, in so far as it made a break in the consciousness, and repressed the activity of the consciousness of the apostles, and caused a mightier spirit to control their spirit and organ of speech. This speaking in tongues falls under the category of inspiration only in so far as it establishes the fact, that an inspiring mind (auctor mentalis) *outside of them* gave direction to what was heard *from them.* Our space does not allow a closer study of this speaking with tongues, neither does it lie in our way to consider here the charismata in general. Be it simply stated, however, that they belong to the ecstatic phenomena. According to 1 Cor. xiv., the content of the glossolaly could be interpreted, but he who spake did not understand it himself. In so far, therefore, it must be judged by the analogy of the mesmerizer who causes his medium, who knows no Latin, to write Latin words, provided, however, this phenomenon be not taken as being brought about by causing the spirit to sleep, but, on the contrary, as wrought by high exaltation.

Graphical Inspiration

All that has thus far been said of inspiration does not refer at all to the Holy Scriptures as canonical writings. Suppose, indeed, that you knew that from the consciousness of God, by the Holy Spirit, inspiration had taken place in the consciousness of psalmists, teachers of wisdom, prophets, and apostles, what warrant would this be, that what the Holy Scripture offers you, was really taken from the sphere of this inspiration, and had come to you in a sufficiently trustworthy form? What has been said thus far of the means and forms of inspiration refers to the prophetic, psalmodic, chokmatic and apostolic appearance among the people, in the gate, at the temple and in the first Christian circles. The field which this inspiration covered was incomparably larger than that which bounds the domain of the Scripture. Think how much must have been spoken by a man like Isaiah during all the years of his prophetic ministry. Compare with this his small book in our Hebrew Bible, of a little more than four quires, and you will be readily convinced that Isaiah spoke at least ten or twenty times as much again. How little is known to us of the preaching of most of the apostles, even of Peter and Paul, who for many years discharged their apostolic mission. What are thirteen epistles for a man like Paul, whose life was so active, and whose connections were so widely ramified? How much of controversy has been raised about his epistle to the Laodiceans, as though, indeed, that were the only one that was not included in the Scripture? On the other hand, what a large part of Scripture is left uncovered by inspiration, as thus far viewed. Even though you count Samuel and Kings among the prophets, the books of Chronicles, Ezra, Esther and Nehemiah, etc., are still left over. And, in the third place, even if there were not this difference of compass, still what has been thus far treated of could never result in anything more than that such an inspiration had taken place in a whole series of ambassadors of God, while the compilation of what they sang or spake under this inspiration had received no supervision.

With this in mind, we purposely distinguish *graphic* inspiration from the other forms of inspiration; so that by *graphic* inspiration we understand that guidance given by the Spirit of God to the minds of the writers, compilers and editors of the Holy Scriptures, by which these sacred writings have assumed such a form as was, in the counsel of salvation, predestined by God among the means of grace for His Church. To prevent any misunderstanding, we observe at once that in an epistle like that to the Galatians, this graphical inspiration coincides almost entirely with the apostolic inspiration, for in an epistle that was sent, the apostolic inspiration itself bore a graphic character. Nevertheless, the one conception is here not entirely covered by the other; so far, indeed, as there was a choice between several epistles, or between several copies of the same epistle, another factor came into play. Moreover, we grant that it would be more logical, to class that which is not indicated as graphic inspiration as a subdivision under the activity of God with respect to the canon (actio Dei circa Canonem), which in turn belongs under the works of God pertaining to providence (opera Dei, quoad providentiam), and more particularly to special providence (quoad providentiam specialem). For instance, the fact that the Epistle to the Colossians is, and the epistle to the Laodiceans is not, included, may have been caused by the preservation of the one and the loss of the other. There is, then, no question of a choice by men, nor of any inspiration to guide that human choice. It was simply the providence of God which *allowed* one to be lost and the other to be kept. To us it would be even preferable to treat this whole matter under the science of canonics, *disciplina canonica* (which follows later), and much confusion would have been prevented, if this Divine activity in behalf of the Canon had always been distinguished in principle from the real inspiration. Now, indeed, there is a confusion of ideas, which to many renders a clear insight almost impossible. A content like that of the second Psalm was certainly inspired to David, when this song loomed before his spirit and shaped itself in a poetical form. This, however, did not assign it a place in the Scripture, neither did this sanction it as an inspired part of the Holy

Scripture. Since we have been accustomed to pay almost no attention to the original inspiration, and for centuries have applied inspiration indiscriminately to all parts of Scripture, according to their content and form, ecclesiastical parlance does not permit the conception of inspiration to be entirely ignored in the compiling and editing of the books of the Holy Scripture. This is the less necessary, since in this cimpiling and editing an activity from the side of God was exerted upon the spirit of man, which, to some extent, is of one kind with real inspiration. Let it never be lost from sight, however, that this graphic inspiration was merely one of several factors used by God in the "divine activity in behalf of the Canon."

This graphic inspiration is least of all of a uniform character, but it differs according to the nature of the several parts of the Holy Scripture. It is least evident, as observed before, in the apostolic epistles, since these were prepared in writing. Neither can graphic inspiration have been greatly significant in purely lyrical poetic-productions, which were bound to their poetic form, and committed to writing by the poet himself. This simply required such a formulation of the content of his memory, that nothing was changed in it, or, if anything was changed, that this change also took place under the leading of God's Spirit. Then follow those productions of chokmatic, prophetic, or lyric-didactic content, which were digests of longer recitations. As in the case of more than one prophet, the oral author superintended this digest himself, or some other person compiled the content of their Divine charge or teaching and committed it to book-form. With the latter especially graphic inspiration must have been more active, to direct the spirit of the writer or compiler. The working of graphic inspiration must have been still more effective in the description of the apocalyptic vision, especially when this assumed such proportions as the vision of John on Patmos. To obey the order of the "write these things" and in calmer moments to commit to writing what had been seen in ecstasy on the broad expanse of the visionary horizon, required a special sharpening of the memory. And at the same time it was necessary that in the choice of language and expression the writer should be elevated to the heights of his subject. But even this was not the department in which the activity of this graphic inspiration reached its highest point. This took place only in the writing of those books, for which no inspired content presented itself, but which the writer had to compose himself; that is, *the historical books.* With these writings also, as shown by their contents, there was no elimination of those natural data implanted in man for this kind of authorship, and made permanent by *common grace;* on the contrary, graphic inspiration adapts itself wholly to these natural data. The same methods pursued in our times, for the writing of any part of history, were pursued by the historiographers of the Old as well as of the New Testament. Oral traditions are consulted, old chronicles and documents are collected, inquiry is made of those who may have knowledge of the particulars involved, and in this way a representation is formed of what actually took place. Thus Luke (i. 1) himself tells us, (1) that "many have taken in hand to draw up a narrative," (2) that he makes distinction between the things of which he had entire and partial certainty, (3) that he has carefully investigated once more all things from the beginning, (4) that he is particularly guided by the tradition of ear- and eye-witnesses, and (5) that then only he deemed himself competent to write a narrative of these things in good order ($\kappa\alpha\theta\epsilon\xi\hat{\eta}s$). This excludes every idea of a mechanical instillation of the contents of his gospel, and may be accepted as the rule followed by each of the historiographers. Of course the question of the origin of the narrative of the creation cannot be included or classed under this rule. No man was present at the creation. Hence no one but God Himself, who has been present ever since He brought it to pass, can be the author of what we know concerning it. And this is taken entirely apart from the closer distinction, whether the first man had received that insight into the origin of the paradise, of sun, moon and stars, or whether this was granted to the Church at a later period, after the separation from the Heathen. For all those things, on the other hand, which happened to or by man, which were matters of human experience, seen and heard, transmitted by oral tradition, and committed to writing in whatever way, the sacred historiographer followed the ordinary method, and discovered at every turn the still imperfect standpoint at which the historiography of the times stood. In their writings it is seen that they consulted tradition, inserted sections from existing works, examined genealogies and other documents, and collected their material in this entirely natural way. This was the first task of their mind. Then came the second task, of making choice between different traditions and diverging documents. In the third place was added the more important task of understanding the invisible motive of this history, and of observing in it the doings of God. And finally their latest task consisted in committing to writing the representation of the past which in this way had formed itself in their minds. And this brings to light what we mean by graphic inspiration. Even where providentially good tradition and trustworthy documents were within reach, their attention had to be directed to them. They needed guidance in their choice between several, ofttimes contradictory, representations. In the study of the mystical background of this history their mind had to be enabled to perceive the Divine motives. And finally in the writing of what had matured in their mind, their mind and their mind's utterance had to be shaped after the mould of the Divine purpose that was to be realized by the Scripture in His Church. To some extent it can be said that none but natural factors were here at work. It often happens in our times that an author gets hold of a correct tradition, consults trustworthy documents, writes as he ought to write, obtains a just insight into the mysticism that hides in history, thus forms for himself a true representation, and commits this faithfully to writing. But in this case these factors were subject to higher leadings, and upon choice, inventiveness, study of conditions, forming of representations, insight into the mysticism of history, and upon the final writing, the Holy Spirit worked effectively as a leading, directing and determining power; but the subjectivity was not lost. No one single subject could receive in himself the full impression of a mighty event. To see an image from all sides, one must place himself at several points and distances. Hence we find in the Holy Scripture not infrequently more than one narrative of the same group of events, as for instance in the four Gospels; these are no repetitions, but rise from the fact that in the consciousness of one subject the interpretation, and hence also the reproduction, of the incident was necessarily different from those of his fellow-laborer. This is the life of history. It gives no notarial acts, but reproduces what has been received in the consciousness, and does this not with that precision of outline which belongs to architecture, but with the impressionistic certainty of life. This excludes by no means the possibility that the writings thus prepared were afterward reviewed by second or third editors; and here and there enriched by insertions and additions. From their content this very fact is evident. Graphic inspiration must then have been extended to these editors, since they indeed delivered the writings, in the form in which they were to be possessed by the Church. This gives rise to the difficulty, that after the Church had entered upon the possession of such writings, unauthorized editors still tried to introduce modifications, which did not belong to them, and these of course must be excluded. This indeed is related to the general position occupied by the Church over against the Scripture, which tends at no time to allow the certainty of *faith* to be supplanted by the certainty of *intellect*. As soon as it is thought that the holy ore of the Scripture can be weighed in the balance with mathematical accuracy, the eye of faith becomes clouded, and the gold is less clearly seen.

The answer to the question as to our right to accept such a graphic inspiration is given in sections 77 and 78. It is the self-witness ($a\vartheta\tau o\mu a\rho\tau\acute{v}\rho\iota o\nu$) of the Scripture, which it gives of itself in the central revelation of the Christ. Christ indeed gives us no theory of graphic inspiration, but the nature of the authority, which He and His apostles after Him attributed to the Scripture of His times, admits of no other solution. The "all Scripture is theopneustic" is not said of the inspiration of the psalmists, wise men, and prophets, but of the products of *the writers*. This certainly declares that they *remained* writers in the strictest sense, even as compilers and examiners of their material, as compositors and in artistic grouping of the contents, but that in all these functions the Holy Spirit worked so effectively upon the action of their human minds, that thereby their product obtained Divine authority. Of course not in the sense that the content of what they rehearsed obtained thereby a Divine character. When they relate what Shimei said, it does not make his demoniacal language Divine, but it certifies that Shimei spake these evil words; always impressionistically, however, the same as in the New Testament. When in the four Gospels Jesus, on the same occasion, is made to say words that are different in form of expression, it is impossible that He should have used these four forms at once. The Holy Spirit, however, merely intends to make an impression upon the Church which wholly corresponds to what Jesus said. The same is the case with what is written in the Old Testament. The composition of this had taken place under one continuous authority, which justifies citation with an "it is written," such as was done by Jesus, but which modified itself in nature and character according to the claims of the content.

For him who has been brought to the Christ, and who on his knees worships Him as his Lord and his God, the end of all contradiction is hereby reached. When the Christ, whose spirit witnessed beforehand in the prophets, attributes such authority to the Scripture of the Old Covenant, and by His apostles indicates the ground for that authority in the Theopneusty, there is no power that can prevent the recognition of that authority by him who believes in Jesus. Not to recognize it would avenge itself in the representation that in the very holiest things Christ had wholly mistaken Himself. This would imply *the loss of his Savior.* The objection will not do, that one learns to know the Christ from the Scripture, so that faith in the Savior can follow only upon a preceding faith on the Scripture. The reading of the Scripture as such, without more, will never be able to bring one single soul from death unto life. The Scripture by itself is as dull as a diamond in the dark; and as the diamond glistens only when entered by a ray of light, the Scripture has power to charm the eye of the soul only when seen in the light of the Holy Spirit. Christ lives, and by His Holy Spirit He still works upon the heart and in the consciousness of God's elect. Sometimes palingenesis takes place in very infancy. If this were not so, all children dying young should have to be considered as lost. During the period of early bringing up, many children show that the enmity against God was broken in their youthful hearts, before they came to read the Scripture. In fact, it is incorrect to say, that we come to the Scripture *first,* and by the Scripture to Christ. Even when, after having learned to read the Scripture, in later years one comes to Christ as his Savior, the Scripture may cooperate instrumentally, but in principle the act of regeneration ever proceeds from heaven, from God, by His Christ; while, on the other hand, without this ἄνωθεν (from above) the most careful study of the Scripture can never lead to regeneration, nor to a "being planted together" with Christ. Tradition, supported and verified by the Scripture, is surely the ground of a purely historic faith in Christ, but this faith at large fails, as soon as another interpretation of the Scripture gains the day. The outcome shows, that where, on the other hand, the revelation of power from heaven (ἄνωθεν) really has taken place, and transformed the mode of the soul's life and consciousness, even in times of spiritual barrenness, the worship of Christ has again and again revived; and amid general negation, the most learned individuals have bowed again to the authority of the Scripture, in the same way in which Jesus recognized it. The words once spoken by Jesus in the temple at Jerusalem (John vii. 17), "If any man willeth to do his will, he shall know of the teaching, whether it be of God," is truly the canon here. In Christ we only see and handle the Divine, when transformed in our inner being and life, and without this preceding change of heart and our acceptance with Christ, even though an angel were to come down from heaven in visible form, no one would ever subject himself to the word of God. The starting-point must ever lie in our inner *ego,* and without this starting-point in sympathy with the revelation of the Scripture, everything in us tends to disown the authority of the Scripture, and to resist it with all our powers.

That our human *ego,* nevertheless, can be brought to accept and appropriate to itself the special revelation, is a result of the fact that of all the ways and means of inspiration, the self-revealing God has never employed any but those which were present in man by virtue of creation. The whole question of inspiration virtually amounts to this: whether God shall be denied or granted the sovereign right of employing, if so needed and desired, the factors which He Himself created in man, by which to communicate to man what He purposed to reveal respecting the maintenance of His own majesty, the execution of His world-plan, and the salvation of His elect.

Testimonium Spiritus Sancti, or The Witness of the Holy Spirit

The point of view held by our Reformers is (1) that true faith is a gift of God, the fruit of *an operation of the Holy Spirit;* and (2) that true faith, as the Heidelberg Catechism teaches, first of all consists of this, "that I hold for truth all that God has revealed to us in His word." This agrees entirely with what was said at the close of the former section. Not merely historical, but true faith is unthinkable in the sinner, except he embrace "the Christ and all His benefits." This, however, by no means exhausts the meaning of what is understood by the "witness of the Holy Spirit," or the *testimonium Spiritus Sancti.* This goes far deeper. Although it is entirely logical, that he who believes on Christ as God manifest in the flesh, cannot simultaneously reject the positive and definite witness borne by that Christ concerning the Scriptures of the Old Covenant, this proof for graphic inspiration is, and always remains, a proof obtained by inference, and not by one's own apprehension. The two grounds for faith in graphic inspiration must be carefully distinguished, for, though the faith that rests upon the testimony of Christ is more absolute in character, the "witness of the Holy Spirit," though it matures more slowly, is clearer and more in keeping with the freedom of the child of God. It is with this as it was with the people of Sychar, who first believed because of the sayings of the woman, and later believed on the ground of their own sight. The link between these two is the authority of the Church (auctoritas ecclesiae). Although the Reformers rightly contested the auctoritas *imperii,* as they called it, viz. the *imperial authority,* which Rome attributes to the utterance of the ecclesiastical institutions, they never denied the authority of dignity (auctoritas *dignitatis*) of the Church as an organism, nor of the Church as an institution. From the ethical side it has been made to appear, in recent times, that our faith in the Scripture floats on the *faith of the believers,* in distinction from the authority of the Church, and this refers to an important element which was originally too much neglected. An unpardonable mistake, however, was committed, from the ethical side, when this was indicated as the starting-point ($\delta \acute{o}\varsigma$ $\mu o \acute{\iota}$ $\pi o v$ $\sigma \tau \hat{\omega}$) and, worse still, when it was left to this so-called "faith of the believers" to decide what should be accepted from the Scripture, and what was to be rejected from its content. To be *able* to furnish such a testimony, the believers must have an authoritative organ, i.e. it must appear as an instituted body. Thus we would have come back to Rome's shibboleth, "the Church teaches," *Ecclesia docet.* Since, on the other hand, "the faith of the believers" was taken, as it voices itself *without* this organ, all certainty, of course, was wanting, and in the stead of "the faith of the believers," there now appeared the interpretation of "the faith of the believers," as given by A or B. And this resulted in the free use of this pleasing title for all that was held true by individual ministers and their private circles. What thus presented itself as an objective, solid basis, appears to have been nothing but a subjective soil of sand. Moreover, in this wise "the believers" as such were exalted *above* the Christ. For where Christ had testified in the strictest sense to a graphic inspiration of the Old Testament, "the believers" contradicted Him, declared that this interpretation was erroneous, and consequently faith was to be pinned to what was claimed by "the believing circle," and not to what was confessed by Him.

The element of truth in this representation is, that the Church forms a link in a twofold way between faith in the inspiration of the Scripture upon the authority of Christ, and faith in this inspiration on the ground of the testimony of the Holy Spirit. In the first place, it cannot be denied that the Church is one of the factors by which he who formerly stood out of Christ is brought to Christ. "How shall they believe in him of whom they have not heard? and how shall they hear without a preacher?" (Rom. x. 14). However much regeneration may be an act of God in the heart of the sinner, immediately effected, independently of all instrumental help, no conscious faith on Christ can develop itself from this "seed of God"($\sigma\pi\acute{\epsilon}\rho\mu\alpha$ $\theta\epsilon o\hat{v}$) without preaching, which introduces the image of Christ and His work into the human consciousness. Preaching is here taken in the broadest possible sense, not merely as catechization and as preaching of the Word, but as including all communication of man to man, orally or in writing, by which the form of Christ is brought in relief before the seeking eye of faith. So far, therefore, the link of the Church claims our notice, and in proportion as this appearance of the Church is purer or less pure, faith in Christ will be richer or poorer. Augustine's saying, "Evangelio non crederem nisi ecclesiae me moveret autoritas" (i.e. "I could not have believed the Gospel, except as moved by the authority of the Church"), contains something more still. In this saying, the Church appears not merely as the preacher of truth, but as an imposing phenomenon in life which exerts a moral power, and which, itself being a work of Christ, bears witness to the "founder of the Church" (auctor ecclesiae). It is the revelation of the spiritual power of Christ in His Church, which as a spiritual reality takes hold of the soul. For this very reason the interpretation of this word of Augustine by the Romish dogmaticians, as an *auctoritas imperii,* or imperial authority, to be attributed to the instituted Church, is wrong, and it was equally wrong to interpret the Gospel *Evangelium* as the "Inspired Sacred Scripture," for then Augustine should have begun by subjecting himself to this official authority of the Church. Suppose, indeed, that such an arbitrary subjection would have been conceivable, the word *moveret* would have been put to an impossible use. An imperial authority does not move (movet), but commands (iubet) and compels (cogit). What remains of this, therefore, is no other than what we, too, confess; viz. that as a herald of the Gospel (praedicatrix Evangelii) and as an imposing spiritual phenomenon, the Church is one of the factors used by the Holy Spirit in bringing the regenerate to a conscious faith in Christ.

To this is added, in the second place, the very important significance of "the communion of saints." Even though it is not impossible in the absolute sense that faith can be maintained in isolation, isolation, nevertheless, goes against the nature of faith; and it remains a question whether any one but Christ Himself, in that absolute sense, has stood alone in his faith. This is the very profound meaning of Gethsemane. Sin, and hence unbelief, scatters, individualizes, and pulverizes; but grace, and hence faith, restores life in organic connection, viz. the life of each member in the body. And what applies to *being* applies also to the *consciousness;* here it is also an "apprehending with all the saints" (Eph. iii. 18). The power of public opinion shows how mightily this factor inworks upon our own conviction; and as there is a public opinion in the things of the world, there is also a certain *fides communis,* or, if you please, a public opinion in the communion of saints. And in so far the ethical school maintains correctly that "the faith of the believers" supports the faith of the individual, and exercises a certain authority over it. This factor works in a threefold way: (1) in an *historical* sense, in so far as the testimony of the ages comes to us in tradition and writings; (2) in a *catholic* sense, insomuch as the general appearance of the universal Church always includes a certain confession of faith; and (3) in an *empirical* sense, if we ourselves personally come in contact with confessors of Christ, move in the circles of the children of God, and thus experience immediately the influence of the communion of the saints. In this we are not dealing with the Church as an institution, but with the Church as an organism. And though it must be granted that the influence of this public opinion, if untrue, can inwork disastrously upon our conviction, so that spiritual criticism only keeps us in the right path, it is nevertheless entirely true that this *communis fides,* this public opinion among the children of God, this "faith of the believers" as it may be called, imprints in our consciousness the image of Christ as the Saviour of the world, and supports in us faith in the Holy Scripture.

This, of course, cannot be the last point of support, and therefore the Reformers wisely appealed on principle to the "witness of the Holy Spirit." By this they understood a testimony that went out directly from the Holy Spirit, as author of the Scripture, to our personal *ego.* They did not call it an internal (internum) but an external proof (argumentum externum), for the reason that it did not rise from our *ego,* but from without us, from God, it moved itself toward our *ego.* It has often, however, been wrongly represented that by this witness was meant in a magic sense a certain "ecstasy" or "enthusiasm," and that it consisted of a supernatural communication from the side of God, in which it was said to us, "This Scripture is my Word." Thus it has been represented by some who were less well informed, but never by our theologians. On the contrary, they have always protested against this representation; the more since experience taught that all such interpretation led at once to a false mysticism, and thereby undermined the authority of the Scripture. For then, indeed, the revelation of God, which one imagines and declares himself to have received, is placed *above* the Scripture, and in the end the Scripture is rejected. No, the representation of the Reformers was this, that this witness is to be taken as "light so irradiating the mind as to affect it gently, and display to it the inner relations of the truth that had hitherto been concealed." Hence it was a subdivision of the enlightening, but in this instance directed immediately upon the Holy Scripture, and not upon its inspiration, but its Divine quality. First one stood before the Holy Scripture as before a foreign object which did not suit his world of conceptions, and over against which, in his world-consciousness, one assumed essentially not merely a doubtful, but a hostile attitude. If meanwhile the change of our inner being has taken place by palingenesis, from which there has gradually sprung in our sense and in our consciousness a modified view of ourselves, of the things of this world, and of the unseen world, which withdraws itself from our natural eye, this enlightening of the Holy Spirit creates discord between our deepest life-consciousness and the consciousness of the world, which formerly ruled and still presses itself upon us. And in this struggle the Holy Spirit opens our eyes, that in the Holy Scripture we may see a representation of our *ego,* of the world and of the eternal things, which *agrees* with what we seek to defend in the combat against the naturalistic consciousness of the world. Hence a process is here involved. The more deeply we are led by the Holy Spirit into the knowledge of ourselves as sinners, of the unreality of the world, and of the reality of the Divine, the more intense becomes this struggle, and the more evident grows the affinity between the work of the Holy Spirit in us and in that Holy Scripture. Thus the veil is gradually being pushed aside, the eye turns toward the Divine light that radiates from the Scripture, and now our inner *ego* sees its imposing superiority. We see it as one born blind, who being healed, sees the beauty of colors, or as one deaf, whose hearing being restored, catches the melodies from the world of sounds, and with his whole soul delights himself in them.

In this connection the so-called *internal* proof for the Divine character of the Holy Scripture must also be understood. In a later period it has been made to appear that the "heavenly majesty of the doctrines, the marvellous completeness of the prophecies, the wonderful miracles, the consent of all its parts, the divineness of the discourse," and so much more, formed a system of outward proofs able to convince the reason without *enlightenment;* but our first theologians, at least, did not attach such a meaning to them. They taught that these inner relations of the Scripture were understood, and thus were able to serve their real purpose only when, by enlightening, the spiritual understanding had been clarified and purified. He only, who in palingenesis had experienced *a miracle* in his own person, ceased to react against miracles, but rather invoked them himself. He who had observed the fulfilment of several prophecies in his own spiritual life, understood the relation between prophecy and its fulfilment. He who heard the music of the Divine melody of redemption in his own soul was rapt in wonder (rapiebatur in admirationem), as they expressed it, in listening to the Oratorio of Salvation proceeding from the heavenly majesty of doctrine in the Holy Scripture. As the *Confessio Belgica* states in Art. 9, that we even believe the mystery of the Trinity "from their operations, and chiefly by those we feel in ourselves," our faith in the Divine character of the Scripture rests upon the experience of spiritual life that addresses us from that Scripture. That similarity of personal experience fosters affinity, quickens sympathy and opens eye and ear. In by far the greater number of cases this *testimonium Spiritus Sancti* works gradually and unobserved. The "enlightening" increases gradually in intensity, and in proportion as it grows stronger we see more, and see with more certainty, and stand the more firmly. Sometimes, however, this witness of the Holy Spirit becomes more incisive in character. This is especially noticeable in days of general apostasy, and then the child of God is fully conscious of this incisive inworking. Living in a society of high intellectual development, and taking notice of what is contributed by reason without enlightening to enervate the Divine character of the Holy Scripture, inwardly most painful discord is born. Doubt is contagious. When with firm tread you walk along your well-chosen way, and without hesitancy at the cross-road turn to the right, you are involuntarily brought to a standstill, and shocked for a moment in your feeling of assurance, when three or four persons call out after you that you should turn to the left. As in sanctification you are made to err in this way from time to time with respect to the Holy Scripture, you may be led to doubt, and even for a while pursue wrong paths. But this will not be permanent. The work of grace is not left to yourself, but with a firm hand is guided by the Holy Spirit, who in no mechanical way, but by a richer spiritual experience, at length restores you to seeing again what is truly Divine. And when the Holy Spirit enters accusation against us in our own soul that we kick against the pricks, and depend more on our own and Satan's word than on His Word, and moves and implores us with groanings unspeakable that for the sake of the glory of God and our salvation we attach again a greater significance to His Word than to any other, then there comes that incisive, and therefore decisive, moment when the child of God lays the hand on his mouth, and with shame and confusion turns his back upon doubt, in order that in contrition and sorrow he may hearken again to the Holy Spirit as the speaker in His Word. As said before, however, this incisive character is not borne by the witness of the Holy Spirit in every person, nor at all times. As the conversion of many people has taken place almost without observation, which often happens in the quieter walks of Christian life, and the conversion of a few only, who at first wandered far off, is incisive like that of an Augustine, such also is the case here. For the most part this witness works gradually and unobserved, and only in exceptional cases is it as lightning that suddenly flames through the skies.

From the nature of this witness of the Holy Spirit, it follows at the same time, that it begins with binding us simply to the Holy Scripture in its *centrum*. It is the *central* truth concerning our *ego*, concerning the world about us, and of the true reality which is with God, that takes hold of us, convinces and follows after us, until we give ourselves captive to it. This central truth will take hold of one by this, and of another by that utterance, in proportion as our inner life is tuned to it; but the first impressions will *always* cause us to descend into the depths of misery and ascend to the heights of redemption. How far the authority, which from this spiritual centrum obtains its hold on us, extends itself later to those things in the Scripture that lie on the periphery, is a question devoid at first of all spiritual significance. Conditions are conceivable in which, after one is captured centrally by the Scripture, the clashing is continued for many years between our thinking and acting on the one hand, and that which the Scripture lays upon us in the name of the Lord as faith and practice (credena and agenda). Gradually, however, an ever more vitally organic relation begins to reveal itself between the centrum of the Scripture and its periphery, between its fundamental and its derivative thoughts, and between its utterances and the facts it communicates. That authority which at first addressed us from that centrum only, now begins to appear to us from what has proceeded from that centrum. We feel ourselves more and more captivated by a power, whose centrum cannot be accepted without demanding and then compelling all unobservedly an ever more general consent for its entire appearance, and all its utterances. Thus it ends as *Scripture* by imposing sacred obligations upon us, as *Holy Book* by exercising over us moral compulsion and spiritual power. And in the end the connection between its form and content appears so inseparable, that even the exceptional parts of its form appeal to us, and, in form and content both, the Scripture comes to stand before us as an authority from God.

But this process of conviction worked in us by the Spirit, is always a spiritual work, which has nothing in common with the learning of the schools; it is moreover incapable of maintaining itself theoretically and of continuing itself according to a definable system. By itself it tends no further than to bear spiritual testimony to our personal, regenerated ego concerning the Divine character of everything the Holy Scripture teaches and reveals; and without more, the truth, for instance, of *graphic inspiration* can never be derived from it. If, however, an absolute certainty concerning this Divine character of the content of the Scripture has been sealed in the personal consciousness of man by this witness of the Holy Spirit, the effect of this goes back to the two former stages of the public opinion (communis fides), and the cleaving to Christ. With this conviction, which is now his own for good and always, he, who has been set free from the veil that darkly hung between, does not stand alone, but feels himself assimilated by the illuminated consciousness which in the communion of the saints is distinguished from the natural consciousness of the world. This assimilation becomes the stronger, according to the greater vitality of the child of God in him, by which he is evermore being changed into the image of the Son of God. Thus there originates a communion of consciousness not merely with those round about us, but also with the generation of saints of former ages, affinity of life with the saints that have gone before, unity of soul-conceptions with the martyrs, with the fathers of the Church, with the apostles, and so at length with Christ Himself and with the faithful of the Old Covenant. In the life-consciousness of that sacred circle the positive conviction prevails, that we have a graphically inspired Scripture, on which we lean and by which we live; and that this is not contingent, nor accidental, but necessary. This faith in the Scripture is found as an indispensable and an entirely natural component part in the life-consciousness of this circle. And when in experience the riches of the Scripture contents become ever more precious to the heart, resistance is no longer possible. The power of assimilation is too strong, the general *unsanctified* human consciousness loses all its power, and at length the believer must accept the equally general, but now sanctified, human consciousness, including this component part of its content. If then, finally, the believer goes back to the first stage in his Christian life, i.e. to his personal faith in his Saviour, and realizes that Christ himself has presented the Holy Scripture—which the common opinion in the communion of saints has adopted in its world of thought as theopneustic, and of the Divine *truth* of which, thanks to the "Witness of the Holy Spirit," he is himself firmly convinced—as the product of the Holy Spirit, the assurance of his faith on this point is immovably established, and to him the Scripture itself is the *principium,* i.e., the starting-point, from which proceeds all knowledge of God, i.e. all *theology.*

In this sense the Holy Scripture was the *principium* of Theology to our fathers, and in the same sense it is this to us. Hence this principium, as such, can be no conclusion from other premises, but is itself *the* premise, from which all other conclusions are drawn. Of course this does not dismiss the fact, that objections, derived from the common *norma* of our thought, can still be entered against the Holy Scripture and its alleged character; in this, indeed, every one should be left free, and these objections it is the task of Theology squarely to face. This, however, can be considered only in the science of the canon (disciplina canonicae) and the science of the text (ars textualis). We merely observe that on the one hand this critical task should not be impeded in the least, provided it is clearly understood on the other hand that the failure of your first efforts to solve such critical objections can rob you of the certainty of your *principium,* as little as success can strengthen it. Assurance of faith and demonstration are two entirely heterogeneous things. And he who, in whatever department, still seeks to demonstrate his *principium,* simply shows that he does not know what is to be understood by a *principium.*

CHAPTER III

THE METHOD OF THEOLOGY

What is demanded by the Nature of its Principium

The legend is still current that the Reformers intended to represent the Holy Scripture as a sort of a code, in which certain articles were set down in ready form, some as things to be believed, and some as rules for practice (credenda and agenda). According to this representation the Holy Scripture consists of four parts: (1) a notarially prepared official report of certain facts; (2) an exposition of certain doctrines drawn up by way of articles; (3) an instituted law in the form of rules; and (4) an official program of things to come. Over against this legend stands the fact that the content and the character of the Holy Scripture correspond in no particular to this representation, and that psychologically it will not do to attribute such a view of the Holy Scripture to any theologian worthy the name. This legend, however, is not the product of pure invention. The way in which Scholastics used to demonstrate from the Holy Scripture consisted almost exclusively of citations of this or that Bible text. Neither did the Reformers abandon this method entirely; they made free use of it; but no one of them employed this method exclusively. They compared Scripture with Scripture. They looked for an analogy of faith. They were thus led to enter more deeply into the organic life of the Scripture. And he who gives Voetius' treatise *quousque sese extendat S. Scripturae auctoritas?* (Select. Disp., Tom. I, p. 29) even a hasty perusal only, perceives at once that the view-point held by the theologians of that day was very just. The narrator of this legend is so far correct, however, that in the eighteenth and beginning of the nineteenth century, under the influences of pietism and methodism, this unscientific method became ever more popular, and that this grotesque representation of the Holy Scripture found acceptance with the less thoughtful among simple believers. Scripture-proof seemed to them to be presented only by the quotation of some Bible verse that literally and fully expressed the given assertion. This is a severe demand, which, on the other hand, excuses one from all further investigation; and, provided you but quote Scripture, does not inquire whether your citation is borrowed from the Old Testament or the New, whether it was spoken by Job or by his friends, or whether it occurs absolutely, or in application to a given case. This makes the Bible your code, a concordance your register, and with the help of that register you quote from that code as occasion requires.

It needs scarcely be said that this method is utterly objectionable. If this were the true method, the Holy Scripture would have to be an entirely differently compiled book from what it is. As to its facts, it should present an accurate, precise, singular story made up in notarial form. It would have to give the program of things to come with the indication of persons, place, time and succession of the several acts in the drama still to be performed. With respect to *truth,* it ought to present this in the form of a precisely formulated and systematically constructed dogmatic. And as for the *rules of practice,* you ought to find in the Holy Scripture a regular codification of a series of general and concretely applied directions, indicating what you should do and leave undone. This is no exaggeration. The question of the Holy Scripture involves nothing short of the question of a *Divine authority,* which imposes faith in facts and teachings, and subjection to rules and commandments. Hence your demonstration must be unimpeachable. And the method that is applicable only to an authenticated official report, a carefully formulated confession and an accurately recorded law, must be objected to as long as it is not shown that the Scripture, from which the quotation is made, exhibits the character asserted. If such, however, is *not* the case, and if on the contrary it is certain that the whole disposition, nature and character of the Holy Scripture resemble in no particular such an official report and codification, it needs no further comment that this method is altogether useless and has no claim therefore on our consideration.

Nevertheless it would be a mistake to explain the popularity which this objectionable method captured for itself, on the simple ground of a lack of understanding. Call to mind the use made of the Old Testament Scripture by Christ and His apostles, and it not infrequently has the appearance that they freely followed this objectionable method. If it can readily be shown that Christ and His apostles also argue from the Scripture in an entirely different way (see Matt. xix. 8 and Heb. vii.), the fact nevertheless cannot be denied that literal citations from the Old Testament, as "the Scripture" or "it is written," repeatedly occur in the Gospels and in the apostolic discourses and epistles. Hence a distinction here is necessary. If we note in what form the Holy Scripture presents itself to us, it certainly has nothing in common with an official report or a code; but it contains, nevertheless, extended series of definite and positive utterances respecting faith and practice, which utterances leave nothing to be desired either in clearness or in accuracy of formulation. Such utterances stand not by themselves, but occur mostly in organic connection with events and conversations. The flower in bloom that exhales its fragrance is attached to a stem, and as a rule that stem is still joined to the plant. But even so, that utterance is there, and by it positiveness demands a hearing. Hence with reference to such utterances the task of the human mind has been reduced to a minimum. In controversy and exhortation these utterances render most ready service. And this explains the fact that the appeal to this category of utterances has occurred most often, still occurs, and ever will continue to occur. Even in the hour of dying it is this sort of utterances that refreshes and comforts most quickly and soothingly, and with the lowly especially will ever carry the most telling effect. But though we grant this, and though this easily explains the fact that the methodistic idea so quickly gained the day, it should not be admitted for a moment that this use of the Scripture is the general and exclusive method.

The task imposed on us is much more difficult and intricate; and so far from consisting of a mechanical quotation with the help of the concordance, the production of what the Scripture contains demands gigantic labor. Beyond doubt the ectype of the archetypal self-knowledge of God is contained in the Scripture according to human capacity with respect to both fallen and regenerate man (pro mensura humana, respectu hominis lapsi, and pro captu hominis renati); but for the most part in the sense in which it can be said by the mine-owner, that gold is at hand, when with folded arms he looks across the fields, beneath which his gold-mines hide. The special revelation does not encourage idleness, neither does it intend to offer you the knowledge of God as bread baked and cut, but it is so constructed and it is presented in such a form, that the utmost effort is required to reach the desire results. With reference also to this, you eat no bread except in the sweat of your brow. We do not imply that this whole task must be performed by every believer personally. The very best of us would faint beneath its load. But we recall what has been said before, viz., that the subject of science is not the individual, but the consciousness of humanity; and that therefore in the same way the subject of the science of theology is not the individual believer, but the consciousness of our regenerated race. Hence it is a task which is in process century upon century, and from its very nature is still far from being completed. And in the absolute sense it can as little be completed as any other scientific task. In the Holy Scripture God the Lord offers us ectypal theology in an organically connected section of human life, permeated by many Divine agencies, out of which a number of blindingly brilliant utterances strike out as sparks from fire. But the treasures thus presented are without further effort not yet reflected *in* and reproduced *by* the consciousness of regenerated man. To realize this purpose our thinking consciousness must descend into this gold mine, and dig out from its treasure, and then assimilate that treasure thus obtained; and not leave it as something apart from the other content of our consciousness, but systematize it with all the rest into one whole. Christian thinking, i.e. scientific theology, has been at work on this task for eighteen centuries; among all nations; under all sorts of constellations. This had to be so, simply because no single nation represents the absolute consciousness of humanity, but every nation, and every period of time, according to their nature and opportunity, has the power and the capacity to do this in a peculiar way; and because the natural content of the consciousness, with which this knowledge of God must be placed in connection, continually changes.

But amid all these changes the threefold task is ever prosecuted: (1) to determine, (2) to assimilate and (3) to reproduce the contents of the Holy Scripture. This task of *determination* covers, indeed, a broad field, and is, moreover, exceedingly intricate. The pertinent utterances of Scripture are, of course, invaluable aids; but more than aids they are not. The content of the Scripture lies before you in the form of an historic process, which covers centuries, and, therefore, ever presents itself in different forms. The Scripture reveals ectypal theology mostly in facts, which must be understood; in symbols and types, which must be interpreted. All sorts of persons make their appearance in strange comming, one of whom is, and another is not, a partaker of Divine grace. The rule for practice presents itself in numerous concrete applications, from which the general rule can only be derived by dint of logical thinking. Thus what stands written is not merely to be understood as it was meant by the writer, but its significance must be estimated in separation from its accidental connection. The several revelations must be taken in their true unity after the analogy of faith. And, finally, from *behind* the meaning of the writers there must be brought out the things, which often they themselves did not perceive, but which, nevertheless, they were called upon to announce to the world, as the mystery of the thoughts of *God* inworked in *their* thoughts. Hence, the free citation of pertinent utterances is lawful; but the person should be considered who spoke them, the antithesis which they opposed, the cause that invited them, as well as the persons to whom they were directed. If this had been observed, the statement, for instance, "Man shall not live by bread alone, but by every word that proceedeth out of the mouth of God," would never have been misused, to represent the spiritual needs as more important than the material needs. The thoughtless citation of this has been very misleading; and this is the more serious, since such classic utterances are indeed authoritative, and when wrongly interpreted confuse and mislead.

In the second place, follows the task of *assimilating* the ectypal theology offered us in the Scripture. We do not speak now of the action of the spiritual factors required for this, but limit ourselves exclusively to the task of taking up into our human consciousness the content found. This content to be assimilated comes to us in language both symbolical and mystical, which reveals and again conceals. Hence, the purpose must be to analyze this content, to transpose the parts discovered into conceptions, and to reconstruct these conceptions thus found into a synthesis adapted to our thinking. This is the more exceedingly difficult because an analysis made too hastily so readily destroys the mystical element, and thus leads to rationalism, while, on the other hand, the synthesis must be able to enter into *our* thinking. To this the fact is added that in this work no one is able to separate himself from his personal limitation and from his limited personality. This assimilation is, therefore, possible for individuals only in so far as the limits of their spiritual and mental action extends, and still it should ever be our effort to assimilate in such a way as to promote this assimilation-process in others. Otherwise there might, indeed, be a spiritual upbuilding of self, but no scientific study. If there is to be scientific study, one must be able, by giving an account, to objectify the assimilation-process one has himself experienced. This task demands intense application of thought, because it is not enough that we take up in ourselves the loose elements of the revelation, but we must take those elements as constitutive parts of one organic whole, and thus in our thoughts, also, order them in one *system*. This would require great energy of thought in a consciousness otherwise empty; but it does this the more, since our consciousness is already occupied. Now it becomes our duty to expel from our consciousness what is criticised by revelation as untrue, and to weave together what remains with the content of revelation, so that the Unity of our world- and life-view shall not be lost.

And then follows the third part of the task, by which we are called *to reproduce* what is thus acquired. The duty of witness-bearing and confession calls us to this third action, but also, without abandoning this practical end, the claim of science itself. Apart, also, from the maintenance of God's honor in the face of the denier of His truth, God counts it His glory that in the human consciousness which He had disposed to His truth, and which we had applied to the service of error and falsehood, His truth is again reflected. The Scripture offers us *the grain of wheat,* but we may not rest until the golden ears are seen in *the fields,* by which to prove the power potentially hidden in the seed. Hence, it is not enough that the knowledge of God, which, as a flower in the bud, is hidden and covered in the Scripture, is set forth by us in its excellency; but that bud must be unfolded, the flower must make exhibition of its beauty, and scent the air with its fragrance. This can be done spiritually by piety of mind, practically by deeds of faith, aesthetically in hymns, parenetically in exhortation, but must also be done by scientific exposition and description.

No theologian, therefore, can go to work in an empirical or in a speculative manner. He who empirically takes religious phenomena as his starting-point is no theologian, but an ethnological or philosophical investigator of religions. Neither is a speculative thinker a theologian. We do not question the relative right of the speculative method. Conceptions also generate, and rich harvests may be gathered from the fields of logical thought, but he who goes to work in this manner is no theologian. Theology is a positive science, which finds the object of its investigation, i.e. ectypal knowledge of God, in the Holy Scripture, and therefore must draw the insight into its object from the Scripture. The reason why abstract intellectualism is insufficient for this will appear later; but in so far as now we limit ourselves exclusively to this intellectual task, it follows from the nature of the object and from the principium of theology that it must determine, assimilate and reproduce, but with this its task is ended. For the sake of completeness, we may add that this includes the investigation of the instrument of revelation, i.e. the Holy Scripture; which task is the more extensive, as that Scripture has not come to us in autographs, nor in our own language, but in foreign languages and in apographa, which are in many respects corrupt, so that it requires an entirely independent effort of the mind, by the study of criticism and language, so to approach the Scripture as to render an investigation of its content possible. Meanwhile this detracts nothing from the character of *principium* which is possessed by the Holy Scripture as the effective cause of all true theology. In view of the full demonstration of the former chapter, this requires no further emphasis.

The Principium of Theology in Action

Without further explanation the impression would be conveyed, that the method of theological investigation, as described in the preceding section, makes theology to terminate in dogmatics. The more so, since earlier dogmaticians frequently named their dogmatics *"Theologia* Christiana." Even Calvin's *Institutes* is based on such a supposition. It is readily seen, however, that in this way theology as a science would be curtailed. To mention one particular only, we ask, what would become of Church history? In this second section, therefore, we observe that he who investigates a given object, obtains full knowledge of it only by the study of its states both of *rest* and *action*. This applies also to the ectypal knowledge of God, which, in behalf of the Church, is deposited in the Holy Scripture. The Word of God also has its action. It is "quick and powerful and sharper than any two-edged sword," "a hammer that breaketh the rock in pieces." It works also as a living seed that is sown, and which, according to the nature of the soil, germinates and brings forth fruit. Hence the task of the theologian is by no means ended when he has formulated, assimilated and reproduced the content of the Word *in its state of rest;* it is his duty, also, to trace the *working* of this principium, when the fountain is *flowing.* After it was finished, the Holy Scripture was not hidden in some sacred grotto, to wait for the theologian to read and to make scientific exhibition of its content; no, it was carried into the world, by reading and recitation, by teaching and by preaching, in apologetic and in polemic writings. And once brought into the world, it has exerted an influence upon the consciousness-form of the circle which it entered. Both its authority, and the consequent activity which it created, are no mean factors in the rise of an ecclesiastical confession and in the institution of an ecclesiastical communion. The Holy Scripture and the Church, therefore, are no foreign phenomena to each other, but the former should be looked upon as the mother of the latter. Not that the Word by itself was able to found a Church or a church life. The Holy Scripture does not possess such an inherent mystical power, and it is self-evident that the transcendental action of the regeneration of the elect had to go hand in hand with the noetic action of the Word, in order to give rise to the Church and to maintain it. This second element, also, will be explained later. But however much it may be bound to this spiritual antecedent, in itself the church-forming and church-maintaining action of the Word cannot be denied, and, *cum grano salis,* the domain of the Church can be described as the domain within which the Holy Scripture prevails and operates.

From this it follows that he who tries to understand the Holy Scripture, and to reproduce its content in a scientific way, may not pass its action by, nor the product of this action. Theological science, therefore, must also institute an investigation into the Church, into its character, jurisdiction, history, etc. He who neglects this has not investigated his subject fully. It cannot be said, therefore, that church history, church law, etc., are added to the real theological studies as so many loose supplements. On the contrary, in the theological whole they form organic, and therefore indispensable, members. If it is not in itself objectionable to compare the Holy Scripture to a gold mine, this comparison nevertheless fails as soon as an attempt is made to view the method of theology as a whole. Then, indeed, there is not a question of a quiescent, passive gold mine which awaits the coming of a miner, but rather of a power propelled by the Holy Spirit, and propelling the spirits of men, which has drawn its furrows deep in the past, and which, from the living phenomenon of the Church, still appeals to us as a principium full of action. We do not step thus a handbreadth aside from the conception of theology as we found it. Theology remains to us theology in the strictest sense of the word, i.e. that science whose object is ectypal theology, given in the Holy Scripture, which is the principium of theology; but we refuse to eliminate the *action* of this Word from our reckoning. Not only the statics, but also the dynamics must be given a hearing. Hence, as a product of the energy of the Word, the Church may not be cut off, but it must find a place of its own in theological science as a whole. So far as this produces an effect upon the organic system of theologic science, this point will be treated in the last chapter but one of this volume; here it is mentioned only in so far as it produces an effect upon *the method of theology.* In this form it comes nearest to what is generally called the relation of theology to the Church, even though it creates some surprise that this question has almost always been separated from the question *about the method.* If a fixed relation between theology and the Church is to be treated in another than an outward sense, this relation *must* also appear in *the method.*

An *outward* relation between the Church and the practice of theology is surely conceivable, in so far as the Church as an institution has herself taken it frequently in hand through the organ of her appointed theologians. She can bind such theologians to her confession; she can forbid them to publish anything in conflict with it; and by discipline she can prevent them from every effort directed against it. But this outward relation is entirely accidental. Civil government can act along the same lines, and has often done it. Individuals, also, in free institutions can do the same thing. On the other hand, the Church may found a theological school of an entirely different kind, to which it allows entire freedom of faith and doctrine. And therefore we did *not* take our start in these outward and by consequence accidental relations, but in the essential and necessary relation which exists between the Holy Scripture and the Church as its product, in order that from this we might borrow the rule for the relation between the Church and theology which is to appear in its method.

There is, to be sure, a theological illusion abroad, which has its relative right, which conveys the impression that, with the Holy Scripture in hand, one can independently construct his theology from this principium. This position was defended only recently by a Protestant theologian at Vienna, Professor Dr. Bohl (*Dogmatik,* Amst. 1887, p. xiii, v); and it must be conceded to him that in the days of the Reformation, also, it was generally imagined that a leap backward had been taken across fourteen centuries, for the sake of repeating what had once been done by the first Christians; viz. to investigate the Bible, while yet no confession or dogma had been framed. But from the nature of the case this illusion is not for a moment tenable. He who harbors it claims for himself the unattainable honor of doing the work of bygone generations. And besides being unhistoric to this extent, he forgets also that no single person, but thinking, regenerated humanity, is the subject of theology. Isolated investigation can never furnish what can only be the result of the cooperation and mental effort *of all*. Actually, therefore, this illusion is a denial of the historic and the organic character of the study of theology, and for this reason it is inwardly untrue. No theologian, following the direction of his own compass, would ever have found by himself what he now confesses and defends on the ground of the Holy Scripture. By far the largest part of his results is adopted by him from theological *tradition,* and even the proofs, which he cites from the Scripture, at least as a rule, have not been discovered by himself, but have been suggested to him by his predecessors. Thus, it is noteworthy that Calvin, who, undeniably, wrote at times as though affected by this same illusion, appeals constantly to Augustine and Thomas Aquinas, which shows that this illusion did *not* govern his method. The true element in this representation, meanwhile, should not be overlooked. And this is grasped at once if one places at the end of the way what Professor Dr. Bohl has held as truth at its beginning. He makes it to appear as if by making a *tabula rasa* the theologian reverts at once to the Holy Scripture and nothing but the Scripture. The actual course pursued, however, is this. The beginning is made under the influence of all sorts of other factors, while the task is not ended until, at the end of the way, all these factors are made to disappear, so that finally our well-balanced conviction rests *upon nothing but the Holy Scripture.* Then the scaffold is taken away, and we stand on the pinnacle of the temple. This is the final ground that must be reached if the theological motive is to attain to ts point of rest. And it is from the exalted feeling which then inspires the theologian that the illusion objected to above is born.

Without hesitation, therefore, *the factor of the Church* must be included in theological investigation. From the life of the Church it appears, what activity the Holy Scripture occasions, which activity in turn sheds light upon its content. This would not have been the case to so great an extent if there had been only one interpretation of the Holy Scripture prevalent in the Church; for this would have tended to likeness of formulation. But such was not the case. Almost all possible interpretations have been tried; all these interpretations have sought to maintain themselves and to reach fixed forms of expression, and the fruit and effect of these several interpretations are manifest in *history* and in *present conditions.* Hence the domain of the Holy Scripture is no longer unexplored territory, on the contrary it is a variegated highland, crossed in all directions, all the mountain passes and paths of which are known, while the goal of each is freely told by experienced guides. As it would be the height of folly, on one's first arrival in Switzerland, to make it appear that *he* is the first to investigate the Berner Oberland, since common sense compels him on the contrary to begin his journey by making inquiry among the guides of the country, the same is true here. In its rich and many-sided life, extending across so many ages, the Church tells you at once what fallible interpretations you need no longer try, and what interpretation on the other hand offers you the best chances for success. On this ground the claim must be put, that the investigator of the Holy Scripture shall take account of what history and the life of the Church teaches concerning the general points of view, from which to start his investigation, and which paths it is useless to further reconnoitre.

But the influence of this factor does not limit itself to this. The investigator does not stand outside of the Church, but is himself a member of it. Hence into his own consciousness there is interwoven the historic consciousness of his Church. In this historic consciousness of his Church he finds not merely the tradition of theologians and the data by which to form an estimate of the results of their studies, but also the confessional utterances of the Church. And this implies more. These utterances of his Church do not consist of the interpretation of one or another theologian, but of the ripest fruit of a spiritual and dogmatic strife, battled through by a whole circle of confessors in violent combat, which enlightened their spiritual sense, sharpened their judgment, and stimulated their perception of the truth; which fruit, moreover, has been handed down to him by the Church through its divinely appointed organs. It will not do, therefore, to place these dogmatical utterances on the same plane with the opinions of individual theologians. In a much deeper sense than they, they provide a guarantee for freedom from error, and he who belongs to such a Church has himself been moulded in part by them. This gives rise to the demand, that every theologian shall, in his investigations, reckon with all those things that are taught him by the history of the churches concerning well and badly chosen paths in this territory to be investigated; and, also, in the second place, that he shall take the dogmas of his Church as his guide, and that he shall not diverge from them until he is compelled to do this by the Word of God. Hence, one should not begin by doubting everything, and by experimenting to see whether on the ground of his own investigation he arrives at the same point where the confession of his Church stands; but, on the contrary, he should start out from the assumption that his Church is right, while at the same time he should investigate it, and only oppose it when he finds himself compelled to do so by the Word of God. If such prove the case, of course, it must be done; and if it concerns any point of importance, an immediate break with his Church is the necessary result, unless the Church herself should modify her confession agreeably to his view. History, however, teaches that ordinary differences in details of opinion among theologians have implied no departure from essentials, and that the conflict between God's Word and error in the confession has been carried to the end in those great movements only, which have brought about a change in the entire thinking consciousness. Great carefulness is always safe. The proclamation of new discoveries is not always a proof of devotion to the truth, it is sometimes a tribute to self-esteem. Nevertheless, the point of support for theology may never be looked for in the Church. It only finds that point of support when it shows that what the Church has offered it as acquired treasures, were really taken *from* the Scripture and *after the rule* of the Scripture.

This decides at the same time the question, whether the Church should prosecute the study of theology, or whether theology grows on a root of its own. The question cannot detain us here, whether in times of need we are not warranted in establishing church-seminaries, and, in the absence of university training, to provide for a need, whose supply admits of no delay. There is no question here of the education of untrained persons for the ministry of the Word, but *of theology as a science.* And, from the nature of the case, there can be no question of theology outside the pale of the Church, because outside of this pale there is neither palingenesis nor a spiritual enlightening, both of which are indispensable to theology. But from this it does not follow, that, as an *instituted corporation,* the Church itself should study theology. This institution has a *limited official* task, and covers, by no means, the *whole* of our Christian life. Outside of this institution endless factors of our human life are at work within the pale of the Church taken as an organism, upon each of which the Spirit of Christ must exert His influence. One of these factors is science, and so far from proceeding from the instituted Church, science includes the Church in its object, and must be subservient to her in the accomplishment of her task. The subject of Christian science is also the subject of Christian theology; or, how could theology otherwise take a place in the organism of science? The instituted Church can never be the subject of *the* Christian science, and consequently it cannot be this of the science of theology. Hence, the dilemma: Your theology has the instituted Church for its subject, in which case it is no science; or if it is a science, the Church as an institution cannot be its subject.

Relation to the Spiritual Reality

In connection with this there is still another, no less important, factor which both affects theology and is indispensable to it. The Church owes its rise not to the Word alone, but in a deeper sense to the supernatural spiritual workings, which go out among men, and whose central point is palingenesis. In a supernatural sense this creates a spiritual reality, which, in so far as the sphere of the consciousness is concerned, cannot dispense with the Holy Scripture, but which potentially does not proceed from the Scripture, but from the Holy Ghost, or if you please concentrically from Christ. This spiritual reality does not consist merely in the deed and in the thing wrought by palingenesis, but from this central point it radiates also subjectively in those who are sanctified and enlightened, and objectively finds its basis in the presence of the Holy Spirit in the Body of Christ. The preaching of the Word joins itself to this spiritual reality, becomes conscious of its inspiration, imparts to it a conscious form, and the Church, as it actually appears, is not merely the product of the Word of God, but at the same time of this spiritual reality. Not as an institution, but as an organism is she a house of the living God. The purer a revelation the instituted Church is of her hidden, organic, spiritual life, the greater is the authority in the spiritual sense exercised by the Church upon the consciousness of the theologian. But that which on the other hand also is of great importance to the method of theology, is the fact that this spiritual reality alone provides that affinity to the Divine life which is indispensable to the knowledge of God.

The "knowledge of God" is here taken as naturally communicated knowledge, but not in the exclusively intellectual sense. In our self-knowledge and in our knowledge of our fellow-men there is also a component part, which is not obtained by observation and reasoning built on this, but which is of itself revealed in us. Without this working of the sense-of-self and of sympathy, abstract intellectual knowledge of ourselves or of others would be unable to grasp the reality of its object. And in like manner, on the ground of our creation after the Divine Image, a holy affinity and a spiritual sympathy with the life of God must be manifest in our spirit, if the revelations of the Holy Scripture are to be real to us and to refer to an object grasped by us as a real object. Both together are the constituent parts of our knowledge of God. Spiritual affinity to the life of God enables us to grasp the "things of God" as real in our deepest perception. The revelation of the Holy Scripture interprets that reality to our consciousness. There is no conscious knowledge without a mystic knowledge, and there is no mystic knowledge without the light of the Scripture that shines in our consciousness. Alas, that these two should be so rudely separated. For this gives on the one hand an intellectualism, which can do nothing but construe theoretical systems from the Scripture, and on the other hand a mystical attempt to attain unto a vision of God outside and above the Scripture. Violence is done to the method of theology by this intellectualism as well as by this one-sided mysticism. That method must adapt itself to the fact of the actual cooperation of both factors. This is possible only, when this spiritual reality is postulated in the theologian, and demands the consequent union of his spirit and the spiritual reality which exists concretely outside of him, and which allows him to borrow from the Scripture only the *conscious* form for this reality. The first was called of old not incorrectly Theology of our inclinations (theologia habitualis), or Theology of use (theologia utens); we should rather call it the mystical knowledge of God in antithesis with intellectual; but by whatever name it goes, from the nature of the case it assumes *regeneration,* the *photismos* and the *communion of saints,* since by these alone one is brought into this spiritual reality and becomes sufficiently spiritual to grasp in his innermost soul the reality of those things revealed to us in the Scripture. He who is deaf must first be healed from his deafness in order to be placed in true touch with the world of sounds. When this contact has been restored, the study of music can again be begun by him. This is the case with reference to the study of theology. Taken as the knowledge of God it is only conceivable, when the spiritual ear is opened in him who prosecutes the study, and to whom the reality of the unseen discovers itself. Palingenesis, therefore, is a requirement which may not be abandoned. Without palingenesis one stands antipathetically opposed to the object of theology. Hence there is no love to quicken communion. But we may not limit ourselves to this. Regeneration by itself is no enlightening. By regeneration the wheel of life in the centrum of our being (the wheel of nature or of birth, James iii. 6) is merely replaced upon its pivot; but this by itself has not changed the world of our *conscious* life. This occurs only when the Holy Spirit, having taken up His abode in us, transfers His working from this centrum to our *facultates,* to the faculty of the understanding by enlightening and to the faculty of the will by sanctification. If, in a more solemn sense than the ordinary believer, the theologian is called to enter into the revealed knowledge of God with his *understanding,* it is evident that so long as he lacks this enlightening he can make no progress. To regeneration and enlightening, is added in the third place the communion of saints. The theologian is no isolated worker, but in the world of thought he is in his way the organ of restored humanity. The subject of theology presents itself to us in the renewed consciousness of restored humanity, and every individual theologian allows this subject to work its effect *pro parte virili.* The farther he isolates himself from restored humanity the more this action must weaken, while on the other hand its gain in energy keeps pace with his progress in vital communion with this restored humanity. It is and remains an "apprehending with all the saints" (Eph. iii. 18), and the apostles do not hesitate to say, that by this fellowship with them alone does one come to the fellowship of the Father and of the Son (1 John i. 3).

By this we do not claim, that in the field of theological science, intelligent persons, who still lack this palingenesis, photismos and fellowship, cannot furnish results that are productive of lasting good. The labor to be done in the field of theology is by no means all of one kind. This can be distinguished into central and peripheral study. To search out, decipher and compare documents and monuments, for instance, to collect and arrange historical data, the writing of monographs on the Cathedral of Cologne, on some order of monks, or of Wessel Gansfort, etc., is altogether work which lies in the periphery, and which in itself has little to do with the research into the knowledge of God. It is all equivalent to the services which were rendered by Hiram of Tyre for the temple on Sion, but which had next to nothing in common with the sacred ministry behind the veil. These studies are certainly indispensable, even as the work of Hiram was indispensable in order that the High Priest might perform his sacred office, but this did not require in the Tyrian architect what was required in the Minister of the Sanctuary. Spiritual affinity to this centrum is certainly not a matter of indifference in these peripherical studies. What Aholiab and Bezaleel did for the tabernacle, was much more *inspired* work than what Hiram wrought on Sion's mount. And if, instead of Hiram, a master builder of Israel, rejoicing in Jehovah, could have built the Temple of Solomon, the work undoubtedly would have been inspired by a higher impulse of art. Our observation merely tends to do full justice to the intelligence which, without being interwoven with the life of the Holy Spirit, has been expended upon these peripherical studies in the field of theology.

So far as connection with the spiritual reality is merely put as a *requisite* in the theologian, it does not touch the method of theology. But it is not difficult to show how there flows an immediate result from this *requisite* for the method of theology. For fellowship with this spiritual reality is not a constant conception, but it changes and is susceptible to becoming both faint and strong. This fellowship with the Father and with the Son will at one time react strongly, and again weakly in one and the same person, and in the long run a lasting increase will follow. If the person himself were passive in this, and went through these changes merely as nature goes through the changes of heat and cold, it would not affect the method of theology. But this is not the case. He who has been regenerated is a fellow-worker with God, and according as he neglects or practises holy living, his fellowship with the Unseen diminishes or increases. And from this follows the demand of theological method, that the theologian shall be on the alert to feed and to strengthen this fellowship. He who fails in this dulls the spiritual sense by which he must observe what goes on in the sacred domain; while on the contrary he who wants to perfect himself in the accuracy of his observations within this sacred domain, is bound to apply himself to mystical devotion as well as to pietistic practice of holiness. As the pianist must make his fingers supple in order by a greater velocity to accommodate them to the vibrations of the world of sounds, so the theologian must tune his inner being and hold it to that pitch by prayer, meditation, self-denial and daily practice in order to accommodate himself to the sound of heavenly things. Not in the sense that prayer and meditation could ever take the place of alacrity and intelligence or of the "body of doctrine" (copia doctrinae). By his supple fingers the pianist cannot produce a single tone, if he has not the instrument itself at his disposal. But however strenuously we emphasize this intellectual development, unless a spiritual development be its guide, it degenerates of necessity into intellectualism, and becomes cold, barren and unfruitful. Only when the theologian applies himself in harmonious relation to the development of *both,* does he offer himself to the Holy Spirit as a prepared instrument, and is able to reveal even more fully the strength of this instrument.

The Holy Spirit as Teacher
(Spiritus Sanctus Doctor)

In this connection only can it be explained what has been implied in the worship of the Holy Spirit by the Church of Christ as *the Teacher of the Church* (Doctor ecclesiae). This confession must now be considered, because it implies that the action of the human mind, in order to attain to the true "knowledge of God," and thus of all theology, stands subject to his guidance. To understand this well, we must first distinguish between the several sorts of activities that go out from the Holy Ghost. From Him all animation proceeds, as well as the whole creation, and wherever life glows, its flame is ignited by the Holy Ghost. That flame is wanting in the chaotic mass, and then the Holy Spirit moves as yet separate above the chaos. But when the chaos becomes *cosmos,* the fiery flame of the Spirit glows and scintillates throughout the entire creation. In all *conscious* life this working of the Holy Spirit reveals itself more intensively and more definitely in the physchical life of man. Not because the Holy Spirit is here a different one, but because plane of life stands higher, possesses the form of *conscious* life, and is consequently able to cause the energy of the Holy Spirit to appear in a much higher form. In this sense all light in us, in our emotional life as well as in the domain of science and art, is light ignited by the Holy Ghost. But this does not touch the highest sphere of His activity. This is reached only, when from his side the creature places himself in conscious communion with this energy of the Holy Spirit, whereby the Holy Spirit becomes the "Gemeingeist" in the organism of humanity. And this is wanting in the life without palingenesis. There the "Gemeingeist" is sought in a *national* spirit, in a spirit *of the times,* in a *prevailing* tendency of spirits, and this effort sets itself in opposition to the Holy Spirit. But it is different with that tree of humanity upon which the "Edelreis" has been grafted by God. For humanity thus restored is identical with the *body of Christ,* and in this *body of Christ* no other "Gemeingeist" but the Holy Spirit is conceivable. This lies expressed in the Pentecost miracle, by which this indwelling of the Holy Spirit was accomplished. Beautiful confession is made of this by the Heidelberg Catechism, when it speaks of the Holy Spirit as "He who dwells in Christ as the Head and in us as His members." Hence there can be but one thought entertained concerning the subject of restored humanity: viz., that it is led and guided by the Holy Spirit, and this is the profounder sense of what Jesus spake, that the Holy Spirit shall guide into all the truth (John xvi. 13); which utterance by itself simply implies that the Church of Christ should have a guide on her way, and that this guide would lead her ever more deeply into the knowledge of the truth. It is this Holy Spirit, who alone is able to "search all the deep things of God" (1 Cor. ii. 10). It is this same Holy Spirit who reveals these mysteries unto us. And finally, it is this Holy Spirit who, by His communion, makes us spiritual, gives us the mind of Christ, and thereby enables us to judge spiritually (1 Cor. ii. 10-16).

From the nature of the case it is this fact that dominates theology. Theology is studied age after age, among all classes of people and in all kinds of lands, in various circles and under the influence of numerous factors, ecclesiastical and non-ecclesiastical. In itself, therefore, this sundry task would bear a broken and atomistic character. All unity and all growth would be wanting. If it is nevertheless a fact that this growth is not wanting, and that in the midst of changes and variations unity and progress are apparent, then a higher subject, standing outside and above the subjects of individual theologians and dominating them, must have caused these many rills to flow in one bed, and in that bed must have determined the direction of the stream. With the other sciences this higher subject is given of itself in the immanent logica, in the Logos of the object, which corresponds to the Logos in the subject and aids the logical understanding of the object after a fixed law. That higher power which guarantees unity and growth in these sciences is certainly given in Creation. But such is *not* the case with theology. This directs itself to a life, which is the fruit of *re*-creation; of re-creation in *being* as well as in *consciousness;* and therefore only the Holy Spirit, who is the author of this double re-creation, can here give the impulse, guidance and direction to the spirits, and introduce unity in what goes out from the individuals. And this claims a still stronger emphasis, because the development of the re-created consciousness is conditioned by the Holy Scripture, of which the Holy Spirit is the "primary author" (auctor primarius). If it is a fact that the secondary authors (auctores secundarii) intended to convey much less of a meaning in their writings than the Holy Spirit, under whose impulse they went to work, then from the nature of the case the Holy Spirit alone is able to reveal to the Church His rich and full intention regarding the Holy Scripture. Hence there is unity in the theological effort only because it is the selfsame Holy Spirit who gave us the principium of theology and superintends the effect and the application of this principium. The exegesis of the Holy Scripture is correct and complete only when the Holy Spirit interprets that Scripture in the Church of God. And the reflection of the content of the Scripture *in* our consciousness, and the reproduction of it *by* our consciousness, is true and pure and entire only when the Holy Spirit gives command and direction to this activity of the re-created consciousness.

The way in which this is done by the Church, in connection with the office, will be shown in the following section. Even without the influence of the instituted Church, it follows that the individual theologian should always be conscious of this working of the Holy Spirit. This is something both different from and greater than his mystical fellowship with the spiritual reality which was explained in the former section. Without more, this mystical fellowship simply referred to the tenor of his inner life. But it is entirely different when the theologian understands and feels that he is an organ of service, on the ground of which he may confidently expect lasting fruit of his labors so long as he puts himself in the service of the Holy Ghost. This is entirely analogous to the difference between the plodder on his own responsibility and the man of science who labors in the service of the truth. What in every other department of study is service of the truth, is here service of the Holy Ghost. Without this sense of service all study becomes subjectivistic, unhistorical, and arrogant, while, on the contrary, the placing of oneself at the service of the truth, i.e. in this instance of the Holy Ghost, banishes all pride, curbs the desire to be interesting by exhibiting new discoveries, feeds the desire of theological fellowship, and thereby sharpens that historic sense which impels the theologian to join himself to that great work of the Holy Spirit effected in past ages, which at most he may help advance a few paces.

This, however, should not be interpreted in the sense that the service of the Holy Spirit is antagonistic to the service of the truth. The domain of palingenesis is no newly created ground, but the outcome of re-creation. Hence the *natural* life is subsumed in it, the natural *consciousness* also, i.e. those powers, attributes, and laws of being, to which the human consciousness is subject by its nature, in virtue of the creation. As was seen above, the light of the Holy Spirit operates also in this natural consciousness, and of itself this lower light is adopted and included in the higher. If this were not so, theology would be merely a mystical beholding ($\theta\epsilon\omega\rho\iota\alpha$), but for the reason alone that it is so, it appears as an intellectual and rational discipline (disciplina noetica and dianoetica). On this depends also the old question, which from the days of Arius has repeated itself in the Church, even this: whether theology is authorized to draw out by logical sequence what is not written $\alpha\dot{v}\tau o\lambda\epsilon\xi\epsilon\iota$ in the Holy Scripture. Almost every tendency, whose interest it was to attach itself to the *letter* of the Scripture, and to oppose inferences from Scripture, has stated its objections against logical deduction in its polemical writings. Even by Franciscus Veronius from the side of Rome a similar objection was raised against the theology of the Reformers (see Voetius, *Disp. Theol.* I. pp. 5-12). In theory, however, this position has been defended only by some Anabaptists, and later by the Methodists, although they themselves did not strictly adhere to it. This whole conception meanwhile starts out from a mechanical Scripture-view, and is not worthy of refutation. It is of importance only in so far as it may be asked, whether in His revelation the Holy Spirit was bound to logic. In principle this is denied by all dualistic tendencies. They view the spiritual life of palingenesis and the intellectual life of sinful nature as two spheres which do not touch each other. The refutation of this false assertion must be sought in this: (1) in that palingenesis is represented as a re-creation, which implies the subsumption of the natural life; (2) in that the Holy Spirit is the author of the logical in the natural life as well as of the spiritual in the regenerated life; and (3) in that the Holy Spirit Himself, as the "Gemeingeist," leads and directs not merely the mystic-spiritual, but also the logical-dianoetical action of the Church, and therefore also of theology.

The Church and the Office

As the result of the two preceding sections no other inference is possible, than that theological science can only exist in the Church of Christ. Outside of her pale palingenesis is wanting, faith is wanting, and the enlightening, and the fellowship of saints, and the guidance of the Holy Spirit as "Gemeingeist." By this, however, it is by no means meant, that the organ for theological science is given in the instituted Church. The conception of the instituted Church is much narrower than the Church of Christ when taken as the body of Christ, for this includes in itself all the powers and workings that arise from re-creation. There is a Christian disposition and a Christian fellowship, there is a Christian knowledge and a Christian art, etc., which indeed spring from the field of the Church and can flourish on this field alone, but which by no means therefore proceed from the instituted Church. The instituted Church finds her province bounded by her *offices,* and these offices are limited to the ministry of the Word, the Sacraments, Benevolence, and Church government. These are the only offices that have been appointed as special functions in her life. All other expressions of Christian life do not work by the organ of the special offices, but by the organs of the re-created natural life; the Christian family by the believing father and mother, Christian art by the believing artist, and Christian schools by the believing magister. From which it follows that in this domain of palingenesis science also does not come to revelation by organs specially appointed for this purpose, but by the regenerated natural organs. By making an exception of theology here, it is assigned a place outside the organism of Christian knowledge, which prevents it from having one and the same subject in common with the other, Christianly understood, sciences. If then for want of a better school, or in behalf of her own safety, the instituted Church may found a seminary for the education of her ministry, such a seminary is never a scientific institution in its absolute sense. Neither are we authorized, in view of such a seminary, to withdraw ourselves from the obligation of prosecuting the science of theology for its own sake. If preachers are to be not merely Ministers of the Word, but theologians as well, the university training is indispensable.

But from this it does not follow that the instituted Church as such should not be of profound significance to the science of theology. The case indeed is this: sufficient knowledge of God *ad hoc* flows from the Holy Scripture in a threefold way: *personal, ecclesiastical* and *scientific*. If now we consider *scientific* theology first, then it is clear that its beginnings are very slow, that its growth covers the lapse of ages, and that it is not only still very incomplete, but it will *never* be finished, because as a science it can never be at a standstill, but will always advance without ever being able to reach completion. In the earlier ages especially it was very imperfect. If then for the sake of procuring the necessary knowledge of God, the Church, which we referred to in the second place, should have had to wait for the result of this study, generation after generation would have passed away before the Church could have begun her task. And this was not to be allowed. The Church had to be in *immediate readiness*. She could not be held back by any embarrassment, Neither has this taken place. From the very beginning, before there could be so much as a question of science, the Church has borrowed the content of her preaching from the Scripture and thereby has made use of a knowledge of God, which was sufficient *ad hoc*, i.e. for *the life of the Church*. What was needed in the churchly life gradually increased also, but in connection with this the Church unfolded the content of her preaching ever more richly, at the same time profiting by the fruit of scientific theology that gradually arose. Thus churchly confessions originated, which were increasingly rich and full, but these churchly confessions have never announced themselves as the results of science. And it is different again in the third place with the *personal* knowledge of God of each individual. The individual person, whose life is measured by the day, was still less able than the Church, to wait till science had ended her combats and finished her task. In a sense even more definite than the Church each individual must personally be in instant readiness, and have convictions, which for him, *ad hoc,* can alone be obtained by personal faith and personal experience. Every other conception is unmerciful, since it is unable to give the elect, at every given moment, according to his several condition, that knowledge of God which he needs. Distinction meanwhile is readily made between this *personal, churchly,* and *scientific* theology (or knowledge of God). The first tends to supply each child of God his comfort in life and in death. The second, to enable the Church to preach and to maintain her confession in the face of the world. And the third is charged with the introduction of knowledge of God into the human consciousness. The first has for its circle the life's-sphere of the *individual,* the second the circle of the *instituted Church,* and the third the circle of the church taken as an *organism.* In connection with this the form of the knowledge of God is distinguished also in these three ways. Personal faith does not formulate, but, as the fathers since Augustine said, "appropriates and enjoys" (utitur et fruitur). The churchly confession formulates in dogmata. Scientific theology sifts and tries, analyzes and draws inferences, constructs systems and places in connection with what lies outside. And, finally, the first is fruit of *personal* enlightenment and experience; the second, of the *official* activity of the Church, also in her struggles with heresy; and the third is the independent fruit of *study.*

If, now, we bring this in connection with the *guidance* of the Holy Spirit, then this guidance in the case of the personal knowledge of God consists in the providential and spiritual leading, by which the heart of the individual is influenced and his world of thought is formed; in the case of the ecclesiastical knowledge of God it is the guidance of the Holy Spirit bestowed upon the Churches through the office; and in the case of the scientific knowledge it consists in the clarifying of the consciousness. This, however, must not be understood in the sense that these three factors are isolated, and work each by itself. No man is a theologian in a scientific sense unless he is also a partaker of personal enlightenment and spiritual experience. For, unless this is the case, his starting-point is wanting, and he has no contact with the principium of theology. Neither can the theologian stand outside the church relation, and thus outside of personal union with the churchly confession, for then he finds himself outside the historic process, and, in fact, the organic contact is broken with the life-circle, within which his studies must flourish, so far as is possible to him. The personal faith, which simply touches the principium, and which as being entirely individual is an inestimable magnitude, needs receive no further mention here. For the theologian, it is the starting-point; but it is nothing more. It is very different, on the other hand, with the churchly confession. An objective condition lies in this. It is a product of the life of the Church, as in an ever richer form it has revealed itself officially, i.e. in ecclesiastical assemblies, under the special guidance of the Holy Spirit. Two things are contained in this confession. First, the self-consciousness of the Church, as it has developed itself historically, which, consequently, is the result of a spiritual experience and a spiritual struggle that fills in the gap between the present and the first appearance of the Christian Church. And in the second place, the result of the special leading of the Holy Spirit, vouchsafed in the course of ages to the Church, and to the knowledge of God that has developed itself within her pale. For this reason the theologian should not undervalue the confession of his Church, as if in it a mere opinion presented itself to him over against which, with equal if not with better right, he might place *his* opinion. The life of the Church, and the forming and reforming of her self-consciousness, is an action which is uninterruptedly continued. Scientific study unquestionably does and must exert an influence upon this, but for this reason this action should not sacrifice its independent character and motive of its own. A company charged with the public water-works may change the direction of some part of a river-bed by cutting off some needless bend or obstructive turn, but this does not render the company the original creator of the river who causes its waters to flow. In the same way, the scientific theologian may exert a corrective power here and there upon the confessional life of the Church, but this does not constitute him the man who sets this life in motion. That life pursues its own course, the stream of that life creates a bed for itself. To the theologian, therefore, the confession of his Church does not merely possess the presumption of truth; it appears objectively before him clothed with authority: with that authority which the many wield over the individual, with the authority of the ages in the face of ephemeral excitements; with the authority of the office in distinction from personal life; and with the authority which is due to the churchly life by virtue of the guidance of the Holy Ghost. It is not lawful, therefore, for him simply to slight this confessional life of the Church in order, while drifting on his own oars, to construct in his own way a new system of knowledge of God. He who undertakes to do this is bound in the end to see his labor stricken with unfruitfulness, or he destroys the churchly life, whose welfare his study ought to further.

From this, however, it does not follow that his studies are to have no other tendency than to confirm the confession of his Church, as if this were clothed with infallible authority. This was the fault committed by Scholasticism. The guidance of the Holy Spirit truly intends to be immediately effective in its final result; but it compels itself least of all to be this in every part of its action. A guide is given you of whom you know that in the end he will bring you where you want to be, but he does not necessarily lead you along a straight line and at once to that end. You approach this end only by stages; and for the sake of having your own thought and activity develop themselves, this guide allows you to take circuitous routes, and to try roads that run out, from which you will return of your own accord; while amid all these apparently contradictory movements he keeps the end in view, and brings it to pass, that finally you go to it of yourself. And in this very connection scientific theology is of a practical significance to the Church. It carries, indeed, the end in itself, of causing the glory of God's truth to shine also in the world of our consciousness. But it is equally called to examine critically the confessional life of the Church, by ever and anon testing the confession of the Church by the principium of theology, i.e. the Word of God. For which reason the theologian can never be a man of abstract study. Of two things he must do one. As a man of study he must remain in harmonious contact with the Church, whose confession he confirms by his study. Or he must enter an ever dangerous suit against the Church, whose confession he antagonizes in one point or another, on the ground of the Word of God. If now this touches an inferential question, which lies in the most distant circumference of dogma, the character of this struggle is less serious. But if the difference concerns the centrum of the confession, i.e. the real knowledge of God, the Church must either consent to his view and modify her confession, or he must break with the Church, whose confession he has found to be false. In this it is assumed, of course, that both he and his Church stand upon the basis of God's Word. Otherwise either the Church or the theologian who criticises her is wanting, so that there may be a good deal of quarrelling, as the outcome of dishonesty, but there can be no question of a spiritual struggle. But that spiritual struggle is the very thing in question. From both sides it must be carried on for the sake of the truth of God. And even as the martyr, the theologian must have courage to hazard his whole position in this struggle. Either *he* must be convinced, or the Church must be convinced *by* him. If one of these two things does not take place, there is no escape from a final breach. Hence, even when apprehended centrally, theological science owes the Church a bounden duty in service of the Holy Spirit. Not the duty of supplying her with the assurance of the faith; this the theologian must derive from the life of the Church. And a theology which makes it appear that it has to furnish the assurance of faith, cuts away the knowledge of God from its moorings, and builds by the authority of reason. But, in the service of the Holy Spirit, theology is called ever and anon to test the historic, confessional life of the Church by its source, and to this end to examine it after the norm of the Holy Scripture. By itself confessional life tends to petrify and to fall asleep, and it is theology that keeps the Church awake; that lends its aid in times of conflict with oft-recurring heresies; that rouses her self-consciousness anew to a giving of account, and in this way averts the danger of petrifaction.

The Liberty of Scientific Theology

To be able, however, to accomplish this task, scientific theology must be entirely free in her movement. This, of course, does not imply license. Every study is bound by the nature of its object, and subjected to the laws that govern the activity of our consciousness. But this is so far from a limitation of its liberty, that its very liberty consists in being bound to these laws. The railway train is free, so long as the rails hold its wheels in their embrace. But it becomes unfree, works itself in the ground, and cannot go on as soon as the wheels jump the track. Hence there is no question of desiring to free the theologian as such at the bar of his own conscience from his obligation to his subject, his principium, or the historic authority of the Church; what we should object to is, that the study should be prevented from pursuing its own way. That a Church should forbid a minister of the Word the further use of her pulpit when he antagonizes her confession, or that a board of trustees should dismiss a professor, who, according to their view, does not serve the end for which he was appointed, has nothing whatever to do with this *liberty of studies.* A ship-owner, who dismisses a captain because he sails the ship to a different point of destination from what the ship-owner designated, in no wise violates thereby the personal rights of the captain. When a Church appoints a minister of the Word, she and she alone is to determine what she desires of him, and when he is no longer able to perform this, she can no longer retain him in her service. And in the same way, when the curators of a university appoint some one to teach Lutheran dogmatics, and this theologian meanwhile becomes Romish, it is not merely their right but their duty to displace him. Yea, stronger still, a theologian who, in such a case, does not withdraw, is dishonest, and as such cannot be upheld. But these cases have nothing to do with the liberty of studies, and at no time does the churchly liberty of the theologian consist of anything but his right to appeal to the Word of God, on the ground of which he may enter into a spiritual conflict with his Church, and if he fails in this, to withdraw. Thus when the liberty of theology is spoken of, we do not mean theology as attached to any office, but theology as an independent phenomenon. The question simply is, whether, after it has separated itself from this office, and thus makes its appearance as theology only, it is or is not free.

And the answer is, that every effort to circumscribe theology by any obstacle whatever is antagonistic to her nature, and disables her for her calling. The law of thought will not allow you to call the thing black, which you see to be white. As a thing presents itself to you, so does it cast its image in your consciousness. To say that you see a thing in this way, but that you must represent it to yourself in the other way, is to violate the freedom of thought. We grant that a man of study is frequently blinded by superficiality, by want of thoroughness and sobriety, and sometimes even by conceit and arrogance, so that he has a false view of his object. *Formally,* however, this does not alter the case; even when his view is false, he is bound to describe a thing as he sees it. We are concerned here with the same problem as with the erring conscience. When Saul before his conversion worked havoc among the churches of God, his conscience erred, in so far as he deemed this to be his duty to God. If, however, he had remained quiescent and allowed the thing free course which he thought it his duty to oppose, at that moment he would have violated his conscience and have formally sinned. Whoever, therefore, may please to be a theologian, and whatever conclusions he may reach by his investigations, and may publish as results of his study, you must quietly allow. Even when the Church or a curatorium decides that his views disqualify him for the office he may hold, neither his theory nor his liberty of speech or writing may be denied him. Of course he must be willing to risk his office and his position; but what is this, compared to what was risked by the martyrs for *their* conviction? If he is a man of principle, and means what he says, he will not hesitate to make this sacrifice. And how great an influence one may exert upon theology, even without office, has sufficiently been shown by Spinoza. All the theologian can ask is, liberty to investigate, speak and write agreeably to the claims of his conviction. If only he is not impeded in this, he is free. And *that* is the liberty in which he may not be hindered in the least.

We grant that this may give rise to the case, that he who began as theologian will cease to be a theologian, in order that he may speak as a philosopher. He who chooses another object than that of theology and consequently goes out from another principium, and investigates agreeably to another method, may still be a man of learning, but he is no longer a theologian. But even this must be left to the free operation of minds. The persistent heretic must be banished from the Church; a professor, whose presence is a menace to the highest interests of a school, must be dismissed; but from the field of theology no one can disappear, unless he leaves it of his own free will. He may do this consciously by the open declaration: I am no longer a theologian; or, again, the results of his investigations may bring it about, that at length nobody numbers him any more among theologians. But so long as it pleases him to pose as a theologian, no one can prevent him; even when he has undermined, as far as he was able, successively, the object, principle and method of theology. However just, therefore, the people's protest is, when from the pulpit a theologian attacks the confession of the Church which he serves, or when from the platform a professor antagonizes the standards of the school for whose principles he ought to make propaganda, that protest becomes unwarranted and may not be tolerated when it directs itself against the liberty of the man of science. Expression may be given to the *indignation* which smarts under an assault on sacred things; but in his personal liberty the man of science must be respected. And when he shows that for the sake of his scientific conviction there is no sacrifice too great for him, so that he bravely defies opposition from every quarter, praise must not be withheld from him for such heroic strength of character. This praise must be withheld from the man who, for the sake of saving his position, sacrifices his Church or his school; but it is due to those titanic spirits who show, indeed, that they do not contend for their position, but simply for the liberty of science and the liberty of their deepest conviction.

This absolute liberty is, moreover, indispensable, if theology is to discharge her duty to the confessional life of the Church. Not that the Church should yield summarily to every criticism of her confession. The Church may not modify her confession, unless the conviction takes hold of her that some part of her confession cannot stand before the bar of the Word of God. But on the other hand, also, her confession must be alive; in its truth and clearness it must rest upon the Church's consciousness of life itself, and thereby be so firmly rooted, that it cannot stand in fear of criticism. Real gold will court trial; and theology is not able to try, test and criticise, if she is withheld the right to do this freely and radically. The history of Scholasticism shows, that when the expression of free thought is choked, and criticism of the confession becomes a question of life and death, theology fails of her task in many respects. And on the other hand, the Church has nothing to fear from this liberty of studies, provided she but do her duty within her own pale. Of course, she must not permit her confession to be attacked or ignored in her pulpits. The Church undertakes the propaganda of her life and consciousness, and he who does not share her life, or does not think from her world of thought, cannot be *her* organ. She must also apply Christian discipline, in order to keep the purity of confession intact among her members. But provided she is not behind in this, the criticism of theological science can bring her blessings only. For this provides the constant stimulus to turn back from the confession to the Word of God, and so prevents the Church from living on the water in the pitcher, and allowing itself to be cut off from the Fountain whence that water was drawn. A sharp, critical development of theology will ever entail a keener wakefulness of historical-positive theology, to make the Church understand anew the treasure she holds in her creed. In this way also the confessional development of the Church will not be at a standstill, but be ever making advance. And if for a while negative criticism carries the greatest weight, it will not last long, since the theologians who stand outside the life of the Church are bound to lose, sooner or later, their interest in theological studies.

If revelation were given in a dialectically prepared form, so that it consisted of a confession given by God Himself, of a catechism and of a law worked out in detailed particulars; if such a dialectically prepared form were given us in our own language, and if the copy of this lay before us in the original, infallible manuscript: the majesty of God would not invite, but forbid, such criticism and such a liberty of studies. But such was *not* the appointment of God. Revelation was given in a historic and symbolic form to be worked into a dialectic form by us; it was given in a language that is foreign to us; and the manuscripts which are at our disposal are very different from each other and not free from faults. We are offered no bread cut and sliced, but seed-grain, from which, by our labor, wheat grows, in turn to be ground into meal and made into bread. Hence the human factor is not doomed to inactivity, but stimulated to highest action, which action *must* always go through all sorts of uncertainty and commotion. By feeling only we find the way. In doing this our consciousness tries to grasp, assimilate and reproduce its object with the aid of both actions of which our consciousness is capable: viz. *immediate faith* and *discursive thought*. At one time the results of this twofold action coincide, and at another time they antagonize each other, and from this tumult that activity is born by which we make personal, ecclesiastical and scientific advances. There is here no papal infallibility to furnish a final decision, and least of all should this be taken as the continuation of infallible inspiration, since it differs entirely in form, character and tendency from the inspiration of the Scripture. Moreover, such a papal infallibility can have no other result than is actually seen in the Church of Rome; viz. that faith in the rich treasure of revelation is superseded by a faith in the Church, and that the healthy reaction of free theology upon the confessional life of the Church is entirely excluded. Such a papal infallibility aims at an outward, mathematical certainty which is irreconcilably opposed to the whole manner of existence of the revelation of God. To a certain extent it may even be said that in an empirical sense there is *nothing* certain here. There is conflict of opinion concerning the reading of the manuscripts, concerning the interpretation of every book and pericope, concerning every abstraction and deduction, and concerning every formulation and every application of the thought obtained. He who desires notarial accuracy is disappointed at every step in this sanctuary. But when the outcome shows that, notwithstanding all these difficulties, thousands and tens of thousands have obtained full assurance and certainty, to our Protestant consciousness it implies the guarantee that the Holy Spirit has not merely given us a Book and then withdrawn Himself from our human scene of action, but that same Holy Spirit *continues* to be our leader, and in that very freedom of the action of *our* spirit causes *His* dominion to triumph.

CHAPTER IV

THE ORGANISM OF THEOLOGY

Part of an Organism

By the organism of theology we mean what is commonly called "the division of the theological departments." Since, however, theology as an organic whole is itself an organic member of the all-embracing organism of science, for the sake of clearness, a short resume is here necessary of what was treated in our first chapter. Notwithstanding our position that science shows itself in a twofold form, viz. science as prosecuted in the circle outside of palingenesis, and science as studied in the circle ruled over by palingenesis, this antithesis is nevertheless merely empiracal. According to its idea there is but one science, and they who do not reckon with palingenesis naturally refuse to see anything but the result of imagination and obscurantism in what is science to us. And we, in turn, refuse to acknowledge as science the science which is studied outside of palingenesis, this antithesis is nevertheless merely empirical. According to its idea there is which includes all those objects which are not affected by the differentiation of palingenesis, in so far as the investigation of these objects employs no other functions of our mind than those which have remained uninjured by the darkening brought upon us by sin. This embraces, in the first place, everything that is commonly called *sciences* by the English, and *sciences exactes* by the French; at least so far as the exponents of these sciences hold themselves to their task, and do not make cosmological inferences or construct philosophical hypotheses. But in the second place, the subordinate labor of the spiritual sciences also belongs to this, so far as it tends exclusively to collect and determine external, observable data. Hence a very large part of philological study, in the narrower sense, and of historical detail goes on outside of the afore-mentioned differentiation. The fact that a person compares a few codices constitutes him by no means a philologist, nor because he studies a certain part of positive law is he made a jurist, and much less does he become a theologian because he inquires into the history of a monastery. But in doing this, such scholars may readily furnish contributions which are of lasting value to their several departments. So far as the *sciences exactes* rest simply on counting, weighing and measuring, they do not stand very high; neither does this subordinate detail-study of the spiritual sciences bear an ideal scientific character; but they have this in their favor, that universal validity attaches to their results, and for this reason, though unjustly, they are largely credited as being the *only* strictly scientific studies. But this is only self-deception. These studies derive their peculiar character simply from the fact that they do not touch the higher functions of the subject, and are affected by the subject only in so far as, standing outside the influence of sin, it is one and the same in all investigators. Science in the higher sense begins only where these higher functions operate, and then, of course, these two streams *must* separate, because the working of these higher functions, with and without palingenesis, differs. From this it follows, at the same time, that universal validity cannot be attained except in so far as, potentially at least, these higher functions work indentically. The students of science in whom these functions are unenlightened can advance no farther than the recognition of their results in their own circle. And on the other hand, the students of science to whom the enlightening has come can never promise themselves anything more than the recognition of their results in the circle of those who have been enlightened. From the nature of the case this is intended simply in the potential sense. Neither one of these sciences expects an immediate recognition of their results and from all; they simply assume that every one who reaches a logical and complete development within one of these two circles will find the results to be thus and not otherwise. Hence the position is this, that that science which arises from natural data only, subjective as well as objective, asserts, and is bound to assert itself, to be *the* science which originates of necessity from the reflection of the cosmos in the subjective consciousness of humanity. And, on the other hand, that science which reckons with the fact of re-creation, objective as well as subjective, asserts that real science is born only from the human consciousness that has been restored again to its normal self, and therefore cannot recognize as such the fruit of the working of the still abnormal human consciousness. The rule that he who is not born again of water and spirit cannot see the kingdom of God, applies not merely to the domain of theology. Without enlightening, the jurist is not able to open his eyes to see the Justice of God, neither can the philologist observe the course of God in history and in the conscious life of the nations.

But whatever view-point one occupies, science, as it develops itself in each of these two circles, is in either case organically one, because the object forms an organic whole, and the subject in the consciousness of humanity is itself organic, and lives organically in connection with the object. Of course theology falls of itself out of that science which has no other machinery than human data; and since by sin and curse, both objectively and subjectively, a disturbance has been created in the organism, its organic character is bound to exhibit defects, and frequently lead to a *non liquet,* or even to radical agnosticism. But neither the one nor the other renders science, thus interpreted, either mechanical or atomistic. The characteristic of the organism remains recognizable and dominant. And from the nature of the case this applies in a much higher sense to that science which is under the power of re-creation, since it includes theology and possesses the *missing links.* From this organic character of science follows, at the same time, its unity. From our standpoint we do not assert that the subject of theology is those who have been enlightened, and that the subject of all other science is those of the natural mind ($\psi\nu\chi\iota\kappa\acute{o}\varsigma$) but we claim that the only subject of *all* science is the consciousness of regenerate or re-created humanity; and that so large a part of scientific study can be furnished equally well by those who stand outside of this, is simply because this building also admits a vast amount of hod-carrier service which is entirely different from the higher architecture.

In the Organism of Science Theology is an Independent Organ

When Schleiermacher described theology as an agglomerate of a few departments of knowledge, which found their unity in the "guidance and direction of the Church," he actually abrogated theology and her organic existence in the organism of the sciences. An agglomerate is never organic, it is the opposite of organic, and is never made organic by any unity in the purpose of your studies. The organic character of a science carries also in itself a teleological element, but the end alone can never make an organism of that which differs in object and principle. The later effort, therefore, was entirely rational, to regain the unity of object by making *religion* the object of investigation. We do not deny that the science of religion finds an equally organic place in the organism of science, as for instance the science of the aesthetic, moral, or intellectual life of man. It is our conviction that this science got into the wrong track, when by the aid of religious evolution it repealed the antithesis between *true* and *false* religion. But even so, this science is formally an organic part of the organism of science. We simply deny that in this organism the science of religion can ever constitute an *independent* organ. By leading motives the organism of science is divided into a few great complexes, which form as it were special provinces in the republic of the sciences. Each of these complexes divides itself into smaller complexes, and these smaller complexes subdivide into smaller groups; but for this very reason the distinction between the coordinate and the subordinate must not be lost from sight. In our body the nervous system forms a complex of its own; hence everything that is radically governed by the nerves must be subsumed by science under this head. The Veluwe along the Zuyder Zee is indeed a particular region of land, but it should not for this reason be coordinated with the Dutch provinces. Nothing arbitrary therefore can be tolerated in the distribution of the organism of science. There must be a principium of division, and only those parts of the organism are independent which by virtue of this principium are governed immediately by this general, and not by a lower, principium of division. Pathology cannot be an independent science, because it is not formed immediately by the principium of division of science, but is governed by the general conception of the medical science. And this is the case here. As a psychological-historical phenomenon, religion is but one of many psychological phenomena. It is granted that it is the most important, but it is always one of many. It is no genus, but a species under a genus. Hence the science of religion can never claim for itself an independent place. It belongs to the philological faculty, and in this faculty it occurs as a subordinated science, partly under psychology, partly under ethnology, and partly under philosophy.

But it becomes a different matter when, passing by the "Science of Religion," we speak of *Theology* in the sense indicated above. Then we deal with a science which has a single common object (objectum univocum), arises from a single common principle (principium univocum), and develops itself after a method of its own. This cannot be subordinated, either under the natural, juridical, philological, or medical sciences, hence it *must* be coordinated. In scientific research human consciousness pursues the five principally differentiated parts of its total object. It directs itself to *man*, to *nature* about man, and to *God* as man's creator, preserver, and end; while with man, as far as he himself is concerned, logical distinction must be made between his *psychic, somatic* and his *social* existence. These are the five primordial lines which spring immediately from the principium of division, i.e. from the human consciousness in relation to its total object; and this agrees entirely with the division of the faculties, which is the outcome of the increated law of life itself and of its practical needs. And since theology directs itself to the "knowledge of God," it cannot be subordinated, but must be coordinated, and because of its independent *object*, its independent *principium*, and its independent *method*, it claims our homage as an independent organ in the organism of science.

The Boundary of Theology in the Organism of Science

Theology is *not* isolated in the organism of science. It is united with it in an organic way. From this it follows that communication between it and the other four great scientific complexes is not prevented from any one side. Communication, avenues of approach, and points of union extend to all sides. This, however, does not imply that there are no boundaries between theology and the other four coordinates; but as in every other non-mechanical domain, these boundaries here must be measured from the centrum, and not in the periphery. When a centre and the length of a ray are given, the boundary is fixed for the entire surrounding, even though this is not entirely marked out and thus is not discernible outwardly.

This centre here is the revealed ectypal self-knowledge of God. Since, however, it is the revealed and ectypal self-knowledge of God, it is not limited to abstract knowledge of God, taken as an isolated object of thought. The fact that it is ectypal expresses, indeed, a relation of this self-knowledge to man, and that it is revealed assumes logically a dealing with the data, condition and means in which and by which this revelation takes place. The knowledge which God has of Himself includes also the knowledge of His counsel, work and will, and the relation in which He has placed man to Himself, outside of as well as under sin. Since this ectypal knowledge of God is revealed, not in the abstract sense to satisfy our desire for knowledge, but very concretely, as one of the means by which this all-excelling work of re-creation is accomplished, a process is effected by this ectypal knowledge of God, namely the Christian Church, by which, even as a tree by its fruit, this knowledge of God is more particularly known. And so far as in this way the light of this ectypal knowledge of God shines out, and its working is observable, the boundaries of theology extend, or what was called its "compass," including, of course, what we must do in order, in our time also, to let the working of the knowledge of God have free course. As soon, however, as the influence which has been exerted by this knowledge of God outside the sphere created by itself is considered, theology provides contributions (Lehnsatze) for other sciences, but operates itself no longer. Then it concerns the application of its results to other objects, and no longer the product of what is to be applied. As the theologian applies results furnished by logic, but is thereby no creator of logic himself, so the jurist, philologist, medicus and naturalist must deal with the results of theology without themselves being thereby theologians.

So far, on the other hand, as the jurist, the medicus, etc., finds data in revelation which bear not on the way of the knowledge of God, but immediately on his department, he must determine for himself what influence one and another shall exert upon his own investigation. Now we speak of course of the jurist, the philologist, etc., as he should be, i.e. as standing within the pale of palingenesis, and as a Christian bending his knee before the majesty of the Lord and of His Revelation; not being limited by Revelation, but enriched and enlarged by it, seeing what otherwise he would not see, knowing what otherwise would be hidden from him. We do not advocate, therefore, a certain subserviency of the other sciences to theology as the queen of sciences. There can never be a question of such a relation of mistress and servant, in a scientific sense, among the sciences. He who investigates may render no obedience to any but the irresistible impulse of his own conviction. Even where material (Lehnsatze) is borrowed by other sciences from theology, it occurs by no other authority than that by which theology in turn borrows material from other sciences, i.e. under the conviction that by similar investigations one would reach like results. The conflicts which arise from this are therefore no conflicts between theology and the other sciences, but conflicts which the jurist, the physicist, medicus, and philologist faces, each in his own domain, in the same way in which the theologian faces these in his. All these conflicts arise from the fact that re-creation has begun, indeed, potentially, but can be completed with the parousia alone. If re-creation were completed now, every conflict of this nature would be inconceivable. Since now it is not finished, either in ourselves or in the cosmos, of necessity we have to deal with natural and supernatural data. Both these reflect themselves in our consciousness, and this gives rise to the conflict in our consciousness; which conflict is ended only in so far as we succeed in tracing the real connection between these two series of data. And this is by no means accomplished by ignoring any data that present themselves to us, from both series, or from either of the two. This might give us an ostrich wisdom but no human science. In no particular should the naturalist, for instance, be impeded. With the aid of all possible means at his command, he must prosecute his observations, and formulate what he has observed. If, on the other hand, he undertakes to construct a system from his discoveries, or commits himself to hypotheses by which to interpret his observations, the leaving out of account of the factor of Revelation is equivalent to the work of one who, in the biography of his hero, ignores his correspondence or autobiography. Whatever applies, therefore, to the origin and end of things cannot be determined by the laws he has discovered, since every law, when carried logically to its extreme in this matter of origin and end, leads *ad absurdum,* and involves us in antinomies that cannot be solved. If a law is to apply to a kingdom, it is assumed that this kingdom has being. Neither is he able, with his discovered law, to react against the possibility of re-creation. Since he knows, while he himself is affected by palingenesis, that (in order to realize the re-creation) a higher law in God is bound to modify the operation of the law which dominates the natural life. If he does not acknowledge this, he denies in principle the very possibility of re-creation, is without the photismos, and is unable to draw any conclusion. If, on the other hand, standing himself at the view-point of palingenesis, he prosecutes his studies, nothing binds him but his own conviction, and he must try to overcome, if possible, the conflicts that are sure to present themselves. In this, however, he will not always succeed, because the want of the necessary data renders this impossible. And neither can the claim be made that the solution found by him shall be at once accepted by every one else. Even in the scientific circles of Law, History and Philosophy, which do not reckon with palingenesis, differences of tendency and insight prevail, from which definite schools form themselves, which arise only presently to go down again. All this is but owing to the limitation of our power to know, to the paucity of data at our command, and to the usual impossibility of verification. The slow progress made in this direction is chiefly to be attributed to the fact that theologians have studied the above-mentioned conflicts almost exclusively, and that the Christians who have devoted themselves to these studies have for the most part been dualistically constituted, being heathen with the head and Christian at heart. And real advances will be made only when men who are themselves heart and soul alive to the efficacy of regeneration, at the same time devote all their powers of thought to these natural and historical studies, and so face these very conflicts.

The theologian also is familiar with these conflicts in his domain, occasioned by the incongruity which so often appears between natural and revealed theology. The theologian also is concerned with re-creation, and in the very idea of re-creation lies the antithesis between that which is to undergo the re-creative act and that which is established as outcome of that act. Hence there is always a duality: (1) the *old* data, which are present in what shall be regenerated, and (2) the *new* data, which shall constitute the regeneration. The Scripture, therefore, does not hesitate to speak of the "old man" and of the "new man" (Col. iii. 10), by which to indicate what present data must be removed($\dot{a}\pi\epsilon\kappa\delta\dot{v}\sigma a\sigma\theta a\iota$) and what data, brought in from without, must appear ($\dot{\epsilon}\nu\delta\dot{v}\sigma a\sigma\theta a\iota$). By that which must be removed, we are by no means to understand *the structure of our human personality;* this, indeed, *must* remain, since otherwise there would be a new creation and no regeneration. What is meant is simply that which in that structure has been deformed by sin and has become a sinful habit. Consequently, revealed theology distinguishes in man between what is his human structure, in order that it may attach itself to this, and all sinful deformity, in order to exclude it. And since natural theology does not belong to what constitutes the "old man," but on the contrary to the psychical structure of our human essence, revealed theology does by no means exclude this natural theology, but rather postulates it, assumes it, and joins itself to it. For this reason it was so absurd in the last century to place this natural theology as a second principium of Divine knowledge by the side of the Holy Scripture, and so really to furnish two theologies: first, a brief and vague knowledge of God from natural theology, and after that a broad and sharply outlined knowledge of God from Revelation. For sinful man, as he is able in his psychical structure from himself, in connection with his observation of the cosmos, to obtain this natural theology (Rom. i. 19, 20), is the person in all dogma toward whom Revelation directs itself, to whom it is disposed, and whom it takes thus and not otherwise. Hence our older theologians were much nearer the truth when they applied the clear distinctions between man in his original creation, fallen, and restored, to almost every dogma, provided it is carefully kept in view that they did not delineate fallen man to whom the revelation was made after life, but took their copy from the image offered of him by the Scripture. Neither did they do this in order to lose themselves in abstraction, which has nothing in common with life, but to obtain certainty that they did not fall into error in their view of fallen man. If they had gone to work empirically, and had sought from life itself to estimate what sort of a person fallen man might be, all certainty of starting-point would have been wanting; which is seen sufficiently clearly from the several sorts of theories that have been framed concerning it. On the contrary, they allowed the Word of God itself to furnish them this image, and now they knew that they had solid ground under their feet. Sinful man was devoid of an adequate self-knowledge, and by the light of the Word of God alone does he recognize his true appearance. Not as if henceforth he was to take no further account of his essential existence, but because in this way only did he come to know what his essential existence is. Natural Theology, therefore, is not added to the Scripture as a second something, but is taken up in the Scripture itself, and by the light of the Scripture alone appears in connection with the reality of our life. Hence natural theology cannot be explained in dogmatics, except under the category of man in his original righteousness and man in his fall. Every other mode of treatment leads either to rationalism, by placing reason alongside of the Scripture as a second principium, or to mysticism, by assigning the same place to the life of the emotions, in order presently, by logical sequence, to push the Scriptural principium to one side and to destroy it. But if this ends the conflict for the theologian, both formally and with respect to principle, the fact is not taken away that the antithesis is bound to reappear between fallen man, who is to be re-created, and restored man, who is to be looked upon as the fruit of this re-creation. This would not be so if this re-creation were completed in one moment. But it is unavoidable, since it requires sometimes a very long process by which to bring out potential re-creation to actual completion. Hence in the doctrines of the Covenant, of Baptism, of the Church, of Sanctification and in Ethics this conflict reappears again and again, and to this day theology struggles to overcome the conflict, theoretically in her formulation of the things to be believed (credenda), and practially in her teaching of the things to be done (agenda).

This conflict, therefore, exists not merely between theology and natural science, etc., but extends across the entire domain of human knowledge and presents itself to the Christian thinker in *every* department. The reason is plain. Since sin denaturalized the entire cosmic life in and about man, re-creation comes in to restore the entire cosmos, as far as it stands related to man. It is one of the demands of truth, therefore, that both factors of this conflict shall be exhibited as they are. By placing a board covered with flowers across an abyss, the abyss is not filled in. There is no need, however, that the conflict shall be overestimated. If, for instance, the naturalist observes that the deposit of the Nile increases annually so many millimetres, and that it is so many metres high, his conclusion is indisputable, that, *if* this deposit has been constant, the height of 12.47 metres now reached would have required a much longer period of time than is known to our era. But he is *not* able to prove that the deposit has been constant. The required observation lies outside the empiric domain to which he must limit his judgment. This is not cited for the sake of proving the fact that our earth has not existed longer than six thousand years. With reference to this fact Scriptural teaching is by no means exegetically sure. But for the sake of showing in a concrete instance what we understand by an *unlawful* extension of the conflict.

Meanwhile, the relation between Theology and Philosophy deserves separate mention, since the boundary which separates these two sciences is frequently crossed from both sides. This requires a closer analysis of the idea of philosophy. Philosophy embraces two things: on the one hand, the investigation into *man's psychical existence*, and, on the other hand, the effort to put together concentrically the entire *content of the scientific consciousness* in organic connection, and to explain it. Man's psychic existence leads, in turn, to a separate investigation (1) into his psyche $\psi v \chi \acute{\eta}$ as such (psychology), and (2) into the ethical, aesthetical and logical qualities of this psyche (ethics, aesthetics and logic). And finally, Logic, in a broader sense, includes the investigation into the consciousness as such, into the laws which govern our thought, and into the ways which lead to knowledge (*Principienlehre, Logica und Erkenntnisstheorie*). The second task of Philosophy is of an entirely different kind; it is not directed to the conscious and thinking man, but it is the effort of the thinking man himself to reflect the cosmos, which presents itself to him as existing organically, as an organic whole in the mirror of his consciousness. Actually, therefore, two sciences are embraced in Philosophy which evermore separate. Efforts have even been made to give an independent position to the study of thinking man, under the name of "Logic" (taken in a broader sense than now). This plan will probably produce the farther effect of having Psychology appear on a ground of its own, with its quality-doctrine in ethics and aesthetics. This will make Logic consist of the science of thinking man, or, if you please, it will make the Logos in man to be the object of investigation, and Philosophy, in the narrower sense, will be the science which collects the results of all the other sciences concentrically under a higher unity. Thus we may have *Logic* as the science of *thinking* (cogitare), and Philosophy as the science of *being* (esse). Meanwhile, no objection can be raised against classing, as yet, this entire complex of sciences under the common name of the *philosophical sciences,* provided in the discussion of the relations between theology and these sciences, the indicated distinction is kept in view, and we no longer speak of *the* philosophy. As for Logic, the saying that it is an auxiliary to the theologian reduces it by no means to the rank of a handmaid of theology. It renders this service equally to all the other sciences. As far as Logic is concerned, this entire representation of the handmaid (ancilla) was simply a matter of custom. It is, indeed, a patent fact, that in every science man is the thinking agent, and if he shall undertake intellectual pursuits in an accurate and prepared way, and in the full consciousness of self, the knowledge and practice of the faculty of thought are indispensable to him. A theologian who undervalues Logic, as being little necessary to him, simply disarms himself. This was by no means the practice of our older theologians. They always emphasized most strongly the study of formal logic, together with its related arts $(\tau \epsilon \chi \nu a \acute{\iota})$ By saying this, we do not imply that in this field, also, no conflicts may present themselves. These are excluded so long as one confines himself to logic in the narrower sense, but are bound to come up as soon as "die Principien der Erkenntniss," together with the method by which to attain to knowledge, or included under Logic. This appears all too painfully, indeed, from the serious effort of naturalism to apply its method to the spiritual sciences. No doubt, this conflict is least of all a conflict between theology and philosophy, but one born from the differing dispositions of the thinker. If his ideal life is high, he cannot reach the same conclusions as another person, whose mind and tendency confine themselves entirely to the things seen $(\acute{o}\rho a \tau a)$. In the same way, if by regeneration thinking man stands in vital communion with the kingdom of God, he *must* see differently, and consequently judge differently, from the one who stands outside of it. The same applies to psychology and ethics. A Christian philosopher knows his own soul $\psi v \chi \acute{\eta}$ and views the ethical life differently from the philosopher who stands outside of regeneration. The antithesis, therefore, does not consist in the fact that theology offers a Christian ethics and philosophy a neutral one. The Christian philosopher cannot do otherwise than live Christian ethics, and what theology gives is not a Christian, but a *theological ethics,* which will be more fully explained in the discussion of the separate departments.

The real conflict, however, between theology and philosophy begins, when philosophy is taken in the narrower sense, as the science that investigates the principles of *being,* and in virtue of these principles seeks to furnish, from all the results of the other sciences, a concentric-organic life- and world-view. Then we should be on our guard, lest theology degenerate into philosophy, and philosophy capture for itself the place of theology. This has already happened; which fact explains itself from the circumstance, that philosophers for the most part have not reckoned with regeneration, and that theologians' frequently have deemed themselves able to get along without philosophy. From the first it followed, that besides a psychology, an ethics, an aesthetics and a logic, philosophers also tried to furnish *a doctrine of God,* and from the imperfectly interpreted data of the inborn and the acquired knowledge of God, sought to construct a theology, independently of the revealed knowledge of God. Thus they set themselves in hostile array against theology, and in self-defence were bent to oppose real theology, suppress it, and in the end banish it from the arena. On the other hand, this made theologians tend to view philosophy in the narrower sense as a hostile phenomenon, and, since they had no real Christian philosophy of their own, to make war against *all* philosophy. Since, however, it is impossible to live even in the Christian world without certain cosmological conceptions, they attempted to supply this want in their dogmatics, and thus it happened that they furnished not a simple theology but a theology with a philosophical seasoning. To bring this perverted relation to an end, it is necessary, on the one hand, to recognize that philosophy has an entirely different task to accomplish than theology, and, on the other hand, to distinguish sharply between Christian and non-Christian philosophy.

Philosophy has an entirely different task. Theology has no other calling than to take up the ectypal knowledge of God, as it is known from its source the Holy Scripture, into the consciousness of re-created humanity and to reproduce it. Philosophy (now always taken in the narrower sense), on the other hand, is called to construct the human knowledge, which has been brought to light by all the other sciences, into one architectonic whole, and to show how this building arises from one basis. From this it follows, that the need of philosophy is a necessity ($\dot{\alpha}\nu\dot{\alpha}\gamma\kappa\eta$) which arises out of the impulse of the human consciousness for unity, and is therefore of equal importance to those who stand outside, as to those who are in the regeneration. To say that a Christian is less in need of philosophy is only the exhibition of spiritual sloth and lack of understanding. The more the enlightening restores harmony in our consciousness, the stronger must be the awakening of the impulse after an unitous (einheitlich) organic knowledge. While, on the other hand, the richer the data at our service, the better the hope of success in this. Philosophy which reckons only with natural data will always vibrate between a pantheistic, deistic and materialistic interpretation, and will never do more than form schools, while Christian philosophy, whose theistic point of departure is fixed, is able to lead to unity of interpretation within the circle of regeneration. But for this very reason theology will be able to go hand in hand with a Christian philosophy. It is the task of philosophy to arrange concentrically the results of *all* the other sciences, and if non-Christian philosophy ignores the results of theology, as though it were *no* science, theology is in duty bound to enter her protest against this. If, on the other hand, the philosopher himself is regenerate, and is historically and ecclesiastically in union with the life of palingenesis, then of course in his studies he includes the results of theology, together with the results of all the other sciences; and it is his care, architectonically to raise such a cosmological building that of themselves the results of theology also find their place in it.

Self-determination of the Organism of Theology

Theological Encyclopedia includes generally the question of the relation of theology to the *University.* As the matter actually stands in Europe, however, this question concerns the relation of theology to the Government. If the universities were *free corporations,* as formerly they were *intended* to be, and as they are sometimes now (in Belgium, in the Netherlands, America, England and in Switzerland), and as they *ought* to be everywhere, this question would entirely fall away; for then this relation would merely be an item of history. But this question is important because to this day in most countries the most influential universities are *state institutions,* founded, supported and governed by state authorities. Thus the Government determines not merely the number, rank and quality of the faculties; but directs also the organism of theology, as being on a par with the other sciences, by its conditions for every chair, and by its choice of departments, which it unites as a group under one and the same chair. Even in former times this was not right, since it can never be derived from the attributes of the Government, that it shall determine the organism of theology. But this raised no preponderating difficulty, inasmuch as in those times the Government made free-will abdication of every discretionary right, and simply followed custom. Such, however, is not the case now. In Holland indeed it has reached such a point that the Law for Higher Education (of April 28, 1876, Stbl. n. 102), Art. 42, prescribes a tenfold division of the theological departments, which is entirely antagonistic to the nature and character of theology; even to such an extent that dogmatics, which is the heart of all theology, is simply cut out from the body of theology. It can scarcely be denied that this is a violent attack upon the organism of theology. In view of facts such as these, we maintain the right of theology to determine its own organism. No Government *can* do this, since this is not its province; neither does it possess the data for it. Neither is it authorized to do this, since playing the role of dilettante and abusing its power it creates confusion in theology. It is evident that the division of departments and of chairs of itself exerts an influence upon the entire course of studies, upon the association of studies even in the case of the ablest theologians, and darkens insight into the true essence of Theology. Such an interference on the part of the Government is an attack upon the liberty of science, while in Theology, moreover, it amounts to the choice of a confessional party; *in casu* of the modern interpretation of Theology as "the science of religion" instead of "the science of the revealed knowledge of God," which it has always been, in keeping with its origin and principle.

A measure of influence can more properly be accorded to the Church, in so far as the Church may dictate what studies are indispensable to the expression of her life, both with reference to the education of her ministers and to the defence of her faith; in fact, this influence is exerted by the Church in the conditions assigned by her for ecclesiastical examinations. No university can permanently neglect in its theological faculty the departments needed for these examinations. But so far as Theology stands in vital connection with the Church this tie is a *natural* one; beyond this it ceases to exist. Hence even ecclesiastical influence should extend no further. The Church states her need, but the question in what way, in what order, and in what connection this need must be met is encyclopedic and pedagogic. That which exists mechanically can be taken apart and reconstructed differently at will, but this is not possible with organic life. That which lives organically obeys, in its organic development, an inner law of life. It is as it is because it sprang from its germ thus and not otherwise, and because it can assume no proportions except those which it possesses by nature. By violently attacking the life of an organism, you can occasion anaesthesia or hyperaesthesia, atrophy or hypertrophy, of one of the organs, but this does not modify the nature of the organism. That remains the same as before. Concerning the organism of theology, therefore, we cannot but think that all interference on the part of the Government should be most firmly resisted; that the Church both may and must exert an influence by the appointment of those studies which she deems necessary for the maintenance of her life, provided she does not presume to determine in what way her requirement shall be met; and that therefore the construction of the body of theology can be determined by itself alone as it unfolds its organic existence. This does not deny that this organic articulation (Gliederung) is formulated by our *thinking*. But if this task is properly performed, it consists of the simple statement of what kind of organic life we have discovered in the organism of theology.

Organic Articulation of Propaedeutics

The discussion of propaedeutics, as such, is really in place in a *ratio studiorum,* and not in Encyclopedia proper. And yet Encyclopedia cannot afford to pass the propaedeutic studies by in silence. For these studies are not accidental, neither are they chosen arbitrarily, but are indicated of themselves in the organic ties that bind theology to the other parts of the organism of science. Being itself a department of ideal science, theology naturally demands such a general development as is indispensable to all ideal sciences. In the conflict waged as to the precedence of humanistic and naturalistic studies in preparatory schools, the humanistic must be preferred for theological propaedeutics. But it is a mistake to make it appear that the humanistic training, indicated as such historically, is sufficient for the theologian. In the main, if not exclusively, humanistic propaedeutics directed themselves to the beautiful form, and were but little impressed with the importance of philosophy and history. Ancient philosophy was taught, and Greek and Roman history, together with their proper antiquities, but rather as a means for the understanding of the classics than as a proper factor for the forming of the mind. And this is not tolerated by the position of theology in the organism of science. To be sure, theology does not allow neglect of beauty of form. The finer form alone lends to the mind that sensitive discernment which is indispensable to all ideal science, and which in its reproduction is not to be discarded. But with this formal scholarship theology is not satisfied. The too excessive admiration of the world of old Hellas is rather an impediment in the way to the deeper study of her principles. To her the old classic world is simply a link in that great process of development that extends to the present time. Hence she demands a propaedeutic which embraces the entire course of philosophy and history down to our times, and which from first to last is subject to the criticism of Christian principles. For which reason this propaedeutic cannot be ended in the preparatory school, but must reach its completion in academic propaedeutics. Even in itself the limitation of propaedeutics to the gymnasia cannot be approved, since for every truly scientific study a scientific introduction into the scientific treatment of it is indispensable; and this the gymnasium can never give. Theology, moreover, must be able to make use of a critical knowledge of human thought and act (philosophy and history) as its background, such as cannot be taught in the prepaiatory school. This implies at the same time that propaedeutics cannot stand on any other foundation than the study of theology itself. Propaedeutica in the pagan sense, standing outside of palingenesis, denies the organic connection between theology and other studies, and does not prepare for, but leads one away from, theology. Hence the character of preparatory as well as of academic propaedeutics ought to be distinctively *Christian;* which demand is *not* met by the addition of religious instruction (a Religionsstunde) to pagan propaedeutics. It demands that the entire preparation itself, both formal and material, shall keep close reckoning with the principles of a Christian life- and world-view. He who is himself a partaker of palingenesis, and who consequently pays homage to the Cross of Golgotha as the centre of the development of human history, has an entirely different outlook upon the propaedeutic departments from him who as a humanist boasts of a *credat Iudaeus Appella.* And the demand for a proper propaedeutics of theology is only met with the organic relation between the propaedeutical studies and the study of theology in the narrower sense is given full scope to assert itself. Indeed, if closely considered, the name of propaedeutics is not very happily chosen. The theologian does not pass on to theological studies, in order henceforth to ignore all other sciences, but, proportionately to the rate of his progress, he finds himself constantly bound to trace the organic connection between his own and still other studies. Such as, for instance, in the historic and ethnologic studies of the religious differences of non-Christian nations. His own studies are not isolated at a single point, and it only weakens the position of theology to prosecute her studies as though she stood alone. Moreover, later study must be continued with a definite end in view, in those departments which at first seemed as propaedeutics only. Every student of Church History is aware of this with reference to the knowledge of history; the same applies to Philosophy, even Psychology, Philosophical Ethics, and Aesthetics.

Of course this applies to the *scientific* theologian only, and not to every Minister of the Word. Other demands apply to his education, which are made not by the position of theology in the organism of the sciences, but by the conditions with which his office brings him in touch, and which therefore cannot be mentioned here. Only think of what is advocated from many sides about the knowledge of medicine, of agriculture, of common law, of social conditions, of the school question, etc., as being of service to the local pastor. Questions with which, from the nature of the case, Encyclopedia cannot be concerned, since they have nothing to do with the nature of theology and its organic relations. But the more formal propaedeutics deserve, certainly, a brief mention, especially the study of the languages, a matter which is not ended with the study of the two fundamental languages of the Scripture, the Hebrew and the Greek. For then even Latin might safely be omitted. It should rather be insisted upon that the languages be first studied from the general linguistic point of view, and then the question is in order, what are the special languages the knowledge of which is indispensable to the study of theology. Without a clear, general linguistic conception of language, one cannot truly enter into the knowledge of any one language. The phenomenon of language as such is organically connected with theology in its principium, and therefore all sound theology presupposes an historic and critical insight into linguistics, graphistics and the philosophy of grammar. Not, of course, as though we should begin with this. It is indeed the claim of pedagogics to supply the *copia doctrinae* during those years in which the memory is most plastic; but in this review, which does not consider the course of studies, but the organic position of theology in the organism of science, the knowledge of language in general comes first. With respect to individual languages in particular, the mother-tongue follows organically first upon linguistics, because in this alone our immediate consciousness feels the pulse-beat of the life of language; and the other modern languages have little connection with theology, except in so far as they give us access to the products of theologic toil in other lands. Strictly taken, translation might do away with this necessity; since, however, the indiscriminate translation of all detail-study is impossible, theological study is simply inconceivable without the knowledge of modern languages.

The question arises next, whether Latin must be maintained under this title only in theologic propaedeutics. There is certainly no difference of opinion about the necessity to the theologian of the knowledge of Latin. For more than twelve centuries the Christian Church documented her life of thought in almost no language but the Latin. He who is no ready reader of Latin finds himself cut off from the historical life of the Church. It is a different matter, however, whether theology as such is interested in the study of Latin as a means to general training; something which is continually being contested, but which, it appears to us, cannot be abandoned. For this we state two reasons. First, because Latin as a language is classic in its clearness, conciseness and beauty, by which it puts a stamp upon our thinking, such as no other language can do, not even Greek excepted, however much richer it may be. In "common grace" the Latin language occupies a place of its own, and he who neglects her claim impoverishes the forming of the mind. And in the second place, the development of Western thought has acquired a characteristic of its own, first under the influence of ecclesiastical, and after that of humanistic Latin, which is plainly apparent in the formation of many words and in syntax. Entirely apart from the question whether this characteristic should be preserved or abandoned, it follows from this, that a real grasp upon the world of our Western thought is simply impossible without the knowledge of Latin. Upon this ground we desire to see the study of Latin upheld, while we urge, at the same time, that this study shall not be limited to classical Latin.

Latin is also the language of the Western Fathers, the Scholastics, Reformers, and later theologians; but their Latin bears another character, uses other words, follows a different construction, and speaks in new terms. He who understands Cicero cannot for that reason understand Augustine. Virgil's *Aeneid* is no help to understand Thomas's *Summa.* Horace is of little help in the reading of Calvin or Voetius. Hence the organic connection demands that the study of Latin shall not limit itself to the golden age of the classics, but that it shall follow the historical process in the language which, though nationally dead, is still alive in use. The importance of this does not appear to those to whom theology is a mere Science of Religion; but he who would study theology in the real sense of the word, and thus continue the task begun by our older theologians, must begin by understanding them.

A like observation applies in part to Greek, which is organically related to theology in three ways: First, as the language of old Hellas; secondly, as the language of the LXX, of Flavius Josephus, etc., and New Testament; and thirdly, as the language of the Eastern Fathers, taken in their widest sense. As a starting-point, therefore, the knowledge of classic Greek is a necessity; then comes the knowledge of later Greek ($\kappa o \iota \nu \acute{\eta}$), and more especially of the Syrian and Alexandrian, which come nearest to the language of the New Testament. Then follows the language of the New Testament itself, and finally that peculiar development attained by Greek in the Byzantine Christian world. They who pass on from Demosthenes to the New Testament, as is the case with many in our times, without ever having a glimpse of one of the Eastern Fathers in the original, fall short in historic knowledge of Greek. Since the gymnasium is intended for young men of other faculties as well, and is, therefore, not able to give a sufficiently broad introduction into this historical knowledge of the Greek language, academic propaedeutics ought to be directed to this with an eye to theology, more than it has thus far been.

Hebrew and Chaldee occupy a somewhat different position. As a language, the Arabic is linguistically rightly esteemed much more highly than Hebrew; both because of its riches of forms and of the mighty world of thought to which it affords an entrance. Hebrew lies altogether outside the circle of higher culture. If it is of great importance to every literator to be familiar with at least one language of the Semitic trunk, and though Hebrew offers special advantages for this, by the simplicity of its forms as well as on account of its significance to the most potent monument of our higher civilization, it will, nevertheless, probably be the rule, that theologians almost exclusively will apply themselves to Hebrew, not as a linguistic phenomenon, but as an auxiliary to the right understanding of the Old Testament. At the gymnasium it is generally a secondary matter, falling outside the lines of a general training; and at the academy few are willing to train the memory to any great extent. Yet it is an imperative necessity that an improvement shall be made in this direction. In our pulpits the fundamental texts of the Old Testament are spoken of by men who are not able to translate the simplest passage at sight, much less to retranslate into Hebrew. And in this condition of things the study of Hebrew is but a waste of time.

In this connection, however, this question cannot be treated more fully. Only under the heads of *general training* and of *special studies* can Encyclopedia indicate to what other studies and languages theology stands organically related. And it is clearly seen that especially in the study of languages, entirely different claims are made, both by the schedule of the general scientific training and by custom, from what theology must demand of these languages within her pale. The very propaedeutics for Theology demand such natural talents and persevering application to study, that the false notion must be abandoned that all those who are educated for the practical ministry of the Word, can be theologians in the real sense of the word. With the majority, the needed requirements for this are altogether lacking. The effort to have so high an aim realized by all would not develop, but stultify, many persons. Hence the old difference between pastors and doctors must be maintained. Pastors should be sufficiently advanced to be able to take their stand intelligently at the scientific view-point, and to follow scientific development;

but apart from the study of theology as a side issue or as a favorite recreation, the profounder study of theology as a science will ever of necessity be the task of the few, who have extraordinary powers of mind at their disposal, as well as the necessary time and means.

Organic Articulation to Spiritual Reality

Science is no abstraction. It is the reflection of life in our consciousness, and therefore it sustains the same organic relation to reality as the shadow to the body by which it is cast. A single word, therefore, is needed to show the organic articulation of theology to spiritual reality. Thus far this has been suggested in a subjective sense, by the assertion that the mysticism of the Spirit is indispensable to the theologian. But from the nature of the case it is evident that for this subjective necessity there must be an objective ground. If the treatment of the subjective demands required at the hand of the theologian belongs to Hodegetics rather than to Encyclopedia, Encyclopedia nevertheless is bound to indicate the relation of this science to its own reality, from which the necessity of these demands is born. If in real life there were no antithesis between the domain of palingenesis and what lies outside, there would be no special Revelation, and in simple consequence there would be no question of theology other than in the style of Cicero. In like manner, if there were no operative grace, which effects enlightenment, articulation of the science to this spiritual reality would be altogether wanting. "The natural man receiveth not the things of the spirit of God." Now, however, the influence of this reality operates upon theology in a threefold way: First, materially, by the provision of matter which it brings to theology; secondly, by the influence of the Church, so far as that Church propels its confession as a living witness; and thirdly, in the theologian personally, inasmuch as his own spiritual experience must enable him to perceive and understand what treasures are here at stake. Coordinated under one head, one might say that the Holy Spirit guarantees this organic articulation through the agencies of the Holy Scripture, the Church, and the personal enlightenment of the theologian. Hence piety of motive is not enough. Piety is often present with the Buddhist also and the Parsee. But the piety referred to here must bear a stamp of its own, and cannot be identical with that pious impulse which operates also in fallen man, either poetically, heroically, or sentimentally. But it is very definitely that piety worked by God, which is possible only when a new life has been implanted in the sinner, and in which new life has dawned a higher light. In the second place, this piety should not remain isolated, but must manifest itself in the communion of saints; not merely arbitrarily, but organically, hence in union with the Church, which affords a bed to the stream of the ages. And finally, in the third place, in its rise from the root of regeneration and in its union with the Church, this piety should not remain a mere mystical sentiment, but, for the sake of affecting theology, it must interpret *being* into *thought,* in order presently from *thought* to return to *being* by the ethical deed.

Where this articulation, in the sense mentioned, is organically present, so far as it concerns the articulation to reality, the position of theology in the organism of science is what it should be. Without this connection the theologian becomes as one who looks out upon nature through eyes half blind, as one almost deaf who studies acoustics, or as one devoid of all finer taste who devotes himself to aesthetics; the simple result of which is that neither nature, acoustics, nor aesthetics receive their dues. History indeed teaches that where this articulation to spiritual reality is *wanting,* rationalism at once lifts up its head to attack theology in its very heart; or, where this articulation is imperfect, sentiment is bound to prevail, and theology disappears in mysticism or pietism. For this reason the theologians of the best period of the Reformation ever insisted strenuously and convincingly upon the linking together of theology to the Word, to the Church, and to personal enlightenment; for in these three factors together is found the guidance of the Holy Spirit, without which no theology can flourish. The proper relation of these three factors has been considered at sufficient length above. Here it is merely observed that our theologians of the Reformation period were embarrassed by the removal of theology from the seminary to the university. It was apparent in Paris, Louvain, and elsewhere, that the university life brought with it far more diversion and temptation than the secluded life at the seminaries. Now the Reformation in principle abandoned the seminary, and from principle gave theology its place in the university, and it became necessary to insist more strenuously upon piety and asceticism of life in the future theologians. The piety at the seminary was too much like a hot-house atmosphere, and results showed how little these hot-house plants amounted to the moment they became exposed to the less favorable atmosphere of common life. In view of this also they gave their preference to the freer university life. A piety, which there maintained itself and kept its virtue, was much better acclimatized to life in the world. At times they expressed the desire that the academy life should be succeeded by at least one year of seclusion from the world in a more quiet seminary. But this was merely a corrective and a palliative, and their chief strength lay in exhortation, in moral pressure, in the power of the Word, to exhibit ever more clearly the folly and the contradiction of the study of theology without the corresponding fear of the Lord, trembling at His word, and communion with God in Christ. This implied at the same time that these demands of Scriptural, ecclesiastical and personal piety were not exacted from the student only, but from every theologian after graduation from academy life. Because it involved the articulation of theology to the spiritual reality, this claim could not be abandoned at a single point of the whole way. Godliness alone is able to foster, feed and maintain that holy sympathy for the object of theology which is indispensable for success.

There is a difference here also between the studies which touch the centrum of theology and those which lie on its periphery. A point of detail in Church history touches the spiritual reality at almost no single point, so that such a study by itself is not able to stamp a man as a theologian. But when theology is taken as an organic whole, and all its subdivisions are viewed from this central interpretation, the demand made by our fathers may not for a moment be abandoned. "Neither knoweth any man the Father, save the Son, and he to whomsoever the Son will reveal him."

The Organism of Theology in its Parts

If theology lies organically wrought into the organism of science, it must also have an organic existence of its own; which is simply according to the law that the *organizing principle* governs the entire organism in its parts. This brings us to the so-called *division* of the theological departments; an expression which is rightly subject to criticism, since one does not divide an organism, but finds its organic parts there and only needs to exhibit them. Hence there can be no question of drawing up a catalogue of departments, and of dividing these departments into certain classes, arbitrarily or after a rule derived from practice. Whatever is a corpus, and exists as a $\sigma\hat{\omega}\mu\alpha$ brings its own division with it. In the second place, it must be carefully ascertained that one has the real corpus in hand. If, with Schleiermacher, theology is made to consist of a conglomerate of learned departments which find their unity in "the guidance and direction of the Church," the organism is lost, and there can be no more question of an organic division. In fact, Schleiermacher has really no division. In his opinion, theology as a whole has become an historic phenomenon, which he classifies in the historic group; that which precedes it is no theology, but philosophy, and that which follows, as practical parts, and which Schleiermacher takes to be the chief end and aim, is too poor and meagre to save the name of theology. Neither can there be any question of theology with those who, though they still call themselves theologians, actually furnish nothing but a science of religions, and from their point of view are bound to follow more or less the division of Noack, who placed phenomenology as first in order, then ideology, and finally the pragmatology of religion. But Encyclopedia of Theology can have nothing in common either with

Schleiermacher's conglomerate or with the science of religion. Its object of investigation is the body of Theology (corpus theologiae), taken as an organic subdivision of the organism of science; and this alone we are to consider.

Taken in this sense, there is no essential difference of opinion concerning the division of the theological departments. It is held, almost universally, that a first group centres itself about the Holy Scripture, a second group has Church history for its centre, a third group has Christian doctrine for its object, and Homiletics, together with what belongs to it, forms the fourth group. This fourth group may be called one thing by some, another by others; some may differ concerning the order to be observed; the classification of certain departments belonging to each of these four groups may vary; but this does not cancel the fact that a certain common opinion indicates ever more definitely these *four groups,* as proceeding of themselves from the organic disposition of theology. The only divergence from this of any importance that presents itself is, that a division into three groups still appeals to a few, which end is reached by uniting with Francke the so-called practical theology with systematic, or like Bertholdt the historic with the dogmatic, or like Kienlen the exegetical with the historical departments. But this difference need not detain us, since it merely involves a question of coordination or subordination. They who follow the division of three always accept a division of one of the three into two parts, so that actually they also acknowledge the existence of four groups. In itself it cannot well be denied that in the Holy Scripture, the Church, Christian doctrine, and in the functions of office, four separate objects are given, which compel a division into four principal groups. And the reduction of these four into three groups is serious only when, with Gottschick and others, the Bibliological group is denied a place of its own *from principle.* For then the principium of theology is assailed in its independence, and theology itself undermined.

But by itself the assumption that there are four organic groups in the body of Divinity (corpus theologiae) is not enough. To be scientifically established, these four groups must of necessity proceed from a common principium of division. Thus far, however, this principium of division has not been allowed sufficiently to assert itself. This is to be attributed to the fact that each of these four groups has been viewed almost exclusively *from the view-point of the subject,* and no notice has been taken of how they lie *in the object* and how they are taken *from the object* itself. Hence the custom has become almost universal to distinguish these four groups as *exegetical, historical, systematic* and *practical.* But this custom is not logical. Distinction can be made between the exegetical, historical and systematic labors of the human mind, but it will not do to add to these three the *practical* departments as coordinate. The name of *practical* departments is not derived from the labor of the human mind, but from the purpose or object of these departments. For the sake of consistency, therefore, we should speak of the exegetical, historical, systematic and *technical* departments. Even with this method of distinguishing the groups, Encyclopedia cannot be satisfied. For this also locates the principium of division in the subject. It is the human mind that lends itself to the fourfold function of exegesis, of the study of history, of constructing certain data systematically, and of technically deriving from these certain theories. But just because the human mind is the subject of *all* science, there is no proper division of theology obtained thus at all, but simply a passport which, *mutatis mutandis,* is applicable to every science; and it is well known how a similar scheme has been applied to almost all the other faculties. But what is applicable to *all* sciences can never disclose to us the proper organic character of theology; and he who derives his principium of division exclusively from the subject, has no information to give concerning the organic existence of the organism of theology. Better progress would have been made if the example of Hyperius had been followed, which points to the Word, the Church and dogmatics as being the constituent elements. These, at least, are elements taken from the object and not from the subject, and therefore dissect the organism of theology itself.

Even this, however, does not indicate the principium of division which operates from the object. In the subjective division the principium operates out of the human mind, which lends itself to the four above-named functions. If, on the other hand, the organic division is to arise from the analysis of the object itself, then the principium of division must be derived from the object. This objective principium of division must be found in the principium of theology itself. In the development of its germ the plant of itself brings the organic spread of branches and stem. If the *Holy Scripture* is this principium of theology, it is plain that those departments should first be taken in hand which deal with *the Holy Scripture as such;* then as a second group those departments which trace the working *of the Word of God* in the life of the Church; then in a third group the departments should be combined which *reflect* the content of the Scripture *in our consciousness;* and finally a fourth group should arise from those departments which answer the question, how the working of the Word of God, subject to His ordinances, *must be maintained.* Thus the division into four groups is the same, but now it is taken from the object, after a principium of division which lies in the object itself. The Word of God, first *as such,* then in its *working,* after that according to its *content,* and finally in its *propaganda.* This is most accurately repeated when one speaks, first, of a *Bibliological,* then of an *Ecclesiological,* after that of a *Dogmatological,* and finally of a *Diaconiological* group. In the *Bible* you have the Word in itself; in the Church (*Ecclesia*), you see the Word in operation, objectified in the reality; in *Dogma* the content of this Word reflects itself in the sanctified human consciousness; and in the *Diaconia,* i.e. *the office,* the service of the ministry is indicated, which must be fulfilled for the sake of that Word.

It is not by accident that these groups thus indicated correspond to the common division of Exegetical, Historical, Systematic and Practical Theology; but is accounted for by the fact that each of these four organic members of the body of Divinity emphasizes a peculiar function of the human mind. In the investigation of the *Bible* as such *exegesis* stands first and always will. In the investigation into the *Church* the historiological activity of the mind is most fully exercised. With *Dogma,* a systematizing function of the human mind is a first requisite. And with the *Diaconia* you enter upon the practical domain, and an insight is required into technique. If meanwhile it is the organic plan of the object which successively calls into action these several functions of the human mind, the real dividing virtue does not go out from your subject, but from the object; hence the division must be taken so as to correspond to the elements of the object. The subjective division corresponds to this, but must not be put in its place. Moreover, the correspondence is only partial. All labor bestowed upon the Bible as such is by no means exegetical. The historic-critical study of the several books as such is not exegetical. Neither is archaeology exegetical, etc. While, on the other hand, it must be remarked that all exegetical labor is by no means confined to the first group. The exegetical function of our mind is equally engaged in the investigation of Symbolics, of the Fathers, and in consultation with the sources of Church history. From this subjective point of view it was entirely logical on the part of Professor Doedes of Utrecht when he classified Symbolics under this first group. With the more precise analysis of the subdivisions of each group, as given in another volume, it will appear that the objective division leads in more than one particular to a modified division of the special departments. These, however, will not detain us now, since this would occasion a needless repetition. Here we simply inquire after the four principal branches as they appear upon the tree of theology, and we think that we have indicated them in the Bibliological, Ecclesiological, Dogmatological and Diaconiological groups; just by *these* names and in *this* order.

The symmetry of these designations is justified by the fact that it is the human logos each time which seeks an entrance into each of the four elements of the object. With each of the four groups it is ever the action of our logos which makes the knowledge of the object to appear from the object. Then coordination of Bible, Church, Dogma and Diaconia—the last taken in the sense of *office*—is warranted by the fact that each of these four bears a supernatural character: the Bible, because it is the fruit of inspiration; the

Church, because it is the fruit of regeneration; Dogma, because it presents to us the result of the guidance of the Holy Spirit in the consciousness of the Church; and the Diaconia, because the offices are appointed by Christ, and as organs of the churchly organism each office derives its authority exclusively from Christ, the King of the Church. Another name than that of *Diaconia* for *office* would be preferable, because "Diaconia" makes one think almost exclusively of the Diaconate. But we have no choice. Diaconia is the official name for office in the Christian Church, clearly defined for us in the New Testament. For *office* the Greeks used the expressions τὸ ἔργον, ἡ ἐπιμέλεια ἡ ἀρχή, ἡ λειτουργία, and for the office of judge τὸ δικα-υτήριον But no one of these expressions could here be used. Ἀρχή could not be used, because the churchly office differs in principle from the magistratic office as a ministerial service; and it would not do, since the expression *archeological* departments would have occasioned a still greater misunderstanding. Λειτουργία of itself would have been no undesirable term, but the name of *Liturgy* is differently employed, and would have caused more difficulty than "Diaconia." Because of their indefiniteness the other terms could not be considered at all. And thus it seemed by far the safest way to maintain the constant use of Scripture and to adopt again the New Testament expression for the churchly office, viz. Diaconia, notwithstanding the confusion a superficial view of it may occasion. It must indeed be conceded that in 1 Tim. iii. 8, 12 and elsewhere, along with ἐπίσκοπος, the word διάκονος' appears as also indicative of a definite office; but when the question is raised as to what word the New Testament uses to indicate *office* without distinction of function, there is no doubt but that διακονία is the expressly indicated term. In Phil. ii. 17, 30 the word λειτουργία· occurs, but not in an official sense. In verse 17 Paul speaks of the sacrifice and service of your faith θυσία καὶ λειτουργία τῆς πίστεως ὑμῶν which he was to accomplish by his martyrdom, a saying in which it appears, from the additional word "sacrifice," that he by no means refers to his apostolic office. And in the 30th verse he mentions a service (λειτουργία) which he was not to administer in his office to the Philippians, but which, on the contrary, they were to administer to him. But wherever on the other hand the administration of a definite office is mentioned in a technical sense, the word "diaconia" is used and not λειτουργία. In 1 Tim. i 12 Paul declares that he is put *into the ministry*, i.e. into the diaconia, viz. into his apostolic office. In 1 Cor. xii. 5 it is expressly stated that there are diversities of ministrations διαιρέσεις διακο- νιῶν In Eph. iv. 2 we are told that Christ "gave some, apostles; and some, prophets; and some, evangelists; and some, pastors and teachers"; and all these together are called unto the work of ministering (εἰς ἔργον διακονίας) In 'this sense Paul speaks of himself constantly as a *diaconos* of Jesus Christ. Hence we must dismiss the objection that the name of diaconate is now indicative of but one of the offices. The use of it by the New Testament is conclusive. Neither was there an escape from the dilemma by the use of the terms "oeconomical" or "technical" departments. For one reason the symmetry would then be lost from the names of the four coordinates. And, moreover, the word *technical* would have brought us back again to the subjective division, and the word *oeconomic* would refer to the Church organization. *Office* alone stands coordinate with Bible, Church and Dogma as a supernatural element, and this word *office* cannot be applied to any other but to the Diaconiological departments.

Nothing need be said in justification of the name of *Bibliological* departments, and the question of what is or is not to be classed under this rubric must be reserved for later discussion. But we must briefly vindicate the name of *Ecclesiological* departments in the sense indicated above. At first sight it appears that the twofold assertion is contradictory, that the Church in this connection is a supernatural fruit of regeneration, and that in another sense she is the product of the operation of the Word. This contradiction, however, is in appearance only. Even here *thought* may not be divorced from *being*. Without the constant activity of the Holy Spirit the Scripture itself is inoperative, and only when this activity of the Holy Spirit causes the Scripture to be illumined does this fruitful virtue go out from it. Suppose, therefore, that the Holy Scripture were to be carried into the world, without the regenerating and illumining activity of the Holy Spirit to precede, accompany, and to follow it, no church would ever be seen among the nations. But on the other hand also, if the action of the Holy Spirit had remained a pure mystery, and had not been unveiled to the consciousness by the Word, there would have been a hidden life-power in the souls of many people, but that power would never have become operative, would not have led one believer to join himself to another, and thus would never have revealed the Church as an observable phenomenon. In its hidden quality the Church therefore is the product of the regenerating action of the Holy Spirit, but theology cannot observe that action; this remains hidden in mysticism; and theology begins to reckon with it only when it makes itself *outwardly* manifest in word and practice. In this the *Word of God* is the leading power, and the touchstone as well, by which it becomes known whether we have to do with an action of the Holy Ghost, or with a fanatic fantasy or imagination. Hence both are true: in its spiritual essence the Church is a product of the action of the *Holy Ghost,* and the Church, as an object observable by theology, exhibits the operation of *the Word.*

The name of *Dogmatological* departments can only be fully explained in connection with the treatment of the group. Here, however, let it be said that it does not mean a group of departments, in which, independently of the history of doctrine, the investigator is to build up for himself a system of truth from the Holy Scripture. Actually this is never done. Every dogmatist who is a real theologian, voluntarily takes the history of doctrine into account. Care, then, should be taken not to appear to do what in reality one does not do. Independent formulation of faith is nothing but the criticism of an individual mind, which cuts itself loose from the communion of saints, takes its stand proudly over against the power of history, and cherishes faith in its own leading by the Holy Ghost but *not* in the guidance of the Holy Ghost in the Church of Christ. As a protest against this the name of Dogmatological group demands that Dogma, as a result of history, shall be taken as one's starting-point, and that in its central interpretation and in each of its subdivisions this Dogma shall be examined critically and ever again be tested by the Holy Scripture, in order that in this way at the same time its further development may be promoted.

And finally, with reference to the order of succession, opinion can scarcely vary as to which group ought to begin and which group close the series. Of themselves the Bibliological departments take the precedence, because the Holy Scripture is the very principium of theology. And in the same way it is but natural for the *official* departments to come last, since they assume the completion of the Dogmatological departments. But a difference of opinion may arise as to the question, whether the Ecclesiological departments ought to follow or to precede the Dogmatological. Planck, Stäudlin, and Harless put Systematic Theology first, and Historic Theology after it; but without doubt Hagenbach owes the great success of his encyclopedic manual largely to his accuracy of judgment in assigning the first place to the historical departments. Raebiger likewise took the same course, and to us also it is no question for doubt but that logical order demands the Bibliological group to be followed immediately, not by the Dogmatological, but by the Ecclesiological group. Our division admits of no other. Dogma has no existence at first, but it originates only by degrees, and it is unthinkable without the Church that formulates it. If thus we would avoid the mistake of formulating our dogmatics unhistorically directly from the Scripture, but rather seek to derive it from the Scripture at the hand of the Church, then the Church as a middle-link between Bible and Dogma is absolutely indispensable. To which, of course, it must be added, that there is an "interaction" between each of the four groups. What man is able to bring any Bibliological department to a satisfactory close without taking the Church into account? How would you be able to understand more than a part of Church history, without keeping account with Dogma and the Office? And how would Dogma be intelligible without the official function, which in councils and synods made their construction a possibility? This, however, applies to any division of any science whatever. In the process of history the fibres of all groups twine themselves about and around each other. To this, however, the organic division cannot adapt itself. The only question to be solved is this: how, in the idea of the organism, the several elements are to be originally distinguished. And so taken, the idea of the organism of theology points out to us four principal branches which divide themselves from her trunk: First, that group which engages itself with the Bible as such; secondly, the group in which the Church appears as the revelation of the operation of the Word; in the third place, the group which ranges itself about Dogma as the reflection of the Word in the consciousness of regenerated humanity; and finally, a fourth group, which has the *office* for its centre, as the means ordained of God to cause His Word continuously to assert itself.

CHAPTER V
HISTORY OF THEOLOGY

Introduction

The historic review of Theology, which closes this volume, cannot undertake to furnish a detailed narrative of the process run by theology in all its ramifications during these eighteen centuries. This process forms, not the subject of an encyclopedic, but of a proper *historical* investigation, which directs itself to a single department, or to a single period, or finally, to theology as a whole (as with Von Zezschwitz, in his *Entwickelungsgang der Theologie als Wissenschaft,* Lpz., 1867). In Encyclopedia, on the other hand, only the result of these investigations can be taken up and put into connection with the encyclopedic course of thought. For the writer, especially, there is less occasion to enter upon details, for the reason that the history of Theological Encyclopedia, which runs so largely parallel with that of Theology, has elsewhere been treated by him more broadly than has heretofore been done, and too much detail in *this* chapter would only lead to needless repetition. The question whether this review should not have been placed before the chapter on the conception of theology is here answered in the negative. It is entirely true that the forming of the conception of theology presumes the knowledge of theology as a historic phenomenon, but the historic knowledge in that sense may be presumed as universally known, and Encyclopedia can accomplish its task of pointing out the right way in this historic process, only when it is ready with its conception. According to the logical course of thought, the history of theology would really have to appear twice. First, a history of the facts should be furnished which should include as fact everything that announced itself as a theological phenomenon, without discrimination or choice, not organically, but atomistically. Then, with these facts in sight, the conception, principle, method and organic nature of theology should have to be determined. And reinforced with this insight, at the end another historic review should have to be furnished, but this time under the criticism of the idea of theology. This double treatment, however, of first recording indiscriminately the "facts," and after that, of indicating with discrimination and selection the course of the process in these facts, could not be justified practically. No single science is capable of encyclopedic treatment, until it has obtained sufficient influence to make its appearance a matter of general knowledge, at least with its own students. This also applies to theology, "the leading facts of the manifestation" of which are to be found in every Church history, so that he who is to treat of them encyclopedically may accept them as being generally known. Encyclopedia discovers no new science, but investigates a science, the phenomena of which are everywhere seen. However much, therefore, such a review of phenomena may form an indispensable link in the course of logical thought, which must ·precede the forming of the conception, Encyclopedia need not furnish that link, since it is of itself present. The second review, on the other hand, may not be omitted, for that is to show how, in connection with the encyclopedic results obtained, the process is to be understood in the phenomena. In this second review, the outline of this process will differ according to the nature of the results obtained by encyclopedic investigation.

This critical review embraces six sections, each one of which covers a proper period. First, comes the period of naivety; then the period of internal conflict; then the period of triumph claimed too prematurely; then the period of multiformity; after this, the period of apparent defeat; and finally, the period of resurrection. Let it be kept in mind, that this review does not concern itself with the history of theology as the knowledge of God, but with the *science* which has this knowledge of God for its object. Hence, this history begins where special Revelation is completed. If the word "Theology" is taken in the sense of science, then there is no theology of Isaiah, Micah, Peter, or Paul, but it arises only when special Revelation has reached its goal, and the task begins of introducing the content of this Revelation into the enlightened consciousness of regenerated humanity, and from this human consciousness to reproduce it. That this was the task imposed upon it, was not understood for a time by regenerated man. Had it depended upon primitive Christianity, intensely satisfied with her great salvation, she would have withdrawn herself in mystical enjoyment of the same, in obedience to the same impulse which, especially in those methodistic circles which originated with the *Reveil,* looks down upon theological effort with a certain spiritual self-conceit. But the Holy Spirit compelled her to undertake this task by the reaction, which in all sorts of ways, from the consciousness of the unregenerate, set itself to dissect and to destroy the content of Revelation, and the Revelation itself. And only when in this way the *need* had rendered this scientific effort a necessity, a taste was created for this work, after the rule of the discendo discere discimus (by learning we learn to learn), and the inclination was fostered which explains the later growth of theology. This, at the same time, exhibits the folly of the desire to explain theology from the instituted Church. As far as the instituted Church herself was concerned, she has almost never known the scientific impulse, but has ever preferred to devote herself to the still enjoyment of her great salvation. Theology, as a science, was, as a rule, more of an hindrance to her than a help; and theology owes its origin, its maintenance, and its guarantee for the future, not to the initiative of the Church, but to the initiative of the Holy Spirit, who was also its guide.

The Period of Naivety

As soon as the Church had freed itself from the swaddling clothes of Israel's national life, the Christian religion went out into the world as a *militant* power. "Think not that I am come," said Christ, "to bring peace on earth, but the sword. For I am come to set man at variance with man." Also, "I am come to send fire on the earth; and what will I, if it be already kindled?" Which sayings but delineate the character of Christian heroism in contrast to a timid irenics, which fills in every gap, and covers up every difference. Conflict might have been in part postponed, if the world of that age had still been confined to the stage of infantile unconsciousness, or if a tabula rasa could have been made of all development attained. But this could not be, since the Christian religion was commissioned to appear in a world which boasted of a very ripe development, and spoke at times of the golden age of emperors, and which, notwithstanding its spiritual dearth, prided itself on great things. This placed the Christian religion as an opposing force over against the historical results of a broad, and, in part, a deep-searching development, which was sufficient unto itself, and which would not readily part with the sceptre of power over the spirits of men. Sooner or later the Christian religion was bound to conflict with the existing state of things at every point, and was forced at once to do this: (1) with the pseudo-religions, which were still dominant; (2) with the world of thought, which it first depopulated, and then undertook to populate with its own content; and (3) with the actual world, both national and social, the whole machinery of which it resolved to place upon another pivot. This threefold antithesis shows itself at once with the appearance of the apostles, who would have been utterly impotent but for their spiritual heroism. Which heroism also, for the most part, they sealed with their blood. From the very beginning the conflict assumed the character of a life and death struggle; on the one side being arrayed the ripest products which unregenerate human nature had thus far commanded, and the richest development the human consciousness had attained to without higher revelation and enlightening; and opposed to this, upon the other side, the "foolishness of the cross," which proclaimed the necessity of palingenesis, prophesied an entirely different condition which was to ripen from this, and at the same time announced a "wisdom" that was to array itself antithetically against the "wisdom of the world." The outbreak could not tarry. What existed and bore rule was rooted too firmly to allow itself to be superseded without a struggle; and the Christian religion, which was the aggressive force, was too heroic in its idealism to be silenced by satire or shame, by the sword or fagot. The conflict indeed has come; for eighteen centuries this strife has never come to a truce except in form; even now the antithesis of principles in this struggle is frankly confessed from both sides, and this contest shall be decided only when the Judge of the living and the dead shall weigh the final result of the development of our human race in the Divine balance.

It was natural that at first the Christian religion should stand most invincible in its attack on religion. In its strength of early youth, aglow with the fires of its first love, it presented a striking contrast to pseudo-religion, aged and worn out, maintained for the most part in forms only, and held in honor among the illiterate more than in the centres of culture and power. Within the religious domain Paganism has almost nowhere been able to maintain itself, and without exaggeration it may be said that almost from the very first the chances for the Christian religion as such were those of a *veni, vidi, vici*. Within the ethical-social and national domain, however, the struggle was far more serious, and it took no less than three centuries of bloody fighting before in Constantine the first definite triumph could be recorded. But much more serious still was the first attack in that strife within the *intellectual* bounds. Here at its first appearance Christianity stood with but a "sling and a stone from the brook" over against the heavily armed Goliath, and thanks to the providential leadings of the Lord, this Goliath also was made at length to eat sand. Christ Himself had drawn this antithesis in the intellectual world, when He said: "I thank thee, O Father, Lord of heaven and earth, that thou hast hid these things from the wise and prudent, and hast revealed them unto babes." And since theology belongs to this domain, and to no other, it is entirely natural, that at its first appearance theology bears the character of *naivety*. Not as though there had not been given in the Revelation of the New Testament itself the clear and entirely conscious tendency of this antithesis also in the full sense of principles involved; but it was reserved for later ages to bring out in all its deductions what was potentially revealed in the Scripture. Even now this task is by no means ended, and our own age has been the first to grasp the antithesis in the higher intellectual world between science within and science outside the sphere of palingenesis.

Hence in this period of naivety there was no question whatever of a theology as an organic science, in the sense in which our age especially understands it. What the apostolic fathers offer is little more than exhortation, pious and serious, but as to principles very imperfectly thought out. From Quadratus to Hegesippus the apologists enter an accidental and fragmentary plea to parry assailants from the side of philosophy or invectives from the lips of public opinion, rather than place over against their world of thought a clearly conscious world of thought of their own. The education at most of prospective ministers of the Word, as well as of the youth of higher rank, was the leading motive at the schools of Asia Minor, Alexandria and North Africa. And in the pseudepigraphical literature tradition and the effort of diverging tendencies are both active to create for themselves an authority to which to appeal. If then, without doubt the attack was made from the side of the Christians in the religious domain, this was not the case in the intellectual domain. Here the pagans themselves took the initiative, either by combating the Christian faith directly, such as was done by Celsus, Porphyry and

Hierocles, or, which was far worse, by introducing the Christian religion as a new phenomenon into their own pantheistic world-view. First with the Gnostics, and shortly after with the Manicheans, the Church of Christ suffered the severest strain, and it is certainly not because of her intellectual superiority that she came out triumphantly from this mortal combat. The strife indeed compelled severe processes of thought, and the deepest principles of life were freely laid bare, but the real character of this antithesis was still so little understood that, with Clement and Origen, the victory was bought at the price of weakness of principle; and the influence of "the knowledge falsely so called," which raises its head in heretical teachings, entered the very pale of the Church already in this first period. If, therefore, the decision in this strife had been reached by a hand-to-hand combat of intellectual powers, there is no doubt but that Paganism would have carried the day. Evidently, therefore, the Church owes the different result to the fact that it soon began to manifest itself as an organizing power, which ethically judged the pagan world, and finally enlisted the political power in its ranks. Hence the severest trial was suffered at the hands of the Manicheans, which is so impressive a phenomenon for the reason that in this an antipodal Church arrayed itself as a religiously organized power in opposition to the Church of Christ, and the false gnosis of Manicheanism assailed the Church with her own weapons. And this Manichean trouble assumed such wide proportions that for a time it seemed as though the Church were on the verge of being swallowed up alive. The flood of this church-like organized gnosis had forced its way from the heart of Asia to the most westerly parts of North Africa. Even Augustine felt the after-pains of it.

If it is asked whether in this first period there was no manifestation of an impulse to apply oneself in a *positive* sense to that intellectual pursuit in which theology finds its appointed task, then be it said that this positive element soon presented itself; for ministers needed to be educated, preaching necessitated exegesis and fixing of ethical standards, the organization of its own power gave rise to the problem of Church government, and, after some time had passed, the need of a review of history became urgent of itself. But for no single moment did these positive studies rise above the primitive water-mark; or where this was the case, as at Alexandria, they made too vain a show of feathers borrowed from pagan speculation, so that almost instinctively the Church perceived at once that this rich development promised more danger than gain. If it takes small pains to observe in this first period of naivety the first buds of almost all the departments of theology, it cannot be said that at that time theology had already mature; as a *self-conscious power* in its organic unity. For this the needed data were wanting; the element of genius was too largely absent from the persons; and where this genius was unmistakably present in men like Origen and in a few teachers in the North African school, it soon showed itself top-heavy, and by its one-sidedness became heretical. The growth was too early and too exuberant, but there was no depth of soil, and because the development in the root was unequal, this element of genius soon outgrew its own strength. There was conflict between a twofold life- and world-view, which undoubtedly governed the general state of things, but the first issue in this struggle with Paganism is owing to *other* factors than intellectual superiority. And in this first period, which was entirely naive, theology neither attained unto a clearly conscious insight of its own position, nor to a clearly perceived antithesis in opposition to "the knowledge falsely so called." Hence, when, after Constantine's appearance, Paganism withdrew, there was almost no one to perceive that the real question of difference on intellectual grounds was still unsolved, much less was it surmised that fifteen centuries later the old assailant would again war against the Church of Christ, and, armed to the teeth, would repulse her from more than half the domain which, through the course of the centuries, had appeared invincibly her own. Naively they lived in the thought that Goliath lay vanquished once and for all time, and that the Lord would return before the antithesis had also been exhibited in the world of intellect, both as a conflict of principles in the lowest depths of our existence, and differentiated above in all the branches.

But however naive this first development of theology may have been, even then it showed potentially all the richness of its colors. In two respects: first, although theology is no abstract speculation, but as a positive science has its origin from life itself, in this first period it furnished a so-many-sided intellectual activity, that to-day there is almost no single department of theology which does not trace its beginnings to this first period. And, secondly, in that in this first period the several tendencies which henceforth were to dominate the study of theology delineate themselves almost completely. Even then dualism asserted itself, and tried to make the Christian religion shine by itself as a *novum quid* apart from the preceding development of our human life, and therefore made its appearance as a tendency which was partly mystical-religious, and partly pietistical-nomistic. In opposition to the one-sidedness of this dualism, which was for the most part apocalyptic, the monistic-syncretistic tendency gained a hearing in this first period, which, while it maintained the unity between the light of nature (lumen naturae) and the light of grace (lumen gratiae), ran the risk of abandoning the specific difference between the two. Similarly also, in this first period, there was seen upon the one side an attempt to find the point of support in the spiritual authority of the Holy Scripture, and, on the other side, to obtain a foothold in the consolidation of ecclesiastical authority. And in those early centuries also the tendency showed itself to combine whatever good there was in each of these four chief points of view in an eclectic and arbitrary way, by a compromise which avoided the conflict of principles. The conflict between the Judaistic and Pagan element should not be coordinated with that between these five tendencies as if it were similar to them, since it falls of itself under the antithesis already named. A separate mention of this specific struggle, however, should be made, in so far as it worked a permanent effect in the Christian Church, both in the pseudo-symbolic stamp of the Romish Church, in Chiliasm so prevalent again in these later times, and in Sabbatism and in all strivings after holiness by works that seek their point of support in the Old Testament. Under all these forms, the antithesis is the same between the real manifestation of Christ and what preceded this manifestation by way of preparation. And while this question, which first presented itself objective-historically, returned subjectively, later on, when Christ became real, to every one who was converted unto Him, it enters too deeply into the life of the Church itself not to be classified under a proper head.

The Internal Conflict

The change brought about by the reign of Constantine the Great is vastly important also in the history of theology. Not that he personally exerted a dominating influence upon theology, but in so far as the change of the religion of the throne offered surest proof that the conflict against Paganism had reached a provisional decision, and had terminated in a complete triumph of the Christian religion. It is indeed noteworthy that, without any direct connection, the ecclesiastical events at Alexandria run almost parallel with the political events. In 313, the very year of the second edict of Milan, Arius was ordained a presbyter in Alexandria. In 321 Arius is condemned by the Synod at Alexandria, while Constantine is at the point of coming over to Christianity in 323. And in 325, at the council of Nice, Arius falls, Athanasius appears upon the scene, and the emperor of the Roman Empire, which was still at the height of its power, casts his influence in the scale of the worship of the Christ as "Begotten, not made, and of one essence with the Father." And with this all other relations are changed. The Christians become polemics, and compel heathen scholars to appear as apologists. Not the Christian religion, but Paganism, is now denied a starting-point in public life. The influence upon public opinion has now passed into the hands of presbyters and bishops. Pagan cult bleeds to death for want of financial support, while Christian ceremonial begins to exhibit pomp and splendor. Moral preponderance is turned entirely to the side of the Christian religion. Henceforth the higher classes follow after the Cross in ever-increasing numbers. Christian schools flourish in proportion as heathen schools wane. And, as is generally observed in such changes in the state of affairs, from now on, talent, the energy of personality, and the power of the word turn their back upon Paganism, and place themselves at the service of the newly arrived religion. And this explains the almost immediate transition from the naivety of the first period, to the almost midlife maturity that marks this second period. The fourth and fifth centuries are contrasted with the second and third almost as light and shadow, and this sudden blossoming of intellectual life and even of genius within the Christian domain is so overwhelming, that already in the sixth century unmistakable signs appear of deterioration, and in the seventh century the decline of the middle ages has already set in. The almost simultaneous appearance of the dominating Fathers in the East, as well as in the West, by which the heroic names of Athanasius and Augustine have been attached to the orthodox development of the Church and theology for all ages,—a fact which finds no explanation from history, nor from psychology, but only from the providential leading of the Creator of spirits and geniuses,—proves of itself, that the change brought about by Constantine marks the beginning of the fundamental period of Christian theology. All that follows after can only be built upon the permanent foundation laid by these gigantic architects. For both these cycles of Patres, which group themselves about Athanasius in the East, and about Augustine in the West, neither lean nor rest upon what went before, but stand entirely upon their own feet, with Atlantic strength to support the development coming after them. This appears most clearly from comparison between the meagre efforts of earlier apologists and the *Civitas Dei* of Augustine. With every earlier apologist it was a mere effort of hands and feet to protect the body against the assailant, but in Augustine we meet with a Herculean figure that destroys the monster with a stroke of the sword and makes the dragon retreat into his hole. Augustine is the Christian triumphator, before whose triumphal chariot are borne the spoils of Paganism and Manicheism as trophies. In him and after him the Christian religion is *dominant,* while nothing remains for Paganism but the convulsions of approaching death. Gloriously has Golgotha been avenged, and the cross, which was once an accursed tree, is now a symbol of honor.

By this, however, theology obtained an entirely different character. Whereas in the first period, it had been chiefly bent upon self-defence against the arch-enemy, that enemy was now vanquished, and thus the antithesis between regenerate and unregenerate human consciousness could no longer be the most conspicuous. When the school, at which Proklus flourished last, was closed at Athens, and the last supporters of classic tradition fled to Persia, there was no more need for a further conflict about this deepest and most incisive antithesis. As an intellectual power, Paganism no longer stood. All intellectual power was now withdrawn within the walls of the Christian Church; consequently, the antitheses which were to impel theology to action could not but have their rise in the heart of that Church itself. Hence it became a conflict within its own bosom.

If the question is raised whether the deepest significance of this conflict is not still stated by the antithesis between *nature* and *grace,* between Humanism and Theism, the answer lies close at hand. It continued of course always the same antithesis, but with this difference, that now the anti-Christian power made its appearance dressed in a Christian and even an ecclesiastical garb. After persecution had ceased and the Christian religion had been duly inaugurated in its career of honor, the transition to Christianity became so colossal, especially among the upper classes, and so largely a matter of fashion, that there could scarcely be any more question of an actual transformation of spirits. People were everywhere baptized, but as baptized members they brought their pagan world-view with them into the Church. Two classes of Christians therefore soon stood arrayed in a well-ordered line of battle over against each other: those who were sincere, who were truly participants of the new principle of life, and were but waiting for the propitious moment in which to work out this principle into a proper world of thought; and on the other side the pseudo-Christians, who from their natural, unregenerate life-principle reacted against the Cross, in order to maintain the old world-view, now exhibited in Christian form. It is this conflict which compelled the Christian Church to awake from her mystical-practical life to energetic activity of spirit, and to create theologically from her own life-principle a correspondingly adequate world of thought. And this was done Christologically and Soteriologically. First Christologically, because the central starting-point of her activity lay in the Christ, so that the just relation between the Divine and human, between nature and grace, had first to be established in the dogma concerning Christ. And after that, Soteriologically, because in the application of the salvation which had appeared in Christ, everything depended upon a correct insight into the true relation between God's action and man's action in bringing about his salvation. In both these questions the sincere Christians proved the stronger, because the conflict was prosecuted from out their own life-principle. As long as it was merely the formal question between the Divine and human factors in the process of attaining certainty in Divine things, the philosophers were their superiors, and their defence could not be one of principle. From the scientific view-point, their apology was weak. But when called upon to formulate dogmatically who Christ was, and how grace operates in the Child of God, the tables were turned. The pseudo-Christians had to deal with a matter foreign to them, while those who were sincere handled what constituted a component part of their own life, the object of their love and worship, the cause of their eternal joy. Thus the sympathy of a holy love sharpened their intellectual capacities, and it explains itself, how these unexcelled Fathers of the Church have caused the stream of theologic life to flow from the rock as with a magic wand, and at the same time have given to theology its inner certainty. Theology could never have substantiated itself by any demonstration from without; and only by starting out from the Christ and the work of grace in the sinner, and, objectively as well as subjectively, formulating accurately the antithesis between the life of nature and the life of grace, did it clear for itself formally also the way to vindicate its view-point.

For this reason the antithesis between philosophy and the Christian religion could not be a stimulant in this period. Already theology feels herself mistress in her own home, and sees in philosophy nothing but a tamed lion, which she harnesses before her triumphal chariot. At Byzantium classic study had obtained a proper place of honor, from the days of Emperor Photius. Boast was made of Plato and of Aristotle. And it was in the footsteps of Aristotle that John of Damascus in his Ἔκδοσις, printed an irremovable dogmatic stamp upon the entire Church of the East. But for theological studies in general, philosophy in all its ramifications offered none but subsidiary services. Centrally theologic development in this period is dogmatic, and the wide exegetical studies have no other tendency than to establish scripturally once for all the truth that had been found. Critically the work done does not extend beyond the content of Scripture, and formally what is attempted is at most to keep in hand good codexes rather than bad. Hermeneutics is established in order, after given rules, to overthrow false exegesis of heretical doctores, and the extent to which Hieronymus busied himself with isagogical questions had merely this object in view—viz. placing at the disposal of the coming clergy all sorts of things worthy of their notice. Thus everything was rendered subsidiary to the development of dogmatics, including even historical studies; and thus dogmatics appeared mostly in the form of polemics, to combat false representations. Time was not yet ripe for the organic construction of a system, which should include all the dogmatic treasures. Even Augustine did not venture upon this. What Origen had too early attempted, served as an example to deter others, and what John Damascene accomplished for the Eastern Church has done much toward the petrifying of that Church; even though it may not be overlooked, that this very early check put upon dogmatic thought saved the Eastern Church from many serious errors, in which at a later date the Western Church lost itself.

But if theology triumphed over heresy in its own bosom during this period, it was not all gold that glittered. This intellectual victory had not been achieved except in union with the ecclesiastical organization; and the Church with her ban had anathematized whoever had been conquered by theology. This effected too close a bond between theology and the Church, which resulted after the death of the coryphaei in a limitation of liberty for theology as a science, even as in the Church everything was compelled to exhibit itself too largely in one mould and move in the same direction. Multiformity of life was lost in the uniformity of the traditional ecclesiastical type, and as soon as opposition ceased, theology lost the spur for action, and almost every reason for existence. Her practitioners were like an army dismissed, since victory had been achieved. The heroic period of the Fathers in the fourth and fifth centuries, therefore, is followed by a period of lassitude and deathlike stillness, which gradually turned into the barrenness of the Middle Ages. At first this baneful uniformity did not make itself so strongly felt. The schools of Antioch and Alexandria, of Nisibis and Edessa, of North Africa and of Rome, were strong with the vigor of youth, each having a theological tendency of its own. But when presently the Eastern schools lost their significance, and the West appeared in the foreground, and in the West Rome's preponderance assumed proportions which became more and more decisive, the distinction was gradually lost sight of between "heretical departure" and "difference of tendency among the orthodox." All differences were looked upon with envy. Unity in the most absolute sense had become the watchword. And when finally this unity was carried off as spoils, it seemed more easy to maintain this unity thenceforth by ecclesiastical decisions than by theologic debate. Theology had done her duty, now the Church was to have the word. Not theology, but the Hierarchy, as early as the sixth century, held the reins of power which are to maintain the principle of the Christian life. And though it is self-evident that there still remained certain variations, and that absolute unity has never been obtained, Rome, nevertheless, preferred to allow these variations sufficient playground within its own organization, and when needed to provide diversion by monastic orders. Especially the removal of the centre of gravity of the Church from the East to the West, from civilized to the still uncivilized nations of the Germanic-Gallic world, materially aided this dismissal of theology from service, and encouraged the withdrawal of study into the convents, as in so many centres of learning in the midst of uncultivated conditions.

Prematurely claimed Triumph

The long period extending across the four centuries which precede and the four centuries which follow the Dark Ages, is of importance for the development of Theology in its second half only. This is not intended to undervalue the rich development of intellectual life in the several monasteries, at the courts of the Carolingian princes, and under Alfred among the Anglo-Saxons, before the night of the Middle Ages set in, but merely to indicate that the great progress of learning rendered no material aid to the development of the conception of theology as such. It brought this development scarcely an indirect good. The study of the better Latin authors was continued, the Church Fathers were read and quoted, series of excerpts from the Fathers (catenae patrum) were compiled for exegesis, chronicles were diligently written, Alcuin prepared even some sort of a dogmatic compendium from the works of Augustine, entitled *De fide sanctae et individuae Trinitatis libri duo,* which was rapidly passed on from hand to hand; but however bright and clear this learning was compared to the night of ignorance that still rested darkly upon Europe's west and north, it produced no scientific results. There were fresh wave-beats in these waters, of momentary duration, as when Elipandus of Toledo and Felix of Urgel advocated adoptionism, Paschasius Radbertus constructed the theological explanation of transubstantiation, and Gottschalk undertook once more to assail the semi-Pelagianism that had crept in on every hand, and the conflict about the *filioque* became necessary as a defence against the Eastern Church; but these efforts effected no enduring results. The Church tacitly giving shape to public thought by her orthodoxy weighed too heavily upon the life of the spirit; and no question was settled scientifically, for after a brief trial it was dismissed by the authority of the ecclesiastical courts. Even an Isidorus Hispalensis, a Venerable Bede, Alcuin, Hrabanus Maurus, or Hincmar of Rheims left no single work of creative genius behind them. And when the ninth century produces an independent thinker in the person of John Scotus Erigena, he distinguishes between affirmative and negative theology (theologia καταφατική and ἀποφατική, and thereby merges real theology into philosophy, and that, a philosophy in which the old sin of Pantheism renews itself in a way more serious than with Origen. So indifferent, however, was his time to these deeper studies that this pantheistical philosopher held his post of honor undisturbed at the court of the Carolingians, surrounded by an orthodox clergy, and his writings were condemned for the first time three centuries afterward by Rome at the mouth of Pope Honorius III as "being full of the vermin of heretical depravity."

This does not imply that these three centuries passed by to no purpose and without important results, but whatever labor did more than protect the inherited theological treasure, directed itself almost exclusively to what was calculated to strengthen the Church in a practical way and civilize the nations of the West. First, the system of monasticism was deeply thought out, carefully ordered and clearly outlined. Then the development of ecclesiastical law took a higher flight, together with the ordering of civil relations, which were included in canonical law. No little effort was made to establish upon a sound footing the cathedral schools, which had been founded by the Carolingian princes, and to provide them with good material for study. And, finally, there was no want during these ages of edifying literature of a pious trend, mystical flavor and sound content. But none of these studies touched upon theology in her nature and being. No thought was expended upon her as such, and there was still less of an effort made to vindicate her relation to the non-theological development or to the reason. The Church was mistress in the entire domain of life. The opposition of ancient Rome's classical development had been silenced by the decline of the culture of the times. Germanic development was still too much in its infancy to renew the old strife, and thus of itself the struggle for principles came to an end; the more because the ever-restless spirit of the Greek came under the pressure of Islam, which prevented it from exerting an influence upon the Church of the West. The Dark Ages, which soon appeared, were but the natural consequence of what went before. The wind blew no longer from any quarter. It was a dead calm. On every hand nothing but stagnant waters were seen. And thus, for want of an animating impulse, the life of study waned.

It was very different, however, in the second part of this long period. In 1096 the first crusade was undertaken. This was an expression of Christian, chivalrous heroism, which not only aroused the peoples from their sleep of death, but also restored to the Church her sense of unity with the Church of the East, and exerted no less mighty an influence upon theology. Here we must retrace our steps to Emperor Justinian I., who closed by a decree the pagan school of Athens, and thereby obliged its scholars to flee to Persia. There these men tried to establish their classical school in safety, and to prosecute their studies; but however much they were disappointed in this, it was nevertheless under Persian, and more especially under Syrian influences, that in the eighth century, under the high protectorate of the Abbasides, the classical studies came to Bagdad, in order there, and presently in Spain, to call into being a scientific life which far surpassed the civilization of Christian Europe at that time. By contact with this rich Mohammedan life the old classics were introduced again in Europe; and when, in competition with Islam, the classical studies were resumed in Byzantium, under Bardas and Photius, the old Greek-Roman world of thought entered Christian Europe simultaneously from these two sides, to recall it from its practical, mystical and ecclesiastically traditional life to a higher development of its self-consciousness.

The new theological activity which was thus called into being bears the name of Scholasticism, which name is derived from *docere in scola,* and for this reason Scholasticism is also connected with the rise of the universities. At first acquaintance the classical world did not stand high in the general esteem. The beautiful in the world of old Hellas and the virility in the world of old Rome was not loved by the Middle Ages and Scholastics. This love flamed up only when the Byzantine scholars fled from Turkish violence into Italy, and when, as a fruit of their activity, Humanism made its entry. No, the Scholastics cared less for Homer, Aeschylus, Virgil and Horace, than for Plato, Aristotle and Cicero. On the first acquaintance with the works of Greece's great philosophers especially, it was soon evident that these men were profounder students than the clergy of the times. And since these Scholastics knew too little Greek to read Aristotle at once in the original, they obtained by their acquaintance with the thinker of Stagira about such an impression as a Zulu negro must receive from a visit to the arsenal at Woolwich. What were the weapons they had thus far used, when compared to the rich supply of arms from the arsenal of Aristotle? And as the Christian knights were inspired to high exploits by crusade upon crusade undertaken against Islam, the sight of this glittering arsenal in the writings of Aristotle made the scholars of those days quickly cast aside the sling and stone and immediately arm themselves with the lances of Aristotle's categories and with the armor of his distinctions, and so to gain trophies for their Christian faith. At the outset they foresaw none of the danger this implied. As yet they perceived nothing of what was to come to light in Abelard, in the Nominalists, and presently in the Humanists. They did not surmise that the Greek-Roman tradition held a spirit peculiar to itself, and that when once called out from its grave this spirit would soon prove able to enlist once more the sympathies of thinking minds, and for a second time let loose against the Church the old enemy which had spoken in Celsus and Porphyry. They thought they were simply dealing with the armor of a buried hero, and that they had a perfect right to appropriate this armor to themselves.

Even thus, however, there was something very beautiful in this impulse. If it lay in the nature of the case that the world of thought of unregenerated humanity must of necessity be different from that of regenerate humanity walking in the light of God's Word, the task of theology was not exhausted in a self-defence against this world of natural thought. She was called, in the first place, to populate her own world of thought and to regulate it. The content of the Divine Revelation had been committed to her, not to possess it as gold in a mine, but to delve it out of that mine, and then to convert that gold into all sorts of ornaments. The content of Revelation had not been given dialectically, nor had it been cast in the form of discursive thought. That which had been revealed of God could therefore not be taken up as such into the human consciousness. It had first to be worked over, and its form be changed so as to suit human capacity. What had been shown to the Eastern mind in images and symbols, had to be assimilated by Western thinking and reproduced intellectually. For this it was indispensable that the believing Christian should also learn how to think, and how to sharpen his powers of thought, in order to grasp the content of his faith, not resting until he had succeeded, from the root of palingenesis and by the light of photismos, in leading the human consciousness to a coherent, comprehensive world of thought entirely its own. And this they failed to do. In the period of naivety the struggle with Paganism had been broken off rather than fought out. Under the inspiration of the Fathers of the Church all the powers of thought had been directed to the establishing of the mysteries, to prevent heresies; but in the following ages they neglected to analyze the further mysteries of the faith to the root. Thus they failed of creating a Christian Philosophy, which should give to the Christian world, to the glory of God, what old Hellas had possessed in Plato and Aristotle, thanks to Socrates' initiative. This want has been felt by the Scholastics, if only feebly. They saw that Aristotle could teach them how to think. They were ashamed of the fact that the scholars of Bagdad and Cordova excelled the Christians in virility of thought. And then they, too, threw themselves upon the world of thought, they worked themselves into it, and became masters in it of the first rank, with a virtuosity which claims our admiration till this day. Suddenly they rise like cedars from the barren tablelands of the Dark Ages. And in so far as they, immovable in their faith, did not shrink before any intellectual labor, however gigantic, they are still our examples as intellectual heroes. He who refuses to consult with Thomas Aquinas weakens himself as a theologian.

However, we have qualified their labor as a triumph grasped prematurely. In the preface of the latest edition of Lombardus' *Sententiae* and Thomas' *Summa,* Paris, 1841, the editor wrote in a high-pitched key of these *Sententiae* and this *Summa:* "Stupendous works indeed, the former of which ruled all Europe for a century and a half and gave birth to Thomas Aquinas, while the latter, being assuredly the very sum of theology, has ruled all Europe for five centuries from the day it was brought to light, and has begotten all succeeding theologians." This flattering speech aims none too high; for after Thomas there has no one arisen who, as a theologian, has thought out the domain of sacred study so comprehensively from all sides, and who has penetrated as deeply to the bottom of all questions so heroically as he; and only the latest development of philosophy has given the stream of theological thought a really new bend. The very rise of this newer philosophy, however, has discovered how greatly Thomas was mistaken, when he thought that he had already hit the mark, when he placed the formal intellectual development of the Grecian world at the service of the Church. Undoubtedly it is since then only that theology within its own ground has come to a richer development, such as it had never known before, which has enabled it to assimilate and to reproduce no mean part of the treasures of Revelation; but the struggle for principles, which theology had to carry on for the vindication of her own right of existence, had scarcely yet begun. Theology and philosophy (taken now in the material sense) are too closely identified by Thomas. He takes too little account of the world of thought of unregenerate humanity as an independent whole. It is with him still too much a subtle gymnastic of intellect, which defends every part of the Church confession of that day by distinctions, and again by distinctions against objections, and vindicates the same as being in harmony with reason. And it was especially serious because thus the foundation of the building of Christian Doctrine was sought by far too much in the subject itself and for the subject in the understanding. For thus finally reason sat in judgment, and though reason appeared in favor of the doctrines of the Church when speaking from the mind of a Thomas, there was no guarantee that this same reason in another subject would not presently arrive at an opposite conclusion, and then where was the triumph of the Christian religion? In Abelard it had already been shown with what fire men were playing. That fire had been extinguished by the holy energy of Bernard of Clairvaux and by the ban of Innocent II. But what was to be done, when presently that same fire should break out again in wider extent and with greater fury? There was an increase of knowledge, but victory had not yet been achieved. The mystical Scholastics were already aware of this, for which reason they offered dialectical proficiency the support of the fervor of devotion and faith. But, of course, in this also there was no lasting security. That security could be regained only when return was made to the Holy Scripture.

Development of Multiformity

The subject in hand is neither Religion nor the Church, but Theology as a science, and therefore in the period preceding the Reformation the emphasis falls upon the unfolding of multiformity. The return to the Holy Scripture as the sole principium was of far-reaching importance. Such men as Thomas Aquinas, etc., fully intended to base their confession upon the Holy Scripture, and on the other hand it is also known that while devoted to the study of the Scriptures, Erasmus held to the confession of Rome till his death. Similarly the motive of the newer development has been sought in the principle of free investigation, but only to be overthrown by the confession of the Reformers themselves, that they never pleaded for a freedom of investigation which lacked all foundation in faith. It is self-evident, moreover, that he who finds the motive of the new evolution of the science of theology too exclusively in the return to the Holy Scripture or too formally in freedom of investigation, excludes thereby Romish theology altogether, and arbitrarily contracts the domain of theology. That the labor of the Romish Church was at first disqualified, is readily understood; but this narrow view has been abandoned a century ago, and in theological circles the learned Jesuits especially are duly recognized again. It certainly cannot be questioned that the Romish theology of the last decenniums can claim the name of theology in the strict sense of the word with far more justice than what is still brought to the market under the name of theology by the men of the Science of Religion or by the speculative or ethical modern tendency. In view of this the point of departure for this period lies for us in the *development of multiformity.* Not as if such a multiformity were intended by Luther or Calvin. This is by no means asserted here. At Wittenberg, as well as at Geneva, the conviction was unassailable for long years that their own confession bore an absolute and exclusive character. Everything that contradicted this was a falsification of the truth, just as in both spheres of the Reformation one's own Church was held to be the purest, not merely by way of comparison, but so as to be actually looked upon as the only lawful continuance of *the* Church of the apostles; and Rome's Church was not only rejected as deformed, but, as a false imitation of the Church, was abhorred by the epigones of the Reformation as the Church of the Antichrist. And this could not be otherwise at first. Notwithstanding the fact that the schism of the Eastern Church had been continued for more than four centuries, men had still refused to consider it anything more than a schism. Age after age they were accustomed to the idea that truth, which of necessity must be absolute, was also bound to maintain this absolute character in the unity of form and expression. And while the rigorous maintenance of the unity of the Church rendered this result possible, the very thought of a certain multiformity for the life of the Church could not commend itself to any one. This conception of unity had entered so deeply into the public consciousness of those times, that while multiformity was already in existence *de facto,* and caused its effects to be felt, they still argued and acted as though there were never anything but the single, uniform Church. It did not enter into the common consciousness of that day that the uniformity of the Church had found its logical expression in the papal idea, and that with the refusal of obedience to the Pope that uniformity was broken forever, never again to be restored. In the days of the interim the dream was still dreamed, to restore by mutual consent, a unity which would also include the papal Church. The numberless conferences between Lutherans and Reformed, and between Reformed and Anabaptists proceeded without distinction, from the desire to unite in the unity of the faith everything that had broken with Rome. The Byzantine spirit, which had come upon the German princes, rejected the ideal of all multiformity in the Church within the boundaries of each, so resolutely and definitely that at length the principle of cuius regio eius religio, i.e. "that the religion of the crown must be the religion of the people," could for a while rule as the leading thought. And when finally, yielding to the force of facts, and compelled by the European-Romish league to political cooperation, the correlation of the Lutheran and Reformed elements could no longer be neglected, their mutual recognition resulted more from the impulse of self-protection than from the impulse of a clearly self-conscious conviction.

That this delusion of unity assumed with the Lutherans forms that were so much more sharply outlined than with the Reformed,—leading first to the rejection of the Reformed exiles on the coast of the North Sea, and finally to the decapitation of Crell in 1601,—cannot be attributed to the fact that the Reformed already occupied on principle a far wider stand-point, but was exclusively the result of their clearer insight in the liberty of the Church. They claimed an autonomous life for the Church under her only King, Christ Jesus, and though later they went so far in granting the State a civil right over sacred things (ius circa sacra), that this liberty of the Church became actually an illusion, yet from the beginning their standpoint was more accurately chosen. In Lutheran lands, the princes, aided by teachers of their appointment acting as *ecclesia docens,* took the guidance of the Church in their hands, while the Reformed demanded that all ecclesiastical questions should be decided by the lawful representatives of the churches, convened in Synod. This is the reason that the State, in Reformed lands, had less interest in the exclusion of those of differing opinions, since it found in these diverging groups a support over against the ever-bolder pretensions of the autonomous churches. Hence the principle, "that the religion of the crown must be the religion of the people," could never gain a foothold in the Reformed lands, the result of which was that from the beginning the ecclesiastical life in these lands exhibited a character of greater multiformity. Exiles, who were refused a shelter elsewhere, found protection in Reformed countries, and thus the idea of the liberty of conscience, which is an immediate result of multiformity, became of itself an established doctrine in the Reformed kingdoms much earlier than in Lutheran and Romish states. He who found himself in trouble for his religion's sake had no standing or chance for life anywhere but in the Reformed lands, viz. in Switzerland and in the Netherlands.

But it cannot be questioned for a moment, that to Luther the honor belongs of having dealt the fatal blow to the false uniformity of the Church. When Luther burned the papal bull, that unity was essentially destroyed. He derived the moral right for this action from no canonical rule, but from the authority of God, by whose Word it was assured unto him in the deepest depths of his conscience. And by this the subjective-religious principle received its right as a power, which, if needs be, could defy churchly authority. And when Luther's initiative found an echo in the hearts of many thousands, and became the point of departure for a separate Church organization, multiformity of churchly life became thereby *eo ipso,* a fact. For if Luther held to the idea that every one who, like himself, broke with Rome, was bound to arrive at like results with himself, from the nature of the case this idea could not be maintained. For so soon as another effort made its appearance by the side of his, which showed itself possessed of the power to be even more efficient in founding churches than his, he might indeed write to Zwingli from Marburg: "You are people of another spirit"; but after the Pope had been renounced, and the State had no power outside of its boundaries, there was no authority to prohibit this third "Church-forming" power from making its appearance and from consolidating itself: 1517 made Luther powerless in 1529. That the Anabaptist and Socinian movements, in their dualistic-mystic and moderate-rationalistic activity, have not produced like results, and still flourish in small groups at most, which have never obtained any universal significance, is not attributable to the fact that these Anabaptists and Socinians were refused the right of existence; for men would fain have treated the Calvinists in the same way, and the Calvinists also barely tolerated the Martinists; but it was the immediate result of their want of "Church-formative" (Kirchenbildende) power. Such then was the lesson of history, viz. that the Church of Christ was bound to reveal herself in more than one form, but, at the same time, that this multiformity of revelation did not depend upon an arbitrary whim or freak, but was determined by the spiritual and forming power which appeared, or did not appear, in the several tendencies that raised their heads.

Gradually, and of itself, this multiformity of the churches led to the recognition of four fundamental types of Church formation, apart from the Armenian, the Koptic, and other churches in the far East; viz. as the fruit of the Reformation the *Lutheran* and the *Reformed,* and by the side of these the *Greek* and the *Romish.* Four principal groups, each one of which exhibits a churchly character of its own, reveals a peculiar effort, assumes a proper form, and as such, also represents a special theological tendency. Without attracting at once attention to itself as such, this multiformity was sealed confessionally in the dogma of the visible Church as the revelation of the invisible Church. So long as the Romish-papal delusion of unity was maintained, it was entirely natural that the visible Church should be identified with the invisible. Where there is only one revelation of the essence, a graded difference may be viewed as an obstacle to the adequateness of the revelation. But Rome removed even this objection by the separation between the Clergy and the Laity. As soon, however, as other church formations arose, each of which pretended to be the revelation of the Church, while they lacked the courage to reject each other's baptism, or to deny salvation in its absolute sense to those of the other confessions, the essence and the revelation of the Church fell of themselves apart. From henceforth what one saw could no longer be *the* Church, the body of Christ, and hence of necessity, simultaneously with the multiformity of church formations, the dogma originated of the visible Church as *not* being adequate to the invisible Church, or to the mystical body of Christ.

With this an entirely different state of things entered in for theology. So long as uniformity maintained itself, there was no other theology conceivable than that which scientifically systematized the confession of the Church. It could take no other point of departure than in the instituted Church, and could arrive at no other result than had been found by the instituted Church. Investigation of the Holy Scripture had no aim when the instituted Church tendered an official Latin translation, and in exegesis prescribed the analogy of faith even to minutest particulars. Everything was known from the start; hence there could be no thirst after truth; to furnish a dialectic proof for the confession of the Church was superfluous for believers, and could serve no purpose for unbelievers, since these were bound to maintain silence for fear of the anathema of the Church. All the benefit, therefore, which one derived from Scholastic Theology was the pleasure, noble enough in itself, which one enjoyed in exhibiting the shining brightness of the Church's confession in all its parts, even when seen by the light of the data of logic. But this, of course, became entirely different when the multiformity of the churches became an established fact. Apologetics over against Paganism, which had gradually become superfluous, was no longer sufficient to answer the needs of the day, but controversy with the confessions of the other Church formations now presented itself. The unity of the Church had to be maintained under the multiformity in its revelation. And no longer able to derive his point of departure from the Church, the theologian had to seek this elsewhere. Thus theology became free, not in the sense of ever being loosened from her object and principium, but so that each of the Church formations expected her to vindicate its effort, and thus from that moment on had to reckon with her criticism. It was self-evident that, resulting from the difference of spiritual disposition and spiritual sphere, the multiformity of the Church formations should also communicate its multiform stamp to theology. But theology as such could never dismiss the problem of how this multiformity was to be brought into harmony with the unity of the body of Christ. It had already been seen that the truth of God was too rich and the great salvation in Christ too aboundingly precious, by reason of the Divine character exhibited in both, for them to be able to reach their full expression in one human form. And though the several nations assimilated one and the same truth and the selfsame salvation, the disposition of the several groups of people was too many-sided not to adopt them in different ways, and to reproduce them in different manners. The claim could never be surrendered that each one for himself should accept and confess the truth in the way in which it appeared most accurate to him and satisfied his needs most fully. But human limitations were at least recognized; and theology could not rest until, together with all the care which she bestowed upon the treatment of one of her concrete forms, she at the same time allowed the relation between the ideal and concrete fully to exhibit itself. She also was not able to make the full content of Divine truth shine forth in a single deduction. She could not be studied except by men, and hence like the Church life itself she remained subject to human limitations. But since the churches could deal only with the concrete result, and thus incurred the danger of communicating a sectarian flavor to their life, and of losing sight of the catholicity of the Church as an organism, it was the mission of theology to raise herself on the wings of the idea above what was exclusively concrete, and from this higher vantage ground to vindicate the good and perfect right of the instituted churches to their confession and life-tendency.

This higher call inspired theology with a zeal such as she had not known since the fourth and fifth centuries. Again she had to fix her point of departure objectively in the Holy Scripture and subjectively in palingenesis, and in the faith awakened by this. Again free access to the Holy Scripture was accorded her. The Vulgate, as the sanctioned translation, fell away. Exegesis became a serious study by which to master the content of the Divine Revelation. In dogma, with the Scripture as the touchstone, distinction had to be made between truth and error. Church history was called upon to point out the several streams of Church life which had been held back under the false papal unity, and to exhibit them as still existing historically. The difference between formation and deformation of churches had become tangible, and it was the task of theology openly to make exhibition of the difference between the two. Thus theology became an independent power, with a task of her own, with a life-purpose of her own, and bound to the claim of truth rather than to any churchly decision.

However energetic and sparkling the life was which characterized this reformative development of theology, it would have been better still if she could have conquered her liberty, in the good sense, at once. But in this she only partially succeeded. Her growth outside of the universities is scarcely worthy of mention, and at the universities, because of the appointment of the professors by the State, she became too greatly subject to the influence of the State. Provisionally this was preferable to being bound to the instituted churches, but it entailed the subsequent loss of separating her too greatly from the life of the Church, and of allowing too great an influence to be exerted upon her by non-theological factors. Since the ministry was educated almost exclusively at the universities, theology, with her diverging tendencies and schools, has undoubtedly exerted a disturbing influence upon the churchly life. And as a reaction against this it has called the narrow-hearted sectarian stream into life, which would prefer to confine theology to an ecclesiastical seminarium. This measure would restore the Romish passion for uniformity, but now without the counterpoise which Rome still furnished in its world-wide organization and in its orders. Compulsion here is of no avail, and since the multiformity of churchly life goes and must go as far as it is postulated by the variations in the organic life of the Church, so likewise, in order to fulfil her mission, theology must be left entirely free, and cannot be limited by any boundary except by such as is indicated in the life-relations themselves. Not the State, as having authority in the sphere of the magistrate, but science and the Church are here to determine the boundary. Theology is inconceivable as a science studied for mere pleasure, and therefore every theological effort, which does not find a corresponding stream in the Church, is bound of itself to bleed to death. Hence for a while it progressed fairly well, i.e. as long as the stream of churchly life propelled itself with power. Both Lutheran and Reformed theology completed their first task when they explained systematically these two new tendencies in the churchly life and in the churchly confession, and thus vindicated them over against Rome as well as over against each other. But so soon as the pulse of the churchly life began to beat more faintly, foreign factors began to undermine the healthful vitality of theology as well. This became evident in the syncretistic and pietistic tendencies, even before Rationalism, as the train-bearer of Philosophy, threw down the glove to her.

In the seventeenth century Syncretism appeared as a natural reaction against the multiformity of churchly life. And it cannot be denied that George Calixtus was actuated by a spiritual motive. The controversy and the separation in churchly life had caused the instituted churches to lose too much from sight their unity in Christ and their sodality as revelations of the body of Christ, and it was against this that Calixtus raised his irenical voice. On the other hand, it must be said that this was accompanied by a certain humanistic indifference to the points of dogma which were in question between the churches. A man like Calixtus did not understand that one could really be concerned because of a controversy about Transubstantiation, Consubstantiation, or the negation of Substantiation. And what was worse, he was not sufficiently acute as a theologian to construct his irenics theologically, so that he saw no other means than to go back to the councils of the first centuries. Hence his effort could *not* be crowned with success. This irenical wave went down as rapidly as it had risen. Not, however, without reminding theology of her vocation to maintain more faithfully the essential unity of the Church in the midst of her multiform tendencies. Holding itself too closely to the instituted Church, theology had departed too widely from the spiritual life of the Church as an organism.

This last fault avenged itself in the movement of the Pietists. Theology had become too abstract. She had found her foundations in the Holy Scripture, but she had taken that Holy Scripture too one-sidedly as a revelation of doctrine, and had thereby lost too much from sight the spiritual reality, and had forgotten that if Luther had found the rock-foundation on which he stood in the Scripture, he had also clung with both hands to that rock. In the end, the inspiring motive for theology must always come from the subject. Without the spiritual alliance between the theological subject and the spiritual reality of which the Holy Scripture brings us the revelation, a barren Scholasticism is conceivable, but no vitalized and living theology. This was felt by Spener; hence the reaction that went forth from him and from his followers against orthodox theology; a reaction, however, which, as is generally the case, wanted to throw out "mit dem Kinde das Bad," i.e. "the bath with the child." At heart Pietism became *anti*-theological. However much of invaluable good it has brought to the life of the churches, it was unable to restore theology from its barrenness to new freshness. It rather cooperated with the syncretistic movement, and so allowed non-churchly factors free play to work destructively upon theology. Reformation theology has not known a second quickening (*elan*) in the higher sense of the word. She has worked out more minutely what was at first treated only in vague terms. She has furnished rich detailed studies. With hair-splitting exactness she has picked apart almost every conceivable antithesis, with the Lutherans as well as with the Reformed. And especially in exegesis and in Church history she has continued to gather her laurels, but as *theology* she has remained stationary; and when the stream of churchly life has flowed away from under her, she has finally proved to be an expanse of ice that could not be trusted, and that broke and sank away the moment Philosophy threw itself upon her with all its weight.

The Apparent Defeat

The reformation movement certainly succeeded in the sixteenth century in exorcising the pagan spirit from Humanism. Whatever gains this revival of the pagan spirit achieved in Italy in the fifteenth and sixteenth centuries, it was not capable of obtaining a solid footing among the nations of Middle and Northern Europe. And when the conflict which Humanism in league with the Reformation had undertaken against the papal power approached its end, it can be said without exaggeration, that the Reformation had become *Herrin im Hause,* and that Humanism had to adapt itself to the performance of all sorts of subsidiary service. Paganism in its humanistic form was bent too much upon the outward world, and was too little animated and too vaguely conscious of being a bearer of a special life-principle, to enable it to place a life- and world-view of its own over against that of the Reformation. But if it subjected itself, this subjection was not sincere, and the theologians soon perceived that children of another spirit cooperated with them in the other faculties. The more Protestantism was interpreted from its negative side, and free investigation was taken as investigation without a spiritual tie, and the more the liberty of conscience, and gradually even that of the press, assisted in the publication of what was thought and pondered, so much the more did a spirit of free thought begin to develop itself among the well-to-do classes in the countries of the Reformation, which impelled individual thinkers to devise philosophical systems, and which among the great masses created an irreligiousness without ideals, that entered into an ever sharper conflict with the mystical and ideal character of the Christian religion. It has by no means been the thorough idealistic systems of Descartes, Spinoza and Leibnitz that have created the greatest commotion. Much more dangerous were the effects worked by Deism, which spread across the Continent from England; by the spirit of the Encyclopedists, which caused its power to be felt from France; and by the so-called

"Aufklarung" (Illumination) which quickly asserted itself in Germany. To some extent the origin of these influences was truly philosophical, if philosophical be taken as antithesis to theological; but as a rule they were of too low an order and of too little exaltation to justify their claiming for themselves the honorable name of philosophical in the higher sense of the word. It was a low moralism, such as plain public opinion loves, which clips every wing, and knows no higher standard than the everyday and common one. Low shrubberies might grow; each oak or cedar, that wanted to lift up its head, was immediately cut down. For the ideal there was nothing to spare but mockery, poetry went down into sentimentalism, admiration was unknown, men were weaned from all higher impulses and laughed at the fools who still persisted in a desire to go up in the balloon. Of course such a time-spirit and the Christian religion stood over against each other as two antipodes. Too bad that in just those days the Christian Church and Christian Theology lacked the holy fire and energy of heroism to withstand with righteous indignation this spirit of dulness and superficiality. But the churches and the universities themselves were caught in the meshes of this unholy spirit, and men soon saw in Rationalism the caricature of what Christian theology ought to be. And this in turn was attacked by Supernaturalism in such a way as to make the entire defeat of Christendom still more humiliating. Pietistic circles, to be sure, were maintained in Lutheran lands, and mystical and methodistical circles in Reformed lands, which hid the salt of the Gospel, lest it should lose its savor, but these spiritually attuned circles failed of exerting any saving influence upon official churches and official theology. The ground on which this Deism and this Aufklarung offered battle was no ground on which the Christian Church or Christian theology could join the battle. The thrusts given did not carry the sting sufficiently deep to reach the deepest life-consciousness. Thus it remained a mere skirmishing, a constant skirmishing on the outer lines, and no one seemed to realize into how shameful a corner they were being pushed. It was no longer the Church against the world, nor theology against the wisdom of Paganism; but it was the world *in* the Church, and it was theology irrecognizably metamorphosed under rationalistic and naturalistic influences into a caricature of itself.

But, however feebly, the antithesis continued to be felt. Rationalism over against Supernaturalism certainly implied that the scientific consciousness of unregenerate humanity refused to undergo the influence of Revelation, and therefore demanded that the treasure of Revelation should first be examined at the frontier by reason. And, on the other hand, the very appearance of Supernaturalism as such implied an effort to make certain demands for the scientific consciousness of regenerate humanity, by which Revelation might escape from testing by the reason. The deepest antithesis between theology and the wisdom of the world was certainly present in this almost fatal conflict; only it received no special emphasis as such from either side. Rationalism did not appear *against* the Church, but *in* the Church, and adapted itself, therefore, to forms which often did not fit in with its principle, and weakened itself by its utter want of piety. But Supernaturalism also was not able to array itself for a conflict of principles. It betrayed somewhat more of a religious sense, but of a kind which never reached the warmth of the mystical life of communion with the Infinite; which, therefore, scarcely noticed the psychological antithesis; and being almost more hostile to Pietism than to Rationalism, it, for the most part, sought strength in sesquipedalian words and in lofty terms; and deemed its duty performed by the defence of faith in the great facts of Revelation, independently of their spiritual significance.

As a result of this wrong attitude, theology lost in less than half a century almost all the authority it had exerted in the circles of science and public opinion. It was no longer thought worth while to continue a conflict which, from both sides, was carried on with so little tact and spirit. It soon became evident that the interval which separated Rationalists and Supernaturalists grew perceptibly less. He who was still bent upon making a name for himself as a theologian, withdrew into some side study of theology, in which at least there were historical and literary laurels to be gathered. The Church life went into a decline. The life of the clergy partook somewhat of the character of the times when "priest laughed at priest" in the days of Imperial Rome. And it was very clear, as early as the middle of the eighteenth century, that theology had nothing more to say with respect to the great problems which were presenting themselves. Thus the French Revolution came, without thinking it worth her while to assume any other attitude toward the Church than that of disdain. The "Italia fara da se," which was a proverb concerning Italy's future in the days of Cavour could then have been prophesied concerning Philosophy: *Filosofia fara da se;* i.e. "Philosophy will have her own way." Theology could exert an influence in three ways: at her frontiers she could give battle to the spirit of Paganism, or she could make a deeper study of the faith of the Christian Church, as had been done in the fourth and sixteenth centuries, or, finally, she could make the mystical and practical life of the Church express itself in conscious action. But when theology did none of these three, but squandered her time in a skirmish, which scarcely touched upon the first antithesis, which went outside of the mysteries of the faith, and had no connection with the mystical-practical life of believers, she herself threw her once brilliant crown down into the dust, and the opponent could not be censured for speaking of theology as an antiquity no longer actual.

The Period of Resurrection

The nineteenth century is far superior to the eighteenth, not merely in a cosmical, but also in the religious sense. Here also action effected reaction. The bent-down spring rebounded at last. And it will not readily be denied, that in our nineteenth century a mystical-religious movement has operated on the spirit, which may be far from comparable to the activity of the Reformation, but which, leaving out of account the Reformation period, seeks to rival it in recent history. Revivals of all sorts of tenets belong to the order of the day, in Europe as well as in America. In spite of its one-sidedness, Perfectionism has gained a mighty following. Methodist and Baptist churches have developed an activity which would have been inconceivable in the eighteenth century, and which affords its masterpiece in the Salvation Army. Missions have assumed such wide proportions, that now they have attained a universal, historical significance. New interests have been awakened in religious and churchly questions, which make manifest how different a spirit had come to the word. Even negative tendencies have found it advisable, in their way, to sing the praises of religion. And, however unfavorably one may judge of Mormonism, Spiritism, etc., it can scarcely be denied that their rise and temporary success would not have been possible, if the problem of religion had not taken a powerful hold upon the general mind. If then, after the shameful defeat of theology in the period of the "Illumination" (Aufklarung), we may affirm an undeniable *resurrection* of theology in the nineteenth century, let it be said that this is owing, first of all, to the many mystical influences, which, against all expectation, have restored once more a current to the religious waters. A breath of wind from above has gone out upon the nations. By the woes of the French Revolution and Napoleon's tyrannies the nations were prepared for a new departure in an ideal direction. The power of palingenesis has almost suddenly revealed itself with rare force. By the very radicalism of the revolutionary theory the sense of a twofold life, of a twofold effort, and of a twofold world-view has come to a clearer consciousness in every department. Moreover, it may not escape our notice, that it has pleased God, in almost every land and in every part of the Church, to raise up gifted persons, who, by Him "transferred from death into life," as singers, as prophets, as statesmen, as jurists, and as theologians, have borne a witness for Christ such as has not been heard of since the days of Luther and Calvin.

It would, however, be a great mistake to explain the resurrection of theology from this powerful revival alone. It may not be overlooked that this mystical-pietistical revival was more than indifferent to theology as such. As far as it called into life preparatory schools for ministers and missionaries, this revival lacked all theological consciousness, and undertook little more than a certain ecclesiastical training for its students; a sort of discipline more bent upon advancing a spirit of piety and developing a power of public address, than upon theological scholarship. It was more the "passion of the Soul," and the desire after religious quietistic enjoyment, that inspired general activity, than the purpose, cherished even from afar, to give battle in the domain of thought, or to maintain the honor of Christ in the intellectual world. The life of the *heart,* or emotions, and the life of *clear consciousness* were looked upon more and more as separate and distinct, and religious activity, which found itself strong within the domain of the emotions, but very weak on intellectual ground, deemed it good tactics to withdraw its powers within the domain within which it felt itself to be invincible. If this *reveil* had been left to itself, the vocation of Christianity to take up the content of Revelation also into the thinking consciousness, and from this to reproduce it, would readily have passed into entire forgetfulness. And it is Philosophy which has been used by the King of the Church as a means of discipline to force His redeemed once again to enter upon that sacred vocation.

It was only when the Christian Church had lost her authority completely and theology lay in the sand as a conquered hero, that in Kant and his epigones the men arose who, anew and more radically than their predecessors, resumed the ancient conflict of the Greek-Roman Philosophy against the Christian religion, which had been broken off rather than decided in the third century. The logic of principles demanded this. Where two contrary principles come to stand over against each other, it is of no avail that the conflict between them is abandoned after the manner of Constantine, or that, as was done in the Middle Ages and in the first period of the Reformation, it is suspended and limited by the preponderance of churchly authority. Such contrary principles but await the first favorable opportunity to take new positions from both sides, and to continue their inevitable conflict, if possible, still more radically. Cartesius, Spinoza and Locke began this conflict from their side at a somewhat earlier date, but without making the Christian religion feel that it was a conflict of life and death. And only when the "Illumination" (Aufklarung) had depleted the Christian religion entirely of her honor, did Philosophy obtain the chance to come forward in full armor. For though it cannot be denied, that with such men as Kant and Fichte, and especially Schelling, and in part also with Hegel, Philosophy did by no means tread the Christian religion under foot, but rather tried in its way to restore the honor of the Christian mysteries, which the Church had shamefully abandoned; yet it would but betray color-blindness if we refused to recognize how the gigantic development of modern Philosophy has revived most radically the ancient and necessary conflict between the unregenerate consciousness and the principium of palingenesis, and with ever greater precision places the pantheistic starting-point over against Christian Theism—even though its first ardor is now followed by a period of exhaustion.

The greatest step in advance effected by this consisted in the fact that Kant investigated the thinking subject, and thereby gave rise to a riper development of the organic conception of science. The principle and method of science had been made an object of study before, but in the sense in which at present we recognize an organic whole of science it was still entirely unknown, even in the days of the Reformation. At that time men still produced piece-work, each in his own domain, and effected certain transitions at the boundaries by the construction of temporary bridges; but the subject, as the organic central point from which went forth the whole activity of science as in so many beams of one light-centre, was not yet apprehended. Hence the earlier theology, however richly furnished within its own domain, makes an impression which is only in part truly scientific. Before Kant, theology had as little awakened to a clear consciousness of itself as any other science, and much less had the position of theology in the organism of science been made clear. However much Kant and his contemporaries and followers intended injury to the Christian religion, the honor is theirs of having imparted the impetus which has enabled theology to look more satisfactorily into the deepest problems that face it. Schleiermacher has unquestionably exerted the most preponderant influence upon this resurrection of theology. This, apart from his titanic spirit, is owing more especially to the fact that in Schleiermacher the mystic-pietistic power of the life of the emotions entered into so beautiful and harmonious a union with the new evolution of Philosophy. At however many points his foot may have slipped, and in however dangerous a manner he cut himself loose from objective Revelation, Schleiermacher was nevertheless the first theologian in the higher scientific sense, since he was the first to examine theology as a whole, and to determine in his way her position in the organism of science. That the result of his work has nevertheless been more destructive than constructive, must be explained from the fact that he did not perceive that the conflict did *not* involve the triumph of Theology over Philosophy, or the victory of Philosophy over Theology; but from each side a first principle was in operation, which necessarily on the one side gave rise to a Philosophy entirely naturalistic, seconded by a religion both pantheistic and mystical, while in opposition to this a proper Christian Philosophy must needs construct its conception of the whole of science, and in this organism of science vindicate the honor of a theistical theology. By this, however, the fact is not altered that Schleiermacher has given theology back to herself, has lifted her out of her degradation, has inspired her with new courage and self-confidence, and that in this formal sense even confessional theology, which may not hide the defeat of his epigones, owes to him the *higher* view-point at present occupied by the whole of theology,—a merit the tribute of gratitude for which has been paid to Schleiermacher by even Romish theology in more ways than one.

It is to be regretted, however, that with the awakened desire to orient itself in the organism of science, theology has suffered so greatly from the want of self-limitation. The intensive power with which theology studied and dissected the content of Divine mysteries in the fourth and fifth centuries, partly also in the thirteenth, but more especially still in the sixteenth century, was entirely exhausted. There have been many who could scarcely imagine how so much ado could have been made over the $\mathring{\eta}\nu$ ὅτε οὐκ $\mathring{\eta}\nu$ of Arius, or over the "This is my body," in the conflict over the sacraments. Is not that which one confesses in common with all Christians, at least with all Protestants, of tenfold greater importance? Moreover, would not the strength of resistance in defence of the Christian religion increase, in proportion as these interconfessional differences are buried deeper in the dust of forgetfulness? Thus, in a sense more dangerous than in Calixtus' days, there arose a syncretistic reaction against the multiformity which, under the ordinance of God, had unfolded itself in the Reformation. This reaction was certain either to force a return to the unity of Rome, or to lead to such an extinction of the conception "Christian," that at length even Buddhism becomes "Christian." It lay in the nature of the case that every "Union" was and could be nothing but a "machine," so that those of a more practical turn of mind could think of no other unity except that which had existed historically before multiformity came into being. While, on the other hand, when the conflict was interpreted as a defence of the good right of religion over against the intellect, piety had to be generalized, till at length all kinds of religious utterances were classed under one and the self-same conception. The result of this has been that a certain Romanizing tendency has met with a wide reception, especially through Schleiermacher's emphasis put upon *the Church,* which led to Romanticism on a large scale in Germany, and in England to *High-Churchism.* A second result was that theology, which ever pursued an arbitrary "Conception of Union," involuntarily entered in the Vermittelungstheologie upon an inclined plane in which it would readily lose all mastership over itself. And as another result no less, a third tendency appeared, which transmuted that which was positively Christian into the idea of the piously religious, and thus prepared the transition of theology into the science of religion.

That this last tendency, even though it is still called theological, furnishes *no* theology, needs no further proof. The science of religion is an anthropological, ethnological, philosophical study, but is in no single respect theology. And when it presents itself as such at the several universities, it plays an unworthy, because untrue, part.

Vermittelungstheologie also is more and more disposed to put away its theological character. We desire in no way to minimize its value, especially in its earlier period. It has furnished excellent results in many ways, and in many respects it has brought lasting gains. But in two ways it has lost ground. Not perceiving that by the side of theology a Christian Philosophy was bound to arise, it has theologized philosophy too greatly and interpreted theology too philosophically. On the other hand, it has sought its point of support too one-sidedly in the mystical life of the emotions, and thus it has deemed itself able to dispense with the objective foundation in the Word of God and in the instituted Church. By virtue of its character, therefore, it occupied no definite view-point. Chameleon-like, it has lent itself to all kinds of divisions into groups and individual variations. But it has never denied its general feature, of feeling stronger in its philosophical premises than in historic theology, and so it has preferred to turn itself irenically to the left, while it shrank from confessional theology as from an unwelcome apparition. It has also prosecuted no doubt the study of history, especially history of dogma, but ever with this purpose in view—viz. to dissolve it, in order presently, by the aid of the distinction between kernel and form, to put its philosophical thought into the dogma. This is the case with the more intellectual, while in other circles of the Vermittelungstheologie the dualism between the emotional and intellectual life has come to so open a breach, that the transition to the school of Ritschl, which has anathematized every metaphysical conception, is already achieved. However widely spread the influence of this Vermittelungstheologie may be, even in Scotland and in America, now that she more and more deserts her objective point of support in the Holy Scripture, sets herself with ever greater hostility against the Confessional churches, and continues ever more boldly her method of pulverizing Christian truth, she can no longer be a theology in the real sense of the word, but turns of necessity into a philosophical and theosophical mysticism. However much she may assert that she still holds fast to Christ, it is nothing but self-deception. As history slips away from her and the self-testimony of the Christ, Christ becomes to her more and more a mere name without a concrete stamp of its own, and consequently is nothing but the clothing of a religious idea, just such as Modernism wills it.

It is entirely different, on the other hand, with confessional theology, such as the Lutheran, Reformed, and Romish theologies, which are beginning to give more frequent signs of life. In its confessional type it continues to bear a concrete and a real historical character, and behind this shield it is safe against the attack which subjectivism in the intellectual and mystical domain is trying to make upon the Christian religion. It holds an objective point of support in the Holy Scripture and in the dogmatic development, which protects it from being overwhelmed in the floods of many waters. And what is of greater significance still, thanks to this very objective-historic character, it is in less danger of being involuntarily annexed by philosophy. It may even now be prophesied, that, while modern theology fades into a science of religion or into a speculation, and Vermittelungstheologie shallows into mysticism, or finds its grave in the philosophical stream, this confessional theology alone will maintain its position. Even now it can be observed how this theology will fulfil a twofold mission: first, a universal one, viz. so to investigate the fundamental questions which are common to all the churches, that the radical difference between the consciousness of regenerate and unregenerate humanity shall ever be more fully exposed to light; and, secondly, to raise the special form of its own confessional consciousness to the level of the consciousness-form of our age. But this confessional theology will only come to a peaceful process of development when the conviction shall be more universally accepted, that the radical difference between regenerate and unregenerate humanity *extends across the entire domain of the higher sciences,* and therefore calls for two kinds of science just as soon as the investigation deserts the material basis and can no longer be constructed without the intermingling of the subjective factor. The exact boundary-line between Theology and Philosophy must not be sought between Christian Theology and pantheistic or pagan Philosophy, but between a Theology and Philosophy, *both* of which, as Keckermann already desired it, *stand at the view-point of palingenesis.*

www.ingramcontent.com/pod-product-compliance
Lightning Source LLC
Chambersburg PA
CBHW060446100426
42812CB00025B/2712